THE VIKING AGE

READINGS IN MEDIEVAL CIVILIZATIONS AND CULTURES: XIV
series editor: Paul Edward Dutton

The Gokstad Ship, built ca 890. Later used for a burial. Now in the Viking Ship Museum, Oslo.

Source: Paul B. du Chaillu, *The Viking Age*, 2 vols. (New York: Charles Scribner's Sons, 1899), vol. 1, frontispiece.

THE VIKING AGE

A READER

edited by

ANGUS A. SOMERVILLE
and R. ANDREW MCDONALD

University of Toronto Press

LIBRARY AND ARCHIVES CANADA CATALOGUING IN PUBLICATION

The Viking age : a reader / edited by Angus A. Somerville and R. Andrew McDonald.
(Readings in medieval civilizations and cultures ; XIV)
Includes index.
ISBN 978-1-4426-0148-2 (pbk). – ISBN 978-1-4426-0147-5 (bound)

1. Vikings. 2. Civilization, Viking. 3. Northmen.
I. McDonald, Russell Andrew, 1965–   II. Somerville, Angus A., 1943–
III. Series: Readings in medieval civilizations and cultures XIV

DL65.V545 2010   948'.022   C2009-906793-5

We welcome comments and suggestions regarding any aspect of our publications – please feel free to contact us at news@utphighereducation.com or visit our Internet site at www.utphighereducation.com.

North America
5201 Dufferin Street
Toronto, Ontario, Canada, M3H 5T8

2250 Military Road
Tonawanda, New York, USA, 14150

ORDERS PHONE: 1-800-565-9523
ORDERS FAX: 1-800-221-9985
ORDERS EMAIL: utpbooks@utpress.utoronto.ca

UK, Ireland, and continental Europe
NBN International
Estover Road, Plymouth, PL6 7PY, UK

TEL: 44 (0) 1752 202301
FAX ORDER LINE: 44 (0) 1752 202333
enquiries@nbninternational.com

This book is printed on paper containing 100% post-consumer fibre.

The University of Toronto Press acknowledges the financial support for its publishing activities of the Government of Canada through the Book Publishing Industry Development Program (BPIDP).

Book design and composition by George Kirkpatrick.
Printed in Canada

For

Barbara, Anna, and Clare

Jacqueline, Emma, and Colin

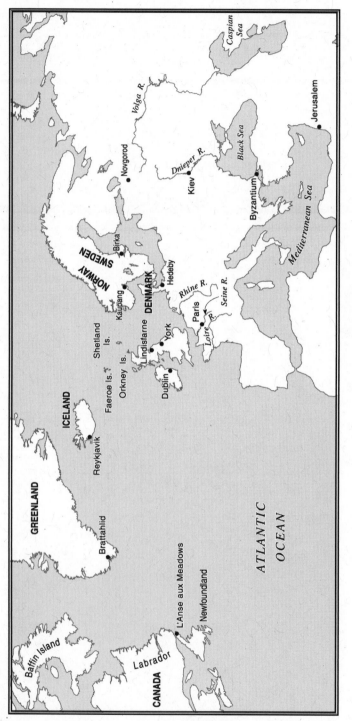

MAP OF THE VIKING WORLD

CONTENTS

CONTENTS

ACKNOWLEDGEMENTS

Our first debt of gratitude is to the many students who have taken our courses over the years and who have provided us with the impetus to produce this book.

We would also like to thank Cathy Bouwers, Erin Hodson, and Trudy Tattersall for their assistance with the preparation of some of the texts, Dr. Behnaz Mirzai for assistance with Arabic texts, and Loris Gasparotto for producing the maps.

We are grateful to the Humanities Research Institute at Brock University for providing funds in support of this project.

At University of Toronto Press we thank Paul Dutton for helpful comments and suggestions, and Natalie Fingerhut for expert editorial assistance.

Unquestionably, however, our biggest debt is to our respective families, who have had to put up with the Vikings for many years. This book is for them: Barbara, Anna, and Clare; Jacqueline, Emma, and Colin.

INTRODUCTION

This book provides a comprehensive and accessible one-volume collection of primary documents that will be of use to instructors and students as well as to the general reader interested in the Viking Age. In assembling, translating, and arranging the materials presented here we have been guided by the principle of providing as much breadth as possible, both in the types of sources presented and in the geographic and chronological coverage of the work. Of course, the vast amount of material available, particularly the corpus of Icelandic saga texts, means that it is impossible to include everything, and we are conscious of omissions. Nevertheless, we hope that the documents presented here will encourage readers to delve further into primary texts dealing with the Vikings and the Viking Age.

Who, When, and Where Were the Vikings?

In the popular imagination, the Vikings are shaggy, unkempt, ax-wielding thugs in horned helmets who raped, pillaged, and plundered their way across Europe in the Early Middle Ages, nearly destroying western civilization in the process. They have been blamed for everything from a decline in learning (thanks to the burning of monasteries, places of learning) to the break-up of the Carolingian empire that dominated Europe in the ninth century. So is the Viking stereotype of the burly, destructive, barbarian even remotely accurate? As usual, the myth is far removed from reality. The shaggy Vikings were not the unkempt louts of popular fiction, but a proud people who were careful about their appearance. The horned helmets associated with the Vikings in popular culture are a romantic invention of the nineteenth century, and no helmets with horns are known from the Viking Age anywhere in Europe. And, while a very small minority of early medieval Viking Age Scandinavians might well have resembled the warriors and bandits of the stereotype, their fellow Norsemen were also renowned merchants, seamen, explorers, mercenaries, and poets, who contributed much to early medieval European civilization.

Understanding the Vikings begins with understanding the word "Viking" itself. In Old Norse (ON), the noun *víkingr* means a sea-borne pirate or raider; *víking* means a sea-borne raid. The word Viking is, then, in the technical sense, a job description, and it was a part-time job at that, since Viking expeditions were undertaken seasonally by farmers, fishermen, merchants, and the like, as a means of supplementing their income. Few Scandinavians of the Viking Age would have thought of themselves, or would have been described by others, as Vikings. In fact, out of all those who suffered at the hands of marauding Scandinavians, only the Anglo-Saxons actually named them *wicingas*. Common designations in contemporary British and Irish, and European, records include the terms "Northmen," "foreigners," and "heathens," the latter a reference to the fact that at the dawn of the Viking Age the Scandinavians had yet to be converted to Christianity. It was not until the nineteenth century, following the "rediscovery" of the Icelandic sagas and eddas and their translation into English, that the term Viking passed into common English use. Today the usefulness of the term is a subject of debate among academics. In this collection, however, we adopt the term in its widely accepted sense as a descriptor for the peoples of Scandinavia in the period from the late eighth to the eleventh centuries, not just for those who undertook sea-borne raiding; we use the terms "Norse" and "Norsemen" in the same sense.

Vikings, then, were raiders, traders, farmers, and, later, settlers; the activities were closely intertwined. In the course of the Viking diaspora, Norsemen (and women) traveled westward across the North Atlantic to North America and eastward down the Russian river systems to Constantinople (modern-day Istanbul) and into the Islamic world. Scandinavian trade flowed through Hedeby in Denmark, Visby and Birka in Sweden, Kaupang in Norway, Novgorod in Russia, Kiev in the Ukraine, York in England, and Dublin in Ireland. Scandinavians were thus important traders from the Caspian Sea to Greenland. Accordingly, this text aims to capture the astonishing geographic scope of the Viking world by including materials relating to all of these regions.

The Viking Age is generally considered to have begun in the late eighth century with the dramatic explosion of Scandinavian raiding parties onto the European stage. The destruction of Lindisfarne Abbey in Northumbria in the summer of 793 horrified Europe and, along with other raids like it, shaped the European perception of the Vikings for many centuries. For several decades Viking raiding parties terrorized most of northern Europe, using hit-and-run tactics to target monasteries where they could lay hands on easily portable wealth, along with captives who could be enslaved or ransomed. But, within about fifty years of the earliest recorded raids, raiding gave way to permanent settlement in Britain, Ireland, and the continent as well as the North Atlantic islands of the Faeroes, Iceland, and Greenland, which were given the names by which they are still known. Around the year 1000, Norsemen were the first Europeans to reach North America, exploring the region they called Vinland the Good, probably the shores of the Gulf of St. Lawrence. Indeed, Norse maritime activity of all kinds was at its height during the so-called medieval warm period of ca 800–ca 1300, and exploration of the North Atlantic was at least partly facilitated by the comparative lack of pack ice in those years.

The end of the period is harder to place. The unification and centralization of the Scandinavian states in the tenth and eleventh centuries have been simultaneously blamed for increases in Viking activity and credited with its cessation. However, a case could be made for regarding some point during the eleventh century as bringing the Viking Age to a close. The Battle of Clontarf (1014) emphasized the waning power of Norsemen to do as they pleased in Ireland. The North Sea empire of Knut (Cnut/Canute) the Great disintegrated with his death in 1035, and his conquests might be seen as the last great expedition of the age of the Vikings. Another possibility is 1066, when King Harald Hardradi of Norway failed disastrously in an attempt to invade England. Harald was killed, and his army destroyed, at the Battle of Stamford Bridge in the north of England. Raiding in England was never more than half-hearted after the death of Harald and the arrival of William the Conqueror.

All of these events may be regarded as stages in a slow process of change. However, Norse activity in the British Isles continued until the death of Hakon IV the Old (d. 1263). His doubtfully successful punitive raid on Scotland was the last serious Scandinavian intervention in the British Isles.

How Do We Know?

One major challenge is the dearth of literary materials from the Vikings themselves in the early part of the Viking Age. It is not quite fair to say, as is sometimes done, that the Vikings were illiterate at the time the Scandinavian expansion began, since they did possess a runic alphabet, the futhark, which was used in carving inscriptions on stone, wood, bone or metal. Runic inscriptions are, by their very nature, not suited to long narrative, however, and their study requires a highly specialized background. Until recently, therefore, our knowledge of the Vikings and their culture was shaped by the accounts of their European enemies, who gave them a very bad press. English and French chronicles are a major source of contemporary narratives of Viking incursions.

However, from the nineteenth century onwards, translation into English of medieval Icelandic sagas added another dimension to the study of the Viking Age, allowing the Vikings to be appreciated from the perspective of their own culture – or at least the culture of their Christianized descendants in thirteenth-century Iceland. The narratives of history and saga-literature frequently overlap, and this has tempted many to find in the sagas a greater degree of historical factuality than is justified. Nonetheless, the sagas are among the major ways in which thirteenth-century Icelanders constructed their own and the wider Scandinavian pasts. They were closer to the events than we are, and we must concede to their writing, if not factuality, a high degree of plausibility.

Two texts appear often in this reader: *Egil's Saga* and Snorri Sturluson's *Heimskringla, a History of the Kings of Norway*. In order to provide cohesiveness across the volume, many topics in the reader are examined in part using *Egil's Saga*, the biography of Egil Skallagrimsson, a notable tenth-century Icelandic Viking and poet. Snorri Sturluson (d. 1241) was a thirteenth-century Icelander of outstanding ability, at once lawyer, diplomat, scholar, and poet. Snorri's *Heimskringla* covers much of Viking Age history, and does so with both clarity and drama. In addition, Snorri interlaces his prose with extensive quotations from court poets contemporary with the events he narrates. While *Heimskringla* is no longer regarded as an absolutely reliable historical source, it is important as a highly skillful blend of history and popular legend. His *Edda*, too, is an indispensable source for the study of Norse mythology and skaldic poetry. It has also been suggested that he wrote *Egil's Saga*.

European and Scandinavian material is complemented by documents from the neighboring civilizations of Byzantium and Islam; in fact, Islamic texts provide some of the most important descriptions of Scandinavians and their customs in the tenth century. Understanding the Vikings, then, necessarily involves the study of many texts and documents from many different regions and periods, and written in many different languages. An important aim of this collection is to highlight this geographic, historical, and linguistic diversity of primary-source materials relating to the Viking diaspora.

Some Notes on the Translations

Unless otherwise noted, all Old Norse and Anglo-Saxon texts are newly translated for this reader. As is usual, the names of persons are anglicized: for example, Egill appears as Egil, and Guðrún as Gudrun.

In Old Norse texts, an individual is often identified as the son or daughter of his or her father: for example, Guðrún Ósvífrsdóttir, anglicized here as Gudrun Osvifrsdaughter, or Egill Skalla-Grímsson, anglicized as Egil Skallagrimsson. A few names, such as Hákon, or Sigurðr have a different form and are anglicized as *Hakonarson* and *Sigurdarson* when used to express the patronymic, as in Hakon Hakonarson or Harald Sigurdarson.

In the headings of chapters and sections of chapters, the titles of Norse texts are given in their original form in parentheses after the customary English translation: for example, *Egil's Saga* (*Egils saga Skalla-Grímssonar*).

Where placenames have well-known English forms, these are generally used: for example, York replaces Jórvík, and Reykjavik replaces Reykjarvík.

Only two symbols from Old Norse are likely to cause confusion on the rare occasions when they are used here: Ð, ð: pronounced th as in that. Þ,þ: pronounced th as in thin.

CHAPTER ONE

THE SCANDINAVIAN HOMELANDS

Written evidence for early medieval Scandinavia is sparse. Some early medieval authors such as Jordanes in the sixth century were clearly well-informed about the contemporary political situation in Scandinavia, but the earliest detailed accounts of the region from inside come from the late ninth-century voyagers Ohthere and Wulfstan, whose narratives are interpolated in the Old English translation of Orosius' Historiae, produced during the reign of Alfred the Great (d. 899). The most important foreign account is that of Adam of Bremen from the last quarter of the eleventh century.

1. THE VOYAGES OF OHTHERE AND WULFSTAN

Ohthere, a Norwegian, explores the coastline from Halogaland in northern Norway to the White Sea and goes on to describe the route from his northern home to the great market town of Hedeby in Denmark. Wulfstan's voyage begins where Ohthere's ends. He recounts his journey eastward through the Baltic Sea from Hedeby to Estland, in the northeastern part of Germany. Both narratives are interpolated in the Old English translations of Orosius's Historiae adversum paganos.

Source: trans. A.A. Somerville, from *Ohthere's Voyages*, ed. Janet Bately and Anton Eglert, *Maritime Culture of the North*, vol. 1 (Roskilde: The Viking Ship Museum, 2007), pp. 1–60.

The Voyage of Ohthere

Ohthere told his lord, King Alfred, that he lived farther north than any other Norwegian. He said that he lived in the north of the country beside the West Sea [the Atlantic]. He said that the land stretches a long way north from there, however, though it is completely unpopulated except for a few places here and there, where Sami live, hunting in winter and fishing by the sea in summer.

He said that on one occasion he wanted to find out how far north the land stretched, and whether anyone lived to the north of the wilderness area. So, he sailed north close to the coastline. For three days, he kept the wilderness to his starboard and the open sea to port. By then he was as far north as the whalehunters ever go. After that, he kept traveling due north as far as he could sail in the next three days. Then the land turned to the east, or the sea curved into the land, he did not know which. But he did know that he waited there for a wind from the west–northwest and afterwards sailed east along the coast as far as he could sail in four days. Then he had to wait there for a north wind, because the land turned due south there, or the sea turned into the land, he did not know which. Next, he sailed south along the coast as far as he could go in five days. There a large river [probably the Dvina] stretched into the land. They turned into the river, not daring to travel beyond it for fear of hostility, because the land on the other side of the river was thickly settled. Until now, he had not come across any populated land since leaving his own home; but all the way there was empty land to starboard except for fishermen, fowlers, and hunters, and they were all Sami and to port there was always the open sea. The Biarmians had settled their land thickly, but they [Ohthere and crew] dared not set foot there. The land of the Ter Sami [southeast Kola Peninsula?], however, was completely uninhabited except for hunters, fishermen, or fowlers.

The Biarmians told him many tales both about their own land and about the lands which lay around them, but he did not know how true these tales were because he did not see anything for himself. It seemed to him that the Sami and the Biarmians spoke much the same language.

In addition to exploring the land, he traveled there mainly for the walrus, because they have very fine bone in their teeth – they brought some teeth for the king – and their hide is very good for ships' ropes. This whale is much smaller than other whales, being no more than seven ells long [an English ell is 1.14 meters]. But the best whale hunting is in his own land where the whales are forty-eight ells long, and the biggest fifty ells in length. He said that he and six other men killed sixty of them in two days.

He was a very well-to-do man, rich in the possessions which comprise their wealth, namely wild beasts. When he visited the king, he still had six hundred unsold animals. These animals are called reindeer. Six of them were decoy reindeer; these are highly prized by the Sami because they catch wild reindeer with them. He was one of the most prominent men in that land, yet he had no more than twenty cattle, twenty sheep, and twenty pigs, and the little that he plowed, he plowed with horses. Their wealth, however, consists mainly of the tribute paid to them by the Sami. This tribute consists of animal hides, bird feathers, whale bone, and ships' cables made from whale and seal skins. Each man pays according to his rank. The highest ranking must give fifteen marten skins, five reindeer hides, a bear skin, ten ambers of feathers, a bear or otter skin coat, and two ships' cables, each sixty ells long, one made from whale skin and the other from seal skin.

He said that the land of the Norwegians is very long and very narrow. All the land that can be grazed or plowed lies beside the sea, and even that is very rocky in places. Above and to the east lie wild, mountainous wastelands, stretching all along the length of the inhabited land. Sami inhabit the wasteland. The inhabited land is broadest to the east [that is, in the south of Norway] and the farther north it lies, the narrower it becomes. To the east, it can be sixty miles broad, or slightly broader, and in the middle, it can be thirty miles or broader. To the north, where it is narrowest, he said, it might be only three miles broad before becoming wasteland. In some places the wasteland is as wide as a man can cross in two weeks; in others, as wide as a man can cross in six days. Alongside the southern part of the land, on the other side of the wasteland, Sweden stretches up to the northern part of Norway, and adjacent to the northern part of Norway is Cwenland [land of the Sami]. Sometimes, the Sami harry the Norwegians across the waste land, and at other times the Norwegians raid them. There are huge freshwater lakes throughout the wastelands; the Sami carry their boats overland to the lakes and raid the Norwegians from there. They have very small, light boats.

Ohthere said that the district where he lived is called Halogaland and that no one lived to the north of him. In the south of that land is a port called Skiringssal [Kaupang]. He said that a man could not sail there in a month if he camped at night and had a favorable wind every day. And all the while, he must sail along the coast, and to his starboard, first there will be Ireland and then the islands [Orkneys and Shetlands] between Ireland and this land [Britain]. Then Britain is to starboard until he comes to Skiringssal and, all the way, Norway is to port. South of Skiringssal, a very large sea cuts deeply into the land; it is broader than anyone can see across. Jutland is opposite on the other side and then Sillende [central and southern Denmark]. The sea flows many hundreds of miles into the land. From Skiringssal, he said that he sailed for five days to the port called Hedeby which stands between the Wends, the Saxons, and the Angles and belongs to the Danes. When he sailed there from Skiringssal, Denmark was on his port side for three days and open sea on his starboard. Then, for two days before he came to Hedeby, Jutland, Sillende, and many islands lay to starboard – the Angles lived in these places before they came to this land [England] – and for these two days the islands that belong to Denmark lay to port.

The Voyage of Wulfstan

Wulfstan said that he traveled seven days and nights from Hedeby before arriving in Truso and that the ship ran under sail the whole way. Wendland [Pomerania] was to starboard and to port were Langeland, Laaland, Falster, and Skåne. These lands all belong to Denmark. Next, Bornholm lay to port, and the people there have their own king. After Bornholm came Blekinge, Möre, Öland, and Gotland; and these lands belong to the Swedes. Wendland was to our starboard all the way to the mouth of the Vistula. The Vistula is a very big river which separates Witland and Wendland, and Witland belongs to the Ests [Estonians]. The Vistula flows out of Wendland and into Frisches Haff, and Frisches Haff is about fifteen miles wide. Then the Elbing comes into Frisches Haff from the east, from the lake on whose bank Truso stands. And these rivers flow together into Frisches Haff, the Elbing from Estland in the east and the Vistula from Wendland in the south. The Elbing then adopts the Vistula's name and flows west and north from the lake to the sea; for this reason it is called the mouth of the Vistula.

Estland is very large. There are a great many towns and in each one there is a king. There is a great deal of honey and fishing. The king and the most powerful men drink mare's milk while the poor and the slaves drink mead. There is much conflict among them. No ale is brewed by the Ests, but there is plenty of mead.

4

It is an Est custom that, when a man dies, he lies indoors uncremated in the midst of his kinsmen and friends for a month, or sometimes two. Kings and other high-ranking men have a longer lying-in, proportionate with the size of their wealth; sometimes they lie uncremated for half a year, above ground in their houses. As long as the corpse is in the house, there must be drinking and entertainment until the day they cremate him. On the day that they intend to carry him to the funeral pyre, they divide up what remains of his property after the drinking and entertainment into five or six parts, and sometimes more, depending on the amount of property. They deposit the largest portion about a mile from the settlement, then the second largest, and then the third until it is all laid out within that single mile. The smallest portion must be closest to the settlement where the dead man is lying. Next, all the men with the swiftest horses in the land must be assembled about five or six miles from the property. Then they all gallop toward it. The man who has the fastest horse comes to the first and largest portion, and so on, one after another, until everything is taken. The smallest portion goes to the man who gallops closest to the settlement to get it. Each man then rides on his way with the property; they may take everything, and that is why fast horses are excessively expensive there. When all the treasure is dispersed, the dead man is carried out and cremated with his weapons and clothes. Almost all of his wealth is used up by the long lying-in of the dead man, and also by the laying out of his property for strangers to gallop toward and take. It is an Est custom that everyone must be cremated there; and if even one bone is found unburned, they must make great atonement for it. Among the Ests there is a group of people who understand the process of freezing. And the reason why the dead men lie there so long without decaying is that they freeze them. If two vessels full of water or ale are set down, they cause one of the two to freeze over, in summer and winter alike.

2. A DESCRIPTION OF THE ISLANDS OF THE NORTH

Adam of Bremen's History of the Archbishops of Hamburg-Bremen *is a history of the diocese and its archbishops, written ca 1072–75/76 and revised down to the early 1080s, when Adam probably died. The archbishops of Hamburg-Bremen were charged with the conversion of the neighboring peoples of the north, including the inhabitants of Scandinavia.*

Source: trans. F.J. Tschan, Adam of Bremen, *History of the Archbishops of Hamburg-Bremen*, with new introduction by T. Reuter (New York: Columbia University Press, 2002), pp. 186–223.

Here, if you please, the fourth book will begin.

1. The country of the Danes, as one also reads in the *Gesta* of Saint Ansgar, is almost all spread out over islands. Now, this Danish land is separated from our Nordalbingians by the river Eider, which rises in the densely wooded highland of the pagans, called Isarnho, which they say, extends along the Barbarian Ocean as far as the Schlei Sea. The Eider flows into the Frisian Ocean, which the Romans in their writings call the British Ocean. The principal part of Denmark, called Jutland, extends lengthwise from the Eider River toward the north; it is a journey of three days if you turn aside in the direction of the island of Fyn. But if you measure the distance direct from Schleswig to Aalborg, it is a matter of five to seven days' travel. That is the highway of the Caesar Otto unto the farthermost sea at Wendila, which sea is to this day called the Ottinsand from the king's victory [Otto II campaigned against Denmark in 974]. At the Eider Jutland is fairly wide, but thereafter it narrows little by little like a tongue to the point called Wendila, where Jutland comes to an end. Thence it is a very short passage to Norway. The soil in Jutland is sterile; except for places close to a river, nearly everything looks like a desert. It is a salt land and a vast wilderness. Furthermore, if Germany as a whole is frightful for its densely wooded highlands, Jutland itself is more frightful in other respects. The land is avoided because of the scarcity of crops, and the sea because it is infested by pirates. Hardly a cultivated spot is to be found anywhere, scarcely a place fit for human habitation. But wherever there is an arm of the sea it has very large cities. This region the Caesar Otto at one time subjected to tribute and divided into three bishoprics. One he established at Schleswig, which also is called Haddeby and is situated on the arm of the Barbarian Sea named by the inhabitants the Schlei, whence also the city derives its name. From this port ships usually proceed to Slavia or to Sweden or to Samland, even to Greece. The second bishopric he founded at Ribe, a city encompassed by another waterway that flows in from the ocean and over which one sails for Frisia, for England or for our Saxony. The third bishopric he planned to fix at Aarhus, separated from Fyn by a very narrow channel that reaches in from the Eastern Sea and extends in a long winding course between Fyn and Jutland northward up to this city of Aarhus. Then one sails to Fyn or Zealand, or Scania, or even to Norway....

3. Now the archbishop consecrated from among his own clerics Rudolf for Schleswig, Wilhelm for Zealand, Egilbert for Fyn. The latter, a convert from piracy, is said to have been the first to find the island Helgoland, which lies hidden in a deep recess of the ocean in the mouth of the Elbe River, and, having built a monastery there, to have made it habitable. This island lies across from Hadeln. It is barely eight miles long by four miles wide, and its people use straw and the wreckage of ships for fuel. Report has it that

whenever pirates plunder there, be the booty ever so slight, they never return home unpunished, either perishing soon after in shipwreck or getting killed by someone. For this reason they are accustomed with great devotion to offer the hermits who live there tithes of their booty. This island produces crops in the greatest abundance and is an exceedingly rich foster mother for birds and cattle. On it there is but one hill and not a single tree. It is hemmed in on all sides by very precipitous crags that prohibit access except in one place, where also the water is sweet. All sailors hold the place in awe, especially, however, pirates. Hence it got the name by which it is called, *Heiligland* [Holy Land, now Helgoland]. From the *Vita* of Saint Willebrord we learned that it was called Fosetisland and that it is situated on the boundary between the Danes and Frisians. There also are many other islands off Frisia and Denmark, but none of them is so noteworthy.

4. Fyn is a fairly important island, lying back of that called Wendila in the entrance of the Barbarian Gulf [Baltic Sea]. It is close to the region named Jutland, from every part of which the passage to Fyn is very short. There is the great city of Odense. Small islands encircle it, all abounding in crops. And it is to be observed that if you pass through Jutland into Fyn, your route is a straight way to the north. But your course faces east in going through Fyn into Zealand. There are two passages to Zealand, one from Fyn, the other from Aarhus; each place is an equal distance from Zealand. The sea is naturally tempestuous and full of two kinds of danger so that, even if you have a fair wind, you can hardly escape the hands of pirates.

5. Zealand is an island, very large in extent, situated in an inner bight of the Baltic Sea. It is very celebrated as much for the bravery of its men as for the abundance of its crops. It is two days' journey in length and almost the same in breadth. Its largest city is Roeskilde, the seat of Danish royalty. This island, equally distant from Fyn and from Scania, may be crossed in a night. To the west of it lies Jutland, with the cities of Aarhus and Aalborg, and Wendila; to the north, where it is also a desert, is the Norwegian strait; to the south, the aforementioned Fyn and the Slavic Gulf. On the east it faces the headlands of Scania, where is situated the city of Lund.

6. There is very much gold in Zealand, accumulated by the plundering of pirates. These pirates, called Vikings by the people of Zealand, by our people, Ascomanni, pay tribute to the Danish king for leave to plunder the barbarians who live about this sea in great numbers. Hence it also happens that the license granted them with respect to enemies is frequently misused against their own people. So true is this that they have no faith in one another, and as soon as one of them catches another, he mercilessly sells him into slavery either to one of his fellows or to a barbarian. In many other respects, indeed, both in their laws and in their customs, do the Danes run

7

contrary to what is fair and good. None of these points appears to me worth discussing, unless it be that they immediately sell women who have been violated and that men who have been caught betraying his royal majesty or in some other crime would rather be beheaded than flogged. No kind of punishment exists among them other than the ax and servitude, and then it is glorious for a man who is convicted to take his punishment joyfully. Tears and plaints and other forms of compunction, by us regarded as wholesome, are by the Danes so much abominated that one may weep neither over his sins nor over his beloved dead.

7. From Zealand to Scania there are many routes; the shortest is that to Helsingborg, which is even within the range of vision. Scania is the province of Denmark fairest to look upon – whence also its name – well provided with men, opulent of crops, rich in merchandise, and now full of churches. Scania is twice as large as Zealand, that is it has three hundred churches, whereas Zealand is said to have half that number, and Fyn a third. Scania is the most remote part of Denmark, almost an island, for it is surrounded on all sides by sea except for one reach of land which, becoming mainland on the east, separates Sweden from Denmark. The densely wooded highlands and very rugged mountains, over which the road from Scania into Götaland necessarily runs, make one doubt whether perils by land are more easily avoided than perils by sea, and whether to prefer the former to the latter....

10. But now, since the subject provides the occasion, it seems appropriate to say something about the nature of the Baltic Sea. Because I drew upon the writings of Einhard when I previously mentioned this sea in connection with the deeds of Archbishop Adaldag, I shall proceed in the manner of a commentator, setting forth for our people in greater detail what he discussed in abridged form. There is a gulf, Einhard says, that stretches from the Western Ocean toward the east. This gulf is by the inhabitants called the Baltic because, after the manner of a baldric, it extends a long distance through the Scythian regions even to Greece. It is also named the Barbarian Sea or Scythian Lake, from the barbarous peoples whose lands it washes. But the Western Ocean apparently is the one which the Romans in their writings called the British Ocean. It is of immense breadth, terrible and dangerous, and on the west encompasses Britain to which is now given the name England. On the south it touches the Frisians and the part of Saxony that belongs to our diocese of Hamburg. On the east there are the Danes and the mouth of the Baltic Sea and the Norwegians, who live beyond Denmark. On the north that ocean flows by the Orkney Islands and then encircles the earth in boundless expanses. On the left there is Hibernia, the fatherland of the Scots, which now is called Ireland. On the right there are the crags of Norway, and

farther on the islands of Iceland and Greenland. There ends the ocean called dark [Arctic Ocean].

11. What Einhard says about the unexplored length of this gulf has lately been proved by the enterprise of the highly spirited men, Ganuz Wolf, a Danish leader, and Harold, the king of the Norwegians [Harald Hardradi, d. 1066]. After exploring the compass of this sea with much toilsome travel and many dangers to their associates, they finally came back, broken and overcome by the redoubled blows of the winds and pirates. But the Danes affirm that many have oftentimes explored the length of this sea. With a favorable wind some have reached Ostrogard in Russia from Denmark in the course of a month. As to its breadth, he asserts that it is "nowhere more than a hundred miles ... and in many places much narrower." This can be seen at the mouth of that sea, the entrance of which from the ocean, between Aalborg or Wendila, the headland of Denmark, and the cliffs of Norway is so narrow that it is an easy trip of one night across by sail. Likewise, on leaving the bounds of Denmark, the sea stretches wide its arms, which come together a second time in the region of the Goths by the side of whom live the Wilzi. The farther one goes, then, the farther do its coast lines spread apart.

12. Many peoples, Einhard says, occupy the shores of this sea. The Danes and the Swedes, whom we call Northmen, hold both its northern shore and all the islands off it. The Slavs, the Esths, and various other peoples inhabit the eastern shore; amongst them the Welatabi, also called Wilzi, are the most important. The Danes and the Swedes and the other peoples beyond Denmark are all called Northmen by the historians of the Franks, although the Roman writers named men of this kind Hyperboreans, whom Martianus Capella extolled with many commendations.

13. At the mouth of the sea mentioned before, on its southern coast facing us, there live as far as the Schlei Sea the first people, the Danes, who are called Jutes. There begins the territory of the diocese of Hamburg, which extends a long way through the midst of the Slavic coastal peoples as far as the Peene River. There are the limits of our diocese. From that place to the Oder River the Wilzi and Leutici have their homes. Across the Oder, as we have learned, live the Pomeranians; beyond them stretches the very extensive country of the Poles, the boundary of which, they say, joins with that of the kingdom of Russia. This is the farthest and largest province of the Winuli, and it also is at the end of that sea.

14. Returning now to the northernmost parts at the entrance of the Baltic Sea, first come the Norwegians; then Scania, which belongs to the Danes, juts out, and beyond it live the Goths in an extensive domain reaching to Björkö. After that the Swedes rule over a spacious region extending to the

land of women [the Amazons]. Beyond them, as far as Russia, are said to live the Wizzi, Mirri, Lami, Scuti, and Turci. In this area that sea again comes to an end. Thus the Slavs possess the southern litoral of that sea; the Swedes, the northern.

15. Those who have a knowledge of geography also assert that some men have passed by an overland route from Sweden into Greece. But the barbarous peoples who live between make this way difficult; consequently, the risk is taken by ship.

16. In this sea [the Baltic Sea] there are many islands, all of which are under the dominion of the Danes and Swedes, though a few are held by the Slavs. Of these islands, at a short distance from one another, the first is Wendila, at the head of this strait, the second is Morsö, the third is Thyholm. The fourth, opposite the city of Aarhus, is Samsö. The fifth is Fyn, the sixth is Zealand, which lies close to it. Of these islands we have made mention before. They say that the seventh, which is very near Scania and Götaland, is called Holm, the most celebrated port of Denmark and a safe anchorage for the ships that are usually dispatched to the barbarians and to Greece. There are, furthermore, close to Fyn on the southeast – although Laaland reaches farther inwards to the confines of the Slavs – seven other smaller islands, which we said above are rich in crops, that is, Möen, Fehmarn, Falster, Laaland, Langeland, and so all the others in their vicinity. These fourteen islands belong to the kingdom of the Danes, and they all are distinguished by the honor of being Christian. There also are other more distant islands that are subject to the authority of the Swedes. Of these islands the largest, the one called Courland, takes eight days to traverse....

21. In going beyond the islands of the Danes there opens up another world in the direction of Sweden and Norway, which are the two most extensive kingdoms of the north and until now nearly unknown to our parts. About these kingdoms the very well-informed king of the Danes [Svein Estridson, 1047–76] told me that Norway can hardly be crossed in the course of a month, and Sweden is not easily traversed in two months. "I myself found this out," he said, "when a while ago I fought for twelve years in those regions under King James. Both these countries are shut in by exceedingly high mountains – higher ones, however, in Norway which encircles Sweden with its alps." About Sweden, too, the ancient writers, Lolinus and Orosius, are not silent. They say that the Swedes hold a very large part of Germany and, besides, that their highland regions extend up to the Rhiphaean Mountains. There, also, is the Elbe River to which Lucan appears to have referred. It rises in the alps before mentioned and courses through the midst of the Gothic peoples into the ocean; hence, also, it is called the Götaälv. The Swedish country is extremely fertile; the land is rich in fruits and honey besides excelling all

others in cattle raising, exceedingly happy in streams and woods, the whole region everywhere full of merchandise from foreign parts. Thus you may say the Swedes are lacking in none of the riches, except the pride that we love or rather adore. For they regard as nothing every means of vainglory; that is gold, silver, stately chargers, beaver and marten pelts, which make us lose our minds admiring them....

22. There are many Swedish peoples excelling in strength and arms, besides being the best of fighters on horse as well as on ships. This also accounts for their holding the other peoples of the North in their power. They have kings of ancient lineage; nevertheless, the power of these kings depends upon the will of the people, for what all in common approve, that the king must confirm, unless it be that his decision, which they sometimes reluctantly follow, seems preferable. And so they enjoy equality at home. When they go to war everyone yields perfect obedience to the king or to the one who, more skilled than the rest, is preferred by the king. Whenever in fighting they are placed in a critical situation, they invoke the aid of one of the multitude of gods they worship. Then after the victory they are devoted to him and set him above the others. By common consent, however, they now declare that the God of the Christians is the most powerful of all. Other gods often fail them, but he always stands by, a surest "helper in due time in tribulation." [Ps. 9:10]

23. Of these Swedish peoples, the so-called Goths live nearest to us; there are other Goths known as eastern. Västergötland, indeed, borders on the Danish territory called Scania, from which they also say it takes seven days to reach Skara, the great city of the Goths. Thence Östergötland extends along the sea, the one they call the Baltic, up to Björkö....

24. Between Norway and Sweden dwell the Wärmilani and Finns and others, who are now all Christians and belong to the Church of Skara. On the confines of the Swedes and Norwegians toward the north live the Skritefingi [Sami], who, they say, outstrip wild beasts at running. Their largest city is Hälsingland ... there are besides countless other Swedish peoples, of whom we have learned that only the Goths, the Wärmilani, and a part of the Skritefingi, and those in their vicinity, have been converted to Christianity.

25. Let us now proceed to give a brief description of Sueonia or Sweden. On the west, Sweden has the Goths and the city of Skara; on the north, the Wärmilani with the Skritefingi, whose chief city is Hälsingland; on the south, the length of the Baltic Sea, about which we have spoken before. There is the great city of Sigtuna. On the east, Sweden touches the Rhiphaean Mountains, where there is immense wasteland, the deepest snows, and where hordes of human monsters prevent access to what lies beyond. There are Amazons, and Cynocephali, and Cyclops who have one eye on their foreheads; there are those Solinus calls Himantopodes, who hop on one foot, and those who

delight in human flesh as food, and as they are shunned, so may they also rightfully be passed over in silence. The king of the Danes, often to be remembered, told me that a certain people were in the habit of descending from the highlands into the plains. They are small of stature but hardly matched by the Swedes in strength and agility. "Whence they come is not known. They come up unexpectedly," he said, "sometimes once in the course of a year or after a three-year period. Unless they are resisted with all one's might, they lay waste the whole region and then withdraw." Many other things are usually mentioned, but in my effort to be brief I have not mentioned them, letting those speak about them who declare they themselves have seen them. Now we shall say a few words about the superstitions of the Swedes....

30. As Nortmannia is the farthest country of the world, so we properly place consideration of it in the last part of the book. By moderns it is called Norway. Of its location and extent we made some mention earlier in connection with Sweden, but this in particular must now be said, that in its length that land extends into the farthest northern zone, whence also it takes its name. It begins with towering crags at the sea commonly called the Baltic; then with its main ridge bent toward the north after following the course of the shore line of a raging ocean, it finally has its bounds in the Rhiphaean Mountains, where the tired world also comes to an end. On account of the roughness of its mountains and the immoderate cold, Norway is the most unproductive of all countries, suited only for herds. They browse their cattle, like the Arabs, far off in the solitudes. In this way do the people make a living from their livestock by using the milk of the flocks or herds for food and the wool for clothing. Consequently, there are produced very valiant fighters who, not softened by an overindulgence in fruits, more often attack others than others trouble them. Even though they are sometimes assailed — not with impunity — by the Danes, who are just as poor, the Norwegians live in terms of amity with their neighbors, the Swedes. Poverty has forced them thus to go all over the world and from piratical raids they bring home in great abundance the riches of the lands. In this way they bear up under the unfruitfulness of their own country. Since accepting Christianity, however, imbued with better teachings, they have already learned to love the truth and peace and to be content with their poverty — indeed, to disperse what they had gathered, not as before to gather what had been dispersed....

31. In many places in Norway and Sweden cattle herdsmen are even men of the highest station, living in the manner of patriarchs and by the work of their own hands. All, indeed, who live in Norway are thoroughly Christian, except those who are removed beyond the arctic tract along the ocean. These people, it is said, are to this day so superior in the magic arts or incantations that they profess to know what every one is doing the world over. Then they

also draw great sea monsters to shore with a powerful mumbling of words and do much else of which one reads in the Scriptures about magicians. All this is easy for them through practice. I have heard that women grow beards in the extremely rough alps of that region and that the men live in the woods, rarely exposing themselves to sight. They use the pelts of wild beasts for clothing and in speaking to one another are said to gnash their teeth rather than to utter words, so that they can hardly be understood by the peoples nearest to them. That mountain region is named by Roman writers the Rhiphaean range, terrible for its perpetual snows. Without these frosty snows the Skritefingi cannot live and in their course over the deepest drifts they fly even faster than the wild beasts. In those same mountains there are such large numbers of big game that the greatest part of the country subsists only on the beasts of the forest. Aurochs, buffalo, and elk are taken there as in Sweden. Bison, furthermore, are caught in Slavia and Russia. Only in Norway, however, are there black fox and hares, white martens and bears of the same color who live under water like aurochs. And since much else may there be seen that is entirely different and strange to our people, we leave it and other things to be more fully described by the inhabitants of that land.

32. The metropolitan city of the Norwegians is Trondheim, which, now graced with churches, is frequented by a great multitude of peoples. In that city reposes the body of the most blessed Olaf, king and martyr [Olaf Horaldsson, d. 1030]. At this tomb the Lord to this very day works such very great miraculous cures that those who do not despair of being able to get help through the merits of the saint flock together there from far-off lands. But the route is of a kind that, boarding a ship, they may, in a day's journey, cross the sea from Aalborg or Wendila of the Danes to Viken, a city of the Norwegians. Sailing thence toward the left along the coast of Norway, the city called Trondheim is reached on the fifth day. But it is possible also to go another way that leads over a land road from Scania of the Danes to Trondheim. This route, however, is slower in the mountainous country, and travelers avoid it because it is dangerous....

34. Beyond Norway, which is the farthermost northern country, you will find no human habitation, nothing but ocean, terrible to look upon and limitless, encircling the whole world. The ocean off Norway contains many considerable islands, of which nearly all are now subject to the rule of the Norwegians and so are not to be overlooked by us because they also belong to the diocese of Hamburg. The first of them are the Orkney Islands, which the barbarians call the *Organae*. Like the Cyclades, they are strewn over the ocean. The Roman writers Martian and Solinus, it appears, wrote about them thus: "Back of Britain, where the boundless ocean begins, are the Orkney Islands, of which twenty are deserted, sixteen are inhabited.

The Orkney Islands, numbering nearly forty, lie close together. In their vicinity, too, are the *Electrides* [the Hebrides?], on which amber originates."
Situated between Norway and Britain and Ireland, the Orkneys, therefore, laugh playfully at the threats of a menacing ocean. It is said that one can sail to them in a day from the Norwegian city of Trondheim. They say, too, that from the Orkneys it is just as far whether you steer toward England or set sail for Scotland. For these same Orkney Islands, although they had previously been ruled by English and Scottish bishops, our primate on the pope's order consecrated Throlf bishop for the city of Birsay, and he was to have the cure of all....

[*There follow descriptions of Iceland, Greenland, Helgeland, and Vinland.*]

39. Archbishop Adalbert of blessed memory likewise told us that in the days of his predecessor certain noble men of Frisia spread sail to the north for the purpose of ranging through the sea, because the inhabitants claimed that by a direct course toward the north from the mouth of the Weser River one meets with no land but only that sea called the Libersee. The partners pledged themselves under oath to look into this novel claim and, with a joyful call to the oarsmen, set out from the Frisian coast. Then, leaving on the one side Denmark, on the other Britain, they came to the Orkneys. And when they had left these islands to their left, while they had Norway on their right, the navigators landed after a long passage on icy Iceland. And as they furrowed the seas from that place toward the farthest northern pole, after they saw behind them all the islands spoken about above, they commended their way and venture to Almighty God and the holy confessor Willehad. Of a sudden they fell into the numbing ocean's dark mist which could hardly be penetrated with the eyes. And behold, the current of the fluctuating ocean whirled back to its mysterious fountainhead and with most furious impetuosity drew the unhappy sailors, who in their despair now thought only of death, on to chaos; this they say is the abysmal chasm – that deep in which report has it all the back flow of the sea, which appears to decrease, is absorbed and in turn revomited, as the mounting fluctuation is usually described. As the partners were imploring the mercy of God to receive their souls, the backward thrust of the sea carried away some of their ships, but its forward ejection threw the rest far behind the others. Freed thus by the timely help of God from the instant peril they had had before their eyes, they seconded the flood by rowing with all their might.

40. No sooner had the mariners escaped the peril of darkness and the land of frost than they unexpectedly came upon an island [possibly Ireland] fortified like a town by very high cliffs which encircled it. When they disembarked there to explore the place, they found men lurking in underground hollows at midday. Before the entrances lay a countless number of vessels of

gold and of metals of a kind considered rare and precious by mortals. When they had taken as much of the treasure as they could carry away, the happy oarsmen returned quickly to their ships. Of a sudden they saw coming behind them the amazingly tall men whom our people call Cyclops. Before them ran dogs exceeding the usual size of these quadrupeds, who in their attack seized one of the comrades and in a twinkling tore him to pieces before their eyes. The rest, however, took to the ships and escaped the peril. The giants, as they said, followed them, with vociferations, almost out to the high sea. Attended by such good fortune, the Frisians came back to Bremen where they told Archbishop Alebrand everything as it had happened and made offerings to the blessed Christ and his holy confessor Willehad for their safe return....

41. This is what we have learned about the nature of the northern regions in order to set it down to the honor of the Church at Hamburg....

CHAPTER TWO

SCANDINAVIAN SOCIETY

While textual material from the Viking Age is scarce, the corpus of later medieval Icelandic literature provides an invaluable source of information on Scandinavian society and its socio-political organization. These sources must be used with care, however. They are rooted in oral tradition, and it is difficult to know to what extent the saga literature is an accurate reflection of the Viking Age, and to what extent it reflects the society of the age in which it was written – mostly the thirteenth and fourteenth centuries.

3. *THE LAY OF RIG* (*RÍGSÞULA*)

The incomplete Eddic poem known as Rígsþula, The Lay of Rig, *relates the mythical origins of the different social orders. Though preserved in a thirteenth-century manuscript, the poem is considerably older. The brief prose introduction to the poem identifies Rig as the Norse god Heimdall, who is said, in* Völuspá *(see docs. 8 and 9), to be the father of the human race.*

Source: *Die Lieder des Codex Regius*, ed. Gustav Neckel; 5th rev. edition, ed. Hans Kuhn (Heidelberg: Carl Winter, 1983), pp. 280–87.

In old tales, men say that one of the Æsir [gods], Heimdall by name, journeyed along a sea-coast, and that he came to a farmhouse, where he went by the name of Rig. This poem tells the story.

1. They said that
long ago,
Rig went striding
along green paths,
a wise god,
powerful, old,
strong and vigorous.

2. More:
he kept
to the middle of the paths,
came to a house,
the door was wide open.
In he went.
A fire burned on the floor;
a grey-haired couple
sat by the hearth:
Greatgrandfather, and
Greatgrandmother in
her old-fashioned head-gear.

3. Rig knew
how to give them advice.
More:
he sat
himself down
in the middle

of the seating area;
on either side
sat the couple
from the homestead.

4. Then Greatgrandmother took
a lumpy loaf,
thick and heavy,
full of bran.
More:
she brought it
placed in the center
of dishes.
There was broth in a bowl;
she placed it on the table.
He rose up from there and
got ready for sleep.

5. Rig knew
how to give them advice.
More:
he lay down
in the middle of the bed.
On either side
lay the couple
from the homestead.

6. He stayed there
three whole nights.
More:
he traveled on
in the middle of the paths.
More:
then nine months passed.

7. Greatgrandmother
gave birth to a dark-skinned baby;
they wrapped him
in linen,
sprinkled him with water,
named him Thrall.

8. He grew and flourished.
On his hands he had
wrinkled skin,
knobbly knuckles,
thick fingers.
Ill-favored was his face,
stooped his back,
long his heels.

9. More:
he began
to exert his strength
binding bast [hemp, jute],
bundling up loads,
carrying home faggots
all the weary day.

10. To the dwelling came
a footloose girl
with muddy soles,
sunburnt arms,
and hooked nose.
Her name was
Thir [Thrallwoman].

11. More:
in the middle
of the seating area
she sat herself down,
the son of the house
sat beside her.
They talked and whispered,
made their bed,
Thrall and Thir,
lived crowded days.

12. They had children,
settled down and were happy.
I think their names were
Bellower and Byreman,
Coarse and Clegg,

Whoreson and Stinky,
Log and Lumpen,
Layabout and Grizzly,
Bent-Back and Leggy.
They built fences,
spread dung on fields,
tended swine,
guarded goats,
cut peat.

13. Their daughters were
Loggy and Lumpy,
Beefy-Calves and Beaky-Nose,
Bustle-About and Serving-Wench,
Stumpy, Raggedy, and Crane-Shanks.
From them are descended
the thrall families.

14. Rig walked by straight ways,
came to a hall.
The door was
closed, but not locked.
In he went;
a fire burned on the floor,
and a couple sat there,
getting on with their work.

15. The man was shaping
wood for a warp-beam [part of a loom].
His beard was trimmed,
the hair of his forehead docked.
His tunic was tight-fitting.
There was planking on the floor.

16. The woman sat there,
twirled her distaff,
stretched out her arms,
getting ready to weave cloth.
On her head was a coif,
a smock on her breast,
a kerchief round her neck,

brooches at her shoulders.
Grandfather and Grandmother
owned the house.

17. Rig knew how
to give them advice.

18. There was boiled veal,
finest of delicacies.
He rose from the table,
got ready for sleep.

19. More:
in the middle of the bed,
he laid himself down;
on either side,
lay the couple from the homestead.

20. Three nights
he stayed there.
More:
then nine months passed.

21. Grandmother gave birth
to a child.
They sprinkled him with water,
named him Karl.
The woman swaddled
the red and ruddy boy
in linen.
His eyes were restless.

22. He grew and flourished,
broke in oxen,
made a plow,
built houses,
put up barns,
made carts,
and guided the plow.

23. Then they brought home
a girl in a goatskin tunic
with dangling keys.
They wed her to Karl;
her name was Snor [Daughter-in-law].
She put on the bridal veil.
They lived as a couple,
exchanged rings,
spread their blankets,
and set up house.

24. They bore children,
settled down and were happy.
Their names were
Manly and Valiant,
Yeoman, Freeman, and Artisan,
Brawny, Farmer, and Sheaf-Beard,
Neighbor and Landholder,
Jut-Beard and Swain.

25. And others yet
were named thus:
Gentlewoman, Bride, Lady,
Haughty, Sparkling,
Dame, Woman, Wife,
Bashful and Bold.
From them are descended
the families of karls.

26. From there Rig walked by straight ways,
came to a hall
with south-facing entry.
The door was closed,
with a ring as door-handle.

27. He entered.
The floor was strewn with straw.
A couple sat,
gazing into one another's eyes,
Father and Mother
twining fingers.

28. The man of the house sat
and twisted bow-strings,
bent the elm-bow,
made shafts for arrows.
The woman gazed at her arms,
smoothed the linen,
pleated the sleeves.

29. Her head-dress rose high;
she wore a brooch at her breast,
a long, trailing gown
and a blue-colored blouse.
Brighter was her brow,
fairer her breast
whiter her neck
than new-fallen snow.

30. Rig knew how
to give them advice.
More:
he settled himself
in the middle of the seating area,
on either side,
sat the couple
from the homestead.

31. Mother took
an embroidered cloth
of white linen,
covered the table.
She took thin loaves,
white and wheaten,
and covered the cloth.

32. She brought to the table
silver-mounted dishes
heaped with
fish, bacon and
roast fowl.
There was wine in a jug
and mounted goblets.

They drank, they talked;
the day passed.

33. Rig knew how
to give them advice.
He rose then,
prepared for bed.
Three nights in all
he was there.
More:
then he went on his way
in the middle of the paths.
More:
then nine months passed.

34. Mother gave birth to a boy,
wrapped him in silk;
they sprinkled him with water,
called him Jarl [Earl].
Blond of hair, bright of cheek,
he had eyes as piercing
as a young serpent's.

35. Jarl grew up there in the hall:
he learned to
brandish a shield,
put on bowstrings,
bend the elm-bow,
make shafts for arrows,
make javelins quiver,
ride horses,
hunt with dogs,
draw swords,
and swim.

36. Rig came walking, walking
from the grove,
taught him runes,
gave him his own name,
recognized him as his son,
bade him seize

freehold lands,
freehold lands,
Long since settled.

37. More:
he rode from there
through dark wood
and rime-clad hills
till he reached a hall.
He brandished his shield,
shook his spear-shaft,
urged on his horse.
He drew his sword,
and stirred up battle.
He reddened the ground,
felled the doomed,
battled for lands.

38. Alone he ruled eighteen estates,
shared out wealth,
gave to all
gifts and treasures,
slim-ribbed horses.
He distributed rings,
cut armlets asunder.

39. Over wet roads
drove messengers,
arrived at the hall
where Hersir [Chieftain] dwelt.
He had a maiden,
slender-fingered, white-skinned, and wise,
named Erna.

40. They asked for her hand,
drove her back home,
gave her in marriage to Jarl;
she put on the bridal veil.
They settled together
and were happy.
They increased their family

and enjoyed life.

41. Boy was the eldest,
Child was second, then
Young One and Noble,
Heir, Youth,
Kith and Kin
– they learned sports –
Son and Lad
– swimming, and board-games.
Another was named Kinsman.
Youngest was King's Kin.

42. Jarl's children grew up there:
broke horses,
shaped shields,
shaved arrow-shafts smooth,
brandished ash-spears.

43. But young King's Kin knew runes,
the wisdom of ages,
the mysteries of life.
More:
he knew how to save men,
how to dull the sword's edge,
how to still the sea.

44. He learned bird-talk,
and how to subdue fires,
soothe the seas
and assuage sorrows.
He had the strength and endurance
of eight men.

45. He bandied runes
with Rig the Jarl,
dealt with him cunningly
and outdid him in knowledge.
Then he gained his inheritance,
and the right to be called Rig
and understand runes.

46. Young King's Kin rode
through brushwood and forest,
launched a bolt,
silenced the birds.

47. Alone on a branch,
a crow spoke:
"Why, young King's Kin,
must you silence birds?
You could instead
be riding on horses,
slaying an army.

48. "Danr and Danpr
have splendid halls,
a finer inheritance
than you have.
They are very skilled
at sailing a ship,
at handling a sword,
and inflicting wounds."

4. POLITICS IN HARALD FINEHAIR'S NORWAY

Egil's Saga is the biography of Egil Skallagrimsson, poet, Viking, and soldier, who lived from ca 910 until ca 990. The story begins in Norway around the year 890, two generations before Egil's, and ends in Iceland with his death at age 80 in the last decade of the tenth century. The following passage from the early part of the saga is set in Norway and shows how Egil's grandfather and uncles respond to the increasing political ambitions of King Harald Finehair, who unified Norway at the cost of driving many people overseas to lands such as Iceland. The family's difficulties appear against a background of social upheaval caused by the struggle for the unification of Norway.

Source: *Egils saga Skalla-Grímssonar*, ed. Sigurður Nordal, Íslenzk fornrit II (Reykjavík, 1933), pp. 3–27.

1. There was a man called Ulf Bjalfason. His mother was Hallbera, daughter of Ulf the Fearless. She was the sister of Hallbjorn Halftroll from Hrafnista, father of Ketil Trout. Ulf was so big and strong a man that no one could equal him. In his youth, he went on Viking voyages, raiding for plunder.

With him in partnership went Kari of Berle, a well-born man, outstanding in strength and courage. He was a berserk. Ulf and he had a common purse and were the closest of friends.

When they gave up raiding, Kari, now a very rich man, went back to his estate at Berle. He had three children: a son called Eyvind Lamb, another called Olvir Snubnose, and a daughter named Salbjorg, a girl of outstanding beauty. Ulf married her and returned to his estate, well-to-do in both land and money. He held the rank of landholder like his forefathers before him and became a powerful man.

People say that Ulf was a first-rate farmer. He was in the habit of getting up early to oversee his farmhands or his skilled workers and to inspect his cattle and fields. Sometimes he would confer with men who wanted his advice, for he was very wise and always gave good counsel. But every day toward evening he became so ill-tempered that few dared speak to him and he usually fell asleep. Rumor had it that he was a shape-shifter; he was called Kveld-Ulf [Evening Wolf].

Kveld-Ulf and his wife had two sons. The elder was named Thorolf, and the younger was called Grim. Both grew up to be big, strong men like their father. Thorolf was a very handsome and accomplished man. Like his mother's kinsmen he was extremely sociable and open-handed, very competitive, and impetuous in all that he did. He was popular with everyone. Grim was a dark and ugly man, who took after his father in both looks and character. He was very hard working and became a fine craftsman, skilled in both woodwork and ironwork. In winter, he often set off in his boat and went herring fishing with nets. Many of the farmhands went with him.

When Thorolf was twenty, he prepared to go raiding and Kveld-Ulf provided him with a longship. Kari's sons Eyvind and Olvir decided to join the expedition with a large company of men and a second longship. In the summer they went raiding and each of them had a large share of the plunder. For several summers they went on Viking expeditions and spent the winters at home with their fathers. Thorolf brought home many valuable objects and gave them to his mother and father. Those were good times for a man in pursuit of plunder and glory. By then, Kveld-Ulf was very old, but his sons were grown men.

2. At this time, Audbjorn was king of Fjordane [a region of Norway]. Hroald was one of his earls, and Thorir was Hroald's son. Another earl, Atli the Slender, lived at Gaular. His children were Hallstein, Holmstein, Herstein, and Solveig the Fair. One autumn when Gaular was crowded for a sacrificial feast, Olvir Snubnose saw Solveig and paid court to her. After a while, he asked for her hand in marriage, but the earl would not give his consent because of the difference in their ranks. After that, Olvir composed

many love poems about Solveig and became so obsessed with her that he gave up raiding. Only Thorolf and Eyvind Lamb continued going on raids.

3. Harald, son of Halfdan the Black, succeeded his father in Vik [region around Oslo Fjord], in the east. He had sworn not to cut or comb his hair until he became sole king in Norway and so he was nicknamed Harald Matted-Hair. First he fought and defeated the neighboring kings; there are long accounts of this. Next, he took possession of Oppland and from there advanced north toward Trondheim, fighting many battles before he became sole ruler of the Trondelag. After this, he decided to go north into Naumdal against the brothers Herlaug and Hrollaug who were kings there. When the brothers heard of his advance, Herlaug and eleven of his men entered a burial mound which they had spent three years building. The mound was then closed up. King Hrollaug, however, gave up his kingdom and adopted the rank of earl. He submitted to the power of King Harald and relinquished his authority. So King Harald came into possession of Naumdal and Halogaland and appointed men to oversee these provinces.

King Harald set out from Trondheim with a naval force and journeyed south to Møre. There he fought and won a victory against King Hundjof who fell in the battle. Then Harald took possession of North Møre and Raumsdal, but Solvi Cleaver, Hundjof's son, escaped to South Møre where he asked King Arnvid for help, saying,

"Though this trouble has befallen us now, it won't be long till the same thing happens to you. For I think that Harald will get here quickly, as soon as he has subdued and enslaved all the people of North Møre and Raumsdal, as he will. You will have the same choice on your hands as we did: either you can defend your property and freedom by risking all the forces you can raise – and I, for my part, will volunteer my men to help against this tyranny and injustice – or your other choice is to follow the example of the men of Naumdal by going voluntarily into bondage and making yourselves Harald's slaves. My father thought it glorious to die with honor on his own throne, rather than to become the underling of another king in his old age. I think that you and other proud and spirited men will think the same."

Convinced by these persuasive words, the king determined to muster troops and defend his kingdom. He and Solvi formed an alliance and sent word to Audbjorn, king of Fjordane, asking for his support. When the messengers reached him and delivered their message, Audbjorn took counsel with his friends. They all advised him to gather together his forces and join up with the men of Møre as requested. So King Audbjorn had a war-arrow sent around his entire realm as a call to war and he summoned his leading men to him by messenger.

When the messengers reached Kveld-Ulf and gave him the message that the king had sent for him and all his men, he answered thus:

"If there's a raid on Fjordane province, the king will think it my duty to go with him and defend his land. However, I consider it no part of my duty to go north to Møre and fight for the defense of their land. Tell your king as soon as you meet him that Kveld-Ulf will sit out this call to arms at home and won't call up his troops or go off to fight against Harald Matted-Hair. For, in my opinion, Harald has a great deal of good luck while our king hasn't even a handful." The messengers returned to the king and told him how their errand had turned out. Kveld-Ulf stayed at home on his farm.

4. King Audbjorn and his followers journeyed north to Møre and met up with Arnvid and Solvi. Together they had a large force. By then, King Harald had arrived from the north with his army, and they met opposite Solskel Island where a great battle took place with heavy loss of life on both sides. Harald lost two earls, Asgaut and Asbjorn, as well as Grjotgard and Heralaug, the two sons of Earl Hakon of Lade, and many other important men. Both King Arnvid and King Audbjorn from the army of Møre were killed, but Solvi Cleaver escaped and afterwards became a great Viking. He frequently inflicted extensive damage on King Harald's kingdom, thus earning himself the nickname Solvi Cleaver.

After that, King Harald subdued South Møre, but Vemund, Audbjorn's brother, hung onto power in the Fjordane district and made himself king over it. Since it was late in the autumn, King Harald's men advised him not to advance south beyond Stad at that time. King Harald put Earl Rognvald in charge of North and South Møre and Raumsdal. He himself returned north toward Trondheim with a large band of followers.

That same autumn, Atli's sons launched a raid against Olvir Snubnose, intending to kill him. They had so large a force that Olvir could not resist and had to take refuge in flight. He traveled north to Møre where he met King Harald and entered his service. In the autumn, he went north to Trondheim with the king and they developed a close friendship. Olvir stayed with the king for a long time and became his skald.

That winter, Earl Rognvald took the inland route across Eid, and south to Fjordane where he received intelligence about King Vemund's movements. One night when Vemund was at a feast in a place called Naustdal, Earl Rognvald went there, attacked the house and burned the king inside with ninety of his men.

After that, Kari of Berle joined Rognvald with a fully manned longship and they both sailed north to Møre. Rognvald commandeered all the ships that King Vemund had owned along with whatever goods he could get his hands on. Then Kari from Berle continued north to Trondheim where he met King Harald and became his man.

The following spring, King Harald sailed southwards along the coast with a large naval force. He subdued Fjordane and Fjalir and appointed his own men to oversee them, putting Earl Hroald in charge of Fjordane province. After he had taken possession of the districts which had newly come under his sway, King Harald kept a watchful eye on the landed men and prominent farmers and anybody else he suspected might rise up against him. Everyone was given three choices – they could enter his service, leave the country, or face harsh treatment, even loss of life. Indeed, some had their hands or feet cut off.

In every district, King Harald took possession of all the inherited estates and all the land, inhabited and uninhabited. He took over the sea and the lakes as well. All farmers had to become his tenants. All foresters, salt-workers, and hunters both on sea and land had to pay him tribute. Because of this oppression, many fled the country and settled in uninhabited places both to the east in Jämtland and Hälsingland, and in Vestrland [British Isles], the Hebrides, the Dublin shire, Ireland, Normandy in France, Caithness in Scotland, the Orkneys, Shetlands, and Faroes. It's at this time that Iceland was discovered.

5. King Harald remained with his army in Fjordane. He sent representatives throughout the land to contact those who had not joined him but whom he felt should. The king's messengers came to Kveld-Ulf and were well received. They delivered the message that the king wanted Kveld-Ulf to come and meet him.

"He has heard tell," they said, "that you are a distinguished man of fine lineage. You will have the opportunity to receive great honors from the king, for he is keen to surround himself with men who are famed for their strength and valor."

Kveld-Ulf answered that he was old and no longer capable of going out in warships. "It's time for me to stay at home and leave off serving kings," he said.

"Then your son should go to the king," replied the messenger. "He is a big, brave fellow. The king will make him a landed man if he enters his service."

"I don't want to be a landed man while my father is alive," said Grim, "for he will be my overlord as long as he lives."

The messengers returned to the king and told him what Kveld-Ulf had said. The king lost his temper and spoke out in no uncertain terms. He said they must be arrogant men and wondered what they were up to. Olvir Snubnose was standing nearby and begged the king not to be angry. "I will go and see Kveld-Ulf," he said. "He'll want to meet you when he knows how much it means to you."

Then Olvir went to Kveld-Ulf and told him that the king was angry. The only way out, he said, was for either father or son to go to the king who would honor them greatly if they paid homage to him. Olvir spoke at length, saying truly that the king was generous to his men and rewarded them with both wealth and honor. Kveld-Ulf said that he had a presentiment, "that neither my sons nor I will have much luck with this king so I won't go to meet him. But if Thorolf comes home in the summer, he will be easily persuaded to go to the king and become his man. Tell the king that I will maintain friendly relations with him and so will all the men who obey me. And if the king wants me to, I shall keep the same right to rule on his behalf as I had from the last king. We'll see later how the king and I get along."

Olvir returned and told the king that Kveld-Ulf would send one of his sons, but that the one who was better suited was not at home. The king let the matter rest. In summer he went across to Sogn, and in autumn he got ready to travel north to Trondheim.

6. In autumn, Thorolf Kveld-Ulfsson and Eyvind Lamb came home from a Viking voyage and Thorolf went to live with his father. While father and son were talking together, Thorolf asked Kveld-Ulf what Harald's men had wanted. Kveld-Ulf replied that the king had sent word that either he or one of his sons should become the king's man.

"What was your answer?" asked Thorolf.

"I said what was on my mind. I made it clear that I would never enter King Harald's service and that neither would you two if it were up to me. I think that we'll all end up dead because of that king."

"It won't go that way at all," said Thorolf. "I have high hopes of earning great honor from him, so I'm determined to go and meet the king and become his man. I know for certain that his court is filled with men of the greatest valor and I am really keen to join that company if they will have me, for those men are better off than anyone else in this land. I have heard that the king is very liberal with gifts of money to his men and that he's quick to bestow advancement and power on those who seem fit for it. I'm told also that those who turn their backs on him and refuse his friendship never amount to anything. Some end up fleeing the country, and others become hired workmen. You are a wise and ambitious man, father, and I'm astonished that you are not delighted to accept the honor the king has offered you. And if you think you can foresee that this king will be our enemy and bring us misfortune, why didn't you fight against him alongside the king you used to serve? I don't think there's any honor at all in being neither his friend nor his enemy."

"My predictions came true," replied Kveld-Ulf. "Those who fought Harald Matted-Hair north in Møre did not have a successful campaign. Likewise you can be sure that Harald will inflict great harm on my kin. But you'll have to make up your own mind, Thorolf. I am quite confident that if you join up with Harald's retainers you will prove yourself up to the mark and equal to any test of courage. Just take care not to be too headstrong, and don't compete with men greater than yourself, though you mustn't give in to them either."

When Thorolf was ready to leave, Kveld-Ulf saw him to his ship. He embraced him, and wished him a fond farewell and a safe reunion.

7. At Torgar in Halogaland there lived a man called Bjorgolf, a landed man, powerful and rich. By descent, he was half mountain-giant, as was clear from his strength and size. He had a son just like himself, Brynjolf by name. Bjorgolf was old and his wife was dead. He had transferred control of all his affairs to his son and had sought a wife for him. Brynjolf married Helga, daughter of Ketil Trout from Hrafnista. They had a son named Bard who, from an early age, was well-built and handsome and developed into a man of outstanding accomplishments.

One autumn Bjorgolf and his son held a feast at Torgar. Many people came, but the father and son were the most distinguished men present. Every evening, as was the custom, people were paired by lot for drinking. At the feast there was a man called Hogni who farmed on Leka. He was very rich, handsome, and clever, but he was of humble birth, a self-made man. He had a very beautiful daughter called Hildirid who drew the lot to sit beside Bjorgolf. They found plenty to talk about in the course of the evening and he thought her an attractive girl. Shortly afterwards, the feast ended.

That same autumn, old Bjorgolf and thirty of his men set sail from home in a ship he owned. He arrived at Leka and went up to the house with twenty men while the other ten guarded the ship. When they reached the farm, Hogni came out to meet him and welcomed him warmly. He invited Bjorgolf and his crew to stay there. Bjorgolf accepted and they went into the living room. When they had taken off their outdoor clothes and put on tunics, Hogni had a large vessel of ale brought in and Hildirid the farmer's daughter served the guests.

Bjorgolf called Hogni to him and said, "I'm here to take your daughter home with me and I want to have an informal wedding with her right now."

Hogni could see no other choice than to let Bjorgolf do what he wanted. So Bjorgolf bought her for an ounce of gold and they went to bed together. Then Bjorgolf took Hildirid home to Torgar. Brynjolf had nothing good to say about the business.

Bjorgolf and Hildirid had two sons, Harek and Hrœrek. Then Bjorgolf died and, no sooner was he carried out for burial, than Brynjolf sent Hildirid and her sons on their way. She went back to her father on Leka and her sons were brought up there. They were handsome men, small in stature and intelligent like their mother's kin. Everyone referred to them as the Hildiridarsons. Brynjolf had little regard for them and allowed them nothing from their father's inheritance, but Hildirid was Hogni's heir, so she and her sons inherited his property. They dwelt at Leka and prospered there. Bard Brynjolfson was around the same age as the Hildiridarsons. For years, Brynjolf and his father Bjorgolf had held the right to travel among the Lapps and levy tribute from them.

North, in Halogaland, there is a fjord called Vefsnfjord and in this fjord lies Alost, a large, fertile island on which there is a farm called Sandness. There lived Sigurd, the richest man in that part of the north. He was a landed man of shrewd intelligence. His daughter, Sigrid, was regarded as the best match in Halogaland as she was an only child and would be her father's heir.

Bard Brynjolfson set off from home with a ship and thirty men. He traveled north to Alost and paid a visit to Sigurd at Sandness. There he made a formal proposal asking for Sigrid's hand in marriage. His suit was well received and Bard was promised the girl. The wedding was arranged for the following summer when Bard was to go north again to fetch his bride.

8. That summer king Harald had sent word to the chief men of Halogaland, summoning to his presence all those who had not yet been to meet him. Brynjolf made up his mind to go and his son Bard went with him. In the autumn, they traveled south to Trondheim where they met the king, who gave them a warm welcome and made Brynjolf a landed man. The king granted him great revenues in addition to those he already had. He gave him the right to travel and trade among the Lapps as well as the stewardship of the mountain areas. Afterwards, Brynjolf went home to his estate, but Bard remained behind and became one of the king's retainers.

Of all his retainers, the king valued his skalds most highly, and they were assigned a place of honor on the second high seat. Closest to the center of the seat sat Audun the Plagiarist, who was the oldest among them and had been skald to Halfdan the Black, King Harald's father. Next to him sat Thorbjorn Hornklofi and his neighbor was Olvir Snubnose. Bard was assigned the place next to Olvir and came to be known as Bard the White or Bard the Strong. Everyone thought well of him and he and Olvir Snubnose became great friends.

That same autumn, Thorolf Kveld-Ulfsson and Eyvind Lamb, Kari of Berle's son, visited King Harald and got a warm welcome. They came in a fast well-manned ship of twenty benches [forty oars] – a ship they had used on Viking raids. They and their followers were assigned places in the guest hall.

They stayed there until they thought it was time to meet the king. Kari of Berle and Olvir Snubnose went with them. They greeted the king and Olvir Snubnose informed him that Kveld-Ulf's son had arrived:

"I told you in the summer that Kveld-Ulf would send him to you," said Olvir. "Kveld-Ulf is a man of his word and you can be sure that he will be an excellent friend to you now that he has sent his son here to enter your service – and what a fine-looking man Thorolf is, as you can see. We all join Kveld-Ulf in asking you to treat Thorolf honorably and give him an important position."

The king replied favorably to this speech and said that he would do what they asked, "as long as I find that Thorolf has the manly qualities his brave appearance suggests."

So Thorolf became one of the king's retainers and joined his household, while Kari of Berle and Eyvind Lamb his son went south in the ship that Thorolf had brought north. After that, Kari returned to his estate and so did Eyvind. Thorolf stayed behind with the king who assigned him a seat between Olvir Snubnose and Bard. The three of them became very close friends. It was the general opinion that Thorolf and Bard were evenly matched for good looks, strength, stature, and abilities, and both of them were now on the friendliest terms with the king.

When winter was over and summer had arrived, Bard asked the king for permission to go and fetch the bride who had been promised to him the previous summer. As soon as the king knew that Bard had urgent business, he allowed him to go home. When he had received this permission, Bard asked Thorolf to travel north with him, declaring that he would meet many noble relatives whom he had never met before or even been aware of. Thorolf thought this was a good idea, so they got the king's consent and outfitted themselves for the journey with a fine ship and crew. Once their preparations had been made, they went on their way.

They arrived at Torgar where they sent a message to Sigurd that Bard would come north to fulfill the promises they had made the previous summer. Sigurd replied that he would honor all their agreements and a date was set for the wedding. Bard and his men were to go to Sandness for the marriage. At the appointed time, Brynjolf and Bard set out and with them went many important people, their relatives by birth and marriage. As Bard had predicted, Thorolf met many relations whom he had not known before. They traveled until they reached Sandness where a most splendid feast was held. When the feast was over, Bard went home with his wife and both he and Thorolf stayed there that summer. In autumn, they went south to join the king and passed another winter with him.

That winter, Brynjolf died. When Bard found out that he had come into his inheritance, he asked leave to go home and the king granted it. Before they parted, Bard was made a landed man, as his father had been, and the king granted him the rights to all the revenues that Brynjolf had enjoyed. Bard went home to his estates and soon became a great leader. Meanwhile the Hildiridarsons received no more of the inheritance than they had got before. Bard and his wife had a son named Grim. Thorolf remained with the king and enjoyed great honors.

9. King Harald assembled a great naval force, gathering together men and ships from far and wide. He left Trondheim and traveled south along the coast. He had found out that a great army had been gathered from Agder, Rogaland, and Hordaland as well as from many other areas of the country, including the inland regions and Vik in the east. Many men of consequence had assembled there intending to defend their land against King Harald. The king headed south with his army, he himself sailing in a large ship manned by his own retainers. In the prow stood Thorolf Kveld-Ulfsson and Bard the White along with Olvir Snubnose and Eyvind Lamb, the sons of Kari of Berle. Behind them in the fore part of the ship were twelve of the king's berserks. The battle took place in the south at Hafrsfjord in Rogaland [ca 872]. It was the most terrible battle King Harald had ever fought and there was great loss of life on both sides.

The king placed his ship in a forward position and that's where the battle was fiercest. It ended in victory for King Harald. Thorir Long Chin, king of Agder, was killed there but Kjotvi the Wealthy fled along with all of his surviving followers who had not surrendered after the battle. When King Harald's troops were counted, many were dead and many were seriously injured. Thorolf was badly wounded and Bard's injuries were even worse. No one on the king's ship forward of the sail was unhurt, except for the berserks, whom weapons did not penetrate.

Then the king had the wounds of his men bound up. He thanked them for their courage and gave them gifts, bestowing most praise on those he thought most deserving and promising to increase their honor. In particular, he mentioned the steersmen, and then the men in the prows and the others stationed forward in the ships. This was the last battle King Harald fought in his own lands. After that he met with no resistance and gained control of the entire country.

The king ordered treatment for those of his men who seemed likely to live and provided burial for the dead, according to the custom of the time.

Both Thorolf and Bard lay wounded, but while Thorolf's wounds began to heal, Bard's became life-threatening. So he asked the king to come to him.

"If I die of these wounds," he said, "then I'd like your permission to dispose of my inheritance myself." When the king had agreed, Bard continued, "I want Thorolf, my companion and kinsman, to inherit everything I own, both land and money. I also want him to have my wife and to bring up my son, because I trust him in these matters more than any other man." He settled these arrangements according to the laws and with the king's leave. Then Bard died. He was prepared for burial and was greatly mourned.

5. HOSKULD BUYS A SLAVE

The Saga of the People of Laxdale *traces the fortunes of the settlers in this region of northwest Iceland and their descendants from the late ninth to the early eleventh century. In this episode, Hoskuld Dala-Kollsson – a godi, or chieftain, in the district – is away from home, in Norway, and casually buys an Irish slave, Melkorka, and takes her as his concubine.*

Source: *Laxdæla saga*, ed. Einar Ól. Sveinsson, Íslenzk fornrit V (Reykjavík, 1934), pp. 22–25.

12. Early in the summer, King Hakon [King Hakon I, the Good, of Norway, ca 920–961] went on a naval expedition east to the Brenney Isles. There, as required by law, an assembly was held every third summer to confirm the peace throughout the land. These meetings were arranged among kings in order to settle those disputes which only they could judge. Attending the assembly was seen as a holiday because men came to it from almost every country in the known world. Hoskuld wanted to attend the assembly since he had not visited the king that winter, so he too launched his ship.

A fair was held at the same time, and the assembly was very crowded. There was plenty of entertainment – drinking, games, and all sorts of amusements – but nothing of particular importance took place. Hoskuld met many of his relatives from Denmark there.

One day, when Hoskuld was on his way to enjoy himself with some companions, he noticed a splendid tent, pitched at a distance from the other booths. Hoskuld walked over and entered the tent; there, in front of him, sat a well-dressed man wearing a Russian hat. Hoskuld asked his name, and he replied that he was called Gilli. "But many people recognize me by my nickname," he said. "I'm called Gilli the Russian."

Hoskuld replied that he had often heard him spoken of as the wealthiest man who had ever belonged to the guild of merchants. "I expect you can sell us anything we want to buy," said Hoskuld.

Gilli asked what he and his companions had in mind. Hoskuld replied that he wanted to buy a slave-woman, "if you have any to sell, that is."

"You thought you'd catch me out by asking for something you didn't expect me to have," replied Gilli. "But whether you're right or not is another matter."

Hoskuld noticed that there was a curtain drawn across the booth, and when Gilli raised the curtain Hoskuld saw twelve women sitting behind it. Gilli invited Hoskuld to go in and take a look, to see if he wanted to buy one of these women. Hoskuld did so. The women were sitting in a row across the booth and Hoskuld scrutinized them carefully. He noticed that one woman was sitting on her own, close to the edge of the tent. She was poorly dressed, but, from what he could see of her, Hoskuld thought she was beautiful.

"How much would you want for this woman if I decided to buy her?" asked Hoskuld. "She would cost you three marks of silver," answered Gilli.

"I would say you're charging rather a high price for this servant," said Hoskuld. "You could get three for that price."

"You're right," answered Gilli. "I do value her more highly than the rest. Choose one of the eleven others and you can have her for a mark of silver; I'll hang on to this one."

"First I'll have to figure out how much silver I have in this purse at my belt," said Hoskuld. He asked Gilli to fetch his scales while he looked into his purse.

"I'm not going to defraud you, Hoskuld," said Gilli. "This woman has a defect, and I want you to know about it before we strike a bargain."

Hoskuld asked what it was. "The woman is mute," replied Gilli. "I've tried many different ways of making her speak, but I've never managed to get a word out of her. It's my firm belief that she doesn't know how to speak."

"Bring out your scales," said Hoskuld, "and let's see how much this purse of mine weighs." Gilli did so; he weighed the silver and the weight came to three marks.

"Then we've got a deal," said Hoskuld. "You take the money, and I'll take the woman. I must say that you have behaved honorably in this affair, because you didn't try to cheat me at all."

Then Hoskuld returned to his booth. That night he slept with the slave-woman. Next morning when it was time to get dressed, Hoskuld said, "Gilli the Rich didn't give you very much in the way of clothing, but I dare say it was more of a problem for him to clothe twelve women than for me to clothe one."

Then Hoskuld opened a chest and took out some fine clothing, which he gave to her. Everyone agreed that she looked good in the clothes. When the chieftains had concluded the business that the law demanded, the assembly came to an end. Then Hoskuld went to see King Hakon and addressed him with respect, as was fitting. The king looked at him and said, "We would have accepted your greeting, Hoskuld, even if you had delivered it a little sooner, but we shall accept it even now."

6. HOW THE HERSIR ERLING TREATED HIS SLAVES

Erling Skjalgsson was a powerful Norwegian landowner and political operator in the reigns of Olaf Tryggvason and Olaf Haraldsson [Saint Olaf]. His life and political career ended in 1028 when he was captured and killed by Olaf Haraldsson's men. From Saint Olaf's Saga. *A hersir was a local chieftain, or lord.*

Source: Snorri Sturluson, *Óláfs saga helga*, in *Heimskringla*, ed. Bjarni Aðalbjarnarson, Íslenzk fornrit XXVI–XXVIII (Reykjavík, 2002), vol. 2, p. 30.

23. In his household, Erling always had thirty slaves as well as other servants. He allotted day work to his slaves, but allowed time later on to anyone who wanted to work for himself in the twilight or at night. He gave them arable land to sow with corn for their own use and to produce crops for profit. He set a price for freedom on each of them. Many freed themselves in one or two years, and all who were at all prosperous gained their freedom in three years.

With this money, Erling bought other slaves. He put some of his freed slaves to work in the herring fishery and some to other ways of making a living. Some cleared forest land and set up their homes there. He helped all of them to get on in life.

CHAPTER THREE

A GLIMPSE OF NINTH-CENTURY
SCANDINAVIA

One of the most important ninth-century documents relating to Scandinavia is Rimbert's Life of the "Apostle of the North," *St. Anskar (d. 865). Anskar conducted missionary work in Denmark and Sweden, and became the first Archbishop of Hamburg-Bremen in 857. His hagiographer, Rimbert (d. 888), is a shadowy figure about whom little is known, but he was a pupil of Anskar and probably accompanied him on some of his travels. His* Life of Anskar *was written soon after Anskar's death and, although it is concerned principally with early missions to the Scandinavian peoples, it provides valuable insights into Scandinavian society that are almost unparalleled in any other ninth-century text.*

7. THE LIFE OF ANSKAR

Source: trans. C.H. Robinson, *Anskar: The Apostle of the North, 801–865, translated from the Vita Anskarii by Bishop Rimbert his fellow missionary and successor* (London, 1921); revised by P.E. Dutton, *Carolingian Civilization*, 2nd ed. (Peterborough: Broadview Press, 2004), pp. 407–40.

7. After this it happened that a king named Harald [Klak], who ruled over some of the Danes, was assailed by hatred and malignity and was driven from his kingdom by the other kings of the same province. He came to his serene majesty the emperor Louis [the Pious; d. 840] and asked to be thought worthy to receive his help so that he might be able to regain his kingdom. While the emperor kept him at his court [in Ingelheim] he urged him, by personal persuasion and through the agency of others, to accept the Christian faith, because there would then be a more intimate friendship between them and a Christian people would more readily come to his aid and to the aid of his friends if both peoples were worshippers of the same God. At length, by the assistance of divine grace, he brought about his conversion, and when he had been sprinkled with the holy water of baptism he himself received him from the sacred font and adopted him as his son [in 826].

When, after that, [Louis] desired to send [Harald] back to his own land in order that he might, by his assistance, seek to recover his dominions, he began to make diligent inquiry to find a holy and devoted man who could go and stay with him, and who might strengthen him and his people and, by teaching the doctrine of salvation, might induce them to receive the faith of the Lord. At a public gathering of his chief men at which their priests and other good men were present, the emperor raised this matter and earnestly begged all of them to find someone who might volunteer for this difficult and honorable task. When they refused and said that they knew of no one who was possessed of so great a devotion as to be willing to undertake this dangerous journey for the name of Christ, Wala, who was at that time [from 826] the much respected abbot of our monastery, said to the emperor that he knew a monk in his monastery who burned with zeal for true religion and was eager to endure suffering for the name of God. He declared, however, that he did not know whether he would be willing to undertake this journey. Why say more? At the king's command Anskar was summoned to the palace and the abbot explained to him everything that had been done and explained the reason for his being summoned. He replied that as an obedient monk he was ready to serve God in all things that were commanded of him. He was then led into the presence of the emperor, who asked him whether on God's behalf and for the sake of preaching the Gospel among the Danish peoples, he would become the companion of Harald, whereupon he replied that he was entirely willing. When the abbot had further stated that he would by no means impose this upon him as a command, but if of his own free will he chose to do it he would be pleased and would give him his authoritative consent. He replied that he nonetheless chose the task and desired by all means to carry it through.

... The two monks [Anskar and Autbert, who had volunteered to accompany him] were subsequently brought before the king, who was gratified by their willingness and desire to undertake this task and he gave them whatever was necessary for the performance of their ministerial functions, including writing cases, tents and other things that would be helpful and which seemed likely to be needed on their great journey. He bade them go with Harald and commanded them to devote the utmost care to his profession of faith and by their godly exhortations to confirm in the faith both Harald and the companions who had been baptized together with him, for fear lest at the instigation of the devil they should return to their former errors, and at the same time by their preaching to urge others to accept the Christian religion.

Having then been dismissed by the emperor they had none to render them any menial service, as no one in the abbot's household would go with them of his own accord and he would compel no one to go against his will. Harald, to whom they had been committed, was as yet ignorant and untaught in the faith and was unaware how God's servants ought to behave. Moreover, his companions, who had been but recently converted and had been trained in a very different faith, paid them little attention. Having started then with considerable difficulty they arrived at Cologne. At that time there was a venerable bishop there named Hadebald. He had compassion for their needs and presented them with a good boat in which they might place their possessions and in which there were two cabins that had been suitably prepared for them. When Harald saw the boat he decided to remain with them in it, so that he and they could each have a cabin. This tended to promote an increase of friendship and good will between them; his companions also, from this time forward, paid careful attention to their wants.

On leaving the boat they passed through Dorestad and, crossing the neighboring territory of the Frisians, came to the Danish border. As King Harald could not for the time being obtain peaceful possession of his kingdom, the emperor gave him a place beyond the Elbe River so that if it were necessary he might halt there.

8. Accordingly the servants of God, who were with him and who were stationed at one time among the Christians and at other times among the pagans, began to apply themselves to the word of God; and those whom they could influence they directed into the way of truth, so that many were converted to the faith by their example and teaching, and the number of those who should be saved in the Lord increased daily. They themselves, being

inspired by divine love, in order to spread their holy religion, made diligent search for boys whom they might endeavor to educate for the service of God. Harald also gave some of his own household to be educated by them; and so it came about that in a short time they established a school for twelve or more boys. Others they took as servants or helpers, and their reputation and the religion which they preached in God's name were spread abroad. After they had spent two years or more in this good work brother Autbert was overcome with a serious illness. For this reason he was taken to Corvey where, as his weakness increased day by day, at Easter time (as it had been revealed to him earlier by the Lord) he died, passing away happily, as we believe.

9. Meanwhile it happened that Swedish ambassadors had come to the Emperor Louis, and, among other matters which they had been ordered to bring to the attention of the emperor, they informed him that there were many belonging to their people who desired to embrace the Christian religion and that their king so far favored this suggestion that he would permit God's priests to reside there, provided that they might be deemed worthy of such a favor and that the emperor would send them suitable preachers. When the God-fearing emperor heard this he was greatly delighted, and a second time he endeavored to find men whom he might send into those districts, who might discover whether this people was prepared to accept the faith, as the ambassadors had assured him, and might begin to inculcate the observance of the Christian religion. So it came about that his serene majesty began once again to discuss the matter with your abbot and asked him whether by chance he could find one of his monks who, for the name of Christ, was willing to go into those parts; or who would go and stay with Harald while God's servant Anskar, who was with him, undertook this mission. Thus it was that Anskar was summoned by royal command to the palace, and was told that he should not even stop to shave himself before coming into the royal presence....

10. Then, by the good providence of God, the venerable abbot [Wala] found for him among your fraternity a companion, namely the prior Witmar, who was both worthy and willing to undertake this great task. He further arranged that the good father Gislemar, a man approved by faith and good works, and by his fervent zeal for God, should stay with Harald. Anskar then undertook the mission committed to him by the emperor, who desired that he should go to the Swedes and discover whether that people was prepared to accept the faith as their messengers had declared. How great and serious were the calamities which he suffered while engaged in this mission, father Witmar, who himself shared them, can best tell. It may suffice for me to say that while they were in the midst of their journey they fell into the hands of pirates. The merchants with whom they were traveling defended themselves

vigorously and for a time successfully, but eventually they were conquered and overcome by the pirates, who took from them their ships and all that they possessed, while they themselves barely escaped on foot to land. They lost then the royal gifts which they should have delivered there, together with all their other possessions, save only what they were able to take and carry away with them as they left the ship. They were plundered, moreover, of nearly forty books which they had accumulated for the service of God. When this happened some were disposed to turn and go back, but no argument could divert God's servant from the journey which he had undertaken. On the contrary, he submitted everything that might happen to him to God's will and was by no means disposed to return until, with God's help, he could ascertain whether he would be allowed to preach the Gospel in those parts.

11. With great difficulty they accomplished their long journey on foot, traversing also the intervening seas, where it was possible, by ship, and eventually arrived at the Swedish port called Birka. They were kindly received in that place by the king, who was called Biorn [II], whose messengers had informed him of the reason for which they had come. When he understood the object of their mission and had discussed the matter with his men, with the approval and consent of all, he granted them permission to remain there and to preach the Gospel of Christ and offered liberty to any who desired it to accept their teaching.

Accordingly the servants of God, when they saw that matters had turned out propitiously as they had desired, began eagerly to preach the word of salvation to the people of that place. There were many who were well disposed toward their mission and who willingly listened to the teaching of the Lord. There were also many Christians who were held captive among them, and who rejoiced that now at last they were able to participate in the divine mysteries. It was thus made clear that everything was as their messengers had declared to the emperor, and some of them desired earnestly to receive the grace of baptism. These included the prefect of this town named Herigar, who was a counselor of the king and much loved by him. He received the gift of holy baptism and was strengthened in the Catholic faith. A little later he built a church on his own ancestral property and served God with the utmost devotion. Several remarkable deeds were accomplished by this man who afforded many proofs of his invincible faith, as we shall make clear in the following narrative [chapter 19].

12. When the servants of God had spent another half year with them and had attained the object of their mission they returned to the emperor and took with them letters written by the king himself in characters fashioned after the Swedish custom [possibly in runes]. They were received with great honor and good will by the emperor, to whom they narrated all that the Lord

had wrought by them and how in those parts the door of faith was opened by which these peoples were bidden to enter. When the most pious emperor heard this, he rejoiced greatly. And as he recalled the beginning which had been made in establishing the worship of God among the Danes, he rendered praise and thanks to Almighty God, and, being inflamed with zeal for the faith, he began to inquire by what means he might establish a bishop's see in the north within the limits of his own empire, from which the bishop who should be stationed there might make frequent journeys to the northern regions for the sake of preaching the Gospel and from which all these barbarous people might easily and profitably receive the sacraments of the divine mystery. As he was pursuing this matter with anxious care he learned from information provided by some of his trusty companions, that when his father, the emperor Charles, of glorious memory, had subdued the whole of Saxony by the sword and had subjected it to the yoke of Christ, he divided it into dioceses, but did not commit to any bishop the furthest part of this province which lay beyond the Elbe, but decided that it should be reserved in order that he might establish there an archiepiscopal see from which, with the Lord's help, the Christian faith might successively spread to the peoples that lay beyond. He, accordingly, caused the first church that was built there to be consecrated by a Gallic bishop named Amalhar [of Trier]. Later on he specially committed the care of this parish to a priest named Heridac, as he did not wish that the neighboring bishops should have any authority over this place. He had further arranged to have this priest consecrated as a bishop, but his speedy departure from this life prevented this being done.

After the death of this memorable emperor, his son Louis, who was placed on his father's throne, acting on the suggestion of others, divided into two that part of the province which lies beyond the Elbe and entrusted it, for the time being, to two neighboring bishops for he paid no attention to the arrangement which his father had made in regard to this matter, or, possibly, he was altogether ignorant of it. When the time came that the faith of Christ began, by God's grace, to bear fruit in the lands of the Danes and Swedes and his father's wish became known to him, he was unwilling that this wish should remain unaccomplished and, acting with the approval of the bishops and a well attended synod, he established an archiepiscopal see in the town of Hamburg, which is situated in the farthest part of Saxony beyond the Elbe. He desired that the whole church of the Nordalbingia should be subject to this archbishopric and that it should possess the power of appointing bishops and priests who for the name of Christ might go out into these districts.

To this see, therefore, the emperor caused the holy Anskar, our lord and father, to be consecrated as archbishop by the hands of Drogo, the bishop of Metz and at that time principal chaplain at the imperial court. He was assisted by Ebbo, the archbishop of Rheims, Hetti of Trier, and Otgar of Mainz, while many other bishops who had gathered for the imperial assembly were present. The bishops Helmgaud and Willerick, from whom Anskar took over the above-mentioned parts of this ecclesiastical district, approved and took part in his consecration.

Inasmuch as this diocese was situated in dangerous regions and it was to be feared that it might come to an end in consequence of the savagery of the barbarians by which it was threatened, and because its area was small, the emperor handed over to his representatives a monastery in Gaul, called Turholt, to be always at its service.

13. In order that these arrangements should be permanently established the emperor sent Anskar to the apostolic see and, by his messengers the venerable bishops Bernold and Ratold and the illustrious count Gerold, he caused the whole matter to be made known to Pope Gregory [IV] so that it might receive his confirmation. The pope confirmed this not only by an authoritative decree, but also by the gift of the pallium in accordance with the custom of his predecessors and he appointed him [in 834] as his legate for the time being among all the neighboring races of the Swedes and Danes [and] also the Slavs and the other races that inhabited the regions of the north, so that he might share authority with Ebbo, the archbishop of Rheims, to whom he had before entrusted the same office. At the tomb of the holy apostle Peter he publicly committed to him authority to evangelize. And, for fear lest anything that he had done should prove ineffectual in time to come, he smote with his curse any who should resist, or contradict, or in any way attempt to interfere with the holy intentions of the emperor and committed such a one to everlasting vengeance and the companionship of devils.

As we have already said, the same office of legate had before been entrusted by Pope Paschal [I, 817–824] to Ebbo, the archbishop of Rheims. Ebbo himself, inspired by the Spirit of God, burned with eager desire to draw to the Christian fold the non-Christian races and especially the Danes whom he had often seen at the palace and who, as he grieved to see, had been led astray by the wiles of the devil. In order to promote their salvation he longed to sacrifice himself and all that he possessed. The emperor had given him a place situated beyond the Elbe, which was called Welanao, so that whenever he went into those parts he might have a place in which to stay. Accordingly he frequently went to this place and distributed much money in the northern districts in order that he might win the souls of the people; and he attached many to the Christian religion and strengthened them in the Catholic faith.

14. After the consecration of the holy Anskar, our Lord and father, those who shared the office of legate conferred together and decided that it was necessary that an assistant bishop should be consecrated who might exercise

the episcopal office among the Swedes, inasmuch as the chief bishop could not be expected to be present so far away and Anskar himself could not be in both places. With the consent, then, and approval of the emperor, the venerable Ebbo sent to Sweden a relation of his own named Gautbert, who had been chosen for this work and had been given the honorable rank of a bishop. He supplied him in abundance with all that was wanted for his ecclesiastical office and for his necessary expenditure at his own cost and that of the emperor. Having himself undertaken, by apostolic authority, the office of an evangelist, he appointed Gautbert to act as legate on his behalf among the Swedes. To him, too, the emperor, at the suggestion of the same bishop Ebbo, gave the monastery which he had himself built at Welanao, to serve as a place of refuge, in order that the performance of his task might be rendered permanent and secure. This Gautbert, who at his consecration received the honored name of the apostle Simon, went to Sweden, and was honorably received by the king [Biorn II] and the people; and he began, amidst general good will and approval, to build a church there and to preach the faith of the Gospel and there was great rejoicing among the Christians who were living there and the number of those who believed increased daily.

15. Meanwhile our lord and master diligently executed his office in the diocese that had been committed to him and in the country of the Danes and by the example of his good life he incited many to embrace the faith. He began also to buy Danish and Slav boys and to redeem some from captivity so that he might train them for God's service. Of these he kept some with him, while others he sent to be trained at the monastery of Turholt. There were also with him here belonging to your order some of our fathers and teachers, as a result of whose teaching and instructions the divine religion has increased among us.

16. While these events, which brought praise and honor to God, were taking place in both directions, pirates suddenly arrived and surrounded the town of Hamburg. As this happened suddenly and unexpectedly, there was no time to collect the people in the villages; moreover, the count who at this time was prefect of the place, namely, the illustrious Bernhar, was absent. The bishop who was there and those who remained in the city and its suburbs, when the first news of their coming arrived, desired to hold the place until further help might reach them. But when the country people put pressure upon him and the town was already besieged, he perceived that resistance was impossible and accordingly made preparations to carry away the sacred relics. As for himself, when his clergy had been scattered and had fled in various directions, he with difficulty escaped without even a cloak to cover his body. The people left the town and wandered here and there; and, while most fled, some were caught and of these the greater part was killed.

The enemy then seized the town and plundered it and its immediate neighborhood. They had come in the evening and they remained that night and the next day and night. When everything had been burned and destroyed they departed. The church there, which had been built in a wonderful manner under the guidance of the bishop, and the monastery, which was also of marvelous construction, were reduced to ashes. The bible which the emperor had given to our father, and which was beautifully transcribed, together with many other books, was lost in the fire. Everything which was used in the services of the church and all his treasures and possessions were lost by pillage or by fire during the enemy attack. This attack left him practically naked as nothing had previously been taken away, nor was anything removed at the time except that which each fugitive was able to carry away. By none of these things was our holy father distressed, nor did he sin with his lips, but when in a moment of time he lost almost everything that he had been able to gather together or to collect for purposes of building, he repeated again and again the words of Job: "The Lord gave, the Lord has taken away; the Lord's will has been done. Blessed be the name of the Lord."

17. After these occurrences the bishop continued with his people in their distress and misfortune, while the brothers belonging to his order traversed various districts and wandered here and there taking with them the holy relics; and nowhere did they find rest, owing to the devices of the wicked one.

It happened, too, at this time, at the instigation of the devil, that the Swedish people were inflamed with zeal and fury, and began by insidious means to persecute Bishop Gautbert. Thus it came about that some of the people, moved by a common impulse, made a sudden attack upon the house in which he was staying with the object of destroying it; and in their hatred of the Christian name they killed Nithard [not the historian] and made him, in our opinion, a true martyr. Gautbert himself and those of his companions who were present they bound and, after plundering everything that they could find in their house, they drove them from their territory with insults and abuse. This was not done by command of the king, but was brought about by a plot devised by the people.

18. The long suffering mercy of God did not allow this crime to go unavenged, but almost all who were present were soon afterwards punished, though in different ways. Concerning these much might be said, but, lest we weary our readers, we mention the case of a single individual in order that the destruction which overtook him may show how the rest were also punished and their crimes avenged. In that country there was a certain influential man whose son had joined with the others in this conspiracy and who had collected in his father's house the booty that he had captured at that place. Thereafter his possessions began to decrease and he began to lose his flocks

and his household possessions. The son himself was stricken by divine vengeance and died and, after a brief interval, his wife, his son, and his daughter also died. When the father saw that he had become bereft of all that he had possessed with the exception of one little son, he began, in his misery, to fear the anger of the gods and to imagine that he was suffering all these calamities because he had offended some god. Thereupon, following the local custom, he consulted a soothsayer and asked him to find out by the casting of lots which god he had offended and to explain how he might appease him. After performing all the customary ceremonies, the soothsayer said that all their gods were well disposed toward him, but that the God of the Christians was much incensed against him. "Christ," he said, "has ruined you. It is because there is something hidden in your house which had been consecrated to him that all the evils that you have suffered have come upon you; nor can you be freed from them as long as this remains in your house." On hearing this he considered anxiously what it could be and he remembered that his son had brought to his house as part of that booty a certain book. On this account he was stricken with horror and fear and, because there was no priest at hand, he did not know what to do with this book and, as he dared not keep it any longer in his house, he at length devised a plan and showed the book openly to the people who were in the same hamlet and told them what he had suffered. When they all said that they did not know how to advise him in regard to this matter and were afraid to receive or keep anything of the kind in their houses, he feared greatly to retain it in his own house, and [so] he fastened it up carefully and tied it to a fence with a notice attached stating that whoever wished might take it. For the offense that he had committed he promised also to make voluntary amends to the Lord Jesus Christ. One of the Christians took the book thence and carried it to his own house. This we ascertained from his own statement. Later on he showed such faith and devotion that when with us he learned to say the psalms without reading them. In like manner were the rest punished either by death or plague, or by the loss of their property, and it was made manifest to all that they had received due punishment from our Lord Jesus Christ because they had presumed to outrage and plunder God's holy bishop and his companions.

19. For nearly seven years afterwards there was no priest in this place [in Sweden], and for this reason our lord and pastor Anskar was afflicted with great sorrow. As he could not bear that the Christian religion which had begun to be established there should perish and because he grieved greatly for his dear son Herigar, whom we have already mentioned, he sent a hermit named Ardgar into those parts and specially directed him to attach himself to Herigar. On his arrival he was courteously received by Herigar and his presence brought great joy to the Christians who were there. These began again

to do as they had done before, namely to search diligently for the things of God and to observe with a willing mind the customs of the Christian religion. None of the unbelievers was able to withstand his preaching, because they remembered with fear the punishment that had come upon those who had expelled God's servants from this place. On the suggestion of Herigar and with the command and permission of the king who was then reigning, he began to celebrate the divine mysteries in public.

This most faithful man [Herigar] endured many reproaches at the hands of unbelievers during the time when there was no priest present there, but by the help of divine grace and as a result of his prayers the true faith was proclaimed and accompanied by signs from heaven. Some of these, in accordance with our promise, we have added to our narrative in order that his invincible fidelity may be made manifest.

On one occasion he himself was sitting in an assembly of people, a stage having been arranged for a council on an open plain. In the course of a general discussion some praised their own gods, by whose favor they had secured great prosperity, while others heaped reproaches upon him because he alone, by accepting a worthless creed, had separated himself from all of them. He then, being fervent in spirit, is said to have replied, "If there be such great uncertainty in regard to the divine majesty, which nevertheless ought not to be called into doubt by anyone, let us prove by miracles who is the more powerful, the many beings whom you call your gods or my one Almighty Lord Jesus Christ. Look, rain is at hand," – a shower was then imminent. "Call upon the names of your gods and ask that no rain fall upon you, and I will ask my Lord Jesus Christ that not a drop of rain touch me and he who on this occasion has regard to those who call upon him let him be God." This was mutually agreed, and as all the rest sat on one side, he and one small boy sat on the other side, and each of them began to invoke his own god, while he invoked the Lord Christ. Thereupon a great stream of rain descended and they were so completely soaked that it seemed as though they and their garments had been thrown into a river. Even the foliage from the branches with which their meeting place had been constructed fell upon them and thereby proved to them that it was by divine power that they were overcome. On himself and the boy who was with him not a single drop fell. When this happened they were confused and astonished. "You see," said Herigar, "who is God. Do not, unhappy men, try to draw me away from his worship, but rather be confounded and, renouncing your errors, learn the way of truth."

On another occasion it happened that Herigar was suffering great pain in his leg, so that it was impossible for him to go out of his place except when he was carried. When he had endured this distress for some time, many persons came to visit him, some of whom urged him to sacrifice to the gods in order to regain his health, while others assailed him with jeers, saying that his illness was due to the fact that he had no god. When this had occurred on several occasions and he had strenuously resisted their evil suggestions, and when at length he could no longer bear their reproaches, he replied that he would not seek aid from vain images but from his Lord Jesus Christ who, if he wished, could cure him in a moment of his sickness. He then summoned his servants and told them to carry him to his church. When he had been placed there he poured out his supplications to the Lord in the presence of all the bystanders and said:

> My Lord Jesus Christ grant to me, your servant, now my former health
> in order that these unhappy men may know that you are the only God
> and that there is none beside you, and in order that my enemies may
> behold the great things that you do and may turn in confusion from
> their errors and be converted to the knowledge of your name. Accom-
> plish, I beseech you, that which I ask for the sake of your holy name,
> which is blessed for evermore, that they who believe in you may not be
> confounded, O Lord.

Having said this he was forthwith healed by the grace of God, and was made completely well. He, accordingly, left the church unaided and rendered thanks to God for his health and, strengthened in the faith of Christ, he more and more confounded those who disbelieved.

About the same time it happened that a certain Swedish king named Anound had been driven from his kingdom and was an exile among the Danes. Desiring to regain what had once been his kingdom he sought aid from them and promised that if they would follow him they would be able to secure much treasure. He offered them Birka, the town already men-tioned, because it contained many rich merchants and a large amount of goods and money. He promised to lead them to this place where, without much loss to their army, they might gain that which they wanted. Enticed by the promised gifts and eager to acquire treasure, they filled twenty-one ships with men ready for battle and placed them at his disposal; moreover he had eleven of his own ships. These left Denmark and came unexpectedly upon the above mentioned town. It so happened that the king of the town was absent and the chiefs and people were unable to meet together. Only Herigar, the prefect of that place, was present with the merchants and people who remained there. Being in great difficulty they fled to a neighboring town and began to promise and offer to their gods, who were demons, many vows and sacrifices in order that by their help they might be saved in so great a peril. But inasmuch as the town was not strong and there were few to offer resistance, they sent messengers to the Danes and asked for friendship and alliance. The king [Anound] commanded them to pay a hundred pounds of silver in order to redeem Birka and to obtain peace. They forthwith sent the amount asked and it was received by the king. The Danes resented this agreement, because it was not in accord with their arrangement and they wanted to make a sudden attack upon them and to pillage and burn the place because they said that each individual merchant in that place had more than had been offered to them and they could not endure that such a trick should be played upon them. As they were discussing this and were preparing to destroy the town to which the others had fled, their design became known to those in the town. They gathered together then a second time and, as they possessed no power of resistance and had no hope of securing refuge, they exhorted one another to make vows and to offer greater sacrifices to their own gods. Herigar, the faithful servant of the Lord, was angry with them and said:

> Your vows and sacrifices to idols are accursed by God. How long will you serve devils and injure and impoverish yourselves by your useless vows? You have made many offerings and more vows and have given a hundred pounds of silver. What benefit has it been to you? See, your enemies are coming to destroy all that you have. They will lead away your wives and sons as captives, they will burn your city and town [Birka] and will destroy you with the sword. Of what advantage are your idols to you?

As he said this they were all terrified and, as they knew not what to do, they replied all together: "It is for you to devise plans for our safety and whatever you suggest we will not fail to perform." He replied: "If you desire to make vows, vow and perform your vows to the Lord God omnipotent, who reigns in heaven, and whom I serve with a pure conscience and a true faith. He is the Lord of all and all things are subject to his will, nor can anyone resist his decree. If then you will seek His help with your whole heart you shall perceive that his omnipotent power will not fail you." They accepted his advice and in accordance with custom, they all went out of their own accord to a plain where they promised the Lord Christ to fast and to give alms in order to secure their deliverance. Meanwhile the king proposed to the Danes that they should inquire by casting lots whether it was the will of the gods that this place should be ravaged by them. "There are there," he said, "many great and powerful gods and in former time a church was built there, and there are many Christians there who worship Christ, who is the strongest of the gods and can aid those who hope in him, in any way that he chooses. We must seek to ascertain therefore whether it is by the will of the gods that we are urged to make this attempt." As his words were in accord with their custom they could not refuse to adopt the suggestion. Accordingly they sought to discover the will of the gods by casting lots and they ascertained that it would be impossible to accomplish their purpose without endangering their own welfare and that God would not permit this place to be ravaged by them. They asked further where they should go in order to obtain money for themselves so that they might not have to return home without having gained that for which they had hoped. They ascertained by the casting of the lot that they ought to go to a certain town which was situated at a distance on the borders of the lands belonging to the Slavonians. The Danes then, believing that this order had come to them from heaven, retired from this place and hastened to go by a direct route to that town. Having made a sudden attack upon its people, who were living in quiet and peace, they seized it by force of arms and, having captured much spoil and treasure, they returned home. Moreover the king who had come with the object of plundering the Swedes, made peace with them and restored the money that he had recently received from them. He remained also for some time with them as he wished to become reconciled to their peoples. Thus did the good Lord, on account of the faith of his servant Herigar, free the people of this place from the attack of their enemies and restore to them their possessions. After these occurrences Herigar brought forward a proposal in a public assembly and advised that they should try more earnestly to ascertain who was God. He said:

> Alas, wretched people, you now understand that it is useless to seek for help from demons who can not succor those who are in trouble. Accept the faith of my Lord Jesus Christ, whom you have proved to be the true God and who in his compassion has brought solace to you who have no refuge from sorrow. Seek not any more after superstitious worship or to appease your idols by useless sacrifice. Worship the true God, who rules all things in heaven and earth, submit yourselves to him, and adore his almighty power.

His own faith having been strengthened by the abounding goodness of the Lord, he was the more ready to come forward both publicly and otherwise, and at one time by reproach, at another time by persuasion, he declared to them the power of the Lord and the benefits resulting from faith in him. And thus he continued the good fight even to the end of his life.

When at length his good deeds were complete and his weakness had increased, having been commended to the mercy of God in the presence of the priest Ardgar, and having received the Holy Communion, he departed this life happily in Christ. Much more might be said concerning the constancy of his faith, but this must suffice, inasmuch as we desire our narrative to be brief.

20. At that time there was among the Swedes a very pious matron, whom the forwardness of wicked men had been unable to turn aside from the true faith. It was frequently suggested to her, when she was placed in any difficult position, that she should, in accordance with their custom, offer sacrifices to idols. But she remained unmoved and did not abandon the performance of her religious duties. She declared that it was useless to seek for help from dumb and deaf images and that she thought it detestable to do again the things that she had renounced in her baptism and to fail to perform the promise that she had made to Christ. If it be an evil thing to lie to men, how much worse is it to lie to God? And if it be a good thing that faith should be preserved among people, how much greater is the obligation that rests upon one who receives the faith of the Lord to continue firm and not to mingle falsehood with truth? "The Lord," she said, "even my Jesus Christ, is omnipotent, and if I continue to believe in him, he can give me health and everything that I need according to his good pleasure." This devout woman, whose name was Frideburg, who was deserving of praise for the goodness of her life and the constancy of her faith, continued even to old age.

When she believed that the day of her death was approaching and no priest had come there since the death of Gautbert, desiring the due performance of the ceremony which she had heard was the "viaticum" of Christians, she caused some wine that she had bought to be reserved in a certain vessel. She further requested her daughter, who was also a devout woman, that when her last moments came, as she had not the [proper] sacrifice she should drop some of the wine into her mouth and thus commend her departure to the mercy of the Lord. She kept this wine with her for nearly three years by which time the priest Ardgar had arrived there. After his appointment she performed her religious duties as long as she retained her strength and she sought at his hands the customary rites and helpful admonition. Meanwhile weakness overtook her and she became sick. Being anxious in view of her death, she caused the priest to be summoned and, having received from his hand the viaticum, she departed with joy to the Lord.

She had ever been intent on almsgiving and, as she was rich in this worldly goods, she had enjoined her daughter Catla that, after her departure from this life, she should distribute all that she possessed among the poor. "And because," she said, "there are here but few poor, at the first opportunity that occurs after my death, sell all that has not been given away and go with the money to Dorestad. There [you will find] many churches, priests, and clergy, and a multitude of poor people. On your arrival seek out faithful persons who may teach you how to distribute this, and give away everything as alms for the benefit of my soul."

After the death of her mother, the daughter diligently accomplished everything that she had ordered. She took her journey to Dorestad, and on her arrival she sought out some devout women who accompanied her to the holy places in the town and told her what to give to each person. On a certain day as they were visiting the holy places for the purpose of distributing charity, when half had already been distributed, she said to her companion, "We are already weary; we had better buy some wine wherewith to refresh ourselves so that we may accomplish the work that we have begun." She provided, therefore, four denarii for this purpose, and having recovered their strength they finished their task. When it was completed and she was returning to her lodging, she placed the empty bag which had contained the money in a certain spot, but, as a result of divine intervention, when she came again to the spot she found that the bag was as full as it had been before. Amazed at so great a miracle, she summoned the devout women who had gone with her and explained to them what had happened to her. In their presence she reckoned up the money that was in the bag and found that it was exactly the sum that she had brought there with the exception of the four denarii. At their suggestion she went to priests who seemed reputable in that place and told them what had happened. They rendered thanks to God for his great goodness and said that the Lord had thus repaid her toil and her good intention. They said:

Forasmuch as you have obeyed your mother and have kept your pledge to her unimpaired and, by undertaking this toilsome journey, have accomplished her generous purpose, the Lord of all good, who repays and rewards, has given you this in order to supply your own needs. He is almighty and self-sufficient and is in need of nothing. He will repay in his heavenly kingdom everything that is distributed by his faithful followers to supply the needs of the poor and of his servants. The Lord has deigned to assure you by a miracle that this is so, lest you should doubt or repent having distributed your treasure. By this same sign be assured that your mother is safe with the Lord and, admonished by this miracle, fear not to give up your property for the sake of Christ, knowing that the Lord will repay you in heaven. This is God's gift to you and it is for you to distribute in accordance with your own will. That which you have taken and used for your own purposes he would not restore, for in his kindness he gave back only that which out of love for him had been distributed among the poor.

The priest Ardgar, after the death of Herigar, then moved by the desire to lead a solitary life as he had formerly done, departed from those parts and sought again his own place. Thus were the Christians who lived here deprived once again of the presence of a priest. In this way it became clearly manifest that the hermit Ardgar had been providentially sent to these parts in order that he might strengthen the faith of Herigar and of the matron [Frideburg] and might commend their departure to the mercy of God and that, in accordance with their constant desire, they might receive the sacrament of the Holy Communion to serve as their final viaticum.

21. While the events related above were occurring, it came to pass by divine ordering that the emperor Louis of happy memory departed this life [in June 840]. When, after his death, a great disturbance arose in connection with the division of the kingdom, the status of our pastor as an [imperial] delegate was weakened. For when the monastery of Turholt had come into the possession of King Charles [the Bald], he set it free from the servitude which his father had ordained and gave it to Raginar, who is well known to you. On this account his brothers, the most noble kings, and many others also besought him frequently, but he refused to heed their requests and our father began to be worried by many needs and distresses. Thus it came about that your brothers, who were with him here [in Hamburg] at that time returned to your society and many others also left him because of poverty. He, however continued to live as best he could with the few who remained with him; and, though he was very poor, he would not abandon the task that had been assigned to him.

22. When the Lord beheld his humility and his patient courage he stirred up (inasmuch as the heart of the king is in the hand of the Lord) the mind of our most gracious lord and ruler, King Louis [the German], who took charge of the kingdom after his father's death, and incited him to discover how he might secure for [Anskar] a comfortable subsistence, so that he might accomplish the trust committed to him. And because [Louis] possessed no monastery in this province suitable for this purpose he arranged to give him the bishopric of Bremen, which was near at hand and was at that time [after 845] without a pastor. Accordingly, at a public meeting of bishops and of his other faithful servants he discussed with them whether canonical law would allow him to do this. For our lord and pastor, fearful lest this should prove dangerous to himself and in order to guard against being blamed by any for covetousness, did not readily assent to this arrangement. By command of the king this matter was threshed out in the council of bishops. They showed by many precedents that it could easily be done, inasmuch as the diocese to which he had been ordained was very small; it had only four churches in which baptisms were held. Moreover, this diocese had been many times

devastated by the incursions of barbarians and on this account they urged that it should be joined to the diocese of Bremen in order to afford him relief. But in order that the bishop of Verden might not suffer injury if he [Anskar] were to retain, in addition to the whole of the Bremen diocese, that part of his own diocese which lay beyond the Elbe and which had been taken away, they decided that, as there had been the two dioceses of Bremen and Verden in the time of the emperor Louis, these should be restored and that Anskar should keep Bremen out of which the greater part of his own diocese had been taken, the diocese of Bremen being at that time bereft of a pastor.

When this decision had been confirmed by the bishops he undertook, at the command of the kings to govern the diocese of Bremen, while Waldgar, the bishop of Verden, took over that part of his own diocese which lay beyond the Elbe. After this had been settled the matter was again carefully discussed in a council of bishops [at Mainz in October 848] which thought that it was not right that the episcopal see to which he had been ordained should be held by another bishop, for Hamburg had at that time fallen to the share of Waldgar. They said, moreover, that it was within the king's rights to extend a small diocese and one which had been devastated, but that a place to which archiepiscopal rank had been attached by apostolic authority ought, on no account, to be transferred. With the approval of the most pious king Louis, the bishops who were present there unanimously decided that our father Anskar should receive the see to which he had been consecrated and that, if he retained any territory beyond the Elbe that belonged to the diocese of Verden, he should make restitution to the bishop of that diocese out of the diocese of Bremen. This was carried into effect by the command of the king and by the decree of the episcopal synod with the approval and consent of Waldgar, the bishop of Verden.

23. When these things were being done, the town of Cologne, to which the diocese of Bremen was subject, was at that time without a bishop. And as this had been the case for some time, this matter had to be decided without the presence of a bishop from this place. When later on the venerable Gunther had been consecrated as bishop of this place [in May 850], our lord and father desired to put the matter before him so that it might be confirmed by his authority. Gunther, however, was opposed to this scheme. For this reason, at a council held by the two kings Louis and Lothar at Worms, at which there were present many bishops belonging to both kingdoms, including our venerable father, the same matter was brought forward. When this decision had been universally approved they all asked Bishop Gunther to confirm and sanction it. He was at first strenuously opposed to them and declared in many words that it was not right that a suffragan see should be transformed into an archbishopric or that the dignity of his own see should

be in any respect diminished. At length, however, when the kings and all the bishops present besought this of him, saying that it was lawful because it was necessary, he replied that he would ratify the proposal provided that it were supported by apostolic authority. When this reply had been received and all his suffragans had agreed, King Louis, who desired to extend the charitable purpose of his father and that the arrangement which he had made should be completely established, sent the most reverend Bishop Salomon, the bishop of Constance, to the apostolic see in order to promote this object. With him our lord and father Anskar, as he could not go himself, sent his son, our brother, the priest Nordfrid. These were most kindly received by the most holy pope, Nicholas [I, 858–867], and to him they explained fully and clearly the mission with which they had been entrusted. He considered with wisdom and care the things that they told him and, as he perceived by the help of God that this arrangement would be conducive to the winning of the souls of these races, he confirmed by his own authority [on 31 May 858] the wish expressed by our king. In order that we may explain more clearly the matter, which was carefully elucidated by him, we have decided to supply his own words. After he had fully and at the same time briefly recapitulated the reason for the sending of the messengers by the king, and other matters which we have included in our previous account, he went on to say:

> The text recording the authority of the delegation and to the reception of the pallium, which was sent to us by our son Louis by the hand of the most holy bishop Salomon, was authenticated in accordance with the custom of the holy Roman Church.
>
> From the contents of this text we find that matters are just as the pious king made known to us by his trusty messenger Bishop Salomon. We, therefore, following in the steps of our predecessor, the great bishop [that is, pope] Gregory and recognizing that the arrangements made by his foresight were deserving of divine approval, have decided to sanction the wish expressed by the great chiefs, namely, the emperor Louis [the Pious] of sacred memory and his most excellent son, who bears the same name, by an edict bearing apostolic authority and by the presentation of the pallium, in accordance with the custom of our predecessors. In order that Anskar may be authoritatively established as the first archbishop of the Nordalbingians and that his successors, who strive for the salvation of peoples, may be enabled to resist the attack of the evil one, we appoint our son Anskar as our legate among all the surrounding races of Swedes, Danes and Slavs, and among all others living in those parts, wherever the grace of God may open a way, and we grant him authority to preach the Gospel openly.

We decree also that Hamburg, the see of the Nordalbingians, which has been dedicated to our holy Savior and to Mary his undefiled mother, should henceforth be an archiepiscopal see. We call God to witness that we decree this in order that after the death of the great preacher, Archbishop Anskar, there may ever hereafter be chosen persons worthy of this great office. But inasmuch as King Charles, the brother of Louis, after the death of his father the emperor Louis of pious memory, took away from Hamburg the monastery called Turholt, which his father had given to the bishop and his clergy in order to supply them with food and other necessities, all those who ministered at the altar began to leave the place, because, after the division of the kingdom between the two brothers, it appeared to lie within his kingdom, being situated in western Francia.

When the necessary funds were no longer available they left these races, and the mission to them which had been carried on in this way ceased; even the metropolis, Hamburg, was nearly deserted. While these events were taking place the bishop of Bremen, the diocese of which is said to be contiguous to this see, died. When the king perceived that this diocese was without a bishop and that the newly instituted diocese had been weakened and that, in addition, the churches in both dioceses had been enfeebled by the savagery displayed by the barbarians, he began to ask whether the diocese of Bremen might be united and made subject to the new archiepiscopal see and whether his project might be authorized by our decree. Accordingly this matter was referred to us by his messenger Salomon, the venerable bishop of Constance, in order that we might approve it and we were asked to confirm the same by our authority. We therefore, after carefully weighing and considering the proposal, think that it will be advantageous in view of the pressing need and in order to win souls among the heathens. For we do not doubt that all things that are proved to be profitable to the church and which are not opposed to divine ordinances are lawful and ought to be done, especially in a district in which the faith has so recently been introduced and in which many different issues are likely to arise. Wherefore, by the authority of Almighty God and the blessed apostles Peter and Paul and by this our decree, we decide, in accordance with the wish of King Louis, that these dioceses of Hamburg and Bremen shall henceforth be called not two dioceses but one diocese and that they shall be subject to the see which was raised to archiepiscopal rank by the decree of our predecessor, provided that the diocese of Verden receive back from the church of Bremen that territory which before had been taken away. No archbishop of Cologne shall henceforth lay claim to any power in this diocese. Moreover we exhort him and all who accept the true faith to assist and support those who carry out this commission, so that for their good deeds they may deserve to receive full reward from him who said: "Go and teach all the nations," and "whosoever receives you receives me." We confirm by our authority therefore, all the wishes expressed by our beloved son King Louis relating to this important matter. And inasmuch as what has happened in the past renders us cautious for the future, we smite with the sword of our anathema anyone who opposes, or contradicts, or tries to interfere with this our desire, and we condemn him to share with the devil everlasting vengeance. We do this in accordance with the custom of our predecessors and in our pious zeal for God, in order that we may render the exalted apostolic see more secure against the attack of all enemies.

By the decrees and dispositions of the holy pope Nicholas, the church of Bremen was joined and united to the see of Hamburg, which had formerly been made a metropolitan see and now became an archbishopric.

24. But inasmuch as we have spoken in advance concerning the arrangements that were made relating to this diocese (for a long time elapsed after Anskar had undertaken the government of this see before it was settled by apostolic authority) let us now go back to the events of an earlier period. For after he took over the diocese of Bremen and became possessed of some resources he began once more to desire fervently that, if it were possible, he might labor on Christ's behalf among the Danes. For this reason he paid frequent visits to Rorik, who was at that time the sole monarch of the Danes, and endeavored to conciliate him by gifts and by any possible kinds of service in the hope that he might gain permission to preach in his kingdom. On several occasions he was sent to him as an ambassador of the king and sought strenuously and faithfully to bring about a peace that should be advantageous to either kingdom. His fidelity and goodness having been so recognized, King Rorik began to regard him with great affection and to make use of his advice and to treat him in every respect as a friend, so that he was allowed to share his secrets when with his fellow counselors he was dealing with matters relating to the kingdom. Concerning matters that had to be arranged in order to establish an alliance between the people of this land, that is the Saxons, and his own kingdom, the king only desired that it should be guaranteed by his pledge, as he said that he had complete confidence in regard to everything that he approved and promised. When Anskar had thus gained his friendship he began to urge him to become a Christian. The king listened to all that was reported to him out of the Holy Scriptures and declared that it was both

good and helpful and that he took great delight therein, and that he desired to earn the favor of Christ.

After he had expressed these desires our good father suggested to him that he grant to the Lord Christ that which would be most pleasing to him, namely permission to build a church in his kingdom where a priest might always be present who might commit to those who were willing to receive them the seeds of the Divine Word and the grace of baptism. The king most kindly granted this permission and allowed him to build a church in a part belonging to his kingdom, called Sliaswich, which was specially suitable for this purpose and was near to the district where merchants from all parts congregated; he gave also a place in which a priest might live, and likewise granted permission to anyone in his kingdom who desired to become a Christian.

When our lord bishop obtained this permission he at once did that which he had long desired. And when a priest had been established there, the grace of God began to bear much fruit in that place, for there were many who had already become Christians and had been baptized in Dorestad or Hamburg, among whom were the principal people of the place, who rejoiced at the opportunity afforded them to observe their religion. Many others also, both men and women, followed their example, and having abandoned the superstitious worship of idols, believed in the Lord and were baptized. There was, moreover, great joy in that place as the men of this place could now do what was before forbidden and traders both from here [Hamburg] and from Dorestad freely sought to visit this place, and an opportunity was afforded for doing much good there. And while many who were baptized there have survived, an innumerable host of those who were clothed in white [those who delayed baptism until the hour of death] have ascended to the heavenly kingdom. For they were willingly marked with the sign of the cross in order to become catechumens, and that they might enter the church and be present at the sacred offices; but they deferred the reception of baptism, as they judged that it was to their advantage to be baptized at the end of their lives, so that, having been cleansed by water unto salvation, they might without any delay enter the gates of eternal life as those who were pure and spotless. Many also among them, who were overcome with sickness, when they saw that their sacrifices offered to idols in order to secure their recovery were of no avail and when their neighbors despaired of their getting well, took refuge in the Lord's mercy and vowed that they would become Christians. When a priest had been summoned and they had received the grace of baptism, by divine help they forthwith recovered their health. In such a manner did the divine compassion spread in that place and a multitude of people were converted to the Lord.

25. Meanwhile our lord and master Anskar, being greatly distressed on behalf of the Swedish race because it was at that time without a priest, begged King Rorik, who was his intimate friend, to help him make an effort to reach this kingdom. The king received this request with the utmost good will and promised that he would do everything to help. Accordingly the bishop began to negotiate with Bishop Gautbert [who died in 845] saying that a further attempt must be made to discover whether this race, having been divinely admonished, would permit priests to dwell among them, so that the Christian faith, which had been established in those parts, might not perish in consequence of their neglect. Bishop Gautbert, who is also called Simon, replied that, as he had been expelled from that country, he would not venture to go there again and that the attempt could not be advantageous, but would on the contrary be dangerous, should those who remembered what happened before raise a disturbance about him. He said that it seemed to him to be more fitting that he should go who was the first to undertake this mission and who had been kindly treated there, and that he would send with him his nephew [Erimbert] who might remain there, should he find an opportunity for preaching, and might perform the duties of a priest among the people. When they had so decided, they came to King Louis and told him the reason for their action and begged that he would permit them to do this. He asked whether they themselves had come to an agreement, whereupon the venerable Bishop Gautbert replied: "We are in the service of God and always have been united and it is our unanimous desire that this should be done." Accordingly, the king, who was ever ready to further God's work, enjoined this mission upon our holy father in accordance with the terms they had agreed among themselves and, on his part, entrusted to the bishop injunctions addressed to the king of Sweden as his father had done previously.

Our good father then began to prepare for this journey and became the more eager to accomplish it with the utmost speed. Moreover he believed that he was commanded by heaven to undertake it, as he was influenced by a vision which he had seen earlier. For in that vision he thought that he was anxious in view of this very journey and it seemed to him that he came to a place where there were large buildings and dwellings of different kinds. A certain man met him there and said:

> Do not be too distressed about the journey over which you are anxious, for there is a certain prophet in this place who will inform you concerning all these matters. And lest in regard to this matter any hesitation should take possession of your mind, I will tell you who this prophet is: Adalhard, the once famous abbot, is the prophet whom the Lord hath sent to you to tell you the things that are to come to pass.

Being greatly encouraged by what he heard in his vision, Anskar replied: "Where shall I find him, O Lord?" "You will find him," was the reply, "by your own effort; and no one may bring him to you." Then it seemed to him that he passed round the dwellings seeking for him and at the same time he said to himself, "If without my asking him he shall tell me what is in my mind, then I shall be satisfied that he is a true prophet." He went on then to a bright and beautiful dwelling and saw him sitting on his chair and recognized him forthwith. He [the prophet] looked upon him and said immediately:

Hear, O islands, and give ear you peoples from afar. The Lord has called you from the womb and from your mother's belly; he has remembered your name, and he has made your mouth as a sharp sword and has covered you with the shadow of his hand and has made you like a choice arrow. He has hidden you in his quiver, and has said unto you, "You are my servant, for in you I will be glorified."

Having said this he stretched out his arm and lifted his right hand to him. When Anskar saw this he advanced to his knees hoping that he would be willing to bless him. But he added these words:

Now says the Lord that formed you from the womb to be his servant, I have given you to be a light to the Gentiles that you may be present to them for salvation even to the ends of the earth. Kings shall see and princes shall rise up together and they shall worship the Lord your God, even the Holy One of Israel, for he shall glorify you.

God's servant, having beheld this vision long before he set out on his journey, was assured that he was summoned by a divine command to go to those parts, and specially by the word that had been spoken "Hear, O islands," because almost all that country consisted of islands; and by that which had been added, "You shall be present to them for salvation even to the ends of the earth," because in the north the end of the world lay in Swedish territory. Finally the word quoted from the end of Jeremiah's [that is Isaiah's] prophecy: "For he shall glorify thee," encouraged his eager desire, as he thought that this referred to the crown of martyrdom that had once been promised to him.

26. As he was then about to set out on this journey he took with him the message and the token given him by King Rorik, who directed him to give the message to the Swedish king named Olaf and to say that the messenger

whom King Louis had sent to his kingdom was well known to him and that he had never before in his life seen so good a man, nor had he ever found any other human being so trustworthy. In recognition of his goodness he had allowed him to do whatever he wished in his kingdom in the interests of the Christian religion and King Louis begged that he would permit him to establish the Christian religion in his own kingdom, as he desired, for he would do nothing that would not be good and right.

Anskar accomplished the journey on which he had set out and after spending nearly twenty days in a ship, he arrived at Birka where he found that the king and many of the people were perplexed by grievous errors. It happened, at the instigation of the devil, who knew beforehand of the coming of this good man, that someone had come there and said that he had been present at a meeting of the gods, who were believed to be the owners of this land, and had been sent by them to make this announcement to the king and the people:

> You, I say, have long enjoyed our good will, and under our protection the land in which you dwell has long been fertile and has had peace and prosperity. You have also duly sacrificed and performed the vows made to us, and your worship has been very pleasing to us. But now you are keeping back the usual sacrifices and are slothful in paying your voluntary offerings; you are, moreover, displeasing us greatly by introducing a foreign god in order to supplant us. If you want to enjoy our good will, offer the sacrifices that have been omitted and give greater vows. And do not receive the worship of any other god, who teaches that which is opposed to our teaching, nor pay any attention to his service. Furthermore, if you desire to have more gods and we do not suffice, we will agree to summon your former king, Eric [III] to join us so that he may be one of the gods.

This devilish announcement, which was publicly made on the arrival of the bishop, disturbed the minds of all and their hearts were deceived and disquieted. For they had resolved to have a temple in honor of the late king and had begun to render votive offerings and sacrifices to him as to a god. When, then, the bishop came there, he asked his friends, the ones he had formerly known there, how he might speak to the king on this matter. They all, with one accord, disagreed with him doing so and said that for the time being this mission could effect nothing, and that if he had anything of value with him he should give it to the king so that he might escape with his life. He replied, "For the saving of my life would I give nothing, for, if my Lord shall

so ordain, I am ready to submit to torments and to suffer death for his name."
Being in great uncertainty in regard to this matter, he acted on the advice
that he received, and invited the king to partake of his hospitality. Then, as
a fellow-guest, he offered what gifts he could and gave him the things with
which he had been entrusted, for the cause of his coming had already been
explained to the king by Rorik's messenger and by the bishop's friends who
resided there. The king was delighted with his kindness and liberality, and
said that he gladly agreed to what he had proposed. He said:

> In former times there have been clergy who have been driven out by
> a rising of the people and not by the command of the king. On this
> account I have not the power, nor do I dare, to approve the objects of
> your mission until I can determine our gods by the casting of lots and
> until I can determine the will of the people in regard to this matter.
> Let your messenger attend with me the next assembly and I will speak
> to the people on your behalf. And if they approve your desire and the
> gods consent, that which you have asked shall be successfully carried
> out, but if it should turn out otherwise, I will let you know. It is our
> custom that the control of public business of every kind should rest
> with the whole people and not with the king.

When our good pastor received the king's reply he turned to the Lord for
refuge, gave up his time to fasting and prayer, and with heartfelt contrition
he humbled himself before God.

27. While he was in this difficult position and the time for the assembly
drew near, he was one day engaged in the service of the Mass and, while the
priest was standing by the altar and was blessing the sacred mysteries, a divine
inspiration came upon him as he prostrated himself on the ground. Strengthened, then, by the gift of the Holy Spirit and adorned with the most complete
confidence, he recognized that all would turn out as he desired. Accordingly,
when the Mass was finished, he declared to this same priest, who was his
most intimate associate, that he ought to have no fear, for God himself would
be his helper. When the priest asked how he knew this he replied that his
knowledge was divinely inspired. The brother was able to recognize this
divine illumination, as he knew that he had been divinely inspired in many
previous instances, and the result quickly justified his confidence.

As soon as his chiefs were assembled the king began to discuss with them
the mission on which our father had come. They determined that an enquiry
should be made by the casting of lots in order to discover the will of the gods.
They went out, therefore, to the plain, in accordance with their custom, and
the lot decided that it was the will of God that the Christian religion should

be established there. When this happened, one of the chief men, who was a friend of the bishop, told him at once and advised him to be comforted, and said, "Be strong and act with vigor, for God has not denied your wish nor rejected your mission." He was then full of courage and rejoicing in spirit exulted in the Lord. When the day for the assembly which was held in the town of Birka drew near, in accordance with their national custom the king caused a proclamation to be made to the people by the voice of a herald, in order that they might be informed concerning the object of their mission. On hearing this, those who had before been led astray into error, held discordant and confused opinions. In the midst of the noise and confusion one of the older men among them said:

> Listen to me, O king and people. In regard to the worship of this God
> it is well known to many of us that he can afford much help to those
> who place their hope in him. For many of us have proved this to be
> the case on several occasions when in peril from sea and in other crises.
> Why, then, do we reject that which we know to be both needful and
> serviceable? Some of us who have on various occasions been to Dores-
> tad have of our own accord adopted this form of religion, believing it
> to be beneficial. Our way there is now beset by those who lie in wait
> for us and is rendered dangerous by the attacks of pirates. Why then do
> we not take that which is brought to us and which, when it was at a
> distance, we sought eagerly to obtain? We have frequently proved that
> the help afforded by this God can be useful to us. Why should we not
> gladly agree to continue as his servants? Consider carefully, O people,
> and do not cast away that which will be to your advantage. For, inas-
> much as we cannot be sure that our gods will be favorably disposed,
> it is good for us to have the help of this God who is always and under
> all circumstances able and willing to succor those who cry out to him.

When he had finished speaking all the people unanimously decided that the priests should remain with them and that everything that pertained to the performance of the Christian mysteries should be done without objection or hindrance. The king then rose up from among the assembly and forthwith directed one of his own messengers to accompany the bishop's messenger and to tell him that the people were unanimously inclined to accept his proposal and at the same time to tell him that, while their action was entirely agreeable to him, he could not give his full consent until, in another assembly, which was to be held in another part of his kingdom, he could announce this resolution to the people who lived in that district.

Once again, then, our good father sought, as was his custom, for divine assistance, and eagerly besought God's mercy. When the time for the assembly came and the king had caused to be proclaimed by the voice of a herald the object for which the bishop had come and all that had been said and done at the previous assembly by divine providence, the hearts of all became as one, so that they adopted the resolution passed by the former assembly and declared that they too would give their entire and complete assent.

28. When this had been done the king summoned the bishop and told him what had occurred. The king accordingly, with the good will and approval of all, determined that churches might be built among the people and that priests might come to them and that whoever so desired might become a Christian without objection or hindrance. Our lord and pastor then commended to the care of the king, Erimbert, the nephew of the venerable Bishop Gautbert, in order that, with his help and protection, he might there perform the sacred mysteries and to him the king granted permission to build a hall to serve as a place of prayer in the town already mentioned; the bishop also bought another courtyard, together with a house in which the priest might live. The king displayed further his affectionate regard for the lord bishop and promised that in every district he would show the utmost kindness to his companions who were concerned with the observance of the Christian religion. When, then, by the Lord's grace everything had been duly accomplished the bishop returned to his own house.

29. While preparations were being made for his journey [to Sweden] our good father foresaw in advance, by divine revelation, the mental anguish which he afterwards endured during his journey. For one night he saw, as in a vision, that it was the time of our Lord's passion and that he was himself present when the Lord Jesus Christ was led from Pilate to Herod and again from Herod to Pilate. When [Christ] endured the spitting and insults at the hands of the Jews and the soldiers, it seemed to him that he himself was scourged all over because he would not suffer him to be so punished, but came forward and gave his back to the scourgers and received on his own body the blows that were inflicted on [Christ], [Christ's] head only being excepted because, being taller of stature, he seemed to reach beyond [Anskar] and he could not, therefore, protect his head. Christ's invincible soldier did not understand what this meant until, on his return from this journey, he considered how much insult and derision he had borne and in what great straits he had been placed and what blasphemies against God he had endured there. For, insofar as he was himself concerned, he undoubtedly suffered there on Christ's behalf and Christ in his servant bore again the reproaches that were directed against himself. Furthermore, he thought that the fact that he was not able to protect [Christ's] head signified that the head of Christ is God and the sufferings, which the saints endure in this world on Christ's

behalf, pertain in part to the majesty of God who, in virtue of his sympathy, endures them for a time, but will some day severely judge, even as it is written: "Vengeance is mine, I will repay, says the Lord."

30. Nor should we omit to mention how, after the completion of this journey, the power of the Lord was manifested to the Swedes. For a certain people named the Cori had in former times been in subjection to the Swedes, but had a long while since rebelled and refused to be under subjection. The Danes, being aware of this, at the time when the bishop had come into Swedish territory, collected a large number of ships and proceeded to this country, eager to seize their goods and to subject them to themselves. Their kingdom contained five towns. When the inhabitants knew of their coming they gathered together and began to resist vigorously and to defend their property. Having obtained the victory they massacred half the Danes and plundered their ships, obtaining from them gold and silver and much spoil.

On hearing this, King Olaf and the Swedes, who wished to win for themselves the reputation that they could do what the Danes had not done and because this people had formerly been subject to them, collected an immense army and proceeded into those parts. In the first instance they came to a town in their kingdom called Seeburg. This town, which contained seven thousand fighting men, they ravaged and despoiled and burned. They left it with strengthened hopes and, having sent away their ships, set out on a journey of five days and hastened with savage intention to another of their towns called Aputra in which there were fifteen thousand fighting men. When they reached it, these were shut up in the town, and while the one party vigorously attacked the town from outside, the other party defended it from within. In this manner eight days went by with the result that, though they fought and waged war from morning until night, and many fell on both sides, neither side obtained the victory. On the ninth day the Swedes, being exhausted by the daily slaughter, began to be distressed, and in their terror considered only how they might get away. "Here," they said, "we effect nothing and we are far from our ships." For, as we have said, it was a journey of five days to the port which contained their ships. As they were greatly disturbed and did not know what they should do, they resolved to inquire by casting lots whether their gods were willing to aid them either to obtain a victory or to get away from the place where they were. Having cast lots they failed to discover any god who was willing to aid them. And when this was announced to the people there arose much outcry and lamentation in their camp and all their courage left them. "What," said they, "shall we, unhappy people, do? The gods have departed from us and none of them will aid us. Where shall we flee? Our ships are far away and if we flee [those in the city] will follow after us and will utterly destroy us. What hope have we?"

When they were in this great difficulty some merchants, who remembered the teaching and instruction given by the bishop, offered them advice. "The God of the Christians," they said, "frequently helps those who cry to him and his help is all powerful. Let us inquire whether he will be on our side and let us with a willing mind promise offerings that will be agreeable to him." Accordingly, at their unanimous request, lots were cast and it was found that Christ was willing to help them.

When this had been publicly announced, the hearts of all were once so greatly encouraged that they wished to proceed immediately to make a bold attack on the town. "What," said they, "have we now to fear or dread? Christ is with us; let us fight and behave like men; nothing can withstand us, nor shall we fail to secure certain victory, for we have the mightiest of the gods as our helper." When all were gathered together with courage and joy to attack the town and they had surrounded it and were eager to commence the fight, those inside asked that an opportunity for speech be afforded them, and when the Swedish king had agreed, they immediately said:

> We desire peace rather than fighting, and we wish to enter into an agreement with you. In the first place we are prepared to give you for the sake of securing an agreement all the gold and the arms that we took as spoil from the Danes last year. Furthermore, we offer half a pound of silver for each individual man now in this town, and in addition we will pay you the tribute that we formerly paid and will give hostages, for we desire henceforth to be subject and obedient to your rule as we were in former times.

When this offer had been made, the passions of the young men could not be assuaged, but, being eager for action and devoid of fear, they desired only to fight and said that they would destroy by force of arms the town and all that the people possessed, and would carry them off as captives. The king, however, and his chief men, were of a wiser opinion and, having accepted their offer and entered into an agreement with them, they gladly returned home, taking with them countless treasures and the thirty hostages that were provided.

When at length peace had been established between the two peoples, the Swedes extolled with utmost zeal the omnipotence and glory of Christ our Lord and declared that he was greater than all other gods. They began also to ask with solicitude what they ought to give to him from whom they had obtained so great a victory. At the suggestion of some Christian merchants who were present at the time they promised that they would observe a fast that would be acceptable to the Lord Christ and accordingly, when they returned, after spending seven days at home they all abstained from eating flesh for another seven days. Moreover, when forty days had elapsed they unanimously agreed to abstain from eating flesh for the following forty days. This was done and all who were present carried out their resolve with willing minds. After this, many in their reverence and love for Christ began to lay stress upon the fasts observed by Christians and upon almsgiving, and they began to assist the poor because they had learned that this was pleasing to Christ. Thus with the good will of all did the priest Erimbert accomplish among them things that pertained to God and, while all applauded the power of Christ, the observance of the divine religion from that time forward increased in these parts and encountered opposition from no one.

31. Meanwhile [in 854] it happened by divine judgment that King Rorik was killed in war in a disturbance caused by pirates while his kinsmen were attempting to invade his kingdom. Together with him all the chief men of that land, who had formerly been acquaintances and friends of the bishop, perished by the sword. When at length the younger Rorik had been established in the kingdom, some of those who were then his chief men and had not been so well known to the bishop, tried to persuade him that the church that had been built among them should be destroyed and that the Christian religion should be abolished. For they said that their gods were angry and that these great evils had come upon them because they had accepted the worship of another and an unknown god. Accordingly the headman [or count] of the village of Sliaswich, whose name was Hovi, who was particularly opposed to this religion, urged the king to destroy the Christian faith, and he ordered the church that had been built there to be shut and prohibited the observance of the Christian religion. On this account the priest, who had been [in charge] there, was forced to withdraw because of the bitter persecution.

32. On this account the lord bishop was very anxious and not a little sad because of the friends whom he had formerly attached to himself by generous gifts. There were none at the court of the younger Rorik through whom he might win over [the king] to do the Lord's will. Being then deprived of human aid, he hastened, as was his custom, to seek for divine assistance. Nor did this hope fail him, for the Lord strengthened him with spiritual consolation and he became assured that the religion which had begun to be established [in Sweden] would not perish, as the enemies of Christ were planning. By the help of the Lord, matters turned out in the following way soon afterwards. When on this account he was arranging to go to the king, the Lord anticipated his action and the headman was expelled from the village and had no prospect of being received back into favor, whereupon the king kindly sent his messenger to the bishop and asked him to send back his priest to his church. He at the same time declared that, no less than the elder

Rorik [had], he desired to secure Christ's favor and to gain the friendship of the bishop. When our venerable pastor came into the presence of the king, having as his helper the most noble Burghard, who had formerly assisted the elder Rorik in all matters and had great influence with both kings because he was their relative, the king showed his pleasure in receiving him by permitting him immediately to do everything connected with the Christian religion which his predecessor had formerly allowed to be done. Moreover, he agreed that there should be a bell in the church, the use of which the pagans regarded as unlawful. In another village called Ripa, situated within his kingdom, he likewise gave a site for the erection of a church and granted permission for a priest to be present there.

33. While these things were being done the venerable Bishop Gautbert [the bishop of Osnabrück] sent to the Swedes a priest called Ansfrid, who was of Danish descent and had been trained by Ebbo for the service of the Lord. When he came there he and the priest Erimbert, who had returned thence, continued there for three or four years and won the respect of all. But when he heard of the death of Gautbert, he returned, and having spent some time with us was seized with sickness, and after suffering much pain he died. Whereupon the bishop, who would not allow the Christian faith that had arisen there to perish, arranged to send there a priest named Ragenbert. He was specially suited to this task and was most willing to undertake the journey, but while he was on his way to the port of Schleswig, where there were ships and merchants who were to make the journey with him, by the contrivance of the devil it happened that he was waylaid by Danish robbers and despoiled of all that he had and on the day of the Assumption of Saint Mary he too, while endeavoring to carry out his good intentions, made a happy end. His death caused great distress to the bishop, but he could in no wise be hindered from carrying out his purpose, and soon afterwards he ordained for this work a priest named Rimbert [probably not the hagiographer and bishop, but another Rimbert], whose ancestors were of Danish extraction. When he had sent him in Christ's name to those parts he was kindly received there by the king and the people and with the help of the Lord he celebrated without restraint the divine mysteries in their midst. To him, as to all the other priests whom he had before appointed to live among the pagans, Anskar gave strict orders that they should not desire nor seek to obtain the property of anyone, but he affectionately exhorted them that after the example of the apostle, Saint Paul, they should labor with their hands and be content with food and raiment. He, however, gave them and those who followed them in abundance out of his own possessions all that they wanted and in addition whatever they needed to give away in order to secure friends.

34. Furthermore, amid the many and varied difficulties which, as we have

said, he endured in connection with this mission, although he was constantly strengthened by divine inspiration, which prevented him from abandoning the task that he had undertaken, the piety and spiritual fervor of Ebbo the archbishop of Rheims, who had first received the members of the mission, afforded him no little comfort. For Ebbo, being inflamed with the desire to render effective the religious call of the non-Christian races, urged him to carry the blessings of the faith into those parts and impressed upon him that he should not abandon what he had begun. The good bishop [Anskar], stirred by his exhortations and his enthusiasm on behalf of this cause, accomplished unhesitatingly the duties of the task that had been entrusted to him, nor could he be diverted from it by any trouble or inconvenience. Among the many words of advice and admonition uttered by the archbishop by which the bishop was gladdened and encouraged, he always remembered the last conversation that they had when they conversed concerning this mission. When our bishop had enumerated the many troubles that had befallen him and asked Ebbo what he thought of the mission, and eagerly demanded whatever consolation he could offer, Ebbo replied with a prophet's inspiration:

Be assured that what we have begun to do in the name of Christ will bear fruit in the Lord. For it is my faith and I firmly believe, nay I know to be true, that although for the time being on account of our sins a hindrance may arise, the work that we have begun among these peoples will never be entirely obliterated, but by the grace of God will bear fruit and prosper until the name of the Lord reaches unto the ends of the earth.

This too, was the faith of the others; with this purpose they set out to visit the distant peoples; in their love for this religion they strove on behalf of the Lord, from whom they will, without doubt, receive the reward of their toil. Such love and devotion were ever present in the mind of our lord and father, nor did he ever cease to pray for the salvation of these peoples.

On the contrary, when the pirates, who came from those people, were continually attacking and the whole of his diocese was being devastated and his household was being plundered, he nevertheless prayed earnestly for those who opposed and laid wait for him, and ceased not to entreat the mercy of God for those who ill-treated him and to pray that their sin might not be reckoned to them, because, being ignorant of God's justice and being deceived by the devil, they had shown themselves to be enemies of the Christian religion. His anxiety on their behalf was so keen that in his last illness, even until his last breath, he never failed to concern himself with and to plan on behalf of this mission. Possessed by this ardent zeal for religion he was taken from this mortal life and we believe that on the resurrection day he will pass with honor and joy into the celestial kingdom accompanied by a great multitude of believers whom he had won for the Lord from among the Danes and Swedes and by the divine mercy will receive the reward for the good contest that he waged.

CHAPTER FOUR

EARLY RELIGION AND BELIEF

A pendant representing Thor's hammer, Mjolnir, made of silver in ninth-century Öland, Sweden.

Source: Paul B. du Chaillu, *The Viking Age*, 2 vols. (New York: Charles Scribner's Sons, 1899), vol. 1, p. 354.

Our knowledge of Norse mythology depends heavily on the work of Snorri Sturluson (see Introduction). His Edda *is an extraordinary compilation of myth and poetry. Without it, we would know significantly less about the subject. A second source for Norse myth and religion is the late thirteenth-century Icelandic manuscript known as the* Codex Regius, *which anthologizes heroic and mythological Norse poems known collectively as the* Poetic Edda. *Without these and accounts in various sagas and histories, the world of pre-Christian Norse beliefs would be largely closed to us.*

8. THE NORSE CREATION-MYTH

Snorri Sturluson's Gylfaginning *is a powerful retelling of many Norse myths. Snorri gives his work the form of a dialogue between Gylfi, a legendary king of Sweden, and Odin, who is presented here as a trinity: Hárr (High One), Jafnhárr (Just as High), and Thridi (Third). Their responses to Gylfi's questions contain much of what we know about Norse mythology. To conceal his identity, Gylfi adopts the pseudonym Gangleri.*

Source: Snorri Sturluson, Edda. Gylfaginning, ed. Anthony Faulkes (London: Viking Society for Northern Research, 1988), pp. 8–19.

3. This is how Gangleri began his questioning: "Who is the oldest and most exalted of all the gods?"

The High One said, "He is called All-Father in our language, but in old Asgard, he had twelve names...."

"Where does this god live?" asked Gangleri. "What power does he have, and what great deeds has he done?"

"He endures throughout all ages," replied the High One. "He rules over all his kingdom and he has power over all things, both great and small."

Then Just as High said, "He made heaven and earth, the sky, and everything in them."

"But his greatest achievement," said Third, "was to create man and give him a soul that will live and never perish, even though his body molders to dust or is burned to ashes. And all men who are virtuous will live, and they will dwell with him in Gimli or Vingof, but evil men will go to Hel and from there to Niflheim, which is down in the ninth world."

"What did he do before the creation of heaven and earth?" asked Gangleri.

"At that time, he dwelt with the Frost Giants," replied the High One.

4. "How did everything begin? What started it all? What was there before?" asked Gangleri. The High One replied, "As *Völuspá* says,

> In earliest times
> nothing existed;
> there was no sand,
> no sea, no chilly wave;
> earth did not exist,
> nor heaven overhead;
> a great void yawned
> and no grass grew."

Then Just as High spoke, "Many ages before the earth was created, Niflheim was formed. In the middle of Niflheim, there is a spring called Hvergelmir out of which flow the rivers Svol, Gunnthra, Fjorm, Fimbulthul, Slid and Hlid, Sylg and Ylg, Vid, Leipt, and Gjoll, which is next to the gates of Hel."

"But first," said Third, "there was the world in the south, called Muspell – a bright, hot place, blazing with fire and inaccessible to outsiders who are not born there. A being named Surt is stationed at the border to defend the land. He has a fiery sword, and, at the end of the world, he will go forth and wage war, defeating all the gods and destroying the whole world with fire. Thus says *Völuspá*,

> Surt travels from the south
> with the scorcher of trees;
> from his sword flashes
> the sun of the slaughter-gods;
> rocks crash
> and witches rove;
> men tread Hel's road
> and heaven is split asunder."

5. Gangleri asked, "What were things like before the various races came into being, and mankind increased and multiplied?"

"There were rivers called the Elivagar [the Ice-waves] and when these rivers had flowed some distance from their source, their poisonous streams began to harden like slag from a forge and turned into ice," said the High One. "And when the ice ceased flowing and came to a stop, the moisture arising from the poison froze and hardened into rime, and the rime built up layer by layer, in Ginnungagap [the Yawning Void]."

"The north-facing part of Ginnungagap filled up with thick, heavy ice and rime, and from that direction there came drizzling rain and gusting wind," said Just as High. "But the southern part of Ginnungagap was brightened by the sparks and glowing embers flying out of Muspellsheim."

Then Third said, "Just as everything that emerged from Niflheim was cold and grim, so everything that faced toward nearby Muspellsheim was hot and bright, and Ginnungagap was mild as a windless sky. And when the warm breeze met the rime, it began to thaw and drip and, through the power of heat, these flowing drops were quickened into life and assumed the shape of a man. That man was named Ymir, but he is called Aurgelmir by the Frost-giants, and they are all descended from him, as the *Short Völuspá* tells us,

All seeresses
stem from Vidolf,
all wizards
from Vilmeid,
all sorcerers from
Svarthofdi,
and all giants
from Ymir.

And this is what Vafthruthnir the giant tells us:

When poisonous drops
sprayed up from Elivagar,
they grew until a giant emerged;
our kin are all
descended from him;
and so they are always fierce."

"How did the various races evolve from him?" asked Gangleri, "How did more men come into being? Or do you believe that Ymir is a god?"

The High One replied, "We do not regard him as a god at all. He was evil like all his kin, whom we call Frost-giants. The story goes that he fell asleep and began to sweat, and a man and a woman grew under his left arm, and one of his legs begot a son with the other. Their offspring are the Frost-giants; but the original Frost-giant is called Ymir."

6. "Where did Ymir live, and what did he live on?" asked Gangleri.

"The next thing to emerge from the dripping rime was a cow called Authumla. Four streams of milk flowed from her udder, and she fed Ymir."

"What did the cow live on?" asked Gangleri.

"She licked the rime-covered stones, which were salty," replied the High One. "On the first day that she licked the stones, a man's hair emerged toward evening. On the second day, his head appeared, and on the third day, the whole man was visible. His name was Buri and he was a big, strong, handsome man. He fathered a son named Borr, who married Bestla, the daughter of the giant, Bolthorn. They had three sons: the first was called Odin, the second Vili, and the third Ve. And it is my belief that this Odin (and his brothers) must be the ruler of heaven and earth; we think that he should be given the name ruler, for that is what we call the greatest and worthiest man we know, and you would be well-advised to call him that too."

7. "How did they get on with one another? Which side was more

powerful?" asked Gangleri. "Borr's sons killed Ymir the giant," replied the High One, "and when Ymir died, such a torrent of blood gushed from his wounds that they drowned the whole race of Frost-giants in it, all except for one, called Bergelmir, who escaped with his household. He and his wife boarded their ark and were saved, and it is from them that the Frost-giant families are descended, as it says here in *Vafþrúðnismál*,

> Numberless winters
> before the world was created,
> Bergelmir was born;
> what I recall first is
> how that clever giant
> took refuge on his ark."

8. "What did Borr's sons do then to make you regard them as gods?" asked Gangleri.

"There's a lot to be said about that," replied the High One. "They picked Ymir up and carried him to the middle of Ginnungagap where they created the earth from his body. They made the sea and the lakes from his blood, the land from his flesh, and the mountains from his bones; rocks and boulder-fields were made out of his teeth, his molars, and any broken bones."

"They made the sea from the blood that flowed and gushed freely from his wounds" added Just as High. "Then, when they had formed the earth and firmed it into shape, they encircled it with the sea, which most men will regard as impossible to cross."

Then Third said, "They also took Ymir's skull and made the sky out of it, raising it up over the earth at four corners, and setting a dwarf under each of them. These dwarfs are called: East, West, North, and South. Next, they collected the sparks and glowing embers that had been hurled out of Muspellsheim and were flying about freely. They placed these throughout the vast heavens to light up the sky above and the earth below. They allotted positions to all these burning masses. Some were fixed in the firmament, while others moved about, but it was Borr's sons who assigned their positions and directed their courses. And thus, according to ancient lore, it became possible to distinguish one day from the next and reckon up the years; *Völuspá* tells us that this is what things were like above the earth before that time,

> The sun did not know
> where her dwelling was,
> the moon did not know

> his own might and
> the stars did not know
> where they should stand."

"These are important events I'm hearing about," said Gangleri. "The heavens are an astonishingly large creation, and skillfully made. How was the earth constructed?"

The High One replied, "The earth is circular. Around it lies the deep sea, and along the shore of this sea, Borr's sons gave the giants lands to live on. But further inland, they built a fortification around their world as a defense against attack by the giants. They made this fortification out of Ymir's eyebrows and called it Midgard. They also tossed Ymir's brains into the sky and made clouds from them, as is said in *Grímnismál*,

> From Ymir's flesh
> the earth was formed,
> from his blood the sea,
> from his bones the mountains,
> from his hair trees,
> and from his skull the heavens.

> And from his brows
> the blessed gods
> made middle-earth
> for the sons of men;
> and from his brains
> all the sullen clouds
> were created."

9. "It seems to me that Borr's sons achieved a great deal when heaven and earth were created, and the sun and the stars put in place, and day divided from night. Now where did the people who live in the world come from?" asked Gangleri.

The High One answered, "When Borr's sons were walking along the shore, they found two trees and created people from them. The first son gave them breath and life, the second gave them intelligence and feeling, and the third gave them form, speech, hearing, and sight. They also gave them clothes and names. The man was called Ash, and the woman Elm, and they begot the human race, which was given a home in Midgard. Next Borr's sons built themselves a city in the centre of the world and named it Asgard, though we call it Troy. The gods and their descendants settled there and from then on many incidents and events took place both on earth and in heaven.

"In Asgard, there is a place called Hlidskjalf and when Odin sat there in his high-seat, he looked out over the whole world and saw what everyone was doing, and understood everything that he saw. His wife was called Frigg Fjorvins-daughter, and from their family line come the Aesir, a race of divine descent that lived in old Asgard and the kingdoms belonging to it. Thus Odin may truly be called All-Father for he is the father of all the gods and of men, and of everything else that was brought into being by him and his might. Earth was both his daughter and the wife by whom he sired his first son, Thor of the Aesir. Through his power and strength he is master of all living things.

10. "Norfi or Narfi was a giant who lived in Jotunheim [Giant-Land]. He had a daughter called Night who was swarthy and dark like all her family. She was given in marriage to a man called Naglfari and they had a son called Aud. Next she was married to someone named Annar [Second] and their daughter was called Earth. Her last marriage was to Delling, who was one of the Aesir. Their son was Day and, like his father, he was bright and beautiful. Then All-Father took Night and her son Day and gave them two horses and two chariots and set them in the heavens to ride around the Earth every day. Night rides ahead with the horse called Hrimfaxi [Frost-Mane] and every morning he bedews the Earth with the foam from his bit. Day's horse is called Skinfaxi [Shining-Mane] and he lights up all the Earth and the sky with his mane."

11. Then Gangleri asked, "How does All-Father regulate the course of the sun and the moon?" The High One replied, "There was a man named Mundilfoeri who had two children. They were so beautiful and fair that he called his son Mani [Moon] and his daughter Sol [Sun]. The gods, infuriated by his arrogance, seized the brother and sister and placed them in the heavens. They made Sol drive the horses that pulled the chariot of the Sun. The gods had fashioned this chariot from the glowing embers that flew out of Muspellsheim, in order to illuminate the worlds. The horses are called Arvak [Early-Waker] and Alsvid [All-Burning]. To keep them cool, the gods placed two bellows under their shoulder-blades; in some sources these are called 'iron-coolers.' Mani directs the course of the Moon and controls its waxing and waning. From earth, he carried off two children named Bil and Hjuki as they were leaving a well called Byrgir, carrying between them on their shoulders a bucket called Soeg, on a pole called Simul. These children, the offspring of Vidfin, can be seen from earth as they follow Mani."

12. Then Gangleri said, "Sol travels fast, almost as if she were afraid; indeed, she could not hurry along her course any faster even if she were in fear of death."

"It's hardly surprising that she moves so quickly," replied the High One, "for she has a pursuer hard on her heels and flight is her only means of escape."

"Who is causing her this anxiety?" asked Gangleri.

"It is two wolves," replied the High One, "The one pursuing her is called Skoll. She is terrified of him, and he will catch her. The one running ahead of her is called Hati Hrodvitnisson. He is eager to seize hold of the Moon; and that too will happen."

"What family do the wolves belong to?" asked Gangleri.

The High One replied, "A giantess lives to the east of Midgard in a forest called Ironwood; in that forest live trollwomen, called the Ironvidjur. The old giantess bears many giant sons, all of whom are shaped like wolves, and it is from this line that these wolves are descended. It is said that this family will produce a mighty wolf called Managarm [Hound of the Moon], who will fill himself up with the blood of everyone who dies. Then he will gulp down the Moon and shower all the heavens and the sky with blood, causing the Sun to lose its brightness, and blustery winds to blow hither and thither. As *Völuspá* says,

> The old woman lives eastward
> in Ironwood
> and there gives birth to
> Fenrir's brood;
> one will emerge,
> one from among them all,
> who, in troll's skin,
> will snatch the Moon.
>
> He devours the flesh
> of doomed men;
> he reddens the gods' home
> with crimson gore;
> the Sun's rays will grow black
> in the summers that follow,
> the weather will always be wretched.
> Do you wish to know more? And what?"

13. Then Gangleri asked, "What is the route from earth to heaven?"

"That question isn't too clever," answered the High One, with a laugh. "Hasn't anyone told you that the gods built a bridge called Bifrost between earth and heaven? You must have seen it; maybe it's what you call a rainbow.

It is tri-colored and very strong, for it was fashioned with more skill and knowledge than other constructions. But strong as it is, the bridge will collapse when Muspell's men come riding across it...."

15. Then Gangleri said, "Where is the chief holy place of the gods?"

"It's at the ash tree called Yggdrasil," answered the High One. "That's where the gods must sit in judgment every day."

"What is known about this place?" asked Gangleri.

Just as High answered him, "The ash is the greatest and best of all trees. Its limbs spread out over the whole world and stretch across the heavens. The tree is supported by three of its roots and these extend for a very long way: one reaches to the Aesir, a second to the Frost-giants, in what was once Ginnungagap [the Yawning Void], and the third extends over Niflheim [Land of Fog]. The serpent Nidhogg gnaws at the base of that root and under it is a spring called Hvergelmir. But under the root which stretches toward the Frost-giants lies Mimir's Well, in which wisdom and understanding are kept. The well-keeper is called Mimir; he is full of wisdom because he drinks well-water from the Gjallarhorn [Bellowing Horn]. All-father went there and asked for a single drink from the well, but he did not get it until he had laid down his eye as a pledge. Thus says *Völuspá*,

> Odin, I know all about
> where you hid your eye
> in Mimir's famous well;
> every morning, Mimir drinks
> mead from Odin's forfeit.
> Do you wish to know more? And what?

The third root of the ash reaches to heaven and beneath it is a very holy well called Urd's [Fate's] well, where the gods have their court. Every day the Aesir ride there over Bifrost, which is also known as the Aesir's bridge...."

Then the High One said, "Under the ash, beside the well, there stands a beautiful hall, and out of this hall come three maidens, whose names are Urd [What Has Been], Verdandi [What Is], and Skuld [What Will Be]. These maidens, who shape the course of men's lives, are called norns. There are also other norns, who come to each man at birth to shape his life. These norns are descended from the gods, but others are of elf origin, and a third group is descended from dwarfs, as it says in *Fafnismál*,

> The norns, I know,
> have numerous origins,
> are not of the same family;

> some are descended from gods
> and some are from the elf-tribe,
> some are daughters of dwarfs."

Then Gangleri said, "If the norns control the fates of men, then they allot these fates very unfairly, for some people have a successful and prosperous life, while others get little honor or affluence. Some men have a long life, while others have a short one."

"Good, well-born norns shape good lives," said the High One, "but the people who suffer misfortune are controlled by evil norns."

16. "Is there anything else of note to be said about the ash?" asked Gangleri.

"There is still a great deal to be said," replied the High One. "In the branches of the ash sits an eagle, which is knowledgeable about many things, and between its eyes sits a hawk, called Vedrfolnir. A squirrel named Ratatosk runs up and down the ash, carrying insults between the eagle and Nidhogg. Four harts called Dain, Dvalin, Duneyr, and Durathror run among the branches, eating the leaves. And, in Hvergelmir, there are so many serpents in addition to Nidhogg that no tongue can count them. As *Grimnismál* puts it,

> The ash, Yggdrasil,
> endures more anguish
> than humankind knows;
> above, a hart bites,
> at the side, it rots; Nidhogg
> gnaws from below.

Grimnismál also says,

> More serpents
> squirm under Yggdrasil
> than old fools imagine;
> Goin and Moin
> – they are the sons of Grafvitnir –
> Grabbak and Grafvollud,
> Ofnir and Svafnir
> will forever, I think, tear
> at the tree's twigs.

"It is said also that the norns who live beside Urd's well take water from it every day, along with some of the surrounding clay, and pour it over the ash tree so that its limbs will not wither or decay. The water is so holy that whatever comes into contact with it becomes as white as the skin that lines the inside of an eggshell. As *Völuspá* puts it here,

> There stands an Ash,
> Yggdrasil by name,
> a tall tree, sprinkled
> with moist, white soil;
> from it come the dews
> that fall in the dales;
> evergreen, the Ash stands
> above the well of Urd.

The dew which falls from the tree to the earth is known among men as honeydew and bees feed on it. Two birds feed in Urd's well. They are called swans, and all the birds of that species are descended from them."

9. RAGNAROK: THE DOOM OF THE GODS

The Poetic Edda *(sometimes called the* Elder Edda*) is a collection of mythological and heroic poems put together in thirteenth-century Iceland. The manuscript, the* Codex Regius, *is considerably later than the arrival of Christianity in Iceland, though much of the material is certainly older than the Codex itself. The following passage comes from* Völuspá [The Seeress's Prophecy]. *The poem is the seeress's reply to Odin's implicit questions about the future. Snorri used a version of this poem as a source for his* Edda.

Source: *Die Lieder des Codex Regius*, ed. Gustav Neckel; 5th rev. edition, ed. Hans Kuhn (Heidelberg: Carl Winter, 1983), pp. 10–15.

> 43. The golden-combed cock
> crowed above the Æsir,
> waking the warriors
> at the Warfather's home;
> and another crows
> under the earth,
> in the halls of Hel,
> a cock dark red in hue.

44. Loud barks Garm
before Gnipahel [Gnipa Cave],
fetters will break
and the wolf run free;
she knows much old lore,
but I see further into the future
to the doom of the gods,
the bitter doom of the victorious gods.

45. Brothers will fight
brothers to the death,
sisters' sons will corrupt
their kinship;
in a harsh world
whoredom is widespread;
ax age, sword age –
shields are shattered,
wind age, wolf age –
till the world collapses.
No man will show
mercy to another.

46. While Mim's sons revel
fate is roused,
fired up by a blast
from old Giallarhorn;
Heimdall blows loud,
with horn raised high;
Odin speaks to
Mim's severed head.

47. The upright ash,
Yggdrasil, trembles;
the ancient tree groans
and the giant breaks free;
all walk in fear
on the way to Hel
until Surt's kinsman,
Fire, consumes all.

48. What disturbs the Æsir?
What alarms the Elves?
all Giantland is in uproar,
the Æsir are in council;
Dwarves groan
before their stone doors,
knowing the nature of their steep rock.
Do you wish to know more? And what?

50. From the east drives Hrym,
hoists his shield before him;
Jormungand [World-Serpent] writhes
in giant's rage;
the serpent roils the waves
and the eagle screams,
pale-beaked, rends corpses;
Naglfar [Nail-Ship] breaks loose.

51. A ship sails from the east.
Muspell's folk
will come by sea
with Loki steering;
the giant's sons
all journey with the wolf,
and Byleipt's brother [Loki]
bears them company.

52. Surt travels from the south
with the scorcher of trees;
from his sword flashes
the sun of the slaughter-gods;
rocks crash
and witches rove;
men tread Hel's road
and heaven is split asunder.

53. Then Hlin [Frigg]
suffers a second sorrow,
when Odin goes forth
to fight the wolf,
and Beli's bright slayer [Frey]

goes against Surt;
then will Frigg's
beloved [Odin] fall....

55. Then comes forward
the Father of Victory's tall son,
Vidar, to give battle
to the murderous brute;
with his hand he thrusts
his sword into the heart
of the son of Hvedrung;
then his father is avenged.

56. Thor, Earth's splendid son
steps forward,
the son of Odin goes forth
to fight the serpent;
Middle-Earth's guardian strikes
with great spirit,
all heroes will forsake
their homestead, earth;
the son of Fjorgyn falls back
nine steps from the serpent,
dying, but undismayed
by its hostility.

57. The Sun darkens,
earth sinks into the sea,
the bright stars
disappear from the sky;
fumes war
with fire,
flames, surging high,
lick against heaven itself....

59. For a second time
she sees the surfacing
of earth from the sea,
green as ever it was;
rivers flow,
the eagle flies overhead

among the hills
hunting fish.

60. The Aesir meet
on Idavoll
and speak of the mighty
World-Serpent;
they bring to mind
momentous events
and the ancient runes
of heaven's great ruler.

61. Once again they will find
fine gold
gaming pieces
in the grass,
pieces they had owned
in ancient days.

62. Unsown fields
will flourish,
all ills will be remedied;
Baldr will return;
Hod and Baldr will dwell
in Hropt's victory halls,
shrine of the gods of the slain.
Do you wish to know more? And what?

63. Then Hœnir will select
the prophetic sticks
and the sons of both brothers
will settle in the wide
land of the winds.
Do you wish to know more? And what?

64. She sees a hall standing
fairer than the sun,
gold-roofed
at Gimlé;
there shall the worthy
warriors live

and all their days
experience delight.

65. At the gods' judgment day
the great one comes
from above, the mighty
master of all.

66. There flies the dusky dragon,
darkly gleaming,
up from the moonless mountains;
flying over the moors,
Nidhogg carries
corpses among his feathers.
And so she will now
sink down.

10. A PROPHETESS IN GREENLAND

The Gudrid mentioned here is Gudrid Thorbjornsdaughter, who married Thorfinn Karlsefni and traveled to Vinland. From Eirik the Red's Saga. *(See docs. 75 and 76.)*

Source: *Eiríks saga Rauða*, in *Eyrbyggja saga*, ed. Einar Ól. Sveinsson and Matthías Þórðarson, Íslenzk fornrit IV (Reykjavík, 1935), pp. 206–8.

4. At that time, there was a serious famine in Greenland. Those who went out hunting found slim pickings and some didn't come back at all. In the settlement there lived a woman called Thorbjorg. She could see into the future and was nicknamed the Little Prophetess. She had had nine sisters, all with the gift of prophecy, but she was the only one still alive. In winter it was her custom to attend banquets, and she was invited mostly by people who were curious about their own destiny or the outlook for the coming season. Since Thorkel was the leading farmer there, people thought that it was up to him to find out when the present lean times would end. Thorkel invited the prophetess to his home and gave her a fine reception as was customary when this sort of woman was received. A high seat was prepared for her and on it was a cushion that had to be stuffed with hen feathers.

She arrived in the evening with the man who had been sent to fetch her and this is how she was dressed: she was wearing a blue cloak that was fastened with ties, and decorated with stones from top to bottom. Around her neck, she had glass beads and, on her head, she wore a hood of black lambskin with an inner lining of white catskin. She carried a staff in her hand. On it was a knob, decorated with brass and set with stones. Attached to her belt was a large skin purse where she kept the charms she needed for her craft. On her feet she wore calfskin shoes with the hair still on them. They had long, tough laces with large tin knobs on the ends. Her gloves were catskin with white fur inside. When she came in, everyone thought it was fitting to address her respectfully. She received these greetings according to how much she esteemed the person giving them. Thorkel the Farmer took the wise woman by the hand and led her to the seat that had been prepared for her. He asked her to run her eyes over his household, herd, and house. She hadn't much to say about anything. The tables were set up in the evening and this is the food that was prepared for the prophetess. She had porridge made from kid's milk and, as a meat dish, she had hearts from all the various kinds of beasts on the farm. She ate with a brass spoon and a knife with a walrus-tusk handle, mounted with a double ring of brass; the knife had a broken point.

When the tables were put away, Thorkel the Farmer went over to Thorbjorg and asked her whether the house and the manners of the household were to her liking. He asked how quickly she would know the answer to his question, adding that everyone wanted to know. She replied that she would not speak until the following morning, after she had slept the night there.

Late in the following day, she was supplied with everything she needed to perform her magic. She asked for women who knew the chants called *vardlokkur* [spirit summoners] that she needed for her witchcraft. However, no such women were to be found. So a search was made throughout the farm for anyone with this knowledge.

Then Gudrid said, "I'm neither skilled in magic nor a prophetess, but Halldis, my foster-mother in Iceland, taught me chants that she called *vardlokkur*."

"Then you know more than I thought," said Thorbjorg. "I have no intention of taking part in this sort of ceremony," said Gudrid, "because I am a Christian woman."

"Maybe you could help the people here and be no worse a woman for it," said Thorbjorg. "Anyway, I will leave it to Thorkel to provide what's needed." Thorkel now pressured Gudrid and she agreed to do as he wished. Thorbjorg sat on the witch's dais and the women formed a circle around it. Then Gudrid sang the songs so well and beautifully that none of those present thought that they had ever heard finer singing.

The prophetess thanked Gudrid for her songs and said that there were now many spirits present who had listened to them with pleasure. "Before this," she said, "these spirits wanted nothing to do with us and would not obey us. Now many things are clear to me which before were concealed both from me and from others. I can tell you that this famine won't last much longer and the year will improve with the spring. The sickness that has lasted so long will clear up faster than expected.

"I'll reward you right away, Gudrid, for the help you have given us, for your whole future is now clearly visible to me. You will make a most honorable match here in Greenland, though the marriage won't last long, for your path in life points toward Iceland. There, your lineage will be long and distinguished and on your descendants a bright light will shine. Now, daughter, go safely and well."

11. ODIN'S WISDOM AND ARTS

The Saga of the Ynglings *opens Snorri's* Heimskringla *and tells of the arrival of the gods in Scandinavia from their former home in the east. The gods are treated euhemeristically as a noble tribe with an uncommon knowledge of the magical arts. They were worshipped because of the power that their magical skills gave them. The following passage introduces some of Odin's attributes and powers.*

Source: Snorri Sturluson, *Ynglinga saga*, in *Heimskringla*, ed. Bjarni Aðalbjarnarson, Íslenzk fornrit XXVI–XXVIII (Reykjavík, 2002), vol. 1, pp. 18–20.

7. Odin was a shape-shifter. When he changed shape, his body lay as if he were asleep or dead, while he took on the form of a bird, or a deer, or a fish, or a serpent and went, in the twinkling of an eye, to distant lands on his own or other men's business....

With words alone he was able to quench fire, calm the sea, and turn the winds in whichever direction he pleased.... Odin possessed Mimir's head which told him a great deal about what was happening in other worlds. Sometimes, he raised the dead from the earth or sat down under men who had been hanged. For that reason, he became known as Lord of the Ghosts, or Lord of the Hanged. He had two ravens, which he had trained to speak. They flew far and wide over the world and brought him many reports of events elsewhere.

By these means, he grew immensely wise, and he taught all these arts with the aid of runes and songs called *galdrar*, or magical chants. And that is why the Æsir are known as Galdrar-makers. Odin also knew and practiced the most powerful of the arts, which is called *seid*, or sorcery. By means of sorcery, he could foresee men's fates and predict the course of future events.

He could also inflict death, ill fortune, or sickness on people, and take one person's intelligence or strength and give it to someone else. Since the performance of this kind of witchcraft brings on an effeminate weakness, it is considered shameful for a man to practice the art, and it is usually priestesses who are taught it.

Odin knew the whereabouts of every hidden treasure and he also knew spells that would open up the earth, hills, rocks, and burial mounds. He could transfix whoever was inside with spells and then he was free to enter and take whatever he wanted.

Through the practice of these arts he became very famous. His enemies feared him, but his friends trusted him and had faith in him and his powers. He taught most of his arts to his sacrificial priests, and they were the ones who came closest to equaling him in wisdom and witchcraft. But many other people took up sorcery too, and the practice of witchcraft spread far and wide and survived for a long time. People sacrificed to Odin and the twelve chieftains [the Æsir]; they regarded them as their gods, and believed in them for a long time afterwards. The name Audun is derived from Odin, and many men give their sons that name, just as the name Thor is the basis for Thorir and Thorarin, or is combined with other words, as in Steinthor or Hafthor, or is altered in a variety of ways.

12. ODIN WELCOMES EIRIK BLOODAX TO VALHALLA

Odin is presented in "Eirik's Poem" ("Eiríksmál") as the ruler of Valhalla, where he welcomes warriors slain in battle. The warrior welcomed here is Eirik Bloodax, king of Norway and son of Harald Finehair. Eirik was deposed by his brother Hakon and later became king of Northumbria in England. The poem was probably commissioned by Queen Gunnhild, Eirik's wife, after his death at the Battle of Stainmore in England in 954. The poem is incomplete, but it offers a contemporary glimpse of pre-Christian beliefs. Both Eirik and Gunnhild were at least nominally Christian.

Source: *Ágrip af Noregskonunga Sögum: Fagurskinna – Noregs Konunga Tal*, ed. Bjarni Einarsson, Íslenzk fornrit XXIX (Reykjavik, 1985), pp. 77–79.

1. Odin said:
"What are these dreams?
At dawn, I saw myself
clearing Valhalla
for the coming of the slain;

I awoke the Einherjar,
told them to get up,
to put straw on benches,
and to wash out beer-mugs,
told Valkyries to bring wine,
as if a warlord was coming;
from the home of man
I await heroes,
noble-hearted men
to gladden my heart."

Odin rides to Valhalla on Sleipnir. Picture stone from Tjängvide, Gotland, eighth century. Odin's eight-legged horse, Sleipnir, was borne by the god Loki while he was disguised as a mare.

Source: Paul B. du Chaillu, *The Viking Age*, 2 vols. (New York: Charles Scribner's Sons, 1899), vol. 1, p. 58.

2. Bragi said:
"What thunders there
as though thousands are on the move,
as though a mighty host comes?
Benches creak and groan
as if Baldr is coming home
to Odin's hall."

3. Odin said:
"Don't talk nonsense,
wise Bragi; you know
very well that all
this uproar is for Eirik,
who's on his way here
to be a warrior in Odin's hall.

4. "Sigmund and Sinfjotli,
rise swiftly, and go
to meet the king.
Make him welcome
if it is Eirik;
I'm anxious to see him."

5. Sigmund said:
"Why hope to meet Eirik
rather than other kings?"
Odin said:
"Because in many countries
he has carried and reddened
his blood-crimsoned sword."

6. Sigmund said [?]:
"Why rob him of victory
if you think him valiant?"
Odin said:
"Since no one can tell
when the grey wolf
will look grimly
at the home of the gods."

7. Sigmund said:
"Hail to you, Eirik,
welcome here!
Enter the hall, wise king;
I must hear
what warriors follow you,
fresh from the fight."

8. Eirik said:
"Five kings
follow; I'll tell you
All their names.
I am the sixth."

13. ODIN HANGS ON YGGDRASIL

Sayings of the High One (Hávamál) *is a wisdom-poem that forms part of the*
Poetic Edda. *The poem contains Odin's advice on various topics, including sugges-*
tions on how to survive in a dangerous world, how to behave as a guest, and how to
behave as a host. Other parts of the poem are more broadly ethical in content, while the
closing section is composed of magical charms. In the following passage, Odin tells of
his suffering when he was suspended from Yggdrasil (Horse of Odin), the World-Tree.

Source: *Hávamál*, ed. David A.H. Evans (London: Viking Society for Northern Research,
1986), pp. 68–70.

138. I hung, I know,
on the wind-tossed tree
for nine nights in all,
suffered the spear wound,
was offered to Odin,
– myself to my self –
tormented on the tree
which rises from roots
hidden from human kind.

139. No one brought me bread,
drink was denied me,
groundward I gazed,
raised up the runes,

screaming I sought them,
but fell back from there.

140. Nine savage spells
I fetched from the famous son
of Bolthorn, Bestla's father,
and I drank deep
of poetry's precious mead,
the outpourings of Odrer.

141. I began to bear fruit,
and welcome wisdom,
began to burgeon and flourish;
word after word
led me to more words,
work after work
led me to more works.

142. Learn to recognize runes,
cleverly ordered characters,
signs with great significance,
characters of colossal power
woven by the wisest one,
made by the greatest gods,
engraved by Odin the god.

143. Odin cut them for the Æsir
Dain etched them for the elves
Dvalin for the dwarfs
Asvid etched them for the giants,
I myself made some [for mankind?].

144. Do you comprehend how runes are cut?
how to comment on the characters?
how the characters must be colored?
how to test their truth?
how prayer is to be practiced?
do you understand how offerings are made?
how the sacrifice is sent on its way?
how the sacrifice is slaughtered?

14. ODIN AND HUMAN SACRIFICE

(a) The Death of King Vikar

Part of the legendary Gautrek's Saga *tells the strange story of the hero Starkad and his involvement in the sacrifice to Odin of Vikar, king of Agder. Starkad is led to a council of the gods by his foster-father, Grani Horsehairs, who turns out to be Odin in disguise. Odin demands Starkad's participation in the sacrifice of Vikar in return for his help before the council. This passage contains a grim account of the Norse gods and their very human capacity for vindictiveness. Adam of Bremen also writes of human sacrifice at Uppsala (see doc. 16).*

Source: *Gautreks saga,* in *Fornaldarsögur Norðurlanda,* ed. Guðni Jónsson, 4 vols. (Reykjavík, 1959), vol. 4, pp. 28–31.

7. ... King Vikar sailed north from Agder to Hordaland with a large fleet of ships. They lay idle in a group of islands for a long time because of unfavorable winds. Using augury, they discovered that Odin wanted them to hang a man, chosen by lot from the army, in order to raise a fair wind. So they drew lots, and King Vikar's number came up. This took them aback, and they decided to have a council meeting next day to discuss the difficulty.

In the middle of the night, Grani Horsehairs woke up his foster son Starkad and told him to come with him. They took a small boat and rowed to another island, closer to the shore. They landed there and went up through the forest until they came to a clearing where a large crowd of men were holding a meeting. Eleven men were sitting on chairs, but the twelfth chair was empty. They joined the meeting, and Grani Horsehairs sat down in the twelfth chair. Then everyone hailed him as Odin, and he declared that the judges [the Æsir, the gods] must decide the fate of Starkad.

Then Thor spoke: "Starkad's father's mother, Alfhild, chose a wise giant to be father of her son, rather than Thor of the Æsir," he said. "So, what I have in mind for Starkad is that he shall never have a son or a daughter, and that his line will end with him."

Odin responded: "I shall grant that his one life will be as long as three."

Thor said: "He will perform a shameful act in each life."

Odin answered: "I decree that he will have the finest weapons and clothes."

Thor said: "I decree that he will have neither land nor homestead."

Odin said: "I grant him money." Thor said: "And I, that he will never feel he has enough."

Odin answered: "I give him victory and prowess in every battle."

Thor said: "I declare that he will be wounded in every battle."

Odin said: "I confer on him the gift of poetry, and the ability to compose as fast as he speaks." Thor said: "He will never remember what he composes."

Odin said: "I decree that the noblest and best men will think him estimable."

Thor said: "He will be loathed by everyone else."

Then the judges confirmed that Starkad should have everything that Odin and Thor had given him and, on that note, the meeting broke up. Starkad and Grani Horsehairs made their way back to their boat, and Grani said, "You must now reward me well, foster-son, for the help I have given you."

"Fine," replied Starkad. "You must now send King Vikar to me," said Grani Horsehairs, "and I'll tell you what to do." Starkad agreed, and Grani Horsehairs put a spear in his hand, saying that it would look like a reed to everyone else. They returned to the fleet at daybreak.

In the morning, the king's advisers held a meeting to consider the problem and they all thought that the sacrifice should be symbolic. Starkad told them what to do. Nearby grew a solitary fir tree and near that stood a tall tree-stump. Low on the fir tree was a thin branch which reached up into the foliage. It was the time of the day when the servants prepared food for the men, and a calf had been slaughtered and disemboweled. Starkad had the calf's guts fetched. Then he mounted the tree stump, pulled the thin branch down, and tied the calf's guts to it. He addressed King Vikar:

"Your gallows is ready, king, and it doesn't seem all that dangerous. If you come over here I'll put the noose around your neck."

"If this contraption is no more dangerous than it appears," said the king, "it won't do me any harm. But if things turn out differently, so be it."

The king mounted the tree-stump, and Starkad placed the halter around his neck. Then Starkad stepped down from the stump to the ground, thrust at the king with the reed, and saying, "Now I give you to Odin," let go of the fir branch. The reed turned into a spear and went right through the king. The tree-stump fell away from under his feet. The calf's entrails became a strong rope, and the branch sprang up and lifted the king to the top of the tree. The islands are now called Vikar's Islands.

This piece of work did not go down well with most of the people, and Starkad was exiled from Hordaland. He fled from Norway and went east to Sweden, where he stayed for a long time with the kings of Uppsala, Eirik and Alrik, the sons of Agni Skjalfarbondi, and went on raids with them.

(b) The Deaths of Domaldi and Olaf Tretelgja

Kingship was not a sinecure in The Saga of the Ynglings, *as the fate of the following monarchs makes plain.*

Source: Snorri Sturluson, *Ynglinga saga*, in *Heimskringla*, ed. Bjarni Aðalbjarnarson, Íslenzk fornrit XXVI–XXVIII (Reykjavík, 2002), vol. 1, pp. 31–32, 74.

15. Domaldi succeeded his father, Visbur, and became ruler of his lands. During his reign, there was famine and starvation in Sweden, so the Swedes held large sacrifices at Uppsala. The first autumn, they sacrificed oxen, but despite that the harvest was no better. The following autumn, they sacrificed men, but the harvest was as bad, or worse. The third autumn, when it was time for the sacrifices, the Swedes flocked to Uppsala in great numbers. The chieftains held a meeting and agreed unanimously that Domaldi, their king, was the cause of the famine, so they decided to attack and kill him and sacrifice him for a good harvest. And that is what they did. They reddened the altars with his blood....

43. Many people were banished from Sweden by King Ivar. They heard that Olaf Tretelgja [Woodcutter] had good land in Varmaland and they thronged there in such large numbers that the land could not support them all, and there was much famine and misery. They blamed the king for this, for the Swedes used to hold their king responsible for years of plenty and famine alike.

King Olaf did not sacrifice much, and this displeased the Swedes, who believed that the famine was caused by the king's laxity. So they mustered an army and marched against him. Taking him by surprise, they burned him alive in his house and gave him to Odin as a sacrifice for a good year. These events took place near Lake Vannen.

15. SIGURD, THE EARL OF LADE, SACRIFICES TO THE GODS

Though King Hakon the Good of Norway, ca 920–961, was Christian, he was never able to force Christianity on his kingdom. From The Saga of Hakon the Good *in* Heimskringla.

Source: Snorri Sturluson, *Hákonar saga Góða*, in *Heimskringla*, ed. Bjarni Aðalbjarnarson, Íslenzk fornrit XXVI–XXVIII (Reykjavík, 2002), vol. 1, pp. 167–68.

14. Sigurd the Earl of Lade was very fond of offering up sacrifices, as was Hakon, his father, before him. Sigurd always presided, on the king's behalf, over sacrificial feasts in the Trondelag [the district around Trondheim]. When there was to be a sacrifice, it used to be the custom that all the landowners would bring with them to the temple whatever food they would need during the festivities. They all had to have ale for the feast too. All sorts of cattle, including horses, were slaughtered there. The blood that was drained from them was called *hlaut,* and the bowls to contain it were known as hlautbowls. Hlautsticks were used to sprinkle the whole altar with blood. The walls of the temple, both inside and out, and the people there were sprinkled with blood too. The meat, however, was cooked and eaten at the banquet.

Fires were lit in the middle of the temple floor and cauldrons were suspended over them. A full goblet was carried around the fire and the chief who was responsible for the feast blessed the goblet and all the sacrificial meat. The first goblet was Odin's and was drunk for the victory and power of the king. Next, Njord's goblet and Freyja's were drunk for a prosperous year and peace. Then it was the custom to drink toasts. People also drank goblets for relatives who had died; these were called memorial cups.

Earl Sigurd was a very generous man who is renowned for mounting an enormous sacrificial festival at Lade, entirely at his own expense. Kormak Ogmundarson says this in *Sigurd's drápa* [*Sigurd's Praise-poem*]:

> No one brought baskets of food
> or vats of ale when visiting
> the lordly earl, so lavish with his
> goods. *The gods deceived Thiazi* [read with line 8].
> all must treat the temple's
> priest with due deference,
> please the provider of
> gold. *Gramr fought for gold* [read with line 4].

16. THE TEMPLE AT UPPSALA

Pre-Christian religious activity took place in a wide range of cult-places. According to Tacitus (100 CE) Germanic tribes worshiped in the open air in sacred groves. Worship could also be conducted in farmhouses or chieftains' halls. Specific cult houses are also known. Here, Adam of Bremen provides a graphic description of what he called a temple at Uppsala, Sweden, and some of the ritual that occurred there, from Book Four of his History of the Archbishop of Hamburg-Bremen *(see doc. 2). Adam's temple has been reinterpreted as a large feasting hall in which seasonal rites took place.*

Source: trans. F.J. Tschan, Adam of Bremen, *History of the Archbishops of Hamburg-Bremen,* with new introduction by T. Reuter (New York: Columbia University Press, 2002), pp. 207–8.

26. That folk [the Swedes] has a very famous temple called Uppsala, situated not far from the city of Sigtuna and Björkö. In this temple, entirely decked out in gold, the people worship the statues of three gods in such wise that the mightiest of them, Thor, occupies a throne in the middle of the chamber; Wotan and Frikko have places on either side. The significance of these gods is as follows; Thor, they say, presides over the air, which governs the thunder and lightening, the winds and rains, fair weather and crops. The other, Wotan – that is, the Furious – carries on war and imparts to man strength against his enemies. The third is Frikko, who bestows peace and pleasure on mortals. His likeness, too, they fashion with an immense phallus. But Wotan they chisel armed, as our people are wont to represent Mars. Thor with his scepter apparently resembles Jove. The people also worship heroes made gods, whom they endow with immortality because of their remarkable exploits, as one reads in the *Vita* of Saint Ansgar they did in the case of King Eric.

27. For all their gods there are appointed priests to offer sacrifices for the people. If plague and famine threaten, a libation is poured to the idol of Thor; if war, to Wotan; if marriages are to be celebrated, to Frikko. It is customary also to solemnize in Uppsala, at nine-year intervals, a general feast of all the provinces of Sweden. From attendance at this festival no one is exempted. Kings and people all and singly send their gifts to Uppsala and, what is more distressing than any kind of punishment, those who have already adopted Christianity redeem themselves through these ceremonies. The sacrifice is of this nature; of every living thing that is male, they offer nine heads, with the blood of which it is customary to placate gods of this sort. The bodies they hang in the sacred grove that adjoins the temple. Now this grove is so sacred in the eyes of the heathen that each and every tree in it is believed divine because of the death or putrefaction of the victims. Even dogs and horses hang there with men. A Christian seventy-two years old told me that he had

seen their bodies suspended promiscuously. Furthermore, the incantations customarily chanted in the ritual of a sacrifice of this kind are manifold and unseemly; therefore, it is better to keep silence about them.

17. A TEMPLE IN ICELAND

Like several other sagas, The Saga of the People of Eyri *(Eyrbyggja saga) begins with the unification of Norway under Harald Finehair and ends in the eleventh century with the death of Snorri Godi (the priest, chieftain) in 1031. In this passage, an early settler, Thorolf Mostrarskegg (Bearded man from Most, Most-Beard), builds a temple.*

Source: *Eyrbyggja saga*, ed. Einar Ól. Sveinsson and Matthías Þórðarson, Íslenzk fornrit IV (Reykjavík, 1935), pp. 7–10.

4. Thorolf Mostrarskegg offered a great sacrifice and asked his dear friend Thor whether he should make his peace with the king, or leave the country and find himself a new future. In answer to his question, Thor directed Thorolf to Iceland, so he bought a large ocean-going ship and got it ready for the journey. He took his household and household property with him, and many of his friends decided to accompany him to Iceland. He dismantled the temple and took with him most of the wood from the building, as well as earth from beneath the pedestal where Thor had sat.

Then Thorolf put to sea. He had a favorable wind and when he reached Iceland, he steered along the south coast and then west around Reykjaness. After that the wind dropped and they saw that there were large fjords cutting into the land. Thorolf threw overboard the high-seat pillars which had stood in the temple; Thor was carved on one of them. Thorolf declared that wherever Thor brought the pillars ashore, that's where he would settle in Iceland. As soon as he threw the pillars overboard, they drifted toward the western fjord, seeming to travel more quickly than might be expected. Then a sea breeze arose and they sailed around Snaefellsness and into the fjord which, they saw, was very broad and long and surrounded by high mountains. Thorolf called the fjord Breidafjord [Broadfjord]. Half way along the south side of the fjord, he made for land and moored his ship in a bay which was afterwards called Hofsvag [Temple Bay]. They explored the land and discovered that Thor and the pillars had come ashore at the point of a headland to the north of the bay. Afterwards, the headland was called Thorsness.

Next, Thorolf carried fire around the boundaries of his land claim, from Stafa [Staf River] in the west, inland to the river called Thorsa [Thor's River] in the east. He settled his crew there, but he himself built a large house near

Hofsvag and called it Hofstad [Templestead]. There he had a temple built. It was a large structure with a door on one of the side walls close to the end of the building. Inside, in front of the door, stood the high-seat pillars, studded with nails called god's nails. Beyond the pillars the whole interior was a sanctuary and at the inner end there was an area resembling what we call a choir in churches nowadays. In the middle of the floor stood an altar-like structure, and on it lay a ring weighing twenty ounces, which had been formed without a joint. All oaths were sworn on it, and the temple priest had to wear it on his arm at every public meeting. A bowl for sacrificial blood always stood on the altar, and in the bowl lay a twig [or aspergillum] for sprinkling *hlaut*, which is the blood of living creatures sacrificed to the gods. The gods were arranged around the altar in the innermost, or choir-like, part of the temple.

All men had to pay a tax to the temple and were obliged to support the temple *godi* [priest] in all his undertakings, just as nowadays Thingmen [a man who owed support to a chief, especially at assemblies] have obligations to their chiefs. The *godi* was responsible for the upkeep and maintenance of the temple, and for holding sacrificial feasts there.

Thorolf named the headland between Vigrafjord and Hofsvag, Thorsness. On this headland stands a mountain for which Thorolf had such reverence that no one was permitted to look at it without washing first. Also nothing was to be killed there, neither man nor beast, unless it came down from the mountain of its own accord. He called the mountain Helgafell [Holy Mountain] and believed that he and all his relatives from Thorsness would go there when they died.

Thorolf designated Thor's landing place at the point of the headland as the site for the settlement of lawsuits. He established the local thing [assembly, judicial and deliberative] there too. The area was so holy that he did not want it polluted in any way, either by bloodshed or by human waste; a skerry called Shit Skerry was set aside for the waste.

Thorolf became a wealthy farmer and maintained a large household because in those days the islands and the sea were an abundant source of food.

18. KING HARALD GORMSSON AND THE LAND-SPIRITS

Landvættir, *Land-Spirits, are guardians of particular places or countries. The Book of Settlements* (Landnámabók) *(see doc. 70b) states that the dragon-prows of ships must be removed close to land for fear of disturbing these spirits. Egil Skallagrimsson left a scorn-pole (*niðstöng: *a pole topped by a horse's head and inscribed with threatening runes) in Norway in the hope of upsetting them so badly that they would drive*

Eirik Bloodax from his kingdom; within a year, Eirik was gone, deposed by his brother Hakon. Clearly, these are beings to be reckoned with, as Harald Gormsson, king of Denmark, discovers in this passage from Olaf Tryggvason's Saga.

Source: Snorri Sturluson, *Óláfs saga Tryggvasonar*, in *Heimskringla*, ed. Bjarni Aðalbjarnarson, Íslenzk fornrit XXVI–XXVIII (Reykjavík, 2002), vol. 1, pp. 270–72.

33. Then the king of the Danes decided to sail with his fleet to Iceland to take revenge for the derision which all the Icelanders had heaped on him. For a law had been passed in Iceland that there was to be one lampoon composed about the Danish king for every person in the land. The reason for this was that an Icelandic ship had been wrecked in Denmark, and the Danes had seized the entire cargo, calling it flotsam. The man who was responsible for this was the king's steward, Birgir, and a lampoon was composed against both him and the king. This is part of it:

> When murderous minded
> Harald from the south
> mounted the mare, stallion-like,
> the Wend-Killer [Harald] became soft as wax;
> but the base Birgir
> – loathed by the Land-Spirits –
> stood mare-like,
> ready with his rear.

King Harald ordered a sorcerer to go to Iceland in animal-shape and find out whatever information he could. He went in the form of a whale and, when he reached Iceland, he swam west around the north of the country. He saw that all the mountains and hills were full of Land-Spirits, some large and some small. When he came to Vapnafjord, he entered the fjord, intending to go ashore, but a huge dragon came down the valley, followed by many serpents, toads, and lizards that breathed poison at him. So he swam away and went west along the coast all the way to Eyjafjord. When he entered the fjord, there came toward him a bird so huge that its wings reached to the mountains on either side of the fjord; with it were many other birds, both large and small. Leaving there, he continued west along the coast, and then went south to Breidafjord, which he entered. There, a huge bull came toward him, wading into the sea and bellowing horribly; a horde of Land-Spirits followed it. So he left and went south around Reykjaness, intending to land at Vikarskeid, but there he was accosted by a mountain-giant with an iron staff in his hand. The giant's head was higher than the mountains, and with him were many other giants. From there he headed east all the way along the coast.

"There was nothing but sands," he said, "and a harborless coast with heavy surf offshore; and the sea between Norway and Iceland is so wide that it's not possible for longships to cross it." After that, King Harald turned his fleet south and went back to Denmark.

19. NORSE FUNERAL PRACTICES

Burial chamber of the Gokstad ship burial. The ship was built in the late ninth century.

Source: Paul B. du Chaillu, *The Viking Age*, 2 vols. (New York: Charles Scribner's Sons, 1899), vol. 1, p. 336.

(a) An Arab Description of a Viking Funeral

There are several accounts from the Islamic world relating to the Vikings. One of the most famous is that of Ibn Fadlān, a member of an embassy sent by the caliph of Baghdad to the king of the Bulgars on the Volga River in the early 920s. His first-hand account, known as the Risāla (Writing), *described the journey and the peoples with whom the embassy came into contact, including a group of Swedish Rūs merchants. About one-fifth of Ibn Fadlān's surviving text is devoted to these Rūs, including this spectacular description of a funeral (see also doc. 62).*

Source: trans. Albert S. Cook, "Ibn Fadlān's Account of Scandinavian Merchants on the Volga in 922," *Journal of English and Germanic Philology* 22 (1923): 59–63.

I was told that the least of what they do for their chiefs when they die, is to consume them with fire. When I was finally informed of the death of one of their magnates, I sought to witness what befell. First they laid him in his grave – over which a roof was erected – for the space of ten days, until they had completed the cutting and sewing of his clothes. In the case of a poor man, however, they merely build for him a boat, in which they place him, and consume it with fire. At the death of a rich man, they bring together his goods, and divide them into three parts. The first of these is for his family; the second is expended for the garments they make; and with the third they purchase strong drink, against the day when the girl resigns herself to death, and is burned with her master. To the use of wine they abandon themselves in mad fashion, drinking it day and night; and not seldom does one die with the cup in his hand.

When one of their chiefs dies, his family asks his girls and pages: "Which one of you will die with him?" Then one of them answers, "I." From the time that he utters this word, he is no longer free: should he wish to draw back, he is not permitted. For the most part, however, it is the girls that offer themselves. So, when the man of whom I spoke had died, they asked his girls, "Who will die with him?" One of them answered, "I." She was then committed to two girls, who were to keep watch over her, accompany her wherever she went, and even, on occasion, wash her feet. The people now began to occupy themselves with the dead man – to cut out the clothes for him, and to prepare whatever else was needful. During the whole of this period, the girl gave herself over to drinking and singing, and was cheerful and gay.

When the day was now come that the dead man and the girl were to be committed to the flames, I went to the river in which his ship lay, but found that it had already been drawn ashore. Four corner-blocks of birch and other woods had been placed in position for it, while around were stationed large wooden figures in the semblance of human beings. Thereupon the ship was brought up and placed on the timbers above mentioned. In the meantime the people began to walk to and fro, uttering words which I did not understand. The dead man, meanwhile, lay at a distance in his grave, from which they had not yet removed him. Next they brought a couch, placed it in the ship, and covered it with Greek cloth of gold, wadded and quilted, with pillows of the same material. There came an old crone, whom they call the angel of death, and spread the articles mentioned on the couch. It was she who attended to the sewing of the garments, and to all the equipment; it was she, also, who was to slay the girl....

When they came to the grave, they removed the earth from the wooden roof, set the latter aside, and drew out the dead man in the loose wrapper [winding-sheet] in which he had died. Then I saw that he had turned quite black, by reason of the coldness of that country. Near him in the grave they had placed strong drink, fruits, and a lute; and these they now took out. Except for his color, the dead man had not changed. They now clothed him in drawers, leggings, boots, and a *kurtak* [tunic] and *chaftan* [cape] of cloth of gold, with golden buttons, placing on his head a cap made of cloth of gold, trimmed with sable. Then they carried him into a tent placed in the ship, seated him on the wadded and quilted covering, supported him with the pillows, and, bringing strong drink, fruits, and basil, placed them all beside him. Then they brought a dog, which they cut in two, and threw into the ship; laid all his weapons beside him; and led up two horses, which they chased until they were dripping with sweat, whereupon they cut them into pieces with their swords, and threw the flesh into the ship. Two oxen were then brought forward, cut in pieces, and flung into the ship. Finally they brought a cock and a hen, killed them, and threw them in also.

The girl who had devoted herself to death meanwhile walked to and fro, entering one after another of the tents which they had there. The occupant of each tent lay with her, saying, "Tell your master, 'I [the man] did this only for love of you.'"

When it was now Friday afternoon, they led the girl to an object which they had constructed and which looked like the framework of a door. She then placed her feet on the extended hands of the men, was raised up above the framework, and uttered something in their language, whereupon they let her down. Then again they raised her, and she did as at first. Once more they let her down, and then lifted her a third time, while she did as the previous times. They then handed her a hen, whose head she cut off and threw away; but the hen itself they cast into the ship. I inquired of the interpreter what it was that she had done. He replied: "The first time she said, 'Lo, I see here my father and mother'; the second time, 'Lo, now I see all my deceased relatives sitting'; the third time, 'Lo, there is my master, who is sitting in Paradise. Paradise is so beautiful, so green. With him are his men and boys. He calls me, so bring me to him.'" Then they led her away to the ship.

Here she took off her two bracelets, and gave them to the old woman who was called the angel of death, and who was to murder her. She also drew off her two anklets, and passed them to the two serving-maids, who were the daughters of the so-called angel of death. Then they lifted her into the ship, but she did not yet admit her to the tent. Now men came up with shields and staves, and handed her a cup of strong drink. This she took, sang over it, and emptied it. "With this," so the interpreter told me, "she is taking leave of those who are dear to her." Then another cup was handed her, which she also took, and began a lengthy song. The crone admonished her to drain the cup without lingering, and to enter the tent where her master lay. By this time, as it seemed to me, the girl had become dazed; she made as though she would enter the tent, and had brought her head forward between the tent and the ship, when the hag seized her by the head, and dragged her in. At this moment the men began to beat upon their shields with the staves, in order to drown the noise of her outcries, which might have terrified the other girls, and deterred them from seeking death with their masters in the future. Then six men followed into the tent, and each and every one had carnal companionship with her. Then they laid her down by her master's side, while two of the men seized her by the feet and two by the hands. The old woman known as the angel of death now knotted a rope around her neck, and handed the ends to two of the men to pull. Then with a broad-bladed dagger she smote her between the ribs, and drew the blade forth while the two men strangled her with the rope till she died.

The next of kin to the dead men drew near, and, taking a piece of wood, lighted it, and walked backwards toward the ship, holding the stick in one hand, with the other placed upon his buttocks (he being naked), until the wood which had been piled up under the ship was ignited. Then the others came up with staves and firewood, each one carrying a stick already lighted at the upper end, and threw it all on the pyre. The pile was soon aflame, then the ship, finally the tent, the man, and the girl, and everything else in the ship. A terrible storm began to blow up, and thus intensified the flames, and gave wings to the blaze.

At my side stood one of the Northmen, and I heard him talking with the interpreter who stood near him. I asked the interpreter what the Northmen had said, and received answer: "You Arabs," he said, "must be a stupid set! You take him who is to you the most revered and beloved of you and cast him into the ground, to be devoured by creeping things and worms. We, on the other hand, burn him in a twinkling, so that he instantly, without a moment's delay, enters into Paradise." At this he burst out into uncontrollable laughter, and then continued: "It is the love of the Master [God] that causes the wind to blow and snatch him away in an instant." And, in very truth, before an hour had passed, ship, wood, and girl had, with the man, turned to ashes.

Thereupon they heaped over the place where the ship had stood something like a rounded hill, and, erecting on the centre of it a large birchen post, wrote on it the name of the deceased, along with that of the king of the Northmen. Having done this, they left the spot.

(b) Snorri's History of Burial Practices

Cremation was the usual funerary practice in the early Viking Age; the dead were burned on pyres along with their possessions, and their ashes scattered or buried in urns. Burial replaced cremation later in the Viking Age, except in Sweden, where cremation persisted. Graves might be marked by simple stones, or by stones arranged in ship-patterns. The graves of the notable dead were sometimes marked by a mound, on occasion containing a ship (as at Oseberg and Gokstad). The dead were often accompanied, not only by the personal possessions they would need in the hereafter, but also by horses and the occasional servant or handmaid. Snorri lived before the age of archaeology, but his account of funerary practices follows this general outline, even though some of his details may be questionable. From the Prologue of Heimskringla.

Source: Snorri Sturluson, *Heimskringla*, ed. Bjarni Aðalbjarnarson, Íslenzk fornrit XXVI–XXVIII (Reykjavík, 2002), vol. 1, pp. 4–5.

The first age was called the age of burning, for in those days the dead had to be burned and standing stones were raised in their memory. But after Freyr had been buried in a burial mound at Uppsala, many chieftains erected mounds as often as standing stones in memory of their relatives. The age of burial mounds began in Denmark when King Dan the Proud had a mound built for himself and gave orders that after his death he was to be laid in it with his regalia and armor, his horse and harness, and many other precious objects. Many of his lineage were buried in the same way. The age of burning lasted for much longer among the Norsemen and the Swedes.

(c) Odin Orders Cremation and Becomes a God

From The Saga of the Ynglings.

Source: Snorri Sturluson, *Ynglinga saga*, in *Heimskringla*, ed. Bjarni Aðalbjarnarson, Íslenzk fornrit XXVI–XXVIII (Reykjavík, 2002), vol. 1, pp. 20–23.

8. The laws which Odin established in his country were those which the Æsir had observed earlier. He decreed that the dead were all to be cremated along with their possessions and said that everyone should arrive in Valhalla

with the riches from his funeral pyre, and with the treasures he had hidden in the earth.

The ashes were to be taken out to sea or buried in the ground. Burial mounds would be built to commemorate outstanding men, and memorial stones would be erected for all men who had manly qualities; this custom was observed for a long time.

There was to be a sacrifice at the beginning of winter for a bountiful year, another at midwinter for good crops, and a third in the summer for victory. Throughout Sweden, the people were to pay Odin a tax of a penny per head, and in return he was to protect their land against attack, and make a sacrifice on their behalf for a good year....

9. Odin fell mortally ill in Sweden and, when he was close to death, he had himself marked with a spear-point and he claimed as his own all men who were killed in combat. He said that he would go to the home of the gods and make his friends welcome there. But the Swedes got it into their heads that he had gone to the ancient Asgard and that he would live there forever. So they renewed their faith in Odin and said prayers to him. They believed that he often appeared to them before great battles, granting victory to some, and inviting others to join him. Either fate was thought desirable.

After his death, Odin was cremated, and the burning was carried out in princely style, for it was their belief that the greatness of the deceased was in proportion to the treasure burned with him, and that the higher the smoke rose, the loftier was his position in heaven.

(d) The Death of Baldur the Good

Baldur, son of Odin, was associated with light and beauty in Norse mythology. His death, which is greatly mourned by the Æsir, is momentous in that it begins the process that will end with Ragnarok (the Doom of the Gods). However, after Ragnarok, Baldur will rise again from the kingdom of Hel to rule a bright new world together with the sons of Thor.

The following passage is from Gylfaginning.

Source: Snorri Sturluson, *Edda. Gylfaginning*, ed. Anthony Faulkes (London: Viking Society for Northern Research, 1988), pp. 45–47.

49. Then Gangleri said, "Have there been any other remarkable happenings among the Æsir?..."

The High One replied, "Here is an event that seemed ... important to the Æsir. The story begins when Baldur dreamt fearful dreams about his life. When he told the Æsir about these dreams, they discussed the matter and resolved to provide Baldur with immunity from all the dangers of life. Frigg received oaths that they would not harm Baldur, from fire and water, from iron and all kinds of metal, from rocks and soil, from trees and illnesses, from animals and birds, from poison and snakes.

When that was done and everyone had heard about it, the Æsir entertained themselves by having Baldur stand up at assemblies and allow the others to shoot at him, to cut at him, and to pelt him with stones; and, no matter what they did to him, he was not harmed. Everyone thought this was a real marvel.

But when Loki Laufeyarson saw that Baldur was not hurt, he was displeased, so he adopted the shape of a woman and went to Fensala, Frigg's palace. Frigg asked this woman if she knew what the Æsir were up to at their assembly. She replied that they were all pelting Baldur with things without doing him any harm.

"Weapons and trees will not hurt Baldur," said Frigg. "I have received oaths from all of them."

"Have absolutely all things sworn oaths not to harm Baldur?" asked the woman.

"A little tree called mistletoe is sprouting to the west of Valhalla," answered Frigg, "and I thought it was too young to be asked to swear the oath."

At that, the woman went away, and Loki pulled up the mistletoe and went to the meeting. Because he was blind, Hod stood alone outside the circle of men who were throwing objects at Baldur. Loki asked him, "Why aren't you throwing things at Baldur?"

"Because I can't see where Baldur is, and, anyway, I haven't anything to throw," answered Hod.

"You should do what the others are doing and show Baldur the same respect. I'll lead you to where he's standing, and you can throw this twig at him," said Loki.

Hod took the mistletoe and threw it at Baldur with guidance from Loki. The twig pierced Baldur, and he fell to the ground, dead.

When Baldur fell, the Æsir were speechless and they couldn't stir themselves to lift him up. They looked at one another, and no one had the least doubt about who had done the deed, but no one could take revenge since their meeting place was such an important sanctuary. When the Æsir attempted to speak, they were so overcome by weeping that no one was able to express his grief in words. But Odin's anguish was the most painful, for he understood best how great a disaster for the Æsir the death of Baldur was.

When the Æsir recovered themselves, Frigg asked who among them wanted to win all her affections and favor by riding the road to Hel to look for Baldur and offer Hel a ransom if she would permit him to return to

Asgard. Odin's son Hermod was the one who undertook the journey. Then Odin's horse Sleipnir was caught and led forward; Hermod mounted the horse and galloped off.

Next, the Æsir lifted Baldur's body and moved it to the sea where lay his ship Hringhorni, the finest of vessels. The gods wanted to launch the ship and build Baldur's funeral pyre on board, but Hringhorni would not move an inch. So a summons was sent to Jotunheim [Giants' Land] for a giantess called Hyrrokkin. She arrived riding on a wolf with a venomous snake for reins. She leapt from her mount, and Odin ordered four berserks to look after it, but, until they had thrown it to the ground, they were unable to control it. She went to the ship's prow and launched it with her first shove, which made the rollers burst into flames, and caused the world to shake. Thor was furious; he seized his hammer, intending to shatter her head, but all the gods begged him to spare her.

Now Baldur's body was carried out to the ship. When Baldur's wife, Nanna Nep's daughter, saw this, she was overcome by grief and died. She too was carried to the pyre which was then set alight. Next, Thor stepped up to consecrate the pyre with Mjollnir, his hammer. But a dwarf called Litr ran in front of his feet, so Thor kicked at him and shoved him into the fire where he burned.

People of many nations attended this cremation. To mention Odin first, he came with Frigg, the valkyries, and his ravens. Freyr came in his carriage with the boar called Gullinbursti [Gold-Mane] or Slidrugtanni [Terribly-Tusked]. Heimdall rode the horse called Gulltopp [Gold-Tuft]. Freyja came drawn by her cats. There was also a great crowd of ice-giants and mountain-giants. On the pyre, Odin placed a gold ring called Draupnir which had the property of producing eight equally valuable rings every ninth night. Baldur's horse was led to the pyre with all its harness.

(e) Gunnar's Burial Mound

For the heroic death of Gunnar in Njal's Saga, *see doc. 81. From* Njal's Saga.

Source: *Brennu-Njáls saga*, ed. Einar Ól. Sveinsson, Íslenzk fornrit XII (Reykjavík, 1954), pp. 191–92.

78. Njal was very upset by the killing of Gunnar, and so were the Sigfussons. They asked Njal if he thought they had any right to bring a lawsuit for the manslaughter of Gunnar. Njal replied that this wasn't possible when a man had been declared an outlaw. He thought that it would be better to disgrace Gizur and his men by killing a few of them in revenge for Gunnar.

They raised a burial mound for Gunnar and placed him inside in a sitting position. Rannveig didn't want Gunnar's halberd taken into the mound. She said that only a man willing to avenge Gunnar should pick up the weapon. No one touched it. Rannveig treated Hallgerd [Gunnar's wife] so harshly that she came close to killing her, saying that she was to blame for her son's death. Hallgerd fled to Grjota with her son Grani. The property was divided; Hogni was to have the land and farmstead at Hlidarend and Grani was to have the land that was rented out.

20. THE LIVING DEAD

(a) Gunnar's Posthumous Poem

Although he stays in his mound, Gunnar appears to have a ghostly afterlife. From Njal's Saga.

Source: *Brennu-Njáls saga*, ed. Einar Ól. Sveinsson, Íslenzk fornrit XII (Reykjavík, 1954), pp. 192–94.

78. ... On one occasion, a strange event occurred at Hlidarend. A shepherd and a servant-woman were driving livestock near Gunnar's burial mound; it seemed to them that Gunnar was in good spirits and reciting verses in the mound. They went home and told Gunnar's mother, Rannveig, what had happened. She asked them to tell Njal. So they went to Bergthorshval and told him and he made them repeat the story three times. Afterwards, he and Skarphedin spoke in private for a long time.

Then Skarphedin picked up his ax and returned with the servants to Hlidarend. Hogni and Rannveig were delighted to see him and welcomed him warmly. Rannveig invited him to pay a long visit and he promised that he would. He and Hogni were always together, both indoors and out. Hogni was a fine, bold man. He was also skeptical, so they did not dare tell him about the apparition.

One evening, Skarphedin and Hogni were outside, to the south of Gunnar's mound. The moon shone brightly though, from time to time, it was hidden by clouds. The burial mound appeared to be open and Gunnar had turned so that he was looking directly at the moon. They thought they saw four lights burning in the mound, and these lights cast no shadows. They saw that Gunnar was happy and cheerful-looking. He recited a poem so loudly that they could have heard it clearly even if they had been further away.

The great-hearted gold-giver,
Bold in bloody battles,
Daring in deeds, Hogni's
Splendid father spoke:
The shade of the shield-warrior
Called yielding cowardly,
Preferred to fall in the fight,
A hero in his helmet,
Preferred to fall in the fight.

Then the burial mound closed up again.

"Would you have believed this if anyone had told you about it?" asked Skarphedin. "I would have believed it if Njal had told me," replied Hogni, "for it is said he never lies."

"An apparition like this has great significance," said Skarphedin. "When Gunnar himself appears and tells us that he would rather die than give in to his enemies, he is teaching us what we should do."

"I won't manage to do anything unless you help me," said Hogni. "I won't forget how Gunnar acted after the death of your kinsman, Sigmund," said Skarphedin. "I'll give you all the help I can. My father promised Gunnar that he would give you or Rannveig whatever help you needed." Then they went back to Hlidarend.

(b) Grettir's Fight with Glam

Frequently, the dead insist on hanging around and making themselves extremely un-pleasant. In this passage from Grettir's Saga, *the hero meets the* draugr *(walking dead, ghost), Glam, in a fight to the death.*

Source: *Grettis saga Ásmundarson*, ed. Guðni Jónson, Íslenzk fornrit VII (Reykjavík, 1936), pp. 107–23.

32. There was a man named Thorhall who lived at Thorhallsstead in Forsaeludale [Shadow Valley], south of Vatnsdale. He was the son of Grim, who was the son of Thorhall, who was the son of Fridmund, who was the first settler of Forsaeludale. Thorhall married a woman called Gudrun, by whom he had a grown-up son and daughter, Grim and Thurid. Thorhall was a very prosperous man. The bulk of his wealth was in livestock and no one else had as many animals as he did. Though he was not a chieftain, he was a respectable landowner.

His farm was haunted, so he had difficulty finding a competent shepherd. He asked many experienced men what he should do, but no one could give him any useful advice. Thorhall had good horses, and rode to the Althing every summer. One year at the Althing, he visited the booth of Skapti Thoroddson, the law-speaker. Skapti was a very knowledgeable man who gave good advice to those who consulted him. The difference between Skapti and his father was that Thorodd had the second sight and it was rumored that he was not to be trusted, whereas Skapti gave everyone whatever advice he thought would serve them best, as long as they followed it. For this reason, Skapti was called 'His Father's Better.'

Thorhall went into Skapti's booth. Skapti knew that Thorhall was a prosperous man, so he welcomed him warmly and asked for his news. "I want your advice," said Thorhall. "I'm not too great at giving advice," replied Skapti. "But what's your problem?"

"My problem is this," said Thorhall. "I don't have much luck keeping shepherds. Some get hurt; others don't stay to finish their contracts. Now, no one who's aware of the situation will take on the job."

"There must be some threatening presence about the place if men are more reluctant to look after your cattle than other people's," said Skapti. "But since you've asked my advice, I'll get you a shepherd. His name is Glam and he's a Swede from Sylgsdale who came to Iceland last summer. He's big and strong, but not very popular."

Thorhall said that that wasn't a problem as long as Glam looked after the sheep properly. Skapti added that there wasn't much prospect of finding another shepherd if someone as strong and brave as Glam didn't work out. After that, Thorhall left the booth; this was toward the end of the Althing.

Thorhall noticed that two of his pale-colored horses were missing, so he went out looking for them and because he went himself, people thought he was a man of little importance. His search took him up toward the Sletha Ridge and then south along Armannsfell mountain. There he saw a man coming down from Godi's Wood with a load of firewood on his horse. When they met, Thorhall asked him his name and the man said he was called Glam. He was a big, odd-looking man with grey, staring eyes, and wolf-grey hair. Thorhall was taken slightly aback when he saw him, but he realized that this was the very man who had been recommended to him.

"What kind of work are you best at?" asked Thorhall. Glam answered that he was good at taking care of sheep in winter.

"Will you look after my sheep?" asked Thorhall. "Skapti has placed you at my disposal."

"You'll get the best work out of me if I'm my own boss," said Glam, "for I'm bad-tempered when I don't get my way."

"That won't bother me," said Thorhall. "I'm anxious for you to come to my farm." "That's fine by me," said Glam, "but are there any problems?"

"The place seems to be haunted," replied Thorhall. "I'm not afraid of ghosts," said Glam. "Besides, they'll make life more interesting."

"That's the sort of attitude you'll need," said Thorhall. "And it's just as well you're not a weakling." They agreed that Glam would come at the beginning of winter and with that they parted. Thorhall found his horses just where he had been looking for them. Then he rode back and thanked Skapti for his assistance.

As summer passed, Thorhall heard not a word of his shepherd, and no one knew anything about him, but at the agreed time he showed up at Thorhall's farm. The farmer greeted him warmly, but no one else took to him, least of all Thorhall's wife. Glam took charge of the sheep. This wasn't much of an effort for him, since he had a deep, resonant voice and the sheep flocked together whenever he shouted "hoh."

There was a church at Thorhallsstead, but Glam wouldn't go near the place, because he disliked the chanting and was not a believer. He was ill-tempered and malicious and was universally detested.

Now, when Christmas Eve came around, Glam got up early and demanded his food. "It's not customary for Christians to eat today," replied Thorhall's wife. "Tomorrow is the first day of Christmas, and so today it's our duty to fast."

"You have lots of superstitions that don't add up to anything, as far as I can see," said Glam. "And people don't seem to be doing any better now than they were before when they didn't bother with this sort of stuff. In my opinion, our way of life was better when people were called heathens. I want my food now, so don't give me the runaround."

"I know for certain," said Thorhall's wife, "that you're in for something terrible today if you commit this sin." Glam told her to bring the food immediately or it would be the worse for her. She didn't dare say no. Afterwards, when he had eaten, he stormed out.

The weather was poor. There was a general gloom and the air was filled with blowing snow, driven by a howling gale. Conditions got worse as the day went on. The shepherd's voice could be heard in the morning, but less clearly later on. The snow began to drift and in the evening a blizzard blew up. People went to mass and night fell, but there was no sign of Glam. They talked about mounting a search for him, but because of the snowstorm and the utter darkness, no search took place.

Glam failed to come home on Christmas Eve. So, when the service was over and there was sufficient daylight, some men set out to look for him. They found sheep scattered far and wide in the snow drifts; some had been injured in the storm, while others had run off into the hills. High up in the valley, they came across a large area where the ground had been trampled. It seemed as though there had been a violent struggle, for rocks and earth had been kicked up all over the place. They looked around carefully and saw Glam lying a short way off. He was dead. His body was as black as hell, and bloated to the size of an ox. They were repelled by the sight and shuddered with horror. Even so, they tried to carry him to the church, but they could get no further than the edge of a gully a little way down.

So they left the body where it was and went back to tell the farmer what had happened. He asked them what could have killed Glam. They said that they had followed some footprints as big as barrel bottoms. The footprints led from the trodden area to the crags at the head of the valley, and large splatters of blood dotted the trail. They concluded that Glam had been killed by the creature which had haunted the farm earlier, and that he had wounded it. The wound must have been fatal for the creature was never seen again.

On the second day of Christmas, they made another attempt to move Glam's body to the church. Draft animals were harnessed to the corpse, but when the land leveled off and ceased to slope downwards, they couldn't move it at all. Again, they left the body where it was and went home.

On the third day of Christmas a priest went with them but, though they searched all day, they couldn't find Glam. The priest wouldn't go looking a second time and, as soon as he left, the shepherd was found. So they gave up the struggle to carry him to the church and buried him where he was under a pile of stones.

Before long, people became aware that Glam was not resting in peace. This had terrible repercussions; many men fainted at the sight of him, and some were driven out of their minds. Soon after Christmas, the farm-folk thought that they saw Glam around the farm again. They were terrified, and many fled from Thorhallsstead. Next, he took to sitting astride the roofs at night and riding them so violently that he nearly wrecked them with his heels. Then he started walking about both by day and night. People hardly dared go up the valley, even if they had urgent business. The local people thought that this was a great affliction.

33. In the spring, Thorhall hired new servants and started farming his land again. As the days lengthened Glam appeared less frequently; and so time passed until midsummer. That summer, a ship put in at Hunavatn. On board, was a foreigner called Thorgaut who was big and powerful, with the strength of two men. He was alone in the world, with nothing to tie him down, and he was also penniless, so he was looking for work. Thorhall rode to the ship and asked Thorgaut if he would work for him. Thorgaut said he would, and added that he wasn't choosy about the kind of work he did.

"You'll have to be ready to encounter the ghosts who have been hanging around my farm for some time," said Thorhall. "I don't want to mislead you; this job isn't for weaklings."

"I can't see myself being upset by a few little ghosts," replied Thorgaut. "If *I'm* afraid, then no one's going to find this an easy job. I won't break my agreement just for that." So they quickly struck a deal and Thorgaut was hired to look after the sheep during the winter. The summer passed and winter began. Thorgaut took charge of the sheep and everyone liked him. Glam kept coming back and riding the roofs, but Thorgaut thought this was hilarious.

"The rogue will have to come closer if I'm to be frightened," he said. Thorhall warned him not to say too much. "It will be best if the two of you avoid confrontation," he said.

"One thing's for sure," said Thorgaut, "you people have had all the nerve shaken out of you. I'm not going to drop dead some night because of idle chatter like this."

Winter passed and soon it was Christmas again. On Christmas Eve when the shepherd was on his way out to see to his sheep, Thorhall's wife said, "Let's hope there won't be a repetition of what happened last year."

"Don't worry about that," said Thorgaut. "If I don't come back, then there will be something worth worrying about." After that, he went back to his sheep.

The weather was cold and it was snowing heavily. Thorgaut usually returned at dusk, but on this occasion he didn't come back at the expected time. The people went to church as usual, but everyone had the feeling that events were taking a familiar course. Thorhall wanted to search right away, but the others refused, saying that they wouldn't risk falling into the hands of trolls at night. The farmer didn't dare go out either, so there was no search.

On Christmas Day, after a meal, searchers went out to look for the shepherd. They went first to Glam's grave, for they thought that the shepherd's disappearance must have been his doing. When they reached the grave, they saw a dreadful sight. There was the shepherd with his neck broken and every bone in his body shattered. They carried Thorgaut to church, and afterwards he caused no one any harm. Glam, on the other hand, went from strength to strength; he caused so much havoc that everyone abandoned Thorhallsstead, except the farmer and his wife.

Thorhall's cowherd had been with him for a long time and he didn't want to lose him, partly because he liked the man and partly because he did his job well. The cowherd was old, and thought that moving would be too much of an effort. He realized, too, that the farmer's possessions would all be ruined if no one was there to look after them.

One morning after midwinter, the farmer's wife went out to the byre to milk the cows at the usual time. By then it was broad daylight, for no one dared go outside earlier than that except the cowherd, who went out at first light. She heard a huge crash and a hideous bellowing in the cowhouse, so she ran back indoors shrieking that something dreadful was going on in the byre. The farmer went out and saw that his cattle were goring one another. This looked bad enough, but when he went into the byre, he found the herdsman lying on his back with his head in one stall and his feet in another. Thorhall went over to the cowherd, felt him, and discovered right away that he was dead; his back had been broken on the stone wall between the stalls. The farmer now realized that he couldn't stay there any longer, so he fled from his farm taking with him whatever he could. Glam killed all the livestock that was left behind and afterwards he traveled around the whole valley, laying waste to every farm as far as the Tung River. Thorhall stayed with relatives for the rest of the winter. No one dared go up the valley with a horse or a dog, for it would be killed straightaway.

In spring, when the days grew longer, the hauntings became fewer. Thorhall wanted to go back to his land and, though he had trouble finding servants, he started farming again at Thorhallsstead. Everything happened exactly as it had before; when autumn returned, the hauntings increased. The farmer's daughter was the main target of the haunting, and finally she died of it. Many measures were tried, but none worked. Everyone thought that all Vatnsdale would be deserted if no remedy could be found.

34. Now the story returns to Grettir Asmundarson. He stayed at home in Bjarg that autumn after he had parted from Killer-Bard at Thoreyargnup. When winter was very close, Grettir set off north over the ridges to Vididale and spent the night at Audunarstead. Audun and Grettir settled all their differences. Grettir gave Audun a fine ax and they agreed to be friends. Audun lived at Audunarstead for a long time and was blessed with many descendants. His son was Egil who married Ulfheid, the daughter of Eyolf Gudmundarson. Their son was Eyolf, who was killed at the Althing; Eyolf was father of Orm, Bishop Thorlak's chaplain.

Grettir rode north to Vatnsdale and paid a visit to his maternal uncle, Jokul Bardarson, who lived at Tung. Jokul was a big, strong man and extremely overbearing. He was a seafarer, and a man of some importance, but very quarrelsome. He welcomed Grettir, who stayed there for three nights. Glam's hauntings were the main topic of conversation. Grettir asked detailed questions about everything that had happened and Jokul told him that the stories were all true.

"Are you interested in going there?" asked Jokul. Grettir said that he was, but Jokul asked him not to.

"You would be pushing your luck to the limit, and your relatives have a lot to lose as well," said Jokul. "For, at the moment, we don't seem to have any young man to equal you. Only evil can come from having to do with the likes of Glam; it's much better to take on human beings than monsters like him."

Grettir said that he really wanted to visit Thorhallsstead to find out what was going on. "I see there's no point in trying to stop you," said Jokul. "But it's a true saying that luck and talent don't always go together."

"There's trouble at your own door once it enters your neighbor's house," said Grettir. "You should be thinking about what could happen to you before this is over."

"It may be," replied Jokul, "that we can both see into the future, but neither one of us can change it." With that, they parted; neither was pleased with the other's prophecies.

35. Grettir rode to Thorhallsstead. The farmer welcomed him warmly and asked him where he was off to. Grettir replied that he'd like to spend the night there if the farmer had no objection. Thorhall said that he would be grateful for Grettir's presence.

"Not many people think that staying here for any length of time is a good idea," said Thorhall. "You must have heard talk about our misfortune here, and I don't want you getting into trouble on my account. Even if you get away safely yourself, I know for sure that you will lose your horse because no one who comes here can keep his animal safe."

Grettir answered that there were plenty more horses, if anything happened to this one. Thorhall was delighted that Grettir wanted to stay and welcomed him with open arms. Then Grettir's horse was locked up securely in the stable and they both went to bed. The night passed without a visit from Glam.

"Your stay has clearly done some good," said Thorhall, "because every night, as you can see, Glam usually rides the roofs or breaks down doors."

"Then there are two possibilities," said Grettir. "Either he won't restrain himself much longer, or he'll hold off for more than one night. So I'll stay on for another night and see how it goes." Then they went to check Grettir's horse, and found it unharmed. The farmer thought that everything was pointing in the same direction.

So Grettir stayed for a second night and the creature did not return. Thorhall thought that this was a promising sign. He went to look at Grettir's horse, but when he got to the stable, it had been broken into. The horse had been dragged outside and every bone in its body was broken. He told Grettir what had happened and begged him to save himself.

"If you wait for Glam, you're dead," said Thorhall.

"A look at the creature is the least I can expect as compensation for my horse," Grettir said. The farmer replied that he would gain nothing from seeing Glam.

"For he doesn't look at all human," said Thorhall. "But every hour you are willing to stay here is a blessing to me."

The day passed and when bedtime came, Grettir didn't take off his clothes but lay down on the raised wooden floor [a low platform used for sitting and sleeping] opposite the farmer's closet-bed. He covered himself with a shaggy fur cloak, tucking one end under his feet and the other end behind his head so that he could look out through the neck-hole. He braced his feet against a sturdy plank which ran along the edge of the raised floor where he was lying. The frame of the outer door had been wrenched away and a hurdle had been tied roughly in place as a makeshift door. The partition which had once divided the hall from the entry-way had been broken away, both above and below the cross-beam. All the bedding had been scattered about, and the place looked uninhabitable.

That night, they kept a light burning in the hall. About a third of the way through the night, Grettir heard a terrific racket outside. Something climbed onto the house and rode on the hall roof, beating it with its heels till every beam in the house groaned. This went on for a long time. Then the something came down from the roof, moved toward the door, and thrust the hurdle aside. Grettir saw the creature sticking its head into the house. The head was a monstrous size with gargantuan features.

Glam advanced cautiously through the doorway, straightening up when he got inside; he towered all the way to the roof. Turning toward the hall, he rested his arms on the crossbeam and thrust his head into the room. Thorhall didn't make a sound because he thought he'd heard quite enough noise coming from outside. Grettir lay still and didn't move a muscle. Glam saw something lying in a heap on the raised floor, so he made his way into the hall and snatched the cloak violently. Grettir braced his feet against the partition and did not give way. Glam pulled a second time with much more force and still the cloak did not move. The third time he heaved so hard with both hands that he pulled Grettir up from the floor and the cloak was torn in two between them. Glam looked at the torn piece in his hand and wondered who could have pulled against him so strongly. At that instant, Grettir darted under Glam's arms, grabbed him around the waist, and pressed against his backbone as hard as he could, hoping to bring Glam to his knees. But Glam wrestled against Grettir's arms so violently that Grettir had to release his grip and retreat. He fled from one bed-space to the next. In the pursuit, all the planking was wrenched from its place and everything in their path was demolished.

Glam wanted to get outside, but Grettir resisted by digging in his heels wherever he could. In the end, however, Glam managed to drag him out of the hall. Then they had a tremendous struggle because the creature wanted to haul him out of the farmhouse, but Grettir saw that, however difficult it was to deal with Glam indoors, it would be worse outside, so he struggled with all his strength against going out. When they got to the entry way, Glam strained with all his might and pulled Grettir toward him. Realizing that resistance was getting him nowhere, Grettir threw himself as hard as he could into the creature's arms, and at the same time thrust with his feet against a stone embedded in the ground at the doorway. Glam was taken completely by surprise. He had been pulling hard, trying to drag Grettir toward him, but now he buckled at the knees and flew backwards out through the door. His shoulders tore the lintel away and the roof fell apart, both the beams and the frozen thatch.

· So Glam fell out of the door, flat on his back, with Grettir on top of him. The Moon was shining brightly, but was hidden now and again by thick clouds. At the very moment when Glam fell out of the house, the clouds cleared and he glared up fiercely at Grettir. Grettir himself has said that this was the only sight that ever terrified him. Then everything got too much for Grettir. What with his own weariness and the horrible rolling of Glam's eyes, he felt so faint that he could not draw his short sword but lay there suspended between this world and the next. Glam showed that he had more evil power than other ghosts when he spoke these words:

"Grettir, you have put a lot of effort into finding me, but don't be surprised if it doesn't bring you much luck. Let me tell you something: you have now achieved only half the strength and vigor that would have been yours in the future if you had not met up with me. I can't take away the strength you already have, but I can make sure that you will never be stronger than you are now, though you are quite strong enough, as many will find to their cost. Until now, your deeds have brought you fame, but in the future they will lead to outlawry and slaughter, and almost everything you do will bring you bad luck and misfortune. You'll be an outlaw, and your fate will be to live shelterless and alone forever. And now I lay this curse upon you: these eyes · of mine will always be before you, so you will find it intolerable to be alone, and that is what will kill you."

When the creature had finished speaking, the weakness that had overcome Grettir left him. He drew his short sword, beheaded Glam, and placed the head down at his crotch. Then the farmer came outside. He had got dressed while Glam was talking, but did not dare come any nearer till he was dead. Thorhall praised God and thanked Grettir for defeating this foul spirit. Then they went to work and burned Glam to ashes. Afterwards, they carried the ashes away in a leather bag and buried them far from pastures and thoroughfares. After that, they went home in the early dawn.

Grettir lay down as he was very stiff, but Thorhall sent for men from the nearest farms to show and tell them what had happened. Everyone who heard about Grettir's deed was overawed by it. The general opinion was that Grettir Asmundarson had no equal in the entire country for strength, courage, and every other accomplishment. Thorhall sent Grettir on his way with costly gifts. He gave him a good horse and fine clothes because the ones he had been wearing had been torn to shreds. They parted on very friendly terms.

Grettir rode to As in Vatnsdale where Thorvald welcomed him warmly and asked him for all the details of his fight with Glam. Grettir told him everything and said that he had never experienced such a trial of strength as their long struggle had been. Thorvald told him to behave with restraint.

"If you do, you'll be alright; if you don't, you'll come to grief."

Grettir said that his temper hadn't improved; he had less self-control than before and took offence more readily now. In this way, too, he was changed: he was so afraid of the dark that he didn't dare go anywhere alone at night, for all sorts of monsters appeared to him then. Since that time, it has become a common saying that people are "lent Glam's eyes" or "given Glam's sight" when they see things otherwise than as they are.

CHAPTER FIVE

WOMEN IN THE VIKING AGE

The legal and social position of women was not straightforward in the Viking Age. The rise of Christianity is sometimes regarded as having deprived women of earlier liberties. This may be partly true, in the matter of divorce for example, but the Church did teach that marriage required the consent of the woman. In theory, at least, this removed some of the power of male relatives over women. Nevertheless, both before and after the appearance of Christianity, women suffered severe legal disabilities. The saga literature suggests, however, that the situation of women may have been considerably less constrained than the surviving law books imply.

21. UNN THE DEEP-MINDED TAKES CONTROL OF HER LIFE

The Saga of the People of Laxdale contains some of the most vivid female characters in all of Icelandic literature. The saga begins with the adventures of Unn the Deep-Minded, the daughter of Ketil Flatnose, a nobleman who fled to Scotland rather than submit to Harald Finehair. After the deaths of her male relatives in Scotland and Ireland, Unn courageously gathers together her household and followers for a migration to Iceland. Unn the Deep-Minded presents an alternative to the largely masculine tales of Iceland's foundation.

Source: *Laxdæla saga*, ed. Einar Ól. Sveinsson, Íslenzk fornrit V (Reykjavík, 1934), pp. 6–15.

4. Ketil Flatnose sailed to Scotland where he was well received by men of good family because he was famous and nobly born. They invited him to stay there on whatever terms he pleased, so Ketil settled with the rest of his family except for Thorstein the Red, the son of his daughter Unn, who immediately went raiding. He made forays all over Scotland and was always victorious. At length, he made a treaty with the Scots. By this he gained half of Scotland and became king there. He married Thurid Eyvindsdaughter, the sister of Helgi the Lean. The Scots did not keep their agreement for long, but betrayed Thorstein during the truce [ca 880–890]. Ari Thorgilsson the Wise [author of the *Book of the Icelanders*] records that he was killed in Caithness.

Unn the Deep-Minded was in Caithness when her son Thorstein was killed. When she heard that he was dead, and since her father had also died, she recognized that she wouldn't have much of a future there. So, she had a cargo ship built secretly in the forest and, when it was ready, she loaded the ship with great riches and prepared it for sailing. She took with her all the members of her family who were still alive. Everyone agrees that it is hard to find another case of a woman escaping with so much property and so many followers in the midst of such hostilities. She was obviously an amazing woman. Unn was also accompanied by many noteworthy and well-born men. A man named Koll was one of the most outstanding in Unn's band, mainly because of his birth; he had the title of *hersir* [local chieftain, lord]. On the journey, too, was a well-born and distinguished man by the name of Hord.

When her preparations were completed, Unn steered for the Orkneys where she stayed for a short time and married off Gro, the daughter of her son, Thorstein the Red.... The son of that marriage was Hlodver, the father of Earl Sigurd whose son was Earl Thorfinn, and from this line are descended all the earls of Orkney. Then Unn made for the Faeroes and stayed there for a while. In the Faeroes, she arranged a marriage for another of Thorstein's daughters, Olof; from her marriage are descended the Gotuskeggjar, the best known family in the Faeroes.

5. Unn prepared to leave the Faeroes and announced to her crew that she intended to head for Iceland. Along with her went Olaf Feilan, the son of Thorstein the Red, as well as Olaf's unmarried sisters. She put to sea and, after a good voyage, arrived at Vikrarskeid in the south of Iceland, where they suffered shipwreck, but all hands survived and no property was lost.

With twenty of her men she went to visit her brother Helgi. When she arrived, he came out to meet her and invited her to stay along with nine of her men. Angrily, she answered that she hadn't known he was so mean-spirited. She left, intending to visit her brother Bjorn at his home in Breidafjord. When Bjorn heard about her approach, he went to greet her with a large band of men. He welcomed her warmly and invited her to stay with him and to bring her entire company, for he understood his sister's expansive nature. This pleased her and she thanked him for his generosity. She remained there all winter and was treated splendidly as provisions were abundant and no expense was spared.

In spring, she crossed Breidafjord and arrived at a headland where she and her companions had their morning meal, *dogurthr.* Thereafter, the place was called Dogurness; it juts out from Medalfellsstrand. Then she sailed in along Hvammsfjord and came to another headland where she rested for a while and lost her comb. Since then the headland has been called Kambsness. Next, she traveled all over the Breidafjord Valleys and took as much land as she pleased. She sailed to the head of Breidafjord. Her high-seat pillars had been washed ashore there, so she thought this was clearly where she should make her home [high-seat pillars were decorated pillars flanking the master of a household's seat; they had religious significance]. Then she built the farm that was afterwards known as Hvamm and settled there. In the same spring as Unn established herself at Hvamm, Koll married Thorgerd, the daughter of Thorstein the Red. Unn met the costs of the wedding and gave Thorgerd the whole of Laxdale for her dowry. Koll built a farm to the south of the Lax River and was a very important man. Their son was Hoskuld.

6. Then Unn gave some of the land she had taken to other people. To Hord she gave all of Hordadale as far as the Skramuhlaup River. He lived at Hordabolstad and was a man of considerable note as well as being fortunate in his offspring. His son was Asbjorn the Wealthy who settled at Asbjornstad in Ornolfsdale. He married Thorbjorg, the daughter of Skeggi from Midfjord. Their daughter was Ingibjorg who married Illugi the Black and their sons were Hermund and Gunnlaug Serpent's Tongue. This family is known as the Gilsbekki clan.

Unn addressed her men: "You must have a reward for your work now that we have the means to repay your efforts and good will. You know that I have given freedom to Erp, the son of Earl Meldun, for the last thing I want is that a man of such a noble family should bear the name of slave."

Then Unn gave him land at Saudafell between the Tungu River and the Mid River. His children were Orm and Asgeir, Gunnbjorn and Halldis whom Alf of the Dales married. To Sokkolf she gave Sokkolfsdale, and he lived there till old age. One of Unn's freedmen was a Scot called Hundi. She gave him Hundadale. Vifil was Unn's fourth slave, and he received Vifilsdale.

The fourth daughter of Thorstein the Red was Osk. She was the mother of Thorstein the Black, known as the Wise. It was he who inserted an extra week to correct the calendar [since the solar year and the calendar had got out of step]. Thorstein the Red's fifth daughter was Thorhild. She was mother of Alf of the Dales from whom many men trace their ancestry. His daughter was Thorgerd, the wife of Ari Masson, son of Atli, son of Ulf the Squint and Bjorg Eyvindsdaughter, sister of Helgi the Lean. From this line come the people of Reykjaness. The sixth daughter of Thorstein the Red was Vigdis from whom are descended the people of Hofdi in Eyjafjord.

7. Olaf Feilan was the youngest of Thorstein the Red's children. He was a big, strong man, good-looking, and very accomplished. Unn thought more highly of him than of any other man and declared publicly that she intended Olaf to inherit all her property at Hvamm after her death. When Unn was becoming very weary with age, she called Olaf Feilan to her and said to him, "It strikes me, kinsman, that you should settle down and get married."

Olaf was amenable and said that he would trust her judgment in the matter. Unn replied, "I really think that your wedding should take place late this summer, because it's easiest to get hold of all the necessary provisions at that time of year and I'm sure that a great crowd of our friends will be there as this is the last feast I intend to give."

"That is generously said," answered Olaf. "However, I won't marry any woman who will rob you of either your property or your authority."

The same autumn, Olaf Feilan married Alfdis and their wedding took place at Hvamm. Unn spent a great deal on the feast as she had sent invitations to well-born men of other districts far and wide. She invited her brothers Bjorn and Helgi and they came with many followers. Her grandson-in-law, Koll of the Dales, came as did Hord of Hordadale and many other prominent men. There were a great many wedding guests, though nowhere near as many showed up as Unn had invited because it was a long journey for the people of Eyjafjord.

Old age had taken its toll on Unn so that she didn't get up before the middle of the day and went to bed early. She allowed no one to consult her from the time she went to bed till the time when she was up and dressed and she answered irritably if anyone asked how she was. On the day of the wedding, Unn slept longer than usual, but she was up and about when the wedding guests arrived. She went out to meet them and welcomed her relatives and friends honorably. She said that those who had come a long way had shown her particular affection.

"I single out Bjorn and Helgi for this, but I thank all of you who have come."

Then Unn went into the hall with a large company. When the hall was full, everyone was amazed at the splendor of the feast. Then Unn said, "I call on you my brothers, Bjorn and Helgi, and my other relatives and friends, to witness that I am handing over to my kinsman, Olaf, the possession and management of this dwelling and of all the household goods that you can see."

After that, Unn stood up and said that she was going to her sleeping chamber. She bade them enjoy themselves in whatever way they pleased, and said that there should be enough ale to give everyone a good time. People say that Unn was both tall and stout. She walked quickly along the hall and people said that she was still a splendid woman.

They drank throughout the evening until they thought it was bedtime. Next day, Olaf went to his grandmother Unn's sleeping chamber. When he entered the room, she was sitting upright against the pillows, and she was dead. Olaf returned to the hall and announced what had happened. Everyone thought it was wonderful how Unn had retained her dignity until her dying day. Now they celebrated both the wedding of Olaf and the funeral feast of Unn. On the last day of the feast, Unn was moved to the burial mound that had been prepared for her. In the mound, she was placed in a ship and much valuable property was laid beside her. Then the burial mound was closed up.

Olaf Feilan took over the possession and management of Hvamm with the consent of all the relatives who had come to visit. When the feast came to an end, he presented expensive gifts to the most important guests before they went away. Olaf became a great man and a powerful chieftain. He lived at Hvamm till his old age.

22. QUEEN GUNNHILD HAS HER WAY
WITH HRUT

Njal's Saga *is marked by the presence of strong women such as Queen Gunnhild, the widow of Eirik Bloodax, king of Norway. Her sons are frequently referred to as the Gunnhildarsons rather than as the* Eirikssons. *In this selection, she dominates her son, King Harald Greycloak, and uses her power to the advantage of Hrut, an Icelander with whom she has an affair.*

Source: *Brennu-Njáls saga*, ed. Einar Ól. Sveinsson, Íslenzk fornrit XII (Reykjavík, 1954), pp. 11–21.

3. Harald Greycloak [Harald II, d. 976] was king of Norway. He was the son of Eirik Bloodax [r. 930–934, d. 954], the son of Harald Finehair. His mother was Gunnhild, the daughter of Ozur Toti. Harald and Gunnhild had their residence at Konungahella [King's Rock, near Viken] in the east of the country.

Now word spread that a ship from the west had arrived in Vik. As soon as Gunnhild heard the report, she asked what Icelanders were aboard. She was told that one of the Icelanders was a man called Hrut, the nephew of Ozur.

"I know what he's here for," Gunnhild said. "He wants to claim his inheritance, which has been seized by a man called Soti."

She called for her servant, Ogmund: "I'm sending you to Vik to meet Ozur and Hrut," she said. "Tell them that I'm inviting both of them to spend the winter with me and that I wish to be their friend. If Hrut follows my advice, I'll take care of his financial business and anything else he undertakes. I shall also bring him to the notice of the king."

Ogmund left and went to meet Ozur and Hrut who received him warmly when they learned that he was one of Gunnhild's servants. Ogmund gave them Gunnhild's message in secret and, afterwards, Ozur and Hrut discussed their options in private. Ozur remarked to Hrut, "I think, kinsman, that our minds have been made up for us because I know what Gunnhild is like. If we don't go to her, she will quickly drive us out of the country and seize all our property, but if we do go to her, she will treat us honorably just as she has promised."

Ogmund returned home and when he met Gunnhild, he told her that his errand had been successful; Hrut and Ozur would come. "That is just what I expected," said Gunnhild, "for Hrut is said to be a clever and sensible man. Now keep a lookout and tell me when they reach town."

Hrut and his men traveled east to Konungahella. When they arrived, their kinsfolk and friends came to meet them and gave them a friendly welcome. They asked if the king was in residence and were told that he was. A little later, they met Ogmund, who passed on Gunnhild's greetings, adding that she would not invite them to her house until they had met the king, for fear that people would gossip and say that she was making too much of them. She would, however, do whatever she thought fit on their behalf and Hrut, for his part, should speak boldly to the king and ask to be one of his retainers.

"Here are some splendid robes that she has sent you, Hrut," said Ogmund. "You must wear them when you go before the king." Then he went away.

Next day, Hrut said, "Let's go before the king." "Right," replied Ozur.

Twelve men, all kinsmen and friends, went together in a group. When they reached the hall where the king sat drinking, Hrut led the way and greeted him. The king looked carefully at this well-dressed man and asked him his name. Hrut told him.

"Are you an Icelander?" asked the king. Hrut answered that he was.

"What brought you here to visit us?" the king asked.

"I was anxious to see your magnificence, my lord," said Hrut. "Also, I am laying claim to a large inheritance in this country and I will need your support if I am to have justice."

"I have promised justice to everyone in this land," said the king. "Have you any other reason for coming to see us?" "My lord," said Hrut, "I ask your permission to join your retinue and become one of your followers." The king was silent. Then Gunnhild spoke.

"I think that this man is offering you a great honor," she said. "In my opinion, if there were many men like him in your retinue, it would be well manned."

"Is he an intelligent man?" asked the king. "He is both intelligent and energetic," said Gunnhild.

"I gather that my mother wants you to have the position you asked for. Out of respect for our dignity and the customs of the land, however, you must come back again in two weeks time, and then you will become a member of my retinue – until then, my mother will look after you."

"Go with them to my house," said Gunnhild to Ogmund, "and prepare a splendid feast for them." They went out with Ogmund, who led them to a stone-built hall, decorated with the finest tapestries. Gunnhild had her high seat there.

"Now you will see that I told you the truth about Gunnhild," said Ogmund. "Here is her high seat. You may sit on it, and you may stay sitting on it even when she herself comes in." Then Ogmund provided a feast for them. They had barely sat down when Gunnhild came in. Hrut was about to leap up and greet her.

"Sit down," she said. "As long as you are my guest you must always sit on this seat." Then she sat down beside Hrut and they drank together. In the course of the evening, Gunnhild said, "Tonight you shall lie with me in the upper chamber – there will be just the two of us."

"You are the one who must make that decision," he said. Then they went to bed and she locked the room from the inside. They slept there that night and in the morning they drank together. For the whole two weeks, the two of them lay on their own in the upper room. Then Gunnhild said to the people in her household, "Your days will be numbered if you say a word about Hrut and me."

Hrut gave Gunnhild a hundred ells of cloth [a Norwegian ell is 62.8 centimeters] and twelve fur cloaks. She thanked him for the gift. Hrut kissed her and thanked her. Then she wished him farewell and off he went. Next day, Hrut came before the king with thirty men and greeted him.

"Now, Hrut," said the king, "you must want me to make good on my promise."

Then Hrut became a member of the retinue.

"Where shall I sit?" asked Hrut.

"My mother will decide that," replied the king.

4. In the spring, Hrut heard that Soti had traveled south to Denmark, taking the inheritance with him. So he went to Gunnhild and told her about Soti's journey.

"I will give you two fully manned longships," said Gunnhild, "and, in addition, I'll give you Ulf the Unwashed, who is a very brave man and the head of our spies. But go and see the king before you leave."

Hrut did so, and when he came before the king, he told him about Soti's movements, and told him too that he intended to go in pursuit of him. "What assistance has my mother given you?" asked the king.

"Two longships and Ulf the Unwashed to command the force," replied Hrut.

"That is a splendid gift," said the king. "Now I will give you two more ships. You will need this large a force." Later, the king accompanied Hrut to his ship and wished him farewell. Then Hrut sailed south with his forces.

[In chapter 5, Hrut defeats some pirates on his way to Denmark. Soti evades Hrut and appears in Norway, where he is captured and killed by Gunnhild's son, Gudrod. Hrut receives his inheritance from Gunnhild and gives her half of it.]

6. Hrut spent the winter with the king and enjoyed great favor. But when the spring arrived, he became very quiet. Gunnhild noticed this and, when they were alone she asked: "Are you depressed, Hrut?"

"As the saying goes," said Hrut, "things are always better at home than abroad."

"Do you want to go back to Iceland?" she asked. "I do," he replied. "Have you got a woman out there?" she asked. "No," replied Hrut. "I'm sure you do," she said and, at that, they broke off the conversation.

Hrut presented himself to the king and greeted him. The king asked: "What do you want, Hrut?" "My lord, I wish to ask you for leave to return to Iceland," said Hrut. "Will you be more honored there than here?" asked the king.

"No," replied Hrut, "but everyone must do what he is destined to do."

"You're in a tug-of-war with a strong man," said Gunnhild. "Give him permission to travel wherever he wants." It had been a bad year in Norway, but even so the king gave Hrut as much flour as he wanted.

Then he and Ozur prepared for the journey to Iceland and, when they were quite ready, Hrut went to see the king and Gunnhild. She led him aside for some words in private: "Here is a gold ring I want to give you," she said, and slipped it onto his arm.

"I have received many fine gifts from you," replied Hrut.

She put her arms around his neck, kissed him, and said, "If I have as much power over you as I think I do, then I cast this spell on you: you will be unable to achieve sexual satisfaction with the woman you have chosen in Iceland, though you will be able to perform with other women. Now we're both going to be miserable because you weren't open and honest with me." Hrut laughed and went away....

Gunnhild's spell works: Hrut's first marriage is a disaster and ends in divorce.

23. THE PROWESS OF FREYDIS, DAUGHTER OF EIRIK THE RED

Eirik's ruthless and adventurous spirit reappears in his daughter, Freydis, who becomes joint leader of an expedition to Vinland the Good (in North America) around the year 1000. She displays a deviousness and cruelty to equal the major male players in the sagas – Egil Skallagrimsson, for instance. This passage comes from The Saga of the Greenlanders *(see docs. 75 and 76).*

Source: *Grænlendinga saga*, in *Eyrbyggja saga*, ed. Einar Ól. Sveinsson and Matthías Þórðarson, Íslenzk fornrit IV (Reykjavík, 1935), pp. 264–68.

7. Once again there was talk of a voyage to Vinland, for such a trip seemed a great way to gain both riches and reputation. In the same summer as Karls-efni came back from Vinland, a ship arrived in Greenland from Norway. The

skippers were two brothers, Helgi and Finnbogi, Icelanders by birth, from the Eastfjords. They wintered over in Greenland.

The story goes on to say that Freydis Eiriksdaughter traveled from her home in Gardar and went to meet the brothers Helgi and Finnbogi. She asked them if they would accompany her to Vinland with their ship and share equally with her all the profits they made there. They agreed to this. Next, Freydis went to see her brother Leif and asked him to give her the houses he had built in Vinland. Leif replied as before that he would lend the houses, but not give them.

Freydis and the brothers agreed that each ship should carry thirty men who were capable of fighting, as well as some women. Immediately, Freydis broke the agreement by bringing along five extra men whom she hid. The brothers had no idea of this until they reached Vinland.

So they put to sea after agreeing beforehand to sail in convoy if possible. However, though they kept close, the brothers arrived a little earlier and had carried their cargo up to Leif's houses before Freydis landed. Her men unloaded her ship and carried the freight up to the houses.

"Why did you put your things in here?" Freydis asked. "Because we thought that you would honor the whole of our agreement," they replied.

"Leif lent the houses to me, not you," she said. "We brothers will never come close to you in nastiness," Helgi replied.

They carried the cargo outside and built themselves a house on a lakeside further inland. They made themselves comfortable there. Freydis, in the meantime, had a shipload of timber felled.

Now winter set in and the brothers suggested that they should hold games and have some entertainments. These amusements continued for a while until relations became strained and the two parties fell out. The games ceased and there was no more coming and going between the houses; this situation lasted for much of the winter.

Early one morning, Freydis got out of bed and put on her clothes except for her shoes. Outside, a heavy dew had fallen. She dressed in her husband's cloak and went to the door of the brothers' house. Someone had just gone out and left the door half-open. She opened it fully and stood in the entry for a time without saying anything. Finnbogi was lying at the far end of the hall. He was awake and said, "What do you want here, Freydis?"

She replied, "I want you to get up and come outside with me because I'd like to have a talk with you." He did as she asked and they walked to a tree trunk lying near the wall of the house and sat down. "How are things going?" she asked.

"I like the land well enough," he answered, "but I don't like the hostility between us. In my opinion, it has arisen out of nothing."

"Very true," she said. "That's my opinion too. But my reason for coming to see you is that I want to swap ships with you and your brother, since yours is bigger than mine, and I want to leave here." "That will be fine with me if it's fine by you," he said.

On this note, they parted. Finnbogi went back to bed and Freydis went home. When she climbed into bed, her feet were so cold that Thorvard woke up and asked why she was so cold and wet. She answered angrily, "I went to ask the brothers if I could buy their ship as I wanted a bigger one and this made them so angry that they beat me and treated me abusively. But you, you miserable creature, won't avenge either my shame or your own. Now I know for sure that I'm not in Greenland and if you won't avenge this, I'll divorce you."

Unable to put up with her abuse, Thorvald ordered his men to get up right away and fetch their weapons. They did so and went straight to the brothers' house, bursting in on them while they were still asleep. They seized them, tied them up, and brought them out one by one. Freydis had each one killed as he came out. Soon all the men were dead and only the women were left. No one wanted to kill them. Then Freydis said, "Hand me an ax."

This was done. She attacked all five women and left them dead. After this terrible deed, they returned to their own house, and it was only too clear that Freydis thought she had acted very cleverly.

"If we ever get back to Greenland," she said to her companions, "I'll kill anyone who talks about what has happened. Our story must be that they stayed behind here when we left."

Early in the spring, they loaded up the brothers' ship with as large a cargo as they could get together and the ship could hold. Then they put to sea. They had a good voyage and sailed into Eiriksfjord early in the summer....

8. Freydis returned to her farm which had survived her absence without harm. She heaped rewards on her entire crew since she wanted her crimes kept secret. After that, she remained on her farm. However, not everyone was close-mouthed enough to keep silent about her wicked behavior and stop it from getting out. After a while, her brother Leif heard the story. He thought it was dreadful. Leif captured three of Freydis's men and tortured them until they confessed what had happened; their stories confirmed one another.

"I can't bring myself to deal with my sister Freydis as she deserves," said Leif, "but I prophesy that their descendants will never thrive." And that's how things turned out: after that, everyone thought badly of her and her family....

24. A WARRIOR-WOMAN

Saxo Grammaticus's History of the Danes, *written in Latin, covers the period from the mythical, pre-Christian past up to the historical present in sixteen books, and was completed around 1216. Much of Book 9 is concerned with the exploits of the semi-legendary Danish warrior-king Ragnar Lodbrok. Saxo includes the story of Ragnar's infatuation with a Norwegian warrior-woman named Ladgerda. Modern scholarship is skeptical about the existence of such warrior-women.*

Source: trans. Oliver Elton, *The Nine Books of the Danish History of Saxo Grammaticus* (New York: Norroena Society, 1905), pp. 231–32; revised by A.A. Somerville and R.A. McDonald from Saxo Grammaticus: *Gesta Danorum*, ed. J. Olrik and H. Ræder (Hauniae: Levin Munksgaard, 1931), pp. 251–52.

... At this time Fro (Frey?), the king of Sweden, after slaying Siward, the king of the Norwegians, put the wives of Siward's kinsfolk in bonds in a brothel, and delivered them to public outrage. When Ragnar heard of this, he went to Norway to avenge his grandfather. As he came, many of the matrons, who had either suffered insult to their persons or feared imminent peril to their chastity, hastened eagerly to his camp in male attire, declaring that they would prefer death to outrage. Nor did Ragnar, who was to punish this reproach upon the women, scorn to use against the author of the infamy the help of those whose shame he had come to avenge. Among them was Ladgerda, a skilled female warrior, who, though a maiden, had the courage of a man, and fought in front among the bravest with her hair loose over her shoulders. All marveled at her matchless deeds, for her locks flying down her back betrayed that she was a woman. Ragnar, when he had justly cut down the murderer of his grandfather, asked many questions of his fellow soldiers concerning the maiden whom he had seen so forward in the fray, and declared that he had gained the victory by the might of one woman. Learning that she was of noble birth among the barbarians, he steadfastly wooed her by means of messengers. She spurned his mission in her heart, but feigned compliance. Giving false answers, she made her panting wooer confident that he would gain his desires; but ordered that a bear and a dog should be set at the porch of her dwelling, thinking to guard her own room against all the ardor of a lover by means of the beasts that blocked the way. Ragnar, comforted by the good news, embarked, crossed the sea, and, telling his men to stop in Gaulardale, as the valley is called, went to the dwelling of the maiden alone. Here the beasts met him, and he thrust one through with a spear, and caught the other by the throat, wrung its neck, and choked it. Thus he had the maiden as the prize of the peril he had overcome. By this marriage he had two daughters, whose names have not come down to us, and a son Fridleif....

Afterwards, changing his love, and desiring Thora, the daughter of the King Herodd, to wife, Ragnar divorced himself from Ladgerda; for he thought ill of her trustworthiness, remembering that she had long ago set the most savage beasts to destroy him....

25. GUDRUN DRIVES HER SONS TO TAKE REVENGE

Excluded from the masculine political world, women often found private means of making their influence felt. The heroic poem, The Goading of Gudrun (Guðrúnarh-vöt), gives legendary expression to the power of women to incite men to action. The poem is an episode from the story of the Nibelungs and distantly recalls events of the fourth and fifth centuries, involving figures such as Attila the Hun and Ermaneric the Ostrogoth. From the Poetic Edda.

Source: *Die Lieder des Codex Regius*, ed. Gustav Neckel; 5th rev. edition, ed. Hans Kuhn (Heidelberg: Carl Winter, 1983), pp. 263–68.

About Gudrun [a prose introduction]

When she had killed Attila [Attila the Hun, 406–453], Gudrun went to the sea and waded in, wishing to drown herself. She could not sink, and the sea swept her across the fjord to the land of King Jonakr, who married her.

Their sons were Sorli, Erp, and Hamdir. Svanhild, Sigurd's daughter [by Gudrun], was raised there. She was given in marriage to Ermaneric the Great [king of the Ostrogoths, d. 376]. Bikki was one of his retainers. He advised Randver, the king's son, to take her for himself. Bikki then informed the king of this. The king had Randver hanged and Svanhild trampled under horses' hooves. When Gudrun heard of this, she addressed her sons.

> 1. Then I heard
> a most fearful tirade,
> words forced
> into speech by terrible woe,
> when with fierce words
> cruel-hearted
> Gudrun urged her sons
> to the slaughter.

2. "Why do you sit still,
why sleep your lives away?
Why does it not grieve you
to talk cheerfully?
When Ermaneric
has trampled your sister,
still in her youth,
on the highway with horses
white, black, and grey,
the steady-paced horses of the Goths.

3. "You have not turned out
like Gunnar,
still less are you as bold
as Hogni was;
you would have
tried to avenge her
if you had the fierce spirit
of my brothers,
or the stern heart
of the Hunnish kings."

4. Then said Hamdir
the great-hearted:
"Little would you have praised
Hogni's valor
when they wakened Sigurd
from sleep,
when your costly bed-sheets,
blue and white,
were reddened in your husband's blood,
Soaked in the blood of the slain.

5. "Revenge for your brothers
became cruel and painful for you
when you murdered your sons.
All of us,
being of one mind,
could have taken vengeance
on Ermaneric
for our sister.

6. "Bring out the treasures
of the Hunnish kings;
you have goaded us
to settlement by the sword."

7. Laughing, Gudrun
turned to her storehouse,
from chests chose
the crested helmets of kings,
long coats of mail,
and brought them to her sons.
Boldly, they leapt
onto the backs of their horses.

8. Then said Hamdir
the great-hearted:
"It may happen
that the spear-warrior,
brought low
in Gothic lands,
will come back
to visit his mother
so that you may drink
at a funeral feast
for all of us,
for Svanhild,
and for your sons."

9. Weeping,
Gudrun, Gjuki's daughter,
went in sorrow
to sit at the entry,
and to tell,
with tears on her cheeks,
tales of savagery
over and over.

10. "Three fires I have known,
three hearths I have known,
three times been taken
to a husband's house;

best of all for me
was Sigurd,
whom my brothers
did to death.

11. "I have not seen or known
a more terrible wound;
but they intended
to hurt me more,
when the princes
gave me to Attila.

12. "I called my lively bear-cubs [her sons]
for secret talk;
I could not get
redress for my misfortunes
till I cut off the heads
of the Nibelungs.

13. "I went to the shore,
furious with the norns [Fates];
I wished to be rid
of their grievous afflictions;
but high waves bore me,
did not drown me,
so I set foot on land,
obliged to live.

14. "For the third time
– I had intended better for myself –
I went to the bed
of a great king.
I bore children,
rightful heirs,
rightful heirs,
Jonakr's sons.

15. "Then still round Svanhild
sat her maidservants;
I loved her best
of my children.

In my hall,
Svanhild was as
glorious to look upon
as a ray of the sun.

16. "I bestowed on her gold
and splendid clothes,
before I gave her
to the Gothic people.
For me the cruelest
of my griefs
is over Svanhild's
blond hair;
they trampled it in mud
under their horses' hooves.

17. "But the sorest was
when they killed my Sigurd,
robbed of victory,
in his bed.
And the most terrible
when those gleaming snakes
slithered toward Gunnar
to end his life.
And the sharpest
when they cut to the heart
the fearless king
while he still lived.

18. "I remember
many misfortunes....
Sigurd, harness
your black horse,
your fleet-footed steed,
let it race here.
Neither daughter
nor daughter-in-law
sits here
to give precious gifts to Gudrun.

19. "Do you recall, Sigurd,
what we said
when we lay
in bed together,
that you, fierce hero,
would visit me,
from hell,
and I would come to you from the world.

20. "Pile up, lords,
the oak-wood pyre,
let it be
highest under heaven.
May fire burn up
the grief-stricken breast.
May sorrows melt away
That oppress the heart."

21. For all lords,   may their fortune improve,
For all ladies,   may their sorrow lessen,
Now that this tale of woe   has been told.

26. GUDRUN OSVIFRSDAUGHTER'S INCITEMENT OF HER SONS

A tenth-century Gudrun follows her namesake's example in The Saga of the People of Laxdale.

Source: *Laxdæla saga*, ed. Einar Ól. Sveinsson, Íslenzk fornrit V (Reykjavík, 1934), pp. 179–81.

60. A few days after her return, Gudrun called her sons to the vegetable garden for a talk. When they got there they saw linen clothes spread on the ground; there was a shirt and a pair of trousers and they were covered with blood.

Gudrun said, "The clothes you see here challenge you to avenge your father. I'm not going to say much; it's not to be expected that speechifying will move you in the right direction if you aren't moved by tokens and reminders like these."

The brothers were shocked by what Gudrun said and answered that they had been too young to take revenge and had no one to lead them. They said that they had no idea how to make plans, either for themselves or for others. "But we certainly haven't forgotten what we have lost."

Gudrun said that in her opinion they were much more interested in horsefights and sports. After that the brothers went away, but that night they could not sleep. Thorgils noticed this and asked them what was wrong. They related to him the whole exchange between themselves and their mother; they said, too, that they could not bear their own sorrow or their mother's taunting any longer. "We want to try for revenge," said Bolli. "We brothers are old enough now for people to reproach us if we don't lift a finger."

The following day Thorgils and Gudrun had a talk and Gudrun began like this:

"I think, Thorgils, that my sons have had enough of doing nothing and making no attempt to avenge their father. Till now, the main reason for delay has been my feeling that Thorleik and Bolli were too young to be plotting against men's lives. However, there has been good reason to talk about this long before now."

"It's no use discussing this business with me," Thorgils replied, "when you have flatly refused to marry me. My thoughts on the matter are the same as they were when we discussed it before. If I can persuade you to marry me, then it won't bother me a bit to kill one or both of the men most involved in the slaying of Bolli."

Gudrun said, "I know that Thorleik thinks no one is better suited than you to take the lead when there is work to be done that requires boldness. I won't conceal from you the fact that the boys intend to take aim at Helgi Hardbeinsson, the berserk, who lives on his farm at Skorradal and is not afraid of anything."

Thorgils answered, "It makes no odds to me whether he goes by the name of Helgi or has some other name, because I don't think it's beyond my powers to deal with Helgi or anyone else. This will be my last word on the subject, so long as you promise before witnesses that you will marry me if I help your sons get their revenge."

Gudrun said that she would honor any agreement she made, even if there were few people to witness it. She said, too, that Thorgils's terms would be acceptable. Gudrun asked to have Thorgils's foster-brother Halldor and her sons called as witnesses. Thorgils asked for Ornolf to be called too, but Gudrun said there was no need for this. "I have more suspicions about Ornolf's loyalty to you than you seem to have yourself," she said.

Thorgils left the decision to her. The brothers then arrived to join Gudrun and Thorgils; Halldor was there talking to them. Gudrun now explained to them how things stood: "Thorgils has promised to lead my sons in a foray against Helgi Hardbeinsson as vengeance for Bolli. He has stipulated that, in return, I will marry him. Now I call upon you to witness my promise to Thorgils that I will marry no man in this land except him, and I don't plan to marry in another country."

This seemed quite satisfactory to Thorgils and he didn't see through it. The parley broke up with full agreement that Thorgils was to take on the exploit. He prepared to leave Helgafell with Gudrun's sons. First they went to Thorgils's home at Tung and afterwards they rode into the Dalir district.

27. THE GOADING OF HILDIGUNN

Hildigunn had not long been married to Hoskuld, Njal's foster son, when he was murdered by Njal's own sons in the seemingly endless chain of revenge that overshadows Njal's Saga. In this passage, Hildigunn attempts to shame Flosi Thordarson, her kinsman, into taking revenge on Hoskuld's murderers.

Source: *Brennu-Njáls saga*, ed. Einar Ól. Sveinsson, Íslenzk fornrit XII (Reykjavík, 1954), pp. 289–318.

116. Hildigunn was outside in the yard. "I'd like all my menfolk to be waiting out here when Flosi arrives," she said. "The women are to clean the house, hang up the tapestries, and get the high seat ready for Flosi." Later on, when Flosi rode into the homestead, Hildigunn went to meet him and said, "Welcome, kinsman, it does my heart good to see you."

"We'll have a meal here with you, before riding on," replied Flosi. Then their horses were tied up. Flosi went into the main room and, as he sat down, he shoved the high seat onto the floor. "I'm not a king or an earl," he said, "so I don't need to have a high seat under me. And there's no need to make fun of me either."

Hildigunn was standing nearby and replied, "It's a pity you're not pleased, because we acted with the best of intentions."

Flosi answered, "If you mean well, your good intentions will speak for themselves: if you mean ill, your evil intentions will condemn themselves."

Hildigunn laughed bitterly. "This is just the beginning," she said. "We'll grapple more closely before this is over." She sat down beside Flosi and they talked quietly for a long time.

After a while the tables were set up, and Flosi and his men washed their hands. Flosi looked at the hand towel; it was in tatters and torn at one end. Not wishing to dry himself with it, he flung it down on the bench. Then he hacked a piece from the tablecloth, dried himself on that, and threw it to his men. After that, Flosi sat down at the table and told his men to eat.

Hildigunn came into the room. She walked over to Flosi, pushed the hair back from her eyes and wept. Flosi said, "You are downcast, kinswoman, so you are crying. But it is good to weep for a good man."

"What legal action will you take on my behalf?" she asked. "What help will you give me?

"I will prosecute the case to the full extent of the law," Flosi said, "or I'll arrange a settlement which good men will regard as being honorable in every respect."

Hildigunn replied, "If Hoskuld had been obliged to take up your cause, he would have avenged you."

"You're a cruel woman," answered Flosi. "It's clear what you want." Hildigunn replied, "Arnor Ornolfsson from Forsarskogar committed less of an offence against Thord Freysgodi [priest of Frey], your father, yet your brothers, Kolbein and Egil, killed him for it at the Skaftafell Thing."

Hildigunn went into the hall and opened up her chest. She took out the cloak which Flosi had given to Hoskuld, the cloak he had been wearing when he was killed. She had kept it there with all its dried blood. She returned to the main room with the cloak and walked up to Flosi without saying a word. He had eaten his fill and the table had been cleared. Hildigunn draped the cloak around Flosi's shoulders; the blood showered all over him. Then she said, "You gave this cloak to Hoskuld, Flosi, and now I give it back to you. He was killed in it. In the name of God and good men I urge you to avenge all the wounds he suffered in death – or be known by everyone as the lowest of the low. I urge this by all the powers of your Christ and by your manhood, and your courage."

Flosi tore off the cloak and threw it in her face. "You are a real monster," he said. "You want us to do things that will turn out very badly for all of us. The counsels of women are cold."

Flosi was so infuriated that his face was by turns red as blood, pale as ashes, and black as hell. He and his men went to their horses and rode off. He rode to Holtsvad where he waited for the Sigfussons and some other friends....

124. ... Flosi said, "Now I'll tell you all I have in mind: when we've gathered there, we'll all ride in a group to Bergthorshval and attack the Njalssons with fire and iron...."

28. BETROTHALS FROM THE SAGAS

(a) The Betrothal of Olaf Hoskuldsson

Though marriage negotiations were generally carried on by fathers, the sagas suggest that daughters often had some say in the decision. For example, in The Saga of the People of Laxdale, *Egil Skallagrimsson consults his daughter about her betrothal to Olaf Peacock, who is Hoskuld's illegitimate son by an Irish slave-woman (see doc. 5).*

Source: *Laxdæla saga*, ed. Einar Ól. Sveinsson, Íslenzk fornrit V (Reykjavík, 1934), pp. 62–65.

22. ... Olaf spent the winter in Iceland and, in the spring, he and his father discussed his prospects. "Olaf," said Hoskuld, "I want you to make a good marriage and take over your foster-father's farm at Goddastead. There's still a lot of property there, and you can manage the place with my help."

"I haven't given it much thought before this," answered Olaf, "and I don't know where there's a woman who would bring me much luck in marriage. You can be sure that I'll set my sights high when I look around for a wife. But, for certain, you wouldn't have brought up the topic without knowing where it would come down."

"You've got that right," said Hoskuld. "There's a man called Egil Skalla-grimsson living at Borg in Borgarfjord. He's got a daughter called Thorgerd; she's the best bet in Borgarfjord, or further afield for that matter, and I'm going to ask for her hand in marriage for you. Another benefit is that your position will be strengthened by having the men of Myrar as your relatives."

"I'll trust your foresight about this," replied Olaf, "for this marriage will please me well enough, if it comes off. But you can be sure of this, father, if this business begins and then gets nowhere, I'll be really displeased."

"We can count on bringing it off," said Hoskuld. Olaf told him to decide for himself. The time for the meeting of the Althing was drawing near, so Hoskuld got ready to leave with a large group of people, his son Olaf among them. When they arrived at the assembly, they covered their booth against the weather. The meeting was crowded and Egil Skallagrimsson was there. Everyone who saw Olaf was talking about what a handsome and distin-guished man he was. He was well provided with weapons and clothes.

23. One day, Hoskuld and Olaf left their booth to pay a visit to Egil Skal-lagrimsson. Egil gave them a warm welcome as he and Hoskuld were old acquaintances. Hoskuld opened the courtship on behalf of Olaf and asked for Thorgerd as his son's wife. She herself was at the Althing. Egil was delighted by the offer, saying that he had heard good things about the father and son.

"I know, Hoskuld," said Egil, "that you are of an excellent family and very worthy in your own right, and Olaf's journey [to Ireland] has made him famous. It's only natural that men like you should aim high, and Olaf has both family and good looks. But now this has to be discussed with Thorgerd, because she's not going to fall into any man's hands unless she wants to."

"Then I want you to discuss this with your daughter, Egil," said Hoskuld. Egil agreed and went to have a talk with Thorgerd.

He said, "There's a man called Olaf – he's the son of Hoskuld and he's very well-known. His father has brought up the question of marriage on his son's behalf, and has asked for your hand. I've put the whole business completely in your hands, and I want your answer now; I think an approach like this deserves a favorable response, because it's an excellent match."

"I've heard you say that you love me best of your children," answered Thorgerd. "But now I think that you weren't telling the truth, if you want to give me to a slave-woman's son, even if he is good-looking and dressy."

"You aren't as well-informed about him as you are about other things," said Egil. "Haven't you heard that his mother is the daughter of Myrkjartan, king of Ireland? He is much better born on his mother's side than on his father's, and even that would be a good enough match for us." But Thorgerd didn't let herself be persuaded and they parted, with rather different views on the subject.

Next day, Egil went to Hoskuld's booth and Hoskuld gave him a friendly welcome. They began talking together, and Hoskuld asked how the courtship business had gone. Egil spoke unhappily about it and told him how things developed. Hoskuld said that the business looked impossible, "But I think you've behaved well."

Olaf didn't take part in the conversation, but when Egil left, he asked how the marriage negotiations had gone. Hoskuld said that they were going slowly on her side.

"Father," said Olaf, "I told you I would be upset if I got an embarrassing reply, and that's just how it is. This was begun mostly on your advice, but now I'm going to manage the courtship myself to make sure that it doesn't collapse here. It's true what they say: 'Wolves make a hash of hunting for another.' So now I'm going straight over to Egil's booth."

Hoskuld told him to do as he pleased. Olaf got dressed in the scarlet clothes given to him by King Harald [Greycloak], and he wore the gilded helmet and sword which he had received from King Myrkjartan. Now Hoskuld and Olaf went to Egil's booth, with Hoskuld in the lead and Olaf right behind him. Egil gave them a warm welcome. Hoskuld sat down beside Egil, but Olaf remained standing, looking about him. He saw a woman sitting on the bench at the end of the booth. She was beautiful, distinguished in appearance, and well-dressed. Olaf was sure that she must be Thorgerd, the daughter of Egil, so he walked over to the bench and sat down next to her. She greeted him and asked him who he was. Olaf gave his own name and his father's. "You must think it's bold of a slave-woman's son to dare sit beside you," said Olaf.

"And you must be thinking," she answered, "that you've done things you consider braver than talking to a woman." Then they fell into conversation with one another. They talked for the whole day, but no one could hear what they were talking about. Before they ended their conversation, Hoskuld and Egil were called over to them, and discussion of Olaf's offer of marriage began afresh, for Thorgerd had come around to her father's way of thinking. The negotiations were quickly concluded, and they were betrothed on the spot. Out of respect for the family at Laxdale, the bride was to be brought to their home, and not the other way around. They announced that the wedding would take place at Hoskuldstead after the seventh week of summer.

(b) How Unn Mordsdaughter Found Herself Betrothed

In this passage from Njal's Saga, *betrothal is treated as a matter of business by Hoskuld and Unn's father, Mord. Unn is not consulted, and her prospective husband leaves the Althing (the Icelandic national assembly) apparently without talking to her.*

Source: *Brennu-Njáls saga*, ed. Einar Ól. Sveinsson, Íslenzk fornrit XII (Reykjavík, 1954), pp. 7–9.

2. On one occasion, the brothers Hoskuld and Hrut rode to a crowded meeting of the Althing. Hoskuld said, "Brother, I want you to improve your way of life and look for a woman to marry."

"That's been on my mind for a while," replied Hrut, "but there have always been two ways of looking at it. But I'll do whatever you think I should. Where are we going to look?"

Hoskuld replied, "there are plenty of chiefs here at the Thing, and you have plenty of choice. But I've settled on one particular place where you can make your offer. There's a woman called Unn, she's the daughter of Mord Fiddle, and you can take a look at her if you like."

Next day, as people were making their way to the law court, the brothers saw some well-dressed women outside the booths of the men from the Rang river valley. Hoskuld said to Hrut, "There's Unn now, the one I was talking to you about. How does she look to you?"

"She looks fine," said Hrut, "but I don't know if we'll get on well together."

So they went on to the law court where Mord Fiddle was discussing legal business as usual and when he finished, he returned to his booth. Hoskuld and Hrut got up, went over to Mord's booth, and entered. Mord was sitting on the innermost seat of the booth, and when Hoskuld and Hrut addressed him, he stood up to meet them. He took Hoskuld's hand and placed him in the seat next to his own, while Hrut sat next to Hoskuld. They discussed various matters before they got down to Hoskuld's business.

"I want to talk business with you," said Hoskuld. "Hrut wants to be your son-in-law, and pay the price for your daughter. I'll do all I can to make sure the deal happens."

"I know you're an important chieftain," answered Mord, "but I don't know a thing about your brother."

"Hrut's got more going for him than I have," replied Hoskuld.

"You'll have to pay out a lot for him because she'll inherit everything I have," said Mord.

"You won't have to wait long to hear what I'll promise with him," answered Hoskuld. "He'll have Kambsness and Hrutstead, and the land as far up as Thrandargils. He also has a trading ship at sea."

"Mord," said Hrut, "my brother has given me far too much credit out of his affection for me. Bearing that in mind, if you want to make an agreement, I want you to decide the terms of the deal."

Mord replied, "I've considered the terms. She will have six hundreds [of homespun cloth, used as a means of exchange] outright, and a third of that in your house. If the pair of you have heirs, you and she will have equal shares in the property."

Hrut answered, "I accept these terms, and now we have to witness the deal."

Afterwards, they stood up and shook hands and Mord betrothed his daughter Unn to Hrut. The wedding feast was to be held at Mord's house two weeks after midsummer. Then both parties rode away from the Thing....

29. DIVORCES FROM THE SAGAS

(a) How Gudrun Divorced Thorvald

While surviving (Christian) law codes are ambivalent about divorce, the sagas suggest a situation in which divorce appears to have been easily available to either partner in a marriage, as is the case in this passage from The Saga of the People of Laxdale.

Source: *Laxdæla saga*, ed. Einar Ól. Sveinsson, Íslenzk fornrit V (Reykjavík, 1934), pp. 93–94.

34. There was a man called Thorvald, the son of Halldor the Godi [chieftain] of Garpsdal. He lived in Garpsdal at Gilsfjord and was a prosperous man, but not very brave. He asked to marry Gudrun Osvifrsdaughter at the

Althing when she was fifteen years old. The offer was not badly received but Osvifr remarked that as far as marriage went, he and Gudrun were not evenly matched. Thorvald responded mildly and said that he was asking for a wife, not money. So Gudrun was betrothed to Thorvald and, on his own, Osvifr drew up a contract by which it was agreed that Gudrun would have sole control of their property as soon as they occupied one bed, and that she would own half their property no matter how long or short a time they lived together. Thorvald was also obliged to buy costly possessions for her so that no woman of equal wealth would have better and he was to keep up the stock on his farm despite these expenses. Then everyone rode home from the Thing.

Gudrun wasn't asked about this arrangement and she was miserable about it, but didn't make a fuss. The wedding feast took place at Garpsdal in the fifth month of summer [late August, early September]. Gudrun cared little for Thorvald and was extravagant in making expensive purchases. There were no costly items in the West Fjords that Gudrun didn't think she ought to have and she scolded Thorvald if he didn't buy them, however expensive they were.

Thord Ingunnarson became very friendly with Thorvald and Gudrun and stayed with them for long periods. There was a lot of talk about the intimacy between Gudrun and Thord. On one occasion, when Gudrun asked Thorvald to buy her something expensive, he said that her demands were insatiable and slapped her on the face. Then Gudrun said, "You have given me a feature we women think it is very important to have in good measure, and that is a high color. And you have persuaded me not to pester you with excessive demands."

When Thord arrived that evening on a visit, Gudrun told him about the insult and asked how she should repay it. With a smile, Thord said, "I know a good way of doing it. Make him a shirt with an opening shamefully wide for a man and declare yourself separated from him because of that effeminacy." Gudrun said nothing against the idea and they ended their conversation.

The same spring, Gudrun declared herself separated from Thorvald and went back to Laugar. Later, their property was divided, and Gudrun got half, though the property was now worth more than before. They had lived together for two years.

(b) Vigdis Divorces Thord Goddi

When a relative, Thorolf, seeks Vigdis's protection from the consequences of a murder, her husband, Thord, fails to act as she thinks a man ought to, and she declares herself divorced from him, in this selection from The Saga of the People of Laxdale.

Source: *Laxdæla saga*, ed. Einar Ól. Sveinsson, Íslenzk fornrit V (Reykjavík, 1934), pp. 30–37.

14. ... The news of Hall's murder spread throughout the islands and was taken very seriously because, although he was not a lucky man, Hall belonged to a noble family. Now Thorolf fled from the islands, for he knew no one there who would shelter him after such a terrible deed. He had no relatives from whom he could hope for protection, whereas there were powerful men in the neighborhood who could certainly be expected to plot against his life, men like Ingjald the Godi [chieftain] of the South Islands, the brother of Hall.

Thorolf got a passage to the mainland. He traveled wearing a large hood on his head and there is no account of his journey until he arrived at Goddastead one evening. Vigdis, the wife of Thord, was some sort of relation of Thorolf's and that is why he turned up at that house. Thorolf had already heard about how things stood there, in particular that Vigdis was more tough-minded than her husband Thord. On the evening of his arrival, Thorolf went straight to tell Vigdis his troubles and ask for her help.

Vigdis gave him this answer: "I won't deny our kinship, and what you have done does not seem to me to have made a worse man of you. I think that anyone who protects you will risk both his life and property considering the stature of the men who will be in pursuit of you. But," she said, "my husband Thord isn't much of a fighting man, and the advice of us women is always wanting in judgment, if anything is needed. But I can't bring myself to turn you away out of hand, since you have decided to come here for help."

After that, Vigdis led him to a farm building and told him to stay there. She locked the door when she left. Later, she approached Thord. "A man has come here looking for a place to stay for the night," she said. "His name is Thorolf, and he has some sort of kinship with me. I think that he will need to stay for longer, if you're willing."

Thord answered that he didn't like having people to visit, but said that he could stay for the next day, so long as he wasn't in trouble. Otherwise he should be on his way as soon as possible.

Vigdis answered, "I have already offered to let him stay and I won't go back on my word even though he may not be equally friendly with everyone."

Then she told him about the murder of Hall and that his murderer, Thorolf, was the man who had arrived at their house. Thord was angry about this, and said that he knew for certain that Ingjald would make him pay heavily for the protection already given to Thorolf, now that the door had been locked behind him.

"Ingjald won't take your money for giving Thorolf one night's shelter," said Vigdis, "because he's staying here for the whole winter."

"You can trump me completely, but I'm really annoyed that such an unlucky man is here," complained Thord. Nonetheless, Thorolf stayed there over the winter.

This reached the ears of Ingjald, who was prosecuting his brother's murder. Ingjald got ready for his journey to the Dales district in late winter and launched a ferry that he owned. He and eleven others sailed from the west before a sharp north-westerly wind and landed at the mouth of the Lax river in the evening. They beached the ferry and traveled to Goddastead during the evening. Their arrival was expected and they received a warm welcome.

Ingjald drew Thord aside for a talk and told him his business, saying that he had heard that his brother's killer, Thorolf, was there, but Thord denied that this was so. Ingjald told him not to deny it.

"Let's make a deal," he said, "You give up the man to me and save me trouble and I've got three marks of silver here for you in return. And I won't prosecute the charges you have brought on yourself by sheltering Thorolf."

Thord thought the money looked good and there was also the promise of the abandonment of the charges, which he had greatly feared would lead to a serious loss of property. "I know that I'll be criticized by people because of our dealings, but our bargain will stand," said Thord. They slept for much of the night until an hour before day.

15. Then Ingjald and his men got up and dressed. Vigdis asked Thord what he and Ingjald had been talking about during the evening. He replied that they had discussed a lot, and had agreed that the place should be ransacked, so they would be out of trouble if Thorolf wasn't found. "So I had my slave Asgaut take him away," said Thord.

Vigdis said that she had no time for lying and declared that she didn't fancy having Ingjald poking about in her house, but told him to get on with it. Ingjald ransacked the place, but didn't find Thorolf there. At that moment Asgaut came up and Vigdis asked him where he had parted from Thorolf. "I took him to the sheep-house as Thord told me to," replied Asgaut.

"Could anything be closer to Ingjald's path when he returns to his ship?" said Vigdis. "I'm not going to take the risk that this is what they cooked up yesterday evening. I want you to go right now and take him to Saudafel to meet Thorolf Raudnef [a different Thorolf]. If you do as I ask you, there will be something in it for you. I'll give you your freedom and some money so that you will be able to go wherever you want." Asgaut was all for this and went to the sheep-house where he found Thorolf and told him to get away as quickly as possible.

At that moment Ingjald was riding away from Goddastead intent on getting his money's worth and when he had come down from the farm, he and his men saw two men walking toward them: they were Asgaut and Thorolf. It was early in the morning, so there wasn't much daylight. Asgaut and Thorolf had got themselves into a very tight spot, with Ingjald on one side, and the Lax river on the other. The river was in flood and there were huge masses of ice on both sides, but the middle of the river was flowing and it looked dangerous to cross.

"We seem to have two choices facing us," said Thorolf to Asgaut. "First, we could wait for them here beside the river and defend ourselves as long as our resolve and courage hold out, but it's more than likely that Ingjald and his men will kill us straight off. The other choice is to try the river, and that seems to have its own risks." Asgaut told Thorolf to decide, and declared that he wouldn't part from him now, whatever he decided to do. "Let's head for the river," said Thorolf.

They did this and lightened their equipment as much as possible. After that, they climbed down to the masses of ice and threw themselves into the water. Because these men were brave, and longer life was in their destiny, they managed to cross the river and climbed up onto the heaped ice on the other side. They were no sooner across than Ingjald and his followers reached the side of the river. Ingjald addressed his men: "What are we going to do? Will we try the river or not?" They told him to decide and said that they would trust his judgment, though the river seemed impassable to them. "We'll turn back and leave the river alone," said Ingjald.

When Thorolf and Asgaut saw that Ingjald and his men were not going to attempt the crossing, they wrung out their clothes first of all and got ready for their journey. They walked all day and in the evening reached Saudafell where they had a warm welcome beacause anyone was allowed to stay there overnight. In the course of the evening, Asgaut went to see Thorolf Raudnef and outlined to him all the circumstances of their errand. He explained to Thorolf Raudnef that the man who had arrived with him had been sent there by his kinswoman Vigdis for support and protection. He gave an account of all that had gone on between Thord Goddi and his wife and presented the identification sent by Vigdis to Thorolf Raudnef.

"I'm not going to question this identification," said Thorolf Raudnef. "Of course I'll take in this man at Vigdis's request. I think she has behaved coura-geously in this business, and it's a great pity that a woman like her has made such a wretched marriage. Asgaut, you can stay here as long as you like."

Asgaut replied that he wouldn't stay there any longer. Then Thorolf

Raudnef received his namesake and made him one of his followers. Thorolf and Asgaut parted as good friends and Asgaut made his way home.

As for Ingjald, he turned back to Goddastead when he and Thorolf had parted company. By that time, no fewer than forty-two men from neighboring farms had shown up at the request of Vigdis. When Ingjald and his men got back to the farm, Ingjald called Thord over to him.

"You haven't behaved like a gentleman about our agreement," said Ingjald. "We know for sure that you got the man away." Thord replied that he truly had no part in the affair, but the whole story of the agreement between Ingjald and Thord came out. Now Ingjald wanted to get back the money he had given to Thord. Vigdis was standing nearby during their conversation and remarked that they had got what they deserved. She told Thord it was unmanly to keep the money. "Because, Thord, you got hold of the money dishonorably," she said. Thord said that she should do whatever she wanted with it.

With that, she went indoors to Thord's chest and found a fat money-bag at the bottom of it. She picked up the bag and took it out to Ingjald and told him to take the money. Ingjald brightened up with that and stretched out his hand toward the money-bag. Vigdis heaved up the bag and struck him on the nose with it, and immediately his blood gushed to the ground. Along with the bag, she hurled a few choice epithets at him, said that he would never get his money back again, and told him to be on his way. Ingjald saw that the best idea was to be off as soon as he could and that's what he did, without stopping till he got home. He wasn't happy about his trip.

16. As soon as Asgaut got back home, Vigdis gave him a warm welcome and asked him how good the hospitality had been at Saudafell. He reported that it had been excellent and repeated Thorolf Raudnef's parting words to her. She was very pleased about that and said to Asgaut,

"You have shown real guts and loyalty, and I'll tell you right now what your reward is going to be: I am giving you your freedom, and from today you will be called a free man; you will have the money Thord accepted in return for the life of my kinsman; the money has found a better home." [The grateful Asgaut moves to Denmark where he becomes a successful farmer.] ...

Vigdis felt such hostility because of the plot between Ingjald and Thord Goddi that she declared herself divorced from Thord. She went back to her relatives and told them what had happened. Thord Gellir, their chief, was not happy about the divorce, but there was no fuss. Vigdis took no more from Goddistead than her own valuables. The people of Hvamm announced that they intended to take half the property owned by Thord Goddi....

(c) How Aud Dealt with Her Humiliating Divorce

Gudrun Osvifrsdaughter becomes involved with Thord Ingunnarson, who, unfortunately, is already married to Aud. The resourceful Gudrun suggests a pretext by which Thord can get a divorce from her. Aud does not simply fade away but exacts an ironic revenge on Thord for her humiliation. From The Saga of the People of Laxdale.

Source: *Laxdæla saga*, ed. Einar Ól. Sveinsson, Íslenzk fornrit V (Reykjavík, 1934), pp. 95–98.

35. … Gudrun Osvifrsdaughter rode to the Althing and Thord Ingunnarson went with her. One day, as they were riding across Blaskogarheath in fine weather, Gudrun asked,

"Is it true, Thord, that your wife, Aud, always wears men's breeches and leg-bands that reach almost to her shoes?" He replied that he hadn't noticed.

"There can't be much truth to the rumor if you haven't noticed it," said Gudrun. "But why else is she called Aud-in-Breeches?"

"I don't think she can have been called that for long," said Thord.

"What's really important is how long the name sticks," replied Gudrun.

After that, people arrived at the Althing: nothing of much importance happened there. Thord spent a lot of time in Gest's booth and was forever talking with Gudrun. One day, he asked her what would be the consequences for a woman who always wore trousers like a man. Gudrun answered, "A woman who does this should face the same penalty as a man who has so large an opening in his shirt that his nipples are exposed. Both are grounds for divorce."

Thord said, "Do you think I should announce my divorce from Aud here at the Althing, or at home in my own district where I'll have the backing of more supporters? For the men who are likely to take offence at this are proud and touchy."

After a moment, Gudrun answered, "The timid postpone their lawsuits till evening." Then Thord sprang up and went to the Law Rock. He named witnesses and declared that he was divorcing Aud, on the grounds that she wore gored breeches as though she were a man.

Aud's brothers were not at all happy about this, but they took no action. Thord rode from the Thing with the Osvifrssons. When Aud heard the news, she said:

> It's as well to know
> I'm deserted so.

Later, Thord and eleven others rode west to Saurby for the division of the estate. This went without a hitch as Thord made no difficulties about how the property was split up. Then he went back to Laugar with a great number of livestock and asked for Gudrun's hand in marriage. His request was granted willingly by Osvifr, and Gudrun didn't object. The wedding was to take place at Laugar ten weeks before the end of summer. The feast was splendid and Thord and Gudrun were happy in their marriage. The only reason that Thorkel Whelp and Knut [Aud's brothers] did not bring a lawsuit against Thord Ingunnarson was that they had no support for it.

The following summer Aud and the men of Hol were at their shieling [a summer pasture, usually with a cottage] in Hvammsdal. The men of Laugar had their shieling in Lambadal, which runs west into the mountains from Saelingsdal. Aud asked the fellow who looked after their sheep how often he ran into the shepherd from Laugar. He said that was always happening, not surprisingly, as only a single ridge separated the shielings. Aud said,

"Go and meet the shepherd from Laugar today and find out for me who is at the shieling and who has stayed behind at the main farm. Talk about Thord in a very friendly fashion, just as you ought to."

The boy promised to do as she asked and when he came home in the evening, Aud asked for his news. The shepherd replied, "I've heard news you're going to like. There's quite a distance just now between the beds of Thord and Gudrun, for she's at the shieling and he's working himself to death building a house. He and Osvifr are the only two at the home farm."

"What a great job of spying you've done!" said Aud. "When everyone goes to bed, have two horses saddled."

The shepherd did as she asked and shortly before sunset Aud mounted her horse. On this occasion she was definitely wearing breeches. She pressed on so hard that the shepherd on the other horse could barely keep up with her. She rode south across Saelingsdal Heath and didn't come to a halt until she got to the fence around Laugar farm. There she dismounted and told the shepherd to watch the horses while she made her way to the house. Aud went up to the entry and found the door open. She entered the main room and walked toward the bed closet where Thord lay asleep. The door was shut but not bolted. She entered the bed-closet and found Thord sleeping on his back. Then Aud woke Thord and he turned toward the door when he realized that a man had come in. She drew a short sword and thrust at Thord, wounding him seriously in the right arm and cutting across both nipples. She thrust so hard that the sword lodged itself in the wooden bed. After that, Aud went back to her horse, leapt into the saddle, and rode home.

Thord tried to spring to his feet when he was wounded, but he couldn't as the loss of blood had weakened him. Awakened by the noise, Osvifr asked what had happened and Thord told him that he had been wounded. Osvifr got up and saw to Thord's wounds. He asked him if he knew who had done this to him. Thord said he thought that Aud had done it. Osvifr offered to ride in pursuit of her. He said she was likely to have come without many companions and so her punishment would be assured. Thord declared he was far from wishing any such thing and that Aud had just done what she had to do.

When Aud arrived home at dawn, her brothers asked where she had been. She answered that she had been to Laugar and told them what she had done there. They were delighted but said that she had not gone far enough. Thord's wounds kept him in bed for a long time. Though the injuries on his chest healed well, his arm was never the same again....

CHAPTER SIX

VIKING WARRIORS AND THEIR WEAPONS

Ax from a grave in Mammen, Denmark, late tenth century. The blade has an elaborate silver and gold inlay. The Mammen style of Viking art takes its name from this piece.

Source: Paul B. du Chaillu, *The Viking Age*, 2 vols. (New York: Charles Scribner's Sons, 1899), vol. 2, p. 88.

30. THE ACCOMPLISHMENTS OF A VIKING WARRIOR

These excerpts from saga texts illustrate the appearance, accomplishments, and character of several famous Viking warriors.

(a) Earl Rognvald Kali on Being a Gentleman

Rögnvald Kali Kolsson (ca 1100–58) became earl of Orkney in 1129. He began the construction of St. Magnus's Cathedral, where he was buried after his assassination in 1158. He was later canonized. From Orkneyinga saga, *a history of the earls of Orkney from the tenth to the thirteenth centuries.*

Source: *Orkneyinga saga*, ed. Finnbogi Guðmundsson, Íslenzk fornrit XXXIV (Reykjavík, 1965), p. 130.

Kali was a very promising man with many accomplishments. He was middle-sized and had well-formed limbs and light brown hair. He was very popular and had more physical abilities than most other men. He composed this verse:

> I know nine arts, for
> I'm a demon at draughts
> and rarely go wrong with runes;
> I read at times, use my hands at times;
> I can slide on skis,
> shoot bows and row boats;
> I know how to harp
> and how poems are made.

(b) Gunnar Hamundarson, the Ideal Warrior

Gunnar's strengths and his nobility do not save him from the cycle of violence and revenge that dominates the saga. From Njal's Saga.

Source: *Brennu-Njáls saga*, ed. Einar Ól. Sveinsson, Íslenzk fornrit XII (Reykjavík, 1954), pp. 52–53.

19. There was a man called Gunnar Hamundarson who lived at Hlidarend in Fljotshlid. Gunnar was tall and strong and more skilled in the use of weapons than any other man. He could strike or shoot with whichever hand

he pleased and he could swing his sword so rapidly that there seemed to be three swords in the air at once. Gunnar was a very fine bowman who never missed his target. He could jump higher than his own height in full armor and was able to leap as far backwards as he could forwards. He swam like a seal and there was no sport in which anyone had any hope of competing with him. It has been said that he had no equal.

Gunnar was a handsome man with a fair complexion and a straight nose that turned up at the end. He had flashing blue eyes, rosy cheeks and a fine head of golden hair. He was an extremely courteous man, but tough-minded in everything. He was open-handed and even-tempered; slow to make friends, but loyal to those he made. He was very well off....

(c) Olaf Tryggvason, King of Norway

Olaf Tryggvason (960–1000) had an eventful life. In childhood, he narrowly escaped capture by Harald Greycloak, king of Norway, who saw him as a rival for the throne. Crossing the Baltic, he was captured by pirates who sold him into slavery. Olaf was bought from slavery by Valdimar, king of Novgorod, and eventually killed the man who had enslaved him. After an adventurous life as mercenary and Viking, he seized the throne of Norway and began the bloody Christianization of that country (see doc. 85). He ruled from 995 until 1000, when he was defeated and killed by a confederacy of his Scandinavian rivals (see doc. 38b). From The Saga of Olaf Tryggvason.

Source: Snorri Sturluson, *Óláfs saga Tryggvasonar*, in *Heimskringla*, ed. Bjarni Aðalbjarnarson, Íslenzk fornrit XXVI–XXVIII (Reykjavík, 2002), vol. I, p. 333.

85. King Olaf was more skilled in every kind of athletic exercise than any other Norwegian of whom we have accounts. He was stronger and more agile than anyone else and many stories have been written about his prowess. One is that he climbed the Smalsarhorn and planted his shield on the topmost crag. Another is that he helped one of his retainers who had climbed up the mountain until he came to a place where he could neither go up nor come down. The king got to him, took him under his arm, and carried him to level ground. King Olaf could also run across the oars outside the ship while his men were rowing the *Serpent* [Olaf's flagship]. He could juggle three daggers, so that one was always in the air and the hilt of another was always in his hand. He could strike equally well with both hands and could throw two spears at once.

King Olaf was the most cheerful and high-spirited of men. He was agreeable and sociable, impetuous and generous. He dressed showily and was braver in battle than any other man. When he was angry, he was very savage and tortured many of his enemies. Some he burned; some he had torn to pieces by wild dogs; some he had maimed, or thrown from high cliffs. For these reasons, his friends loved him and his enemies feared him, and he was very successful because some obeyed him out of affection and friendship, while others obeyed him out of fear.

31. BERSERKERS AND THE BERSERK RAGE

Berserkers or berserks were ferocious warriors who were able to fall into a battle-frenzy in which they fought without regard for their own safety and, reputedly, could not be harmed by weapons. The berserks were particularly associated with the god Odin, and with shape-shifting, and one etymology for the word proposes that it is related to the German bär (= bear) *plus* serkr, shirt, *meaning one who wears a bear skin. Another etymology proposes that the word is derived from* berr, bare, *plus* serkr, *meaning one who fights without armor.*

(a) Odin's Berserks

The Saga of the Ynglings *opens Snorri's* Heimskringla *and recounts the arrival of the gods in Scandinavia. This passage introduces the berserks.*

Source: Snorri Sturluson, *Ynglinga saga*, in *Heimskringla*, ed. Bjarni Aðalbjanarson, Íslenzk fornrit XXVI–XXVIII (Reykjavík, 2002), vol. I, p. 17.

6. When Odin of the Aesir and the Diar [judges, priests] who came with him arrived in the northlands, they introduced and taught the arts which men practiced there for a long time afterwards. Odin was the cleverest of all, and the others learned the arts from him, because he knew them first and, besides, he knew more than anyone else.

The reasons why Odin was so highly honored are these: when he sat among his friends, his appearance was so handsome and noble that everyone's spirits were raised. But when he was with his army, he appeared fearsome to his enemies. This was because he knew the art of changing his appearance and shape in whatever way he pleased. Another reason was that he spoke so eloquently and smoothly that all who heard him thought that his words alone were true. He spoke everything in rhyme just as we recite what is now called poetry. He and his priests are known as songsmiths because the art of poetry in the northlands began with them. In battle, Odin knew how to make his enemies blind, or deaf, or terrified, and how to make their weapons no sharper than twigs. His men advanced without coats of mail, as mad as dogs or wolves. They bit their shields and were as strong as bears or bulls. They slaughtered men, but neither fire nor iron harmed them. This is called the berserk frenzy.

(b) The Rage of Skallagrim and Egil

Father and son display a berserk's rage when they take games too seriously.

Source: *Egils saga Skalla-Grímssonar*, ed. Sigurður Nordal, Íslenzk fornrit II (Reykjavík, 1933), pp. 98–102.

40. Skallagrim took great delight in trials of strength and sports and he loved talking about them. Ball-games were played in those days. At that time there were plenty of strong men, but no one came near Skallagrim in strength, even when he was advanced in years.

Grani of Granistead had a young and very promising son called Thord who was deeply attached to Egil Skallagrimson. Egil was a great one for wrestling as well as being extremely headstrong and hot-tempered. Everyone knew to warn their sons not to win against Egil.

At the beginning of winter, a large number of people held a ball-game at Hvitarvellir; they came from all over the district, including many from Skallagrim's household. Thord Granison was the most eager amongst them. Egil asked Thord if he could go with him to the game; he was seven years old then. Thord agreed and carried Egil on his back.

When they arrived, the men were divided up for the game. Lots of boys had come as well. They set up another game, and they formed groups for that too. Egil drew as his opponent a boy called Grim, son of Hegg from Heggstead. Grim was eleven or twelve years old, and strong for his age. When they played, Egil proved the weaker and Grim put all that he had into the effort. Egil lost his temper, raised the bat, and struck him with it. Grim seized him and gave him a really bad fall; he said that he would hurt Egil seriously if he didn't behave himself.

When Egil got to his feet, he left the game, and the boys laughed at him. Egil went looking for Thord Granison and told him what had happened. Thord said, "I'll go with you and we'll get our own back on him." Thord handed him a skeggax [one-handed ax] which he had with him. They walked to where the boys were playing. Grim had the ball and was running off with it; the other boys were in pursuit. Egil leapt at Grim and drove the ax into his head so that it penetrated the brain. Egil and Thord immediately returned to their people. The men from Myrar seized their weapons; indeed, both sides did so. Oleif Hjalti ran with his followers to join the men of Borg, so that they were much the larger group; then the two sides separated.

This caused bad blood between Oleif and Hegg and they fought at Laxfit near Grimsa [Grim's River]. Six men died there; Hegg was mortally wounded and his brother, Kvig, died too.

When Egil came home, Skallagrim paid little heed, but Bera said that he was likely to become a great Viking and that a warship would be in store for him when he was old enough. Egil recited a poem:

> She would buy me, said my mother,
> a fast ship with splendid oars;
> I would travel away with Vikings,
> stand watch at the prow,
> steer my fine ship;
> I would make for harbor,
> cut down one man and another.

At the age of twelve, Egil was so well-developed that few grown men, however big and strong, could beat him at games. In the winter he turned twelve, Egil competed frequently in games; he and Thord Granason, a strong twenty year old, were often pitted against Skallagrim. On one occasion late in the winter, a ball game [Knattleikr] was held at Sandvik, south of Borg. Egil and Thord were playing against Skallagrim and the game was going in their favor because Skallagrim was tiring. However, in the evening, the going got tougher for Egil and Thord since, after sunset, Skallagrim became stronger. He grew so strong that he was able to pick Thord up and throw him to the ground so hard that every bone in his body was broken and he died instantly. Then Skallagrim seized Egil.

One of Skallagrim's slave-women, Thorgerd Brak, had nursed Egil in his childhood. She was a big woman, as strong as a man, and very skilled in magic.

"Skallagrim," she said, "you're raging like a berserk against your own son." Skallagrim let Egil go and grabbed at her, but she broke away and took to her heels with Skallagrim right behind her. They ran to the very tip of Digraness where she leapt from the cliff into the sea. Skallagrim pitched a huge rock at her. The rock struck her between the shoulder-blades and neither she nor the rock ever resurfaced. The place is now called Brak's Sound.

When they got back to Borg later that evening, Egil was in a rage and, when Skallagrim and the others sat down at the dinner-table, he didn't take his place. Then he strode into the room and went straight up to the man who managed Skallagrim's workers and estate; this man was very dear to Skallagrim. Egil killed him with a blow and then went to his seat. Skallagrim said nothing and the matter rested there. But afterwards Egil and Skallagrim had not a word, either good or bad, to say to one another, and this state of affairs lasted all winter.

(c) Egil Fights a Berserk

Fighting berserks comes to be expected of saga-heroes. Here, Egil obliges. In the sagas, the berserks are often seen as thugs and bullies rather than as members of a warrior class. They are little more than social nuisances.

Source: *Egils saga Skalla-Grímssonar*, ed. Sigurður Nordal, Íslenzk fornrit II (Reykjavík, 1933), pp. 201–6.

64. ... All evening, Egil was very cheerful but Frithgeir and his household were a bit subdued. Egil saw an attractive, well-dressed girl there and was told that she was Frithgeir's sister. The young woman was miserable and cried incessantly all evening. Egil and his men thought this was really odd.

They stayed there overnight. Next morning the wind was so strong that putting to sea was out of the question. Moreover, to leave the island, they needed a ship. Both Frithgeir and Gytha, his mother, went to Egil and invited him to stay there with his men until the weather was favorable for sailing. They also offered to give him whatever transport and provisions he needed for the journey. Egil accepted the offer and he and his men stayed there, weather bound, for three nights. They were treated very hospitably.

Then the weather improved, so Egil and his men got up early in the morning and prepared to leave. They gathered their things together, and then sat down to have something to eat and ale to drink. After the meal, Egil rose and thanked Frithgeir and Gytha for their hospitality. Then everyone went outside.

The farmer and his mother came to see them on their way. Then Gytha began a whispered conversation with her son, Frithgeir. While Egil stood waiting for them, he spoke to the young woman.

"Why are you crying, my girl?" he asked. "I have never seen you looking happy."

She couldn't answer, and cried all the more. Frithgeir said to his mother in a loud voice, "I'm not going to ask them to do this now that they're ready for their journey."

So, Gytha went over to Egil and said, "I'll tell you what's happening here, Egil. There's a man called Ljot the Pale, a berserk and a duelist, whom everyone dislikes. He came here and asked to marry my daughter, but we gave him short shrift and turned down his offer. So he challenged my son,

Frithgeir, to a duel and tomorrow he's coming to fight him on Valdero island. Egil, I'd like you to go to the duel with Frithgeir. If my brother, Arinbjorn [a close friend of Egil], were here in Norway, we certainly wouldn't have to put up with bullying from the likes of Ljot."

"Lady," said Egil, "for Arinbjorn's sake, I'm duty bound to go with your son, if he thinks I can help at all."

"You're doing a fine thing, Egil," she replied. "Let's go back inside and spend the day together." Egil and his men went into the living room and sat there drinking all day. In the evening, they were joined by some of Frithgeir's friends who had volunteered to go with him. The house was crowded that night and there was a splendid feast.

Next morning, Frithgeir got ready for the journey. With him, he had Egil and a large crowd of men. The weather was perfect for sailing, so they went on their way and got to Valdero island. Close by the sea, there was a pleasant field where the duel was to take place. The dueling ground itself was marked out by stones which were laid around it. Now Ljot arrived with his men and prepared for the duel. He was a huge, strong-looking man, armed with a sword and shield. As he advanced through the field to the dueling ground, he went into a berserk's rage, uttering terrible howls, and biting his shield. Frithgeir was a small, slender man, handsome but not strong, and he had no experience of fighting. When Egil saw Ljot, he recited this poem:

> We shall go to the island, warriors,
> defend the maiden from this man;
> Frithgeir must not fight,
> battle against the shield-biter
> who gives offerings to the old gods,
> battle against the storm-fierce fighter,
> who rolls his eyes unnervingly
> and is doomed to death.

Ljot saw Egil standing there and heard his words. "If you're so keen to fight me, big man," said Ljot. "come on over to the field and we'll put one another to the test. It will be much fairer than fighting Frithgeir, for my self-esteem won't be improved even if I send him to his grave."

Then Egil recited:

> It's wrong to reject
> Ljot's little request;
> I'll swing my sword against
> the wan-faced warrior;

> ready for the fierce fight,
> I'll mete out no mercy;
> here in Møre, warlike man,
> you and the skald will skirmish.

Then Egil got ready for the duel with Ljot. He was carrying the shield he always used; at his waist he was wearing the sword called Adder, and in his hand he held Dragvandil [Slicer, a sword given to Egil by Arinbjorn]. When Egil entered the dueling ground, Ljot was not yet ready, so Egil brandished his sword and recited this poem:

> Let cutting swords clash,
> let steel strike shield,
> and test its toughness;
> let's bathe swords in blood;
> we'll dock Ljot's life,
> play harshly with the pale one,
> silence the bold warrior with our weapons,
> let the eagle feed on his flesh.

Then Ljot stepped forward into the dueling ground and they attacked one another. Egil slashed at Ljot, who parried with his shield, but Egil's blows came so fast that Ljot couldn't get in a return blow. He drew back to give himself room to strike, but Egil stayed right with him, delivering blows ferociously until Ljot fled beyond the marker stones and ran far into the field. That is how the first round went. Then Ljot asked for a break, and Egil acquiesced. So they stopped and, while they rested, Egil recited:

> Greedy for gain, Ljot,
> the scatterer of sword's fire,
> the hapless hero
> falls back in fear;
> bloodied, he balks at battle,
> fails to stand firm,
> flees far afield from
> the bald-headed bard.

According to the rules of dueling in those days, when one man challenged another, the challenger would receive whatever was in dispute as the prize of victory if he won. But, if he lost, he had to pay an agreed amount as ransom. If he died in the duel, he forfeited all his property and the man who had killed him inherited it. It was also the law that if a foreigner died without heirs in the country, his inheritance went into the king's treasury.

Egil told Ljot to get ready. "Let's fight this duel to a finish," he said. Then, Egil ran at Ljot, struck him, and pressed up so close to him that he fell back, and his shield slipped to the side. Immediately, Egil struck Ljot just above the knee and cut off his leg. Ljot fell down dead on the spot. Egil went over to Frithgeir and the others and they thanked him profusely for what he had done. Then Egil recited:

> The skald severed Ljot's leg;
> the doer of evil deeds died,
> fell to feed wolves.
> The poet gave Frithgeir peace;
> I sought for myself
> no gold-giver's gift,
> but fought the pale-faced foe
> for the noisy sport with spears.

Few people lamented Ljot's death for he had been a very violent man. His family was Swedish and he had no relatives in Norway, but he had gone there and made a fortune from dueling. He had killed many good farmers after challenging them for their farms and ancestral lands. This had made him exceptionally rich both in land and money.

After the duel, Egil went home with Frithgeir and stayed with him for a short time before going south to Møre. Frithgeir and Egil parted on the friendliest terms; Egil commissioned Frithgeir to claim the land that had been owned by Ljot. Then he went on his way and arrived in Fjordane.

(d) Grettir Fights a Berserk

Source: *Grettis saga Ásmundarson*, ed. Guðni Jónson, Íslenzk fornrit VII (Reykjavík, 1936), pp. 135–37.

40. At Yule, Grettir came to the farm of a landowner called Einar. He was a wealthy man who had a wife and a daughter of marriageable age, named Gyrid. Gyrid was a beautiful woman and was regarded as an excellent match. Einar invited Grettir to stay with him over the Yule season and Grettir accepted.

In those days, over much of Norway, there were bandits and criminals who would emerge from the forests and challenge men to fight for their women. They would also seize their property by force when there weren't enough men to resist them. One day in Yule, a gang of these ruffians turned up at Einar's. Their leader, Snaekoll, was a great, big berserk. He challenged Einar to hand over his daughter, or defend her, if he thought he was man enough. Now Einar was past the prime of life and not used to fighting. He knew that he had a serious problem on his hands and asked Grettir in private what he would advise.

"For you have a great reputation," he said. Grettir told Einar not to consent to anything that he thought dishonorable.

The berserk was sitting on his horse, wearing a helmet with the cheek-guards unfastened, and carrying an iron-rimmed shield. His demeanor was terrifying.

"Be quick. Make your choice one way or the other," he said to the land-owner. "What does that big fellow standing beside you advise? Does he want some sport with me?"

"Farmers like Einar and me are much of a muchness," said Grettir. "For neither of us is keen on fighting."

"You'll be really terrified of fighting me if I get angry," said Snaekoll. "We won't know that till we put it to the test," said Grettir.

The berserk thought that all this talk was just a delaying tactic, so he began to howl loudly and bite the rim of his shield. Raising the shield to his mouth, he grimaced horribly over the rim as though he was mad. Grettir hurled himself forward until he drew level with the berserk's horse. Then he kicked the bottom of Snaekoll's shield so hard that it ripped through his mouth, shattering his jaw; the jaw bones fell down to his chest. At one and the same time, Grettir grasped the Viking's helmet with his left hand and pulled him off his horse, while with his right hand he drew his short sword, struck the berserk on the neck, and beheaded him. When Snaekoll's follow-ers saw what had happened, they fled in all directions. Grettir didn't bother to chase them because he could see that they were a spiritless bunch.

Einar thanked Grettir for what he had done and so did many other people. Everyone thought that he had acted with presence of mind and courage in the affair. Grettir stayed there all through Yule, and was entertained hand-somely. When he left, Einar gave him many gifts. Then Grettir traveled east to Tunsberg where he met Thorstein, his brother. Thorstein welcomed him warmly and asked about his adventures, particularly about his killing of the berserk. Grettir recited a poem:

> A quick kick
> shoved the shield
> straight into Snaekoll's
> menacing mouth;
> the iron-bound buckler

tore the tooth-wall in two;
the jaw's broken bones
dropped down to his breast.

Thorstein said, "You'd be successful in all sorts of ways, Grettir, if you weren't hounded by bad luck."

"Still, what I've done will be remembered," replied Grettir.

32. WEAPONS

Viking warriors were equipped in much the same way as their contemporaries elsewhere in Europe and possessed no inherent edge in weapons technology. The ensemble of a wealthy Viking might include an iron helmet and mail shirt (byrnie), a sword, spear, knife (sax) or battleax, and a shield. The kit of a lesser man might comprise only a single weapon like a spear, knife, or ax and perhaps a shield; leather armor and caps might also have been utilized. Swords were prestige items and could have been afforded only by the élite. Swords might be named, and could be passed down for generations. Their histories may be traced through sagas and other texts.

(a) King Magnus Barelegs Dresses to Kill

Magnus Barelegs was king of Norway from 1093 until 1103, when he died in battle in Ireland. The following passage gives an account of his appearance and behavior in that last battle. From The Saga of King Magnus Barelegs *in* Heimskringla.

Source: Snorri Sturluson, *Magnúss saga Berfœtts*, in *Heimskringla*, ed. Bjarni Aðalbjarnarson, Íslenzk fornrit XXVI–XXVIII (Reykjavík, 2002), vol. 3, pp. 234–35.

24. King Magnus positioned men to protect Dublin and readied his ships, with the intention of sailing east to Norway. He lay off Ulster with his entire fleet ready to sail. As they thought they needed provisions, King Magnus sent word to King Myrjartak telling him to send cattle. Magnus fixed the day before Bartholomew's Day [24 August] as the day for their arrival, provided that his messengers got to King Myrjartak safely. However, by the eve of Bartholemew's mass, the cattle had not shown up. So at sunrise on the feast day itself, King Magnus went ashore with the bulk of his army, intending to look for his men and the cattle.

The day was windless and sunny. Their way passed through bogs and fens; paths had been cut through the marshes and there was scrub on both sides of the road. When they went further, they arrived at a high hill from which they had a good view. They saw a large cloud of dust in the distance and wondered whether it was the Irish army or their own men with the cattle. They halted there.

Then Eyvind Elbow said, "King, what are your plans for this journey? The men think you're advancing incautiously. You know that the Irish aren't to be trusted, so work out some plan for your army."

"Let us draw up our men," said the king, "and we'll be ready if this is treachery."

When the lines were drawn up, the king and Eyvind took up position in front of them. King Magnus wore a helmet and had a red shield with a gold lion on it. He was girt with an excellent weapon, the sword called Legbiter, which had an ivory hilt and a handle wound with gold. He had a halberd in his hand and, over his tunic, he wore a red silk doublet with a lion embroidered in gold silk, both front and back. It was the general opinion that no one had seen a braver or more gallant man. Eyvind also had a red silk doublet in the same style as the king's. He, too, was a tall, handsome, warlike man.

(b) The Sword Skofnung

(1) Hrolf Kraki and Skofnung

Hrolf Kraki belonged to the Danish Scylding dynasty. He was nephew of King Hrothgar in whose hall Beowulf killed the monster Grendel. This passage from The Saga of Hrolf Kraki *recounts Hrolf's last battle and his burial with his sword, Skofnung.*

Source: *Hrólfs saga kraka*, in *Fornaldarsögur Norðurlanda*, ed. Guðni Jónsson, 4 vols. (Reykjavík, 1959), vol. 1, pp. 98–105.

50. King Hrolf leapt up from the high seat after he and his champions had been drinking for a while. They left their good drink and went outside at once, all except Bothvar Bjarki. No one saw him and they wondered about his absence; they thought that he had probably been captured or killed somewhere else.

As soon as they got outside, a dreadful battle broke out. King Hrolf himself rushed forward with the standards and on either side of him were his champions; the entire garrison was there but, though they were numerous, they contributed little to the battle. Terrible blows could be seen there, striking helmets and mail-shirts. Many swords and spears could be seen in the air, and there were so many dead that they covered the entire battlefield.

Brave-hearted Hjalti spoke: "Though many a mail-shirt has been shredded, many a weapon broken, many a helmet shattered, and many a brave horseman has been thrust from the saddle, our king is in great spirits, for he is just as happy now as when he was drinking his fill of ale. He always attacks with both hands, and he is very different from other kings in battle, for it seems to me he fights with the strength of twelve kings and kills many brave men. Now King Hjorvard [a legendary Danish king] can see that Skofnung bites, and that it clangs against their skulls, for it is Skofnung's nature to sing aloud whenever it tastes bone."

The battle grew so hot that nothing could stand against King Hrolf and his champions. It was wonderful to see how King Hrolf wielded Skofnung; they wrought such havoc on King Hjorvard's army that his soldiers fell in heaps....

52. King Hrolf defended himself as a warrior should and his bravery was incomparably greater than the courage of other men. The best troops of Skuld [wife of Hjorvard] and King Hjorvard surrounded the king and pressed him hard. Skuld now arrived at the battle and eagerly urged her ruffians to attack King Hrolf, for she saw that his champions were not near him. Bothvar Bjarki was enraged because he could not help his lord, and the other champions shared Bjarki's rage since they were now as eager to die with their king as they had been to live with him in the flower of their youth. By this time, King Hrolf's entire retinue had fallen – not one was left on his feet – and most of the champions had been fatally wounded, as was only to be expected.

Now such a great storm was brought about by spells that the champions began to fall one on top of the other. Hrolf himself was outside the shield-wall, almost dead from exhaustion. There is no need to prolong the story: King Hrolf and all his champions died there with great glory. A burial mound was built for King Hrolf, and the sword Skofnung was laid beside him. A mound was also raised for each of the champions, and each had his weapons beside him. Here ends the saga of King Hrolf Kraki and his Champions.

(2) Skeggi and Skofnung

The Book of Settlements (Landnámabók) *is an account of the settlement of Ice-land in the ninth and tenth centuries (see doc. 70b).*

Source: *Landnamabók*, ed. Jakob Benediktsson, Íslenzk fornrit I (Reykjavík, 1986), p. 212.

S. 174. In Norway, there was a distinguished man called Skeggi from Skautad. His son was called Bjorn, nicknamed Bjorn the Skin because he had traveled to Novgorod in Russia [as a fur trader]. When he grew tired of trading-journeys, he went to Iceland and settled Midfjord and Linakradal. His son was Skeggi from Midfjord, a brave man and a traveler, who fought in Russia. When he returned from the east, he went to Saeland in Denmark where he broke into the burial mound of Hrolf Kraki and stole Skofnung, King Hrolf's sword, as well as Hjalti's ax, and many other treasures, but he didn't find Laufi, the sword of Bothvar Bjarki.

(3) Kormak and Skofnung

In Kormak's Saga, Kormak, an Icelandic poet, attempts to use Skofnung in a duel. The passage illustrates the magical properties of the sword.

Source: *Kormak's Saga*, in *Vatnsdœla saga*, ed. Einar Ól. Sveinsson, Íslenzk fornrit VIII (Reykjavík, 1939), pp. 234–42.

9. ... Kormak told his mother, Dalla, how he had got on. "Our luck's not going to improve much, the way your life's going," she said. "You've turned down an excellent match and you don't stand a chance in a fight against Bersi, for he's a brave man with fine weapons."

Bersi's sword was called Hviting, a sharp sword with a healing stone in the hilt; he had carried it in many life-threatening fights. "Where will you find weapons to use against Hviting?" asked Dalla.

Kormak answered that he would have a big, sharp ax. Dalla suggested that he should visit Skeggi of Midfjord and ask him for the loan of his sword, Skofnung. So Kormak went to Reykir, and explained his predicament to Skeggi. He asked him to lend Skofnung, but Skeggi was reluctant, saying that Kormak and Skofnung had entirely different temperaments.

"Skofnung is slow and deliberate whereas you are rash and impatient," said Skeggi. Kormak rode away; he wasn't very pleased. When he got home to Mel, he told his mother that Skeggi would not lend the sword. Now, Skeggi looked after Dalla's business affairs and there was a warm friendship between them.

"He will lend the sword," said Dalla, "though he may not give in quickly."

"It's not fair if he'll lend the sword to you, but not to me," said Kormak.

Dalla said that her son was an ill-tempered man. Some days later, Dalla told Kormak to go to Reykir. "Skeggi will lend you the sword now," she said. So Kormak went to see Skeggi and asked for Skofnung.

"You'll find the sword difficult to handle," said Skeggi. "There's a pouch attached to it, and you must leave that alone. The sun mustn't shine on the pommel, and you must never carry the sword unless you're getting ready for a fight. When you get to the scene of the fight, wait until you are sitting alone before drawing the sword; then hold the blade out in front of you, blow on it and a little serpent will wriggle out from under the pommel; then turn the sword over to allow the serpent to wriggle back under the pommel."

"You sorcerers put on quite a show," said Kormak. "Nonetheless," said Skeggi, "everything must be done just so."

After this, Kormak rode home and told his mother how he had got on, remarking that her wishes carried great weight with Skeggi. He showed her the sword and tried to draw it, but it wouldn't come out of the scabbard. "You're too headstrong, my son," said Dalla. Then Kormak put his feet on the hilt of the sword and tore off the pouch. Skofnung howled, but stayed in the sheath.

Time passed and the appointed day arrived. Kormak rode from home with fifteen men, and Bersi, too, rode to the island with an equal number of men. Kormak arrived first and told Thorgils that he wanted to sit on his own. Then he sat down and took off the sword. However, he made no effort to keep the pommel out of the sunlight, and had actually been wearing it outside his clothes. He tried to draw the sword but wasn't able to until he stood on the hilt. The little serpent came out, but it wasn't handled properly. So, the spell was broken, and the sword came from the sheath groaning.

10. After that, Kormak rejoined his companions. By then, Bersi and his men had arrived, and many others had come to watch the fight. Kormak picked up Bersi's shield and hacked at it so that sparks flew. A cloak was now spread on the ground for them to stand on.

"Kormak, you have challenged me to a formal duel, but I'm offering you single combat instead," said Bersi. "You are a young and inexperienced man, and duels are a complicated business, but single combat is straightforward."

"Fighting in single combat won't be any better," said Kormak. "I'll take my chances and consider myself your equal in everything." "Just as you like," said Bersi.

The laws of dueling required that the cloak laid on the ground should be five ells square and have loops at each corner. Pegs with heads at one end should then be driven into each loop: these pegs are called *tjosnur*. Whoever sets this up must approach the pegs in such a way that he can see the sky between his legs and he must hold the lobes of his ears while saying the prayer used later in the sacrifice called the *tjosnur* sacrifice. Three squares, each a foot wide, must be measured around the cloak and, at the outer edges of these squares, there must be four poles, called *hazels*. When these steps are complete, the field is called a "hazeled field."

Each man was to have three shields and when all three were destroyed, he was to get onto the cloak, even if he had been driven from it before, and from then on he was to defend himself there using his weapons alone. The one who had been challenged was to strike the first blow and if either was wounded so that blood fell on the cloak, there was no obligation to go on fighting. If a man stepped outside the hazel poles with one foot, he was said to be "falling back on his heel," but if both feet went outside, he was said to be "running." Each of the two fighters was to have a companion to hold his shield in front of him, and the man who was the more seriously wounded was to pay a dueling ransom of three marks of silver.

Thorgils carried the shield in front of his brother, Kormak, and Thord Arndisarson did the same for Bersi. Bersi struck the first blow and split Kormak's shield. Kormak struck back just as aggressively. Each wrecked the other's three shields. Then it was Kormak's turn to strike and he swung at Bersi who warded off the blow with Hviting. Skofnung broke the point from Hviting right where the gutter-ridge ended. The sword-point flew onto Kormak's hand, wounding his thumb. The joint was cut open and blood dropped onto the cloak. After that the men were separated and prevented from fighting on. "This is a shabby victory that Bersi has won," said Kormak. "He owes it to my bad luck, and yet we have to part now."

Kormak threw Skofnung down and it hit Bersi's shield. Sparks were struck from the shield and a notch was gouged from Skofnung. Bersi asked for the dueling-ransom and Kormak replied that it would be paid. With that, they parted.

11. ... After that, Kormak went home to Mel and visited his mother. She healed his hand; the wound became ugly and the flesh swelled up around it. They tried to smooth the notch in Skofnung, but the more they tried, the larger it grew. Then he went back to Reykir and threw the sword at Skeggi's feet and recited this verse:

> I bring back to you,
> Skeggi, this sword
> broken-edged, blunt-toothed;
> truly, their might outdid mine;
> no fault falls to me
> who fought fiercely
> for the girl guarded
> by the singing of swords.

(4) Thorkel Eyolfsson and Skofnung

Thorkel reaps the benefits of Skofnung's magic properties. From The Saga of the People of Laxdale.

Source: *Laxdæla saga*, ed. Einar Ól. Sveinsson, Íslenzk fornrit V (Reykjavík, 1934), pp. 170–74, 221–22.

57. ... At that time, there was a man named Thorkel Eyolfsson who was involved in trading voyages. He was a well-known man of noble family and a great friend of Snorri Godi. When he was in Iceland, he always stayed with his kinsman, Thorstein Kuggason.

Once, when Thorkel had a ship laid up at Vail on Bard strand, the son of Eid of As was killed in Borgarfjord by the sons of Helga of Kropp. Grim was the man who did the killing along with his brother, Njal. Njal drowned in the Hvita [White River] shortly afterwards and Grim, who was condemned to outlawry for the killing, hid out in the hills after he was outlawed. Grim was a big, strong man when all this happened, but Eid was very old and that is why the case was not followed up vigorously. However, people were very critical of Thorkel Eyjolfsson for not pursuing the case.

In the spring, after he had fitted out his ship, Thorkel traveled south across Breidafjord. There, he got himself a horse and rode alone without stopping until he reached the home of his relative Eid at As; Eid gave him a warm welcome. Thorkel explained that he intended to find the outlaw, Grim, and asked Eid if he had any idea where Grim's hideout was.

"I don't like this one bit," replied Eid. "I think you're risking a great deal taking on a devil like Grim. But, if you're determined to go, take plenty of men with you, so that you'll have the upper hand."

"I don't think there's much glory in taking a whole body of men against a single man," said Thorkel. "I'd like you to lend me the sword Skofnung and then I'm sure I'll be able to deal with a lone outlaw, no matter how resourceful he is."

"Have it your own way," said Eid. "It won't surprise me, though, if you come to regret your willfulness. But, since you seem to think you're doing this for my sake, I won't refuse your request, for I'm sure that Skofnung will be in good hands when it's with you. However, Skofnung has special properties because of which the sun must never shine on the hilt, and it must never be drawn when there are women present. Also, if someone is wounded by the sword, the wound won't heal unless it's rubbed by the healing stone that is mounted on the sword."

Thorkel said that he would be careful to bear all these instructions in mind. Then he took up the sword and asked Eid to show him the way to Grim's hideout. Eid thought that Grim had a den in the north at Tvidag [Two-Day Heath] near Fiskivatn [Fish Lake]. So Thorkel rode north across the heath, following Eid's directions, and when he had traveled quite a distance into the heath, he saw a shed near a large lake and headed toward it.

58. Thorkel approached the shed and saw a man with a cloak over his head fishing at the mouth of a stream which flowed into the lake. He dismounted, tethered his horse by the wall of the shed, and walked over to the lake where the man was sitting. Grim saw Thorkel's reflection in the water and leapt up quickly, but by then Thorkel had got very close to Grim and struck him. The blow caught Grim on the arm just above the wrist, but the wound was not serious. So right away, Grim ran at Thorkel and they started wrestling. The difference in strength told immediately and Thorkel fell with Grim on top of him. Grim then asked him who he was, but Thorkel replied that it didn't matter.

"Things haven't gone quite as you intended," said Grim, "for your life is in my hands now." Thorkel answered that he would not ask for mercy. "It's just my bad luck," he said.

Grim replied that he had enough problems already without looking for more.

"Your fate lies elsewhere; you're not going to die here in a fight with me, for I'm going to give you your life, and you can repay me however you like."

They both got up and walked back to the shed. Thorkel noticed that Grim was becoming weak from loss of blood so he rubbed Grim's wound with Skofnung's healing stone and then tied it to his arm. Immediately, the stone removed all the pain and swelling from the wound. They stayed there overnight; in the morning Thorkel got ready to leave and asked Grim if he wanted to come with him. Grim said yes.

[*The story of Skofnung and Thorkell is resumed after a considerable absence from the saga.*]

76. Early in the morning of Maundy Thursday [Thursday before Easter], Thorkel got ready for his journey, but Thorstein tried his best to dissuade him. "The weather looks unsettled," he said. Thorkel replied that the weather would suit him just fine. "You're not going to stop me, kinsman," said Thorkel, "because I want to get home for Easter."

Thorkel launched the ferry and loaded it with timber, but Thorstein unloaded the cargo just as quickly as Thorkel and his crew got it aboard. "Give it up, Thorstein," said Thorkel. "Stop trying to delay our journey; you won't get your way this time."

"Then," said Thorstein, "the person least suited to make the decision will get his way, and this journey will have terrible consequences." Thorkel and his crew sailed along Breidafjord all that day; there were ten men aboard. The weather blew up a gale which became a major storm before letting up again, but being very brave men they pressed on regardless. Thorkel had Skofnung with him in a chest. They sailed on until they came to Bjarnarey [Bjorn's Island] – people were watching them from both shores – but when they got to the island, a squall caught the sail and capsized the ship. Thorkel and all the men with him were drowned, and the cargo of timber was driven far and wide among the islands. Skofnung, which had got stuck in the ribs of the ship, came ashore at Skofnung's Island.

(5) Gellir Thorkelsson and Skofnung

Skofnung finally disappears from history. From The Saga of the People of Laxdale.

Source: *Laxdæla saga*, ed. Einar Ól. Sveinsson, Íslenzk fornrit V (Reykjavík, 1934), p. 229.

78. ... Thorkel's son Gellir lived at Helgafell until his old age and many remarkable stories are told about him. He appears in many sagas though he is not much mentioned in this one. He built a fine church at Helgafell, which Arnor Jarlaskald [earls' poet] describes in detail in the mourning poem he wrote about Gellir.

When Gellir was in late old age, he left Iceland on a journey. First, he went to Norway. He didn't stay there long, but left almost immediately and traveled south to Rome to visit the holy apostle, Peter. This was a lengthy trip, but eventually he traveled north to Denmark where he fell ill and was confined to his bed for a long time. He received the last rites and afterwards he died; now he lies buried in Roskilde. Gellir had the sword Skofnung with him and it has never been seen since. It had been taken from the burial mound of Hrolf Kraki in Denmark.

(c) Sigmund, Sigurd, and the Sword Gram

The Saga of the Volsungs *is a prose version of the history of the Volsung family, the descendants of King Volsung, the legendary great-grandson of Odin. The saga includes the legends of Sigurd, Brunhild, and the Nibelungs. The tale of the Nibelung family is the focus of Richard Wagner's operatic cycle* The Ring of the Nibelungs. *This excerpt culminates in the slaying of Fafnir by Sigurd.*

Source: *Völsunga saga,* in *Fornaldarsögur Norðurlanda,* ed. Guðni Jónsson, 4 vols. (Reykjavík, 1959), vol. I, pp. 113, 135–47, 150–56.

3. Once there was a king called Siggeir who ruled over Gothland in Sweden. He was a powerful king with a large following. He went to visit King Volsung and asked for the hand of his daughter, Signy. The king and his sons were pleased by the proposal, but Signy was reluctant, though she asked her father to decide this matter as he did everything else that concerned her. The king thought that it was expedient to give her in marriage, so she was betrothed to King Siggeir. King Siggeir was to come to King Volsung's court for the wedding banquet and the wedding itself. King Volsung put his best efforts into preparing for the banquet and, when everything was ready, King Volsung's guests and King Siggeir's guests arrived on the appointed day; many noble men accompanied King Siggeir.

It is said that many large fires were lit all along the hall, and in the middle stood the great tree, as has been mentioned already. The story tells that when people were sitting at the fires in the evening, a solitary man whom no one recognized walked into the hall. The man wore a spotted coat with a hood, his feet were bare, and his legs were covered by linen breeches. He had a sword in his hand, a wide hat on his head, and he approached the tree in the middle of the hall. He was tall, old, and one-eyed. He drew the sword and thrust it into the tree trunk so that it sank in all the way to the hilt. No one offered any greeting to the man. However, he began to address them.

"The man who draws this sword from the tree will receive it as a gift from me and he will find truly that he has never had a better sword than this in his hand." After that, the old man left the hall, and no one knew who he was or where he went.

Then they got up, and there was no hesitation about trying to take the sword because they thought that whoever tried first would win. The noblest men went up to the tree first, and then the others, one after another. No one who approached the tree won the sword, for it didn't give an inch when they laid hold of it. Then Sigmund, the son of King Volsung, seized the sword and drew it from the tree trunk as though he had found it loose. The weapon seemed so excellent to everyone that they thought they had never seen its equal. Siggeir offered three times its weight in gold for the sword, but Sigmund replied, "You could have taken the sword from its place just as I did, if it had been fitting for you to carry it, but you will never do that now that the sword has come into my possession, even if you offer all the gold you possess."...

11. Once there was a king called Eylimi, a ruler both powerful and noble. His daughter, Hjordis, was the most beautiful and wisest of women. King Sigmund heard that she was a match for him, if anyone was, so he went to the home of King Eylimi who wished to honor Sigmund with a feast, provided that he was not coming to make war. Messages passed between them, and it was established that Sigmund's journey was peaceful and that he had no hostile intentions. King Eylimi had only the best provisions for his banquet, which was attended by a large number of guests. Markets were set up everywhere for King Sigmund and he was provided with whatever provisions or equipment he needed for his journey.

They arrived at the feast, and the two kings shared one hall. Also at the feast was King Lyngvi, the son of King Hunding, and he, too, wanted to marry King Eylimi's daughter, Hjordis. King Eylimi saw that they had come on a single errand and he also knew that there would be difficulties with the loser.

So, the king spoke to his daughter. "You are a wise woman," said Eylimi, "and I have told you that you must choose whom you marry. Choose between these two kings; your decision will be mine."

"This seems a difficult problem," she answered. "However, I choose the more famous king, and that is Sigmund, though he is stooped with age." Accordingly, she was promised to Sigmund and Lyngvi went away. Then Sigmund married Hjordis and from one day to the next the festivities grew better and more splendid.

Later, Sigmund, accompanied by his father-in-law, returned to Hunland and took care of his kingdom. But King Lyngvi and his brothers gathered an army against King Sigmund because they had always come off worst, and the present instance was even more irritating, so they wanted to humble the glory of the Volsungs. They advanced into Hunland and sent word to King Sigmund that they did not want to take him unawares, and that they did not expect him to flee. King Sigmund said that he would meet them in battle and gathered his army. Hjordis was moved to the forests with a maid-servant and a great deal of treasure. She remained there while the fighting continued.

An overwhelming army of Vikings leapt from their ships. King Sigmund and King Eylimi set up their standards and horns were sounded, but King

Sigmund had sounded his father's horn to encourage his men; Sigmund had by far the smaller army. A fierce battle developed and, though he was an old man, Sigmund fought hard and was always at the forefront of his men. Neither shield nor mail-shirt could withstand him and, that day, he was so constantly engaged with his enemies' army that no one could tell how the conflict would turn out. Many spears and arrows were in the air, but his guardian spirits protected him so that he was unwounded and no one could tell the number of those who fell at his hands; both his arms were bloodied to the shoulder.

After the battle had gone on for some time, a man with a broad hat and a blue cloak entered the battle. He was one-eyed and carried a spear. The man approached King Sigmund and thrust his spear at him. When King Sigmund swung hard, his sword struck the spear and broke in two. Then the tide of battle turned, for King Sigmund's luck had deserted him, and many of his men fell all around him. Yet the king defended himself and urged on his men but, as the saying goes, there's no arguing with numbers. In this battle, King Sigmund and King Eylimi, his father-in-law, fell at the head of their troops, most of whom perished.

12. Now King Lyngvi went to the king's residence, intent on capturing Hjordis there, but he was disappointed for he found neither the woman nor the treasure. He traveled all over the country and divided the kingdom among his followers. He thought that he had exterminated the whole race of the Volsungs and that there was no cause to fear anything from that direction.

That night, after the battle, Hjordis searched among the dead and found where King Sigmund was lying. She asked whether he would recover. "Many who are hardly expected to live survive," he answered, "but my luck has deserted me, so I won't allow myself to be healed and Odin doesn't want me to raise the sword that has been broken. I won battles as long as it pleased him."

"I would be happy," she replied, "if you got better and avenged my father." "That's another man's destiny," answered Sigmund. "You are carrying a man-child. Raise him well and carefully, and the boy will be noble and the foremost of our family. Take care of the sword-fragments, for a good sword called Gram may be made from them and our son will carry it. The many great deeds he performs with Gram will never be forgotten, and his name will be renowned while the world lasts. Let that satisfy you for now. I am exhausted by my wounds and I'm going to visit our relatives who have gone before me."

Hjordis sat with him until he died and by then it was daybreak. She saw that many ships had reached land and said to her maid-servant, "We must change clothes, and you will go by my name and say that you are the king's daughter." They did so. The Vikings were looking over the many dead when they saw two women heading for the forest. The Vikings realized that great events had taken place and leapt from their ships.

The leader of this force was Alf, son of Hjalprek, king of Denmark, who was sailing along the coast with his army. Then they arrived where the dead lay, and they saw that there had been a great slaughter. The king gave orders for the women to be brought before him, and this was done. He asked who they were, and the answer was given by the maid-servant, who recounted the deaths of King Sigmund, King Eylimi, and many other great men; she explained, too, who had done this. King Alf asked if they knew where the treasure of King Sigmund was hidden.

"It is to be expected that we would know," replied the maid-servant. She showed the way to the treasure, and they found it was a vast amount of wealth. No one recalled ever having seen so large a treasure or so many precious objects gathered together in one place. All of this property was carried to Alf's ships; Hjordis and the maid-servant followed too. He traveled home to his own kingdom and said that the most famous kings had fallen there. The king stayed at the steering oar, while the women sat just before the quarter deck. He talked to them, and found their opinions worth listening to.

King Alf, the most accomplished of kings, arrived back in his own kingdom with the treasure. When they had been there for a little while, the king's mother asked, "Why has the more beautiful of these women fewer rings and inferior clothes? In my estimation, you have ranked the better woman as inferior."

"I have suspected," he replied, "that she did not have the bearing of a maid-servant, and when we met, she greeted honorable men with ease. We'll put them to the test." One day, when they were drinking, the king started a conversation with the women and asked, "How do you recognize that it is daybreak and the night has gone if you see no sun in the sky?"

The servant answered, "When I was young, I used to drink a great deal at dawn; I've given up the habit, but I still waken because of it, and that is how I recognize morning." The king laughed at that answer and said, "Poor behavior for a King's daughter!"

He turned to Hjordis and asked her the same question. "My father gave me a little ring," she answered, "and it had the property of turning cold on my finger at dawn."

"A lot of gold for a maid-servant to carry," he said. "You have hidden yourself from me for long enough. I would have treated you as if we had been children of the same king if you had told me this from the beginning. But I shall treat you even more honorably, for you will be my wife and I shall pay you a dower when you bear me a child." In reply, she told him the whole truth about her condition and she stayed there in great honor and seemed the most worthy of women.

13. At this point in the story, Hjordis gave birth to a boy, and the child was taken to King Hjalprek. The king was delighted when he saw the boy's bright eyes and declared that there would never be anyone like him, or equal to him in any way. The child was sprinkled with water and named Sigurd. Everyone had the same opinion: that there was no one to match him in character or physique. He was brought up by King Hjalprek with great affection, and whenever the noblest men and kings are named in the old sagas, Sigurd always comes first for his strength, his accomplishments, his energy, and his valor; he was more highly endowed with these qualities than anyone else in the northern regions of the world. So, Sigurd grew up with King Hjalprek and King Hjalprek betrothed Hjordis to his son, King Alf, and paid the bride-price.

Regin, son of Hreithmar, was Sigurd's foster father. He taught Sigurd the accomplishments that were expected of kings' sons: how to play chess, how to read runes, how to speak several languages, and many other things as well. One day when they were together, Regin asked Sigurd if he knew how much property his father had owned and who was managing it. Sigurd replied that the kings were looking after it.

"Do you trust them completely?" asked Regin. Sigurd answered, "It's only right that they should look after it until I am fit to do so, for they know how to take care of it better than I do."

On another occasion, Regin approached Sigurd and said, "It's odd that you don't mind being the kings' stable boy and going about like a tramp." "That's not how things are," said Sigurd. "We talk over everything together, and I get whatever I want." "Ask for a horse, then," said Regin. "I'll get one the minute I want it," answered Sigurd.

Then Sigurd went to the king. "What do you want?" asked Hjalprek. "I would like a horse to ride," replied Sigurd. "Then choose yourself a horse and anything else of mine that you'd like," said the king.

So next day, Sigurd went to the forest where he met an old man with a long beard. The stranger asked Sigurd where he was off to. "I have to choose a horse," said Sigurd. "Can you give me any advice?"

"Let's go and drive the horses to the river Busiltjorn," said the old man. So they drove the horses deep into the river. All but one of them returned to land, and that was the one Sigurd chose. The horse was a young gray, big and handsome – no one had ever ridden him.

"This horse is descended from Sleipnir," said the bearded man, "and he must be carefully reared, for he will be better than any other horse." With that, the man vanished. Sigurd called the horse Grani, and it was the best horse ever.... Odin was the old man whom he had met.

On another occasion, Regin said to Sigurd, "You haven't got nearly enough money, and it upsets me to see you running about like a peasant boy. But I can tell you where there's a great treasure to be found; you'll gain fame if you go looking for it, and even more if you get hold of it." Sigurd asked where it was and who was guarding it.

"The guardian of the treasure is called Fafnir," replied Regin, "and he lives not far from here at a place called Gnitaheath. When you get there, you'll have to admit that you have never seen more gold in one place. You will never need more even if you live to be the oldest and most famous of kings."

"I may be young," said Sigurd, "but I have heard what sort of dragon this is, and I have also heard that no one dares to attack him because of his size and his malevolence."

"That's not so," answered Regin, "he's only about the size of a heath-snake, but he's made out to be much bigger than he really is – that's what your ancestors would have thought. But even though you are one of the Volsungs, it doesn't look as if you have their spirit and courage, for their reputation for heroic deeds is unsurpassed."

"Perhaps I don't have much of their courage and prowess," replied Sigurd, "but there's no need to taunt me. I'm scarcely more than a child. Why are you goading me like this?"

"There's a story about that," said Regin, "and I'll tell it to you." "Let me hear it," said Sigurd.

14. "The story begins with my father, Hreithmar," said Regin. "He was a great man and a wealthy one, and he had three sons: the first was Fafnir, the second was Otter, and I was the third. I was the least handsome and accomplished of the sons, but I knew how to work with iron, silver, and gold, and I could make a variety of useful items. My brother, Otter, had a different nature and occupation. He was a first-rate huntsman – much better than anyone else – for during the day he assumed the shape of an otter and was constantly in the river, catching fish and carrying them ashore in his mouth. He brought his catch to his father, and it was a great help to him. My brother spent much of his time in otter-shape; then he would come home late and eat alone with his eyes closed, for he could not see on dry land. Fafnir was by far the biggest and fiercest of the three of us, and he coveted everything for himself.

"There was a dwarf named Andvari," continued Regin, "who spent all his time in a waterfall called Andvari's waterfall. There, he took on the shape of a pike and caught his food, for fish were plentiful. Otter, too, was always in that waterfall, catching fish in his mouth and laying them on the bank, one at a time.

"Odin, Loki, and Hoenir were on a journey and came to Andvari's waterfall just when Otter had caught a salmon and was eating it on the river bank with his eyes closed. Loki hurled a stone at him and killed him. The Aesir were delighted with their catch and flayed the otter's pelt. That evening, they visited Hreithmar and showed him what they had caught. At the sight of the skin, he seized them and demanded compensation and ransom for Otter. They were to fill his skin with gold and then cover it up completely with more gold. Loki was sent to procure the gold, so he went to Ran and stole her fishing net. Then he went to Andvari's falls and cast the net in front of the pike. The pike leapt into the net and Loki said:

> 'What fish is this
> that swims in the river
> and cannot protect itself?
> redeem your head,
> from death,
> find gold for me.'

> 'I am Andvari;
> my father is Oinn;
> I frequent waterfalls;
> long ago
> a wretched norn [one of the Fates]
> shaped my fate,
> made me swim in water.'

"Then Loki was shown Andvari's gold, and Andvari handed it all over, except for one ring. But Loki took this ring from him, too. Then the dwarf retreated to a cave, warning that the ring and all the rest of the gold as well would spell death for whoever owned it.

"The Aesir brought the gold to Hreithmar and stuffed the otter's hide with it. Then they stood the hide on its feet and covered it up with gold. When that was done, Hreithmar went over to the skin. He noticed a single whisker sticking out and ordered the Aesir to cover it up too. So Odin drew the ring, Andvari's Gift, from his hand and covered the whisker. Then Loki said:

'Gold is now given;
you have a large
payment for my head.
But happiness
is not fated for your son;
the gold is death for both of you.'

"Later," said Regin, "Fafnir murdered his father. I got none of the gold, for Fafnir became so mean that he took to lying outside and would allow no one but himself any share in the treasure. Eventually, he became a terrible dragon and, to this day, still lies on the treasure. After a while, I made my way to the king and became his smith. The upshot of my story is that I lost both the inheritance from my father and the compensation for my brother. And it's because of this story that gold has been known ever since as 'Otter's Ransom.'"

"You have lost a great deal," said Sigurd, "and your kinsmen have been very wicked. But now, if you wish me to kill that mighty dragon, use all your skill to make me a sword of matchless quality so that I can perform great feats with it if my courage is equal to the task." "I'll do it," said Regin, "and I'm confident you'll be able to kill Fafnir with the sword."

15. Regin forged a sword and placed it in Sigurd's hands. Sigurd took the sword and saying, "*This* is your forging, Regin!", he struck the anvil and shattered the sword. Then he threw the sword away and ordered Regin to forge a better one. So Regin made another sword and brought it for Sigurd's inspection.

"This sword should please you," said Regin, "even though you're a hard taskmaster." Sigurd tested the sword, but it broke just like the first one. "You're just like your kinsmen before you," said Sigurd to Regin. "You can't be relied on."

Sigurd now went to see his mother. She greeted him joyfully, and they talked and drank together. Then Sigurd asked, "Is the rumor true? Did King Sigmund give you the sword, Gram, in two pieces?"

"It's true," she replied. "Give the pieces to me," said Sigurd. "I want them." So she gave him the sword, saying that he would probably win fame with it.

Sigurd went to Regin and told him to make the best sword he could from the pieces. Regin was angry – he felt that Sigurd was concerning himself too much with the forging. Nevertheless, he went into the smithy with the pieces and made a new sword out of them, and when he drew it from the hearth it seemed to his workmen that fire was blazing from its edges. Regin told Sigurd to take the sword, saying that he didn't know how else to make him a sword if this one broke. So Sigurd took it and struck the anvil and split it all the way down to the base without breaking or shattering the sword itself. Sigurd was full of praise for the sword. He went down to the river with a lock of wool and threw it in against the current. The wool sheared in two when it met the sword.

Sigurd went home happy. Then Regin said to him, "Now that I have made you a sword, you must fulfill your promise to kill Fafnir." "I will," said Sigurd....

18. Now Sigurd and Regin rode across the heath to the path which Fafnir usually slithered along when he went to the water. People say that the cliff on which Fafnir lay down to drink was thirty fathoms above the water. "Regin, you told me that this dragon was no bigger than a heath-snake," said Sigurd, "but his tracks seem huge to me."

"Dig yourself a hole and sit in it," said Regin, "and when he crawls to the water, strike him to the heart and kill him. You'll win a lot of glory that way."

"But what will happen if I get in the way of the dragon's blood?" asked Sigurd.

"There's no point in giving you advice if you're afraid of everything," said Regin. "You don't have the courage of your kinsfolk."

Sigurd rode to the heath, but Regin, who was very frightened, turned back. Then Sigurd dug a hole, and, as he was doing so, an old man with a long beard came up to him and asked what he was doing there. Sigurd told him. "That's not a great idea," replied the old man. "You should dig several holes for the blood to run into; then you can sit in one of them and strike at the serpent's heart."

With that, the old man vanished and Sigurd dug the holes as he had been advised.

When the dragon slithered toward the water, the earth quaked violently and the ground shook all around him. He blew out poison all over the path in front of him, but Sigurd was neither frightened nor dismayed by the din. As soon as the serpent crawled over his hole, Sigurd thrust his sword under its left shoulder and it went in right up to the hilt. Then Sigurd leapt up from his hole and pulled out the sword; his arms were bloodied right up to the shoulder. When the great serpent felt its death wound, it lashed out with head and tail, and everything in its path was destroyed.

After he had received his death wound, Fafnir asked Sigurd, "Who are you? Who is your father and who are your kinsfolk that you are brave enough to take up weapons against me?"

"No one knows who my family is," answered Sigurd. "I am called 'Noble Beast'; I have neither father nor mother and I have come here all alone."

"If you have neither father nor mother," said Fafnir, "what miracle produced you? You know that you are lying, although you won't tell me your name on this my dying day."

"My name is Sigurd," he replied, "and Sigmund was my father." "Who goaded you into doing this deed," asked Fafnir, "and why did you allow yourself to be persuaded? Hadn't you heard that everyone is afraid of me and my helmet of terror? Bright-eyed youth, you had a brave father."

"My own fierce courage incited me to this deed and helped me to carry it out," replied Sigurd. "So too did this strong arm and this keen sword with which you are now familiar. Few men are brave in maturity who have been timid in their youth."

"I know that you would have been able to fight in anger if you had grown up surrounded by your family," said Fafnir, "but I find it strange that a captive would have had the courage to attack me, for few prisoners-of-war are brave in a fight."

"Are you reproaching me for being far from my kinsmen?" said Sigurd. "I may have been a captive, but I was never in fetters – you yourself have found out that I was free."

"You are taking offence at everything I say," said Fafnir, "but, beware, the treasure that was mine will be the cause of your death too." "Everyone wishes to keep all his treasure till his dying day," said Sigurd, "but everyone has to die sometime."

"You won't pay much attention to my advice," said Fafnir, "but, if you put to sea unwarily, you will be drowned, so stay on land until the weather is calm." Then Sigurd said, "if you are so wise, Fafnir, tell me this: who are the norns who deprive mothers of their sons?"

"There are many norns," replied Fafnir, "and they are not all alike: some are of Aesir race, some are of Elf race, and some are daughters of Dvalin."

"What is the name of the island where Surt and the Aesir will mingle their blood?" asked Sigurd.

"Its name is Oskapt [Uncreated]," answered Fafnir. Then he continued, "My brother, Regin, has brought about my death, and it gratifies me that he will bring about your death too, for things are going to happen just as he wished."

Fafnir went on, "When I was lying on my brother's inheritance, I wore a helmet of terror to instill fear in everyone and I spewed poison all around me so that no one dared approach. I feared no weapon, and however mighty were the men I encountered, I always knew that I was much the stronger; everyone was afraid of me."

"The helmet of terror that you mentioned gives victory to few," said

Sigurd, "because anyone who comes into contact with lots of other people, will find out sooner or later that no one man is braver than all the rest."

"My advice to you is to get on your horse and ride away as quickly as possible," said Fafnir, "for it's often the case that someone who receives a death wound will avenge himself."

"Keep your advice," said Sigurd. "I've got other plans. I'm going to ride to your den and seize the great treasure that belonged to your kinsmen."

"Ride there then," replied Fafnir, "and you will find enough gold to last you for the rest of your days, but that same gold will kill you and anyone else who owns it."

Then Sigurd stood up and said, "I would ride home and give up that great treasure if I knew that I would live forever, but every brave man wants to enjoy as much wealth as possible till his dying day. As for you, Fafnir, lie there in your death throes until Hel [goddess of death] carries you off." Then Fafnir died.

19. After that, Regin came to Sigurd. "Hail, my lord," he said, "you have won a great victory by defeating Fafnir, for before you came along, no one was brave enough to lie in wait in his path. This heroic act will be remembered as long as the world lasts." After that, Regin stood staring at the ground for a long time; suddenly, he spoke with great passion.

"You have killed my brother," he said, "but I can hardly be considered guiltless."

Sigurd took his sword, Gram, wiped it dry on the grass, and said, "Regin, you fled a long way off while I carried out this deed and tested this sharp sword with this strong arm. I had to contend with the might of the dragon while you were hiding in the heather, not knowing whether you were in heaven or on earth."

"This dragon might have lain in his den for a long time if you had not made use of the sword I made for you with my own hands," said Regin, "and without the sword, neither you nor anyone else would have managed to kill him yet."

Sigurd replied, "When it comes to fighting, a man is better off with a stout heart than a sharp sword." Then Regin said to Sigurd with great sorrow, "You have killed my brother, but I can hardly be considered guiltless."

Afterwards, Sigurd cut out the dragon's heart with a sword called Ridil. Regin drank Fafnir's blood and said, "Do me a small favor, Sigurd: take the heart to the fire, roast it, and let me have it to eat."

Sigurd roasted the heart on a spit, and when the juices began to run, he tested the meat with his finger to see if it was done. Then he put his finger in his mouth and as soon as the blood from the serpent's heart touched his tongue, he was able to understand the speech of birds. He heard some nut-hatches chirping in the nearby bushes.

"There sits Sigurd roasting Fafnir's heart," said one. "He should eat it himself and then he would be wiser than anyone else." "There lies Regin, intending to betray the man who trusts him," said the second. "Sigurd should cut his head off," said the third. "Then he would be sole owner of all that gold." The fourth said, "Sigurd would be wise to follow this advice. Afterwards he should go back to Fafnir's lair, get hold of the treasure, and ride up to Hindarfell where Brunhild is sleeping. He will gain great wisdom there. He would be wise to take this advice and consider his own needs. For, when I see a wolf's ears, I expect a wolf." "He isn't as wise as I thought, if he spares the man whose brother he has just killed," said the fifth. "It would be a good idea for Sigurd to kill Regin and became sole owner of the treasure," said the sixth.

"It won't be my ill fate to be killed by Regin," said Sigurd. "Instead, both brothers will go the same way." With that, he drew the sword, Gram, and cut off Regin's head.

Afterwards, he ate some of the dragon's heart, and saved the rest. Then he leapt on his horse and followed Fafnir's tracks to his den, which stood open; all the doors and the door fastenings were made of iron, and the beams were iron too. The lair itself had been dug down into the earth. There, Sigurd found a huge quantity of gold and the sword, Hrotti. There, too, he got the helmet of terror, a gold mail-shirt, and many other precious objects. In fact, he found so much gold that he doubted whether two or even three horses could carry it away. He took all the gold and put it into two large chests. Then he took his horse, Grani, by the reins, but the horse would not budge and it was useless to whip it. Then Sigurd realized what the horse wanted: he leapt onto its back, pricked it with the spurs, and the horse ran as if it had no load.

(d) Saint Olaf's Sword, Hneitir

This passage recounts the sword's history after the death of Saint Olaf at Stiklestad. From The Saga of Hakon the Broadshouldered.

Source: Snorri Sturluson, *Hákonar saga Heiðibreiðs*, in *Heimskringla*, ed., Bjarni Aðalbjarnarson, Íslenzk fornrit XXVI–XXVIII (Reykjavík, 2002), vol. 3, pp. 369–71.

20. It has already been recounted that King Olaf threw away the sword Hneitir when he was wounded at the battle of Stiklestad. A certain Swede, who had broken his own sword, picked up Hneitir and fought with it. This man

survived the battle and escaped with other fugitives. When he got back to Sweden, he returned to his farm. He owned the sword all his life as did his son after him, and so on from one kinsman to another. Always, when the sword passed from one owner to the next, the earlier owner told his successor the name of the sword and also where it had come from.

Much later, in the days of Kirjalax [Kurios Alexios, the emperor Alexius I], the emperor of Mikligard [Constantinople], there were large companies of Varangians in the city. One summer, the emperor was on a campaign and his soldiers were living in tents, with the Varangians, the emperor's guard, stationed in the open ground outside the camp keeping watch. They changed guard during the night and the men who had been on duty previously lay down and slept, all of them fully armed. It was customary for each man, when he lay down to sleep, to have his helmet on his head, his shield over him, and his sword under his head, with his right hand on the hilt.

One of these fellow-soldiers, whose lot it had been to stand guard in the latter part of the night, woke at dawn to discover that his sword was missing. When he looked for it, he saw the sword lying on the ground at a great distance from him, so he got up and fetched it. He thought that his comrades who had been on watch must have filched the sword as a practical joke, but they denied it. The same thing happened for three nights in a row. He himself was greatly puzzled, as were the others who saw or heard what was going on. He was asked what these events signified, and he replied that the sword, which was called Hneitir, had been owned by St. Olaf, who had carried it himself at the battle of Stiklestad. He also recounted how the sword had changed hands since then. When, later, the emperor, Kirjalax, heard about it, he summoned the sword's owner and gave him three times its value in gold. The emperor had the sword carried to St. Olaf's church, which the Varangians supported. There, it was placed above the altar.

Eindrid the Young was in Mikligard when these events took place and he told the story when he returned to Norway, as Einar Skulason affirms in the drapa [heroic praise-poem] he composed for Saint Olaf, where this event is related.

(e) Viking Age Swords

Sword hilts and pommels from Sweden.

Source: Paul B. du Chaillu, *The Viking Age*, 2 vols. (New York: Charles Scribner's Sons, 1899), vol. 2, pp. 69, 74, and 78.

CHAPTER SEVEN

FJORD-SERPENTS: VIKING SHIPS

The icon of the Viking Age is the Viking ship. Praised by poets and the writers of sagas, depicted in art and graffiti, and even taken to the grave by members of the elite, these vessels were certainly the most important means of transport in the maritime societies of Scandinavia, but they were also symbols of power, wealth, and prestige. Viking ships and parts of ships of varying sizes and designs have been discovered and excavated since the mid-1800s throughout the regions settled by Scandinavians. Among the most important ships are those from the burials at Tune, Gokstad, and Oseberg in Norway, but other ship burials are known from Iceland to Orkney, and the remains of five scuttled Viking Age vessels were recovered from Roskilde fjord in Denmark in the early 1960s. Representations of ships are to be found on memorial stones (particularly from Gotland in Sweden), coins, tapestries (such as the Bayeux Tapestry), and graffiti from Dublin, Shetland, and Norway. Sagas, poems, and law codes also provide important information. Modern reconstructions of Viking Age ships offer insights into the construction and sailing characteristics of the originals. This chapter presents some of the literary evidence for Viking ships, as well as for sea-battles.

33. KING OLAF TRYGGVASON BUILDS THE
LONG SERPENT

One of the most famous ships of the entire Viking Age is King Olaf Tryggvason's Long Serpent, *constructed near Nidaros/Trondheim, Norway, in the winter of 999–1000. The* Long Serpent *was probably about 40 meters in length, belonging to the class of vessels known as* drekkar *or dragon. The* Long Serpent *was King Olaf's ship at the battle of Svold in 999/1000, where the most intense fighting of the entire battle took place on the fore- and after-decks of this ship (see doc. 38b). From* The Saga of Olaf Tryggvason *in* Heimskringla.

Source: Snorri Sturluson, *Óláfs saga Tryggvasonar,* in *Heimskringla,* ed. Bjarni Aðalbjarnarson, Íslenzk fornrit XXVI–XXVIII (Reykjavík, 2002), vol. 1, pp. 335–36.

88. During the winter after his return from Halogaland, King Olaf Tryggvason built a ship at Hladhamar. This ship was bigger than any other in the country and the stocks on which it was built survive as visible proof of this. Thorberg the Woodcarver was responsible for the stem and stern, but there were many others involved in the work as well. Some of them felled trees; some shaped the wood; some forged nails; and some hauled timber. All the materials used were of the best quality, and the ship was constructed with large timbers. It was long and broad and stood high above the water.

Just as the sides were being built, Thorberg had to go back to his farm on pressing business. He stayed there for some time and when he returned, the sides had reached their full height. That evening, the king and Thorberg went out right away to see how work on the ship was progressing, and everyone agreed that such a large and beautiful longship had never been seen before.

Then the king returned to town, but, early next morning, he and Thorberg went back to the ship again. The workmen had already arrived, but they were all standing around doing nothing. When the king asked them what the problem was, they replied that the ship had been vandalized; someone had gone from stem to stern, cutting one deep notch after another all down one side of the ship.

When the king drew near and saw the truth for himself, he swore that the man who had damaged the ship so maliciously would die, if he could be found. "There will be a substantial reward for anyone who can provide me with information," he said. Then Thorberg spoke up. "I can tell you who did this, king," he said.

"I'm not surprised," replied the king, "that you're the man who's lucky enough to find this out and tell me about it."

"I'll tell you who did it, king," repeated Thorberg. "I did it." "Then you'll make it as good as new," said King Olaf, "or pay for it with your life."

Thorberg went and shaved down all the planks to the same depth as his ax-cuts. The king and everyone else agreed that the ship was much more elegant on the shaved side, and King Olaf asked Thorberg to finish the other side in the same way. Then he thanked Thorberg profusely and appointed him head shipwright until construction was completed.

The ship was a warship built on the same lines as the *Serpent*, which King Olaf had brought from Halogaland, but the new ship was much bigger and more splendidly finished throughout. King Olaf named it the *Long Serpent* and called the other one the *Short Serpent*.

The *Long Serpent* had thirty-four rooms, or rowers' benches [giving a total of sixty-eight oars]. The dragon's head at the prow and the coiled tail at the stern were both heavily gilded and the sides stood as high above the water as those of ocean-going ships. The *Long Serpent* was the best and most costly ship ever built in Norway.

34. HARALD SIGURDARSON'S SPLENDID SHIP

Another famous saga-ship was the one constructed in the early 1060s by King Harald Sigurdarson Hardradi. It was modeled on King Olaf's Long Serpent *and was constructed for an expedition against Denmark. From* Harald Sigurdarson's Saga *in* Heimskringla.

Source: Snorri Sturluson, *Haralds saga Sigurðarsonar*, in *Heimskringla*, ed. Bjarni Aðalbjarnarson, Íslenzk fornrit XXVI–XXVIII (Reykjavík, 2002), vol. 3, pp. 141–43.

59. King Harald spent the winter in Nidaros and, that same winter, he had a ship built out at Eyrar. The ship was of the *Buss* type [a large, broad warship]. It was as large as the *Long Serpent*, and great care was lavished on every detail of its construction. At the bow was a dragon's head and at the stern were the coils of its tail; both stem and stern were decorated with gold. The ship had thirty-five rowers' benches [seventy oars] and was very spacious as well as being very beautiful. The king had the finest equipment made for the ship, from the sail and its rigging to the anchor and its cable. In the winter, King Harald sent a message south to King Svein [Svein Forkbeard] of Denmark asking him to come north to the River Elf in the spring. They could then fight it out to establish how their lands should be divided and which one of them should rule both kingdoms.

60. That winter, King Harald called up a full levy throughout Norway

and, when spring came, a large army assembled. Then King Harald had the great ship launched in the River Nid and had the dragon carvings mounted in place. Thjodolf the skald [poet, court poet] said:

> Fair maid, I saw the ship slide
> from the river's side to the sea.
> Behold the planks of the proud dragon
> lying off the land.
> Over the ship shines the
> serpent's mane, streaming light;
> bow and stern bore pure gold
> as she sped from the slipway.

Then King Harald fitted out the ship and, when everything was ready for his journey, he steered the ship out of the river. The men rowed in perfect unison, as Thjodolf says:

> The army's leader cast the long
> awning aside that Saturday;
> the proud serpent-ship sails
> as women watch from the town.
> West, the powerful young warrior
> steered his shining new ship
> from the river; the rowing warriors
> sliced their oars through the sea.

> Lord Harald's army lifts
> the straight oars from the sea;
> the women stand and wonder at the
> men's mastery of the oars.
> We'll pull pitch-blackened oars
> until they split asunder,
> or oars may rest from rowing
> when peace prevails.

> The army will suffer sorrows
> before oars rest, raised
> from the swift sea where
> the seventy-oared ship sails.
> Norsemen row the iron-nailed
> serpent over hail-swept seas;

it moves under oars
like an eagle with wings spread wide....

35. KING SVERRIR'S *MARIASUD*

Great ships took on new significance in the turbulent era of Norwegian politics of the late twelfth and early thirteenth centuries. King Sverrir of Norway had the Mariasud *constructed in the early 1180s, and the ship played an important role in the battle of Fimreite (Norafjord) in 1184 (see doc. 38e). From* Sverrir's Saga.

Source: *Sverris saga*, ed. Þorleifur Hauksson, Íslenzk fornrit XXXV (Reykjavík, 2007), pp. 123–25.

80. During the summer in which King Sverrir captured the ships in Bergen, the building of the *Mariasud* was completed, and King Sverrir came north in the autumn to have it launched. The ship had been built above the town and many people said that it could not be launched without demolishing some of the houses. People also said that, in building the ship, the king had behaved arrogantly and ostentatiously and that nothing good would come of it. However, when the ship was launched, it turned out that the king had foreseen the problem and had planned the launch in such a way that there was no need to demolish any houses or buildings.

When the ship shot forward from the stocks into the river, some of its joints sprang open. This happened because, while Sverrir was south in Møre during the winter, the ship was being built in Kaupang and, by the time the king returned, nine rows of planks had been completed on each side. When the king saw what had been done, he said, "This ship is much smaller than I'd anticipated. Take it apart and insert a piece twelve ells long in the middle of the keel [a Norwegian ell was 62.8 cm]."

The shipwright objected, but the king was adamant. As a result, there were many joints at the bottom of the ship and, when it was launched, some of them opened up. King Sverrir was aboard the ship when it hit the water.

"Praise be to God, the Virgin Mary, and St. Olaf that this ship has got into the water safely without harming anyone," said the king. "As for the many people who bad-mouthed me, may God forgive them. I don't imagine that many here have seen as big a longship as this afloat on the water. This ship will be a great defense against our enemies if good luck goes with it. I entrust this ship to the protection and safe-keeping of the Virgin Mary. I name it *Mariasud* and pray that the Blessed Virgin will defend and guard it. As a token of this, I will bestow on Mary vestments that the archbishop can wear when he is splendidly dressed for solemn feasts, treasures fit for the service of God. I hope that she will look favorably on these gifts and grant support and good fortune to the ship, the crew, and everyone on board."

The king had holy relics inserted in the carved prow and stern of the ship. He distributed the vestments, sending the cope to the Mariakirk, the gown to Helgaset, and everything else to Nunnaset at Bakki.

The *Mariasud* was not an elegant ship. The prow and the stern were small in proportion to the mid-section, mainly because the ship had been length-ened. The king had repairs done to the damage caused by the launch. During the winter, he had more longships built and others refitted. All the work was carried out to the highest standards. Thorolf Rympill's ship, the *Hjalp*, was built at this time. It had twenty-six rooms [rowers' benches]. Ulf from Laufness's ship, the *Vidsja*, was also built at this time, and had almost as many rooms as the *Hjalp*.

81. After Easter, King Sverrir got ready to travel south from Kaupang with thirty-three ships, most of which were large. With him went his brother Eirik, Ulf from Laufness, Ulf Fly, Bard Guthormsson, Ivar Selki, and Havard Earlsson. Together, they made up a large and splendid force. The king com-manded the *Mariasud* with two hundred and eighty men aboard. He had three chests sent out to the ship and each chest had to be carried by four men; no one knew what was in them. The king's son Eirik was in command of the *Oskmey*, a ship which had about twenty-five rooms....

They headed to the Herey Islands and there the king held another council at which he said exactly the same things as he had said before. From the Herey Islands, he sailed south past Stad, but a sharp wind blew up and they ran into rough weather. This put a great strain on the *Mariasud*, causing its seams to open, so the king turned in to Ulf's Sound. When they anchored there, the men found out what was in the big chests, for ship's nails were taken out of them and distributed among the ships. The king gave nails to the men in each half-room [rowing space] and told them to keep their eyes open and use the nails whenever necessary. Then Sverrir sailed on his way to Sogn....

36. THE GREAT SHIPS OF KING HAKON IV

By the middle of the thirteenth century, Norwegian politics had grown more tranquil, and the demand for the construction of massive ships like the Mariasud *dwindled. However, for campaigns in Denmark and an expedition to Scotland in 1263, King Hakon IV had three great ships built which were said to have been the biggest ever constructed in Norway. The* Saga of Hakon the Old *was written in the 1260s by the Icelandic historian and chieftain Sturla Thordarson (1214–84), nephew and pupil of Snorri Sturluson. Hakon's son, Prince Magnus, is said to have commissioned the saga from Sturla. This saga is the main source for Norwegian history from 1217 to 1263. Sturla's historical writings are unusual in that they frequently record events contemporary with the writer (see doc. 102).*

Source: trans. A.A. Somerville from *Icelandic Sagas and Other Historical Documents Relating to the Settlements and Descents of the Northmen of the British Isles*, vol. II, *Hákonar Saga, with Fragment of Magnus Saga, with Appendices*, ed. G. Vigfusson (Rolls Series: London, 1887), pp. 175–76, 273, 293–94.

197. Next morning, after he had heard mass, King Hakon sailed along the coast of Jadar. As they approached Hvin, the steering oar on the king's ship broke, and almost the whole blade snapped off, but by using the gangplanks and the oars, they steered the ship south around the headland. When they had cleared the headland, they laid aside the gangplanks and steered into Skerdadarsound using the remains of the steering oar as well as the regular oars. The damaged steering oar was brought ashore when they came into port, and it seemed astonishing that such a large ship had been steered by such a small fragment of rudder....

277. ... Then a great force flocked to King Hakon, from around the Vik and from the north of the country. King Hakon was aboard the *Olafssud* and the young king had the *Dreki* [Dragon]. Earl Knut brought the *Dragsmark*, Sigurd the king's son had the *Rygjabrand*, Peter from Gizki had the *Borgundarboat*, and Ogmund Kraekidance [Crow-dance] had the *Gunnarsboat*. Bard from Hestby commanded a large ship and there were also many other good-sized ships. King Hakon headed into Hervidar Sound, and most of his forces joined him there.

From Hervidar Sound, he set out for Hrafnsholt. There, on its stocks, stood the great ship built on his instructions by his kinsman, Gunnar. The ship was one of the biggest ever built in Norway. The king had her launched, and the launch went well. In an eloquent speech, the king named the ship *Krosssud*. After the ceremony, King Hakon left some men behind to fit out the ship, while he himself went to join the rest of his fleet. Then he sailed south to Ekrey, where he ordered most of the fleet to lie at anchor.

The kings and most of the landed-men boarded small ships and headed in to the Elf River, anchoring at a place called Lindisholm. Then King Hakon heard that Earl Birgir had arrived with the Swedish army, just as they had planned earlier....

278. King Hakon sent his son, Prince Magnus, and Gaut from Mel to fetch the *Krosssud* from the north and sail her to join the other large ships at Ekrey.

When they arrived in the north, they completed whatever preparations were still needed to fit out the ship. Before they sailed from Hrafnsholt, the prince made his first official speech, and everyone admired its eloquence and the maturity of its delivery.

Then they headed for Ekrey. When they entered the harbor and dropped anchor, the momentum of the ship was so great that fire broke out in the windlass around which the cable was wound. The fear was that the rope would burn, so they soaked an awning, intending to stifle the fire with it, but Prince Magnus was much quicker and more resourceful. He lifted up a tub full of drink, poured it over the windlass, and cooled down the cable.

When the *Krosssud* was berthed alongside the other ships, her sides were as high as the awning pole of the *Olafssud*. The sides of the *Krosssud* stood nine ells [a Norwegian ell was 62.8 cm] above sea-level, and she was by far the biggest of all the ships there. The general opinion was that this number of great ships had never been seen together in one harbor. Many terrible tales about this levy and fleet spread all over Danish territory, and resistance seemed out of the question. Sturla puts it this way:

> Sea-King, I speak of how you repaid
> the strife of the Danes in the south.
> Far and wide from fir-rollers
> your people launched lithe ships;
> many conscripts were called out
> by your freemen, ruler of fleets,
> for long campaigns along the coast.
> It was the largest of levies.
>
> The renowned ruler's men
> rushed to their rowlocks.
> You sailed south,
> lord, with a large fleet;
> the folk of Halland feared
> your power, ring-giving prince.
> Fear of Norway's king filled
> the Jutish lord's land.

291. King Hakon got ready to travel from Tunsberg to Denmark aboard the *Mariasud*, a dragon-ship with thirty rowers' benches. She was the most elegant ship ever built in Norway with gilding on the animal heads and on the bow and stern. The sail was decorated with beautiful pictures. King Hakon

had many other splendid, well-built ships, and, in the sunshine, it seemed as though the beaks, weather vanes, and the gilded shields next to the bows and sterns were on fire. As Sturla said:

> Glorious pictures in fiery gold
> were seen on your sail, Gold-giver.
> The bright gold beaks
> shone above your dragon-ship;
> beaten gold burned from
> the shields on your ships;
> across the gilded fleet, gold
> reddened shields at stem and stern.

When everything was ready, King Hakon and his army sailed from Tunsberg, east across the Fold [Oslo Sound] and a large force joined him from the eastern side of the fjord. While Hakon was sailing east, the ship belonging to Thorir Grepsson and Bard Groson collided with Archbishop Einar's ship, and the collision swept away everything on Einar's ship between the stern and midships. The decorated stern and the shields next to it finished up in the sea, but the weather vanes stuck in the sail of the other ship, which sailed away with them. The archbishop sent out a boat to pick up the stern and the shields. The stern was fixed securely in place and the shields were put back on the sides of the ship. Then he sailed south to Ekrey to meet the king. When the king discovered that the archbishop's ship had been damaged, he was very displeased. However, some people said that the ship had been less damaged than the archbishop's men claimed. When the archbishop heard about this, he had the stern removed and it drifted along the coast....

37. ANIMAL HEADS ON THE PROWS OF SHIPS

The thirteenth-century Icelandic Book of Settlements (see doc. 70b) contains information concerning the use of animal heads on the prows of ships.

Source: *Landnamabók*, ed. Jakob Benediktsson, Íslenzk fornrit I (Reykjavík, 1986), p. 313.

H. 268. The heathen laws began by forbidding people to go to sea with animal heads on the prows of their ships. However, if they did, they should remove the heads before coming in sight of land so that they did not approach with gaping heads or yawning snouts which might frighten the guardian spirits of the country.

38. SEA-BATTLES IN THE SAGAS

The sagas contain many references to sea-battles, the nature of which is summed up by Snorri Sturluson in The Saga of Harald Finehair *in* Heimskringla: *"It was then customary when men fought on board ships to tie them together and fight in the prows." Unlike naval engagements of later centuries, Viking Age sea-battles were not fought under sail. Masts were usually lowered before battle, and the ships, which might be lashed together, were essentially used as floating fighting platforms. The aim was to grapple enemy vessels with hooks and anchors and drag them closer for hand-to-hand fighting on board ship.*

(a) A Hard-Fought Sea-Battle at Bute

Thrand and Onund flee Harald Finehair after the Battle of Hafrsfjord, where Onund lost a leg; they settle on the Hebridean island of Barra. Meanwhile, two Vikings who have found Ireland too difficult a target begin raiding in the Hebrides. Thrand and Onund track them down in Bute, where they win a decisive victory although the Vikings have the larger force.

Source: *Grettis saga Ásmundarson*, ed. Guðni Jónson, Íslenzk fornrit VII (Reykjavík, 1936), pp. 10–13.

4. There were two Vikings from the Hebrides called Vigbjod and Vestmar who stayed at sea both winter and summer. They had eight ships and pillaged mostly in Ireland where they committed many atrocities until Eyvind the Easterner took over the defense of the country. After that, they retreated to the Hebrides. They plundered there and all the way into the firths of Scotland.

Thrand and Onund went in pursuit of them and, when they heard that they had sailed to the island of Bute, they went there themselves with five ships. When the Vikings saw how many ships Thrand and Onund had, they decided that their own force was large enough for an attack, so they seized their weapons and sailed toward them. Onund ordered his ships to take up position in a channel between two cliffs. This channel was narrow and deep and could be attacked from only one direction by no more than five ships at once.

Onund, who was a cunning man, sailed his five ships into the channel and positioned them so that they could back out quickly whenever they wished, because there was plenty of open sea behind them. On one side of the channel lay an island. Onund sent a ship there, and the crew carried a large quantity of rocks to the cliff-top, where they could not be seen from the ships.

The Vikings attacked boldly, thinking that they had caught Onund's ships in a trap. Vigbjod asked: "Who are these people that are so hemmed in?" Thrand replied that he was the brother of Eyvind the Easterner. "And my companion here is Onund Treefoot," he said.

The Vikings laughed and said:

> May trolls take all of Treefoot,
> May trolls take all of them.

"We don't often see men going into battle who can't even stand on their own two legs," they said. Onund answered, "You never know till you try."

After that, the ships came together and a mighty battle began. Both sides advanced bravely and, when the fighting was at its fiercest, Onund let his ship drift toward the cliff. Seeing this, the Vikings assumed that Onund was trying to get away, so they made for his ship, getting as close to the cliff as they could. At that moment, the men who had been stationed on the cliff moved forward to the edge and threw such huge rocks down onto the Vikings that they could not put up any resistance. Many Vikings were killed; others were injured and were unable to bear arms.

The Vikings tried to escape, but they could not, for by then their ships had reached the narrowest part of the channel and they couldn't maneuver there because of the enemy ships and the strong current. Onund and his men attacked Vigbjod energetically, while Thrand set on Vestmar, with little success. When Vigbjod's crew had been reduced in numbers, Onund and his men attempted to board the ship. Vigbjod saw what was happening and urged his men on furiously. Then he turned to face Onund; most of Onund's men gave way before him, but Onund, who was a very strong man, ordered his men to wait and see what happened between Vigbjod and himself. They shoved a tree-stump under his knee so that he stood quite steady.

The Viking made his way forward along the ship until he reached Onund. He slashed at him with his sword, but the sword struck Onund's shield, hacked a piece off, and embedded itself in the tree-stump under his knee. As Vigbjod leaned forward to pull his sword free, Onund hit his shoulder with an ax and cut off his arm. That put Vigbjod out of the fight. When Vestmar realized that his fellow Viking had fallen, he leapt onto the outermost ship and fled, as did everyone else who could get aboard. After that, Onund and his men searched among the bodies. Vigbjod was very near death; Onund went up to him and said:

> Do you see your bloodied body?
> Did you see me flinch or flee?
> One-footed Wooden Foot

sustained not a scratch from you.
Many a man is more
boastful than brave;
the battle-ax breaker
was not fearless in the fight.

They took a lot of booty and went back to Barra in the autumn.

(b) Olaf Tryggvason at the Battle of Svold

*In response to Olaf's territorial ambitions, Svein Forkbeard, king of Denmark, Olaf
Eiriksson, king of Sweden, and Eirik, earl of Lade, formed a confederation against him,
though Snorri suggests that Svein Forkbeard encouraged the alliance for more personal
reasons. In 1000, as he sailed home from an expedition to Wendland (Pomerania), Olaf
was intercepted by the combined fleets of his enemies. The location of Svold is uncertain,
but most authorities place it in the western Baltic Sea. From Olaf Tryggvason's Saga.*

Source: Snorri Sturluson, *Óláfs saga Tryggvasonar*, in *Heimskringla*, ed. Bjarni Aðalbjarnarson,
Íslenzk fornrit XXVI–XXVIII (Reykjavík, 2002), vol. I, pp. 348–68.

97. King Olaf traveled south along the coast [of Norway] with his fleet. He
was joined by many of his friends and by other powerful men who were
ready and willing to make the journey. The most important of these was his
brother-in-law, Erling Skjalgsson, who brought a large, well-equipped ship
of sixty oars. The king's brothers-in-law, Hyrning and Thorgeir, also joined
him, each with a large ship, and many other great men followed him too.
When he left Norway, the king had sixty longships. He sailed south toward
Denmark, through Eyrarsund and on to Wendland [Pomerania] where he
arranged to meet King Burislaf.

When the kings met, they discussed the property claimed by King Olaf.
The talks went well and King Olaf's claims were settled quickly. Afterwards,
he stayed on for much of the summer and met many of his friends there.

98. Svein Forkbeard, king of Denmark, was married to Sigrid the Proud,
as has already been related. Sigrid was very hostile to King Olaf Tryggvason
because he had broken his engagement to her, and had struck her in the face.
She was continually urging King Svein to go to war with Olaf Tryggvason,
saying that he had a good enough reason seeing that King Olaf had married
Svein's sister, Thura, without his permission. "None of your ancestors would
have put up with that," she said.

Queen Sigrid kept making remarks like this. As a result of her pressure,
King Svein was quite willing to fall in with this plan of action.

Early in the spring, King Svein sent messengers to his brother-in-law, King Olaf of Sweden [ca 980–ca 1022], and to Earl Eirik [Eirik Hakonarson, ca 960–ca 1020] to let them know that Olaf, king of Norway, had gathered men and ships and intended to travel to Wendland in the summer. Svein went on to suggest that the king of Sweden and Earl Eirik should call out an army and meet up with him so that together they could make war on Olaf Tryggvason. The king and the earl were quite ready to take part in this expedition. They assembled a large fleet in Sweden and, with this force, they went south to Denmark. When they arrived there, King Olaf Tryggvason had already sailed east. Halldor the Heathen tells of this in his poem about Earl Eirik:

> King-destroying Eirik came with
> his army south from Sweden;
> the storm-strong earl ordered men
> to the sword-blaze of battle.
> Warriors, the feeders of wound-wasps,
> followed Earl Eirik;
> flesh-feeding fowls
> sipped blood at sea.

The king of Sweden and Earl Eirik sailed to meet the king of the Danes and together they had a huge army.

99. After he had called out his army, King Svein dispatched Earl Sigvald to Wendland to keep an eye on Olaf Tryggvason's movements and to lure him into an encounter with Svein and his allies. Earl Sigvald made his way to Wendland. He came first to Jomsborg and then went to meet King Olaf Tryggvason. Their conversation was very friendly and the earl ingratiated himself with the king. Sigvald's wife, Astrid, was the daughter of King Burislaf. She was a close friend of Olaf Tryggvason mainly because of their earlier ties when King Olaf was married to her sister, Geira. Earl Sigvald was a wise and cunning man and, when he had worked his way into King Olaf's confidence, he found various reasons for delaying the king's journey back to Norway. Olaf's men took this very badly for they were anxious to get home; they were ready to sail, and the wind was favorable.

Sigvald received secret intelligence from Denmark that the armies were ready and that Svein, Olaf, and Eirik would come east to Wendland, where they would lie in wait for King Olaf at an island called Svold. Sigvald was to lure King Olaf into an encounter with them there.

100. A rumor reached Wendland that Svein, king of the Danes, had mobilized his army and that he meant to attack King Olaf Tryggvason. But Earl Sigvald said to the king, "Given the size of your force, King Svein won't be

planning to fight against you with the Danish army alone. Still, if you are at all suspicious that you may be heading into trouble, I'll follow you with my fleet. Rulers have always thought it an advantage to have the Jomsvikings on their side. I can offer you eleven well-manned ships."

The king agreed to this and, as there was a light but favorable wind, he ordered the fleet to cast off and had the signal blown for departure. The sails were hoisted. The small ships all got underway quickly and put to sea ahead of the others. But Earl Sigvald sailed close to the king's ship and hailed him.

"Follow me," he said. "I know where the sounds between the islands are deepest and you will need depth for the big ships."

So the earl took the lead with his eleven ships, and the king followed with his large ships, which were also eleven in number; but the rest of the fleet sailed out to sea. When Earl Sigvald came near Svold, a cutter rowed out to meet him. The crew told the earl that the Danish fleet was lying in the harbor there. At that, the earl ordered the sails of his ships to be lowered, and his fleet rowed close in to the island. Halldor the Heathen says this:

> From the south sailed King Olaf
> with seventy-one warships.
> The sword of the sea-king
> was bloodied in battle;
> Eirik summoned ships from Slaney,
> called their fleet to the fight;
> peace fell apart
> and war was awakened.

The poem relates that King Olaf and Earl Sigvald had seventy-one ships when they sailed from the south.

101. Svein, king of the Danes, King Olaf of Sweden, and Earl Eirik were at Svold with their whole fleet. The weather was fine, and the sun shone brightly. All the chieftains and their retinues landed on the island and surveyed the vessels sailing close together out at sea. Then they saw a large and splendid ship. Both kings said, "That ship is big and very beautiful. It must be the *Long Serpent*."

In reply, Earl Eirik said that it was not the *Long Serpent*, and he was right. That ship belonged to Kindred of Gemstar. Shortly afterwards, they saw another ship, much bigger than the first. King Svein said,

"Olaf Tryggvason must be afraid now, for he doesn't dare sail with the figurehead on his ship."

"That's not the king's ship," replied Earl Eirik. "I know that ship and its striped sail. That's Erling Skjalgsson. Let them sail by. It's better for us if a well-equipped ship like that goes on its way; it will reduce the strength of Olaf's fleet."

Later, they recognized Earl Sigvald's ships heading toward the island. Then they saw three other ships sailing by, and one of them was very large. King Svein said that this was the *Long Serpent* and ordered them to embark.

"They have many other great and splendid ships besides the *Long Serpent*," said Earl Eirik. "Let's wait a while."

"Earl Eirik won't fight to avenge his father," many men said. "That is a disgrace, for everyone will hear about it if we sit here with such a large fleet while King Olaf sails right past us."

After discussing this for a while, they saw four ships sailing up, and one of them was a huge warship, its dragon's head heavily decorated with gold. Then King Svein stood up and said, "The *Long Serpent* will carry me high tonight, for I shall steer it."

Many men declared that the *Long Serpent* was a truly mighty and splendid ship, and that only a great man would have built such a magnificent vessel.

Earl Eirik said, loudly enough for people to hear him, "Even if King Olaf had only that one ship, King Svein could never capture it with the Danish army alone."

The men then rushed to their ships and took down the awnings. While the leaders were talking together, as has just been related, they saw three large ships sailing by, with a fourth bringing up the rear; this was the *Long Serpent*. As for the great ships, which they had mistaken for the *Long Serpent* as they sailed by before, the first was the *Crane* and the second was the *Short Serpent*. But when they saw the *Long Serpent*, everyone was quite certain that Olaf Tryggvason must be aboard such a vessel, so they went down to their ships and prepared for the attack.

The three leaders – Earl Eirik, Olaf of Sweden, and King Svein – agreed that each of them would have a third of Norway, if they brought down King Olaf Tryggvason and that whichever one of them was first to board the *Long Serpent* would get the ship and all its contents. Also, each of them would keep whatever ships he himself put out of action. Earl Eirik had a very large warship which he was accustomed to take on Viking raids. At the top of both the prow and the stern, there were iron spikes and below these there was thick iron plating, as wide as the keel, which extended all the way down to the water-line.

102. When the commander of the *Crane*, Thorkel Dyrthil, and the steersmen of the accompanying ships saw that Earl Sigvald's fleet had rowed close in to the island, they lowered their sails and rowed after him. They hailed Sigvald's men and asked why they had turned in this direction. The earl replied that he wanted to wait for King Olaf.

"I suspect that there's trouble ahead of us," he said.

They let their ships drift there until Thorkel Nefja came up in the *Short Serpent*, along with the three ships that were following him. They were told the same tale, so they lowered their sails, hove to, and waited for Olaf Tryggvason. As soon as the king sailed in toward the island, the whole enemy fleet rowed out into the sound to meet him. When his men saw this, they urged the king to stay on course and avoid battle with such a large fleet. The king was standing on the quarter-deck and answered in a loud voice,

"Lower the sails. My men will never think of fleeing, and I have never fled from a battle. God may do as he wants with my life, but I'll never run for it." The king's orders were carried out. Hallfred relates it thus:

> Let me recall the king's words:
> it is said the mail-clad man,
> spoke spiritedly
> on the brink of battle;
> the conquering King Olaf
> forbade the thought of flight;
> the prince, beloved of his people,
> spoke warrior's words that endure.

103. King Olaf Tryggvason had the trumpets blown to summon his ships together for battle. The king's ship was in the center of the line, with the *Short Serpent* on one side, and the *Crane* on the other. When they began to tie the ships together for battle, they lashed the prows of the *Long Serpent* and the *Short Serpent* together. Seeing this, King Olaf called to his men in a loud voice and ordered them to position the big ship further forward, so that it wouldn't stretch out behind the other ships. Ulf the Red replied,

"If we line up the sterns, then the *Long Serpent* will jut out far in front of the other ships, and we'll have a rough time of it in the bows."

"I didn't know that I had a man in the bows as yellow as he's red," said King Olaf.

"Just you make sure to defend the stern, as well as I will defend the bow," replied Ulf the Red. The king laid an arrow to his bow and aimed at Ulf. "Shoot it somewhere else where it will do more good," said Ulf. "What I do, I do for you, king."

104. King Olaf stood on the quarter-deck of the *Long Serpent*. He was a conspicuous figure. His gilt shield and helmet made him clearly recognizable, as did the short scarlet tunic that he wore over his chain mail. He noticed that the enemy ships were forming up and that the chiefs opposing him had raised their standards.

"Who is leading the group directly opposite us?" he asked. One of his men told him that it was King Svein Forkbeard with the Danish army. "We're not afraid of these cowards," said King Olaf. "The Danes are not noted for their courage. But whose standards are those to the right of the Danes?"

He was told that they belonged to King Olaf of Sweden. "He and his men would be better off at home licking their sacrificial bowls instead of rowing in under a hail of weapons to attack the *Serpent*," said Olaf Tryggvason. "But who owns those large ships on the port side of the Danes?"

"Earl Eirik Hakonarson," was the answer. "He must certainly think he has good reason to fight us," said King Olaf, "and we can expect a fierce battle with that lot, for they are Norsemen, like ourselves."

105. Then the kings prepared for the attack. King Svein steered his ship toward the *Long Serpent*. King Olaf of Sweden sailed out to one side and engaged the outermost ship in Olaf Tryggvason's line, while Earl Eirik attacked on the other side. A savage fight broke out, but Earl Sigvald just moved his ships to and fro and did not join the battle. Skuli Thorsteinsson, who was with Earl Eirik at that time, says this about the battle:

> I followed Eirik, the Frisians' foe,
> and Sigvald to where spears sang out;
> we brought bloody swords
> south to Svold
> to meet the wielder of iron weapons
> in the deadly din of battle.
> Young then, I found fame,
> but now all see I'm growing old.

Hallfred also speaks about this event:

> Many turned tail
> and you, who brought on the battle,
> sorely missed the support
> of Trondheim's troops;
> a single brave sovereign
> battled two bold kings,
> and Earl Eirik as a third;
> it is a fine custom to tell such tales.

106. This fight was very bitter and bloody. The men at the bows of the *Long Serpent*, the *Short Serpent*, and the *Crane* threw anchors and grappling hooks into King Svein's ships. They hurled weapons down on the men below

them and cleared everyone off the ships they grappled. King Svein and the survivors of his army fled to other ships and got themselves out of weapon range as quickly as they could. And so Svein's army fared just as badly as King Olaf Tryggvason had said it would. Then King Olaf of Sweden moved into King Svein's place but, as soon as he came close to the great ships, his force suffered as badly as Svein's had done. They lost many men and some of their ships and, given the circumstances, they withdrew.

Meanwhile, Earl Eirik laid his ship, the *Ironbeard*, alongside the outermost ship in Olaf Tryggvason's line. He cleared the ship of men and cut it free from the ropes connecting it with the fleet. Then he moved on to the next ship and fought until it, too, was cleared. Now the men began to leap from the small ships to the larger ones, and the earl cut loose each ship as soon as it was put out of action. Then the Danes and the Swedes moved back into shooting range on all sides of Olaf Tryggvason's ships. But Earl Eirik was constantly alongside the enemy ships and was always engaged in close fighting, and, as soon as men died on his ships, they were replaced by Danes and Swedes. As Halldor says:

> The clash of keen swords
> spoke loud on the *Long Serpent*,
> gold-worked spears sang out
> while warriors tore peace apart;
> Earl Eirik led,
> Danes and Swedish forces followed
> into close combat
> in the south, at Svold.

Then the battle reached its crisis, and many men fell. Finally, all of King Olaf's ships were cleared except the *Long Serpent*, and all his men who were still able to fight gathered on board this one ship. Then, Earl Eirik brought the *Ironbeard* alongside the *Long Serpent* and hand-to-hand fighting broke out. As Halldor says:

> Last year, the *Long Serpent*
> encountered cruel trials;
> sword struck sword,
> shields were shattered.
> Earl Eirik laid *Ironbeard*
> alongside the *Long Serpent*;
> he won the war of weapons,
> at Svold in the south.

107. Earl Eirik was standing near the stern of his ship where he and his men were protected by a shield-wall. They were fighting with swords and axes; they were throwing spears and anything else that could be employed as a missile. Some used bows; others used their hands to hurl weapons. The *Long Serpent* was now completely surrounded by warships and there was such a hail of weapons and spears, and such a dense rain of arrows that the men on the *Serpent* could scarcely protect themselves with their shields. King Olaf's men grew so frantic that they leapt up onto the sides of their ship, trying to kill their antagonists with sword strokes. But few of the enemy ships lay close enough to the *Serpent* for sword fights and most of Olaf's men, behaving as though they were fighting on dry land, simply kept on going and went over the side and sank under the weight of their weapons. Thus says Hallfred:

> Warriors wounded in the spear-fight
> sank down from the *Long Serpent*;
> but they did not flinch from the fight,
> mighty in their ringed-mail;
> wherever the *Long Serpent* sails,
> even guided by the greatest of steersmen,
> she will long lack
> king and crewmen like these.

108. Einar Thambarskelf, the strongest archer there, was wielding his bow just below the quarter-deck of the *Long Serpent*. He shot at Earl Eirik and hit the top of the rudder just above his head with such force that the arrow-head was completely embedded. The earl looked in Einar's direction and asked if anyone knew who had fired the arrow. He had no sooner spoken than another arrow flew between his side and his arm and struck the steersman's headboard so hard that the point came through on the other side. Then the earl spoke to a man called Finn who was a first-rate archer:

"Shoot that big man standing next to the quarter-deck." Finn shot and the arrow hit the middle of Einar's bow just as he was drawing it for a third time. The bow split in two.

"What broke with so much noise?" asked King Olaf.

"Norway from your grasp, king," answered Einar.

"It wasn't as big a break as that," said the king. "Take my bow and use it." The king threw the bow to Einar who caught it. But the moment he drew it, the wood of the bow flexed beyond the arrow-point. "Too weak, too weak for a king's bow," he cried. He threw the bow back and fought with his sword and shield.

109. King Olaf Tryggvason stood on the quarter-deck of the *Long Serpent* and spent most of the day shooting, sometimes with his bow and sometimes with spears, which he always threw two at a time. He cast his eye the length of his ship and noticed that his men were swinging their swords and slashing vigorously, but the swords were not inflicting many wounds.

"Why are you striking so feebly with your swords?" asked the king in a loud voice. "I can see that they aren't doing much damage."

"They're blunt and badly hacked," someone replied. The king got down from the quarter-deck and opened the chest under the high seat. He took many sharp swords from it and handed them out. But when he reached down with his right hand, his men noticed that blood was running out from under his mail sleeve. No one knew where he was wounded.

110. Aboard the *Long Serpent*, the fiercest and bloodiest defense came from the men stationed just below the quarter-deck and from those fighting in the bow, for in both places the men were specially selected, and the ship was high above the water. The men amidships had fallen first. When only a few of them were left standing around the mast, Earl Eirik decided to board the *Serpent*, and fourteen men went with him. They were attacked by Hyrning, King Olaf's brother-in-law, and a group of his followers. The ensuing fight was fierce and ended with Eirik's retreat to *Ironbeard*. Some of the men who accompanied him were killed, others were wounded. Thord Kolbeinsson says:

> Blood-showered were the shields
> of the helmeted host.....
> ....
> ....
> Protecting his prince
> with his steel sword,
> Hyrning gained glory that will last
> till the hall of the high hills [heaven] falls.

The fight grew even more bitter and many men died aboard the *Long Serpent*. When the defenders of the *Serpent* had been thinned out, Earl Eirik decided to board for the second time, but again he met with stiff resistance. When the men at the bows of the *Serpent* saw the boarding, they made their way aft and mounted a desperate defense against the earl. Aboard the *Long Serpent*, so many men had fallen that the sides of the ship were almost undefended. Seeing this, the earl's men boarded in large numbers, while all the defenders of the *Serpent* who were still on their feet joined the king in the stern. Halldor the Heathen says that Earl Eirik urged on his men:

> Olaf's men fled aft,
> back among the benches,
> as Earl Eirik urged on
> his battle-tough band.
> Eirik the gold-giver's fleet
> encircled King Olaf's ship;
> all around the enemy of the Wends [Olaf]
> was the deadly din of battle.

111. Kolbjorn, the king's marshal, who was the best and bravest of men, went up to the quarter-deck and approached King Olaf. The two men were similarly clothed and armed. Ferocious fighting was still going on in the stern. As many of Earl Eirik's men as could find room on the *Serpent* had now boarded her, and his ships had surrounded her. So, although the defenders were both strong and brave, they were too few in number to resist such a large force, and most of them fell in a very short time. King Olaf and Kolbjorn both jumped overboard, one on each side of the ship. The earl's men had positioned small boats around the *Long Serpent* and were killing everyone who took to the water. But when the king himself jumped overboard, they tried to capture him and take him to Earl Eirik. King Olaf, however, held his shield above his head and plunged down into the water. Kolbjorn, on the other hand, thrust his shield beneath him to protect himself against spears thrown from the surrounding ships. He landed in the water with his shield beneath him so that he stayed on the surface long enough for them to seize him and pull him aboard a boat. Thinking he was the king, they took him to Earl Eirik, but Eirik recognized him as Kolbjorn and spared his life. At the same moment, all of King Olaf's men who were still alive jumped over the side of the *Serpent*. Hallfred says that Thorkel Nefja, the king's brother, was the last to dive overboard:

> Heroic Thorkel, happy
> to have bloodied his spear in battle,
> saw the *Long Serpent*, the *Short Serpent*,
> and the *Crane*, empty and adrift.
> Then the wise warrior Thorkel,
> brave in battle,
> firm in fierce fight,
> swam away from the *Serpent*.

112. As has been written, Earl Sigvald joined King Olaf in Wendland. The earl had ten ships at Svold, as well as an eleventh aboard which his wife,

Astrid, King Burislaf's daughter, had her men. When King Olaf jumped overboard, the whole army raised a shout of triumph. Then Earl Sigvald and his men put their oars into the water and rowed toward the battle. Halldor the Heathen says:

> The Wendish warships came
> from afar to the fight.
> Then the sharp ax, the shield's foe,
> gaped and grinned with iron-mouth.
> There was the clash of swords on the sea,
> and ravenous eagles ripped men's flesh.
> The worthy leader of warriors
> fought, but many fled.

However, the Wendish longship with Astrid's men on board rowed straight back to Wendland. Immediately, a rumor sprang up that Olaf Tryggvason had struggled out of his mail shirt in the sea and had swum underwater away from the longships out to the Wendish vessel, which took him to land. Afterwards, many tales were told about King Olaf's travels; Hallfred says this:

> Shall I praise a living lord,
> or praise the raven's prey?
> Shall I praise the shield-warrior
> alive, or lost to death?
> Men talk of both as true,
> but truth is hard to tell.
> Whatever fate befell him,
> the warrior was surely wounded.

But, whatever the truth of the matter, King Olaf Tryggvason never returned to his kingdom in Norway.

(c) Rognvald and Thorfinn the Mighty Fight It Out in the Orkneys

For many years, Earl Thorfinn the Mighty (1009?–1064) was sole ruler of the Orkneys. Late in the 1030s, his nephew, Rognvald Brusason, with the support of Magnus the Good (king of Norway 1035–47), claimed his father's share of the Orkneys. Thorfinn was obliged to accept the claim, and the two ruled side by side until the arrival of Kalf Arnason (uncle of Thorfinn's wife) caused strain between them. In the ensuing war,

Rognvald was supported by Magnus the Good, who provided him with ships and men. From Orkneyinga saga, *a history of the earls of Orkney from the tenth to the thirteenth centuries.*

Source: *Orkneyinga saga*, ed. Finnbogi Guðmundsson, Íslenzk fornrit XXXIV (Reykjavík, 1965), pp. 65–70.

26. Earl Rognvald sailed west from Norway to the Orkneys. He landed in the Shetlands first and gathered forces there. Then he went south to the Orkneys, where he sent for his friends and recruited reinforcements. Earl Thorfinn was in Caithness and it wasn't long before he heard about Earl Rognvald's movements and raised troops in Scotland and the Hebrides. Earl Rognvald immediately forwarded King Magnus's message to Kalf Arnason [that Kalf's property would be restored and he would be permitted to live in Norway], and Kalf was satisfied with everything the king had said.

Earl Rognvald gathered his army together in the Orkneys, intending to cross over to Caithness, and he had thirty large ships when he came into the Pentland Firth. There he came up against Earl Thorfinn with sixty ships, most of which were small; they met off Robery, and the fighting began immediately. Kalf Arnason turned up with six large ships, but did not join the battle. The fighting grew ferocious as the earls urged on their men, but after a while, the casualties began to mount on Earl Thorfinn's side, mainly because of the difference in height of their ships. Thorfinn himself had a large, well-equipped ship and he pressed forward courageously, but, when his smaller ships had been disabled, his own ship was attacked from both sides. This was a perilous situation; many of his crew were killed or seriously wounded. Then Earl Rognvald exhorted his men to board Thorfinn's ship, but when Thorfinn realized the danger he was in, he gave orders for his ship to be cut loose from the others and rowed ashore.

There, he had seventy bodies carried from his ship. He also put ashore all those who were too badly wounded to fight. Then he asked Arnor Jarlaskald [Poet of Earls] to disembark too; Arnor was one of his retainers and was held in high regard. So Arnor went ashore and composed this poem:

Unwilling is this warrior
to battle with Brusi's son;
It is excellent to serve one's earl,
– I do not deny that;
so when earls are eager
to attack each other,

it's a hard choice I have
– A tough trial of friendship.

Earl Thorfinn manned his ship with the best men he had left. Then he went
to Kalf and asked for his help. He told Kalf that he was unlikely to win back
King Magnus's friendship after being driven out of Norway.

"If you weren't safe while you were on good terms with the king," said
Thorfinn, "do you think that you'll be welcome here if Rognvald defeats
me, and he and King Magnus extend their authority to this side of the western sea? But if we are victorious, you won't lack for anything that it's in my
power to give you, and if we're both of one mind, we won't be at anyone's
mercy on this side of the sea. Surely you won't want to have it on your conscience that you were lurking here like a cat in its den while I was fighting
to keep both of us free? Besides, our family ties oblige us to help each other
when we're up against strangers."

Goaded into action by Thorfinn, Kalf called his men together and ordered
them into battle beside the earl. Bjarni Gullbrarskald composed this verse:

> Kalf, we have heard how
> you followed Finn's kinsman,
> sailed your snake-ships
> eagerly against the earl:
> quelled the rash courage
> of Brusi's bold son;
> when, mindful of former malice,
> you hastened to help Thorfinn.

Now Kalf and Earl Thorfinn both rowed to the attack, but by the time they
reached the battle, Thorfinn's fleet was poised to flee, for many of his men
had been killed. Thorfinn steered straight for Rognvald's ship and a terrible
fight took place. Here is how Arnor describes it:

> My grief grew
> as I saw both benefactors
> slaughter each other's soldiers,
> fighting in Pentland Firth;
> stained was the sea, as
> dark gore seeped through seams
> of ships, and shield –
> boards sweated blood.

Kalf attacked the smaller of Rognvald's ships; he was able to clear them quickly since his own ships had a considerable advantage in height. When the soldiers levied in Norway saw the ships near them being cleared, they cut the ropes that linked their own ships and fled. Soon there were hardly any ships left to support the earl, and at that point the battle turned against him. As Arnor Jarlaskald says:

> The battle-eager earl could
> have taken the old territory,
> – there was less loss of life
> among his men –
> if Kalf and his crews
> had sailed with the sea-king;
> but they showed Shetland's
> lord little loyalty.

Now that the main part of Rognvald's army had fled, Kalf and Earl Thorfinn attacked his ship together and killed many of his men. When Earl Rognvald realized what straits he was in, and that he could not defeat Thorfinn and Kalf, he had his ship cut loose from the coupling ropes and fled. The day was far gone by then, and it was growing dark. That very night, Earl Rognvald put to sea and sailed east to Norway. He did not break his journey until he reached King Magnus. As before, the king made him welcome and invited him to stay. Earl Rognvald remained there for some time.

27. The following morning, Earl Thorfinn sent his men rowing all around the Orkneys in search of fugitives. Many of them were killed, while others were spared. Earl Thorfinn gained control over all the Orkneys and ordered everyone to accept his authority, even those who had sworn oaths to Rognvald. He established himself in Orkney with a large entourage and brought provisions over from Caithness. He also sent Kalf Arnason to the Hebrides to strengthen his position there....

(d) Earl Rognvald Kali in the Mediterranean

In the early 1150s the Earl of Orkney, Rognvald Kali Kolsson, embarked upon a pilgrimage/crusade to Rome and the Holy Land. Orkneyinga saga *describes an encounter in the Mediterranean between the Orcadian crusaders and a Muslim vessel called a dromond.*

Source: *Orkneyinga saga*, ed. Finnbogi Guðmundsson, Íslenzk fornrit XXXIV (Reykjavík, 1965), pp. 222–28.

87. ... One morning, the mist lifted, and the men stood up and looked around them. They saw two islands but, when they looked again later, one of the islands had vanished. They told the earl what they had seen.

"It can't have been islands you saw," he said. "It must have been ships. The ships that people have out here in this part of the world look as big as islands; they're called dromonds. A sea breeze must have blown up where the one of the dromonds was lying and now it has sailed away. The people on board must be traveling men of some sort, probably merchants."

After that, the earl summoned the bishop and all the captains to a meeting.

"Lord bishop," he said, "and Erling my kinsman, I've called you here to ask if you can think of any ruse or strategy for defeating the people aboard the dromond?"

"Your best plan would be to grapple the bulwark with battle-axes," replied the bishop, "but you'll find it difficult to bring your ships alongside the dromond because they'll have sulphur and boiling pitch that they can shower you with from head to toe. A man as wise as you, earl, must see how dangerous it would be to expose himself and his men to such a great risk."

Then Erling spoke up. "Lord bishop," he said, "you're probably right. Attacking them may well prove futile. But to my way of thinking, if we get in close to the dromond, and lie broadside to it, most of their weapons will fall beyond our ship. And if things don't work out that way, we can always sail away quickly, for the people on the dromond aren't going to chase us."

"Well said," declared the earl. "That's just what I think. Now I want the captains and crews to be clear about this: every man is to go to his place and arm himself with his best equipment. Then we'll attack. If they turn out to be Christian merchants, we can make peace with them, but if they're heathens, as I think they are, then almighty God in his mercy will give us victory. We'll give the poor every fiftieth penny of whatever booty we take."

At that, the men seized their weapons, put up battle-walls on the bulwarks of their ships, and made ready as best they could with the equipment they had. The earl decided where each ship should head. Then they rowed to the attack as fast as possible.

88. When the people aboard the dromond saw ships rowing toward them and realized that they were under attack, they took their fine materials and valuables and carried them to the sides of the ship. They began shouting loudly as though goading the earl's men to approach the dromond. Earl Rognvald positioned his ship toward the stern of the dromond on the starboard side; Erling was at the stern, too, but on the port side. Jon and Aslak lay toward the bow, one on either side of the dromond, while the others were amidships on the port and starboard sides. All of the ships lay broadside on. When they came alongside the dromond, it stood so high out of the water

that they could not reach the bulwarks with their weapons. The crew of the dromond began pouring burning sulphur and pitch over them, but most of it fell beyond the ships as Erling had predicted, and so they had no need to shield themselves from it.

As they were getting nowhere with their attack, the bishop withdrew his own ship and two others. They concentrated their archers aboard these ships and then they moved within range of the dromond and opened fire. This attack was very effective. The people on board the dromond were so busy protecting themselves that they paid little attention to what the Norsemen at the sides of their ship were up to. Earl Rognvald ordered his men to take their axes and hack at the side of the dromond where it was least protected by iron-plating, and, when the crews of the other ships saw what the earl's men were doing, they followed suit.

Where Erling and his men had come alongside, there was a huge anchor hanging down from the dromond. Its fluke was hooked over the gunwale and its shank pointed down toward Erling's ship. His bowsman, Audun the Red, was lifted up onto the anchor-stock and he hauled up other men until as many men as possible were crammed onto the stock. There, far above the other ax-wielders, they hacked at the planking as hard as they could and when they had cut a big enough hole, they boarded the dromond. The earl and his men got into the lower hold, while Erling and his men got into the upper one, and when both groups were aboard, there was much hard fighting.

The men on the dromond were Saracens, whom we call Mohammed's heretics. There were many black men too, and they put up the strongest resistance. As Erling was jumping aboard the dromond, he received a serious neck-wound right at the shoulder. This wound healed so badly that he carried his head to one side ever after, and that's why he was nicknamed Erling Wry-Neck. As soon as the earl and Erling joined forces, the Saracens retreated before them toward the bows, but the earl's men kept pouring onto the ship one after another, pressing the enemy hard as their numbers increased. The Norsemen noticed that one man aboard the dromond was taller and handsomer than the others and they thought for sure that he must be their leader. Earl Rognvald ordered them not to use weapons against this man if they could take him some other way. So the Norsemen hemmed him in with their shields and that is how he was captured. He and a few of his companions were taken aboard the bishop's ship, but everyone else was killed. The Norsemen seized lots of money and many valuables, and when most of the work was done, they sat down and rested. The earl recited this verse:

> Bloody our banners, when the
> famous fighter, glorious Erling,

> strongest spearman, advanced
> victorious against the vessel.
> Brave were the warriors who bloodied
> sharp swords and spilled enemy
> blood from stem to stern,
> when we felled the black men's best.

and this:

> Desperate to take the dromond,
> warriors stained their swords
> early in the action;
> this was a slaughter for sure; from the
> south northwards, and from the north
> to Narbonne, the lady will hear news
> of the awful loss of life inflicted
> on the heathen by our host.

They talked about what had taken place, and each man recounted his own version of the events. Then they got into an argument about who had boarded the dromond first, and they couldn't agree on this point. Some of them declared that it was absurd to have several versions of such a great event. So they agreed that Earl Rognvald should settle the dispute and that they would all go along with his decision. The earl spoke:

> Hell-bent on booty,
> Audun the Red rushed
> first with fierce courage
> aboard the dark dromond;
> there we wet our weapons
> in black men's blood;
> dark bodies fell to the decks
> as the god of men granted.

Then they cleared the dromond, and set it ablaze. When the tall man they had captured saw this, he started and grew pale and agitated. They tried to make him talk, but no matter how much they threatened or cajoled, he didn't say a word or make a sign. When the dromond was completely ablaze, they saw something that looked like a burning stream flowing into the sea. This greatly affected their prisoner. They concluded that they hadn't searched carefully enough for treasure and that metal, either gold or silver, had melted as the fire took hold.

(e) The Battle of Fimreite (Norafjord), 1184

This battle secured the throne of Norway for King Sverrir (1145/51–1202). The "Birkibeins" (birch-legs) were the rebellious supporters of the pretender Sverrir in his struggle against King Magnus Erlingsson (1156–84), whose supporters were known as the Heklungs. From Sverrir's Saga. *(See doc. 35).*

Source: *Sverris saga*, ed. Þorleifur Hauksson, Íslenzk fornrit XXXV (Reykjavík, 2007), pp. 136–44.

88. ... Then King Sverrir ordered his men to take down the awnings and row the ships into the fjord, close to shore. "I want a cutter to row as rapidly as possible to Soknadale with orders for our ships there to join us," said Sverrir. "Then we'll row out to meet the enemy. In every ship, one man from each half-room is to sit at the oar, the second is to row ashore in a small boat to fetch stones, while the third man, as well as anyone else who is free, is to get the ships ready and put up the battle-walls [upward extensions of a ship's sides]."

They carried out the king's orders and used the nails he had given them to fasten loops of walrus rope all round the inner surface of the ships' sides. Then they fitted supports into the loops and used them to prop up the battle-walls securely. Everyone was busy now and the Birkibeins were obviously used to work like this.

When the crew of the cutter rowed up the fjord, they met their comrades rowing down and they passed on the rumor about King Magnus's fleet. The sailors on the longships leapt into action, put their oars into the water and rowed for all they were worth. As they approached King Sverrir's ships, they got into a race and rowed so close to one another that several oars were broken. At that, the king said, "We have more serious business on hand than breaking one another's oars."

He ordered them to make for the shore and wait there for King Magnus. Then they brought as many rocks as they wanted out to the ships and raised up the battle-walls. After that, the king ordered his men to haul the stern mooring-ropes aboard all the ships. He also ordered them to turn the ships' bows to face away from the shore and to place their oars in the rowing position. The king's ship lay close to shore and was nearest to the mouth of the fjord. Then the king ordered his men to arm themselves and take their places in the rooms....

"We're not going to lash our ships together," said King Sverrir. "We must rely on the height of our ships' sides and the courage of our battle-hardened army to gain whatever advantage we can. There's only one course of action open to us, and that is to defeat our enemies, for neither running away nor begging for peace will do us any good. Be careful with your weapons and don't throw them at the enemy until you have to. Look after yourselves first, and one another next! May God protect us all!"

Then he had the standards raised. Close to their ships, a small headland jutted out into the sea, almost blocking their view of the entrance to the fjord. So the king had a cutter row out to watch for King Magnus's fleet, but when they had gone only a few strokes from land, they rowed quickly back and announced that the enemy fleet was heading toward them. Immediately, the trumpet was sounded and the Birkibeins started rowing all their ships to the attack, raising a war cry as they went. Thord, brother of Fingeir, was steersman on the *Mariasud*.

89. King Magnus now sailed into the fjord in search of the Birkibeins. When he and his men realized that the fleets were not far apart, they lowered their sails and went forward under oars, staying close together as they advanced....

King Magnus addressed his men: "These large merchant ships of ours are not designed for rowing. We shall lash them together between Orm's ship and mine. Then we'll head for King Sverrir's big ship and attach our ships to it. I don't want the ships separated until either we clear theirs of men or they clear ours...."

Then King Magnus's brother, Orm, said, "My lord, my advice is that we should attack the small ships first because they won't offer much resistance, but I think it will be hard to overcome the big ship as long as they have plenty of men and ships to support it."

King Magnus replied, "It seems to me that all the ships will be taken if the big ship is taken." The king's words were decisive. The four biggest ships were lashed together and the king's ship sailed closest to the southern shore of the fjord....

91. Now it is time to recount some of the events which took place in the encounter between the two kings. We have already touched on this, and now the story returns to the Birkibeins who (as previously mentioned) rowed out from the land as soon as they saw King Magnus's fleet heading their way. In front of this fleet they saw what looked like heavy rain, the sort of shower that is seen at sea in calm weather. This shower, which passed quickly overhead, was, in fact, a hail of arrows; shields had to be used against them.

They tried to bring the *Mariasud* about to face the enemy, but her turning circle was so wide that the ships crashed together before she could complete the turn. Magnus's ships collided with the side of the *Mariasud*, striking her near the bow with their prows. The *Skeggi* [one of Magnus's ships] lay at the *Mariasud*'s forward pump-room, and the other ships were lined up side by side from there to the prow.

A fierce battle followed. King Magnus's men fought with great vigor, but the Birkibeins hung back defensively. In the meantime, the ships were all drifting toward the shore together, coming very close to the land. At first, the Birkibeins were unable to go on the offensive because the *Mariasud* lay between them and King Magnus's ships. So King Sverrir and one other man leapt aboard a boat and rowed out to his son Eirik's ship. Sverrir called out to them that their behavior was weak and unmanly. He ordered them to row around the big ship and head toward the smaller enemy ships and see how they got on there. The king rowed among his ships, encouraging his men and telling them where to attack. Heartened by the king's words, his men attacked bravely and put up a fierce fight, but their enemies gave as good as they got. Both sides let fly with all the weapons they had.

As the king rowed back to his ship, an arrow struck the prow of the boat just above his head; immediately afterwards, another arrow hit the side of the boat above his knees. The king sat still and didn't flinch. His companion said, "Dangerous shots, my lord."

"They come as near as God wills," replied the king.

Then the king realized that the hail of weapons and stones falling on the *Mariasud* was so dense that he couldn't get aboard again, and so he rowed away toward the land. Munan Gautsson [a Heklung] and his men also steered their ship to land. They leapt ashore and fetched great stones to hurl at the *Mariasud*. They bombarded her from the rowing space at the stern all the way forward to the pump room, and the men in those areas endured terrible slaughter. It was the men stationed in the bow, however, who were most exposed to the attack and the shower of weapons. They told one another that it was now time to pay the king for their mead and their fine clothing.

The men at the stern ordered the starboard oarsmen to row forward. By doing so, they pulled the *Mariasud* forward till the *Skeggi* was level with the aft pump-room. Now the men on the port side and in the rowing place at the stern had their hands full because fourteen ships lay along one side of the *Mariasud*. Then the Heklungs [King Magnus's men] launched missiles, even halberds and blocks of whetstone that they had brought west from Skida; these were very dangerous weapons. They also threw pikes and short swords, but they couldn't get close enough for hand-to-hand fighting. The Birkibeins took cover since they could do nothing else. Even so, many of them died and nearly all of them were wounded by weapons and rocks. They were so worn out and had taken such a beating that some men died of exhaustion even though they were just slightly wounded, or not wounded at all. The Heklungs hung back from boarding the *Mariasud* because they had difficulty in attacking over the prows of their own ships. If they had lain broadside to the *Mariasud*, then one side would have boarded the other much sooner.

92. Now, anyone listening to this story will find its account of the end of the battle improbable. For now the tale goes on to recount what (apart from good luck) caused the victory to take such an unlikely turn.

As the story said earlier, King Sverrir's son, Eirik, rowed around the big ship with the thirteen ships not engaged in the fight. He made for the thirteen of the Heklungs' ships that were furthest from the shore and were not lying next to the *Mariasud*. The ships met broadside on and a fierce battle broke out. The Birkibeins had larger ships and more men and they mounted a hard and vigorous attack. However, the Heklungs put up a stubborn resistance and defended themselves with such spirit that no one could tell whether the battle would be decided by this fight or by the clearing of the *Mariasud*. The men of Sogn had a flotilla of boats within firing range of the Birkibeins and shot at them.

Eirik the king's son brought his ship broadside against the outermost of the ships that were lashed together. His ship had much higher sides, and there was heavy fighting, for the Heklungs resisted strongly. However, after a period of hand-to-hand fighting, they were overwhelmed by numbers. Some of them died and others abandoned their half-rooms.

Then the Birkibeins set about boarding the enemy ship. Eirik's standard-bearer, a man called Benedikt, went first and was followed by the men from the bow. Seeing this, the Heklungs launched a violent attack and killed Benedikt and most of the boarding party. The rest were driven back. Then the king's son encouraged his men to attempt a second boarding. This time, they recaptured their standard and attacked so fiercely that the Heklungs retreated and leapt aboard the nearest ship, with the Birkibeins hard on their heels. What happened next is what always happens in battle, when men are overcome by panic or the desire for flight; they are seldom anxious to face the enemy a second time, even if they resisted courageously at first. The Heklungs put up less of a fight on the second ship than on the first and soon they all retreated from that ship to the next. And so they fled from one ship to another with the Birkibeins in pursuit, uttering war-cries, and shouting encouragement to their comrades. They cut down and killed everyone in their path.

As the crowd of fleeing men surged onto the big ships, people jumped overboard from King Magnus's ship since it was closest to shore. But the other four large ships sank under the weight of so many men. These were the ships commanded by Orm, Asbjarn, and Gesta-Flei.

93. King Sverrir was ashore and when he saw these decisive events, he went down to his boat with Bishop Hroi's son, Peter. At that moment some men rowed up in a cutter, intending to come ashore. The king called out to them, "Go back! Don't you see they're running away?"

The men turned back, and seeing the scene just described, they dipped their oars into the water and rowed off down the fjord. "Did you know these men?" asked Peter. "Why did you say what you did?"

"I would have said the same thing whoever they were," replied King Sverrir.

Then the king went straight to his ship and walked aft to the quarter-deck. There he began to sing the Kyrie to celebrate his victory, and all his men joined in. But King Magnus and all his men jumped from his ship and a whole host of them perished there. The Birkibeins hurried ashore to intercept anyone who tried to reach land. Only a handful of men made it, though a few cutters rowed down the fjord and escaped. The Birkibeins rowed out in small boats. They killed some of the men who were swimming, but spared others. All those who managed to reach King Sverrir were given quarter; and the commanders of Sverrir's ships also gave quarter to their relatives and friends.

CHAPTER EIGHT

"SUDDEN AND UNFORESEEN ATTACKS OF NORTHMEN"

As the eighth century waned, Europe began to experience what one contemporary described as "sudden and unforeseen attacks of Northmen." The ninth-century Anglo-Saxon Chronicle *describes what may be the earliest recorded raids in its entry for 789, when three ships of Northmen landed in the south of England and killed a king's officer, and when Lindisfarne was sacked on 8 June 793. Irish annals recorded the first appearance of the Northmen in the islands off the west coast of Britain and in Ireland from 795, and in 799 there is the first reference to Viking activity off the Continent. By the 830s and 840s, Viking fleets had penetrated far inland up waterways such as the Shannon, the Loire, the Seine, and the Rhine. By the mid-840s and 850s some intrepid leaders were even reaching the Mediterranean and the Rhône River. Such sea-borne raids instilled fear in contemporaries and have inspired modern historians to distinguish a "First Viking Age" or a period of "Reconnaissance" characterized by raiding and plundering, lasting from the 790s until the middle of the ninth century, when raiding intensified and eventually gave way to over-wintering and settlement (see chapter 9).*

39. ON THE CAUSES OF THE VIKING EXPANSION

Dudo, dean of St. Quentin (died before 1027), wrote his De moribus et actis primorum Normanniae ducum *(On the Customs and Deeds of the First Dukes of Normandy) at the behest of Count Richard I (d. 996). The work was composed between about 996 and 1015 and covered events between the 850s and the death of Count Richard. The first book includes one of the few attempts by a medieval writer to explain the sudden advent of the Northmen as anything other than the wrath of God. Modern scholarship is quite skeptical about the historical value of the work, but it is important as an early formulation of the Norman origin myth.*

Source: trans. E. Christiansen, Dudo of St. Quentin, *History of the Normans*, (Woodbridge, Suffolk: Boydell, 1998), pp. 15–17.

1.1 Now the cosmographers who have surveyed the world's whole mass, and have cunningly measured the perimeter and the surface of the land, have taken a bearing by the cardinal points of the four-cornered sky, and have divided the whole of the land, hedged round on all sides by the endless girdle of Ocean, into three parts; and these parts are reckoned to be Asia, Europe, and Africa. Of these, Europe is threaded by the courses of very many rivers, and marked out into various provinces, and divided up into countries within its "separating boundary." And of these, the most spacious and the most affluent of all, owing to the many uncountable throngs of its people, is called Germany. Within which, the river *Hister* rises at the top of mount *Abnoba*, grows vastly bigger fed by sixty tributaries, and wanders boisterously from the south to the east (having separated Germany from Scythia) up to the point where it is received into the Scythian Sea; it is usually called the Danube.

Spread out within the huge space between the Danube and the edge of the Scythian Sea, there dwell savage and barbarous peoples, which are said to have sprung forth in various different ways from the island of Scanza [Scandinavia], hemmed in on both sides by the Ocean, like a swarm of bees from a hive, or like a sword from a scabbard; as barbarians will. For there lies the region of the great multitudes of Alania, the exceedingly fertile site of Dacia, and the far-extended reaches of Getia. Of which, Dacia stands in the middle, looking like a crown, or resembling a city fortified by enormous Alps. And wild peoples, warlike and "foreboding Mars" inhabit this extensive corner; that is, the Getae (also called Goths), the Sarmatians, and the Amacsobii, the Tragoditae, and the Alans, and many other peoples who dwell in and cultivate the Maeotid Marshes. Now these people burn with too much wanton lasciviousness, and with singular depravity debauch and mate with as many women as they please; and so, by mingling together in illicit couplings, they generate innumerable children.

When these have grown up, they clamor fiercely against their fathers and their grandfathers, or more frequently against each other, for shares of property; and, as they are over-many, and the land they inhabit is not large enough for them to live in, there is a very old custom by which a multitude of youths is selected by lot and expelled into the realms of other nations, to win kingdoms for themselves by fighting, where they can live in uninterrupted peace. That is what the Getae did, who are also called Goths, after they had laid waste almost the whole of Europe as far as where they live now.

1.2 Besides, at one time they used to complete their expulsions and exits by making sacrifices in honor of their god Thor. And to him they would offer no single beasts, nor herds of cattle, nor "gifts of Father Liber, nor of Ceres," but men's blood, which they deemed to be the most precious of all holocausts; because him whom a soothsaying priest would determine beforehand, they struck with one fatal blow on his head, [as with] a pair of oxen. And then, when the head of the one chosen by lot had been struck a single blow by each man, he was laid out on the ground, and they would search for "the tube of the heart" on the left-hand side; that is, for the aorta. And it was their custom to smear their own and their followers' heads with the blood that was drained out; and then they would quickly hoist the sails of their ships into the winds, thinking to placate those [winds] by such a procedure, and would briskly ply the oars of their ships.

But if, on the other hand, the lot they drew was for going out on horseback, they would raise the martial standards of battle, and so escape from their own confines and pursue the policy of "falling upon other nations with" deadly "force." For they are exiled by fathers, boldly to batter kings. They are sent away without wealth from their own people, that they may enrich themselves out of the plenty of foreigners. They are deprived of their own lands, that they might be settled undisturbed on those of others. They are expelled as exiles, that they may be rewarded as warriors. They are thrust out by their own people, that they may share with aliens. They are separated from their own nation, that they may rejoice in possessing others. They are abandoned by their fathers, perhaps never again to be seen by their mothers. The ferocity of the young men is aroused, and the nations are destroyed. The native land is liberated, having been purged of its own numerous enemy. So they lay waste everything which stands in their way. Along the sea-shores they sail, to win for themselves the despoiling of lands. What they seize from one kingdom they remove to another. They make for "peace-protected" ports in order to make a profit from their loot.

40. VIKING RAIDS ON ENGLAND, 789–850/1

One of the most important sources for this period is The Anglo-Saxon Chronicle, *which records the annals of England from 60 BCE until 1154.* The Anglo-Saxon Chronicle *is not the title of a single document, but refers collectively to a group of nine manuscripts, none of which is the original copy. The following translation relies mainly on the version known as* The Peterborough Chronicle. *This selection covers the period from the first appearance of Vikings off the south coast of England to the year 851, in which the "great army" of the Danes wintered in England instead of heading back home. Dates in the chronicle are often out by one or more years. Correct dates are supplied in brackets.*

Source: trans. A.A. Somerville from David Dumville and Simon Keynes, general eds., *The Anglo-Saxon Chronicle: A Collaborative Edition* (Cambridge: D.S. Brewer, 1983–), vol. 7; MS E, ed. Susan Irvine (Cambridge: D.S. Brewer, 2004), pp. 41–46.

787 [789]. This year, King Beorhtric [of Wessex] married Eadburg, Offa's daughter. And in his days there came for the first time three ships of North-men, from Hordaland [in Norway]. Then the Reeve rode to meet them; he intended to have them go to the king's town because he did not know what they were. They killed him. These were the first Danish ships to attack the land of the English people....

793. In this year, terrifying omens appeared over Northumbria, and the people were wretchedly afraid. There were huge flashes of lightning and fiery dragons were seen flying in the air. A great famine followed these signs, and shortly after that, on the sixth day before the Ides of January of the same year [8 January], the miserable raiding of the heathens destroyed God's church on the Isle of Lindisfarne through plundering and murder. Also, Sicga [a Northumbrian nobleman] died on the seventh day before the Calends of March [23 February].

794 [796]. In this year, Pope Hadrian and King Offa [of Mercia] died. King Athelred of Northumbria was killed by his own people on the thirteenth day before the Calends of May [19 April]. Also, the bishops Ceolwulf and Eadbald left the country. Ecgferth succeeded to the kingdom of Mercia and died the same year. Eadbriht came to power in Kent; his other name was Præn. Athelheard the alderman died on the Calends of August [1 August]. The heathens raided in Northumbria and plundered Ecgferth's monastery at Jarrow. And there one of their leaders was killed. Also, some of their ships

were wrecked in a storm, and many of them drowned. Some of them got to the river bank alive; they were promptly killed at the mouth of the river....

832 [835]. In this year, heathen men ravaged Sheppey.

833 [836]. In this year, King Ecgbriht [of Wessex] fought against the men from twenty-five ships at Carhampton. After great slaughter the Danes were left in possession of the battlefield. Hereferth and Wigferth, two bishops, died as did the aldermen Duda and Osmod.

835 [838]. This year, a great Danish fleet came to the West Welsh [Cornishmen]. The Welsh and the Danes joined forces and began fighting against Ecgbriht, king of the West Saxons. He moved against them and fought them at Hingston. There he put to flight both the Welsh and the Danes.

837 [840]. This year, Alderman Wulfheard fought against the men from thirty-three ships at Southampton. He slaughtered a great number and won the victory, but he died the same year. Alderman Athelhelm fought the Danes at Portland in Dorset. The alderman was slain and the Danes won control of the battlefield.

839 [842]. In this year, there was much slaughter in London, Canterbury, and Rochester.

840 [843]. This year, King Athelwulf fought the men from thirty-five ships at Carhampton, and the Danes won possession of the battlefield.

845 [848]. In this year, Alderman Ceorl with the men of Somerset, Bishop Ealhstan, and Osric with the men of Dorset fought the Danes at the mouth of the Parret and won the battle there with great slaughter.

851 [850 or 851]. In this year, Alderman Ceorl and the men of Devonshire fought against heathens and, after huge slaughter, defeated them. The heathens stayed in Thanet over the winter. The same year, three hundred and fifty ships arrived at the mouth of the Thames. The heathens stormed Canterbury and routed Brihtwulf, king of the Mercians, and his army. Next, the heathens went south across the Thames where King Athelwulf [of Wessex] and Athelwulf his son with the West-Saxon host fought them at Oakley. This battle was the greatest massacre of a heathen army we have ever heard tell of. King Athelwulf and his forces were victorious there. That same year, King

Athelstan and Alderman Ealhere fought in their ships and massacred a large heathen force at Sandwich. They captured nine ships and drove off the rest.

41. ALCUIN'S LETTER TO KING ATHELRED, 793

The sack of the monastery of Lindisfarne on the east coast of England on 8 June 793 (described in the Anglo-Saxon Chronicle, *doc. 40 above) prompted the churchman and scholar Alcuin (d. 804) to write a series of letters in which he criticized the Northumbrian king, people, and churchmen for misconduct, which, he argued, had brought the wrath of God upon them.*

Source: *English Historical Documents c. 500–1042*, ed. D. Whitelock (London: Eyre & Spottiswoode, 1955), pp. 775–77.

To the most beloved lord King Ethelred and all his chief men, Alcuin the humble deacon, sends greeting.

Mindful of your most sweet love, O men my brothers and fathers, also esteemed in Christ the Lord; desiring the divine mercy to conserve for us in long-lasting prosperity our land, which it once with its grace conferred on us with free generosity; I do not cease to warn you very often, my dearest fellow-soldiers, either with words, when present, if God should grant it, or by letters when absent, by the inspiration of the divine spirit, and by frequent iteration to pour forth to your ears, as we are citizens of the same country, the things known to belong to the welfare of an earthly kingdom and to the beatitude of an eternal kingdom; that the things often heard may be implanted in your minds for your good. For what is love in a friend, if it is silent on matters profitable to the friend? To what does a man owe fidelity, if not to his fatherland? To whom does he owe prosperity, if not to its citizens? We are fellow-citizens by a two-fold relationship: sons of one city in Christ, that is, of Mother Church, and natives of one country. Thus let not your kindness shrink from accepting benignly what my devotion is eager to offer for the welfare of our country. Do not think that I impute faults to you; but understand that I wish to avert penalties.

Lo, it is nearly 350 years that we and our fathers have inhabited this most lovely land, and never before has such terror appeared in Britain as we have now suffered from a pagan race, nor was it thought that such an inroad from the sea could be made. Behold, the church of St. Cuthbert spattered with the blood of the priests of God, despoiled of its ornaments; a place more venerable than all in Britain is given as prey to pagan peoples. And where first, after the departure of Saint Paulinus from York, the Christian religion in our race took its rise, there misery and calamity have begun. Who does not fear this? Who does not lament this as if his country were captured? Foxes pillage the chosen vine, the heritage of the Lord has been given to the Gentiles; the holy festivity has been turned to mourning.

Consider carefully, brothers, and examine diligently, lest perchance this unaccustomed and unheard-of evil was merited by some unheard-of evil practice. I do not say that formerly there were no sins of fornication among the people. But from the days of King Ælfwold fornications, adulteries, and incest have poured over the land, so that these sins have been committed without any shame and even against the handmaids dedicated to God. What may I say about avarice, robbery, violent judgments? – when it is clearer than day how much these crimes have increased everywhere, and a despoiled people testifies to it. Whoever reads the Holy Scriptures and ponders ancient histories and considers the fortune of the world will find that for sins of this kind kings lost kingdoms and peoples their country; and while the strong unjustly seized the goods of others, they justly lost their own.

Truly signs of this misery preceded it, some through unaccustomed things, some through unwonted practices. What portends the bloody rain, which in the time of Lent in the church of St. Peter, prince of the apostles, in the city of York, which is the head of the whole kingdom, we saw fall menacingly on the north side from the summit of the roof, though the sky was serene? Can it not be expected that from the north there will come upon our nation retribution of blood, which can be seen to have started with this attack which has lately befallen the house of God?

Consider the dress, the way of wearing the hair, the luxurious habits of the princes and people. Look at your trimming of the beard and hair, in which you have wished to resemble the pagans. Are you not menaced by terror of them whose fashion you wished to follow? What also of the immoderate use of clothing beyond the needs of human nature, beyond the custom of our predecessors? The princes' superfluity is poverty for the people. Such customs once injured the people of God, and made it a reproach to the pagan races, as the prophet says: "Woe to you, who have sold the poor for a pair of shoes," that is, the souls of men for ornaments for the feet. Some labor under an enormity of clothes, others perish with cold; some are inundated with delicacies and feastings like Dives clothed in purple, and Lazarus dies of hunger at the gate. Where is brotherly love? Where the pity which we are admonished to have for the wretched? The satiety of the rich is the hunger of the poor. That saying of our Lord is also to be feared: "For judgment without mercy to him that hath not done mercy." Also we read in the words of the blessed Peter: "The time is that judgment should begin at the house of God."

Behold, judgment has begun, with great terror, at the house of God, in which rest such lights of the whole of Britain. What should be expected for other places, when the divine judgment has not spared this holy place? I do not think this sin is theirs alone who dwell in that place. Would that their correction would be the amendment of others, and that many would fear what a few have suffered, and each say in his heart, groaning and trembling, "If such great men and fathers so holy did not defend their habitation and the place of their repose, who will defend mine?" Defend your country by assiduous prayers to God, by acts of justice and mercy to men. Let your use of clothes and food be moderate. Nothing defends a country better than the equity and godliness of princes and the intercessions of the servants of God. Remember that Hezekiah, that just and pious king, procured from God by a single prayer that a hundred and eighty-five thousand of the enemy were destroyed by an angel in one night. Likewise with profuse tears he averted from him death when it threatened him, and deserved of God that fifteen years were added to his life by this prayer.

Have decent habits, pleasing to God and laudable to men. Be rulers of the people, not robbers; shepherds, not plunderers. You have received honors by God's gift; give heed to the keeping of his commands, that you may have him as a preserver whom you had as a benefactor. Obey the priests of God; for they have an account to make to God, how they admonish you; they as interceders for you, you as defenders of them. But, above all, have the love of God in your hearts, and show that love by keeping his commandments. Love him as a father, that he may defend you as sons. Whether you will or not, you will have him as a judge. Pay heed to good works, that he may be propitious to you. "For the fashion of this world passeth away"; and all things are fleeting which can be seen or possessed here. This alone from his labor can a man take with him, what he did in alms-giving and good works. We must all stand before the judgment-seat of Christ, and each must show what he did, whether good or evil. Beware of the torments of hell, while they can be avoided; and acquire for yourselves the kingdom of God and eternal beatitude with Christ and his saints in eternal ages.

May God both make you happy in this earthly kingdom and grant to you an eternal country with his saints, O lords, my dearest fathers, brothers and sons.

42. AN ENGLISH GOSPEL BOOK RANSOMED FROM THE VIKINGS

The Canterbury Codex Aureus (also known as the Stockholm Codex Aureus) is a splendidly decorated book of Gospels, produced in England (probably at Canterbury) in the eighth century. Stolen by Vikings in the ninth century, the codex was ransomed by Alderman Alfred and handed over to Christ Church, Canterbury. Alfred's pious deed is remembered in an Anglo-Saxon inscription added to the first page of St. Matthew's Gospel. The codex now resides in the Swedish Royal Library, Stockholm.

Source: trans. A.A. Somerville from *A Second Anglo-Saxon Reader: Archaic and Dialectal*, ed. Henry Sweet, rev. T.F. Hoad (Oxford: Clarendon Press, 1978), p. 115.

In the name of our Lord Jesus Christ, I Alderman Alfred and Werburg my wife obtained these books from the heathen army with our money; the purchase was made with pure gold. We did this for the love of God and the good of our souls, and because we did not want these holy books to remain any longer in the possession of heathens. And now we wish to present these books to Christ Church for the praise, glory, and honor of God, and in thanks for his sufferings, and for the use of the religious brotherhood who offer praise to God in Christ Church every day – on condition that they are read every month, as long as God sees fit that baptism should be performed in this place, for the sake of Alfred, Werburg, and their daughter Alhthryth, for the eternal salvation of their souls. Also, I Earl Alfred and Werburg beg and beseech in the name of God Almighty and all his saints that no one should be so bold as to give away or remove these holy books from Christ Church as long as baptism is performed there.

Alfred.   Werburg.   Alhthryth their daughter.

43. VIKING RAIDS ON IRELAND, 795–842

The Annals of Ulster is one of the most important sources of early Irish history. It is a record of medieval Irish affairs, covering the period from the fifth to the early sixteenth centuries, surviving in two late manuscripts. The annals drew on earlier sources, and by the Viking period they were contemporary with the events they chronicle; they have been described as "substantially accurate accounts" of Viking activity, though this is debated. The chronology of the annals is off by one year for the section reproduced here; corrected dates are provided in parentheses. Because of limited space, only entries pertaining to the Vikings are reproduced here; the culling of the text in this manner has the effect of removing much contextual material that illustrates, among other things, that Irish society was extremely violent before the arrival of the Vikings.

Source: ed. and trans. S. MacAirt and G. MacNiocaill, *The Annals of Ulster (to A.D. 1131),* (Dublin: Institute for Advanced Studies, 1983), pp. 251–301, excerpts.

AD 794 [795]

3. The burning of Rechru [Rathlinn, Co. Antrim, or Lambay, Co. Dublin] by the heathens, and Scí [possibly Skye, but more likely scrin: shrine, or reliquary] was overwhelmed and laid waste.

AD 797 [798]

2. The burning of Inis Pátraic [St. Patrick's Island] by the heathens, and they took the cattle-tribute of the territories, and broke the shrine of Do-Chonna, and also made great incursions both in Ireland and in Alba [Scotland].

AD 801 [802]

9. Í Coluim Chille [Iona, in the Hebrides] was burned by the heathens.

AD 805 [806]

8. The community of Í [Iona], to the number of sixty-eight, was killed by the heathens.

AD 806 [807]

8. The heathens burned Inis Muiredaig and invaded Ros Comáin.
9. A battle between the community of Corcach and the community of Cluain Ferta Brénainn, among whom resulted a slaughter of a countless number of ordinary ecclesiastics and of eminent men of the community of Corcach.

AD 811 [812]

8. A slaughter of the heathens by the men of Umall. A slaughter of the Conmaicne by the heathens.
11. A slaughter of the heathens in Mumu, viz. by Cobthach son of Mael Dúin, King of Loch Léin.

AD 812 [813]

4. The slaughter at Umall by the heathens in which fell Coscrach son of Flannabra and Dúnadach, king of Umall.

AD 820 [821]

3. Étar was plundered by the heathens, [and] they carried off a great number of women into captivity.

AD 822 [823]

8. Heathens invaded Bennchor the great [Bangor, Co. Down].

AD 823 [824]

2. The heathens plundered Bennchor at Airtiu [?], and destroyed the oratory, and shook the relics of Comgall from their shrine....

9. Étgal of Scelec [Skellig Michael, a tiny, jagged, mountain of rock off the southwest coast of Co. Kerry on which was a small monastic community] was carried off by the heathens, and died shortly afterwards of hunger and thirst.

AD 824 [825]

9. Dún Lethglaise was plundered by the heathens.

10. Mag Bile with its oratories was burned by the heathens.

11. The Ulaid inflicted a rout on the heathens in Mag Inis, in which very many fell.

12. The heathens inflicted a rout on the Osraige.

15. The plundering of Inis Daimle by the heathens.

17. The violent death of Blamac son of Flann at the hands of the heathens in Í Coluim Chille [Iona; see doc. 44].

AD 826 [827]

3. Lusca was plundered by the heathens and burned; and Cianacht was invaded as far as Uachtar Ugán; and also a plundering of the foreigners of the East.

9. An encampment of the Laigin was overwhelmed by the heathens, and Conall son of Cú Chongalt, king of the Fortuatha, and countless others fell there.

AD 827 [828]

3. A great slaughter of porpoises on the coast of Ard Cianachta by the foreigners; and the violent death of the anchorite Teimnén.

4. The mortal wounding of Cinaed son of Cumuscach, king of Ard Cianachta, by the foreigners; and Lann Léire and Cluain Mór were burned by them.

5. A battle-rout [was inflicted] on the heathens by Lethlobar son of Loingsech, king of Dál Araidi.

6. Another battle-rout [was inflicted] on the heathens by Cairpre son of

Cathal, king of Uí Cheinnselaig, and by the community of Tech Munnu.

AD 828 [829]

3. Diarmait, abbot of Í, went to Scotland with the halidoms [relics] of Colum Cille [St. Columba d. 597]. [This is thought to have been in response to the frequent raiding of Iona by the Vikings.]

AD 830 [831]

6. Conaille was invaded by the heathens, and Mael Brigte, its king, and his brother Canannán, were taken prisoner and taken away to the ships.
7. The heathens defeated the community of Ard Macha in a battle at Aignig, and great numbers of them were taken captive.

AD 831 [832]

1. The first plundering of Ard Macha by the heathens three times in one month.
2. The plundering of Mucnám, Lugbad, Uí Méith, Druim Moccu Blae, and other churches.
3. The plundering of Dam Liac and the sept [division of a clan] of the Cianacht with all their churches by the heathens.
4. Ailill son of Colgu was taken captive by the heathens.
5. Tuathal son of Feradach was taken away by the heathens, and Adamnán's shrine from Domnach Maigen.
6. Ráith Luraig and Connaire were plundered by the heathens.

AD 832 [833]

4. Niall and Murchad routed the foreigners in Daire Calgaig.
5. Cluain Dolcáin was plundered by the heathens.
11. Druim Inasclainn was burned by the heathens.

AD 833 [834]

8. Dúnadach son of Scannlán, king of Uí Fhidgeinte, won a battle against the heathens, in which many fell.
9. Glenn dá Locha was plundered by the heathens. Sláine and Finnubair Abae were plundered by the heathens.

AD 834 [835]

5. Ferna and Cluain Mór Maedóc were plundered by the heathens.
11. Mungairit and other churches of Iarmumu were burned by the heathens.
12. The foreigners plundered Druim Ing.

AD 835 [836]

5. Cell Dara was plundered by heathens from Inber Dea, and half of the church was burned.

7. The first prey was taken by the heathens from southern Brega, i.e. from Telcha Dromáin and Dairmag of the Britons; and they carried off many prisoners, and killed many and led away very many captive.

10. A most cruel devastation of all the lands of Connacht by the heathens. The heathens inflicted a slaughter in a battle won over the Déis Tuaisceirt.

AD 836 [837]

3. A naval force of the Norsemen sixty ships strong was on the Bóinn, and another one of sixty ships on the river Life. Those two forces plundered the plain of Life and the plain of Brega, including churches, forts, and dwellings. The men of Brega routed the foreigners at Deoninne in Mugdorna of Brega, and six score of the Norsemen fell.

4. The heathens won a battle at Inber na mBárc against the Uí Néill from the Sinann to the sea, in which an uncounted number were slaughtered, though the principal kings escaped.

5. Inis Celtra was plundered by the heathens.

6. The churches of all Loch Éirne, including Cluain Eóis and Daiminis, were destroyed by the heathens.

9. Saxolb, chief of the foreigners, was killed by the Cianacht.

AD 837 [838]

9. The heathens won a battle against the Connachta, in which Mael Dúin son of Muirgius and many others fell.

AD 838 [839]

7. A raiding party of the foreigners were on Loch nEchach, and from there they plundered the states and churches of the north of Ireland.

9. The heathens won a battle against the men of Foirtriu, and Eóganán son of Aengus, Bran son of Óengus, Aed son of Boanta, and others almost innumerable fell there.

10. Ferna and Corcach were burned by the heathens.

AD 839 [840]

1. Lugbad was plundered by the heathens from Loch nEchach and they led away captive bishops and priests and scholars, and put others to death.

8. In this year below the Norsemen first came to Ireland, according to the senchus [Senchus Fer n-Alban (History of the Men of Scotland), written in the tenth century].

AD 840 [841]

1. The heathens were still on Loch nEchach.

4. There was a naval camp [longport] at Linn Duachaill from which the peoples and churches of Tethba were plundered. There was a naval camp at Duiblinn from which the Laigin and the Uí Néill were plundered, both states and churches, as far as Sliab Bladma.

AD 841 [842]

2. The heathens still at Duiblinn.

5. Mael Dúin son of Conall, king of Calatruim, was taken prisoner by the heathens.

6. Cluain Moccu Nóis was plundered by heathens from Linn Duachaill.

7. Biror and Saiger were plundered by heathens from Duiblinn.

8. A naval force of the Norsemen was on the Bóinn at Linn Rois. There was [also] a naval force of the Norsemen at Linn Sailech in Ulaid.

9. Mórán son of Indrechtach, abbot of Clochar Mac nDaiméni, was taken prisoner by the foreigners of Linn, and later died on their hands.

10. Comán, abbot of Linn Duachail, was fatally wounded and burned by heathens and Irish.

11. Dísert Diarmata was plundered by heathens from Cael Uisci.

44. THE MARTYRDOM OF BLATHMAC, 825

Walafrid Strabo (d. 849) was a Carolingian court scholar and abbot of the monastery of Reichenau. One of his works was a Latin poem on the martyrdom of the Irish warrior-aristocrat turned monk Blathmac, who joined the monastic community on Iona in order, it would seem, deliberately to seek martyrdom at the hands of Scandinavian raiders.

Source: ed. and trans. A.O. Anderson, *Early Sources of Scottish History A.D. 500 to 1286*, 2 vols. (Edinburgh: Oliver and Boyd, 1922; reprinted Stamford: Paul Watkins, 1990), vol. 1, pp. 263–65.

A certain island appears in the shores of the Picts, rising above the wave-driven sea; it is called Iona, and there the saint of the Lord, Columba, rests in the flesh. To this island came Blathmac, wishing to endure Christ's scars, because there many a pagan horde of Danes is wont to land, armed with malignant greed. And the saint of the Lord purposed in his mind [decided] to tempt these lions, and stripped his mind of empty dread; but armed with the shield of faith, and the helmet of salvation, he feared not the arms of wicked men. He might have sung with the wisdom-speaking prophet, "I have God as my helper, let base fear depart." Already too by wars of states he had been taught to despise the servants of the devil, since he had fitly overthrown their lord, and alone defeated him in all his weapons.

The time arrived, when God's great clemency disposed to associate his servant with the shining bands above the stars, and to bestow upon the good conqueror his certain crown: when the holy man's mind, foreknowing events, learned in advance by exalted sense that the approaching wolves were hastening to divide the members of the pious sheep. He said, "You, my friends, search within yourselves with active minds whether you have courage to endure suffering with me for the name of Christ; you who are able to await it, I ask to arm your manly minds; but those whose frail hearts are afraid, let them hasten their flight, to avoid the impending danger, and arm their hands in a better cause; close to us stands the experience of certain death. Let strong faith be watchful, supported by hope in the future; let the prudent precaution of flight save the weaker."

Upon these words the company was stirred, and in this mood they decided upon what they saw was possible; some, with courageous breast, to face the sacrilegious hands; and they rejoiced with tranquil minds to have submitted their heads to the violent sword: but others, not yet induced to this by their confidence of mind, took to flight by a footpath through regions known to them.

Golden dawn shone forth, parting the dewy dusk, and the brilliant sun glittered with beautiful orb, when this holy teacher, celebrating the holy service of mass, stood before the sacred altar as a calf without blemish, a pleasing offering to God, to be sacrificed by a threatening sword. The others of the company were prostrate, commending to the Thunderer [God] with tears and prayers their souls, about to depart from the burden of the flesh. See, the violent cursed host came rushing through the open buildings, threatening cruel perils to the blessed men; and after slaying with mad savagery the rest of the associates, they approached the holy father, to compel him to give up the precious metals wherein lie the holy bones of St Columba; but [the monks] had lifted the shrine from its pediments, and had placed it in the earth, in a hollowed barrow, under a thick layer of turf; because they knew then of the wicked destruction [to come]. This booty the Danes desired; but the saint remained with unarmed hand, and with unshaken purpose of mind; [he had been] trained to stand against the foe, and to arouse the fight, and [was] unused to yield[ing].

There he spoke to thee, barbarian, in words such as these: "I know nothing at all of the gold you seek, where it is concealed in the ground or in what hiding place it is concealed. And if by Christ's permission it were granted me to know it, never would our lips relate it to thy ears. Barbarian, draw thy sword, grasp the hilt, and slay; gracious God, to thy aid I commend me humbly."

Therefore the pious sacrifice was torn limb from limb. And what the fierce soldier could not purchase by gifts, he began to seek by wounds in the cold bowels [of the earth]. It is not strange, for there always were, and there always reappear, those that are spurred on by evil rage against all the servants of the Lord; so that what Christ's decision has appointed for all, this they all do for Christ, although with unequal deeds.

Thus [Blathmac] became a martyr for Christ's name; and, as rumor bears witness, he rests in the same place, and there many miracles are given for his holy merits. There the Lord is worshipped reverently with fitting honor, with the saints by whose merits I believe my faults are washed away, and to whom as a suppliant I have sent up gifts of praise. Christ refuses nothing to these – they have brought him the greatest gains – and he reigns forever with the good Father and the Holy Spirit, and is exalted without end in everlasting splendor.

45. IRISH RESISTANCE TO THE NORSEMEN

The War of the Irish against the Foreigners (Cogad Gáedel re Gallaib) *is an account of the ninth- and tenth-century Scandinavian invasions of Ireland, and of the resistance to them by the Dál Cais dynasty of Munster. It was compiled in the early twelfth century for the grandson of the famous Dál Cais king Brian Boru, whose victory over the Dublin Vikings at the battle of Clontarf in 1014 forms the climax of the work (see doc. 99). It is, therefore, a dynastic propaganda text and by no means an accurate or impartial version of events, but it remains valuable for the attitudes toward the Vikings that it presents. The first part of the work, from which the excerpts below are taken, recounts the arrival of Viking fleets in different parts of Ireland. The historicity of the "Turgeis" mentioned as the leader of a great royal fleet in section 9 is debated by scholars; some regard him as a real member of the Norwegian royal house, others as nothing more than a legend.*

Source: trans. J.H. Todd, *The War of the Gaedhil with the Gaill, or The Invasions of Ireland by the Danes and Other Norsemen* (London: Longmans, Green, Reader and Dyer, 1867), pp. 5–15.

4. It was in the time of Airtri son of Cathal, and of Aedh son of Niall, that the foreigners first began their devastation of Erinn; for it was in their time that the foreigners came into Camas ó Fothaidh Tire – namely, a hundred and twenty ships, and the country was plundered and devastated by them, and Inis Labrainn and Dairinis were burned by them. And the Eoganachts of Loch Lein gave them battle, when four hundred and sixteen men of the foreigners were killed. This was the year after that in which Diman of Aradh was killed, and ten years after the death of Airtri, son of Cathal [812].

5. There came another fleet after that – namely, in the second year after the accession to the throne of Feidhlim, son of Crimthann, and they plundered Corach, and Inis Temhni; and Bennchair, and Cluain Uamha, and Ros Maelain, were plundered by them. Scelleg Michil was also plundered by them; and they took Edgall with them into captivity, and it was by miracles he escaped, and he died of hunger and thirst with them [824].

6. There came, after that, another fleet into the north of Erinn, four years after the death of Aedh, son of Niall, at Ath-dá-Fert; and they plundered Bennchur of Uladh [Bangor], and brake the shrine of Comhgall, and killed its bishop, and its doctors, and its clergy: they devastated also the plain [Co. Down].

7. Another fleet came to Ui Cennselaigh, and they plundered Teach Munnu, and Teach Moling, and Inis Teoc. They afterwards went into Osraighe, and the country was devastated by them. The Osraighe gave them battle; and one hundred and seventy of them were killed there. [They] demolished Dun Dermuighe and Inis Eoganain, and Disert Tipraiti; and they devastated Leas Mor, and burned Cill Molaisi, and Cluan-ard Mubeoc; Lann Leri, also, and Cenn Slebhi were plundered by another party of them. [They] plundered also Sord-Colum-cilli, and Damliag Chianain, Slaini, and Orlla-saile, and Glenn-dá-Locha, and Cluain Uamha, and Mungairt, and the greater part of the churches of Erinn.

8. Another fleet came into the harbor of Luim-nech; and Corco-Baiscinn, and Tradraighe, and Ui Conaill Gabhra were plundered by them. The Ui Conaill defeated them at Senati, under Donnchadh, son of Scann-lan, king of Ui Conaill, and Niall, son of Cennfaeladh, and it is not known how many of them were slain there.

9. After that a great royal fleet came into the north of Erinn, with Turgeis, who assumed the sovereignty of the foreigners of Erinn; and the north of Erinn was plundered by them, and they spread themselves over Leth Chuinn [the northern half of Ireland]. A fleet of them also entered Loch Eathach, and another fleet entered Lughbudh, and another fleet entered Loch Rai. Moreover, Ard Macha was plundered three times in the same month by them; and Turgeis himself usurped the abbacy of Ard Macha, and Farannan, abbot of Ard Macha, and chief comharba of Patrick, was driven out, and went to Mumhain, and Patrick's shrine with him; and he was four years in Mumhain, while Turgeis was in Ard Macha, and in the sovereignty of the north of Erinn, as Berchan prophesied, chief prophet of heaven and earth, –

> Gentiles shall come over the soft sea;
> They shall confound the men of Erinn;
> Of them there shall be an abbot over every church;

Of them there shall be a king over Erinn.
Seven years shall they be; nor weak their power,
In the high sovereignty of Erinn.
In the abbacy of every church
The black Gentiles of Dubhlinn.
There shall be of them an abbot over this my church,
Who will not attend to matins;
Without Pater and without Credo;
Without Irish, but only foreign language.

Colum Cille also foretold the same thing when he said –

This fleet of Loch Rai,
By whom are magnified the Gaill-Gentiles;
Of them there shall be an abbot over Ard Macha;
It shall be the government of a usurper.

10. The old Ciaran, of Saigher, foretold also the same – namely, that Danars would three times conquer Erinn; that is, a party of them [in punishment] for the banishment of Colum Cille; a party of them for the insult to [Ciaran] himself at Tailltin; and a party for the fasting of the Apostles in Temhair. And it was said of this poet and prophet Bec-mac-De sang, as he said –

When the bell was rung in warm Tailltin,
Ciaran the Old, the wealthy, of Saigher,
Promised [to Erinn] that three times there should be
Parties of Danars of the black ships.

And now these three predictions came to pass, and the prophecies were fulfilled....

11. There came [now Turgeis, of Ard Macha, and brought] a fleet upon Loch Rai, and from thence plundered Midhe and Connacht; and Cluain Mic Nois was plundered by him, and Cluain Ferta of Brennan, and Lothra, and Tir-dá-glas, and Inis Celtra, and all the churches of Derg-dheirc, in like manner; and the place where Ota, the wife of Turgeis, used to give her audience was upon the altar of Cluain Mic Nois. The Connacht-men, however, gave them battle, in which Maelduin, son of Muirghes, royal heir apparent of Connacht, was slain.

12. After this came three score and five ships, and landed at Dubhlinn of Athcliath, and Laghin was plundered to the sea by them, and Magh Bregh.

But the Dal Riada met them in another battle, in which Eoghan, son of Oengus, king of Dal Riada was slain.

13. After this there came great sea-cast floods of foreigners into Erinn, so that there was not a point thereof without a fleet. It was by these that Bri-Gobhann was plundered, and Tressach, son of Mechill killed. A fleet came to Ciarraighe Luachra, and all was plundered by them to Cill Ita and Cuil Emhni; and the Martini of Mumhain were plundered by the fleet of Luimnech, who carried off Farannan, Comharba of Ard Macha, from Cluain Comairdi to Luimneach, and they broke Patrick's shrine.

14. It was in this year [845] that Turgeis was taken prisoner by Maelsechlainn; and he was afterwards drowned in Loch Uair, namely, in the year before the drowning of Niall Cailli, and the second year before the death of Fedhlimidh, son of Crimthann, and it was in the time of these two that all these events took place. Now, when Turgeis was killed, Farannan, abbot of Ard Macha, went out of Mumhain [to Ard Macha], and the shrine of Patrick was repaired by him....

46. FRANKS AND VIKINGS, 800–829

The Royal Frankish Annals *covers the period 741 to 829. Written at the royal Frankish court, it has been described as the single most important source for the reign of Charlemagne (768–814). It is regarded as an official court source and demonstrates detailed knowledge of contemporary events. Military activities are to the forefront, and the annals provide contemporary evidence of relations between the Carolingians and the Northmen; later entries are very well-informed on Scandinavian affairs.*

Source: trans. B.W. Scholz and B. Rogers, *Carolingian Chronicles: Royal Frankish Annals and Nithard's Histories*, (Ann Arbor: University of Michigan Press, 1970), pp. 78–125, excerpts.

800. [Charlemagne] left the palace of Aachen in the middle of March and traversed the shore of the Gallic sea. He built a fleet on this sea, which was then infested with pirates, set guards in different places, and celebrated Easter at St. Riquier in Centulum....

804. The emperor spent the winter at Aachen. But in the summer he led an army into Saxony and deported all Saxons living beyond the Elbe and in Wihmuodi [east of the Weser, near Verden] with wives and children into Francia and gave the districts beyond the Elbe to the Obodrites [a Slavic people who controlled Holstein and Mecklenburg-Schwerin].

At the same time Godofrid, king of the Danes, came with his fleet and the entire cavalry of his kingdom to Schleswig on the border of his kingdom and Saxony. He promised to show up for a conference with the emperor, but was made wary by the counsel of his men and did not venture any closer. Instead he communicated through envoys whatever he wanted to say. The emperor stayed at Hollenstedt on the River Elbe and sent an embassy to Godofrid to discuss the return of fugitives. About the middle of September he returned to Cologne. After dismissing the army he went first to Aachen and then into the Ardennes. He devoted himself to the chase and then returned to Aachen.

808. The winter was extremely mild and unhealthy at that time. When spring came, the emperor went to Nijmegen. After spending Lent and celebrating Holy Easter there, he returned again to Aachen.

Since he was informed that Godofrid, the king of the Danes, with his army had crossed over into the land of the Obodrites, he sent his son Charles with a strong host of Franks and Saxons to the Elbe, with orders to resist the mad king if he should attempt to attack the borders of Saxony. Godofrid set up quarters on the shore for some days and attacked and took a number of Slavic castles in hand-to-hand combat. Then he withdrew, suffering severe casualties. He expelled Thrasco, duke of the Obodrites, who did not trust the loyalty of his countrymen, hanged on the gallows Godelaib, another duke, whom he had caught by treachery, and made two-thirds of the Obodrites tributary. But he lost the best and battle-tested of his soldiers. With them he lost Reginold, his brother's son, who was killed at the siege of a town along with a great number of Danish nobles. But Charles, the son of the emperor, built a bridge across the Elbe, and moved the army under his command as fast as he could across the river against the Linones and Smeldingi. These tribes had also defected to Godofrid. Charles laid waste their fields far and wide and after crossing the river again returned to Saxony with his army unimpaired.

On this expedition Godofrid had as his allies the Slavs called Wilzi, who joined his forces voluntarily because of their ancient conflicts with the Obodrites. When Godofrid returned home, they also went home with the booty which they had been able to capture from the Obodrites. But Godofrid before his return destroyed a trading place on the seashore, in Danish called Reric, which, because of the taxes it paid, was of great advantage to his kingdom. Transferring the merchants from Reric he weighed anchor and came with his whole army to the harbor of Schleswig. There he remained for a few days and decided to fortify the border of his kingdom against Saxony with a rampart, so that a protective bulwark would stretch from the eastern bay, called Ostarsalt, as far as the western sea, along the entire north bank of the river Eider and broken by a single gate through which wagons and horsemen would be able to leave and enter. After dividing the work among the leaders of his troops he returned home.

809. ... When Eardwulf, king of the Northumbrians, had been taken back to his kingdom and the envoys of emperor and pontiff were returning, all crossed without mishap except one of them, the deacon Aldulf, who was captured by pirates and taken to Britain. But he was ransomed by one of King Cenwulf's men and returned to Rome....

In the meantime Godofrid, king of the Danes, sent word by some merchants that he had heard of the emperor's wrath against him because he had led an army against the Obodrites the year before and revenged himself for injuries done to him. Godofrid added that he would like to purge himself of the charges made against him and that the Obodrites had broken the peace first. He also requested that a meeting between his counts and the emperor's should take place beyond the Elbe near the borders of his kingdom. There they would establish what both parties had done and determine what redresses were to be made. This the emperor did not refuse. A conference was held with Danish nobles beyond the Elbe at Badenfliot. Both sides brought up and elaborated on a number of matters and then departed, leaving the entire question unsettled. But Thrasco, duke of the Obodrites, first surrendered his son as a hostage to Godofrid as Godofrid demanded, and then gathered an army of his people. Supported by the Saxons, he attacked the neighboring Wilzi and laid waste their fields with fire and sword. Returning home with immense booty and with even more help from the Saxons, he conquered the largest city of the Smeldingi. By these successes he forced all who had defected from him to join him again....

Since he had heard much of the arrogance and pride of the Danish king, the emperor decided to build a castle on the other side of the Elbe and to garrison it with a Frankish force. For this purpose he gathered men in Gaul and Germany equipped with arms and all other necessities, and ordered them to be taken by way of Frisia to their destination. In the meantime Thrasco, duke of the Obodrites, was treacherously killed by Godofrid's men at the trading place of Reric. When the location for the founding of a castle had been explored, the emperor appointed Count Egbert to be responsible for this matter, ordering him to cross the Elbe and to occupy the site. This place is located on the River Stör and is called Esesfelth. Egbert and the Saxon counts occupied it and began to fortify it about March 15.

810. ... While the emperor was still at Aachen, considering an expedition against King Godofrid, he received the news that a fleet of two hundred ships from Denmark had landed in Frisia, that all the islands off the coast of

Frisia had been ravaged, that the army had already landed and fought three battles against the Frisians, that the victorious Danes had imposed a tribute on the vanquished, that already one hundred pounds of silver had been paid as tribute by the Frisians, and that King Godofrid was at home. That, in fact, is how things stood. This information aroused the emperor so much that he sent out messengers everywhere to gather an army. Leaving the palace without delay, he decided first to go and meet the fleet, then to cross the Rhine at Lippeham and wait for the troops which had not yet arrived.... When the troops had finally assembled, the emperor hastened to the Aller at the greatest possible speed, set up camp where it flows into the Weser, and then waited for what would come of King Godofrid's threats. Inflated by the vain hope of victory, this king boasted that he wished to fight the emperor in open battle.

But while the emperor had his quarters in the place mentioned, news of various matters was brought to him. It was reported that the fleet which ravaged Frisia had returned home and King Godofrid had been murdered by one of his retainers; that the castle of Hohbuoki on the Elbe, with Odo, the emperor's envoy, and a garrison of east Saxons had been captured by the Wilzi; that his son Pepin, the king of Italy, had died on July 8, and that two embassies to make peace had arrived from different countries, one from Constantinople, the other from Cordova. When the emperor had received all these reports, he settled the affairs of Saxony as far as circumstances at that time permitted and returned home....

After the death of Godofrid, king of the Danes, Hemming, the son of his brother, succeeded to his throne and made peace with the emperor.

811. ... The peace announced between the emperor and Hemming, the king of the Danes, was only sworn on arms because of the severity of the winter, which closed the road for traveling between the parties. Only with the return of spring and the opening of the roads, which had been closed because of harsh frost, did twelve magnates of each party and people, that is, of Franks and Danes, meet on the River Eider at Heiligen and confirm the peace by an exchange of oaths according to their customs....

[Following a general assembly at Aachen and campaigns beyond the Elbe, in Pannonia, and Brittany] the emperor himself went to the port city of Boulogne in order to inspect the fleet whose construction he had ordered the year before. There the ships in question had assembled. At Boulogne he restored the lighthouse constructed a long time ago to guide the course of sailors and had a fire lit on its top at night. From Boulogne he came to the River Scheldt at Ghent and inspected the ships built for the same fleet. About the middle of November he came to Aachen. The envoys of King Hemming, Aowin and Hebbi, came to meet him and brought presents and assurances of peace....

812. Not much later the news arrived that Hemming, king of the Danes, had died. Sigifrid, the nephew of King Godofrid, and Anulo, the nephew of Heriold and of the former king, both wished to succeed him. Being unable to agree on who should be king, they raised troops, fought a battle, and were both killed. The party of Anulo won, however, and made his brothers Heriold and Reginfrid their kings. The defeated party of necessity had to go along with Anulo's party and did not reject the brothers as their kings. They say that ten thousand nine hundred and forty men died in that battle....

Also a fleet of the Norsemen landed in Ireland, the island of the Scots, and in a battle with the Scots many of the Norsemen were killed, and the fleet returned home after shameful flight....

Heriold and Reginfrid, kings of the Danes, sent an embassy to the emperor, asking for peace and requesting that their brother Hemming be released.

813. [A general assembly at Aachen.] From this assembly several Frankish and Saxon nobles were sent beyond the Elbe to the borders of the Norsemen. They came to make peace, at the request of the Danish kings, whose brother they intended to return. When an equal number – they were sixteen – of Danish magnates met them at the stipulated place, peace was sworn by mutual oaths and the brother of the kings was returned. The kings themselves at this time were not at home but had marched with an army toward Westarfolda [in southern Norway], an area in the extreme northwest of their kingdom across from the northern tip of Britain, whose princes and people refused to submit to them. When they returned after conquering the Britons and received their brother, who had been sent from the emperor, the sons of King Godofrid gathered troops from everywhere and made war upon the kings. The sons of King Godofrid were assisted by not a few of the Danish nobles who for some time after leaving their homeland had been in exile with the Swedes. Since hosts of their countrymen joined the sons of Godofrid from all over the land of the Danes, they easily drove the kings from the kingdom after a battle.

814. [The annals record the death of Charlemagne, the succession of Louis, and summarize diplomatic affairs.] Heriold and Reginfrid, kings of the Danes, had been defeated and expelled from their kingdom the year before by the sons of Godofrid, against whom they regrouped their forces and again made war. In this conflict Reginfrid and the oldest son of Godofrid were killed. When this had come to pass, Heriold despaired of his cause, came to the emperor, and put himself under his protection. The emperor received him and told him to go to Saxony and wait for the proper time when he would be able to give him the help which Heriold had requested.

815. The emperor commanded that Saxons and Obodrites should prepare for this campaign, and twice in that winter the attempt was made to cross the Elbe. But since the weather suddenly turned warm and made the ice on the river melt, the campaign was held up. Finally, when the winter was over, about the middle of May, the proper time for the march arrived. Then all Saxon counts and all troops of the Obodrites, under orders to bring help to Heriold, marched with the imperial emissary Baldrich across the River Eider into the land of the Norsemen called Silendi [in eastern Schleswig]. From Silendi they went on and, finally, on the seventh day, pitched camp on the coast at.... There they halted for three days. But the sons of Godofrid, who had raised against them a large army and a fleet of two hundred ships, remained on an island three miles off the shore and did not dare engage them. Therefore, after everywhere laying waste the neighboring districts and receiving hostages from the people, they returned to the emperor in Saxony, who at that time was holding the general assembly of his people at Paderborn....

817. ... Because of Heriold's persistent aggression, the sons of Godofrid, king of the Danes, also sent an embassy to the emperor, asked for peace, and promised to preserve it. This sounded more like hypocrisy than truth, so it was dismissed as empty talk and aid was given to Heriold against them....

When the news of the revolt of the Obodrites and of Sclaomir arrived, he ordered through his envoys that counts be stationed for the defense on the River Elbe to protect the borders assigned to them. The cause of the revolt was that Sclaomir was to share with Ceadrag, son of Thrasco, the royal power over the Obodrites which Sclaomir had held alone after the death of Thrasco. This matter exasperated Sclaomir so much that he solemnly declared he would never again cross the Elbe and come to the palace. He at once sent an embassy across the sea, made friends with the sons of Godofrid, and coaxed them to send an army into Saxony beyond the Elbe. Their fleet came up the Elbe as far as the castle of Esesfeld and ravaged the entire bank of the River Stör. Gluomi, commander of the Norse border, led his foot soldiers overland with the Obodrites to the same castle. But since our people offered them violent resistance, they gave up the siege of the castle and departed.

819. ... On the emperor's order Heriold was taken to his ships by the Obodrites and sailed back to his homeland to take over the kingdom. Two of the sons of Godofrid are said to have made an alliance with him to share the throne; two others were driven out of the country. But this is believed to have been done by trickery.

820. ... From the land of the Norsemen ... thirteen pirate vessels set out and tried to plunder on the shores of Flanders, but were repelled by guards. But because of the carelessness of the defenders, some wretched huts were burned down and a small number of cattle taken away. When the Norsemen made similar attempts on the mouth of the River Seine, the coast guards fought back, and the pirates retreated empty-handed after losing five men. Finally, on the coast of Aquitaine they met with success, thoroughly plundered a village by the name of Bouin, and then returned home with immense booty.

821. Everything was quiet on the Danish front in this year, and Heriold was received as partner in the rule by the sons of Godofrid. This is believed to have caused peaceful relations among them at this time....

823. ... Also Heriold came from Nordmannia, asking for help against the sons of Godofrid, who threatened to drive him out of his country. To explore this matter more thoroughly Counts Theothari and Hruodmund were sent to the sons of Godofrid. Traveling ahead of Heriold they carefully studied the dispute with the sons of Godofrid as well as the condition of the whole kingdom of the Norsemen and informed the emperor of all that they could find out in those lands. They returned with Archbishop Ebbo of Reims, who had gone to preach in the land of the Danes on the counsel of the emperor and with the approval of the Roman pontiff and had baptized many converts to the faith during the previous summer.

826. ... the emperor left Aachen in the middle of May and arrived at Ingelheim about June 1. He held an assembly there that was heavily attended, receiving and dismissing many embassies from various countries.... The envoys of the sons of Godofrid, king of the Danes, had also been sent there to make peace and clinch an alliance....

At the same time Heriold came with his wife and a great number of Danes and was baptized with his companions at St. Alban's in Mainz. The emperor presented him with many gifts before he returned home through Frisia, the route by which he had come. In this province, one county was given to him, the county of Rüstringen, so that he would be able to find refuge there with his possessions if he were ever in danger....

827. ... In the meantime the kings of the Danes, that is, the sons of Godofrid, deprived Heriold of his share in the kingship and forced him to leave Nordmannia....

828. ... Near the border of Nordmannia in the meantime negotiations were planned to ratify the peace between Norsemen and Franks and to discuss the affair of Heriold. For this business counts and margraves came from almost all of Saxony. But Heriold was too thirsty for action. He broke the peace that had been agreed upon and confirmed by hostages, and burned and pillaged some small villages of the Norsemen. Upon hearing this the sons of Godofrid immediately gathered troops. Our people were stationed on the bank of the River Eider, not expecting any trouble. The sons of Godofrid advanced toward the march, crossed the river, and attacked the Franks, driving them out of their castle and putting them to flight. They took everything from them and retreated with all their forces to their camp. Then they deliberated how to ward off revenge for this action. They dispatched an embassy to the emperor and explained that need had compelled them against their will to do this, that they were now ready to give satisfaction, and that it was entirely up to the emperor how amends should be made in order to preserve the peace between the two parties....

829. ... The emperor, delayed by various affairs, remained at Aachen until July 1. He finally decided to depart with his retinue for the general assembly to be held at Worms in August. But before he left he received the news that the Norseman planned to invade Saxony on the far side of the Elbe and that their army was approaching our borders. On hearing this he sent into all parts of Francia, ordering the general levy of his people to follow him as fast as they could to Saxony. He announced at the same time that he planned to cross the Rhine at Neuss about the middle of July.... But when he found out that the rumor about the Norsemen was false, he came to Worms in the middle of August, as had been planned before....

47. THE NORTHMEN IN FRANCE, 843–865

The Annals of St-Bertin *covers the years 830 to 882 and is an important source for the ninth-century Carolingian world. This set of annals was produced in the 830s as a court chronicle under Louis the Pious and was later continued by Prudentius of Troyes and Hincmar of Rheims. This selection illustrates the scope and intensity of Viking activities on the Continent, as well as the responses of Carolingian kings, local rulers, and even peasants.*

Source: trans. Janet L. Nelson, *The Annals of St-Bertin. Ninth-century histories*, vol. 1, (Manchester and New York: Manchester University Press, 1991), pp. 55–129, excerpts.

843. Northmen pirates attacked Nantes, slew the bishop and many clergy and lay people of both sexes, and sacked the *civitas* [city]. Then they attacked the western parts of Aquitaine to devastate them too. Finally they landed on a certain island [probably Noirmoutier], brought their households over from the mainland and decided to winter there in something like a permanent settlement.

844. The Northmen sailed up the Garonne as far as Toulouse, wreaking destruction everywhere, without meeting any opposition. Then some of them withdrew from there and attacked Galicia, but they perished, partly because they met resistance from missile-throwers, partly because they were caught in a storm at sea. Some of them, though, got to the south-western part of Spain, where they fought long and bitterly with the Saracens, but were finally beaten and withdrew to their ships.

845. A very hard winter. In March, 120 ships of the Northmen sailed up the Seine to Paris, laying waste everything on either side and meeting not the least bit of opposition. Charles [the Bald] made efforts to offer some resistance, but realized that his men could not possibly win. So he made a deal with them: by handing over to them 7,000 lb [of silver] as a bribe, he restrained them from advancing further and persuaded them to go away....

Horic, king of the Northmen, sent 600 ships up the Elbe in Germany against Louis [the German]. The Saxons opposed them, and when battle was joined, by the help of our Lord Jesus Christ, emerged victorious. The Northmen went away from there, and attacked and captured a certain *civitas* of the Slavs [possibly Hamburg]....

The Northmen went back down the Seine to the open sea. Then they devastated all the coastal regions, plundering and burning. God in his goodness and justice, so much offended by our sins, had thus worn down the lands and kingdoms of the Christians. Nevertheless, so that the pagans should no longer go unpunished in falsely accusing the most all-powerful and most provident Lord of improvidence and even powerlessness, when they were going away in ships loaded with booty from a certain monastery [St. Germain] which they had sacked and burned, they were struck down by divine judgment either with blindness or insanity, so severely that only a very few escaped to tell the rest about the might of God. It is said that their king Horic was so disturbed when he heard about this that he sent envoys to King Louis for peace talks, and was ready to release all the captives and make every effort to restore the stolen treasures....

The Danes, who had ravaged Aquitaine the year before, returned and attacked Saintonge. They won the fight, and settled down there to stay quietly for a while.

846. Danish pirates went to Frisia, extracted as large a tribute as they wanted and then fought a battle which they won. As a result they gained control of the whole province....

847. The Danes came to the western region of Gaul where the Bretons live, defeated them in three battles, and completely overpowered them. Nominoë [leader of the Bretons], beaten, fled with his men; later he softened up the Danes with bribes and got them out of his territories....

The Irish, who had been attacked by the Northmen for a number of years, were made into regular tribute-payers. The Northmen also got control of the islands all around Ireland, and stayed there without encountering any resistance from anyone....

Danes attacked and plundered the coastal regions of Aquitaine. They laid siege to the town of Bordeaux for a long time. Another group of Danes occupied and took possession of the *emporium* [trading center, market town] called Dorestad and the island of Betuwe [just south of Dorestad].

848. Charles attacked the contingent of Northmen who were besieging Bordeaux and manfully defeated them.... In Aquitaine some Jews betrayed Bordeaux to the Danes: having taken the town, they ravaged and burned it.

850. Horic, king of the Northmen, was attacked by two of his nephews and war ensued. The nephews were induced to make peace by a partition of the realm. Roric, the nephew of Harald, who had recently defected from Lothar, raised whole armies of Northmen with a vast number of ships and laid waste Frisia and the island of Betuwe and other places in that neighborhood by sailing up the Rhine and the Waal. Lothar, since he could not crush Roric, received him into his allegiance and granted him Dorestad and other counties. Another band of Northmen plundered the inhabitants of Mempisc, Thérouanne and other coastal districts, while yet others attacked the island of Britain....

851. ... Danish pirates ravaged Frisia and the inhabitants of Betuwe. Running amok right up to the monastery of St-Bavo which they call Ghent, they burned the monastery and then after reaching Rouen they proceeded on foot as far as Beauvais which they burned. On their way back, they were

intercepted by our forces and some of them were killed [these events are dated to 852 by other sources].

852. Godefrid, son of Harald the Dane who had once been baptized at Mainz in the emperor Louis's time [826], now defected from Lothar and took himself off to his own people. He collected a strong force from among them, and attacked Frisia with a large number of ships, then went to the area around the River Scheldt, and finally to the Seine. Lothar and Charles came up to meet him with their whole army, and blockaded him from either bank of the Seine.

853. During this blockade they celebrated Christmas. But the men in Charles's contingent did not want to fight, so he had to withdraw having achieved no advantage at all. Charles got Godefrid to make peace with him on certain agreed conditions. But the rest of the Danes settled down there right through March without needing to feel the least anxiety: they ravaged, burned and took captives all the more savagely for being completely unrestrained....

In July the Danes left the Seine and went to the Loire where they sacked the town of Nantes and the monastery of St-Florent and its neighborhood....

On 8 November Danish pirates from Nantes heading further inland brazenly attacked the town of Tours and burned it, along with the church of St-Martin, and other neighboring places. But because the attack had been known about beforehand with complete certainty, the body of St-Martin had already been taken away to the monastery of Cormery and the treasures of his church to the *civitas* of Orléans.

854. The Danes stayed on the Loire. They sailed up as far as the stronghold of Blois which they burned. Their aim was to reach Orléans and wreak the same havoc there. But Bishop Agius of Orléans and Bishop Burchard of Chartres got ready ships and warriors to resist them; so the Danes gave up their plan and headed back to the lower waters of the Loire. Other Danish pirates also laid waste the part of Frisia next door to Saxony.

The Danes fought amongst themselves in a civil war. They battled like madmen in a terribly stubborn conflict lasting three days. When King Horic and other kings with him had been slain, almost the entire nobility perished too. Pirates of the Northmen came up the Loire again and burned the *civitas* of Angers.

855. Lothar gave the whole of Frisia to his son Lothar, whereupon Roric and Godefrid headed back to their native Denmark in the hope of gaining royal power....

The Northmen attacked Bordeaux, a *civitas* in Aquitaine, and moved about all over the countryside at will....

The Northmen sailed up the Loire. They left their ships and tried to reach Poitiers on foot. But the Aquitanians came up to meet them and beat them so soundly that hardly more than 300 of them escaped. Roric and Godefrid, on whom success had not smiled, remained based at Dorestad and held sway over most of Frisia.

856. On 18 April, Danish pirates came to Orléans, sacked it and went away again without meeting any opposition....

In mid-August, other Danish pirates again sailed up the Seine. They ravaged and plundered the *civitates*, monasteries and *villae* [farms] on both banks of the river, and even some *civitates* further away. Then they chose a place on the bank of the Seine called Jeufosse, an excellent defensive site for a base camp, and there they quietly passed the winter.

857. On 28 December [856] Danish pirates attacked Paris and burned it. Those pirates who were based in the region of the lower Loire sacked Tours and all the surrounding districts as far as the stronghold of Blois....

The Danes who were coming up the Seine ravaged everything unchecked. They attacked Paris where they burned the church of Sts-Peter and Genevieve and all the other churches except for the cathedral of St-Stephen, the Church of Sts-Vincent and Germain and also the church of St-Denis: a great ransom was paid in cash to save these churches from being burned. Other Danes stormed the *emporium* called Dorestad and ravaged the whole island of Betuwe and other neighboring districts....

As the Danes attacked his *civitas*, Frotbald bishop of Chartres fled on foot and tried to swim across the river Eure but he was overwhelmed by the waters and drowned.

858. Bjørn, chief of one group of the pirates on the Seine, came to King Charles at the palace of Verberie, gave himself into his hands and swore fidelity after his own fashion. Another group of those pirates captured Abbot Louis of St-Denis along with his brother Gauzlin, and demanded a very heavy fine for their ransom. In order to pay this many church treasuries in Charles's realm were drained dry, at the king's command. But even all this was far from being enough: to bring it up to the required amount, large sums were eagerly contributed also by the king, and by all the bishops, abbots, counts and other powerful men....

The Danes attacked Saxony but they were repulsed....

In July, King Charles came to the island of Oissel in the Seine [just south of Rouen], to besiege the Danes ensconced there. There the Young Charles, his son, arrived from Aquitaine and along with him came Pippin, now a layman.... In August too, King Lothar hastened to that same island of Oissel, to bring help to his uncle. They stayed there till 23 September, without making any progress in the siege. Then they went home....

859. The Danes ravaged the places beyond the Scheldt. Some of the common people living between the Seine and the Loire formed a sworn association amongst themselves, and fought bravely against the Danes on the Seine. But because their association had been made without due consideration, they were easily slain by our more powerful people....

Danish pirates made a long sea-voyage, sailed through the straits between Spain and Africa and then up the Rhône. They ravaged some *civitates* and monasteries, and made their base on an island called the Camargue....

Danes launched new attacks [in the autumn], and laid waste, by firing and plundering, the monastery of St-Valery [sur-Somme], the *civitas* of Amiens, and other places round about. Others of them also attacked with the same fury the island in the Rhine called Betuwe.

Those who were still on the Seine made a night attack on the *civitas* of Noyon. They took captive Bishop Immo along with other nobles, both clerics and laymen, and after laying waste the *civitas* carried the prisoners off with them and slew them on their march. Two months earlier, they had also killed Ermenfrid bishop of Beauvais at a certain *villa*, and the previous year they had slain Baltfrid, bishop of Bayeux.

For fear of those same Danes, the bones of the blessed martyrs Denis, Rusticus, and Eleutherius were removed to Nogent [sur-Seine], one of the *villae* belonging to St-Denis in the Morvois district. There on 21 September the bones were reverently placed in reliquaries.

860. King Charles, deceived by the empty promises of the Danes on the Somme, ordered a tax to be levied on the treasures of the churches and on all *mansi* [small farms] and on traders – even very small-scale ones: even their houses and all their equipment were assessed so that the tribute could be levied on them. For the Danes had promised that if 3,000 lb of silver, weighed out under careful inspection, were handed over to them, they would turn and attack those Danes who were busy on the Seine and would either drive them away or kill them....

The Danes on the Somme, since the above-mentioned tribute was not paid to them, received hostages, and then sailed over to attack the Anglo-Saxons by whom, however, they were defeated and driven off. They then made for other parts. The Danes who were still on the Rhône got as far as the city of Valence, ravaging as they went. There they destroyed everything around, and then returned to the island on which they had made their base....

The Danes who had been on the Rhône made for Italy, where they took Pisa and other *civitates*, sacked them and laid them waste.

861. In January, the Danes burned Paris and with it the church of Sts-Vincent the Martyr and Germain the Confessor. Also, traders who were fleeing back up the Seine by ship were chased and captured. Other Danish pirates came to the district of Thérouanne and ravaged it....

The Danes had lately come back from the English and burned Thérouanne. Under Weland's command, they now sailed up the Seine with over 200 ships, and besieged the fort built by the Northmen on the island of Oissel with those Northmen inside it too. To support the besiegers, Charles ordered a levy to be raised from his realm to bring in 5,000 lb of silver and a large amount of livestock and corn, so that the realm should not be looted....

Meanwhile the other group of Danes with sixty ships sailed up the Seine and into the *Tellas* and from there they reached those who were besieging the fort, and joined up with them. The besieged were forced by starvation, filth, and general misery to pay the besiegers 6,000 lb made up of gold and silver and to make an alliance with them. So they sailed away down the Seine as far as the sea. But they were prevented from putting out to sea by the winter now coming on. So they split up according to their brotherhoods [possibly kin-groups] into groups allocated to various ports, from the sea-coast right up to Paris. Weland with his company came up the Seine to the fort of Melun. Former occupants of the besieged fort, with Weland's son, now occupied the monastery of St-Maur-des-Fossés.

862. ... Charles arrived at Senlis, where he waited, expecting the people to assemble there so that troops could be positioned along both banks of certain rivers, namely the Oise, Marne, and Seine, and defensive measures taken to stop the Northmen from coming up to plunder. But Charles now received word that a select force of Danes, picked from amongst those encamped at Fossés, was making for Meaux with a few ships. Charles made all speed in that direction with those men whom he had with him. But he could not catch up with them, because the bridges had been destroyed and the ships taken over by the Northmen. He therefore followed some indispensable advice and rebuilt the bridge across to the island by Trilbardou, thereby cutting the Northmen's access to the way down the river. He also assigned squadrons to guard both banks of the Marne. The Northmen, now tightly hemmed in by

these moves, gave hostages chosen by Charles, and on his orders: the conditions were that they should return without any delay all the captives they had taken since sailing up the Marne, and either, on some prearranged assembly-date, should withdraw from the Seine with the other Northmen, and should seek the open sea, or, if the others would not withdraw with them, should unite with Charles's army to attack those who refused to go. Thus, when ten hostages had been given, they were allowed to return to their own people. About twenty days later, Weland himself came to Charles and commended himself to him, while he and the men he had with him swore solemn oaths in their own way. Then he returned to the ships and with the whole Danish fleet sailed down the Seine to Jumièges, where they decided to repair their ships and await the Spring equinox. When the ships had been repaired, the Danes made for the open sea, and split up into several flotillas which sailed off in different directions according to their various choices. Most of them made for the Bretons, who live in Neustria with Salomon as chief; and these Danes were joined by the ones who had been in Spain. Salomon hired twelve Danish ships for an agreed fee, to use against Robert. These Robert captured on the river Loire and slew every man in the fleet, except for a few who fled into hiding. Robert, unable now to put up with Salomon any longer, made an alliance against Salomon with the Northmen who had just left the Seine, before Salomon could ally with them against him. Hostages were exchanged, and Robert paid them 6,000 lb of silver.

Weland with his wife and sons came to Charles, and he and his family became Christians.

... Charles caused all the leading men of his realm to assemble about 1 June, with many workmen and carts, at the place called Pîtres, where the Andelle from one side and the Eure from the other flow into the Seine [Pont-de-l'Arche, dep. Eure]. By constructing fortifications on the Seine, he closed it off to ships sailing up or down the river. This was done because of the Northmen....

863. In January Danes sailed up the Rhine toward Cologne, after sacking the *emporium* called Dorestad and also a fairly large *villa* at which the Frisians had taken refuge, and after slaying many Frisian traders and taking captive large numbers of people. Then they reached a certain island near the fort of Neuss [near Xanten]. Lothar came up and attacked them with his men along one bank of the Rhine and the Saxons along the other and they encamped there until about the beginning of April. The Danes therefore followed Roric's advice and withdrew by the same way they had come....

[After 25 October] two Northmen who had recently left their ships with Weland and come asking to be baptized as Christians now revealed – and it afterwards turned out to be true – that this had been a trick, and they accused Weland of bad faith. So, according to the custom of their people, one of the Northmen challenged him to single combat in King Charles's presence, and killed him in the fight.

Meanwhile he [King Charles] received news that the Northmen had come to Poitiers, and though the city was ransomed, they had burned the church of the great confessor Saint Hilary....

864. Charles arranged his troops and ordered the Aquitanians to advance against the Northmen who had burned the church of St-Hilary....

The Northmen got to Clermont where they slew Stephen, son of Hugh, and a few of his men, and then returned unpunished to their ships. Pippin, son of Pippin [II, king of Aquitaine], who had changed back from being a monk to become a layman and an apostate, joined company with the Northmen and lived like one of them [he was later captured and executed].

Lothar, son of Lothar, raised 4 *denarii* [denarius, a silver coin] from every manse in his whole kingdom, and handed over the sum in cash, plus a large quantity of flour and livestock and also wine and cider, to the Northman Rodulf, son of Harald, and his men, all this being termed a payment for service [these were probably the Northmen who sailed up the Rhine in 863]....

Northmen sailed to Flanders with a large fleet, but when they met with resistance from the local people, they sailed up the Rhine and laid waste the neighboring regions of the kingdoms of Lothar and Louis on both banks of the river....

... Then Charles ordered fortifications to be constructed there [at Pîtres] on the Seine to prevent the Northmen from coming up the river....

Robert, count of Anjou, fought against two companies of Northmen who were based on the Loire. Of one, he slew every man, except for a few who got away; the other larger group attacked from behind, and Robert was wounded, and having lost a few of his men, he decided to withdraw....

865. ... Northmen based on the Loire made their way up the river with a favorable wind, divine judgment thus making it easy for them, to launch a full-scale attack. They reached the monastery of St-Benedict known as Fleury and burned it. On their way back they burned Orléans and the monasteries both in the *civitas* and round it, except for the church of the Holy Cross which, despite great efforts on the part of the Northmen, the flames proved unable to consume. So they sailed back down the river and after ravaging all the neighboring districts they returned to their base....

From Attigny [in mid-July] Charles marched to resist the Northmen who had sailed up the Seine with fifty ships....

The Northmen on the Loire made their way on foot to Poitiers without meeting any resistance, burned the *civitas* and returned to their ships unscathed. But Robert slew more than 500 of these Northmen based on the Loire, without losing any of his own men, and sent to Charles the standards and weapons captured from the Northmen.

Charles, for his part, came up to the place called Pîtres where the Northmen still were. Now there were bridges over the Oise and the Marne at two places called Auvers and Charenton, but the local people who had built them long ago could not repair them because of the attacks of the Northmen. On the advice of his faithful men, Charles therefore ordered these bridges to be repaired by men drafted from more distant regions to perform labor services in order to complete the fortifications on the Seine, but on condition that this was treated as a special case of urgent need and that the men who would now repair these bridges should never at any future time suffer any disadvantage through performing labor services on this particular job. Guards were assigned to keep watch on both banks of the Seine. Then in mid–September, Charles moved to the *villa* of Orville to do some hunting. But the guards still had not taken up their positions on this [the east] bank of the Seine, so those Northmen dispatched about 200 of their number to Paris to get wine. Failing to find what they sought there, they came back to their people who had sent them, without suffering any losses. More than 500 of them planned to advance from there beyond the Seine to sack Chartres, but they were attacked by the troops guarding the west bank of the Seine and after losing some men killed and some wounded, they retreated to their ships....

[Charles] received news [while en route from Cologne to Quierzy] ... that on the 18 October, Northmen had got into the monastery of St-Denis, where they stayed for about twenty days, carrying off booty from the monastery to their ships each day, and after much plundering without encountering resistance from anyone at all, they returned to their camp not far from the monastery.

Meanwhile Northmen on the Loire joined forces with Bretons and attacked Le Mans. They sacked it without opposition, and sent back to their ships. The Aquitanians fought with Northmen based on the Charente under their leader Sigfrid, and slew about 400 of them: the rest fled back to their ships.

48. THE ANNALS OF ST-VAST, 882–886

The Annals of St-Vast, written at that monastery near Corbie, are an important window into the events of the late ninth century. The entries for this period are particularly concerned with the activities of the Northmen and recount the siege of Paris by the Vikings in 885–86; they may be compared with Abbo's poem on this event (see doc. 49).

Source: trans. P.E. Dutton, *Carolingian Civilization: A Reader*, 2nd ed. (Peterborough, ON: Broadview Press, 2004), pp. 507–512.

882. The [eastern] Franks raised an army against the Northmen, but at once turned and ran, and there Walo, the bishop of Metz, died. The Danes set that most famous palace of Aachen on fire [and also] some monasteries. They also set cities on fire – the most noble city of Trier and Cologne – also the palace of kings and villas, with the inhabitants of the place having been killed. The emperor Charles [the Fat] raised a huge army against them and besieged them at Elslo [in the Netherlands]. King Godefrid came over to [Charles] and the emperor gave him the kingdom of the Frisians which Rorik the Dane once held. He gave Gisela, the daughter of King Lothar [II by Waldrada] to him in marriage and he made the Northmen depart from his kingdom.

King Louis [III, of west Francia] sought out the Northmen on the Loire and hoped to eject them from his kingdom and to receive Hasting as his friend, which he did....

In the month of October the Northmen established themselves at Condé and bitterly ruined the kingdom of Carloman. King Carloman and his army resided on the Somme at Barleux, but the Northmen did not stop their robbery and all the inhabitants of that place who remained fled to the other side of the Somme. Whence with their forces making a trip through La Thiéarche they crossed over the Oise. King Carloman pursued them and he caught up with them at Avaux. A battle broke out and the Franks were superior; almost a thousand Northmen died there. But this battle in no way tamed them. Carloman went to the palace of Compiègne, while the Northmen took to their boats and returned to Condé. From there they devastated with fire and sword the entire kingdom up to the Oise. Defenses were pulled down, monasteries and churches were demolished, and the servants of the [Christian] religion were killed by the sword or by hunger or they were sold abroad, and the inhabitants of the countryside were killed. No one resisted them.

Abbot Hugh [of St-Martin of Tours], hearing of these things, raised an army and came to the king. The Northmen were returning from the region of Beauvais where they had been plundering. Hugh and the king chased them into the woods of Vicogne [near Condé], but the Northmen scattered here and there and, few of them having been killed, they returned to their ships....

883. Fulk, an admirable man in all things, succeeded Hincmar in the episcopal see [of Rheims]. After this the Northmen set the monastery and church of Saint Quentin afire. At the same time they set fire to the church of the Mother of God in the city of Arras. Again Carloman pursued the Northmen, but he did nothing either successful or useful [against them]. At this time Rotgarius, the bishop of Beauvais, died and was succeeded by Honoratus. In the springtime the Northmen departed from Condé and sought out lands along the sea. Returning there through the summer, they forced the Flemings to flee from their own lands. All around they furiously laid waste to things with their swords and with fire. Around autumn, in order to protect the kingdom, King Carloman established his army in the region of Vithmau at the villa of Miannay [near Abbeville] opposite to Lavier. At the end of October the Northmen came to Lavier with cavalry and infantry and supplies. Ships also entered the Somme by the sea and forced the king and all his army to flee and made them pass over the Oise. Then the Northmen prepared to winter at the city of Amiens. Next, with no one resisting them, they devastated all the land up to the Seine and around the Oise and they burned both the monasteries and churches of Christ. Then the Franks, seeing that things grew ever better for the Northmen, sent a certain Christian Dane by the name of Sigfried, who carefully worked to save the kingdom, to [the Northmen]. He came to Beauvais and then proceeded to Amiens to do the business enjoined upon him.

884. Then Engelwin, the bishop of Paris, died and Abbot Gauzelin replaced him. The Northmen did not stop from capturing and killing Christians or from destroying churches, pulling down fortifications, or putting villas to fire. The corpses of clerics, laymen, nobles, women, young people and children were lying in every street. There was no street or place in which the dead did not lie and lamentation and sadness filled everyone, seeing that Christians were massacred.

Meanwhile, because the king was still a young man, all the magnates gathered in Compiègne to determine what they should do. After they had discussed the matter, they sent Sigfried, the Danish Christian, who was loyal to the king and the nephew of Rorik, [to the Northmen]. He was supposed to deal with the chiefs of his people to see if they would accept tribute and leave the kingdom. He undertook to fulfill the assignment given to him and went to Amiens. [There] he repeated his mission to the chiefs of his people who were present. After a lengthy discussion, delayed in part by much back and forth activity, by repeating now these things, now those, in the end [the Northmen] imposed on the king and the Franks a tribute of 12,000 pounds of silver calculated according to their way of weighing things. Once hostages had been exchanged, those who lived beyond the Oise began to feel safer. Thus from the day of the Purification of Saint Mary [2 February] until the month of October [884] this freedom from attack was granted to them.

But the Northmen, raiding as usual beyond the Scheldt, devastated with fire and sword churches, monasteries, cities and villages, and slaughtered people. After holy Easter [19 April] the [people] began to pay the tribute. Churches and church properties were ruthlessly stripped [of wealth]. Finally, when the tribute had been paid, the Franks gathered together to resist the Northmen in case they intended to break their agreement. The Northmen burned down their camps and withdrew from Amiens. The king and the Franks pursued them on a slow march beyond the Oise. The Danes on their journey came to Boulogne-sur-Mer and there deliberated what they should do. A group of them crossed the sea, another group came to Louvain in the kingdom that once belonged to Lothar and there they set up camps in order to spend the winter. The Franks who were with Carloman returned to their own land; a few young men remained with him to hunt in the Bezu forest [where he was killed in a hunting accident].

885. The emperor Charles, having received the news [of Lothar's death], made a rapid march and came to Ponthion, and there all the men who lived in Carloman's kingdom came to him and placed themselves under his rule. Thus the emperor Charles returned to his own land, ordering those who lived in the kingdom [that was formerly] Carloman's to proceed to Louvain to fight the Northmen. On the agreed upon day both armies came together at that place, except Abbot Hugh, who held back from this outing because of a foot ailment. But [these armies] accomplished nothing successful there, and returned to their own lands in great shame. The Danes laughed at the Franks who came from Carloman's kingdom: "So why did you come to [see] us? It was not necessary. We know how you are and [what] you want, so let us visit you. Let us do that [for you]."

At the same time [in May] Godefrid the Dane, because he was undertaking to break his pledge with the crafty help of his vassal, Gerulf [of Frisia], was killed by Duke Henry.... On the eight Kalends of July [24 June] [the Northmen] with their entire army entered Rouen and the Franks pursued them to the same place. Since their ships had still not come there, they crossed the Seine in ships found along the river and then they fortified a camp there. While this was taking place, all those who lived in Neustria and Burgundy assembled and, when an army had been raised, they approached as if to make war upon the Northmen. But, though they should have fought, [when] Ragnold, the duke of Le Mans, fell with a few of his men, they all returned to their own lands in great sadness, having accomplished nothing useful.

Then the Northmen began to rage with fire and to thirst for slaughter. They killed and captured Christians, demolished churches, and no one resisted them. Once again the Franks prepared themselves to resist, not in war, but rather by constructing fortifications to impede the progress of their ships. They constructed a castle on the river Oise at a place [now] called Pontoise, and they entrusted Aletramnus with guarding it. Bishop Gauzelin built fortifications at Paris. But in the month of November, the Northmen set out upon the Oise and surrounded with a blockade the castle at Pontoise. They stopped those who were shut up in the castle from drawing water from the river, for they had no other water to draw upon. But those who were in the castle began to be pressed by their lack of water. Need I say more? They sued for peace, seeking only to leave there alive. Once hostages were exchanged on both sides, Aletramnus and his men set out for Beauvais. The Northmen set fire to the castle and stole everything that was left there, for those who abandoned the castle left everything there except for their arms and horses. It was under this condition that they had been allowed to leave.

Wildly excited by their victory, the Northmen approached Paris and, with great energy immediately attacked a tower. They thought that they could take it without any great delay, because it was not yet fully strengthened. But Christians defended it with great vigor and the battle lasted from morning till evening. Night interrupted the battle and so the Northmen, that night, returned to their ships [26 November]. Bishop Gauzelin and Count Odo labored all through the night with their men to fortify the tower in preparation for [the coming] battle. The following day [27 November] the Northmen again rushed back to the battle at the same tower and a fierce battle went on until sunset. But the Danes, having lost many men, returned to their ships. Then they set up a camp for themselves opposite the city and they laid siege to the city, constructed machines [of war], employed fire, and used all their ingenuity to capture the city. But the Christians fighting bravely against them were superior in everything.

886. On the eighth Ides of February [6 February] a grave crisis arose for the inhabitants of the city, since a very serious rise in the water level of the river smashed the smaller bridge [running to the south from the Ile de la Cité].

When the bishop learned of this event, he selected some strong and noble men to guard the tower that night so that, in the morning, they might restore the bridge. None of this was hidden to the Northmen. They rose before dawn with all their men and rushed to that tower and laid siege to it and they began to attack before help from the city could arrive. Those men in the tower resisted bravely and the shouting of the multitude [of them] lifted up to heaven. The bishop stood on the wall of the city with everyone who was in the city crying intensely because they could not come to the assistance of their people and because there was nothing they could do [to help]. [Gauzelin] entrusted them to Christ's care. The Northmen approached the gate of that tower in [full] force and tried to set fire to it. Those men inside the tower, worn down by wounds and defeated by fire, and to the dishonor of Christians, were killed in various ways and their bodies were flung into the river. Then the Northmen demolished the tower. After these things [had occurred], they did not cease their attack upon the city.

The bishop's heart was broken over this grave loss. He sent letters to Count Herkenger [of Melun], commanding him to go as quickly as he could to eastern Francia and to search out Henry, the duke of Austrasia, so that he might come to the assistance of the bishop and the Christian people [as a whole]. What was commanded, Herkenger at once carried out and he convinced Henry with his army to come to Paris, but Henry accomplished nothing there and returned to his own territory. But Gauzelin, who was anxious to help his Christian people in every way, reached a cordial understanding with Sigfried, the king of the Danes, to free [Paris] from the siege.

While these things were taking place, the bishop fell gravely ill, died [on 16 April] and was buried in the city. His death was not a secret to the Northmen who, before the fact was known to the citizens [of Paris], shouted from outside the city that he was dead. The people, touched by the death of their bishop and by the siege, were immensely depressed, but the illustrious Count Odo fortified them with his encouraging words. Nevertheless the Northmen daily attacked the city and many people on both sides were killed, many were laid low with wounds, and food began to grow scarce in the city.

Then [on 12 May] Hugh, the venerable abbot, died and was buried in the monastery of Saint German of Auxerre. But Odo, seeing the people fall into despair, went out of the city secretly to seek help from the chief man of the kingdom and to send word to the emperor that Paris would soon perish if it did not receive assistance. Returning to Paris after his absence, Odo discovered a great deal of sadness, but he did not enter the city without an astonishing incident, for the Northmen, knowing in advance of his return, blocked off the gate of the tower to him. But even with his horse dead, Odo slashed at his enemies left and right and, entering the city, made his sad people happy. No one can count the dead, what dangers they faced there, how many thousands of people on both sides fell there in various skirmishes. For, without any cessation, those [warriors] struck that city with a varying complement of arms, machines [of war], and battering rams. But with great persistence they begged God [for help] and were delivered. But in the eight or so months before the emperor could come to [Paris], the struggle continued in various ways.

49. AN ACCOUNT OF THE SIEGE OF PARIS, 885–886

Abbo was a monk of St-Germain-des-Prés near Paris and wrote a Latin poem about the Norse assaults on Paris in 885–86 and 896.

Source: trans. F.A. Ogg, *A Source Book for Mediaeval History: Documents Illustrative of European Life and Institutions from the German Invasions to the Renaissance* (New York: American Book Company, 1908), pp. 168–71; revised by P.E. Dutton, *Carolingian Civilization: A Reader*, 2nd ed. (Peterborough, ON: Broadview Press, 2004), pp. 514–16.

885. [The Northmen] came to Paris with 700 sailing ships, not counting those of smaller size which are commonly called barques. At one stretch the Seine was lined with the vessels for more than two leagues, so that one might ask in astonishment in what cavern the river had been swallowed up, for nothing was visible there, since ships covered that [river] as if with oak trees, elms, and alders. On the second day after the fleet of the Northmen arrived under the walls of the city, Sigfried, who was then king only in name but who was in command of the expedition, came to the dwelling of the illustrious bishop. He bowed his head and said: "Gauzelin, have compassion on yourself and on your flock. We beseech you to listen to us, in order that you may escape death. Allow us only the freedom of the city. We will do no harm and we will see to it that whatever belongs either to you or to Odo shall be strictly respected." Count Odo, who later became king, was then the defender of the city. The bishop replied to Siegfried, "Paris has been entrusted to us by the Emperor Charles, who, after God, king and lord of the powerful, rules over almost all the world. He has put it in our care, not at all that the kingdom may be ruined by our misconduct, but that he may keep it and be assured of its peace. If, like us, you had been given the duty of defending these walls, and if you should have done that which you ask us to do, what treatment do you think you would deserve?" Siegfried replied, "I should deserve that my head be cut off and thrown to the dogs. Nevertheless, if you do not listen to my demand, on the morrow our war machines will

destroy you with poisoned arrows. You will be the prey of famine and of pestilence and these evils will renew themselves perpetually every year." So saying, he departed and gathered together his comrades.

In the morning the Northmen, boarding their ships, approached the tower and attacked it. [The tower blocked access to the city by the so-called Great Bridge, which connected the right bank of the Seine with the island on which the city was built. The tower stood on the present site of the Châtelet.] They shook it with their engines and stormed it with arrows. The city resounded with clamor, the people were aroused, the bridges trembled. All came together to defend the tower. There Odo, his brother Robert, and the Count Ragenar distinguished themselves for bravery; likewise the courageous Abbot Ebolus, the nephew of the bishop. A keen arrow wounded the prelate, while at his side the young warrior Frederick was struck by a sword. Frederick died, but the old man, thanks to God, survived. For many this was their last moment of life, but they inflicted bitter blows on many of the enemy. At last the enemy withdrew, carrying off a vast number of Danish dead. Now Apollo, having followed Olympus, turned toward the west, to further Thule and the southern regions [i.e., the evening came].

No longer did the tower appear as fine as it once did, but its conditions were still solid and it delighted a little in the windows that had been opened up to the sun. The people spent the night repairing the holes with boards. By the next day, on the old citadel had been erected a new tower of wood, a half higher than the former one. In the morning the sun and the Danes fell on the tower together. They engaged the [Christians] in violent skirmishes. On every side arrows sped and blood flowed. With the arrows mingled the stones hurled by slings and war-machines; the air was filled with them. The tower which had been built during the night groaned under the strokes of the darts, the city shook with the struggle, the people ran hither and thither, the bells jangled. The warriors rushed together to defend the tottering tower and to repel the fierce assault.

Among these warriors two, a count and an abbot [Ebolus], surpassed all the rest in courage. The former was the redoubtable Odo who never experienced defeat and who continually revived the spirits of the worn-out defenders. He ran along the ramparts and hurled back the enemy. On those who were secreting themselves so as to undermine the tower he poured oil, wax, and pitch, which, being mixed and heated, burned the Danes and tore off their scalps. Some of them died; others threw themselves into the river to escape the awful substance....

Meanwhile Paris was suffering not only from the sword outside but also from a pestilence within which brought death to many noble men. Within the walls there was not ground in which to bury the dead.... Odo, the future king, was sent to Charles, emperor of the Franks, to implore help for the stricken city.

One day Odo, powerful with his arms, suddenly appeared on Montmartre in splendor in the midst of three bands of warriors. The sun made his armor glisten and greeted him before it illuminated the country around. The Parisians saw their beloved chief at a distance, but the enemy, hoping to prevent his gaining entrance to the tower, crossed the Seine and took up their position on the bank. Nevertheless Odo, his horse at a gallop, got past the Northmen and reached the tower, whose gates Ebolus opened to him. The enemy pursued fiercely the comrades of the count who were trying to keep up with him and get refuge in the tower.... [The Danes were defeated in the attack.]

Now came the Emperor Charles [the Fat], surrounded by soldiers of all nations, even as the sky is adorned with resplendent stars. A great throng, speaking many languages, accompanied him. He established his camp at the foot of the heights of Montmartre, near the tower. He allowed the Northmen to have the country of Sens to plunder; and in the spring he gave them 700 pounds of silver on condition that by the month of March they leave France for their own kingdom. Then Charles returned [home], destined to an early death.

50. VIKINGS IN THE IBERIAN PENINSULA

Spanish and Islamic sources provide information on ninth- and tenth-century Viking activities in the Christian kingdoms of Galicia and Asturias and in the Islamic Umayyad Emirate of Cordoba in the Iberian Peninsula, which experienced Viking raids in 844–45, 859–61, 964–66, and 968–71. Ibn al-Kutia (d. 977) lived in Cordoba and was the author of a historical work on the History of the Conquest of Andalusia, *which dealt with the period from the Islamic conquest to the early tenth century. Little is known of the life of Ibn Idhari, a Moroccan whose history of the Maghreb and Iberia of ca 1300 contains important information extracted from earlier works now lost. The Vikings were known in Al-Andalus (Islamic Spain) as* madjus, *in reference to their polytheistic religion. The following passages use the Islamic calendar, which numbers the years from the migration of the Prophet from Mecca to Medina (622 CE). Gregorian dates are given in parentheses.*

Source: trans. J. Stefánsson, "The Vikings in Spain. From Arabic (Moorish) and Spanish Sources," *Saga Book of the Viking Club* VI, Pt. 1 (Jan. 1909), pp. 33–36, 37–39.

(a) Ibn al-Kutia. Year 230 (17 September 844–1 October 845)

Abd al-Rahman [II, Umayyad Emir of Cordoba, 822–852] built the great Mosque in Seville, and when the walls of this city had been destroyed by Madjus in 230 he rebuilt them. The arrival of these barbarians struck terror into the heart of the inhabitants. All fled and sought a refuge, partly in the mountains of the neighborhood, partly in Carmona. In all the west there was none who dared to meet them in battle. Therefore the inhabitants of Cordoba and the nearest districts were called to arms as soon as Madjus had landed on the coast in the farthest west, and had seized the plains of Lisbon. Our leaders with their troops took up a position at Carmona, but, as the enemy was uncommonly brave, they dared not attack them before the arrival of soldiers from the border.... The border chieftains demanded news of the movements of the enemy, and the commander answered that Madjus sent every day detachments toward Firrich, Lacant, Cordoba, and Moron. They [the chieftains] then asked, if there were not, near Seville, a place where they could lie in ambush without being seen. The commander told them of the village Quintos-Maâfir, south-east of Seville. They moved there in the middle of the night, and sat in ambush. One of their men, with a bundle of faggots, was set to keep watch from the tower of the village church. At sunrise the guard made known that a host of 16,000 Madjus was marching on Moron. The Moslem let them pass, cut them off from Seville, and cut them down. Then our leaders advanced, entered Seville, and found its commander besieged in the castle. They joined forces, and the inhabitants returned to the city in multitudes.

Besides the host that had been cut down, two other hosts of Madjus had moved out, one toward Lacant, the other toward the quarter of the tribe of Beni-'l-Laith in Cordova. But when the Madjus who remained in Seville saw the Moslem army coming, and heard of the disaster that the detachment marching on Moron had met with, they suddenly embarked. When they were sailing up the river toward a castle, they met their countrymen, and when these had also embarked, they all together began to sail down the river, while the inhabitants of the country poured on them curses and threw stones at them. When they had arrived a mile (league) below Seville, Madjus shouted to the people, "Leave us in peace, if you wish to buy prisoners of us." People then ceased to throw stones at them, and they allowed everybody to ransom prisoners. A certain sum was paid for most of them, but Madjus refused both gold and silver. They took only clothes and food.

After this the Emir Abd al-Rahman took measures of safety. He built an arsenal in Seville, ordered ships to be built, and gathered sailors on the coasts of Andalos; to these he gave very high wages, and provided them with war engines and naphtha. When Madjus returned next, in 244 [19 April 858–7 April 859], during the reign of Emir Mohammed, battle was given them at the mouth of the river [Guadalquivir], and when they had been beaten and several of their ships burnt, they departed.

(b) Ibn Adhari. Year 229 (30 September 843–17 September 844)

In the year 229 a letter arrived in the capital [Cordoba] from Wahballah ibn-Hazm, governor at Lisbon. He wrote therein that Madjus had been seen on the coast of his province, in 54 ships, and in the same number of smaller vessels. Abd al-Rahman gave to him, as to other governors in provinces adjoining the sea, authority to take all needful measures.

Madjus arrived in about 80 ships. One might say they had, as it were, filled the ocean with dark red birds, in the same way as they had filled the hearts of men with fear and trembling. After landing at Lisbon, they sailed to Cadiz, then to Sidona, then to Seville. They besieged this city, and took it by storm. After letting the inhabitants suffer the terrors of imprisonment or death, they remained there seven days, during which they let the people empty the cup of bitterness.

As soon as Abd al-Rahman had news of this, he gave to the Hadjib [Prime Minister] Isâ ibn-Chohaid the command of the cavalry. Moslems hastened to gather under the banner of this general, and to join him as closely as the eyelid is joined to the eye. Abjullah ibn-Kolaib, Ibn Wasim, and other great chieftains also joined the cavalry. The commander-in-chief made Axarafe [a high hill near Seville] his headquarters, and wrote to the governors all round to command them to call their men to arms. They went to Cordoba, and the eunuch Nasr took them to the army.

But Madjus continually received reinforcements, and, according to the author of the book, *Bahdja, an-n-afs*, they continued for thirteen days to kill men and drag women and children into slavery. Instead of thirteen days, the author of *Dorar al-Kalayid* says seven days, and we have followed him above. After some skirmishes with Moslems they [Madjus] went to Kaptel [an island in the Guadalquivir] where they stayed three days. They then entered Caura [Coria], twelve miles from Seville, where they murdered many people. Then they took Talyata, two miles from Seville. There they spent the night, and were seen next morning at Al-Fakkharin [Alfarache]. Then they re-embarked and joined battle with Moslems, who were put to flight and lost so many men that they could not be numbered. After returning to their ships, Madjus sailed to Sidona, and then to Cadiz, after Abd al-Rahman had sent his generals against them and fought them, sometimes successfully, sometimes with loss. At last, when war engines were used against them, and reinforcements had arrived from Cordoba, Madjus were put to flight. They [the Moors] killed about 500 of their men, and took four of their ships with all their cargoes. Ibn-Wazim had these burnt, after selling all that was found in them. Then they [Madjus] were defeated at Talyata on the 25 Safar of this year [11 November 844]. Many were killed, others hanged at Seville, others hanged in the palm trees of Talyata, and thirty of their ships were burnt. Those who escaped from the bloodshed embarked. They went to Niebla, and then to Lisbon, and were no more heard of. They arrived at Seville on the 14 Moharram, 230 [1 October 844], and forty-two days had passed from the day when they entered Seville until those of them who were not put to the sword departed. Their general was killed. To punish them for their crimes, God gave them to our sword and destroyed them, numerous as they were. When they had been annihilated, the government made this happy event known through all the provinces, and Abd al-Rahman also wrote to the Cinhadja tribe in Tanger, to tell them that with God's help he had succeeded in destroying Madjus. At the same time he sent them the heads of the general, and of two hundred of the noblest Madjus warriors.

CHAPTER NINE

"THE HEATHENS STAYED":
FROM RAIDING TO SETTLEMENT

By the middle of the ninth century, chroniclers in Ireland and England began to observe with a certain amount of surprise and shock that parties of Vikings were beginning to overwinter in those regions. This ushered in the beginning of a new phase of activity characterized by the establishment of a permanent Scandinavian presence in the British Isles and continental Europe. Many scholars regard this period of settlement as a "Second Viking Age" quite distinct from the "First Viking Age" of raiding. Settlement did not occur at the same time or in the same way, in the same concentration, or with the same effect across Europe, and it is much better documented in some regions than in others.

51. VIKING ACTIVITIES IN ENGLAND, 851–900

*Danish Vikings overwintered on the Isle of Thanet at the mouth of the River Thames
in 850 and again on Sheppey in 854, marking the transition from seasonal raiding to
a more permanent Viking presence in England. But the real turning point came with
the arrival of what is usually translated as the Great Army (Anglo-Saxon: micel
here) in 866, including as its leaders the sons of Ragnar Hairy-Breeches, Ivar and
Halfdan. The size of the Great Army is hotly debated, as is its precise nature. This
selection ends with the death of King Alfred at the end of the century. See doc. 40 on
the* Chronicle.

Source: trans. A.A. Somerville, from David Dumville and Simon Keynes, general eds., *The
Anglo-Saxon Chronicle: A Collaborative Edition* (Cambridge: D.S. Brewer, 1983–), vol. 7; MS E,
ed. Susan Irvine (Cambridge: D.S. Brewer, 2004), pp. 46–53.

851 [850/851]. In this year, Alderman Ceorl and the men of Devonshire
fought against heathens and, after huge slaughter, defeated them. The heathens stayed in Thanet over the winter. The same year, three hundred and
fifty ships arrived at the mouth of the Thames. The heathens stormed Canterbury and routed Brihtwulf, king of the Mercians, and his army. Next, the
heathens went south across the Thames where King Athelwulf [of Wessex]
and Athelwulf, his son, with the West-Saxon host fought them at Oakley.
This battle was the greatest massacre of a heathen army we have ever heard
tell of. King Athelwulf and his forces were victorious there. That same year,
King Athelstan and Alderman Ealhere fought in their ships and massacred a
large heathen force at Sandwich. They captured nine ships and drove off the
rest.

852 [853]. In this year, Burgred, king of the Mercians, subdued North Wales
with the help of King Athelwulf [of Wessex]. In that year, too, Ealhere and
Huda with the hosts of Kent and Surrey fought a heathen army at Thanet.
Many were killed and drowned on either side. Both aldermen were among
the dead. King Burgred of Mercia married the daughter of Athelwulf, king
of the West Saxons.

855. In this year, heathens spent the winter on Sheppey. In the same year,
King Athelwulf made over a tenth of his property throughout his kingdom
for the glory of God and for his own eternal welfare. That year, he went to
Rome with great honor and stayed there for two years. On his way back, he
married the daughter of Charles, king of France. He arrived home safely and
died about two years later. His body lies in Winchester. He was the son of

Ecgbriht, and ruled for nine years. Then his two sons took power: Athelbald ruled Wessex and Surrey for five years.

860. This year, King Athelbald [of Wessex] died and his body lies at Sherborne. His brother Athelbriht succeeded to the entire kingdom. In his days, a large fleet arrived and ravaged Winchester. Alderman Osric with the Hampshire host, and Alderman Athelwulf with the force from Berkshire took on the army and put it to flight; they were left in possession of the battlefield. Athelbriht reigned for five years and his body rests at Sherborne.

865. In this year, the heathen army occupied Thanet and made peace with the people of Kent. The Kentishmen promised money in return for peace. Taking advantage of the promise of money, the heathen army stole up by night and raided the whole of east Kent.

866 [probably 865]. In this year, Athelred, Athelbriht's brother, took over the rule of the West Saxons. That year, too, a great heathen army invaded the land of the Angles and established winter quarters and procured horses there. They made peace with the East Anglians.

867 [866]. This year, the heathen army advanced from East Anglia across the mouth of the River Humber as far as York in Northumbria. The Northumbrians were seriously at odds with one another. They had recently overthrown their king, Osbriht, and had accepted as king, Ella, a man with no claim to the throne. However, late in the year they submitted again to Osbriht and then fought against the heathen army. They gathered an immense host and attacked the heathens at York. They penetrated the fortifications and some of them got inside. There was a huge slaughter among the Northumbrians, some inside the city and others outside. Both Northumbrian kings were killed. The survivors made peace with the heathen army. The same year, Bishop Ealhstan died after holding the bishopric of Sherborne for fifty years. He is buried in the town.

868 [867]. In this year, the heathen army moved to Nottingham in Mercia and took up winter quarters there. King Burgred of Mercia and his council begged King Athelred of Wessex and his brother Alfred to help them in their fight against the great army. They led the West Saxon host into Mercia as far as Nottingham where they encountered the heathen army at the fortifications and laid siege to the city. However, there was no serious fighting, so the Mercians made peace with the army.

869. In this year, the heathen army returned to York and stayed there for a year.

870 [869]. In the course of this year, the Danish army crossed Mercia on its way to East Anglia where they took up winter quarters at Thetford. The king of East Anglia, Saint Edmund, fought them, but the Danes won the battle and killed the king. They overran the whole land and destroyed all the monasteries they came to. At that time, they stormed and burned Medesh-amstede, where they killed the abbot and the monks. They destroyed every-thing they found there and reduced to nothing a place that had formerly been very prosperous. Archbishop Ceolwulf died this year.

871 [870]. In this year, the heathen army rode to Reading in Wessex. Three days later, two earls arrived. Alderman Athelwulf encountered them at En-glefield where he fought and beat them. One of the Earls, Sidrac by name, was killed there. Four days later, King Athelred and his brother Alfred ar-rived at Reading, leading a large host. They fought with the heathen army and there was great carnage on both sides. Alderman Athelwulf was killed and the Danes remained in possession of the battlefield.

Four days later, King Athelred and his brother Alfred fought against the entire army at Ashdown. The Danish army was drawn up in two divisions, in one of which were Basecg and Halfdan, the heathen kings, while the two earls were in the other. King Athelred fought against the division of the two kings and King Basecg was killed. Alfred took on the earls' division. Earl Sidrac the Elder and Sidrac the Younger were both killed there, as were the earls Osbjearn, Fræna, and Harold. Both divisions of the army were put to flight and many thousands were slain. Fighting continued until nightfall.

A fortnight later, King Athelred and his brother Alfred fought the heathen army at Basing, where the Danes won. Two months after this, King Athelred and his brother Alfred fought the heathen army at Marden [?]. The armies were arranged in two divisions, and each side drove back the other, and both had successes for a long time during the day; there was much slaughter on both sides, but the Danes were left in possession of the battlefield. Bishop Hæhmund was killed along with many good men. After this battle, the men from a large Danish summer-fleet came to Reading.

After Easter, King Athelred died after a reign of five years; his body rests in Wimborne Minster. Then his brother, Alfred son of Athelwulf, ruled Wessex. A month later, King Alfred, with a small force, met the whole Dan-ish army in battle at Wilton, and he had them on the run for much of the day, but the Danes remained in possession of the battlefield. During this year, nine major battles were fought against the Danish army in the kingdom to the south of the Thames, not to mention minor raids carried out by Alfred, aldermen, or king's thanes which were not regarded as important. Nine earls and a king were killed in this year. Also, the West Saxons made peace with the Danish army in the same year.

872 [871]. This year, the Danish army moved from Reading to London, where they established winter quarters. The Mercians made peace with the army in the same year.

873 [872]. [This year, the Danish army went to Northumbria and] set up winter quarters in Torksey.

874 [873]. This year saw the army move from Lindsey to Repton, where they stayed for the winter. And they drove King Burgred [of Mercia] overseas after he had ruled for twenty-two years. They overran the country, while Burgred went to Rome and lived there. His body lies in the church of Saint Mary in the English College. The same year, the Danes gave the throne of Mercia to a foolish king's thane called Ceolwulf. He gave them hostages and swore oaths that the kingdom would be theirs whenever they wished. He swore, too, that he and all who followed him would be ready to meet the army's needs.

875 [874]. This year, the army moved from Repton. Halfdan led part of the army to Northumbria and settled for the winter beside the River Tyne. The army overran that district and often carried out raids on the Picts and the Welsh of Strathclyde. The three Danish kings, Guthrum, Oscytel, and Anwend, left Repton for Cambridge, which they occupied for a year with a large army. That summer, King Alfred went to sea with a fleet and fought against seven Danish ships, capturing one and putting the rest to flight.

876 [875]. In this year, the Danish army stole into Wareham, a fort belonging to the West Saxons. Later, the king made peace with the army. They gave King Alfred as hostages the finest men in the army, and swore oaths on their holy ring – something they had never before done for any people – that they would leave his kingdom immediately. Taking advantage of this, their cavalry left the fort surreptitiously and entered Exeter. That year, Halfdan divided up the land of Northumbria; the raiders became tillers of the land as well. Rollo and his men invaded Normandy and he ruled for fifty-three years.

877 [876]. In this year, the Danish army arrived at Exeter from Wareham. Their fleet sailed round the west coast and ran into a powerful storm at sea. They lost 120 ships at Swanage. King Alfred pursued the cavalry with his forces as far as Exeter but could not overtake them before they reached the fort where no one could get at them. They gave King Alfred as many prominent hostages as he wanted and swore many oaths to keep the peace. The army moved into Mercia at harvest time; they took some of the produce and gave some to Ceolwulf.

878. In this year, the Danish army moved surreptitiously to Chippenham in the middle of winter, after twelfth night. They reached Wessex and occupied it. They drove many of the people overseas, but subdued most of them, except for King Alfred and a small body of men, who were, despite hardships, keeping to the forests and areas protected by marshes. The same winter, the brother of Ivar and Halfdan entered Wessex and Devonshire where he and 840 men were killed. This year the battle-standard called the Raven was captured. At Easter, King Alfred, with his small force, built a fort at Athelney from which he attacked the Danish army with support from the part of Somerset which is closest. In the seventh week after Easter, King Alfred rode to Ecgbrihtesstone [?] to the east of Wealwudu [Selwood?] and he was met there by all the people of Somerset, Wiltshire, and the part of Hampshire on this side of the sea; they were all happy to see him. He traveled for one night to Æglea [Hey?] and one more night to Eddington where he fought with the whole army and put them to flight. Then King Alfred rode after them as far as the fort and stayed there for a fortnight. Then the Danish army gave hostages and swore many oaths that they would leave his kingdom. They promised that their king would accept baptism; they kept that promise. Three weeks later, [Danish] King Guthrum arrived at Aller [?] near Athelney with thirty of the noblest men in the army. At that time, the king received baptism; his chrysmal [baptismal] robe was removed at Wedmore. Guthrum stayed with King Alfred for twelve days, and King Alfred honored Guthrum's companions with rich gifts.

879 [878]. This year the army moved from Chippenham to Cirencester and remained there for the winter. That year, a band of Vikings gathered and occupied Fulham beside the Thames. That same year the sun went dark for an hour.

880 [879]. In this year, the Danish army moved from Cirencester to East Anglia which they occupied and divided up. In the same year, the army

occupying Fulham crossed the sea to Ghent in the land of the Franks and stayed there for a year.

881. This year, the Danish army moved deeper into the land of the Franks, and the Franks fought them. After the battle, the Danish army acquired horses.

882 [881]. This year, the Danish army traveled up the River Maas in the land of the Franks and stayed there for a year. That same year, King Alfred took a fleet to sea and fought four Danish ships. He captured two and killed their crews. The other ships surrendered to him, but not before their men were badly knocked about and wounded.

883 [882]. In this year, the Danish army traveled up the Scheldt to Condé and stayed there for a year. Also, Pope Marinus sent a fragment of the true cross to King Alfred. In the same year, Sighelm and Athelstan took to Rome the alms that had been promised by King Alfred. They also took alms for Saint Thomas and Saint Bartholemew in India. At that time, King Alfred besieged the Danish army at London, and there, God be thanked, their prayers were largely fulfilled after they had made their vows.

884 [883]. This year, the army went up the Somme to Amiens and stayed there for a year.

885 [884]. This year, the Danish army, mentioned above, divided into two parts. One part went east while the other went to Rochester and laid siege to it. The Danes built defensive works for themselves, but the defenders of the castle held out until King Alfred came up with the host. Then the Danes took to their ships, abandoning their defensive works. They were also deprived of their horses there, and soon after went overseas.

That same year, King Alfred sent a fleet from Kent to East Anglia. As soon as they entered the mouth of the Stour, they encountered sixteen Viking ships which they fought and captured, killing the crews. Traveling home with their spoils, they met a large Viking fleet. They fought the same day and the Danes won.

At midwinter, Charles [Carloman II], king of the Franks, died, killed by a wild boar. The year before, his brother [Louis III] had died. He, too, had ruled the western kingdom and died in the year of the eclipse. He was son of the Charles whose daughter King Athelwulf of Wessex married [Carloman II was the son of Louis II; Charles the Bald was actually his grandfather].

That year, the good Pope Marinus died. He had given liberty to the English College at the request of Alfred, king of Wessex. The pope sent King Alfred the splendid gift of a fragment of the cross on which Christ suffered. That same year, the Danish army advanced on East Anglia and broke the peace treaty with King Alfred.

886 [885]. This year, the Danish army which had earlier gone east in the land of the Franks came back west along the River Seine and took winter quarters in the city of Paris. That same year. King Alfred occupied London and the entire English people came to him, except for those who were in the power of the Danes. Then he entrusted the city to the care of Athelred the alderman.

887 [886–87]. This year, the Danish army crossed the bridge at Paris and followed the Seine as far as the Marne. Then they went along the Marne to Chézy and the Yonne, and occupied both positions for two winters.... In the same year as the army crossed the bridge at Paris, Athelhelm the alderman took the alms of the West Saxons and of King Alfred to Rome.

888. In this year Beocca the alderman took the alms of the West Saxons and of King Alfred to Rome. Also, Queen Athelswith, King Alfred's sister, died and her body lies in Pavia.... In the same year, Archbishop Athelred and Alderman Athewold died in the same month.

889. In this year, no one traveled to Rome except two couriers who were sent with letters by King Alfred.

890 In this year, Abbot Beornhelm of Wessex took the alms of Wessex and King Alfred to Rome. Guthrum, king of the Northmen, died. His baptismal name was Athelstan and he was King Alfred's godson. He lived in East Anglia where he had first settled. That year, the Danish army on the Seine moved to Saint-Lô, which is situated between the Bretons and the Franks. The Bretons fought them and won. The Danes were driven into a river, where many of them drowned. At this time, Plegmund was chosen as archbishop by the pope and the whole people.

892. This year, the army which we have already spoken about moved back westwards to Boulogne where they boarded ships and crossed all at once with their horses and equipment. They arrived at the mouth of the Limne in 250 ships. The mouth of the Limne is in the east of Kent, at the eastern end of the great forest we call Anderida. This forest runs from east to west

112 miles or longer and is thirty miles broad. The river we are speaking about flows from the Weald. They towed their ships up this river as far as the Weald, four miles from the estuary of the river. There, in a fen, they destroyed a hastily built fort with a few common men in it. Soon after this, Hastein sailed into the mouth of the Thames with eighty ships. He built a fortification at Middletown and the other army did the same at Appledore. This year, Wulfhere, archbishop of Northumbria, died.

What follows is taken from MS A of the Chronicle.

Source: trans. A.A. Somerville, from David Dumville and Simon Keynes, general eds., *The Anglo-Saxon Chronicle: A Collaborative Edition* (Cambridge: D.S. Brewer, 1983–), vol. 3; MS A, ed. Janet Bately (Cambridge: D.S. Brewer, 1986), pp. 59–61.

896. Then King Alfred ordered the building of longships to oppose the Danish ships. Some had sixty oars and others more. The new ships were nearly twice as long as the others as well as being faster, steadier in the water, and higher. These ships were modeled neither on Frisian nor Danish lines, but according to what seemed most useful to King Alfred.

Later in the same year, six Danish ships came to the Isle of Wight and did a lot of damage in the area, in Devon and nearly everywhere else on the seacoast. Then King Alfred ordered out nine of the new ships. They closed off the river mouth, denying the Danes access to the open sea. Then the Danes sailed out against them with three ships, while the other three were beached further up the river mouth because their crews had gone ashore. Two Danish ships were captured and their crews killed at the outer part of the river mouth. The third ship escaped with only five of its crew still alive. This ship escaped because the English ships had gone aground in an awkward position; three had gone aground on the same side of the channel as the Danish ships. The rest were on the other side so that none of them could reach the others, for the tide had ebbed many furlongs from the ships. Then the Danes from the three beached ships approached the three English ships which had been grounded on their side of the river. They fought. Lucumon, the king's reeve was killed, and so were Wulfheard the Frisian, Ebbe the Frisian, Athelhere the Frisian, and Athelferth the king's herdsman. Sixty-two of the English and Frisians died and a hundred and twenty of the Danes.

However, the flood tide reached the Danish ships before the Christians could shove out their own. So the Danes rowed away, but they were so badly wounded that they could not row beyond the Sussex coast. Two of their ships were driven ashore there. The crews were taken to the king in Winchester, and he hanged them. The remaining Danish ship made it to East Anglia with its badly wounded crew. That summer, no fewer than twenty ships and their crews were lost along the south coast....

900 [899]. In this year, Alfred Athulfing [son of Athelwulf] died six days before All Saints' Day. He was king over all England except for the part under Danish control. He ruled that kingdom for twenty-eight and a half years....

52. THE VIKINGS IN IRELAND, 845–917

By the middle of the ninth century, Scandinavians had established permanent settlements in Ireland, including that at Dublin (Áth Cliath). The Annals of Ulster *(see doc. 43) for the years 845 to 917 is crucial for shedding light on Viking activities in this period. Settlement made the Vikings more vulnerable to Irish attack and also saw them drawn into Irish politics, especially dynastic warfare. Powerful Viking rulers, styling themselves kings, emerged, notably Amlaíb (Olaf) and Ímar (Ivar) in the 850s to early 870s. These men were successful Viking leaders whose influence was felt on both sides of the Irish Sea: Ímar (Ivar) has been identified as one of the sons of Ragnar Hairy-Breeches, and he is mentioned in the* Anglo-Saxon Chronicle *as one of the leaders of the Great Army in England (see doc. 51).*

Some terms used in the Annals *are problematic and require clarification. The "Norse-Irish" or Gall-goídel mentioned in 856 and 857 seem to have been a group of mixed Norse and Gaelic blood who were notorious for their violence. The terms "dark foreigners" and "fair foreigners" (Dubgaill and Finngaill), mentioned in 851 and elsewhere, are used only in Irish and Welsh sources of the ninth and tenth centuries, and their meaning is the subject of much modern scholarly discussion. It was once believed that these descriptions were used to distinguish Norwegians and Danes, but such ethnic labels have been rejected and the terms are now seen as a means of distinguishing successive groups of Vikings or rival Viking dynasties or warbands.*

Source: trans. S. MacAirt and G. MacNiocaill, *The Annals of Ulster (to A.D. 1131),* (Dublin: Institute for Advanced Studies, 1983), pp. 305–67, excerpts.

AD 844 [845]

1. Forannán, abbot of Ard Macha, was taken prisoner by the heathens in Cluain Comarda with his halidoms [relics, sacred items] and following, and was brought to the ships of Luimnech.

2. Dún Masc was plundered by the heathens, and there were killed there Aed son of Dub dá Crích, abbot of Tír dá Glas, and Cluain Eidnig, Ceithernach son of Cú Dínaisc, prior of Cell Dara, and many others.

3. There was an encampment of the foreigners under Tuirgéis on Loch Rí,

and they plundered Connacht and Mide, and burned Cluain Moccu Nóis with its oratories, and Cluain Ferta Brénainn, and Tír dá Glas and Lothra and other monasteries....

6. Niall son of Aed inflicted a battle-rout on the heathens in Mag Ítha....

8. Tuirgéis was taken prisoner by Mael Sechnaill and afterwards drowned in Loch Uair....

12. An encampment of the foreigners of Áth Cliath [Dublin] at Cluain Andobuir....

AD 845 [846]

2. Baislec was plundered by the heathens....

6. The foreigners won a battle against the Connachta, in which fell Rígán son of Fergus, Mugrón son of Diarmait and Aed son of Cathrannach and many others....

AD 846 [847]

3. Mael Sechnaill destroyed the Island of Loch Muinremor, overcoming there a large band of wicked men of Luigni and Gailenga, who had been plundering the territories in the manner of the heathens.

AD 847 [848]

4. Mael Sechnaill won a battle against the heathens at Forach in which seven hundred fell.

5. Ólchobor, king of Mumu, and Lorcán son of Cellach, with the Laigin, won a battle against the heathens at Sciath Nechtain, in which fell the jarl [earl] Tomrair, *tanist* [heir] of the king of Lochlann, and two hundred about him.

6. Tigernach inflicted a rout on the heathens in the oakwood of Dísert Do-Chonna, and twelve hundred fell there.

7. The Eóganacht of Caisel inflicted a rout on the heathens at Dún Maíle Tuile, in which five hundred fell.

AD 848 [849]

6. A naval expedition of seven score ships of adherents of the king of the foreigners came to exact obedience from the foreigners who were in Ireland before them, and afterwards they caused confusion in the whole country.

7. Indrechtach, abbot of Í [Iona], came to Ireland with the halidoms of Colum Cille [St. Columba, d. 597].

AD 849 [850]

3. Cinaed son of Conaing, king of Cianacht, rebelled against Mael Sechnaill with the support of the foreigners, and plundered the Uí Néill from the

Sinann to the sea, both churches and states, and he deceitfully sacked the island of Loch Gabor, leveling it to the ground, and the oratory of Treóit, with seventy people in it, was burned by him....

AD 850 [851]

3. The dark heathens came to Áth Cliath [Dublin], made a great slaughter of the fair-haired foreigners, and plundered the naval encampment, both people and property. The dark heathens made a raid at Linn Duachaill, and a great number of them were slaughtered.

7. Eochu son of Cernach, king of Fir Rois, was killed by the heathens.

AD 851 [852]

2. Ard Macha was laid waste by the foreigners of Linn on the day following Summer-Lent.

3. The complement of eight score ships of fair-haired foreigners came to Snám Aignech, to do battle with the dark foreigners; they fought for three days and three nights, but the dark foreigners got the upper hand and the others abandoned their ships to them. Stain took flight, and escaped, and Iercne fell beheaded.

8. A slaughter was inflicted on the foreigners at the islands of eastern Brega, and another slaughter of them at Ráith Alláin by the Cianacht in the same month.

AD 852 [853]

2. Amlaíb [Olaf], son of the king of Lochlann, came to Ireland, and the foreigners of Ireland submitted to him, and he took tribute from the Irish.

6. Cathmal son of Tomaltach, one of two kings of Ulaid, was killed by the Norsemen.

AD 855 [856]

3. Great warfare between the heathens and Mael Sechnaill, supported by Norse-Irish.

4. The oratory of Lusca was burned by the Norsemen.

5. Aed son of Niall inflicted a great rout on the Norse-Irish in Glenn Foichle and a vast number of them were slaughtered by him.

6. Horm, chief of the dark foreigners, was killed by Rhodri son of Mervyn, king of Wales....

AD 856 [857]

1. Ímar [Ivar] and Amlaíb inflicted a rout on Caitil the Fair and his Norse-Irish in the lands of Munster.

AD 858 [859]

2. Amlaíb and Ímar and Cerball led a great army into Mide.

4. Mael Guala, king of Mumu, was killed by the Norsemen.

AD 860 [861]

1. Mide was invaded by Aed son of Niall with foreigners.

AD 861 [862]

2. Aed son of Niall went with [?] the kings of the foreigners into Mide, and plundered Mide with Flann son of Conaing.

AD 862 [863]

3. Muirecán son of Diarmait, king of Nás and eastern Life, was killed by the Norsemen.

4. The caves of Achad Aldai, and of Cnodba, and of Boadán's Mound above Dubad, and of Óengoba's wife, were searched by the foreigners – something which had never been done before. This was the occasion when three kings of the foreigners, i.e. Amlaíb and Ímar and Auisle, plundered the land of Flann son of Conaing; and Lorcán son of Cathal, king of Mide, was with them in this.

AD 863 [864]

2. Conchobor son of Donnchad, one of two kings of Mide, was put to death in water at Cluain Iraird by Amlaíb, king of the foreigners.

AD 865 [866]

1. Amlaíb and Auisle went with the foreigners of Ireland and Scotland to Fortriu [one of the provinces of Pictland in northeastern Scotland], plundered the entire Pictish country, and took away hostages from them....

4. Aed son of Niall plundered all the strongholds of the foreigners, i.e. in the territory of the North, both in Cenél Eógain and Dál Araidi, and took away their heads, their flocks, and their herds from camp by battle [?]. A victory was gained over them at Loch Febail and twelve score heads taken thereby....

AD 866 [867]

6. Auisle, one of three kings of the heathens, was killed by his kinsmen in guile and parricide.

7. The dark foreigners won a battle over the northern Saxons at York, in which fell Aelle, king of the northern Saxons.

8. Amlaíb's fort at Cluain Dolcáin was burned by Gaíthíne's son and Mael

Ciaráin son of Rónán, and the aforesaid commanders caused a slaughter of a hundred of the leaders of the foreigners in the vicinity of Cluain Dolcáin on the same day....

AD 867 [868]

4. Aed son of Niall won a battle at Cell Ua nDaigri against the Uí Néill of Brega, and the Laigin, and a large force of the foreigners, i.e. three hundred or more; and Flann son of Conaing, king of all Brega, and Diarmait son of Etarscéle, king of Loch Gabor, fell therein; and in this battle very many of the heathens were slaughtered; and Fachtna son of Mael Dúin, heir designate of the North, and many others, fell in the counter-attack of the battle....

AD 868 [869]

4. Mael Ciaráin son of Rónán, royal champion of eastern Ireland, a warrior who plundered the foreigners, was killed....
6. Ard Macha was plundered by Amlaíb and burned with its oratories. Ten hundred were carried off or killed, and great rapine also committed.

AD 869 [870]

6. The siege of Ail Cluaithe [Dumbarton, the stronghold of the Britons of Strathclyde on the River Clyde, near Glasgow] by the Norsemen: Amlaíb and Ímar, two kings of the Norsemen, laid siege to the fortress and at the end of four months they destroyed and plundered it....
7. Mael Sechnaill, son of Niall, one of the two kings of the southern Brega, was treacherously killed by Ulf the dark foreigner.

AD 870 [871]

2. Amlaíb and Ímar returned to Áth Cliath from Alba [Scotland] with two hundred ships, bringing away with them in captivity to Ireland a great prey of Angles and Britons and Picts.
3. The storming of Dún Sobairche, which had never been achieved before: the foreigners were at it with the Cenél Eógain.
4. Ailill son of Dúnlang, king of Laigin, was killed by the Norsemen....

AD 872 [873]

3. Ímar, king of the Norsemen of all Ireland and Britain, ended his life....

AD 873 [874]

5. Cell Mór of Mag Enir was plundered by the foreigners.

AD 874 [875]

3. The Picts encountered the dark foreigners in battle, and a great slaughter of the Picts resulted.

4. Oistín son of Amlaíb, king of the Norsemen, was deceitfully killed by Albann....

AD 876 [877]

3. Rhodri son of Merfyn, king of the Britons, came in flight from the dark foreigners to Ireland.

5. A skirmish at Loch Cuan between the fair heathens and the dark heathens, in which Albann, king of the dark heathens, fell.

AD 877 [878]

9. The shrine of Colum Cille and his other halidoms arrived in Ireland, having been taken in flight to escape the foreigners.

AD 878 [879]

6. Mael Coba son of Crunnmael, superior of Ard Macha, and the lector, i.e. Mochta, were taken prisoner by the foreigners.

AD 880 [881]

3. The oratory of Cianán was destroyed by the foreigners, and many people were taken from it. Afterwards Barith, a great despot of the Norsemen, was killed by [St.] Ciannán.

AD 881 [882]

1. Flann son of Mael Sechnaill led an army both of foreigners and Irish into the North. He camped at Mag eter dí Glais, and Ard Macha was invaded by him.

AD 887 [888]

5. The foreigners inflicted a battle-rout on Flann son of Mael Sechnaill and there fell there Aed son of Conchobor, king of Connacht, and Lergus son of Cruinnén bishop of Cell Dara, and Donnchad son of Mael Dúin, superior of Cell Delca and other monasteries....

9. Sigfrith son of Ímar, king of the Norsemen, was deceitfully killed by his kinsman....

AD 892 [893]

4. A great dissension among the foreigners of Áth Cliath, and they became

dispersed, one section of them following Ímar's son, and the other Sigfrith the jarl.

AD 893 [894]

4. Ímar's son came again to Ireland.

AD 894 [895]

6. Ard Macha was plundered by the foreigners of Áth Cliath, i.e. by Glún Iarainn, and they took away seven hundred and ten persons into captivity.

> Alas, o holy Patrick
> That your prayers did not protect [it]
> [When] the foreigners with their axes
> Were smiting your oratory!

AD 895 [896]

3. Sitriuc son of Ímar was killed by other Norsemen.

7. A slaughter of the foreigners by the Conaille and Laigne's son, in which Amlaíb son of Ímar fell.

9. Flannacán son of Cellach, king of Brega, was killed by the Norsemen.

AD 901 [902]

2. The heathens were driven from Ireland, i.e. from the fortress of Áth Cliath, by Mael Finnia son of Flannacán with the men of Brega and by Cerball son of Muirícán, with the Laigin; and they abandoned a good number of their ships, and escaped half dead after they had been wounded and broken.

AD 903 [904]

4. Ímar, grandson of Ímar, was killed by the men of Fortriu [in Pictland/ Alba], and there was a great slaughter around him.

AD 912 [913]

5. The heathens inflicted a battle-rout on the crew of a new fleet of the Ulaid, on the coast of England, and many fell, including Cumuscach son of Mael Mocheirgi, son of the king of Leth Cathail.

AD 913 [914]

4. A naval battle at Manu between Barid son of Oitir and Ragnall grandson of Ímar, in which Barid and almost all his army were destroyed.

5. A great new fleet of the heathens on Loch dá Caech.

AD 914 [915]

7. A great and frequent increase in the number of heathens arriving at Loch dá Chaech, and the laity and clergy of Mumu were plundered by them.

AD 915 [916]

3. Ainnle son of Cathán, king of Uaithne of Cliú, was put to death by the foreigners of Loch dá Chaech.

6. The foreigners of Loch dá Chaech continued to harry Mumu and Laigin.

AD 916 [917]

2. Sitriuc, grandson of Ímar, landed with his fleet at Cenn Fuait on the coast of Laigin. Ragnall, grandson of Ímar, with his second fleet moved against the foreigners of Loch dá Chaech. A slaughter of the foreigners at Neimlid in Muma. The Eóganacht and the Ciarraige made another slaughter.

3. Niall son of Aed, king of Ireland, led an army of the southern and northern Uí Néill to Munster to make war on the heathens. He halted on the 22nd day of the month of August at Topar Glethrach in Mag Feimin. The heathens had come into the district on the same day. The Irish attacked them between the hour of tierce and midday and they fought until eventide, and about a hundred men, the majority foreigners, fell between them. Reinforcements [?] came from the camp of the foreigners to aid their fellows. The Irish turned back to their camp in face of the last reinforcement, i.e. Ragnall, king of the dark foreigners, accompanied by a large force of foreigners. Niall son of Aed proceeded with a small number against the heathens, so that God prevented a great slaughter of the others through him. After that Niall remained twenty nights encamped against the heathens. He sent word to the Laigin that they should lay siege to the encampment from a distance. They were routed by Sitriuc grandson of Ímar in the battle of Cenn Fuait, where five hundred, or somewhat more, fell. And there fell too Ugaire son of Ailill, king of Laigin, Mael Mórda son of Muirecán, king of eastern Life, Mael Maedóc son of Diarmait, a scholar and bishop of Laigin, Ugrán son of Cennéitig, king of Laíges, and other leaders and nobles.

4. Sitriuc grandson of Ímar entered Áth Cliath.

53. KETIL FLATNOSE AND HIS DESCENDANTS IN THE HEBRIDES

Scandinavian settlement in the Hebrides, the numerous islands off Scotland's west coast, is undocumented in contemporary sources and must be traced from archaeological and place-name evidence in the first instance, but a significant Scandinavian presence there is not in doubt. From the ninth century a series of rulers with Scandinavian names and backgrounds began to appear in the region. Ketil Flatnose was a prominent Norse sea-king associated with the Hebrides. He appears in several Icelandic sagas, and some scholars believe he should be identified with Caittil the Fair mentioned in the Annals of Ulster under the year 857, while others doubt this association. The Icelandic saga tradition is not entirely in agreement on his role either, but the various sagas that mention him agree that he participated in an expedition to the Western Isles and established himself there. On Ketil and his descendants see doc. 21.

Source: *Eyrbyggja saga*, ed. Einar Ól. Sveinsson and Matthías Þórðarson, Íslenzk fornrit IV (Reykjavík, 1935), pp. 3–4.

1. There was a distinguished hersir [chief, lord] in Norway, called Ketil Flat-nose. He was the son of Bjorn Buna [Club-Foot], who was the son of Grim the hersir from Sogn. Ketil was married to Yngvild, the daughter of Ketil Wether, a hersir from Raumarike. Their sons were called Bjorn and Helgi, and their daughters were Aud [Unn] the Deep-Minded, Thorunn Hyrna [Horned] and Jorunn Manvitsbrekka. Ketil's son, Bjorn, was fostered by Earl Kjallak in Jämtland [Norway]. The earl was a wise and distinguished man, with a son called Bjorn, and a daughter, Gjaflaug.

This was in the days when Harald Finehair came to power in Norway. Because of that turbulence, many noble men fled their ancestral estates in Norway. Some went east over the Kiolen Mountains and others went west across the sea. There were some who wintered in the Shetlands or the Orkneys and raided Norway in the summers, doing great damage in King Harald's kingdom. The farmers complained to the king and asked him to free them from this trouble. The king decided to get an army ready to cross the western sea and said that Ketil Flatnose would be in command. Ketil declined, but the king declared that he had to go. When Ketil saw that the king intended to have his way, he got ready for the journey and took with him his wife and those of his children who were at home.

After he had crossed to the west, Ketil fought several battles and always won. He took control of the Hebrides and made himself ruler there. Then he came to terms with the most powerful chiefs on that side of the western sea and formed alliances with them. He sent the army back east, and, when they met King Harald, they told him that Ketil Flatnose was the ruler of the Hebrides, but declared that they did not know if he would present the king with a kingdom across the western sea. When the king heard that, he seized all that Ketil owned in Norway.

Ketil Flatnose gave his daughter, Aud, in marriage to Olaf the White, who was the most powerful warlord in the west at that time. Olaf was the son of Ingjald, who was son of Helgi; Ingjald's mother was Thora, the daughter of Sigurd Snake-in-the-Eye, who was the son of Ragnar Hairy-Breeches. He married off his daughter, Thorunn Hyrna, to Helgi the Thin, who was the son of Eyvind the Easterner and Raforta, the daughter of Kjarval, king of Ireland.

54. EARL SIGURD AND THE ESTABLISHMENT OF THE EARLDOM OF ORKNEY

Scandinavian settlement in Orkney and Shetland is undocumented in contemporary sources. It is thought that settlement began in the ninth century, after the initial raiding of the late eighth century, though the suggestion has been made that Shetland and Orkney may have been settled earlier and used as bases for the late eighth-century raids. Orkneyinga saga, *composed around 1200 in Iceland, is the main written source for Viking Age Orkney, but its historical value for the settlement period is limited and it has little to say about how the islands were initially settled by Scandinavians. The saga's early chapters contain an account of the establishment of the earldom, but modern scholarship is highly skeptical about King Harald Finehair's expedition. The dating of these events is uncertain; Earl Sigurd probably died ca 892.*

Source: *Orkneyinga saga*, ed. Einar Ól. Sveinsson and Matthías Þórðarson, Íslenzk fornrit XXXIV (Reykjavík, 1965), pp. 7–9.

4. When King Harald Finehair seized Norway, Earl Rognvald was with him, and the king gave him control of North Møre, South Møre, and Raumsdal. Earl Rognvald married Ragnhild, the daughter of Hrolf the Nose, and their son Hrolf conquered Normandy. He was so large that no horse could carry him and, for that reason, he became known as Gongu-Hrolf [Hrolf the Walker]. The earls of Rouen and the kings of England are descended from him. Rognvald and Ragnhild had two other sons whose names were Ivar and Thorir the Silent. Rognvald also had three illegitimate sons called Hallad, Hrollaug, and Einar, who was the youngest.

One summer, Harald Finehair sailed west on a punitive expedition against some Vikings, for he was growing tired of the lawless behavior of these men who were raiding in Norway over the summers and spending the winters in the Orkneys and Shetlands. Harald brought the Shetlands, the Orkneys, and the Hebrides under his control, and then he sailed west as far as the Isle of Man where he laid waste the settlements. He fought many battles there and took possession of lands further west than any Norwegian king has done since. In one of these battles, Earl Rognvald's son Ivar was killed. So when King Harald sailed east again, he gave Earl Rognvald the Orkneys and Shetlands as compensation for the loss of his son. Rognvald gave both territories to his brother, Sigurd, who was the forecastle-man on King Harald's ship. And when the king left for Norway, he gave Sigurd the title of earl, and Sigurd stayed behind in the west.

5. Earl Sigurd became a great chieftain. He formed an alliance with Thorstein the Red, the son of Olaf the White and Unn the Deep-Minded, and together they conquered the whole of Caithness as well as Sutherland, Moray, and Ross. He built a fortress in the south of Moray.

Sigurd and Maelbricht Tooth, earl of the Scots, agreed to hold a meeting at an appointed place to settle their differences. Each of them was to bring forty men. But on the day of the meeting, Sigurd reflected that the Scots were not to be trusted, so he mounted eighty men on forty horses. When Maelbricht noticed this, he said to his men:

"Sigurd has tricked us. I can see the feet of two men on the flanks of every horse, so there must be twice as many men as horses. Let us muster our courage, so that each of us may kill a man before dying ourselves." Then they prepared for battle.

But Sigurd saw what the Scots were up to and said to his men, "When the fighting starts, half of us will dismount and outflank the Scots from the left. Meanwhile the rest of us will ride at them as hard as possible and break up their formation."

And that's what they did; there was some fierce fighting and before long Maelbricht and his men were slain. Sigurd had their heads hung from his horses' cruppers as a sign of his triumph. Then they rode home, boasting of their victory. But on the way, as Sigurd was attempting to spur on his horse, he struck his calf against Maelbricht's protruding tooth and scratched himself. The wound grew swollen and painful, and that's what caused his death. Sigurd the Powerful is buried in a mound beside the River Oykel....

55. RUNIC INSCRIPTIONS FROM MAES HOWE, MAINLAND, ORKNEY

Maes Howe is a Neolithic chambered tomb built some 5,000 years ago on the mainland of Orkney. Although it passed out of use as a burial mound three millennia before the beginning of the Viking Age, Norsemen and women broke into it in the middle of the twelfth century. These visitors left a unique series of some thirty-three runic inscriptions and eight sketches carved inside the burial chamber, most of which are still visible today. Two of the inscriptions refer to "Jerusalem-travelers," which has led scholars to associate them with Earl Rognvald Kali Kolsson and his followers, whose pilgrimage to Rome and Jerusalem between 1150 and 1153 is recounted in Orkneyinga saga. *The saga also tells how Earl Harald Maddadarson and his men sought shelter in a tomb called* Orkahaugr *during a snowstorm in 1153; two inscriptions inside Maes Howe also use the name* Orkahaugr.

Source: K. Holman, *Scandinavian Runic Inscriptions in the British Isles: Their Historical Context* (Trondheim: Tapir, 1996), pp. 252–53.

"That will be true which I say, that treasure was carried away. Treasure was carried away three nights before they broke this mound."

"Ingibjörg, the fair widow. Many a woman has gone stooping in here. A great show-off. Erlingr."

"Þorny fucked. Helgi carved."

"Jerusalem men [crusaders] broke this mound."

"The man who is most skilled in runes west of the ocean carved these runes with that ax which Gaukr Trandilssonr owned in the south of the country [Iceland]."

"Ingigerðr is the most beautiful…."

"Benedikt made this cross."

"This mound was built before Loðrók's. Her sons, they were bold; such were men, as they were of themselves [i.e., they were the sort of people you would really call men]."

"Jerusalem-travelers [crusaders] broke Orkhaugr. Hlíf, the Earl's housekeeper, carved."

"It was long ago that great treasure was hidden here."

56. RUNIC INSCRIPTIONS FROM THE ISLE OF MAN

It was perhaps inevitable that, as a small, fertile island set at a nodal location in the northern Irish Sea basin, the Isle of Man would eventually be colonized by Scandinavians. The process is, however, entirely unattested in historical records and must be recovered through archaeological, linguistic, epigraphic, numismatic, and sculptural evidence. The sculptural evidence includes a large corpus of carved memorial stones, known collectively as the Manx crosses. The tradition of carving such monuments originated in the early Christian era and was taken up by the Scandinavians on the Isle of Man following their conversion to Christianity. The Norse cross slabs added Scandinavian art styles and motifs to the earlier Celtic traditions, and about thirty of these crosses carry runic inscriptions. Most of these are dated on stylistic grounds to the tenth and eleventh centuries. In the absence of any written documents for Scandinavian settlement on the Isle of Man, these late Norse crosses constitute a very important source. Among other things, the mixture of Gaelic and Norse personal names in the inscriptions has attracted the attention of scholars, as has the proportion of crosses erected in memory of women.

Source (for inscriptions): H. Shetelig, ed., *The Viking Antiquities in Great Britain and Ireland*, Part VI of A.O. Curle, M. Olsen, and H. Shetelig, *Civilisation of the Viking Settlers In Relation to Their Old and New Countries* (Oslo: H. Aschehoug & Co., 1954), pp. 184, 189, 191, 193, 200, 206, 207, 209, 216, 217. Some of the personal names have been amended to reflect the recent scholarship of K. Holman, *Scandinavian Runic Inscriptions in the British Isles: Their Historical Context* (Trondheim: Tapir, 1996).

Sandulf's Cross-slab, Andreas (Andreas II; Manx Museum no. 131)
"Sandulf the Black erected this cross after Arinbiorg his wife."

Olaf Liotulfson's Cross, Ballaugh (Manx Museum no. 106)
"Áleif Ljótolfsson erected this cross after Ulf, his son."

Odd's Cross, Braddan (Braddan III; Manx Museum no. 136)
"Odd erected this cross after Frakki, his father, but Tho(rbiorn)...."

Thorleif Hnakki's Cross, Braddan (Braddan IV; Manx Museum no. 135)
"Thorleif hnakki (nape) erected this cross after Fiac, his son, brother's son of Hafr." [Fiac is a Gaelic name, while Thorleif and Hafr are Norse, as is Thorleif's nickname.]

Truian's Cross, Bride (Manx Museum no. 118)
"Druian Dubgall's son erected this cross after A[thmiu] his wife."

57. ROLLO OBTAINS NORMANDY FROM THE KING OF THE FRANKS

The second book of Dudo of St. Quentin's History of the Normans *(doc. 39) concerns the activities of Rollo, the ancestor of the Norman dukes, who, exiled from Dacia by a tyrannous king, plundered Frisia and fought with the Franks before receiving lands at the mouth of the Seine River from the Frankish king Charles the Simple by the treaty of St. Clair-sur-Epte. Dudo places Rollo's baptism in 912, but historians treat the date with skepticism; in fact, no source mentions Rollo before his defeat at Chartres in 910, and his baptism was forced upon him after defeat. In Dudo's* History, *Rollo becomes a sort of Viking Aeneas who develops into a paragon of Christian virtue.*

Source: trans. E. Christiansen, Dudo of St. Quentin, *History of the Normans* (Woodbridge, Suffolk: Boydell, 1998), pp. 46–51.

2.25. As the Franks were unable to put up any resistance to the pagans, and saw that the whole of Francia was verging on annihilation, they came to the king with one accord, and said to him:

"Why will you not come to the aid of the kingdom which you ought to 'preside over and profit' with the scepter? Why not buy peace through conciliation, since we are unable to get it either through war, or by any sort of defensive precaution? The king's honor and the king's power are brought low, and the insolence of the heathen is raised up. The land allotted to the Franks is considered no better than a desert, for its population is either dead through famine or the sword, or is perhaps in captivity. Protect your kingdom: if not by arms, then by counsel."

Then was King Charles enraged, and he spoke these words: "Then give me the counsel which will be salutary and appropriate for the kingdom and for us."

Then said the Franks: "If you will trust us, we will give you advice fitting and wholesome for you and for the kingdom, so that the people, who are all too stricken with want, may have repose. Let the land from the River

Andelle to the sea be given to the pagan peoples; and in addition, join your daughter to Rollo in marriage. And thereby you will be able to grow mightily in power against the peoples who resist you; for Rollo is born of the proud blood of kings and of chiefs; he is very fair of body, a ready fighter, far-sighted in counsel, seemly in appearance, amenable to us, a faithful friend to those to whom he gives his word, a ferocious enemy to those whom he opposes, a constant and amenable vassal in all things, with a shrewd mind, such as we need. He is well-versed in speech, teachable in affairs, kindly in his deeds, honorable in his eloquence, full of manly courage, humble in his manners, most prudent in forensic matters, just in judgment, most careful in keeping of secrets, very rich in gold and silver, strictly attended by a most numerous throng of warriors – nay, he is fully endowed with all kinds of good qualities."

Having consulted these men, Charles at once sent Franco, the archbishop of Rouen, to Rollo, leader of the pagans, As soon as he came to him, he began to address him with gentle words: "Most outstanding of all leaders, and most excellent of all men, do you mean to spend your whole life pursuing your quarrel against the Franks? Will you always be battling against them? What will become of you, should you be snatched away by death before your time? Whose creation are you? Do you think that you are God? Is not a man a thing fashioned from mud? Are you not the food of worms, and dust and ashes? Remember what you are and what you will be, and by whose judgment you will be condemned. It is my belief that 'you will have hell to enjoy'; and after your battles are over, 'you will do no more harm to anyone.' If you wish to become a Christian, you will be able to know peace, now and in future, and to remain in this land as a man of great wealth. The most long-suffering King Charles, led by the advice of his men, is willing to give you this coast-land too often laid waste by Hastings and by you. Moreover, so that peace and agreement and firm, stable, and continuous friendship may endure between you and him for all times, he will give you his daughter, called Gisla, in marriage as your wife. If you will have the joy of offspring through this union, you will hold the kingdom in perpetuity."

2.26. When he had heard this, he called together the Danish chiefs, and told them what the bishop had said to him. And the Danes remembered the interpretations of the dream, and said to Rollo: "This utterly desolated land, bereft of warriors and untilled by the plow, is full of good trees, is intersected by rivers stocked with various sorts of fish; it teems with game, is not unfamiliar with vines, bears fruit in soil worked by the plow, is hemmed in on one side by a sea which will afford an abundant wealth of different commodities, and on the other by the outflow of waters carrying all sorts of goods by ship. It is virtually distinct from the kingdom of Francia, and if it were occupied by a dense population it would be mightily fertile and very rich, sufficient and suitable for us to inhabit. The girl whom he is promising you is lawfully born of the seed of either parent. She is tall enough, and her shape, we have heard, is most rare; she is a most unsullied virgin, provident in counsel, careful in her public dealings, most pleasant in her manner, most affable in her speech, highly skilled in handiwork. Indeed, she is the most outstanding of all virgins, and it is right that she be joined to you in wedded affection. And so the plan which seems to us the best, the most profitable, and proof against any misguided quarreling, is that you should have the king's daughter joined to you in marriage.

"Remember the interpretation of the dream, and its mystical meaning. As we see it, things will turn out better for us within this territory. Enough have we battled and beaten the Franks; it seems right to us that we should take our ease, and quietly enjoy the fruits of the earth. Send the bishop back to the king, so that he may say that you are ready to be at his service if he gives you what he has promised. Give him three secure months of peace, as well, so that if he wants, he may come within the period of truce to meet you in public, and make entirely sure of his words and promises."

Rollo told the bishop forthwith that he was sending him back to the king to say these things to him. When he came to the king, and when the bishops had been convoked with a gathering of counts and abbots, he said: "Rollo, the leader of the Northmen, will offer you his hands in submission as a token of fealty, and he pledges love and inviolable friendship toward you, and even his service, if you will give him your daughter, as you have said, to be his wife, and the coast-land as a perpetual possession for the progeny of his progeny; and he will not cease to perform service to you, and you will be able with his help to crush the risings of opponents and rebels against you, and regain your power much strengthened."

When these words had been brought back by the bishop, the Franks wished each other joy, and with one mind proposed to the king that he give his daughter and the land to Rollo. And the king, urged on by the request of the Franks, gave his daughter to the bishop as Rollo's proxy, for a pledge, guaranteed by a jointly sworn oath. When the details of these matters had been worked out, settled and confirmed, and the place and time were determined, and the truce had been arranged, each went back to his own people. Franco, the archbishop of Rouen, went to Rollo and explained to him what he had done in an orderly narrative. And so, when these words had been reported to him, Rollo and his men were filled with great joy, and they called to mind the symbolic interpretation of the dream.

2.27 Now when Duke Robert heard that King Charles would give his daughter to Rollo, and that they would make peace with one another, and that there would be peace for the whole kingdom, he sent a messenger to Rollo with peaceable words to say to him the following words. And when he arrived he spoke to Rollo with words of entreaty: "Robert, duke of the Franks [sends his] faithful service to you. He has heard of the agreement between you and the king, and he rejoices greatly thereat. He says it is right that you and your men should rest, and rebuild the land given to you, and restore the cities and buildings and live in perpetual peace. Enough wars have been waged: enough have you proved your manly skill at arms. Enough have you made known the temper of your valor, enough have you undergone many dangers, enough have you proved your worth as a vassal, enough have you been praised by the whole world. Nay, even the duke himself kneels to you in his mind, and entreats you and charges you that when you have avowed the name of Christ and have been washed in the health-giving font of baptism, you will allow yourself to be raised up by him. From then onwards, if it please you, you two will be firm and inseparable friends, and 'no man will be able to stand against you,' and he will always do you service, and make the king ever look kindly upon you."

When this had been said, Rollo took the advice of bishop Franco and of his counts, and said: "I wish to do as the king and the Franks want: let him come to the appointed meeting and receive me when I have been immersed in the font. Let this man be to me as a father with fatherly love; I will be a son to him, with the love of sons. Let him aid me, if need be, as a father aids a son; I, him, as a son aids a father. Let him rejoice in my prosperity, and sorrow in my adversity. What is in my possession will be his by right, and what is mine by right shall be his possession."

And so the intermediary reported to duke Robert what he had heard.

2.28 And so at the time agreed they came to the appointed place, which is called St. Clair. And Rollo's army sat on this side of the rive Epte, and the king's and Robert's on the other. Without delay, Rollo sent the archbishop to the king of the Franks, to say to him what had to be said: "Rollo cannot make peace with you, because the land you wish to give him is untilled by the plow, altogether bereft of sheep-flocks and herds of cattle, and void of human occupation. Therein is not to be found the means to support life, unless by robbery and raiding. Give him some kingdom from which he can fetch food and clothing for himself until the land which you give him is filled with collected wealth and in time will render to you a harvest in food, men, and beasts. Moreover, he will not be reconciled to you, unless you swear by an oath of the Christian faith, you and the archbishops and the bishops and the counts and abbots of the whole kingdom, that he may hold the land you give him for himself and for his successors, as if it were his private and allodial land [land owned absolutely], in perpetuity: that land from the stream of the Epte as far as the sea."

Then Robert, duke of the Franks, and the counts and bishops who were present along with the abbots, said to the king: "You will not have as honorable a duke as this one, unless you do what he desires. If you will not give him what he asks of you in return for his service, give it to him at least for his adopting the Christian religion, in order that so great a people may be won over to Christ after being ensnared by devilish error; and to prevent the authority of the whole of your realm and of the church from being brought to nothing by the assault of a hostile army, when you hold office as its advocate and protector in lieu of Christ and ought to be the most constant king and advocate."

Then the king wanted to give him the land of Flanders, so that he might live off it; but Rollo would not accept it, on account of the obstructive marshes. Therefore the king undertook to give him Brittany, which was on the frontier of the promised land. Thereupon, Robert and bishop Franco reported everything back to Rollo, and when hostages had been given, they brought him to king Charles under the safe conduct of a Christian oath. And when the Franks gazed on Rollo, who had overrun the whole of Francia, they said to each other: "Great is the power of this leader, great his valor, and great his counsel and his wisdom; and great his labor, too, for having waged so many battles against the counts of this kingdom."

Urged on by the words of the Franks, he immediately put his hands between the hands of the king [in the ceremony of homage], which neither his father, nor his grandfather, nor his great-grandfather had done for any man. And so the king gave his daughter, Gisla by name, to be the wife of that same duke, and he gave the specified territory from the river Epte to the sea as an allod and property; and the whole of Brittany to live off.

2.29 Rollo was unwilling to kiss the king's foot, and the bishops said: "He who accepts a gift such as this ought to go as far as kissing the king's foot." And he replied: "I will never bow my knees at the knees of any man, and no man's foot will I kiss."

And so, urged on by the prayers of the Franks, he ordered one of his warriors to kiss the king's foot. And the man immediately grasped the king's foot and raised it to his mouth and planted a kiss on it while he remained standing, and laid the king flat on his back. So there arose a great laugh, and a great outcry among the people. Apart from that, King Charles and Duke Robert and the counts and nobles swore an oath on the Catholic faith to the patrician Rollo, on their own life and limbs, and by the honor of the whole kingdom, that he should in addition hand on to his heirs the appointed territory as he himself held and owned it, and that the lineage of his sons and grandsons should hold and cultivate it through the course of all time....

2.30 And so, in the 912th year from the incarnation of Our Lord Jesus Christ, archbishop Franco baptized Rollo, after he had been instructed in the Catholic faith of the Holy Trinity; and Robert, duke of the Franks, received him from the font of the Savior, bestowed his name upon him, and honorably enriched him with great rewards and gifts. And Robert, also known as Rollo, had his counts and knights and the whole complement of his army baptized and instructed in the observances of the Christian faith by preaching.

After that, bishop Franco was summoned and asked which churches within his land were held in greater respect, and which should be called the more powerful for the merit and protection afforded by the saints....

So, on the first day of baptism, Robert gave a huge estate to God and to Saint Mary at Rouen church, to be held by the canons in perpetuity. On the second day, to the church of Saint Mary at Bayeux. On the third day, to the church of Saint Mary at Évreux. On the fourth, to the church of the archangel Michael, which is ringed about by the intermittent flooding of the stormy sea, swollen according to the phases of the moon in seven-day patterns. On the fifth, to the church of Saint Peter and Saint Ouen. On the sixth, to the church of Saint Peter and Saint Aicard of Jumièges. On the seventh he gave Berneval with all its dependencies to Saint Denis.

2.31 On the eighth day of his expiation, he took off his baptismal and chrismal vestments, and began to measure out land for his counts by word of mouth, and to enrich his followers. Then, when preparation for a splendid wedding had been made, he married the king's daughter Gisla as his wife, and so reconciled himself to the Franks and made peace. He placed all the nations which desired to remain within his land under his protection. He divided that land among his followers by measure, and rebuilt everything that had been long deserted, and restored it by restocking it with his own warriors and with peoples from abroad. He imposed everlasting privileges and laws on the people, authorized and decreed by the will of the chief men, and he compelled them to dwell together in peace. He raised up churches that had been demolished to the ground, he rebuilt temples that had been ruined by the visitations of the heathens, and he made new and extended the walls and defenses of cities. He subdued the Britons who resisted him, and he amply victualed the whole of the realm that had been granted to him from the Breton food-renders....

CHAPTER TEN

AUSTRVEG: THE VIKING ROAD TO THE EAST

Scandinavian expansion in the East, dominated by the Swedes, was an outgrowth of pre-Viking Age activities in the southeastern Baltic. From about the second half of the eighth century, Scandinavians were living at the trading center at Staraya (Old) Ladoga (known as Aldeigjuborg by the Scandinavians), just off Lake Ladoga on the river Volkhov. With the exception of places where ships had to be portaged to avoid rapids or to get from the headland of one river to another, it was possible to sail by river all the way from the Baltic to the Caspian Sea. This was the austrvegr, the way to the East, or the "Viking road to Byzantium." Trade was the driving force of this eastward expansion. Viking merchants traded furs, honey, wax, walrus ivory, high-grade weapons, and slaves, obtaining in return Arab silver – tens of thousands of coins have been found in Viking Age hoards. Not all Viking voyages to the East were peaceful, however, and commerce was often inseparable from fighting.

Two terms, Rūs and Væringjar (Varangian), are used in Western and Eastern sources to describe the Swedish Vikings in the East. Although this point is contentious, Rūs is probably derived from the Finnish name for the Swedes, Ruotsi, which itself is probably derived from an Old Swedish word meaning something like "rowers" or "seamen." It was the Rūs who gave their name to Russia, although the extent to which they influenced state formation there has been hotly contested by scholars for decades. From the mid-tenth century the term Varangian also came into use. It may be derived from the Old Norse vár (pledge), with reference to the groups of merchant-adventurers who bound themselves into companies and swore to support each other. The term was also used for foreign mercenaries but does not seem to have had specific ethnic associations.

58. THE PIRAEUS LION

In 1687, the Piraeus Lion was looted from Greece and removed to its present location at the Arsenale in Venice. This first- or second-century statue is three meters high and is made of white marble. In the late eleventh century, the lion was visited by some Scandinavians (probably mercenary soldiers), who embellished it with Norse inscriptions in the runic alphabet, or futhark. The inscriptions are now badly worn and difficult to interpret.

Source: Carl Christian Rafn, *Runeindskrift i Piraeus: Inscription runique du Pirée* (København: Société Royale des Antiquaires du Nord, 1856), pp. 2–5.

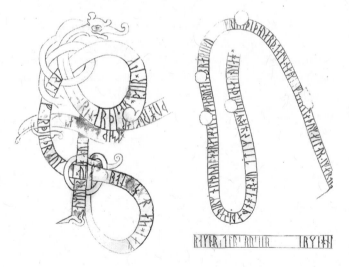

This conjectural transcription is the work of Carl Christian Rafn, a nineteenth-century Danish scholar. Rafn's argument that Harald the Tall is Harald Sigurdarson Hardradi is not persuasive, as the latter's adventures in the East took place considerably earlier than the probable date of the inscription.

Right side of the lion:

ASMUDR : HJU : RUNAR : ÞISAR : ÞAIR : ISKIR : AUK: ÞURLIFR :
ÞURÞR : AUK : IVAR : AT : BON : HARADS : HAFA : ÞUAT :
GRIKIAR : UF : HUGSAÞU : AUK : BANAÞU :

ASMUND CARVED THESE RUNES ALONG WITH ASGEIR AND THORLEIF,
THORD AND IVAR AT THE REQUEST OF HARALD THE TALL, THOUGH THE
GREEKS THOUGHT ABOUT IT AND FORBADE IT.

Left side of the lion:

HAKUN : VAN: ÞIR : ULFR : AUK : ASMUDR : AUK : AURN : HAFN : ÞESA :
ÞIR : MEN : LAGÞU : A : UK : HARADR : HAFI : UF IABUTA : UPRARSTAR :
VEGNA : GRIKIAÞIÞS : VARÞ : DALKR : NAUÞUGR : I : FIARI : LAÞUM :
EGIL : VAR : I : FARU : MIÞ : RAGNARR : TIL : RUMANIU . . . . AUK :
ARMENIU :

HAKON, ALONG WITH ULF AND ASMUND AND ORN, WON THIS SEAPORT.
THESE MEN, WITH HARALD THE TALL, IMPOSED A FINE BECAUSE OF THE
UPRISING OF THE GREEKS. DALK REMAINS AGAINST HIS WILL [CAPTIVE]
IN DISTANT LANDS. EGIL WENT ON A JOURNEY WITH RAGNAR TO
ROMANIA .... AND ARMENIA.

59. THE RŪS

*The Carolingian Annals of St-Bertin (see doc. 47), in its entry for the year 839,
contains the first reference in a European source to the people called the Rūs, and it
links them with Sweden. This excerpt relates how the Byzantine Emperor Theophilus
(829–842) sent envoys to the emperor Louis the Pious.*

Source: trans. Janet L. Nelson, *The Annals of St-Bertin*, (Manchester and New York: Manchester
University Press, 1991), p. 44.

There also came envoys from the Greeks sent by the emperor Theophilus.
They were Theodosius, metropolitan bishop of Chalcedon, and Theophanus
the Spatharius, and they brought gifts worthy for an emperor, and a letter.
The emperor received them with due ceremony on 18 May at Ingelheim.
The purpose of their mission was to confirm the treaty of peace and per-
petual friendship and love between the two emperors and their subjects....

[Theophilus] also sent with the envoys some men who said they – meaning their whole people [*gens*] – were called Russians and had been sent to him by their king, whose name was the Khagan, for the sake of friendship, so they claimed. Theophilus requested in his letter that the emperor in his goodness might grant them safe conducts to travel through his empire and any help or practical assistance needed to return home, for the route by which they had reached Constantinople had taken them through primitive tribes that were very fierce and savage and Theophilus did not wish them to return that way in case some disaster befell them. When the emperor investigated more closely the reason for their coming here, he discovered that they belonged to the people of the Swedes. He suspected that they had really been sent as spies to this kingdom of ours rather than as seekers of our friendship, so he decided to keep them with him until he could find out for certain whether or not they had come in good faith. He lost no time in sending a letter to Theophilus through the same envoys to tell him all this, and to add that he had received them willingly for the sake of his friendship with Theophilus and that if they were found to be genuine, he would supply them with means to return to their fatherland without any risk of danger and send them home with every assistance, but if not, he would send them with envoys of ours back to Theophilus for him to deal with as he might think fit.

60. THE RŪS ATTACK CONSTANTINOPLE

In June of 860, while the emperor Michael III and the army were on campaign against the Muslims, Constantinople was attacked by a Russian fleet numbering two hundred vessels, according to Greek and Slavonic sources. Photius (d. ca 895) was patriarch of Constantinople at the time of the attack and spoke of it in two sermons. The first, quoted here, was delivered in St. Sophia during the attack itself, in the second half of June, and the second probably in early July, following the withdrawal of the Rūs. Although Photius's purpose was not to provide a chronicle or narrative of the attack, but rather to draw moral and religious lessons, his sermons, despite their rhetorical flourishes and moral invectives, represent our best Greek source on the event and constitute important historical evidence, coming as they do from a highly educated and articulate eyewitness.

Source: trans. Cyril Mango, *The Homilies of Photius Patriarch of Constantinople*, (Cambridge, MA: Harvard University Press, 1958), pp. 82–84, 86–92.

Homily III of the Same Most-Blessed Photius, Archbishop of Constantinople, First Homily on the Attack of the Russians.

1. What is this? What is this grievous and heavy blow and wrath? Why has this dreadful bolt fallen on us out of the farthest north? What clouds compacted of woes and condemnation have violently collided to force out this irresistible lightning upon us? Why has this thick, sudden hail-storm of barbarians burst forth, not one that hews down the stalks of wheat and beats down the ears of corn, or lashes the vine-twigs and dashes to pieces the unripe fruit, or strikes the stems of plants and tears the branches apart (which for many has often been the extent of its most grievous damage), but miserably grinding up men's very bodies, and bitterly destroying the whole nation? Why or how have the lees (to call them no worse) of so many and great disasters been poured out on us? Is it not for our sins that all these things have come upon us? Are they not a condemnation and a public parading of our transgressions? Does not the terror of things present indicate the awful and inexorable judgment of the future? Is it not the apprehension of us all, nay the sight before the eyes of each, that not one will have been left any longer to survive, so that not even the fire-tender can escape the calamity to tell the tale? Verily, sins diminish tribes, and sin is like a two-edged sword for those who indulge in it. We were delivered from evils which often had us held; we should have been thankful, but we showed no gratitude. We were saved, and remained heedless; we were protected, and were contemptuous. For these things punishment was to be feared. O cruel and heedless minds, worthy to suffer every misfortune and distress! From those who owed us small and trifling things we made relentless exaction; we chastised them. We forgot to be grateful when the benefit had gone by. Nor did we pity our neighbors because we had been pardoned ourselves. But in being freed from the impending fears and dangers, we became yet more cruel to them, and we neither considered the number and magnitude of our own debts which the Savior had forgiven, nor did we respect the debt of our fellow-servants, tiny as it was, and not to be weighed against our own even in the measure of speech. Having been ourselves mercifully delivered from many great debts, we unmercifully enslaved others for little ones. We enjoyed ourselves, and grieved others; we were glorified, and dishonored others; we grew strong and throve, while waxing insolent and foolish. We became fat, gross and thick, and although we do not forsake God as Jacob of old, yet like the beloved one, we have been filled and we kicked, and like a maddened heifer we raged against the Lord's commandments, and we disdained his ordinances. For this reason there is a sound of war and great destruction in our land. For this reason the Lord hath opened his treasury and brought forth the weapons of his anger. For this reason a people has crept down from the north, as if it were attacking another Jerusalem, and nations have been stirred up from the end of earth, holding bow and spear; the people is fierce and has no mercy;

its voice is as the roaring sea. We have heard the report of them, or rather we have beheld their massed aspect, and our hands have waxed feeble; anguish has seized us, and pangs as a woman in travail....

... I am far from enumerating all the thefts and robberies, the fornications and adulteries, and all those other unspeakable deeds, excellent and durable fuel for this fire that has been kindled and poured around us. I know that now as you revolve these matters, you mourn and look downcast. But time is pressing, the Judge incorruptible, the danger terrible, the mass of sins great, and the repentance insufficient. Often I have sown words of reproof, words of threat in your ears, but, it seems, they grew up amidst thorns. I implored you, I castigated you. Often have I pointed out to you the ashes of the Sodomites, and the flood that went before, when the earth was covered with the waters, and the universal destruction of the human race was effected. Often have I represented the Jewish people, the chosen one, the beloved one, the royal priesthood, for its murmuring, its rebelliousness, its ingratitude, and similar trespasses, being lashed and humbled by the foe it had defeated, and over whom it had itself triumphed – diminished, falling, perishing. Often have I admonished you: be on your guard, mend yourselves, convert yourselves; do not wait for the sword to be furbished: the bow is being bent. Do not take *God's* long-suffering as an occasion for contempt; do not act wickedly in the face of his extreme gentleness. But why do I irritate your hearts which are already inflamed? Surely it is better to castigate you as you are now sorrowing, than to send you away unreproached to suffer punishment from above, and to use the present misfortune as a helper in convicting you, rather than, respecting your plight, leave the disobedient and the sinners unreproved. What now? We have admonished and threatened you, using the name of God: our God is jealous and long-suffering, but when he is angered, who shall withstand him?

2. These things have I been saying, but, it seems, it was like carding *wool* into the fire – a proverb that is timely for me to quote now (would it were not so!). For you have not been converted, nor have you repented, but you have made your ears heavy so that you should not hear the word of the Lord. For this reason his wrath has been poured upon us, and he has kept watch over our sins, and he has set his face against us. "Woe is me, that my sojourning has been too long," will I cry out with the psalmist David, short as it has been. It has been too long because I have not been heard in my entreaties, because I see a cloud of barbarians deluging with blood our city which has been parched by sins. Woe is me that I have been preserved to see these evils, that we have become a reproach to our neighbors, a scorn and derision to them that are round about us, that the unbelievable course of the barbarians did not give rumor time to announce it, so that some means of safety could be

devised, but the sight accompanied the report, and that despite the distance, and the fact that the invaders were sundered off from us by so many lands and kingdoms, by navigable rivers and harborless seas. Woe is me, that I see a fierce and savage tribe fearlessly poured round the city, ravaging the suburbs, destroying everything, ruining everything, fields, houses, herds, beasts of burden, women, children, old men, youths, thrusting their sword through everything, taking pity on nothing, sparing nothing. The destruction is universal. Like a locust in a cornfield, like mildew in a vineyard, or rather like a whirlwind, or a typhoon, or a torrent, or I know not what to say, it fell upon our land and has annihilated whole generations of inhabitants. I deem them happy who have fallen prey to the murderous barbarian hand, because, having died, they have avoided sooner the awareness of the calamities which have seized us unexpectedly. If the departed had any consciousness of these things, then they too would have bewailed with me those who are still left behind for the things they are suffering continually, and because they have taken their fill of so great pain without being relieved of it, and seeking death they find it not. For it is much preferable to die once than to expect continually to die, to be constantly grieved by the sufferings of one's neighbors, and to have one's soul lacerated.

3. Where is now the Christ-loving emperor? Where are the armies? Where are the arms, the engines, the military deliberations and preparations? Is it not an attack of other barbarians which has removed and drawn to itself all these things? The emperor endures long labors beyond the frontier, and the army has marched away to toil with him: whilst we are worn down by the ruin and slaughter before our eyes, which have overtaken some and are about to overtake others. As for this fierce and barbarous Scythian tribe, having crawled out of the very outskirts of the city, like a wild boar it has devoured all round about. Who then will defend us? Who will array himself against the foe? We are deprived of everything, we are helpless on all sides. What lament may equal our misfortunes? What tears will be able to suffice for the magnitude of the calamities that surround us? Come unto me, O most compassionate of prophets, bewail Jerusalem with me – not the ancient one, the metropolis of one nation, which grew up from a root with twelve offshoots, but the metropolis of the entire universe, as much of it as is adorned by the Christian creed, which lords it in antiquity, in beauty, size, splendor, in the multitude and magnificence of its inhabitants. Bewail with me this Jerusalem, not yet captured and fallen down, but standing nigh to being captured, and rocked by the calamities we behold. Bewail with me the queen of the cities, not as she is led away captive, but whose hopes of salvation are in captivity. Seek water for the head and fountains of tears for the eyes, pity her and mourn for her, since she weeps sore in the night, and her tears are on

her cheeks, and there is none to comfort her; since Jerusalem has sinned a sin; therefore has she come into tribulation and those who have been awed by her might have sneered at her; since the Lord has sent fire into her bones, and has made heavy his yoke on our neck, and has laid pains on our hands which we shall be unable to withstand. Weep with me since mine eyes have failed with tears, my belly is troubled, and my heart is turned within me for I am embittered with much bitterness; abroad the sword has bereaved me; and the enemy has opened his mouth against me, and gnashed his teeth, and said: I shall swallow her up. O queenly city, what a throng of evils has poured around thee, as the depths of the sea and the mouth of fire and sword have cast lots according to barbarian custom for the children of thy belly, yea, those settled so splendidly outside the town, and are devouring them. O fair hope of many men, what a calamitous threat and what a mass of horrors have inundated thee all round, and have humbled thy celebrated glory! O city reigning over nearly the whole universe, what an uncaptained army, equipped in servile fashion, is sneering at thee as at a slave! O city adorned with the spoils of many nations, what a nation has bethought itself of despoiling thee! O thou who hast erected many trophies over enemies in Europe, Asia and Libya, see how a barbarous and lowly hand has thrust its spear against thee, making bold to bear in triumph victory over thee! Everything with thee has come to such a pitch of misfortune, that thy unassailable strength has sunk to the dregs of extreme infirmity, and thy enemies, beholding thy infirmity and subjection, display the strength of their arm against thee, and try to bedeck themselves with a glorious name. O queen of queenly cities, who hast saved many others from dangers by thy alliance, who hast with thy arms raised up many that had been forced down to their knees, now lying a prey deprived of helpers! O grace and splendor, size and beauty, elegance and adornment of venerable shrines, O sanctuary of bloodless victims, place inviolate and holy of the dread sacrifice and the mystical table, see how enemies' feet are threatening defilement! O pure veneration, stainless faith, undefiled worship, see how the mouth of the impious and the arrogant is opened wide against us! O white hairs, unction and ministry of the priests! O me, holy shrine of God and God's Wisdom, sleepless eye of the universe! Wail ye virgins, daughters of Jerusalem. Weep ye young men of the city of Jerusalem. Mourn ye also, mothers. Shed tears, ye babes, shed tears; for the magnitude of the calamity forces even you to awareness. Shed tears, for our ills have been multiplied, and there is none to deliver, none to help....

61. ON THE ARRIVAL OF THE VARANGIANS

One of the most important sources relating to the Scandinavians in the East is the so-called Russian Primary Chronicle, *in modern critical literature commonly termed the* Tale of Bygone Years, *after the opening sentence of the text. It covers the period from about 850 to the early twelfth century, but it was compiled only after the mid-eleventh century, and the value of its information before about 1050 is debated. It draws on earlier documents, interweaving historical and legendary material, and its account of the "Calling of the Varangians" is hotly contested. Indeed, the extent to which the Scandinavians had an impact on processes of state-formation in what is today Russia has been vigorously debated by scholars for decades.*

Source: trans. and ed. S.H. Cross and O.P. Sherbowitz-Wetzor, *The Russian Primary Chronicle. Laurentian Text*, (Cambridge, MA: Medieval Academy of America, 1953), pp. 59–60, 64–69, 71–72.

(859) ... The Varangians from beyond the sea imposed tribute upon the Chuds, the Slavs, the Merians, the Ves, and the Krivichians. But the Khazars imposed it upon the Polyanians, the Severians, and the Vyatichians, and collected a squirrel-skin from each hearth.

(860–862) ... The tributaries of the Varangians drove them back beyond the sea and, refusing them further tribute, set out to govern themselves. There was no law among them, but tribe rose against tribe. Discord thus ensued among them, and they began to war one against another. They said to themselves: "Let us seek a prince who may rule over us, and judge us according to the Law." They accordingly went overseas to the Varangian Russes: these particular Varangians were known as Russes, just as some are called Swedes, and others Normans, English, and Gotlanders, for they were thus named. The Chuds, the Slavs, the Krivichians and the Ves then said to the people of Rus [Rus']: "Our land is great and rich, but there is no order in it. Come to rule and reign over us." They thus selected three brothers with their kinfolk, who took with them all the Russes and migrated. The oldest, Rurik, located himself in Novgorod; the second, Sineus, in Beloozero; and the third Truvor, in Izborsk. On account of these Varangians, the district of Novgorod became known as the land of Rus. The present inhabitants of Novgorod are descended from the Varangian race, but aforetime they were Slavs.

After two years, Sineus and his brother Truvor died, and Rurik assumed the sole authority. He assigned cities to his followers, Polotzk to one, Rostov to another, and to another Beloozero. In these cities there are thus Varangian colonists, but the first settlers were, in Novgorod, Slavs; in Polotzk,

Krivichians; at Beloozero, Ves; in Rostov, Merians; and in Murom, Muro-mians. Rurik had dominion over all these districts.

With Rurik there were two men who did not belong to his kin, but were boyars [nobles]. They obtained permission to go to Tsar'grad [Constantinople] with their families. They thus sailed down the Dnieper, and in the course of their journey they saw a small city on a hill. Upon their inquiry as to whose town it was, they were informed that three brothers, Kiy, Shchek, and Khoriv, had once built the city, but that since their deaths, their descendants were living there as tributaries of the Khazars. Askold and Dir remained in this city, and after gathering together many Varangians, they established their dominion over the country of Polyanians at the same time that Rurik was ruling at Novgorod.

(863–866) ... Askold and Dir attacked the Greeks during the fourteenth year of the reign of the Emperor Michael. When the emperor had set forth against the infidels [Muslims] and had arrived at the Black River, the eparch [governor] sent him word that the Russes were approaching Tsar'grad, and the emperor turned back. Upon arriving inside the strait, the Russes made a great massacre of the Christians, and attacked Tsar'grad in two hundred boats. The emperor succeeded with difficulty in entering the city. He straight-away hastened with the patriarch Photus to the Church of Our Lady of the Blachernae, where they prayed all night. They also sang hymns and carried the sacred vestment of the Virgin to dip it in the sea. The weather was still, and the sea was calm, but a storm of wind came up, and when great waves straightaway rose, confusing the boats of the godless Russes, it threw them upon the shore and broke them up, so that few escaped such destruction. The survivors then returned to their native land.

Prince Oleg's Campaign against Constantinople

(904–907) ... Leaving Igor [Igor'] in Kiev, Oleg attacked the Greeks. He took with him a multitude of Varangians, Slavs, Chuds, Krivichians, Merians, Polyanians, Severians, Derevlians, Radimichians, Croats, Dulebians, and Tivercians who are pagan. All these tribes are known as Great Scythia by the Greeks. With this entire force, Oleg sallied forth by horse and by ship, and the number of his vessels was two thousand. He arrived before Tsar'grad, but the Greeks fortified the strait and closed up the city. Oleg disembarked upon the shore, and ordered his soldiery to beach the ships. They waged war around the city, and accomplished much slaughter of the Greeks. They also destroyed many palaces and burned the churches. Of the prisoners they captured, some they beheaded, some they tortured, some they shot, and still others they cast into the sea. The Russes inflicted many other woes upon the Greeks after the usual manner of soldiers. Oleg commanded his warriors to make wheels which they attached to the ships, and when the wind was favorable, they spread the sails and bore down upon the city from the open country. When the Greeks beheld this, they were afraid, and sending messengers to Oleg, they implored him not to destroy the city, and offered to submit to such tribute as he should desire. Thus Oleg halted his troops. The Greeks then brought out to him food and wine, but he would not accept it, for it was mixed with poison. Then the Greeks were terrified and exclaimed: "This is not Oleg, but St. Demetrius, whom God has sent upon us." So Oleg demanded that they pay tribute for his two thousand ships at the rate of twelve *grivnas* [unit of Kievan currency] per man, with forty men reckoned to a ship.

The Greeks assented to these terms, and prayed for peace lest Oleg should conquer the land of Greece. Retiring thus a short distance from the city, Oleg concluded a peace with the Greek emperors Leo and Alexander, and sent into the city to them Karl, Farulf, Vermund, Hrollaf, and Steinvith, with instructions to receive the tribute. The Greeks promised to satisfy their requirements. Oleg demanded that they should give to the troops on the two thousand ships twelve *grivnas* per bench, and pay in addition the sums required for the various Russian cities: first Kiev, the Chernigov, Pereiaslavl, Polotzk, Rostov, Liubech, and other towns. In these cities lived princes subject to Oleg.

[The Russes proposed the following terms:] "The Russes who come hither shall receive as much grain as they require. Whosoever come as merchants shall receive supplies for six months, including bread, wine, meat, fish and fruit. Baths shall be prepared for them in any volume they require. When the Russians return homeward, they shall receive from your emperor food, anchors, cordage, and sails and whatever else is needed for the journey."

The Greeks accepted these stipulations, and the emperors and all the courtiers declared: "If Russes come hither without merchandise, they shall receive no provisions. Your prince shall personally lay injunction upon such Russians as journey hither that they shall do no violence in the towns and throughout our territory. Such Russes as arrive here shall dwell in the St. Mamas quarter. Our government will send officers to record their names, and they shall then receive their monthly allowance, first the natives of Kiev, then those from Chernigov, Pereyaslavl, and the other cities. They shall not enter the city save through one gate, unarmed and fifty at a time, escorted by agents of the emperor. They may conduct business according to their requirements, and without payment of taxes."

Thus the emperors Leo and Alexander made peace with Oleg, and after agreeing upon the tribute and mutually binding themselves by oath, they kissed the cross, and invited Oleg and his men to swear an oath likewise. According to the religion of the Russes, the latter swore by their weapons and by their god Perun, as well as by Volos, the god of cattle, and thus confirmed the treaty.

Oleg gave orders that sails of brocade should be made for the Russians and silken ones for the Slavs, and his demand was satisfied. The Russes hung their shields upon the gates as a sign of victory, and Oleg then departed from Tsar'grad. The Russes unfurled their sails of brocade and the Slavs their sails of silk, but the wind tore them. Then the Slavs said: "Let us keep our canvas ones; silken sails are not made for the Slavs." So Oleg came to Kiev, bearing palls, gold, fruit, and wine, along with every sort of adornment. The people called Oleg "the Sage," for they were but pagans, and therefore ignorant.

A Treaty with Byzantium, 911–912

(912) ... Oleg despatched his vassals to make peace and to draw up a treaty between the Greeks and the Russes. His envoys thus made declaration:

"This is the copy of the treaty concluded under the emperors Leo and Alexander. We of the Rus nation: Karl, Ingjald, Farulf, Vermund, Hrollaf, Gunnar, Harold, Karni, Frithleif, Hroarr, Angantyr, Throand, Leithulf, Fast, and Steinvith, are sent by Oleg, Great Prince of Rus, and by all the serene and great princes and the great boyars [nobles] under his sway, unto you, Leo and Alexander and Constantine, great autocrats in God, emperors of the Greeks, for the maintenance and proclamation of the long-standing amity which joins Greeks and Russes, in accordance with the desires of our great princes and at their command, and on behalf of all those Russes who are subject to the hand of our prince.

"Our serenity, above all desirous, through God's help, of maintaining and proclaiming such amicable relations as now exist between Christians and Russians, has often deemed it proper to publish and confirm this amity not merely in words but also in writing and under a firm oath sworn upon our weapons according to our religion and our law. As we previously agreed in the name of God's peace and amity, the articles of this convention are as follows:

"First, that we shall conclude a peace with your Greeks, and love each other with all our heart and will, and as far as lies in our power, prevent any subject of our serene princes from committing any crime or misdemeanor. Rather shall we exert ourselves as far as possible to maintain as irrevocable and immutable henceforth and forever the amity thus proclaimed by our agreement with you Greeks and ratified by signature and oath. May you Greeks on your part maintain as irrevocable and immutable henceforth and forever this same amity toward our serene prince of Rus and toward all the subjects of our serene Prince.

"In the matter of stipulations concerning damage, we subscribe to the following provisions:

"If clear proofs of tort exist, there shall be a true declaration of such proofs. But if this declaration is contested, the dissenting party shall take oath to this effect, and after he shall have taken oath according to his faith, a penalty shall be assessed in proportion to the apparent trespass committed.

"Whatsoever Russ kills a Christian, or whatsoever Christian kills a Russ, shall die, since he has committed murder. If any man flee after committing a murder, in the case that he is well-to-do, the nearest relatives of the victim shall receive a legal portion of the culprit's property, while the wife of the murderer shall receive a like amount, which is legally due her. But if the defendant is poor and has escaped, he may be under duress until he returns, when he shall be executed.

"If any man strike another with a sword or assault him with any other sort of weapon, he shall, according to Russian law, pay five pounds of silver for such blow or assault. If the defendant is poor, he shall pay as much as he is able, and be deprived even of the very clothes he wears, and he shall also declare upon oath that he has no one to aid him. Thereafter the case against him shall be discontinued.

"If any Russ commit a theft against a Christian, or *vice versa*, and should the transgressor be caught in the act by the victim of the loss, and be killed while resisting arrest, no penalty shall be exacted for his death by either Greeks or Russes. The victim of the loss shall recover the stolen property. If the thief surrenders, he shall be taken and bound by the one upon whom the theft was committed, and the culprit shall return whatever he has dared to appropriate, making at the same time restitution for it.

"If any person, whether Greek or Russ, employs abusive treatment or violence against another and appropriates by force some articles of his property, he shall repay three times its value.

"If a ship is detained by high winds upon a foreign shore, and one of us Russes is near by, the ship with its cargo shall be revictualed and sent on to Christian territory. We will pilot it through every dangerous passage until it arrives at a place of safety. But if any such ship thus detained by storm or by some territorial obstacle cannot possibly reach its destination, we Russes will extend aid to the crew of this ship, and conduct them with their merchandise in all security, in case such an event takes place near Greek territory. But if such an accident befalls near the Russian shore, the ship's cargo shall be disposed of, and we Russes will remove whatever can be disposed of for the account of the owners. Then, when we proceed to Greece with merchandise or upon an embassy to your emperor, we shall render up honorably the price of the sold cargo of the ship. But if anyone on that ship is killed or maltreated by us Russes, or if any object is stolen, then those who have committed such acts shall be subject to the previously provided penalty.

"From this time forth, if a prisoner of either nation is in durance either of the Russes or of the Greeks, and then sold into another country, any Russ or Greek who happens to be in that locality shall purchase the prisoner and return the person thus purchased to his own native country. The purchaser shall be indemnified for the amount thus expended, or else the value of the prisoner's daily labor shall be reckoned toward the purchase money. If any Russ be taken prisoner by the Greeks, he shall likewise be sent back to his native land, and his purchase price shall be repaid, as has been stipulated, according to his value.

"Whenever you find it necessary to declare war, or when you are conducting a campaign, providing any Russes desirous of honoring your emperor shall come at any time and wish to remain in his service, they shall be permitted in this respect to act according to their desire.

"If a Russian prisoner from any region is sold among the Russes, he shall be ransomed for twenty bezants and returned to his native land.

"In case a Russian slave is stolen or escapes or is sold under compulsion, and if a Russ institutes a claim to this effect which is substantiated, the slave shall be returned to Rus. If a merchant loses a slave and institutes a complaint, he shall search for his slave until he is found, but if any person refuses to allow him to make this search, the local officer shall forfeit his right of perquisition.

"With respect to the Russes professionally engaged in Greece under the orders of the Christian emperor, if any of them dies without setting his property in good order and has no kinsfolk there, his estate shall be returned to his distant relatives in Rus. But if he makes some disposition of his goods, the person whom he has designated in writing as his heir shall receive the property of which he thus disposed. Such shall be the due process of inheritance in the case of Russes engaging in trade, of casual travelers in Greece, and of those having debts outstanding there.

"If a criminal takes refuge in Greece, the Russes shall make complaint to the Christian Empire, and such criminal shall be arrested and returned to Rus regardless of his protests. The Russes shall perform the same service for the Greeks whenever the occasion arises.

"As a convention and an inviolable pledge binding equally upon you Greeks and upon us Russes, we have caused the present treaty to be transcribed in vermillion script upon parchment in duplicate. In the name of the

Holy Cross and the Holy and Indivisible Trinity of your one true God, your emperor has confirmed it with his signature and handed it to our envoys. According to our own faith and the custom of our nation, we have sworn to your emperor, who rules over you by the grace of God, that we will neither violate ourselves, nor allow any of our subjects to violate the peace and amity assured by the articles thus concluded between us. We have transmitted this document for the ratification of your Majesty in order to confirm and promulgate the treaty thus concluded between us this second of September, in the year of Creation 6420 [911 CE], fifteenth of the indiction."

A Russian Attack on Byzantium is Beaten Back by Greek Fire, 941

(935–941) ... Igor attacked the Greeks, and the Bulgarians sent word to the emperor that the Russes were advancing upon Tsar'grad with ten thousand vessels. The Russes set out across the sea, and began to ravage Bithynia. They waged war across the Pontus as far as Heraclea and Paphlagonia, and laid waste the entire region of Nicomedia, burning everything along the gulf. Of the people they captured, some they butchered, others they set up as targets and shot at, some they seized upon, and after binding their hands behind their backs, they drove iron nails through their heads. Many sacred churches they gave to the flames, while they burned many monasteries and villages, and took no little booty on both sides of the sea. Then, when the army came out of the east, Pantherius the Domestic with forty thousand men, Phocas the Patrician with the Macedonians, and Theodore the General with the Thracians, supported by other illustrious nobles, surrounded the Russes. After taking counsel, the latter threw themselves upon the Greeks, and as the conflict between them was desperate, the Greeks experienced difficulty in winning the upper hand. The Russes returned at evening to their companions, embarked at night upon their vessels, and fled away. Theophanes pursued them in boats with Greek fire, and dropped it through pipes upon the Russian ships, so that a strange miracle was offered to view.

Upon seeing the flames, the Russians cast themselves into the sea-water, being anxious to escape, but the survivors returned home. When they came once more to their native land, where each one reported to his kinsfolk the course of events and described the fire launched from the ships, they related that the Greeks had in their possession the lightning from heaven, and had set them on fire by pouring it forth, so that the Russes could not conquer them. Upon his return, Igor began to collect a great army, and sent many messengers after the Varangians beyond the sea, inviting them to attack the Greeks, for he desired to make war upon them.

62. A MUSLIM DIPLOMAT MEETS VIKING MERCHANTS

Ibn Fadlān was a member of an embassy sent by the caliph of Baghdad to the king of the Bulgars on the Volga River in the early 920s. His Risāla *(Writing) describes his meeting with a group of Swedish Rūs merchants (see doc. 19a).*

Source: trans. Albert S. Cook, "Ibn Fadlān's Account of Scandinavian Merchants on the Volga in 922," *Journal of English and Germanic Philology* 22 (1923): 54–63.

I saw how the Northmen had arrived with their wares, and pitched their camp beside the Volga. Never did I see people so gigantic; they are tall as palm trees, and florid and ruddy of complexion. They wear neither camisoles [tunics] nor *chaftans* [cloaks], but the men among them wear a garment of rough cloth, which is thrown over one side, so that one hand remains free. Every one carries an ax, a dagger, and a sword, and without these weapons they are never seen. Their swords are broad, with wavy lines, and of Frankish make. From the tip of the finger-nails to the neck, each man of them is tattooed with pictures of trees, living beings, and other things. The women carry, fastened to their breast, a little case of iron, copper, silver, or gold, according to their wealth and resources of their husbands. Fastened to the case they wear a ring, and upon that a dagger, all attached to their breast. About their necks they wear gold and silver chains. If the husband possesses ten thousand dirhems [Islamic silver coins], he has one chain made for his wife; if twenty thousand, two; and for every ten thousand, one is added. Hence it often happens that a Scandinavian woman has a large number of chains about her neck. Their most highly prized ornaments consist of small green shells [or beads, according to a more recent translation], of one of the varieties which are found in the [bottoms of] ships [or, alternatively, which are formed on the polishing stone]. They made great efforts to obtain these, paying as much as a dirhem for a shell, and stringing them as a necklace for their wives.

They are the filthiest race that God ever created. They do not wipe themselves after going to stool, nor wash themselves after a nocturnal pollution, any more than if they were wild asses.

They come from their own country, anchor their ships in the Volga, which is a great river, and build large wooden houses on its bank. In every such house they live ten or twenty, more or fewer. Each man has a couch, where he sits with the beautiful girls he has for sale. Here he is as likely as not to enjoy one of them while a friend looks on. At times several of them will be thus engaged at the same moment, each in full view of the others. Now and again a merchant will resort to a house to purchase a girl, and find her master thus embracing her, and not giving over until he has finally had his will.

Every morning a girl comes and brings a tub of water, and places it before her master. In this he proceeds to wash his face and hands, and then his hair, combing it out over the vessel. Thereupon he blows his nose, and spits into the tub, and, leaving no dirt behind, conveys it all into this water. When he has finished, the girl carries the tub to the man next him, who does the same. Thus she continues carrying the tub from one to another, till each of those who are in the house has blown his nose and spit into the tub, and washed his face and hair.

As soon as their ships have reached the anchorage, every one goes ashore, having at hand bread, meat, onions, milk, and strong drink, and betakes himself to a high, upright piece of wood, bearing the likeness of a human face; this is surrounded by smaller statues, and behind these there are still other tall pieces of wood driven into the ground. He advances to the large wooden figure, prostrates himself before it, and thus addresses it: "O my lord, I am come from a far country, bringing with me so and so many girls, and so and so many pelts of sable [or marten]"; and when he has thus enumerated all his merchandise, he continues, "I have brought thee this present," laying before the wooden statue what he has brought, and saying: "I desire thee to bestow upon me a purchaser who has gold and silver coins, who will buy from me to my heart's content, and who will refuse none of my demands." Having so said, he departs. If his trade then goes ill, he returns and brings a second, or even a third present. If he still continues to have difficulty in obtaining what he desires, he brings a present to one of the small statues, and implores its intercession, saying: "These are the wives and daughters of our lord." Continuing thus, he goes to each statue in turn, invokes it, beseeches its intercession, and bows humbly before it. If it then chances that his trade goes swimmingly, and he disposes of all his merchandise, he reports: "My lord has fulfilled my desire; now it is my duty to repay him." Upon this, he takes a number of cattle and sheep, slaughters them, gives a portion of the meat to the poor, and carries the rest before the large statue and the smaller ones that surround it, hanging the heads of the sheep and cattle on the large piece of wood which is planted in the earth. When night falls, dogs come and devour it all. Then he who has so placed it exclaims: "I am well pleasing to my lord; he has consumed my present."

… It is the custom among the Northmen that with the king in his hall there shall be four hundred of the most valiant and trustworthy of his companions, who stand ready to die with him or to offer their life for his. Each of them has a girl to wait upon him – to wash his head, and to prepare food and drink; and, besides her, he has another who serves as his concubine. These four hundred sit below the king's high seat, which is large, and adorned with precious stones. Accompanying him on his high seat are forty girls, destined for his bed, whom he causes to sit near him. Now and again he will proceed to enjoy one of them in the presence of the above mentioned nobles of his following. The king does not descend from the high seat, and is therefore obliged, when he needs to relieve himself, to make use of a vessel. If he wishes to ride, his horse is led up to the high seat, and he mounts from there; when he is ready to alight, he rides his horse up so close that he can step immediately from it to his throne. He has a lieutenant, who leads his armies, wars with his enemies, and represents him to his subjects.

63. RIVER ROUTES TO CONSTANTINOPLE

The treatise De Administrando Imperio, *compiled and written between 948 and 952 by the Byzantine emperor Constantine VII Porphyrogenitus (r. 945–959), was intended as a confidential manual of kingcraft for his son. It has been called the most important of the Byzantine sources concerned with the Rūs. It contains a detailed account of the so-called Viking Road to Byzantium – the network of waterways, lakes, and portages that led from Scandinavia to Byzantium (Constantinople); the Dnieper River was a key artery of this network.*

Source: trans. R.J.H. Jenkins, Constantine Porphyrogenitus, *De Administrando Imperio*, ed. G. Moravesik (new revised ed.; Washington, DC: Dumbarton Oaks, 1967), vol. I, pp. 57–63.

9. The monoxyla [dugout vessels of varying sizes] which come down from outer Russia to Constantinople are from Novgorod, where Sviatoslav, son of Igor, prince of Russia, had his seat and others from the city of Smolensk and from Teliutza and Chernigov and from Vyshegrad. All these come down the river Dnieper, and are collected together at the city of Kiev, also called Sambatas. Their Slav tributaries, the so-called Krivichians and the Lenzanenes and the rest of the Slavonic regions, cut the monoxyla on their mountains in time of winter, and when they have prepared them, as spring approaches, and the ice melts, they bring them on to the neighboring lakes. And since these lakes debouch into the river Dnieper, they enter thence on to this same river and come down to Kiev, and draw the ships along to be finished and sell them to the Russians. The Russians buy these bottoms only, furnishing them with oars and rowlocks and other tackle from their old monoxyla, which they dismantle; and so they fit them out. And in the month of June they move off down the river Dnieper and come to Vitichev, which is a tributary city of the Russians, and there they gather during two or three days; and when all the monoxyla are collected together, then they set out, and come down the

said Dnieper river. And first they come to the first barrage, called Essoupi, which means in Russian and Slavonic "Do not sleep!"; the barrage itself is as narrow as the width of the Polo-ground; in the middle of it are rooted high rocks, which stand out like islands. Against these, then, comes the water and wells up and dashes down over the other side, with a mighty and terrific din. Therefore the Russians do not venture to pass between them, but put in to the bank hard by, disembarking the men on to dry land leaving the rest of the goods on board the monoxyla; they then strip and, feeling with their feet to avoid striking on a rock.... This they do, some at the prow, some amidships, while others again, in the stern, punt with poles; and with all this careful procedure they pass this first barrage, edging round under the river-bank. When they have passed this barrage, they re-embark the others from the dry land and sail away, and come down to the second barrage, called in Russian Oulvorsi, and in Slavonic Ostrovouniprach, which means "the Island of the Barrage." This one is like the first, awkward and not to be passed through. Once again they disembark the men and convey the monoxyla past, as on the first occasion. Similarly they pass the third barrage also, called Gelandri, which means in Slavonic "Noise of the Barrage," and then the fourth bar-rage, the big one, called in Russian Aeifor, and in Slavonic Neasit, because the pelicans nest in the stones of the barrage. At this barrage all put into land prow foremost, and those who are deputed to keep the watch with them get out, and off they go, these men, and keep vigilant watch for the Pechenegs. The remainder, taking up the goods which they have on board the monoxyla, conduct the slaves in their chains past by land, six miles, until they are through the barrage. Then, partly dragging their monoxyla, partly portaging them on their shoulders, they convey them to the far side of the barrage; and then, putting them on the river and loading up their baggage, they embark themselves, and again sail off in them. When they come to the fifth barrage, called in Russian Varouforos, and in Slavonic Voulniprach, because it forms a large lake, they again convey their monoxyla through at the edges of the river, as at the first and second barrages, and arrive at the sixth barrage, called in Russian Leanti, and in Slavonic Veroutzi, that is "the Boiling of the Water," and this too they pass similarly. And thence they sail away to the seventh barrage, called in Russian Stroukoun, and in Slavonic Naprezi, which means "Little Barrage." This they pass at the so-called ford of *Vrar*, where the Chersonites cross over from Russia and the Pechenegs to Cherson; which ford is as wide as the Hippodrome, and, measured upstream from the bottom as far as the rocks break surface, a bow-shot in length. It is at this point, therefore, that the Pechenegs come down and attack the Rus-sians. After traversing this place, they reach the island called St. Gregory, on which island they perform their sacrifices because a gigantic oak-tree stands there; and they sacrifice live cocks. Arrows, too, they peg in round about, and others bread and meat, or something of whatever each may have, as is their custom. They also throw lots regarding the cocks, whether to slaughter them, or to eat them as well, or to leave them alive. From this island onwards the Russians do not fear the Pecheneg until they reach the river Selinas. So then they start off thence and sail for four days, until they reach the lake which forms the mouth of the river, on which is the island of St. Aitherios. Arrived at this island, they rest themselves there for two or three days. And they re-equip their *monoxyla* with such tackle as is needed, sails and masts and rudders, which they bring with them. Since this lake is the mouth of this river, as has been said, and carries on down to the sea, and the island of St. Aitherios lies on the sea, they come thence to the Dniester River, and having got safely there they rest again. But when the weather is propitious, they put to sea and come to the river called Aspros, and after resting there too in like manner, they again set out and come to the Selinas, to the so-called branch of the Danube River. And until they are past the river Selinas, the Pechenegs keep pace with them. And if it happens that the sea casts a *monoxylon* on shore, they all put in to land, in order to present a united opposition to the Pechenegs. But after the Selinas they fear nobody, but, entering the territory of Bulgaria, they come to the mouth of the Danube. From the Danube they proceed to the Konopas, and from the Konopas to Constantia, and from Constantia to the river of Varna, and from Varna they come to the River Ditzina, all of which are Bulgarian territory. From the Ditzina they reach the district of Mesembria, and there at last their voyage, fraught with such travail and terror, such difficulty and danger, is at an end. The severe manner of life of these same Russians in winter-time is as follows. When the month of November begins, their chiefs together with all the Russians at once leave Kiev and go off on the *poliudia*, which means "rounds," that is, to the Slavonic regions of the Vervians and Drugovichians and Krivichians and Severians and the rest of the Slavs who are tributaries of the Russians. There they are maintained throughout the winter, but then once more, starting from the month of April, when the ice of the Dnieper river melts, they come back to Kiev. They then pick up their *monoxyla*, as has been said above, and fit them out, and come down to Romania....

64. A NORWEGIAN SOLDIER OF FORTUNE IN THE EAST

The names of many Scandinavians who ventured to the East are known, but none is as famous as Harald Sigurdarson, better known as Harald harðráði (Hardradi; Hard-Ruler). A half-brother of Olaf Haraldsson (St. Olaf, d. 1030), Harald was sole ruler of Norway from 1047 until his death in 1066 (see doc. 100). But before becoming king of Norway, Harald's career took him to the East, first in the service of Jaroslav, the ruler of Kiev, and subsequently in the service of the Byzantine emperor as leader of the famous Varangian guard. The most gripping account of Harald's career is his saga in Snorri Sturluson's Heimskringla, *and while some folkloric elements and geographical errors have crept into the saga, Harald's presence and campaigns in the East are also recorded in an eleventh-century Greek text. The saga account provides valuable insight into the employment of Scandinavian mercenaries in the East, though Harald's experiences as a prince must have differed from those of the rank-and-file.*

Source: Snorri Sturluson, *Haralds saga Sigurðarson*, in *Heimskringla*, ed. Bjarni Aðalbjarnarson, Íslenzk fornrit XXVI–XXVIII (Reykjavík, 2002), vol. 3, pp. 71–90.

3. At that time, Queen Zoe the Great [ca 978–1050] ruled over Greece [Byzantine Empire] together with Michael Katalactus [r. 1034–41]. When Harald arrived in Mikligard [Constantinople], he went to see the queen and entered her service as a mercenary soldier. That autumn, he sailed with the galleys that were transporting soldiers to the Greek Sea. He was in charge of a company of his own men.

In those days, the commander of the army was one of the queen's relatives, a man called Gyrgir. But before long the Varangians allied themselves with Harald, and formed up with him and his men whenever there was a battle. Eventually, Harald became leader of all the Varangians. Gyrgir and his army sailed all through the Greek islands, making frequent attacks on corsairs....

6. When Harald arrived in Sicily he went on raiding expeditions and then camped with his army beside a large, populous city. He settled in for a siege, for the city had strong walls, and he didn't think he could breach them.

The citizens had plenty of food and whatever else they needed to withstand a siege. So Harald hit on a plan. He had his fowlers catch some little birds which nested in the city and flew out to the forest during the day to find food. Then he had chips of resinous wood, smeared with wax and brimstone, attached to the birds' backs and set alight. The instant the birds were released, they all flew straight back to the city to seek out their young and their nests in the thatched roofs. The fire then spread from the birds to the house-thatches, which were made of reeds or straw. Even though each bird carried only a small spark of fire, there was soon a huge conflagration as lots of birds brought fire to thatches throughout the city. One house after another burst into flames until the whole city was ablaze.

The inhabitants abandoned the city and begged for mercy, even the ones who had often spoken haughtily and dismissively about the Greek army and its leaders. Harald spared everyone who asked for mercy and took control of the city....

11. Harald spent many years in this sort of warfare, both in the land of the Saracens and in Sicily. Afterwards, he returned to Mikligard with the army, and stayed there for a short while before setting out on a journey to Palestine. He left behind the gold he had got from the Greek king as payment for his services, and so did all the Varangians who went with him. It is said that Harald fought eighteen major battles in the course of his campaigns. Thjodolf says:

> People have heard that Harald
> fought eighteen fierce fights;
> in that prince's presence,
> peace often perished;
> the eagle's grey claws grew
> blood-red and the ravening
> wolf ate well
> before Harald headed home.

12. Harald sailed to Palestine with his army and then went overland to Jerusalem. Wherever he went, every town and castle was surrendered to him. Here is Stuf the skald's account of these events – he heard them related by the king himself.

> From Greece, the great king
> came to conquer Jerusalem;
> without effort he easily
> got control of the country;
> without battle or burnings,
> the whole land laid itself
> under his princely power.
> Joyfully, may the mighty Harald
> [the last line to be read with the last
> line of the next stanza]

Here we are told that the land came under Harald's control without being burned or plundered. Then he went to the River Jordan and bathed in it, as is the custom of pilgrims. He donated great treasures to the Lord's tomb, as well as to the holy cross and other sacred relics in Palestine, and made the road safe all the way to the Jordan by killing robbers and plunderers. Thus says Stuf:

> His wrath being roused,
> the kingly commander
> targeted the treacherous
> on both banks of the Jordan;
> for their evil acts
> the prince punished
> all his enemies.
> live forever with the Lord.
> [the last line to be read with the last line of
> the previous stanza]

Then he returned to Mikligard.

13. When Harald got back to Mikligard from Palestine, he grew anxious to return to his ancestral estates in the Northlands, for he had heard that his nephew Magnus Olafsson had become king of both Norway and Denmark. He declared his intention of ending his service with the king, but when Queen Zoe heard about this, she was furious. She accused Harald of misappropriating valuables, which had been seized as plunder when he was in command of the army, but which rightfully belonged to the Greek king.

Harald had asked for the hand of a beautiful, young girl – Queen Zoe's niece, Maria – but the queen had refused. According to Varangians here in the north who had served as mercenaries in Mikligard, it was the opinion of people in the know there that the queen wanted to marry Harald herself. This, they said, was the real reason for her accusations against him when he wanted to leave Mikligard – though people were led to believe something different. And this explains why the Greek king had Harald arrested and thrown into a dark dungeon. The king at that time was Constantine Monomach [ca 1000–1055], who ruled together with Queen Zoe.

14. As Harald approached the prison, King Olaf the saint appeared to him and said that he would help him. Afterwards, a chapel was built in that street and dedicated to Saint Olaf. It has stood there ever since. The prison consisted of a tall tower, open at the top, and with a door leading into it from the street. Harald was thrown into this prison, along with Halldor and Ulf

[two Icelanders], but the very next night, a rich lady and two of her servants climbed up ladders to the top of the tower. Then they lowered a rope into the prison and pulled up Harald and his men. King Olaf the saint had once cured this lady of a sickness and had appeared to her and asked her to free his brother [Harald].

King Harald went straight to the Varangians, and they all got up and welcomed him. Then they armed themselves and went to the king's bedchamber. There they seized the king and put out both his eyes. Thorarin Skeggjason says in his *drápa*:

> Our king came by
> much gold in Greece;
> but the emperor is eyeless
> after terrible torture.

Thjodolf the skald says:

> The healer of wolves' woes,
> our great lord, gouged
> out the emperor's eyes
> – that was the start of the strife;
> over in the east
> the lord of Agder left
> a cruel mark on a manly king;
> rough was the Greek king's road.

In these two *drápas*, and in many other poems about Harald, it is clearly stated that he himself blinded the Greek king. A chieftain, or an earl, or some other high-born man would have been named if it had been known for sure that he had done it. But this story was spread by Harald himself and by the men who were there with him.

15. The same night, Harald and his men went to the house where Maria slept and abducted her. Then they went to the Varangian galleys, took two of them, and rowed into the Golden Horn until they reached the point where iron chains are stretched across the sound. Harald ordered the crews of both galleys to ply their oars and told all the men who were not rowing to run toward the stern, carrying their leather bags. In this way, they ran the galleys up onto the iron chains, where they stuck fast. Harald immediately ordered his men to run to the bows. This movement tipped Harald's galley forward and pitched it free of the chains with a shudder, but the other galley remained hung up on the chains and broke apart. Some of the crew were pulled from

the water, but many of them drowned there.

That is how Harald escaped from Mikligard and entered the Black Sea, but before he sailed away, he put the young woman ashore and provided her with several attendants to escort her back to Mikligard. Harald told her to point out to Zoe how little control she had over him and how, with all her power, she was unable to prevent him from abducting the girl. Then he sailed north to the mouth of the Dnieper and from there he traveled all over the eastern realm....

16. When Harald came to Holmgard [Novgorod], King Jarizleif [ca 978–1054] gave him a splendid welcome. He stayed there for the winter and took charge of all the gold and the many other treasures that he had sent from Mikligard. No one in the Northlands had ever seen so much wealth in the possession of one man for, while he was in Mikligard, Harald had participated in "palace-pillaging" three times. It was the law there that when a Greek king died, the Varangians had pillaging rights at his palaces. They were permitted to go through all the king's treasuries and each man could help himself freely to whatever he could lay his hands on.

65. RŪS EXPEDITIONS TO THE MIDDLE EAST

Among the otherwise unknown sources incorporated into the historical compilation of the Ottoman writer Ahmad b. Lutfullāh (d. 1702) is an anonymous local history, originally composed in the late eleventh century, of three Muslim lands in the eastern Caucasus, in what today roughly corresponds to Azerbaijan: Al-Bāb (Bāb al-Abwāb or Darband); Sharvān, north of the Kur River; and Arrān, south of the Kur. On the frontiers of the Islamic world, the northern neighbors of these regions included, from the 960s, the Rūs. The first reference to the Rūs in this text occurs in the chapter on al-Bāb under the dates 377/987, with further episodes related in 379/989, 421/1030, and 423/1032.

Source: trans. V. Minorsky, *A History of Sharvān and Darband in the 10th–11th Centuries* (Cambridge: W. Heffer & Sons, 1958), pp. 31–32, 45, 47.

Of the Kings of Sharvān and Bāb al-Abwāb in Two Sections

15. ... Later in the same year [1030] the Rūs entered Sharvan and the sharvanshah Minūchir met them near Bākūya [Baku]. Many of the Sharvanians were killed and Ahmad b. Khāsskīn, one of their notables, lost his life. Then the Rūs went up to the river Kurr and Minuchihr closed the Araxes [al-Rass] in order to stop their progress, but they drowned a party of Muslims. Later

the lord of Janza [Ganja] Mūsā b. Fadl made them disembark. He gave them much money and took them to Baylaqān, whose inhabitants had revolted against him. With the help of the Rūs he captured Baylaqān and seized and killed his brother 'Askariya. Then the Rūs quitted Arrān for Rūm [probably the western parts of the Caucasus controlled by Byzantium] and thence proceeded to their own country.

36. [Amir Ahmad] was succeeded by his son Maymūn b. Ahmad b. 'Abd al-Malik [as ruler of al-Bāb]. He remained in the citadel where his father used to stay, but then was brought down and imprisoned in the "government building" and the inhabitants began to dismantle the middle (transverse) wall of the citadel. The time between its construction and destruction was seven years and one month. Amir Maymūn remained in the government building as a prisoner and all the power was in the hands of the "chiefs." ...

The amir Maymūn secretly sought help from the Rūs against the "chiefs" and in 377/987 the Rūs arrived in eighteen ships. At first they sent one single ship to see whether the amir was eager to employ them. When they brought the amir out of (his confinement), the people of al-Bāb in a joint effort massacred the Rūs to the last man and the remaining ships sailed on to Masqat and plundered it. Thence they proceeded further to Sharvān and Mūqān and to the old river.

In 378/988 the amir Maymūn (re-)built the citadel of al-Bāb and fortified himself in it.

In 379/989 the disturbance of Mūsā al-Tūzī, the preacher from Gīlān, broke out in al-Bāb. This man arrived from Gīlān in the town of al-Bāb, convened a meeting at the cathedral mosque and over 1,000 men made penitence before him. With them he went to the Tower of the Vault and amir Maymūn also took a vow not to drink (wine). Matters went on in such a way that the preacher got control of all government affairs. He requested the amir to surrender his Rūs *ghulāms* [armed retainers] to him so that he might offer them Islam, or kill them. As the Amir refused to do so, disturbances broke out and in 380/990 the amir fortified himself in the citadel against the preacher. Tūzī and the people of al-Bāb besieged him there for twenty-eight days and matters came to such a pass that he asked the preacher for safe-conduct, [on condition] that he should surrender the citadel to him and himself, with his *ghulāms*, depart for Tabarsarān....

38. ... In 423/1032 the amir Mansūr with the ghāzīs of the Islamic "Centres" led a great expedition. This was because the Rūs had raided the territories of Sharvan, ruined and plundered them, and murdered or made prisoner a great mass of the inhabitants. As they were returning, their hands full of booty and captives, the ghāzīs of al-Bāb and the Marches, with the amir Mansūr at their head, occupied the defiles and the roads and put them to the

sword so that few escaped. They took from their hands all the booty, animate and inanimate, which they had captured in Sharvan. Then the Rūs and the Alāns [returned] with the intention of revenge. They gathered together and jointly set off in the direction of al-Bāb and the Marches. First of all, in 424/1033 they moved to al-Karakh where there was only a small group [of warriors] with Khusrau and Haytham b. Maymūn al-Bā'ī (?) chief of the tanners. And [the latter?] fought (them) with the help of the people of Karakh, and God let victory descend on the Muslims and they wrought great havoc among the Alāns and the Rūs. The lord of the Alāns was beaten off from the gate of Karakh, and the infidels' greed for these Islamic "Centres" was extinguished absolutely....

CHAPTER ELEVEN

INTO THE WESTERN OCEAN: THE FAEROES, ICELAND, GREENLAND, AND VINLAND

The colonization of the North Atlantic islands, commonly referred to by modern writers as the North Atlantic Saga, was a significant and lasting accomplishment of the Viking Age. The Faeroes, Iceland, and Greenland may seem bleak and uninviting to modern travelers, but they had much to offer Viking colonists. Apart from some Irish monks in the Faeroes and Iceland, there were no local populations to resist settlement. With their deeply indented fjords, sheltered dales, cliffs, and mountains, these lands were geographically similar to Norway, and Norwegian emigrants would have felt at home here (most of the settlers in the North Atlantic area came from Norway). Although generally not well suited to growing crops, these lands were suitable for pasturing animals, which was more important to the Viking economy. Another attraction was the abundance of resources provided by the proximity to the ocean. Finally, the climate of the Viking Age was also more favorable than either before or after the Middle Ages. This so-called medieval warm period would have had a disproportionate effect on navigation and subsistence in the North Atlantic.

Climatic deterioration from the late thirteenth century onward, on the other hand, led to hard times in both Iceland and Greenland, and probably contributed to the collapse of the Norse Greenland colonies in the fourteenth and fifteenth centuries. Viking contact with North America was a brief affair, seemingly lasting for only a few decades at the start of the eleventh century, but it represented the westernmost limit of Viking expansion.

66. THE ISLANDS IN THE NORTHERN OCEAN,
ca 825

The Irish monk and scholar Dicuil wrote the important geographical work Liber de Mensura Orbis Terrae *[The Book on the Measurement of the Earth] around 825. This work includes a discussion of the islands in the northern ocean, some of which Dicuil says he had visited himself, while for others he had his information from priests who had visited them. Dicuil's work thus seems to demonstrate that Irish hermits had visited and seasonally inhabited the Faeroe Islands as well as Iceland. Thule is generally regarded as Iceland; the modern name Faeroe Islands derives from Faereyjar, "Sheep Islands."*

Source: ed. and trans. J.J. Tierney, *Dicuili Liber de Mensura Orbis Terrae*, (Dublin: Dublin Institute for Advanced Studies, 1967), pp. 73, 75, 77.

7.6. We do not read of islands being found in the sea west or north of Spain. There are islands around our own island Hibernia, some small and some very small. Near the island Britannia are many islands, some large, some small, and some medium-sized. Some are in the sea to her south, and some in the sea to her west, but they abound mostly to the north-west and north. Among these I have lived in some, and have visited others; some I have only glimpsed, while others I have read about.

7. Plinius Secundus [Pliny the Elder, d. 79 CE] in his fourth book informs us that Pytheas of Marseilles states that Thule lies six days' sail to the north of Britain.

8. About the same island, which was always uninhabited, Isidorus [Isidore of Seville, d. 636] says in the same fourteenth book of his *Etymologiae*: Thule is the farthest island of the ocean, and coming to Thule, which shines both by day and by night under the rays of the sun, when he ascends in his chariot to the axes of the zodiac, lighting up the north, with his torch....

11. It is now thirty years since clerics, who had lived on the island [Thule] from the first of February to the first of August, told me that not only at the summer solstice, but in the days round about it, the sun setting in the evening hides itself as though behind a small hill in such a way that there was no darkness in that very small space of time, and a man could do whatever he wished as though the sun were there, even remove lice from his shirt, and if they had been on a mountain-top perhaps the sun would never have been hidden from them....

14. There are many other islands in the ocean to the north of Britain which can be reached from the northern islands of Britain in a direct voyage

of two days and nights with sails filled with a continuously favorable wind. A devout priest told me that in two summer days and the intervening night he sailed in a two-benched boat and entered one of them.

15. There is another set of small islands, nearly separated by narrow stretches of water; in these for nearly a hundred years hermits sailing from our country, Ireland, have lived. But just as they were always deserted from the beginning of the world, so now because of the Northman pirates they are emptied of anchorites, and are filled with countless sheep and very many diverse kinds of seabirds. I have never found these islands mentioned in the authorities.

67. SAILING DIRECTIONS AND DISTANCES IN THE NORTH ATLANTIC

Scholars are in general agreement that instruments and charts were not used in Viking navigation. Instead, an understanding of the sun and stars, landmarks, prevailing wind and wave systems, cloud formations, and the habits of birds and sea mammals was important in aiding navigation. The following passage from the Hauksbók *manuscript of* The Book of Settlements *[Landnámabók] (see doc. 70b) identifies landmarks for navigation across the North Atlantic as well as sailing times between destinations.*

Source: *Landnámabók*, ed. Jakob Benediktsson, Íslenzk fornrit I (Reykjavík, 1986), pp. 33–34.

H. 2. Knowledgeable men say that it is seven days' sailing west from Stad, in Norway, to Horn in eastern Iceland. From Snaefellsness [Iceland], it takes four days at sea to reach Hvarf [Cape Farewell] in Greenland. From Hernar in Norway it is necessary to sail due west to Hvarf in Greenland, passing to the north of Shetland, so that it is just visible, when visibility at sea is good; then the route lies far enough south of the Faroes that the sea is half-way up the mountains, and far enough south of Iceland that there are both birds and whales. From Reykjaness, in the south of Iceland, there are five days at sea to Cape Slyne in Ireland to the south. There are three days' sailing from Langaness in the north of Iceland to Svalbard to the north at the head of the sea [the Arctic Ocean, then regarded as a gulf]. From Kolbeinsey to the uninhabited parts of Greenland is one day's sail northwards.

68. THE WESTERN OCEAN

The King's Mirror [Konungs-Skuggsjá or Speculum Regale] is a didactic work composed in Norway during the reign of King Hakon IV (1217–63) and has been called the most important Norwegian work of the Middle Ages. It takes the form of a dialogue between a father and son in which the father imparts knowledge on a variety of subjects to the son; it was undoubtedly intended for one of the sons of King Hakon. The first part is concerned with material that would be of use to merchants and traders, including proper behavior in foreign lands, descriptions of Ireland, Iceland, and Greenland, and information on the weather.

Source: *Speculum Regale. Konungs-Skuggsjá*, ed. R. Keyser, P.A. Munch, and C.R. Unger (Christiania [Oslo]: Akademiske Collegium ved det kongelike norske Frederiks-Universitet, 1848), pp. 29, 32, 33–40.

Wonders of the Iceland Sea

12. In the seas around Iceland, there is not much that is memorable or worth mentioning, apart from the whales, and these vary considerably in size and species. The most numerous are called dolphins and they grow to a length of twenty ells [Norwegian ell= 62.8 cm], though many of them are much smaller and grow no longer than ten ells. The rest fall somewhere in between and come in various sizes. These fish have neither teeth nor whalebone, and present no danger to ships or men – in fact, they tend to avoid fishermen. Even so, they are frequently rounded up and driven ashore in their hundreds, and wherever they are caught in large numbers, they provide men with an excellent source of food. There are also other kinds of small whales such as the porpoise, which grows no longer than five ells, or the *leiptr* [?] which grows no larger than seven ells....

There is one fish that I haven't mentioned yet and I am reluctant to describe it because of its size which will seem incredible to most people. Very few people are able to say anything definite about this fish since it is very rarely seen. This is because it hardly ever comes close to land and seldom shows itself where fishermen might see it. I do not think that there are many of this sort of fish in the sea. We usually call it *hafgufa* [mermaid] in our language. I cannot speak with certainty about its length because, whenever one has been seen, it has looked more like an island than a fish. I have never heard of any of these fish being caught or found dead; it seems probable that there are only two of them in existence and that they don't reproduce, for I think that we always see the same pair. If they were as numerous as other whales, it would not bode well for other fish, because the *hafgufa* are huge and need vast amounts of food. When they want something to eat, these fish usually emit a huge belch and throw up lots of food so that all kinds of fish in the area, both large and small will crowd up, expecting to find food and good things to eat. In the meantime, this great fish leaves its mouth wide open, and since the opening is as big as a sound or a fjord, the fish cannot prevent themselves from flooding into it in large numbers. As soon as its mouth and stomach are full, the fish closes its mouth, thus trapping and shutting in all the fish which had been looking for food there.

Of Iceland's Fire and Ice

13. As for the ice that is a feature of Iceland, I tend to think that it's the price Iceland has to pay for its proximity to Greenland; and it's no wonder that bitter cold emanates from Greenland, given that it is much more ice-covered than any other land. It is because Iceland absorbs so much cold from Greenland and receives so little warmth from the sun that it has so much ice on its mountain ranges. But I'm not so sure what to say about the surfeit of fire that is to be found there, because it is a strange phenomenon. I have heard that there is a great amount of fire in Sicily and that it burns both earth and vegetation. I have also heard that, in his *Dialogue*, Gregory the Great [Pope Gregory I, 590–604] states that there are places of torment in the fires of Sicily. But men are more likely to believe that there are places of torment in the fires of Iceland because the fires of Sicily consume living things, such as earth and trees. Trees are alive; they grow and produce green leaves.... The earth, too, may be said to be living because it sometimes produces a bountiful harvest and, when that harvest has withered, it produces another. The fires of Sicily, then, burn both trees and earth and are nourished by them. The fires of Iceland, however, do not consume earth or wood, even when those things are thrown into them. Instead, they consume stone and hard rock ... and there is no stone or rock so hard that the fires will not melt it like wax or burn it like fatty oil.... Now, since the Icelandic fire consumes only dead things and rejects what other fires feed on, it may be called dead fire. And so, it is very likely that the fire of Iceland is the fire of hell, because everything in hell is dead.

14. I have no doubt that there are places of torment in Iceland other than in the fires, for the amount of ice and frost in Iceland is as excessive as that of the fire.... There are springs and streams of boiling water.... There are also ice-cold streams which flow from beneath the glaciers. These streams are so powerful that they cause the earth and nearby mountains to tremble, for when water flows so rapidly and with such force, mountains quake because of the overwhelming violence of the torrent.... I am certain that there must be places of torment wherever such great turbulence manifests itself and takes

on such strange forms. God has shown men such fearful phenomena openly here on earth ... as a sign ... that men must expect torments when they leave this world unless they shun evil deeds and wrong-doing while they are alive.

15. ... In Iceland there is a great deal of the ore from which iron is made. Icelanders call it "red ore" in their own language, which is what we call it ourselves. This ore has been found in large quantities one day, only to vanish without trace the following day when people were ready to smelt it and make iron. No one knows what happens to it and, in Iceland, this is called the red-ore mystery.

On the Greenland Sea

16. ... There is yet another marvel in the Greenland Sea, but I don't know much about it. It is called "sea hedges" and it looks for all the world as if every wave and every storm at sea had come together and formed three waves. These waves then form an unbroken wall of water that hedges in the sea. The three waves are higher than mountains and resemble steep precipices. In only a very few instances have men escaped after finding themselves at sea when this phenomenon occurred. These stories must have arisen because God has always spared some of the people who have been exposed to these dangers and their tales have spread from one person to another. We don't know if these stories are exactly the same now as when they were first told, or whether they have grown longer or become shorter. Therefore, we must be cautious in speaking about these matters, for we have come across very few people recently who have escaped to tell the tale....

69. ADAM OF BREMEN ON ICELAND

Adam of Bremen included a description of Iceland among the islands of the North discussed in Book Four of his late-eleventh-century History of the Archbishops of Hamburg-Bremen.

Source: trans. F.J. Tschan, Adam of Bremen, *History of the Archbishops of Hamburg-Bremen*, with new introduction by T. Reuter (New York: Columbia University Press, 2002), pp. 216–18.

Book Four: A Description of the Islands of the North

35. "The island Thule, which, separated from the others by endless stretches, is situated far off in the midst of the ocean, is," they say, "barely known." About it Roman writers as well as barbarians report much that is worth repeating.

"The farthest island of all," they say, "is Thule, in which there is no night at the summer solstice, when the sun crosses the sign of Cancer; and likewise, no day at the winter solstice. This they think, takes place every six months." Bede [Anglo-Saxon, eighth century] also writes that the bright summer nights in Britain indicate without a doubt that at the solstice it is continuously day for six months and, on the contrary, night in the wintertime, when the sun is withdrawn. And Pytheas of Marseilles [Greek explorer, ca 300 BCE] writes that this happens on the island of Thule, six days' sail distant from Britain toward the north. This Thule is now called Iceland, from the ice which binds the ocean. About this island they also report this remarkable fact, that the ice on account of its age is so black and dry in appearance that it burns when fire is set to it. This island, however, is so very large that it has on it many peoples, who make a living only by raising cattle and who clothe themselves with their pelts. No crops are grown there; the supply of wood is very meager. On this account the people dwell in underground caves, glad to have roof and food and bed in common with their cattle. Passing their lives thus in holy simplicity, because they seek nothing more than what nature affords, they can joyfully say with the Apostle: "But having food, and wherewith to be covered, with these we are content." For instead of towns they have mountains and springs as their delights. Blessed, I say, is the folk whose poverty no one envies; and in this respect most blessed because all have now adopted Christianity. They have many meritorious customs, especially charity, in consequence of which they have all things in common with strangers as well as with natives. They hold their bishop as king. All the people respect his wishes. They hold as law whatever he ordains as coming from God, or from the Scriptures, or even from the worthy practices of other peoples. For them our metropolitan returned vast thanks to God that they had been converted in his time, even though before receiving the faith they were in what may be called their natural law, which was not much of accord with our religion. On their petition, therefore, the archbishop consecrated a certain most holy man named Islef [consecrated in 1056]. And when he was sent from that region to the prelate, the latter held him in his company for a while and furthermore bestowed great honor upon him. In the meantime Islef learned in what respects peoples newly converted to Christ can salutarily be instructed. By him the archbishop transmitted letters to the people of Iceland and Greenland, reverently greeting their churches and promising them he would come to them very soon that their joy may be full together. From these words the high purpose which the archbishop had with regard to his legateship can be adduced as, indeed, we also learn the Apostle wished to journey to Spain in order to preach the Word of God, which intention he was unable to carry out. Disregarding the fabulous, these facts about Iceland and the farthest Thule we learned are true.

70. ICELANDIC ACCOUNTS OF THE DISCOVERY AND SETTLEMENT OF ICELAND

(a) The Book of the Icelanders [Íslendingabók] *is a concise, vernacular outline of historical events in Iceland from its settlement in the 870s to the early twelfth century. It was the work of Ari Fróði (the Wise) Thorgilsson (1068–1148), who compiled it between about 1122 and 1133. Little is known of Ari, but he was well educated, and Snorri Sturluson tells us that he was the first Icelander to write Icelandic history in the vernacular. Ari drew on reliable native informants who could remember events stretching back to about the year 1000. He provides precise dates for key events, thereby laying the foundation of early Icelandic chronology. Despite its brevity, Íslendingabók is one of the most important sources for the settlement of Iceland and subsequent historical developments, including the conversion to Christianity.*

Source: *Íslendingabók*, ed. Jakob Benediktsson, Íslenzk fornrit I (Reykjavík, 1986), pp. 4–7.

1. Iceland was first settled from Norway in the days of King Harald Finehair, the son of Halfdan the Black. According to the reckoning of the wisest man I know – my foster-father Teit, son of Bishop Isleif – and of my uncle, Thorkel Gellisson, who remembered a long way back, and of Thurid, daughter of Snorri the Priest, who was both wise and well-informed, the settlement of Iceland took place at the time when Ivarr, the son of Ragnar Hairy-Breeches, had Saint Edmund, king of the English, killed. And according to Saint Edmund's saga, that happened 870 years after the birth of Christ.

The story goes – and it is a true one – that a Norwegian, called Ingolf, traveled from Norway to Iceland for the first time when Harald Finehair was sixteen years old and, again, a few years later. He settled to the south, in Reykjavik. The place where he landed first is called Ingolf's Head, to the east of Minthak's Shoal, and the place where he later settled is Ingolfsfell, which lies to the east of the Olfoss river.

In those days, there were trees growing in Iceland between the mountains and the shore. There were also Christian men here, whom the Norsemen called *papar*, but they left afterwards because they did not want to live alongside heathens. They left behind some Irish books, bells, and croziers, from which it may be deduced that they were Irishmen.

After that, a great number of people began to migrate here from Norway until King Harald banned the practice, fearing that his land would be depopulated otherwise. Then it was agreed that anyone coming here from Norway would have to pay the king five pieces of gold, unless he was granted an exemption. King Harald is said to have been king for seventy years and to have reached the age of eighty.

This is the origin of the tax called Landaurar [Land money]. The tax was sometimes higher and sometimes lower until Olaf the Stout [Saint Olaf, 995–1030] made it definite that anyone traveling between Norway and Iceland had to pay the king half a mark, except for women and the men he exempted. Thorkell Gellisson was our source for this.

2. ... After Iceland had been extensively settled, a Norwegian called Ulfljot brought the first laws here from Norway. Teit was the one who gave us an account of this. The laws were called Ulfljot's Laws.... These laws were largely based on the Gulathing Law or on the judgment of Thorleif the Wise, son of Hortha-Kari, when a law needed to be extended or abolished, or modified in some other way....

Ulfljot's foster-brother was said to be Grim Goat's Hair. On Ulflot's advice, this Grim surveyed the whole of Iceland before the Althing [general assembly] was established. As payment for this, every man in the country contributed a penny to him, and afterwards he gave that money to temples.

(b) The Book of Settlements (Landnámabók, *from* landnám, *land-taking*) *is a detailed account of the discovery and settlement of Iceland in the ninth and tenth centuries and may have originally been compiled in order to ensure the property rights of important Icelandic chieftains. It is arranged in topographical order and preserves the names of about 430 individual settlers, their families, and descendants. Overall, more than 3,000 personal names and about 1,500 farm names appear in it. The text survives in three different medieval redactions, but in its oldest form it is thought to date from the early twelfth century. This translation follows the* Sturlubók [Sturla's Book] *text.*

Source: *Landnámabók* , ed. Jakob Benediktsson, Íslenzk fornrit I (Reykjavík, 1986), pp. 32–46.

S. 1. In his book, *On Time*, the Venerable Bede mentions a certain island called Thule which, in other books, is said to be six days sailing to the north of Britain. He said that there is no daylight there in winter, and no darkness in summer, when the days are longest. For this reason learned men are convinced that Thule must be Iceland, for, in most parts of Iceland the sun shines all night when the days are longest, and does not appear in the daytime when the nights are longest. According to written sources, Bede the Priest died 735 years after the incarnation of our Lord, and more than 100 years before Iceland was settled by Norwegians.

Before Iceland was settled from Norway, men were already living there. The Norwegians called these men *papar*. They were Christians, and it is generally believed that they had come across the sea from the west, because Irish books, bells, and croziers were found, leading to the conclusion that the men were Irish. Moreover, we learn from English books that in those days there was travel between the two countries.

S. 2. When Iceland was discovered and settled from Norway, Adrian was pope in Rome and was succeeded by John, the fifth of that name to occupy the apostolic throne. Louis, son of Louis, was emperor north of the Alps, while Leo and his son, Alexander, ruled over Constantinople. Harald Finehair was king of Norway, Eirik Emundsson and his son, Bjorn, ruled Sweden, and Gorm the Old reigned in Denmark; Alfred the Great and his son, Edward, ruled England, Kjarval ruled Dublin, and Sigurd the Mighty was Earl of Orkney....

S. 3. The story goes that some men set sail from Norway to the Faeroes – people mention Naddod the Viking by name – but they were driven westward out to sea and discovered a great land there. They went ashore at Austfjord. Then they climbed a high hill and gazed all round about, looking for smoke, or any other sign that the land was inhabited, but they saw nothing at all. In the autumn, they set out for the Faeroes, and, as they were sailing away from the land, heavy snow fell on the mountains, so they called the country Snowland. They were full of praise for it. According to Saemund the Wise, the place in Austfjord where they landed is now called Reydarfell.

S. 4. A Swede called Gard Svavarsson went in search of Snowland at the suggestion of his mother, who had the gift of prophecy. He landed to the east of the eastern Horn, where there was a natural harbor in those days. Gard circumnavigated the land, and discovered that it was an island. He spent the winter in the north at Husavik in Skjalfandi and built a house there. In the spring, when he was ready to sail, a man called Nattfari made off in a boat, along with a slave and a servant-woman, and settled in a place that was afterwards called Nattfaravik. Then Gard sailed to Norway where he praised the island highly.... After that, it was called Gardarsholm.

S. 5. There was a great Viking called Floki Vilgerdarson who went in search of Gardarsholm. He set sail from Flokarvard [in Norway], which is situated where Hordaland and Rogaland meet, and sailed first to the Shetlands, where he anchored in Floki's Bay. His daughter, Geirhild, perished there in Geirhild's Loch. On board ship with Floki was a farmer called Thorolf, and another named Herjolf; also on board was a man from the Hebrides, called Faxi.

Floki had taken three ravens to sea with him. When he released the first one, it flew over the stern, back in the direction they had come from. The second one flew straight up into the air, and then returned to the ship. But the third one took off over the bows and flew ahead of the ship toward the place where they found land. They approached Horn from the east and then sailed west along the south coast. As they rounded Reykjaness, the fjord opened up before them so that they could see Snaefellsness.

"This land we've found must be really big to have such broad rivers," said Faxi.

Ever since then, the fjord has been called Faxaoss [Faxi's river-mouth].

Floki and his men sailed west over Breidafjord and landed at Vatsfjord, near Bardastrand. In those days, the fishing in the fjord was so abundant that they neglected the haymaking and all their animals died over the winter. The spring was on the cold side, and when Floki climbed a high hill, he saw a fjord full of drift-ice, to the north beyond the mountains. So they called the land Iceland, and that is what it has been called ever since. Floki and his men intended to leave in the summer, but it was almost winter before they were ready and they could not get round Reykjaness. Then one of the boats broke loose with Herjolf on board. He landed at a place that is now called Herjolf's Haven. Floki spent the winter in Borgarfjord. The following summer, he and Herjolf met up again and sailed back to Norway. When they were asked about Iceland, Floki spoke ill of the place, but Herjolf recounted both the good and the bad. Thorolf said that butter dripped from every blade of grass in the land they had discovered, and for that reason he was called Thorolf Butter....

S. 6. [Two] sworn-brothers, Ingolf and Leif, fitted out a big ship they owned and went looking for the land, by now called Iceland, which Floki of the Ravens had discovered. They found the place and stayed at South Alptafjord in the Eastfjords. They were better pleased with the southern part of the country than with the north. They stayed in the land for a winter and then sailed back to Norway.

After that, Ingolf laid their property aside for a journey to Iceland, but Leif went on a Viking raid in the west. When he was raiding in Ireland, he found a large earth-house. It was dark when he went in, until there was a flash of light from a sword that some man was holding. He killed the man and took the sword and a great deal of money from him. From then on, Leif was called Hjorleif [the Sword]. Hjorleif raided throughout Ireland and collected a lot of property. He captured ten slaves there; their names were: Dufthak, Geirrod, Skaldbjorn, Halldor, and Drafdit; the others are not named. After that, Hjorleif returned to Norway where he met his sworn-brother, Ingolf. He had already married Helga Orn's daughter, the sister of Ingolf.

S. 7. That winter, Ingolf prepared a great sacrifice hoping to find omens regarding his future. But Hjorleif would never make sacrificial offerings. The omens directed Ingolf toward Iceland, so each of the kinsmen fitted out a ship for the journey. On board Hjorleif's ship was his plunder from raiding, while on Ingolf's ship was the property they owned jointly. When everything was ready, they put to sea.

S. 8. That summer, when Ingolf and Hjorleif went off to settle Iceland, Harald Finehair had been king of Norway for twelve years; six thousand and seventy three years had passed since the beginning of the world, and eight hundred and seventy four years had gone by since the birth of Christ.

The sworn-brothers sailed in convoy until they sighted Iceland, but then they got separated. When Ingolf saw Iceland, he threw his high-seat pillars overboard, hoping for an omen, and vowed that he would settle wherever the pillars came ashore. He landed at a place now known as Ingolf's Headland, but Hjorleif was driven west along the coast. He ran out of drinking water, so his Irish slaves began to knead meal and butter together, claiming that this would slake their thirst: they called the mixture *minnthak*. No sooner was it prepared than there was a heavy rain, and they collected water in the awnings. When the *minnthak* grew moldy, they tossed it overboard, and it drifted ashore at the place now called Minnthak's Shoal.

Hjorleif landed at Hjorleif's Head where there was a fjord that cut into the headland. Hjorleif had two halls built there. One of them was eighteen fathoms long, and the other was nineteen fathoms. Hjorleif spent the winter there, intending to sow seed in the spring. Since he had only one ox, he made his slaves draw the plow. While Hjorlief and his companions were busy about the house, Dufthak suggested to the slaves that they should slaughter the ox and say that a bear had killed it. Then they should kill Hjorleif and his companions when they went looking for the bear. So they told this tale to Hjorleif, and when he and his comrades fanned out through the woods in search of the bear, the slaves attacked them one by one and killed them all.... There were as many dead men as there were slaves. Then they fled in the boat, taking with them the wives and property of the murdered men, and sailed to some islands that they had seen to the south-west. They settled there for a while.

Two of Ingolf's slaves were called Karli and Vifil. He sent them west along the coast to look for his high-seat pillars, and, when they got to Hjorleif's Head, they found Hjorlief dead. They went back and broke the news to In-golf, who was greatly upset by Hjorleif's murder. He went west to Hjorleif's Head and, when he saw Hjorleif's body, he said, "It's a sorry fate for a brave warrior to be murdered by slaves. But now I see what happens to people who won't sacrifice."

Ingolf saw to the burial of Hjorleif and his men and took possession of their ship and property. Afterwards, he went up to the headland. He noticed that there were some islands lying to the south-west and, since the boat was missing, it occurred to him that the slaves might have gone there. So they went in search of the slaves, and found them in the islands at a place called Eid. When Ingolf and his men came upon them, they were having a meal and were so panic-stricken that they fled in all directions. Ingolf killed the lot of them. Dufthak died at a place called Dufthak's cliff. Most of the slaves jumped off a precipice that has since been named after them, and the islands where the slaves were killed are now known as Vestmannaeyjar [the Isles of the Westerners] because those who were slain there came from the west [from Ireland]. Then Ingolf and his men returned to Hjorleif's Head, taking the wives of the murdered men with them. Ingolf stayed there for a second winter. The following summer he headed west along the coast and spent the third winter near Ingolfsfell, to the west of the Olfu River. It was at this time that Vifil and Karli found the high-seat pillars down from the heath near Arnarshval [Orn's Hill].

S. 9. In the spring, Ingolf crossed the heath and settled at Reykjavik, where his high-seat pillars had come ashore. The pillars are still standing in the hall there. Ingolf took possession of the land between the Olfu river and Hvalfjord [Whale Fjord] beyond the Brynjudal river. He also took the land from there to the Axe river, and all the headlands in the area. Then Karli said, "There was no point in traveling over all that fine countryside, just to settle on this remote headland."

So he left, taking a servant-woman with him. Ingolf gave Vifil his freedom and he settled at Vifil's Homestead; Vifil's Fell is named after him too. He lived there for a long time and became a respectable man. Ingolf had a hall built at Skali Fell; from it he noticed some smoke near Olfuvatn and found Karli living there.

Ingolf was the most renowned of all the settlers, for he came to this land when it was uninhabited, and was the first to settle it. Afterwards, other settlers followed his example. Ingolf married Hallveig Frodi's daughter, the sister of Lopt the Old. Their son was Thorstein who set up the Thing [assembly] at Kjalarness before the Althing was established.

(c) The Saga of the People of Eyri [Eyrbyggja saga] *tells how Bjorn, son of Ketil Flatnose, settles in Iceland. Like many of the early settlers, Bjorn did not migrate directly to Iceland, but went there only after a stay in the British Isles (see doc. 21).*

Source: *Eyrbyggja saga*, ed. Einar Ól. Sveinsson and Matthías Þórðarson, Íslenzk fornrit IV (Reykjavík, 1935), pp. 5–11.

2. Bjorn, the son of Ketil Flatnose, lived in Jämtland until Earl Kjallak, his foster-father, died. He married the earl's daughter, Gjaflaug. Later, he traveled west across the Kiolen Mountains, arriving first at Trondheim and then going south. He took over the lands his father owned and drove away the stewards who had been put in charge of the property by King Harald. The king was in the Vik when he heard about this. Thereupon, he left for Trondheim, taking the inland route north. When he arrived at Trondheim, he

summoned a Thing from eight districts at which he outlawed Bjorn Ketils-son in Norway and declared that he might be killed or seized wherever he turned up. After that, the king dispatched Hauk Habrok [High-Breeches] and others of his warriors to kill Bjorn wherever they could find him.

When the king's men came south to Stad, Bjorn's friends got to hear about their approach and passed on the information to him. Then Bjorn hurried aboard a small ship that he had, taking his household and portable property with him. He sailed south, hugging the coast because it was the depth of winter and he didn't dare head for the open sea. Bjorn kept going until he reached the island called Most, which lies off South Hordaland. There he was welcomed by a man called Hrolf, the son of Ornolf the Whale-Driver. Bjorn stayed there secretly for the winter. The king's men turned back when they had taken over Bjorn's properties and placed men in charge of them.

3. Hrolf was a great chieftain and a very open-handed man. He looked after the temple of Thor on the island, and was a great friend of Thor. For that reason, he was called Thorolf. He was a tall, strong, handsome man with a big beard, on account of which he was called Most-Beard. He was the noblest man on the island.

In the spring, Thorolf gave Bjorn a ship manned by good men, and sent his son, Hallstein, to accompany him. They sailed west across the sea to visit Bjorn's relatives. When King Harald heard that Thorolf Most-Beard had sheltered Bjorn Ketilsson, his outlaw, he sent men to him and ordered him off his lands to wander as an outlaw, like his friend Bjorn, unless he came and placed his case in the king's hands. This was ten years after Ingolf Arnarson had gone out to settle in Iceland. His journey had become very famous because the men who came from Iceland said that there was a good choice of land out there....

5. Now the story says of Bjorn, the son of Ketil Flatnose, that he sailed west across the sea after he and Thorolf Most-Beard had parted, as was mentioned earlier. He made for the Hebrides and, when he arrived in the west, his father had already died, but he met his brother, Helgi, and his sisters. They offered him a good living with them, but Bjorn became aware that they had adopted a new faith. It seemed mean-spirited to him that they had abandoned the ancient faith their ancestors had followed, so he had no desire to stay, and had no intention of establishing a permanent residence there. However, he stayed for the winter with his sister, Aud [Unn; see doc. 29c], and her son, Thorstein, but when they discovered that he meant to turn a deaf ear to his relatives, they called him Bjorn the Easterner. They took it badly that he did not want to stay there permanently.

6. Bjorn stayed for two years in the Hebrides before he got ready to travel to Iceland. Hallstein Thorolfsson accompanied him. They landed in

Breidafjord and, with Thorolf's advice, Bjorn claimed land between the Staf river and Hraunsfjord. Bjorn lived at Borgarholt in Bjorn's Harbor. He was the noblest of men.

Hallstein Thorolfsson thought it was unmanly to accept land from his father, so he traveled west across Breidafjord and took land there. He lived at Hallsteinsness. A few years later, Aud the Deep-Minded came out to Iceland. For the first winter, she stayed with Bjorn, her brother, and later took all the Dales district in Breidafjord, between the Skraumuhlaups River and the Dogurdar River. She lived at Hvamm. In these days, the whole of Breidafjord was settled, but there is no need to mention the landtakes of men who don't come into this story.

71. SKALLAGRIM'S LANDTAKE IN ICELAND

In Egil's Saga, *the hero's father, Skallagrim, and grandfather, Kveld-Ulf, emigrate to Iceland from Norway to escape the tyrannical rule of King Harald Finehair. Chapters 27 to 29 of the saga provide a glimpse into the nature of landtaking and the natural resources available to early settlers in Iceland.*

Source: *Egils saga Skalla-Grímssonar,* ed. Sigurður Nordal, Íslenzk fornrit II (Reykjavík, 1933), pp. 70–76.

27. ... But when they got further out to sea, Kveld-Ulf's illness worsened until he was close to death. Then he called his crewmen together and told them that he thought it likely they would soon part company. "I have never been sick in my life," he said, "and I'm probably going to die. If that happens, make a coffin for me and throw me overboard. Things won't turn out as I'd anticipated if I don't reach Iceland and settle there. When you see my son, Skallagrim, give him my regards and tell him that if he reaches Iceland, and I'm there before him (unlikely as that may seem), he's to set up house as close as possible to the place where I came ashore."

Shortly afterwards, Kveld-Ulf died and his crew did as he had told them. They put him in a coffin and threw him overboard.

One of the crew was a wealthy man of good family called Grim. He was the son of Thorir and the grandson of Ketil the Keel-Traveler. Grim was an old friend of Kveld-Ulf and Skallagrim and had gone on expeditions with them and with Thorolf; for this reason he had incurred the king's wrath. After Kveld-Ulf's death, he took over the running of the ship. When they reached Iceland, they approached the land from the south. Then they sailed west along the coast because they'd heard that Ingolf had settled there.

When they rounded Reykjaness, they saw a fjord opening in front of them and they steered both ships into it. Then a storm blew up, with driving rain and fog, and the ships were separated. Grim and his men sailed up Borgarfjord past all the rocks and anchored there until the wind dropped and the weather brightened. They waited for high tide and brought their ship to the mouth of a river called the Gufa. After hauling the ship as far upstream as possible, they unloaded their cargo and settled there for the first winter. They explored the land along the coast in both directions, and before they had gone far, they came upon an inlet where Kveld-Ulf's coffin had drifted ashore. They carried the coffin over to the headland where they laid it down and covered it with rocks.

28. Where Skallagrim came ashore, a large headland stretches out into the sea, with a narrow isthmus on the landward side. They unloaded the cargo there and called the place Knarrarness [Shipsness]. Exploring the large stretch of country between the mountains and the shore, Skallagrim found extensive moorlands and wide forests. Both the seal-hunting and the fishing were excellent. When they explored southwards along the coast, they came to a large fjord. They turned into the fjord and kept walking up it until, to their great joy, they came across their companions, Grim from Halogaland and his crewmen.

Grim and his men told Skallagrim that Kveld-Ulf had come ashore there and that they had buried him. They led Skallagrim to the grave, and he thought that the locality would be a good place to build a homestead. Then Grim went back to his crew and the two groups spent the winter where they had come ashore.

Skallagrim took the land between the mountains and the sea: all of Myrar [Moorland] district, west as far as Selalon [Seal Inlet], north to Borgarhraun [Borgar Lava Field], and south to Hafnar Fells; that whole area is divided up by rivers flowing to the sea. The following spring, he moved his ship south to the fjord, and entered the inlet closest to where Kveld-Ulf had come ashore. There Skallagrim established a farm, and called it Borg. The fjord he named Borgarfjord and the surrounding district was called after it. He gave Grim from Halogaland a farm to the south of Borgarfjord; it was called Hvanneyri. Nearby a narrow inlet cut into the land. They found lots of ducks there and so they called the place Andakil [Duck Inlet] and the river flowing into the sea there they named Andakilsa [Duck River]. Grim's land extended from Andakilsa up to Grimsa [Grim's River].

That spring, when Skallagrim was having his cattle driven along the coast, he and his men came to a small headland where they caught swans and so they called the place Alptaness [Swans' Ness].

Skallagrim distributed land to his crew. Ani was given the land between

Langa river and Hafs Creek and he lived at Anabrekka; his son was Onund Sjoni [Keen-Sighted]. Grimolf settled first at Grimolfsstead, and the meadow and stream there are named after him (Grimolsfit and Grimolfsloek). Grim, his son, settled south of the fjord and Grim's son, Grimar, made his home at Grimarstead. Grani settled at Granastead on Digraness. Thorbjorn Krum and Thord Beigaldi got land along the Gufa River. Thorbjorn settled at Krum Hills, and Thord at Beigaldi. The land above Einkunnir as far west as the river Langa was given to Thorir Thurs [the Giant] and his brothers. Thorir Thurs made his home at Thursstead and later on his daughter, Thordis Stang [the Thin], settled at Stangarholt. Thorgeir lived at Jarthlangsstead.

Skallagrim explored the whole district. First, he traveled right to the head of Borgarfjord. Then he and his companions followed the west bank of the river they called Hvita, or White River, because they had never seen water that flowed from a glacier before and they were astonished by the color. They carried on along the Hvita until they reached a river that flowed down from the hills to the north. They named this river the Northra and followed it till they came to a smaller river, which they crossed. Proceeding along the Northra, they soon saw that the small river flowed from a gorge, so they called it the Gljufra, or Gorge River. Then they crossed the Northra, returned to the Hvita and followed the Hvita upstream. Shortly afterwards, another river crossed their path and flowed into the Hvita. This river they named the Thvera, or Cross River. They noticed that every river was full of fish. After this, they went back to Borg.

29. Skallagrim was a very hard worker. He always had numerous men in his household, and they had to collect large amounts of local produce to feed themselves, because they didn't have enough livestock at first to meet the needs of so many people. What animals he had fended for themselves in the woods over the winter.

Skallagrim was an excellent shipbuilder and there was plenty of driftwood west of Myrar. He established a farm and built another dwelling at Alptaness and from there his men rowed out to catch fish, hunt seals, and gather eggs, all of which were plentiful. They also brought him great quantities of driftwood. Whales were grounded here in large numbers and could be shot at will; and all the wildlife in the hunting ground was tame at this time for it was unused to man. He established a third farm by the sea in the western part of Myrar. This was an even better place to look for driftwood. He planted crops there and called the farm Akrar [Cornfields]. Offshore, there lay some islands where whales gathered; they called these islands Hvalseyjar [Whale Islands].

Skallagrim also sent his men up river to fish for salmon and settled Odd the Lone-dweller at the Gljufra river to look after the salmon-fishing. Odd lived at the foot of Einbuabrekkur [Lone-Dweller's Slopes] and Einbuaness is named after him. Skallagrim settled a man called Sigmund by the Northra river. He lived at Sigmundarstead, which is now called Haugar, and Sigmundarness is named after him. Later on, Sigmund moved to Munodarness because it was more convenient for the salmon-fishing.

As Skallagrim's livestock increased in number, the animals started going up to the mountains for the summer. Skallagrim discovered that this made a big difference, for the cattle grew better and fatter when they went up onto the heaths, and the sheep could survive the winter in the mountain valleys without being brought down. So Skallagrim had a dwelling built close to the mountains and set up a sheep farm there. Since a man called Griss was in charge of the farm, Grisartungu is named after him. And so, Skallagrim's wealth flowed from many sources.

72. THE SETTLEMENT OF GREENLAND

(a) *Both* The Book of the Icelanders (Íslendingabók) *and* The Book of Settlements (Landnámabók) *relate that Iceland was fully settled within about sixty years of the initial landtaking in the early 870s. Later colonists were forced to settle on marginal lands, or to seek new lands entirely. One of these was a Norwegian named Eirik Thorvaldsson, better known as* Eirikr rauði [Eirik the Red].

Source: *Íslendingabók*, ed. Jakob Benediktsson, Íslenzk fornrit I (Reykjavík, 1986), pp. 13–14.

6. The land named Greenland was discovered and settled from Iceland. A man from Breidafjord called Eirik the Red traveled there from Iceland and settled in the area later known as Eiriksfjord.

He gave the land its name and called it Greenland, saying that people would be more eager to make the journey there if the land had an attractive name. They discovered human dwellings both to the east and west of the land, as well as fragments of skin-boats and stone tools, from which it could be conjectured that the same kind of people had traveled there as had settled Vinland: Greenlanders call them Skraelings.

He began settling the land fourteen or fifteen years before Christianity came here to Iceland, according to what he told Thorkel Gellisson, who himself followed Eirik the Red out to Greenland.

(b) Landnámabók *provides a more detailed account of the settlement of Greenland than does* Íslendingabók.

Source: *Landnámabók*, ed. Jakob Benediktsson, Íslenzk fornrit I (Reykjavík, 1986), pp. 131–34.

89. ... Eirik told them that he intended to look for the land that Ulf Kraka's son Gunnbjorn saw when he was driven west beyond Iceland and discovered Gunnbjorn's Skerries. He said that he would come back to visit his friends if he discovered land.

Eirik sailed from Snaefellsness and arrived in Greenland at Midjokul, which is now called Blaserk. From there, he traveled south along the coast to find out if there was anywhere to settle in that direction. He spent the first winter in Eiriksey [Eirik's Island], near the middle of the Western Settlement. The following spring, he sailed to Eiriksfjord where he established his home. During the summer, he traveled in the uninhabitable lands in the west, and gave names to places throughout the area. He passed the next winter at Eirik's Holm, near Hvarfsgnip. In his third summer, he went all the way north to Snaefell and into Hrafnsfjord. He claimed that he had then reached the head of Eiriksfjord. He turned back from there and spent his third winter on Eiriksey at the mouth of Eiriksfjord.

The next summer, he sailed to Iceland and arrived at Breidafjord. He spent the winter with Ingolf at Holmslatr. The following spring, Eirik and Thorgest fought and Eirik had the worse of it. Afterwards, there was a reconciliation between them. The same summer, Eirik set off to settle the land he had discovered. He called it Greenland because, he said, people would be much more eager to go there if he gave it an attractive name.

90. Knowledgeable men say that twenty-five ships set out for Greenland from Breidafjord and Borgarfjord, but that fourteen made it out there. Some were driven back, while others were lost. This was fifteen years before Christianity became the law in Iceland.

91. There was a man called Herjolf, son of Bard, who was son of Herjolf, who was a kinsman of Ingolf the settler. Ingolf gave Herjolf and his people land between Vag and Reykjaness. Herjolf the younger went to Greenland when Eirik the Red settled there. Aboard his ship with him was a Hebridean who was Christian. He composed the "Sea-Hedges" poem [see doc. 68]; this is the burden of the poem:

> Sinless master of monks,
> safeguard my sea-journey;
> prince of earth's high hall, hold
> your hand, the hawk's rest, over me.

Herjolf settled Herjolfsfjord and lived at Herjolfsness. He was the finest of men.

92. Then Eirik settled Eiriksfjord and lived at Brattahlid, as did Leif his son after him. The following men went out to Greenland with Eirik and

settled there. Herjolf settled Herjolfsfjord; he lived at Herjolfsness; Ketil settled Ketilsfjord; Hrafn settled Hrafnsfjord; Solvi settled Solvadal; Helgi Thorbrandsson settled Alptafjord; Thorbjorn Glora settled Siglufjord; Einar, Einarsfjord; Hafgrim, Hafgrimsfjord and Vatnahverfi; Arnlaug settled Arnlaugsfjord, and some went to the Western Settlement.

93. There was a man called Thorkel Farserk. He was the son of Eirik the Red's sister and traveled to Greenland with him. He settled Hvalseyarfjord and extensive territory between Eiriksfjord and Einarsfjord. He lived at Hvalseyarfjord and all the people of that district are descended from him. He was a very powerful man. Once, when he wanted to entertain his relative, Eirik, and there was no seaworthy boat available, he swam out to Hvalsey [Whale Island] for an old wether and returned with it on his back. The distance is over half a mile. Thorkel was buried in the home-field at Hvalseyarfjord and he has haunted the place ever since.

73. *THE KING'S MIRROR* ON GREENLAND

The thirteenth-century Norwegian text The King's Mirror (Konungs-Skuggsjá) *(see doc. 68) contains one of the most important medieval descriptions of Norse Greenland.*

Source: *Speculum Regale. Konungs-Skuggsjá*, ed. R. Keyser, P.A. Munch, C.R. Unger (Christiania [Oslo]: Akademiske Collegium ved det kongelike norske Frederiks-Universitet, 1848), pp. 42–44.

17. You ask what men are looking for when they go to Greenland, and why they travel there at such great risk to their lives. The answer lies in the threefold nature of man. One element is competitiveness and the desire for fame, for it is in a man's nature to travel to places where dangers are to be encountered, in order to win renown. Another element is curiosity, for it is in a man's nature to enquire into things that he has heard about and to find out for himself whether what he has been told is true or not. The third element is acquisitiveness, for men will look for wealth wherever they hear they can get hold of it, even though acquiring it involves great danger. But, as you probably know, whatever is imported into Greenland from other lands is expensive, because Greenland is so remote from other countries that people seldom go there. Anything that Greenlanders need to improve their country has to be bought abroad, including iron and all the supplies needed for house-building. In exchange for their goods, men engaged in the Greenland trade bring back goatskin, cowhide, sealskin, walrus-teeth, and the walrus-hide rope we mentioned earlier....

In answer to your question about whether grain is grown in Greenland, I don't think that the Greenlanders derive much gain from that source. Some of the wealthiest and most prominent men have tried sowing grain, but most of the inhabitants have no idea what bread is, for they have never seen it....

18. There aren't many people in Greenland because only a small part of the country is sufficiently ice-free to be habitable; but all the people are Christian, and they have churches and priests. If it were near any other land, Greenland would be considered a third of a diocese; but the Greenlanders have their own bishop now, because they live so far from other lands that this is the only practical arrangement.

You ask what they live on since they don't sow grain. Well, man can live on more than bread alone. Greenland is said to have good pastures and large, productive farms where they raise many cattle and sheep, and make a great deal of butter and cheese. This food accounts for a large part of their diet, along with meat and various kinds of game, such as the flesh of reindeer, whales, seals, and bears. That's what the Greenlanders live on....

74. ADAM OF BREMEN ON VINLAND

Adam of Bremen's History of the Archbishops of Hamburg-Bremen *contains the earliest historical reference to Vinland, an area of eastern North America. Norse explorers found grapes growing there and named it "Vine Land." The precise location of Vinland is uncertain, but the shores of the Gulf of St. Lawrence is a strong possibility.*

Source: trans. F.J. Tschan, Adam of Bremen, *History of the Archbishops of Hamburg-Bremen*, with new introduction by T. Reuter (New York: Columbia University Press, 2002), pp. 219–20.

Book Four: A Description of the Islands of the North

38. He [Svein Estridson, king of the Danes, r. 1047–76, one of Adam's informants] spoke also of yet another island of the many found in that ocean. It is called Vinland because vines producing excellent wine grow wild there. That unsown crops also abound on that island we have ascertained not from fabulous reports but from the trustworthy relation of the Danes. Beyond that island, he said, no habitable land is found in that ocean, but every place beyond it is full of impenetrable ice and intense darkness. Of this fact Martianus [Martianus Capella, fifth century], makes mention as follows: "Beyond Thule," he says, "the sea is congealed after one day's navigation." The very well-informed prince of the Norwegians, Harold [Harald Hardradi, d. 1066], lately attempted this sea. After he had explored the expanse of the Northern

Ocean in his ships, there lay before their eyes at length the darksome bounds of a failing world, and by retracing his steps he barely escaped in safety the vast pit of the abyss.

75. THE NORSE DISCOVERY OF VINLAND

The so-called Vinland Sagas *comprise two separate works,* The Saga of the Greenlanders *and* Eirik the Red's Saga, *both of which contain accounts of several voyages undertaken around the year 1000 by Icelanders and Greenlanders to North America. Both were originally written down in the thirteenth century, though* The Saga of the Greenlanders *is thought to be older than* Eirik the Red's Saga. *The sagas contain two different accounts of these Viking voyages to North America.* The Saga of the Greenlanders *relates a total of five successful voyages and one abortive voyage to Vinland, while* Eirik the Red's Saga *recounts two successful journeys and one abortive attempt. As well as the family of Eirik the Red, the family of Thorfinn Karlsefni and Gudrid Thorbjarnardaughter (see doc. 10) are the principal characters involved in the exploration and exploitation of Vinland. Both sagas mention the descendants of Thorfinn and Gudrid and are thought to reflect family tradition.*

Source: *Grœnlendinga saga*, in *Eyrbyggja saga*, ed. Einar Ól. Sveinsson and Matthías Þórðarson, Íslenzk fornrit IV (Reykjavík, 1935), pp. 244–54

1. Herjolf was the son of Bard Herjolfsson. He was a relative of Ingolf the Settler from whom Herjolf and his people received land between Vag and Reykjaness. Herjolf lived first at Drepstokki. His wife was called Thorgerd and their son was Bjarni, a most promising man. Bjarni traveled abroad from an early age and he increased both his wealth and his reputation. He spent alternate winters overseas or with his father. Soon Bjarni was the owner of a trading ship. During the last year Bjarni spent in Norway, Herjolf got ready for the journey to Greenland with Eirik the Red and gave up his farm.... Herjolf settled at Herjolfsness in Greenland, and was a highly honored man....

The same summer, Bjarni arrived with his ship at Eyrar [in Iceland] when his father had already sailed for Greenland. This news seemed so momentous to him that he did not want to disembark. His crew asked him what he would do, and he answered that he intended to stick to what he usually did, and spend the winter with his father.

"I mean to sail to Greenland, if you're willing to come with me," he said. They all declared that they would fall in with his plans.

"Our journey seems really stupid," he said, "considering that none of us has ever sailed in the Greenland Sea."

Nonetheless, as soon as they were ready, they put out to sea and sailed for three days until the land fell below the horizon. Then the favorable wind fell away and shifted to the north. There was a fog, so that they had no idea of where they were going, and that went on for many days. After a time, they saw the sun and so were able to orientate themselves. They hoisted sail and went on that day until they sighted land. They had a discussion about what land it might be, and Bjarni said that he thought it wasn't Greenland. They asked him if he wanted to sail toward this land or not.

"I think we should sail close to the land," he said. They did so, and saw straightaway that the land had no mountains and was forested, with low hills. So they left the land to port and set the sail with their sheet turned toward the coast.

They sailed on for two days after that until they saw land for a second time. Again they asked if Bjarni thought this was Greenland. He replied that he thought this was no more Greenland than the last place. "For there are said to be massive glaciers in Greenland," he said.

They quickly approached this place and saw that it was flat and wooded. At that point, the favorable wind died away. After some discussion among themselves the crew announced that it would be a good idea to go ashore here, but Bjarni refused. The crew thought that they needed both wood and water.

"You've no shortage of either," said Bjarni and gave his crew the rough side of his tongue. They obeyed his orders to raise the sail and turned the prow out to sea, away from land. For three days they sailed with a southwesterly wind and saw land on the third. This land was high and had a glacier, so they asked Bjarni if he would let them go ashore here, but he said no. "I think this land looks unpromising," he said. They didn't lower the sail and followed the coastline only to discover that it was an island.

Once again they headed out to sea with the same wind behind them. But the wind blew more and more strongly, so Bjarni ordered the sail to be reefed and not to be raised so much that either the ship or its rigging was in danger. They sailed four more days and sighted land on the fourth. Then the crew asked if he thought this was Greenland or not.

"This place is most like what I've been told about Greenland, and we'll head for shore here," said Bjarni. They did so and made land beside a headland in the evening. There was a ship at the headland. Herjolf, Bjarni's father, lived by the headland which took its name from him and ever since has been called Herjolf's Ness. Bjarni went to his father's house. He gave up sailing and stayed with his father while Herjolf lived. After his father's death, he continued living there.

2. Bjarni Herjolfsson traveled from Greenland to meet Earl Eirik. The earl made him welcome, and Bjarni told him about his journey and about the

lands he had seen. However, he had no real information about these places, so people thought he was lacking in curiosity, and he attracted some criticism for this. Bjarni became one of the earl's retainers, and the following summer he returned to Greenland.

Everyone was now talking about voyages of exploration. Leif, the son of Eirik the Red from Brattahlid, went to see Bjarni Herjolfsson and bought his ship. He assembled a crew of thirty-five and invited his father to lead the expedition. Eirik was reluctant, saying that he was getting on in years and could no longer bear the hardships of seafaring as he had done in the past. Leif answered that his father still brought better luck than any of his kinsmen, so Eirik gave in. When everything was ready, he left home on horseback, but a short distance from the ship, his horse stumbled and he was thrown, injuring his foot.

"I'm not destined to discover any other lands than the one where we are living now," said Eirik. "This is as far as we'll be traveling together." Eirik returned to Brattahlid while Leif and his crew of thirty-five carried on to the ship. One of the crew was a southerner, a man called Tyrkir.

When their ship was ready, they set sail, and the first land they came to was the one that Bjarni had discovered last. They made for the coast and dropped anchor. Then they launched a boat and went ashore. There was no grass to be seen, only great glaciers stretching inland with what seemed like a single slab of rock between the glaciers and the shore; this land didn't look as if it would be much use. "At least we've come ashore here, which is more than Bjarni did," said Leif. "Now I'm going to give the land a name. I'll call it Helluland [Flat-Rock Land: Baffin Island?]."

Then they went back to the ship, put to sea, and found a second land. Once again, they sailed toward it, anchored, launched a boat, and went ashore. This land sloped gently to the sea; it was flat and tree-covered, and, wherever they went, there were extensive beaches of white sand. "I'm going to name this land for its resources," said Leif, "and call it Markland [Forest-Land: Labrador?]."

They hurried back to their ship and sailed away with a north-easterly wind behind them. After two days at sea, they sighted land. They sailed toward it and came to an island which lay to the north of the land itself. The weather was fine and they went ashore. Looking about them, they noticed that there was dew on the grass. The first thing they did was to collect the dew on their hands and put it in their mouths; they thought that they had never tasted anything so sweet. Then they returned to their ship and sailed into the sound which separated the island from a headland that stretched north from the mainland. They steered west around the headland, but the water there was very shallow at low tide. Before long they ran aground, and the sea retreated so far that it could hardly be seen from the ship. They were so anxious to get to land, however, that they didn't wait for the sea to float their ship, but ran [a boat] ashore by way of a river that flowed into the sea from a lake. As soon as the tide floated their ship, they rowed out to it in their boat and moved it up the river and into the lake, where they anchored. Then they carried their hide sleeping bags ashore and built sod huts.

Later on, they decided to spend the winter there and built some large houses. There were plenty of salmon in the river and the lake, and they were bigger than any they had ever seen. The land seemed fertile too, and they didn't think they would need winter fodder for their livestock, because there was no frost in the winter and the grass scarcely withered. Day and night were more equal in length than in Greenland or Iceland, for on the shortest day the sun was visible from 8:30 a.m. until 3:30 p.m.

When they had finished building their houses, Leif said to his men, "Now I want to divide our company into two groups so that we can explore the country. Half of you will stay at the houses while the other half explores the land. But don't go so far that you can't get back in the evening, and don't split up."

This is what they did for a time. Leif alternated between staying at home and exploring. He was a big, strong man, very impressive in appearance. He was intelligent, too, and moderate in all things.

3. It happened one evening, that a man went missing, and that man was Tyrkir the southerner. Leif was particularly upset because Tyrkir had lived with him and his father for a long time and had been very fond of Leif when he was a child. Leif gave his men an angry talking to and got ready to go looking for Tyrkir along with twelve of his men. No sooner had they left the house than they met Tyrkir coming toward them. They greeted him warmly, and Leif soon realized that his foster-father was in very good spirits. Tyrkir was a small man with a bulging forehead and squinting eyes in an insignificant little face. He was a poor-looking creature, but expert in all sorts of crafts.

"What kept you, foster-father?" asked Leif. "How did you get separated from the others?" At first Tyrkir spoke only in German, rolling his eyes in all directions and making peculiar grimaces, and for a long time, they couldn't understand a word of what he was saying. Eventually, however, he started speaking in Norse.

"I didn't go much further than you," he said, "but I have something astonishing to tell you: I have found vines and grapes."

"Are you sure about that, foster-father?" asked Leif. "Of course I'm sure," replied Tyrkir. "Where I was brought up there were lots of vines and grapes."

They spent the rest of the night asleep, and, in the morning, Leif said to his men,

"We've got two jobs to do at the moment and we'll work on them day about. One day we'll gather grapes and cut vines; the next we'll cut down trees, to make a cargo for my ship." And that's what they did. The story goes that the ship's boat was crammed with grapes and the ship itself had a cargo of timber.

When spring arrived, they got ready to set sail. Leif named the land Vinland [Wineland] for its produce. After that they put to sea and had a favorable wind until they saw the glacier-clad mountains of Greenland. Then one of the crew said to Leif, "Why are you sailing so close to the wind?"

"I'm watching where I'm going," answered Leif, "but I'm watching something else as well. Do you see anything unusual?" They replied that they couldn't see anything at all out of the ordinary.

"Well, I don't know if it's a skerry or a ship that I'm seeing," said Leif. Now the crew saw something too, and said that it was a skerry. However, Leif was further-sighted than the rest and he could make out people on the skerry.

"I'm going to sail close to the wind so that we can reach these people," said Leif. "If they need our help, we have no choice but to give it to them. And if it turns out that they're unfriendly, the advantage is all on our side, not on theirs."

They approached the skerry, lowered their sail, and anchored; then they launched another small boat they had with them. Tyrkir asked who was in charge of the group. Their leader replied that his name was Thorir and his family was Norwegian.

"And what's your name?" asked Thorir. Leif told him who he was. "Are you the son of Eirik the Red from Brattahlid?" said Thorir. "Yes, I am," replied Leif. "And I'd like to invite all of you aboard my ship with as many of your possessions as the ship can hold."

They accepted his offer and then they all sailed to Eiriksfjord with the cargo. When they reached Brattahlid, they unloaded the ship, and afterwards Leif invited Thorir, Gudrid his wife, and three other men to stay with him. He also found lodgings for all the other men, both his own and Thorir's. Leif rescued fifteen people from the skerry; he was known after that as Leif the Lucky. He had now become both rich and respected. That winter Thorir and his companions came down with a serious illness and Thorir died along with many of his men. Eirik the Red also died that winter.

There was now a great deal of talk about Leif's journey to Vinland. His brother, Thorvald, thought that the land had not been well enough explored, so Leif said to him,

"If you want to go to Vinland, brother, you can take my ship, but first I want to send it to fetch the wood Thorir salvaged on the skerry." And that is what happened.

76. THORFINN KARLSEFNI IN VINLAND

Thorfinn Karlsefni made a serious attempt to settle in Vinland, possibly in what is now the Gaspé region of Canada. His wife, Gudrid, was perhaps the best-traveled woman in the Viking age. She was an Icelander who traveled first to Greenland and then to Vinland. Later in life, she went on a pilgrimage to Rome. From The Saga of the Greenlanders.

Source: *Grœnlendinga saga*, in *Eyrbyggja saga*, ed. Einar Ól. Sveinsson and Matthías Þórðarson, Íslenzk fornrit IV (Reykjavík, 1935), pp. 260–64, 268–69.

6. That same summer, a ship came to Greenland from Norway and the steersman of the ship was called Thorfinn Karlsefni. He was the son of Thord Horsehead who was the son of Snorri Thordarson from Hofdi. Thorfinn Karlsefni was a very prosperous man. He spent the winter with Leif Eiriksson at Brattahlid. Soon, he directed his attentions to Gudrid, and asked her to marry him. She asked Leif to answer for her. Before long, she was engaged to Karlsefni and the wedding took place that winter.

There was the same talk as before about travel to Vinland, and people were eager for Karlsefni to go, Gudrid among others. At length, he decided to undertake the voyage and hired a crew of sixty men and five women. He and his crew agreed that whatever goods they acquired would be shared equally. They took all kinds of livestock with them as they meant to settle the land if they could. Karlsefni asked Leif for the houses he had built in Vinland, and Leif said that he would lend them, but not give them.

Then they put to sea and arrived safe and well at Leif's houses and carried their hammocks up to them. Soon, they got their hands on rich and plentiful provisions when a large, fresh *rorqual* [whale] was stranded on the beach. After they had cut it up, there was no shortage of food. They put their livestock out to pasture and soon the males became ill-tempered and intractable. They had brought a bull with them.

Karlsefni had timber felled as a cargo for his ship. The wood was hewn up and laid on a rock to dry. They had their choice of the available resources of the land – grapes and all kinds of game and produce.

The first winter passed into summer. They became aware that there were Skraelings [Native Americans] about when a large group of them came out of the woods quite close to Karlsefni's cattle. The bull began to bellow and roar furiously, and this so terrified the Skraelings that they took to their heels, carrying their packs full of grey fur, sable, and all kinds of skins. They made for Karlsefni's settlement and tried to get into the houses, but Karlsefni had the doors bolted against them. Neither side understood the other's language.

The Skraelings put their bundles down, opened them and offered to trade, especially for weapons, but Karlsefni forbade his men to part with weapons. Instead, he came up with the following plan. He told the women to take out milk and as soon as the Skraelings saw it, they wanted to buy the milk and nothing else. The upshot of the trading trip was that the Skraelings carried their goods away in their bellies while Karlsefni and his companions kept the bags of skins. After this the Skraelings left. Then Karlsefni had a sturdy fence built around his settlement and they made themselves comfortable there.

About this time, Karlsefni's wife, Gudrid, gave birth to a boy whom they named Snorri.

Early in the second winter, the Skraelings came back again. This time there were many more of them and they brought the same sorts of goods as before. Then Karlsefni said to the women, "Take out the kind of food that was most popular last time, but don't take out anything else." The moment they saw it, the Skraelings threw their bundles in over the fence.

Gudrid was sitting just inside the doorway beside her son Snorri's cradle. A shadow darkened the doorway and in came a woman wearing a black tunic with a ribbon around her light chestnut hair. She was rather short and pale and had the largest eyes ever seen in a human head. She walked to where Gudrid sat.

"What are you called?" she asked.

"I'm called Gudrid. What's your name?"

"I'm called Gudrid [too," she answered.]

Then Gudrid, Karlsefni's wife, stretched out her hand to the woman, inviting her to sit beside her, but at that precise moment there was a great outburst of noise and the woman vanished. At that same moment, a Skraeling was killed by one of Karlsefni's men, for attempting to make off with some of their weapons. The Skraelings cleared off as fast as they could, leaving their clothes and trade-goods behind. No one except Gudrid had seen the woman.

"Now we need to come up with a plan," said Karlsefni, "for I think they'll come back for a third visit, and this time they'll be hostile and more numerous. What we must do is this. Ten men should go over to the headland and show themselves plainly. The rest of us should go into the woods and cut a clearing where we can keep our cattle when the Skraelings come out of the forest. We should take our bull and let him go ahead of us."

The place where they planned to fight the Skraelings was protected by water on one side and by forest on the other.

Karlsefni's plan was adopted. Before long, the Skraelings came to the place Karlsefni had selected for the fight and many of them were killed in the ensuing battle. Amongst the Skraelings, there was a tall, handsome man, and Karlsefni concluded that he must be their chief. One of the Skraelings had picked up an ax. He looked at the ax for a moment, brandished it at one of his comrades and then struck him with it. Instantly he fell down dead. The tall man took the ax and scrutinized it. Then he threw it into the sea as far as he could. After that, the Skraelings fled into the forest as quickly as possible, and that was the end of the hostilities.

Karlsefni and his companions remained there for the whole winter, but in spring, Karlsefni announced that he didn't want to stay there any longer and wished to return to Greenland. So they got ready for the journey and took with them a great deal of produce, such as vines, berries, and skins. They put to sea and arrived safely in Eiriksfjord where they spent the winter....

8. ... Then Karlsefni put to sea and arrived at Skagafjord in northern Iceland where he beached his ship for the winter. In spring, he bought land at Glaumbaer, set up a home and lived there for the rest of his life. He was a highly regarded man, and he and his wife, Gudrid, had many distinguished descendants.

After Karlsefni died, the management of the farm was taken over by Gudrid and her son, Snorri, who had been born in Vinland. When Snorri married, Gudrid left Iceland and traveled on a pilgrimage to Rome. On her return, she stayed with Snorri, who by then had built a church at Glaumbaer. Afterwards, Gudrid became a nun and anchoress, and remained there until she died....

CHAPTER TWELVE

VIKING LIFE AND DEATH

Svein Asleifarson, an Orkneyman of Norse descent, lived a definitely Viking life. Viking raids were part-time and seasonal occupation for him. Following the rhythms of the agricultural year, he alternated sowing and harvesting with forays as far south as Ireland, where he died gloriously on his last autumn raid. Raiding and trading also flow seamlessly together in Egil Skallagrimsson's Baltic adventure. Rather prosaically, Egil himself died comfortably in bed, but many other individuals in this chapter have the opportunity to display the Germanic hero's sang froid in the face of violence and inevitable death. The chapter opens more pacifically with sound advice on sailing and trading, a reminder that Vikings were merchants and explorers as well as warriors.

77. ADVICE FOR SAILORS AND MERCHANTS

The first part of the thirteenth-century Norwegian text Konungs skuggsjá *(Specu-lum* Regale) *or* King's Mirror *(see doc. 68) consists of a father providing all sorts of useful advice to his son. Much of the advice in this section relates to how a prospective merchant should behave when abroad.*

Source: *Speculum Regale. Konungs-Skuggsjá,* ed. R. Keyser, P.A. Munch, C.R. Unger (Christiania [Oslo]: Akademiske Collegium ved det kongelike norske Frederiks-Universitet, 1848), pp. 5–9, 51–53.

3. ... If you are staying in market towns ... and you don't know how buying and selling is done there, observe carefully how those who are reputed to be the best and most successful merchants carry on their trading. When you are buying, take a careful look at the merchandise before clinching the deal, in case it is damaged or flawed in any way. And whenever you seal a bargain, always have a few trustworthy men present to witness the transaction....

You should occupy yourself with business matters until breakfast time, or until mid-day if necessary, and afterwards you should sit down to a meal. Set your table with white cloths, fresh food, and good drink, and eat well if you can afford it. After lunch, take a nap, or go for a walk, either for your own amusement, or to see what other reputable merchants are up to, or to find out if any new goods have arrived in town that you might want to buy. When you get back to your lodgings, take a careful look at the goods you have to sell and make sure that none of them have been damaged while in your possession. If there is any damage and you are going to sell the goods, don't hide the defect from the buyer. Instead, show him the damage and make the best deal you can. That way, you won't get a reputation as a swindler. Set a high price on your goods, one as close as possible to what you think you can get, but don't set the price too high or you'll be regarded as a profiteer.

Whenever you have a spare moment, devote some time to your studies, especially to the study of law.... If you want to be a merchant, you must have a good grasp of all lawcodes, but you'll need to have a more thorough grasp of the Bjarkey code than of any other. If you know the law, no one will be able to use legal trickery against you if you bring lawsuits against your peers, and you will be able to plead according to the law in every case.

Though I am speaking mainly about the law, I don't consider anyone to be well-informed unless he has a thorough knowledge and understanding of the people he is living amongst. If you want to be really erudite, you must learn all languages, especially Latin and French, which are the most widely used languages. Do not, however, neglect your own speech or language.

4. There are some habits that you must guard against and avoid like the devil himself – these are drinking, gaming, whoring, brawling, and betting – for these practices are at the root of the worst evils, and few people can avoid sin or censure for long unless they guard against these habits.

You must observe the movements of the heavenly bodies, and make a careful study of how the sky is illuminated, how night is divided from day, and how day is divided into several time-periods. You must also learn how to monitor the sea-surge and understand the significance of its ebbings and swellings, because that is essential knowledge for seafaring men. And you should make a thorough study of arithmetic, because merchants need to make frequent use of it....

Don't hang onto your trade goods too long, if you can get rid of them at a decent price, for merchants usually buy regularly, and sell on quickly....

If you are getting ready for an overseas trading-trip, and you own your own ship, tar it thoroughly in the autumn, and keep it tarred all winter if you can. But if your ship is laid up on blocks too late to be tarred in the autumn, tar it in the early spring, and then leave it until it dries out completely. Always buy shares in good ships, or don't buy them at all. Keep your ship looking smart, so that able men will choose it, and you'll have a competent crew. Get your ship ready early in the summer and sail when the weather is at its best. Always make sure that the gear on your ship is in good repair, and don't stay at sea late into the autumn, if you can help it....

There are one or two minor points still to be mentioned. Whenever you go to sea, take two or three hundred ells of *vadmal* [homespun woollen cloth] with you – the kind suitable for sail-mending – in case it's needed. Take lots of needles and a good supply of thread and ropes. It may seem trifling to mention these things, but they are often needed on a journey. You should always take along plenty of nails, both large ones and rivets, in the requisite sizes for your ship. And you'll also need good grapnels, adzes, chisels and augers, as well as all the other tools used in ship-building. Whenever you go on a trading voyage in your own ship, you must always remember to take everything I have mentioned....

If you start making a lot of money, divide it up and form partnerships in places that you don't go to yourself, but choose your partners carefully....

If you have a large amount of money invested in trade, divide it into three parts. Use a third of it to buy partnerships with men who are permanent residents of market towns; make sure that these men are trustworthy and experienced in trade. Put the other two thirds into several different trading ventures, for if your money is invested in a variety of ventures, it's unlikely that you will suffer losses in everything at once. The more likely outcome is that you will hold onto your wealth in some of the places where you trade, even though you suffer frequent losses. On the other hand, if you see that your profits from trade are increasing greatly, buy good land with two thirds of it, for money is usually secure in the form of land, whether it's in your own hands or in your kinsmen's hands. Do as you like with the remaining third – leave it in trading, or put it all into land if you want. But if you decide to keep your money invested in trade, you yourself should stop going from land to land on trading voyages, as soon as you have made enough money and have learnt as much as you want about foreign customs....

22. Seas are not all the same size. Small seas present few dangers and may be navigated without risk at any time of the year, for it's only a question of being able to predict favorable winds for a day or two, and that's not difficult for men who understand weather. Also, there are many lands which offer numerous harbors when the coast is reached. So, if men can wait for fair winds in a good harbor, or can be confident of good harbors once the crossing has been made, or if the sea is so small that there is no need to anticipate conditions for more than a day or two, then they may risk crossing such a sea almost at will. But where the sailor meets more difficulties – whether because the sea is broad and full of currents, or because he has set his course for lands where the harbors are dangerous owing to skerries, breakers, shoals, or sandbanks – then he should always exercise great caution and avoid crossing such seas late in the sailing-season.

You asked about suitable times for sailing. I am strongly of the view that it is not really safe to risk crossing the sea after the beginning of October, because after that the seas become very rough and storms grow wilder and wilder as autumn advances and winter comes closer....

23. At the beginning of April it is possible to cross all but the widest seas without risk, for about the middle of March, the days grow longer, the sun is higher in the sky, and the nights become shorter....

78. EGIL IN YOUTH AND OLD AGE

This passage from Egil's Saga *makes clear the connection between trading and raiding in the sagas. Whatever the historicity of this account, it is a splendid example of the narrative art of the saga.*

Source: *Egils saga Skalla-Grímssonar*, ed. Sigurður Nordal, Íslenzk fornrit II (Reykjavík, 1933), pp. 114–27, 294–98.

Egil in Youth

46. Thorolf and Egil spent the winter with Thorir and were treated very hospitably, but in the spring, they got a large longship ready and gathered a crew. During the summer, they raided in the east where they fought a good many battles and acquired a great deal of plunder. Then they made for Courland where they moored offshore and traded peacefully for a couple of weeks. But when they were done with trading, they started raiding again, going ashore at a number of different places.

One day they put in at a broad river mouth close to a huge forest. They decided to land there and then split up into groups of twelve. They went into the forest and before long they came across some settlements where they began looting and killing. The inhabitants fled, so they met with no resistance. Late in the day, Thorolf had the trumpets sounded to recall the men to the beach. So, no matter where they were, they all went back into the forest, because they had to return to the shore before their numbers could be checked. Thorolf got back, but there was no sign of Egil, and as darkness was falling, it seemed pointless to go looking for him.

Egil and his twelve men made their way through the forest until they came to a broad, open plain on which settlements had been built. A farmstead stood nearby, so they headed toward it. As soon as they got there, they rushed into the buildings, and since no one was about, they seized everything of value. This took them quite a while since there were so many buildings. When they left the farmstead, they found that a band of armed men had come between them and the forest, and was advancing to attack them.

There was a high fence stretching all the way from the farm to the forest and Egil ordered his men to follow the line of the fence to prevent the enemy from getting at them from all sides. He himself went first and the rest followed hard on one another's heels so that no one could come between them. The Courlanders attacked them fiercely with spears and arrows, but avoided close combat. Egil and his companions followed along the fence and discovered too late that there was another fence at right angles to the first one, so they could go no further. They were cornered. Some of the Courlanders followed them into the pen formed by the fences, while others attacked from the outside, thrusting their swords and spears between the fence-posts. Still others threw clothes onto their weapons. Egil and his men were wounded and captured. Then they were bound and led back to the farm.

The owner of the farm was a rich and powerful man with a grown-up son. They discussed what to do with the prisoners, and the farmer thought it would be a good idea to kill them all in quick succession, but his son replied that it was growing too dark to get any fun out of torturing them and advised waiting till morning. So, they were thrown into one of the farm buildings and trussed up tightly. Egil had his hands and feet tied to a post. Then the building was locked up securely and the Courlanders went into the main room where they ate and drank with great merriment.

Egil strained and heaved at the post until he pried it loose from the floor. It fell to the ground, and he was able to detach himself from it. Then he untied his hands with his teeth, and when his hands were free, he untied his feet. After that he set his comrades free, and they all looked around for the best way out. The walls of the building were constructed from huge logs, but at one end there was a partition made of flat planking. They took a run at it and broke it down, only to find themselves in another building that also had log walls.

Then they heard voices coming from beneath their feet, so they investigated and found a trap-door in the floor. They opened it and found a deep pit. This was where the men's voices were coming from. Egil asked who was there, and the man who answered said his name was Aki. Egil asked him if he wanted out of the pit, and Aki replied that they were desperate to get out. So Egil and his men took the rope they had been tied with, lowered it into the pit, and hauled up three men.

Aki told them that these were his two sons and that they were Danes who had been captured the previous summer.

"I was treated well during the winter," said Aki, "for I did much of the farm management, but my sons were treated like slaves and they didn't enjoy that at all. In the spring, we decided to run away, but we were caught and imprisoned in this pit."

"You must know how these buildings are laid out," said Egil. "Where's the best place to get out?"

Aki said there was another plank partition. "Break through it, and you'll be in the barn, and you can find your way out of that easily enough."

So Egil and his men broke through the partition into the barn and escaped from there. The night was pitch black, and Egil's men wanted to make for the woods as quickly as possible. But Egil said to Aki, "If you're familiar with the farmstead, you should be able to show us the way to something worth stealing." Aki said that there were lots of valuable items for the taking: "And there's a big loft where the farmer sleeps; there's no shortage of weapons in there."

Egil told his men to go to the loft. When they reached the top of the stairs, they saw that the loft was open. There was a light inside and servants were making up beds. Egil sent some of the group outside to make sure that no one escaped. Then he leapt into the loft and grabbed some of the many weapons. He and his men killed everyone in the loft and equipped themselves with arms. Then Aki pulled open a trapdoor in the floor and told them to go down to the room below. So they took a light and down they went. They found themselves in the farmer's store room that contained many valuable objects and a great deal of silver. Each man gathered up an armload of treasure and carried it off, but Egil picked up a large mead cask and put it under his arm. Then they headed for the woods.

When they got there, Egil came to a halt and said, "This is no way for warriors to behave. We've stolen the farmer's property, but he doesn't know a thing about it — we should be ashamed of ourselves. Let's go back to the farm and tell them what's been happening."

Everyone else was against the idea. They said they wanted to return to the ship, but Egil put down the mead cask and started running toward the farm. When he got there, he saw manservants carrying serving dishes from the kitchen to the main room. He also saw a large fire in the kitchen with cooking pots over it. He went across to the fire. Great logs had been brought in and the fire had been lit, as was the custom there, by kindling one end of a log and letting it burn along its length. Egil grabbed the log and carried it to the main room. He thrust the burning end up under the eaves and into the bark roof where the faggot lining quickly caught fire. He also found some dry wood lying about and piled it outside the door. The drinkers in the main room didn't notice a thing until the roof was ablaze. Everyone rushed for the door, but they couldn't get out because of the piled wood, and because Egil was blocking the doorway. He cut down men both in the doorway and just in front of it. In next to no time, the house was engulfed with flames and collapsed, and everyone inside perished.

Egil ran back to the forest where he was reunited with his companions. They all went back to the ship, and for his share of the plunder Egil claimed the mead cask he had carried off with him … it turned out be full of silver. Thorolf and his men were overjoyed at Egil's return, and they set sail first thing in the morning. Aki and his two sons joined Egil's group. Late that summer, they sailed to Denmark where they lay in wait for merchant ships and plundered whenever they could.

47. At this time, Harald Gormsson had succeeded to the throne of Denmark after the death of his father Gorm. The country was in turmoil, with many Vikings lying off the coast. Aki knew a lot about Denmark; he was familiar with both the land and the seas around it. So Egil often asked him about the best places to plunder. When they entered Eyrarsund, Aki told him that there was a large market town called Lund in the vicinity. There was a

good chance of finding plunder there, though the townspeople would probably resist. The men were asked if they wanted to go ashore. Opinion was divided. Some were all for it, while others were against the idea.

Thorolf was eager to go. Then Egil was asked for his opinion, and he recited a poem:

> We warriors – wolf's prey –
> must make swords glitter;
> and do daring deeds
> in the serpents' season [summer];
> let each of us eagerly
> land here in Lund,
> and before the setting of the sun
> we'll sing the spear-songs.

After that they got ready to go ashore. They made their way to the town, and as soon as the townspeople realized what was happening, they went to meet their attackers. There was a wooden fortification surrounding the town, and men were sent to defend it. Fighting broke out, and Egil was first inside the fortification. The townspeople fled and a great slaughter followed. The attackers sacked and burned the town. Then they went on their way and returned to their ships.

49. The following spring, Thorolf and Egil prepared to go on another Viking trip. When they were ready, they headed east toward the Baltic and when they reached Vik, they sailed south along the coast of Jutland, where they did some raiding. Next they made for Friesland and stayed there for much of the summer. Then they headed toward Denmark, but when they got to the border between Friesland and Denmark, they anchored off the coast.

One night, two men came to Egil's ship just as the people aboard were getting ready to go to sleep. The men said that they had business with Egil, and when they were brought before him, they told him that Aki the Rich had sent them with this message:

"Eyvind Skreyja is lying off the coast of Jutland intending to ambush you when you come north. He has assembled such a large army that you won't stand a chance if you have to face the whole force at once; but he himself is on the move with two light ships, and he's not far away from you at the moment."

When Egil got this news, he ordered his men to take down the awnings and keep very quiet; they did as he asked. At dawn, they came upon Eyvind and his force lying at anchor. Egil's men attacked immediately, hurling rocks and spears. Many of Eyvind's men were killed, but Eyvind himself jumped overboard, and he and the rest of the survivors escaped by swimming to land.

Egil and his men seized their ships, and took all their clothes and weapons. Later that day, they returned to their own ships and rejoined Thorolf. He asked Egil where he had been and where he had got the ships. Egil said that the ships had belonged to Eyvind Skreyja, but they had taken them from him. Then he recited the following poem:

> When we fought in fierce
> combat off Jutland's coast,
> the Viking defender of the Danish
> kingdom fought creditably;
> until Eyvind leapt overboard,
> and, swift to save himself,
> swam for the seashore
> with his whole host.

Thorolf said, "Given what you've done, I don't think it would be a good idea for us to go to Norway this autumn." Egil replied that it might be just as well to find somewhere else to stay....

Egil in Old Age

85. Egil Skallagrimsson became an old man. In old age, he grew stiff in the legs and had difficulty moving. Both his hearing and his sight began to fail. He was living at this time with Grim and Thordis at Mosfell. One day, he was walking outside near the wall, when he tripped and fell.

Some women who saw this laughed at him and said, "You're done for now, Egil, when you can't help falling over."

"Women didn't laugh at us so much when we were younger," said Grim. Then Egil made up this verse:

> My shriveled neck shakes,
> I'm forever falling on my hairless head,
> my pointless prick is moist and soft,
> and I'm hard of hearing.

Egil became completely blind. One cold winter's day, he went to the fire to warm himself. The cook complained that it was shameful for a man of Egil's reputation to be lying about under their feet, keeping them from getting their work done.

"Don't be annoyed if I toast myself by the fire," said Egil. "There should be enough room for both of us."

"Get up," she said. "Go back to your seat and let us get on with our work."

Egil got to his feet and went back to his place. He composed this poem:

> Blind, I must bear
> this eye ailment,
> blunder to the fire, beg
> mercy from a maidservant;
> formerly a fierce king
> warmed to my words;
> the noble lord of lands
> gave me gold as reward.

Another time when Egil went to the fire to warm himself, someone asked him if his feet were cold and warned him not to stretch them too close to the fire. "Alright," said Egil, "but it's hard for me to guide my feet now that I can't see. Being blind is a real pain." Egil composed this poem:

> Life drags,
> lying alone is no fun,
> a decrepit man
> on a down bed;
> my feet are frozen
> like frigid widows,
> ladies chill as ice
> lacking passion's fire.

In the early days of Hakon the Powerful's reign [Earl Hakon Sigurdarson, d. 995], Egil Skallagrimsson was in his eighties. He was still hale and hearty apart from his blindness. One summer, when everyone was getting ready to go to the Althing, Egil asked Grim if he could ride along with him. Grim wasn't too happy about this. When he talked to Thordis, he told her what Egil had asked.

"I want you to find out what's behind this," he said. Thordis went to talk to her kinsman, Egil. At that time, conversation with Thordis was Egil's greatest pleasure. When she met him, she asked,

"Kinsman, is it true that you want to ride to the Althing? I'd like to know what your plans are."

"I'll tell you what I have in mind," he said. "I'm planning to go to the Althing and take with me the two chests King Athelstan [king of England,

ca 895–939] gave me. They're both full of English silver. I intend to have
the two chests carried to the top of the Law Rock when the place is really
crowded and then I'm going to scatter the silver. I'll be surprised if people
share it out fairly. I expect there will be shoving and punching. It might even
end with the whole crowd at the Althing getting into a fight."

"That seems like a great plan," said Thordis, "and one that will be remembered as long as Iceland is inhabited." Then Thordis went to talk to
Grim and told him what Egil intended to do.

"That mustn't happen," said Grim. "He can't go ahead with such a crazy
scheme." So, when Egil approached Grim about going to the Althing, Grim
opposed the idea completely, and Egil stayed at home during the Althing. He
wasn't at all pleased and looked rather sullen.

At Mosfell, the animals were kept at a shieling [summer pasture, usually
with a cottage] and that's where Thordis stayed while the Althing took place.
One evening as the inhabitants of Mosfell were getting ready for bed, Egil
summoned two of Grim's slaves and ordered them to fetch him a horse.

"I want to go to the hot springs," he said. When he was ready, Egil went
out carrying his chests of silver with him. He mounted the horse, rode over
the home field to the slope beyond, and vanished from sight. When the farm
people got up in the morning, they saw Egil wandering about on the hill to
the east of the farm, leading the horse behind him. They went to him and
brought him home, but neither the slaves nor the chests were ever seen again.

There has been much speculation about where Egil hid his treasure. To
the east of the farm at Mosfell, a gully runs down the mountainside, and it
has been noticed that whenever there is flooding following a sudden thaw,
English pennies have turned up in the gully after the water has subsided.
Some people conclude from this that Egil must have hidden his treasure
there. Below the homestead at Mosfell are large and very deep bogs. Many
people are convinced that Egil must have thrown his treasure into them. To
the south of the river there are hot springs, and close by the springs there are
deep pits in the earth. Some think that this is where Egil must have hidden
his money, for the fire that flickers over buried treasure is often seen there.
Egil admitted that he had killed Grim's slaves and also that he had hidden his
treasure, but he told no one where he had hidden it.

Later that autumn Egil fell ill, and the illness carried him off. When he
was dead, Grim had him dressed in fine clothes and moved down to Tjalda-
ness where he had a burial mound built. Egil was laid there with his weapons
and clothes.

79. SVEIN ASLEIFARSON'S VIKING LIFE

One of the most colorful characters in the pages of Orkneyinga saga *is Svein Aslei-farson. Svein's historicity is not in doubt, though* Orkneyinga saga *is virtually the only source for his life and exploits. Svein was by turns confidant, advisor, and rival to several earls of Orkney. He was a farmer, fisherman, and landlord; a warrior, pirate, and mercenary. His exploits extended to Scotland, the Hebrides, the Isle of Man, England, Wales, and Ireland, and his reputation was such that he was celebrated by the author of the saga as "the most outstanding of all the men in the Westlands, either past or present" of similar rank. He died, according to the saga, on a raid to Dublin.*

Source: *Orkneyinga saga*, ed. Finnbogi Guðmundsson, Íslenzk fornrit XXXIV (Reykjavík, 1965), pp. 283–88.

105. After the death of Earl Rognvald [in 1158], Earl Harald [Harald Mad-dadarson, ca 1134–1206] subjugated the islands and made himself sole ruler over all of them. Earl Harald was a great chieftain and a very big, strong man. He married a woman named Afreka, and their children were called Heinrek, Hakon, Helena, and Margret. When Hakon was only a few years old, Svein Asleifarson offered to take him as his foster-son, and he was brought up by Svein on Gareksey [Gairsay]. As soon as Hakon was old enough to travel with the other men, Svein took him raiding every summer and sought to advance his reputation in whatever way he could.

At that time, it was Svein's custom to spend his winters at home in Gareksey, [Gairsay] where he always kept eighty men around him at his own expense. His drinking hall was so large that there was nothing to equal it in the Orkneys. Svein was always very busy in the spring; he had a great quantity of seed planted, attending to much of the work himself. Every spring, when the planting was over, he went on a Viking expedition, raiding in the Hebrides and Ireland. He called this his spring-raid. He returned home after midsummer and stayed at home until the fields were harvested and the grain was stored. Then he went on another Viking trip and did not return until the first month of winter was over. He called this his autumn-raid.

106. Once, Svein Asleifarson was away on his spring-raid, accompanied by Hakon, the son of Earl Harald. They had five large galleys with which they raided in the Hebrides.

The Hebrideans were so afraid of Svein that they buried their property or hid it under rocks. Then Svein sailed as far south as the Isle of Man, but he found little in the way of plunder, so he sailed out to Ireland and began raiding there. As they were heading south to Dublin, they saw two English merchant ships also making for Dublin. They were laden with English cloth and many other valuable goods. Svein accosted the ships and challenged the Englishmen to battle, but they didn't put up much of a fight, so Svein and his men robbed them of every last penny. The Englishmen kept only the clothes they stood up in and some provisions, and afterwards they were allowed to sail away in their own ships.

Then Svein and his fellow-raiders made for the Hebrides where they divided up their plunder. Afterwards, they traveled east in great splendor. Whenever they lay in harbor, they drew attention to themselves by using English cloth as awnings, and when they sailed to the Orkneys, they stitched English cloth to the front of their sails to give the impression that the sails were made from rich material. They called this trip their "cloth-raiding" trip, but Svein had also robbed the English ships of a large quantity of wine and English mead, and he took this home with him to Gareksey.

After Svein had been at home for a little while, he invited Earl Harald to visit and prepared a splendid banquet in his honor. At the banquet, there was much talk about Svein's lavish hospitality. Then the earl spoke.

"I want you to give up raiding now, Svein," he said. "It's good to drive home with a full wagon, and you've certainly supported yourself and your men for a long time by raiding, but most men who live by looting and pillaging die on raids if they don't get out in time."

Svein looked at the earl and answered with a smile, "Friendly words indeed, my lord, and I'm grateful for your advice, though some might argue that you yourself are not the most peaceful of men."

"I shall have to answer for my own deeds," answered the earl. "But that doesn't stop me from speaking my mind."

"You mean well, my lord," said Svein. "So, I'll give up raiding because I find that with age my strength is being drained away by the exertions of war. I'll go on my autumn-raid now, and I hope it will be as glorious as my spring-raid. After that I'll give up raiding."

"It's hard to predict, old friend, whether death or glory will come first," said the earl. After that, the conversation came to an end. Earl Harald left the banquet and was sent on his way with appropriate gifts. He and Svein parted on very friendly terms.

107. Soon after this, Svein got ready for his raiding trip. He had seven longships, all of them large. Again, Hakon, Earl Harald's son, joined him on the journey. First, they steered for the Hebrides but, finding little plunder there, they crossed over to Ireland where they raided extensively.

They traveled as far south as Dublin where they took the townspeople completely by surprise. No one was aware of their presence until they were actually inside the town, seizing a great deal of plunder. The leading townsmen were captured and surrendered the town to Svein, promising to pay whatever ransom he demanded. They also agreed that Svein and his men should occupy the town and rule it, and the people of Dublin swore an oath confirming this. In the evening, the Orkneymen went back to their ships, but next morning, Svein was to occupy the town, receive the ransom, and take hostages from the townsfolk.

Now the story turns to what happened in the town during the night. The leaders in the town held a meeting to discuss the troubles which had befallen them. They had no desire to turn their town over to the Orkneymen, and, worst of all, to the man whom they knew to be the most tyrannical in the Westlands, so they made up their minds to deceive Svein if at all possible. This is the plan they came up with: they dug deep pits just inside the town gates and also in several other places between the houses on the route that Svein and his men were expected to take. They concealed armed men in the nearby houses. Then they covered the pits with wood which would collapse under a man's weight. After that, they spread straw over the wood so that no trace of the pits could be seen. Then they waited for morning.

108. Next morning, Svein and his men got up, armed themselves, and set off for Dublin. When the Orkneymen entered the town, the Dubliners formed a lane of men from the gate to the pits. Svein and his men didn't notice anything amiss and ran straight into the pits. Some of the townsmen immediately stationed themselves in front of the gate while others ran up to the pits, turning their weapons on Svein and his men, who had a hard time defending themselves. And so Svein Asleifarson died there in the pits along with all the other Orkneymen who had entered the town.

The story goes that Svein was last to die and that he spoke these words before his death. "Whether I die today or not, let all men know that I am a retainer of the holy Earl Rognvald and I intend to place my trust in him now that he is with God."

The rest of Svein's men returned to their ships and sailed away. There is nothing more to say about their journey except that they reached Orkney. Now Svein's story is ended. It is the general view that, except for men of higher rank than himself, he was the most outstanding of all the men in the Westlands, either past or present.

80. THE JOMSVIKINGS MEET THEIR END

Supposedly an elite group of Viking mercenaries of the ninth and tenth centuries, the Jomsvikings are described as the greatest of warriors, whose exploits are detailed in the saga bearing their name as well as in other texts. Whether the Jomsvikings were historical or not, in the sagas they represent the embodiment of the heroic ideal. The following passage from Olaf Tryggvason's Saga *in* Heimskringla *shows how they face death at the battle of Hjorundarfjord in 986.*

Source: Snorri Sturluson, *Óláfs saga Tryggvasonar*, in *Heimskringla*, ed. Bjarni Aðalbjaranarson, Íslenzk fornrit XXVI–XXVIII (Reykjavík, 2002), vol. I, pp. 273–86.

35. King Svein [Svein Forkbeard, king of Denmark, ca 960–1014] held a magnificent banquet to which he summoned all the important men in his kingdom so that he could honor his father, Harald, with a funeral feast. Shortly before this, in Skane, Strut Harald had also died as had Veseti in Bornholm: he was father of Bui Digri and his brothers. King Svein sent word to the Jomsvikings that Earl Sigvald and Bui, with their brothers, should come to honor their own fathers at the feast provided by the king. The Jomsvikings came to the feast with all their bravest men. They had forty ships from Vendland and twenty from Skane. A huge crowd of men assembled there.

On the first day of the feast, before he mounted his father's high seat, King Svein drank a memorial toast and took an oath that before three years were over he would invade England with his army and kill King Athelred [Athelred the Unready, ca 968–1016] or expel him from the land. Everyone at the funeral feast had to drink that memorial toast. Then the chiefs of the Jomsvikings were served the strongest drink in the biggest drinking horn available. When they had drunk that toast, then everyone had to drink a toast to Christ and again the Jomsvikings were served the fullest horn and the strongest drink. The third toast was to St. Michael and everyone drank it.

After that, Earl Sigvald drank a memorial toast to his father and swore an oath that before three years were out he would invade Norway and kill Earl Hakon [r. 970–995] or drive him from the country. Then his brother, Thorkel the Tall, swore an oath that he would follow Sigvald to Norway and would not flee the battle as long as his brother was fighting. Next, Bui Digri swore that he would go to Norway with them and would not flee from the battle against Earl Hakon. His brother Sigurd then swore that he would go to Norway and would not run away as long as the majority of the Jomsvikings were fighting. Then Vagn Akason swore an oath that he would go to Norway and that he would not come back until he had killed Thorkel Leire and gone to bed with his daughter, Ingibjorg. Many other chiefs made vows about various other matters. That day, the men drank all through the funeral feast, but, the morning after, when the Jomsvikings were sober, they thought that they had said too much and held a conference to decide how they should proceed. They decided to get their equipment together as quickly as possible and make ready their ships and their army. News of this spread far and wide throughout the land.

36. Hakon's son, Earl Eirik, heard the news when he was in Raumarik. Immediately, he gathered his troops together and then went to Uppland. From there, he continued northwards across the mountains to Trondheim to meet his father, Earl Hakon. Thord Kolbeinsson tells of this in *Eiriksdrápa* [*Eirik's Praise-poem*]:

> From the south there traveled afar
> fierce rumors of war
> and of armored men. Farm-folk
> feared disaster.
> The sea-warrior [Hakon] heard
> of long-planked ships in the south,
> dragged down from the beaches,
> Danish ships sent to sea.

37 . Earl Hakon and Earl Eirik sent a war arrow through the whole Trondelag and dispatched messages to both the Møre provinces and Raumsdal, as well as north to Naumadal and Halogaland. They called for a full levy of both men and ships, as is told in *Eiriksdrápa*:

> The skald's praise-poem swells.
> The shield-warrior has spread on the sea
> his serpent-ships,
> his swift vessels under sail;
> when the great warrior
> went in haste to protect
> his father's land with his shield,
> many ships lay off the coast.

Earl Hakon immediately headed south to Møre to scout and gather troops, while Earl Eirik assembled the army and moved south.

38. The Jomsvikings made for Limafjord with their fleet and from there they sailed out to sea with sixty ships. They arrived at Agder and immediately steered north to Rogaland. As soon as they reached Earl Hakon's territory, the Jomsvikings began to pillage. They sailed north along the coast, plundering as they went.

A man called Geirmund, traveling with a few men in a fast boat, headed north to Møre where he met Earl Hakon. Presenting himself to the earl, he told Hakon the news that there was an army from Denmark in the south of the country. The earl asked if he knew this for certain and Geirmund stretched out one of his arms, which was severed at the wrist. This, he said, was clear evidence that there was an army in the country. Then the earl asked detailed questions about the army. Geirmund said that they were Jomsvikings and that they had killed many people and pillaged far and wide.

"But they are moving quickly and aggressively," he said. "I'm afraid that it won't be long till they show up here."

Then, traveling day and night, the earl rowed into every fjord, going in on one side and coming out by the other. He sent spies to the uplands around Eid, and south to the Fjords, and also to the north where Eirik had gone with his army. It is told thus in *Eiriksdrápa*:

> The war-wise earl
> had longships at sea,
> launched high prows,
> threats to Sigvald.
> Oars quivered, but the prey
> of the predatory raven
> feared no death,
> divided foam with their oarblades.

Earl Eirik hurried south with his army as fast as he could.

39. Earl Sigvald steered his fleet north to the Stad area. The first place he came to was the Herey Islands. Even though the Vikings came across local people, the locals never told them the truth about what Hakon and Eirik were up to. The Vikings laid waste wherever they went. They lay off Hod, went ashore there and raided. They herded both people and cattle to their ships and killed all the men who were able to bear arms. As they were returning to their ships, an old farmer approached them and drew near to Bui's men. The farmer said: "Driving cows and calves to the shore isn't very warlike behavior. You'd do better to trap the bear, now that you're almost at its den."

"What's the fellow saying?" they asked. "Can you tell us anything about Earl Hakon?"

"He rowed into Hjorundarfjord yesterday. He had only one or two ships, three at the most, and he hadn't heard anything about you," the farmer replied. At once, Bui and his men rushed to their ships, abandoning all their plunder. Bui said, "Let's put this information to good use; we're on the brink of victory."

They reached their ships and rowed out immediately. Earl Sigvald called to them and asked what was up. They replied that Earl Hakon was there in the fjord. Sigvald immediately weighed anchor and they rowed north around the island of Hod.

40. The earls Hakon and Eirik lay in Hallkelsvik where their entire fleet of 150 ships had assembled. They had got word that the Jomsvikings had sailed around Hod. So the earls rowed north in search of them. The two sides met at a place called Hjorungavagr and drew up their fleets for the battle. Earl Sigvald raised his standard in the middle of his troops and Earl Hakon marshaled his fleet for the attack. Earl Sigvald had twenty ships, and Hakon had sixty. In Hakon's army were the chieftains Thorir Hjort from Haloga-land and Styrkar from Gimsar. On one wing of Sigvald's fleet were Bui Digri and Sigurd his brother, with twenty ships. Opposite them Earl Eirik, Hakon's son, took up position with sixty ships, and with him were the chieftains Guthbrand the White from the Uplands and Thorkell Leira from Vik. On the other wing of Sigvald's fleet, Vagn Akason positioned himself to the fore with twenty ships, and opposing him was Hakon's son Svein with sixty ships. Among his troops were Skeggi from Uphaug in Yrjar and Rognvald from Ærvik in Stad. As it is told in *Eiriksdrápa*:

> Slender ships glided
> to sea-battle with the Danes;
> the fleet sped
> along the sea-coast;
> at Møre the earl disabled many
> ships of the gold-rich Danes;
> the ships drifted,
> heaped with the warm dead.

Eyvind Skaldaspillir also says this in *Haleygjatal*:

> The meeting was miserable,
> the morning grim for the Ynglings' [Norwegians']
> foes, when the earls urged their fleet
> furiously against the destroying
> Danes, when sword-bearing Hakon
> drove his sea-riding ships
> against the Danish fleet.

Then the fleets joined battle and a fierce fight began. Many men fell on both sides, but far more fell on Hakon's side because the Jomsvikings fought with vigor and daring and their weapons went right through the shields of their opponents. Such a hail of weapons was directed at Earl Hakon that his mail shirt was cut to pieces and he threw it off. Tind Hallkelson says of this:

The splendid mail shirt
that the jeweled woman
had readied for the earl
with her own hands
was riven asunder
in the heat of battle.
There the ringed mail shirt
was stripped from the earl;
(the lord of men still
bears the marks of it).
The warrior threw it off, and the ships
of the mail-clad Danes were cleared.

41. The Jomsvikings' ships were bigger and had higher sides than Hakon's, but both sides fought bravely. Vagn Akason attacked Svein Hakonson's ship so violently that Svein backed up and was on the verge of flight. At that moment, Earl Eirik pressed forward into the battle line against Vagn, who retreated. Now the ships were in the same position as they had been at first. Then Eirik returned to his own ranks where his men had pulled back. Bui had cut the ropes binding his ship to the others in his formation and was bent on pursuing Eirik's men as they fled. Earl Eirik laid his ship broadside to Bui's and a fierce, closely fought battle broke out. Two or three of Eirik's ships came alongside Bui's single vessel.

Then foul weather set in with a hailstorm so severe that a single hailstone weighed an ounce. Sigvald cut the ties between his ship and the others. Then he turned his ship around, intending to flee. Vagn Akason shouted to him and begged him not to go, but Earl Sigvald paid no attention to what he said. Then Vagn threw a spear at him, but hit the steersman. Earl Sigvald rowed off with thirty-five ships, leaving twenty-five behind. Then Earl Hakon brought his ship to the other side of Bui's. Incessant blows fell on Bui's men. Vigfuss, son of Killer Glum, lifted up a pointed anvil which lay on the deck and which someone had just used to rivet the hilt of his sword. Vigfuss was immensely strong. He hurled the anvil with both hands and drove it into Aslak Holmskalli's head so that the point penetrated his brain. Aslak had not been wounded till this moment, but had struck blows to left and right. Aslak was Bui's foster son and was entrusted with the bow position on Bui's ship. Another man there was Havard Cutter. He was the strongest and bravest of men.

During this attack, Eirik's men boarded Bui's ship and headed aft to the raised deck where Bui stood. Then Thorstein Midlang gave Bui a terrible wound across the forehead, shattering his nose-guard. Bui struck Thorstein in the side and sliced him in two at the waist. Then Bui grabbed up two chests filled with gold and shouted loudly:

"Overboard, all Bui's men!"

Bui plunged overboard with the chests and many of his men leapt after him. Many men died aboard the ship because there was no point in asking for mercy. Bui's ship was cleared of men from stem to stern and afterwards the other ships were cleared too, one after another.

Next, Earl Eirik came alongside Vagn's ship. There was fearsome resistance, but, at length, the ship was cleared and Vagn was taken prisoner. He and thirty of his men were tied up and taken ashore. Then Thorkell Leire approached Vagn and said:

"You took an oath to kill me, Vagn, but it looks more likely that I'll kill you."

Vagn and his men sat together on a fallen tree. Thorkell had a great ax and he beheaded the man sitting at the end of the tree-trunk. Vagn and his men were bound together by a rope tied around their legs, but their hands were free. One of them said:

"I have a cloak-pin in my hand. I'll stick it in the earth if I know anything when my head is cut off." When his head was off, the pin fell from his hand.

Next to him sat a handsome man with a fine head of hair. He swept his hair forward over his head and stretched out his neck, saying, "Don't get my hair all bloody."

A man grasped his hair and held it fast. As Thorkell swung the ax, the Viking jerked his head back sharply and the man holding his hair was left in the way. The ax cut off both his hands and embedded itself in the ground.

Then Earl Eirik came up and asked: "Who is this good-looking fellow?"

He replied, "I am called Sigurd and I am Bui's illegitimate son. Not all the Jomsvikings are dead yet."

"For sure, you are a true son of Bui," said Eirik. "Will you accept a pardon?"

"That depends on who's offering it," replied Sigurd.

Eirik answered, "The man offering it is the man with the power to do so – Earl Eirik." "I'll accept," said Sigurd, and he was released from the rope.

Then Thorkell Leire asked: "Earl, even if you mean to give all these men quarter, Vagn Akason isn't going to leave here alive." He rushed forward with his ax raised, but a Viking called Skathi threw himself over the rope and fell in front of Thorkell's feet. Thorkell fell over him, flat on his face. Vagn seized the ax, raised it, and dealt Thorkell his death wound. Eirik said, "Vagn, will you accept a pardon?"

"I will," he replied, "if we all receive one." "Free them from the rope," said the Earl, and it was done. Eighteen men were killed and twelve were pardoned.

42. Earl Hakon and many of his men were sitting on a fallen tree when a bowstring twanged on Bui's ship. The arrow struck Gizur from Valdres, a splendidly dressed landowner, who was sitting next to the earl. Some men boarded the ship and found Havard Cutter standing on his knees by the ship's side, for the lower parts of his legs had been cut off. He held a bow and when the men reached the ship, he asked, "Who fell off the log?"

They answered that it was a man called Gizur. "Then I wasn't as lucky as I wished to be," said Havard. "You've done quite enough damage, and you'll do no more," they replied, and killed him.

Afterwards, the dead were searched, and twenty five of the Jomsvikings' ships were stripped. The booty was carried off and divided. As Tind says:

> Sword bit limb
> when the warlord laid
> the sword's edge
> on the southern host;
> there was danger for the army
> until the sword-bearing earl
> could clear twenty five
> Danish longships.

Then the army was disbanded, and Earl Hakon went to Trondheim. He was not at all pleased that Eirik had given quarter to Vagn Akason. People say that in this battle Earl Hakon had sacrificed his son, Erling, for victory and that, afterwards, the hail storm arose and the tide of slaughter turned against the Jomsvikings.

Earl Eirik went to Uppland and then traveled east to his own territory. Vagn Akason went with him. Then Eirik gave Ingibjorg, daughter of Thorkell Leire, to Vagn in marriage. He also gave Vagn a fine longship, fully equipped and complete with a crew. They parted the best of friends. Then Vagn went south, home to Denmark, and afterwards became a distinguished man; many great men are descended from him.

81. THE DEATH OF GUNNAR

Earlier in the saga, Njal has warned Gunnar that, if he wants to avoid disaster, he should not kill two members of the same family. Unfortunately, in the web of violence and retaliation that surrounds Gunnar, he manages to kill two members of Gizur the White's family. The powerful Gizur has Gunnar banished as an outlaw from Iceland, but Gunnar cannot bear to leave his beloved land. Inevitably, Gizur and his allies come to take their revenge, as the law allows them to do. From Njal's Saga.

Source: *Brennu-Njáls saga*, ed. Einar Ól. Sveinsson, Íslenzk fornrit XII (Reykjavík, 1954), pp. 185–91.

76. In the Autumn, Mord Valgardsson sent word that Gunnar would be home alone, while all his people were down on the islands finishing the haymaking. As soon as they heard this, Gizur the White and Geir the Godi [priest, chieftain] rode east, over the rivers and across the sands, to Hof. Then they sent word to Starkad down at Thrihyrning. All Gunnar's would-be attackers met at Hof to discuss how they should go about the business. Mord said that they would never take Gunnar by surprise unless they seized the neighboring farmer, Thorkell, and forced him to go along with them. Then they could send him on alone to Gunnar's homestead to catch the dog, Sam.

So they traveled east to Hlidarend and sent men in search of Thorkell. They captured him and offered him two choices: be killed or get the dog. He preferred to save his life and went with them. Leading down to the farmyard at Hlidarend was a walled path and here the group stopped. Thorkell the farmer went on to the farmstead. The dog was lying on the housetop and Thorkell enticed him up the lane. As soon as the dog saw the other men, he leapt at Thorkell and bit him in the groin. Onund of Trollaskog struck the dog on the head with his ax. The ax penetrated right to its brain and, with an incredibly loud howl, the dog fell down dead.

77. Inside the house, Gunnar woke up. "Sam my friend," he said, "you have been cruelly treated, and perhaps this is a sign that our deaths won't be far apart." Gunnar's dwelling was built entirely of wood with an outer shell of overlapping planks. Near the ridge-beams were windows protected by shutters. Gunnar slept in a loft in the house along with Hallgerd and his mother.

When Gizur and the others approached, they had no idea if Gunnar was at home so they asked someone to go ahead and find out; the others sat down on the ground. Thorgrim the Norwegian scrambled up onto the roof. Gunnar saw a red tunic passing in front of the window and thrust at the middle of it with his halberd. The Norwegian lost his shield and his footing, and tumbled down from the roof. He went back to Gizur and the others who were sitting on the ground. Gizur looked at him and asked, "So, is Gunnar at home?" "Find out for yourselves," Thorgrim answered. "But I've found out one thing: his halberd is at home." Then he fell down dead.

The rest of them headed for the house. Gunnar showered them with arrows and defended himself so well that they got nowhere. Some climbed onto the buildings intending to attack him from the roof, but Gunnar could get at them with his arrows and they made no headway. The stalemate continued for a while. Then they took a rest and attacked again, but Gunnar kept up his hail of arrows. Once again, they gained no ground and retreated a second time.

Then Gizur the White said, "Let's attack more fiercely; we're getting nowhere." They launched a third attack and kept it up a long time, but again they fell back.

Gunnar said, "One of their arrows is lying outside on the roof. I'll shoot it at them. It will be humiliating for them to be wounded by their own weapons." His mother replied, "Don't do that: you will only provoke them when they have already withdrawn."

Gunnar seized the arrow and shot it at them. It struck Eilif Onundarson, wounding him seriously. He was standing by himself and his companions did not realize that he was wounded.

Gizur said, "Over there, an arm wearing a gold ring reached out and picked up an arrow lying on the roof. They wouldn't be looking for arrows outside, if there were enough inside; we must attack now."

Mord said, "Let's burn him alive inside his house." "Never," said Gizur, "even if my life depended on it. But surely someone with your reputation for cunning can come up with a workable plan."

Lying on the ground were some ropes used to tie down the house. Mord said, "Let's take the ropes and wind them around the ends of the roof-beams. Then we'll fasten the other ends of the ropes to rocks, and winch the roof off the house."

They picked up the ropes and got everything ready. Before Gunnar knew anything about it, they had pulled the whole roof off the house. Gunnar kept shooting with his bow so they couldn't get near him. Then Mord said a second time that they should burn Gunnar alive inside his house. Gizur replied, "I don't know why you keep going on about something that no one else wants to do, something that must never happen."

At that moment, Thorbrand Thorleiksson leapt onto the roof and severed Gunnar's bowstring. Turning quickly, Gunnar seized his halberd with both hands, drove it through Thorbrand, and hurled him off the roof. Then Asbrand, Thorbrand's brother, leapt up and Gunnar thrust at him with his halberd. Asbrand defended himself with his shield, but the halberd ran right through the shield between his upper and lower arm. Gunnar twisted his halberd so that the shield split and both parts of the arm were broken. Asbrand, too, fell from the roof. By this time, Gunnar had wounded eight men and killed two. Then he was wounded twice, but everyone said that he flinched neither at wounds nor at death.

He said to Hallgerd, "Give me two locks of your hair; you and my mother can twist them together to make a bowstring for me."

"Does anything depend on it?" she said.

"My life depends on it," he replied, "for they will never get the better of me as long as I can use my bow."

"Well then," she said, "I'm going to repay you now for the slap on the face you once gave me. And I couldn't care less how long you hold out."

"Everyone wins fame somehow," said Gunnar. "I won't ask you again."

Rannveig said to her, "You are a wicked woman, and your shame will last for a long time."

Gunnar defended himself bravely and well, wounding eight more men so terribly that many were close to death. He fought on until he fell exhausted. His attackers inflicted many serious wounds on him, but even then he escaped from their hands and warded them off for a long time. Finally, however, they killed him. Thorkel Elfaraskald made up this poem about Gunnar's defense:

> They say how the seafaring
> Gunnar, great-spirited in battle,
> hewing with his halberd,
> defended himself to the death;
> sixteen he wounded sorely,
> bearers of shields in battle,
> two he doomed to death,
> killed them south of Kjol.

Gizur said, "We have brought down a great warrior and it has been hard work indeed. His defense will be remembered as long as this land is inhabited."

He walked over to Rannveig and said, "Will you give us some ground here where we can bury our two dead?"

"I'd rather provide ground for all of you, not just for two," she replied.

"You have every excuse for speaking like this," said Gizur. "You have suffered a great loss." He gave orders that there should be no pillaging or destruction. After that, they left.

Then Thorgeir, son of Starkad, spoke, "We can't stay at home on our farms for fear of the Sigfussons unless you, Gizur, or you, Geir, stay here in the south for a while."

"So be it," said Gizur.

They drew straws and it fell to Geir's lot to stay behind in the south. He went to Oddi and settled there. Geir had a son called Hroald. Hroald was illegitimate; his mother was Bjartey, sister of Thorvald the ailing, who was killed near Hestlok in Grimsness. Hroald boasted that he had given Gunnar his death wound. He stayed at Oddi with his father. Thorgeir, son of Starkad, boasted that he too had wounded Gunnar. Gizur remained at home in Mosfell. The killing of Gunnar was denounced in every district. He was deeply mourned by many men.

82. THE BURNING OF NJAL

The alacrity with which Njal's assailants decide to use fire contrasts markedly with Gizur the White's honorable refusal to deal that way with Gunnar. Flosi Thordarson's quarrel is with Njal's sons, and he is willing to let Njal go free, but Njal elects to stay and share their death by fire. Only Kari Solmundarson, a friend of Njal's sons, escapes from the burning. His revenge is the motivating force for the rest of the saga.

Source: *Brennu-Njáls saga*, ed. Einar Ól. Sveinsson, Íslenzk fornrit XII (Reykjavík, 1954), pp. 315–39.

124. Flosi summoned all his men to Almanna Gorge, and he went there himself. By the time he got to the gorge, all one hundred and twenty of his men had arrived. Flosi addressed the Sigfussons, "How can I help you in this affair? What would suit you best?"

Gunnar Lambason replied, "We won't be happy until all the Njalsson brothers are killed."

"I give my word to the Sigfussons," said Flosi, "that I won't turn my back on this business until one side destroys the other. And I'd like to know if there is anyone here who doesn't want to help." They all declared themselves willing to help.

"Then," said Flosi, "let each of you come before me and take an oath that you won't give up on this undertaking." They all went up to Flosi and swore the oaths.

"We must also shake hands," declared Flosi, "as a pledge that anyone who pulls out will forfeit both life and property."...

Flosi said to the Sigfussons, "Someone will have to take charge, so choose a leader. Pick the man who seems best suited to the job."

Ketil answered, "If the choice is up to us brothers, then we'll all choose you. There's a lot to be said in your favor: you are well-born and a great chieftain; you are strong-willed and wise; we also reckon that you are the best man to look after our interests in the affair."

"Clearly, I should agree to your request," replied Flosi, "and now I'll set out our course of action. My plan is for everyone to go home from the Althing and see to his farm during the summer until the haymaking is over.

I will ride home too, and stay there for the summer. On the Sunday eight weeks before winter, I'll have a mass sung for me at home and then I'll ride west across Lomagnup Sand. Each of us must bring two horses. I won't add anyone to our group beyond those who have just sworn the oaths, because there are enough of us if we all keep our word. I'll ride all that Sunday and overnight too and, by the evening of the second day of the week, I'll arrive at Thrihyrning Ridge. All of you who have taken the oath should be there by then. If anyone who has committed himself to this business doesn't show up, he must pay for it with his life, if we're successful.... When we've assembled, we'll all ride to Bergthorshval and attack the Njalssons with fire and iron and we won't quit until they are all dead. You must keep this plan secret; all our lives depend on it. Now let's fetch our horses and ride home.".…

One day, Hrodny, mother of Hoskuld Njalsson, arrived at Keldur. Her brother Ingjald gave her a warm welcome, but she ignored his greeting and asked him to go outside with her. He did so, and they walked out of the farmyard together. Then, she clutched at him and they sat down.

"Is it true," she asked, "that you have sworn to attack Njal and his sons and kill them?" "It is true," he replied.

"What a vile wretch you are," she said, "considering that Njal has saved you from outlawry three times." "But as things stand now," he responded, "I'll pay with my life if I don't keep my word."

"That's not true," she said. "You'll go on living and be reckoned an honorable man if you don't betray the man who deserves most from you."

Then, she took a tattered and blood-stained linen hood from her purse.

"Hoskuld Njalsson was wearing this hood when they killed him," she said. "I think it reflects badly on you to help the people responsible."

"Alright," replied Ingjald. "I won't take sides against Njal whatever the consequences. But I know that they will make trouble for me."

"You could help Njal greatly if you warned him about their plans," said Hrodny.

"I won't do that," he answered, "because I would be despised by everyone if I revealed what was told to me in confidence. I can, though, in all honor pull out of this business, since I know they will take revenge. But tell Njal and his sons that it would be a good idea to be on their guard this summer and to have plenty of men on hand."

After that, Hrodny went to Bergthorshval and related the entire conversation to Njal. Njal thanked her and said she had done well: "For it would be especially wicked for him, of all men, to be against me." She returned home and Njal told his sons what she had said....

126. Two months before winter, Flosi got ready to travel west and summoned all the men who had promised to go with him. Each of them had

two horses and good weapons. They all came to Svinafell and stayed there overnight. Early on Sunday, Flosi had prayers said and then he sat down to eat. He told his servants what work each of them was to do in his absence. After that, he went to his horses.

Flosi and his men rode west to Lomagnup Sand. He ordered them not to ride too fast at first, but told them they would speed up toward the end of the journey. He said that if anyone had to stop, the others should all wait. They rode west to Skogahverf and arrived at Kirkjubae where Flosi asked all his men to come to church and say their prayers. They did so.

Then they mounted their horses and rode uphill as far as Fish Lakes. They rode to the west of the lakes, and then headed west for Maelifell Sand. Keeping Eyjafell Glacier on their left, they made their way down to Godaland, and on to Markarfljot. At the hour of nones [3:00 pm] on the second day of the week, they arrived at Thrihyrning Ridge and waited there until mid-evening. By then, everyone had turned up except Ingjald from Keld. The Vigfussons had harsh words for him, but Flosi asked them not to malign Ingjald in his absence. "However," he said, "we'll make him pay later."

127. Now the tale turns to Njal's farm at Bergthorshval. The brothers Helgi and Grim left Bergthorshval and went to Holar where their children were being fostered. They told their father, Njal, that they would not be back that night. The brothers spent the whole day at Holar. Some beggar women turned up there, saying that they had come a long way. Grim and Helgi asked them if they had any news. The women said they had no real news, but they could tell something unusual was going on. The brothers asked the women what they meant and entreated them not to hide anything. The women said they wouldn't.

"When we were coming down from Fljotshlid," they said, "we saw all the Vigfussons riding fully armed. There were fifteen of them altogether and they were heading up to Thrihyrning Ridge. We also saw Grani Gunnarson and Gunnar Lambason in a group of five all riding in the same direction. It could be said that the whole countryside is on the move at the moment."

"Then Flosi must have arrived from the east," said Helgi Njalson, "and all the others are going to join him. Grim, we should be at home with our brother Skarphedin."

Grim agreed and they returned home.

Meanwhile at Bergthorshval, Bergthora, Njal's wife, spoke to her household, "You must all choose your own food tonight and everyone is to have what he likes best, for this is the last evening I will serve food to my household."

"That won't happen," said the people standing near. "It will happen," she answered, "and I could tell you about a lot more if I wanted to. But this will be a sign: Grim and Helgi will come home this evening before people have finished eating. If this comes true, so will the rest of what I say." Then she carried food to the table.

"This is very strange," said Njal. "It seems to me that I can see all around the room, and it looks as if both gable walls have collapsed; and the table and the food are soaked in blood." This seemed ominous to everyone but Skarphedin. He told them not to despair or indulge in any discreditable behavior that people could talk about. "We have a greater obligation to behave well than other people do," said Skarphedin, "and that's only to be expected."

To everyone's astonishment, Grim and Helgi returned home before the tables had been cleared away. When Njal asked why they had come back so soon, they told him what they had heard. Njal told everyone not to go to bed that night.

128. Now the story turns to Flosi. He said to his men, "We'll ride to Bergthorshval now and get there before supper-time." There is a valley in the knoll on which Njal's farm stands. They rode into the valley, tied up their horses, and stayed there until late in the evening.

"Now we'll go to the farm," said Flosi. "Let's stay close together, and advance slowly until we see what they do."

Njal was standing outside with his sons, and Kari, and all the man-servants; there were nearly thirty men altogether drawn up in the yard in front of the house.

Flosi came to a halt.

"Now we'll have to wait and see what they intend to do," he said, "because I don't think that we'll ever get the upper hand if they stay outside."

"If we don't dare attack them, we've had a wasted journey," said Grani.

"It won't come to that," said Flosi. "We will attack them even if they do stay outside, but we'll pay dearly because not many of us will live to say who wins."

Njal said to his men, "What do you think? How many men have they got?"

"They have a good-sized force of tough-looking men," said Skarphedin. "Even so, they've come to a halt because they think we'll be hard to beat."

"That's not why they've halted," said Njal. "I want everyone to go inside the house, because the men who attacked Gunnar at Hlidarend had a hard time overpowering him, even though he was on his own. The house here is just as well-built as the one at Hldarend, so they won't be able to defeat us."

"That's not the way to go about things," said Skarphedin. "The chieftains who attacked Gunnar were honorable men who would have turned back rather than burn him in his house. But this lot will use fire if they can't defeat us any other way, because they will do anything to get the better of us. They will think, and rightly so, that we'll kill them if we escape. Besides, I'm not keen on being suffocated like a fox in its den."

"As usual, my sons," said Njal, "you're going to ignore my advice and show me no respect. You didn't behave like this when you were younger, and things went better for you then."

"Let's do as our father wishes," said Helgi. "That will be our best plan."
"I'm not so sure about that," replied Skarphedin, "for he's a doomed man now. But, nonetheless, I've no objection to humoring him and being burned inside the house with him, because I'm not afraid of death."

He spoke to Kari, "Let's stick together, kinsman, so that we don't get separated from one another."

"That's what I had in mind," said Kari, "but if fate decrees otherwise, then so be it; there's nothing to be done about it."

"Avenge us," said Skarphedin, "and we'll do the same for you if we survive."

"Agreed," said Kari. Then they all went into the house and took up position at the doors.

"They're finished now that they've gone indoors," said Flosi. "Let's get to the house quickly and form up as closely as possible around the doors. That way we can make sure that no one escapes, neither Kari nor the Njalssons — otherwise we'll end up dead."

Flosi and his followers advanced and surrounded the house in case there was a secret exit. Then Flosi and his own men went up to the front of the house. Hroald Ozurarson ran up to Skarphedin and thrust at him with a spear. Skarphedin chopped the head off the spear-shaft, leapt at Hroald, and swung at him with his ax. The ax struck Hroald's shield and slammed it against his body. The upper point of the ax sliced into Hroald's face and immediately he fell back dead.

"No one gets away from you, Skarphedin," said Kari. "You're the bravest of us all."

"I don't know about that," said Skarphedin and drew back his lips in a grin. Kari, Grim, and Helgi kept thrusting with their spears and wounded many men. Flosi and his men got nowhere.

Flosi said, "Our men have taken a lot of punishment. Many are wounded and the man we can spare least is dead. Several of our men are not fighting as boldly as they said they would and, clearly, we're not going to defeat them with weapons. Now we need to adopt another plan. We have two choices, and neither is attractive. Either we turn back, and that will be the death of us, or we burn them in their house, and for that we'll have to answer to God, for we are Christians. However, that's the step we have to take."

129. Then they laid a fire and built a huge blaze in front of the door. Skarphedin said, "So you fellows are lighting a fire now. Are you planning to cook something?"

"Right. And it will be hot enough for baking," replied Grani Gunnarson.

"This is how a man like you repays me for avenging your father," said Skarphedin. "You value most what you should value least." Then the women in the house threw whey on the fire and extinguished it despite the efforts of Flosi and his men.

"I have an idea," said Kol Thorsteinsson to Flosi. "I spotted a loft above the cross-beams in the hall. Let's build a fire in there and kindle it with chickweed from the pile behind the house."

So they fetched the chickweed and set fire to it. The people inside didn't notice the fire until the hall was completely ablaze above their heads. Then Flosi and his men built huge fires in front of all the doors. The women in the house grew distraught, and Njal said to them, "Take heart, and don't talk about giving up hope, for this is only a passing storm, and it will be a long time before we have another one like it. Have faith in God's mercy; he won't let us burn both in this world and the next." Such were the words of reassurance he gave them, and he made other remarks, too, that were even more encouraging.

Now the whole house began to burn. Njal went to the door and said, "Is Flosi close enough to hear what I have to say?" Flosi said that he could hear, and Njal continued, "Would you make terms with my sons, or let some people leave?"

Flosi answered: "I won't make a settlement with your sons. We're going to finish with them now, and we won't leave until they are all dead. But I will allow women, children, and man-servants to get out."

Njal went in and spoke to his household: "Everyone who has permission to leave must go now. You must go too, Thorhalla Asgrim's daughter, and take with you everyone who is allowed out."

"I never expected to part from Helgi like this," replied Thorhalla, "but I'll persuade my father and brothers to avenge the lives lost here."

"You'll do well," said Njal, "because you are a good woman." Then she went out and many people went with her.

Astrid from Djuparbak said to Helgi, "Come out with me; I'll throw a woman's cloak over you and cover your head with a hood." At first, he was reluctant, but at length he gave in to their entreaties. Astrid wrapped his head in a hood while Thorhild put the cloak over him. He walked out between them accompanied by his sisters, Thorgerd and Helga, and several other people.

When Helgi came out, Flosi said, "Look how tall that woman is, and how broad her shoulders are. Grab her and hang onto her."

When Helgi heard this, he threw off the cloak. He had concealed a sword under his arm and he struck out with it, cutting off the point of a man's shield and his leg as well. Then Flosi came up and slashed at Helgi's neck, beheading him instantly.

Flosi went up to the door and asked Njal and Bergthora to come and talk to him. They did so. Flosi said, "I want to offer you safe passage, because you don't deserve to be burnt in there."

"I'm not coming out," replied Njal, "because I'm an old man, and scarcely fit to avenge my sons, and I don't want to live in shame."

Then Flosi said to Bergthora, "Why don't you come out, Bergthora? The last thing I want is to burn you with the house."

Bergthora replied, "I was young when I was given to Njal, and I promised him that we would share the same fate." Both went back into the house. "What shall we do now?" asked Bergthora. "We'll go to bed and lie down," said Njal.

Then Bergthora said to the boy, Thord Karason, "Someone will take you outside; you mustn't burn in here."

"Grandmother," said the boy, "you promised that we would never be parted, and that's how it will be, because I think it's much better to die here with you."

Then she carried the boy to the bed.

Njal said to his steward, "Pay attention to where we lie down and how we settle ourselves so that you'll know exactly where to find our remains, for I don't intend to stir from here, no matter how much I'm bothered by the smoke and fire."

The steward replied that he would do so. An ox had been slaughtered and its hide was lying close by. Njal told the steward to spread the hide over them, and he promised that he would. Then Njal and Bergthora lay down in the bed with the boy between them. They crossed themselves and the boy, and entrusted their souls to God's hands. Not another word was heard from them. The steward picked up the hide and covered them with it. Then he left the house. Ketil of Mark grabbed hold of him and hauled him out. He questioned the steward closely about his father-in-law, Njal, and the steward told him the whole story. "Terrible sorrow has befallen us; we have so much misfortune to share," said Ketil.

Skarphedin had noticed when his father lay down and what preparations he had made. "Our father has gone to bed early," he said, "and that's only to be expected since he is an old man."

Skarphedin, Kari, and Grim picked up burning fragments as quickly as they fell and hurled them at the people outside. This went on for a while. Then the attackers threw spears at them, but they caught them all in flight and threw them back. Flosi ordered his men to stop the spear-throwing: "Exchanging weapons with them will only go badly for us. It will be better to wait till the fire overcomes them." And so they did. Then huge beams began to fall from the roof.

"My father must be dead by now," said Skarphedin, "and not a groan or a cough has been heard from him." Then they went to the end of the hall where the crossbeam had fallen down at a slant; it was badly burnt in the middle.

Kari said to Skarphedin, "Run up here and jump out. I'll give you a hand and come right behind you. This way we'll both get away, because all the smoke is blowing toward us." "You jump first, and I'll follow you straight-away," Skarphedin replied.

"That's not a good idea," said Kari, "because I'll find another way out, if I don't get out here."

"I'm not having that," said Skarphedin. "You go first, and I'll be hard on your heels." "Every man has a duty to save his own life, and that's what I'm going to do," said Kari. "After we part, we'll never see each other again, for if I once escape from this fire, I won't feel like jumping back in again, and we'll each have to go our own way."

"It's a consolation, brother-in-law, that you will avenge us if you get away," said Skarphedin. Kari seized a burning log and ran up the crossbeam. He flung the log from the roof and it landed on the people outside. They leapt out of the way. By this time, all of Kari's clothes and his hair had caught fire. He threw himself down from the roof and stumbled away under cover of the smoke. One of the men outside said, "Was that a man jumping from the roof?"

"No," replied one of the others. "It was Skarphedin throwing a burning log at us."

After that, they suspected nothing.

Kari ran till he reached a stream; he threw himself in and doused the flames. Then, he ran on, hidden by the smoke, until he reached a hollow where he rested. Ever since, the hollow has been called Kari's Hollow.

130. Now the story tells us that Skarphedin ran up the crossbeam right behind Kari. But when he reached the most badly burnt section, it collapsed under him. Skarphedin landed on his feet. Immediately, he had another try, scrambling up the wall this time, but the main beam gave way and he tumbled back again.

"Now it's clear how things will be," said Skarphedin. Then he walked along by the side wall. Gunnar Lambason jumped onto the wall and saw Skarphedin. "Are you weeping now, Skarphedin?" he asked.

"Not at all," replied Skarphedin, "though it is true that my eyes are smarting. You seem to be laughing; am I right?"

"I am indeed," said Gunnar, "and I haven't laughed once since you killed Thrain."

"Well here's something to remember him by," said Skarphedin. From his purse, he took out a molar that he had hacked from Thrain's mouth and threw it at Gunnar's eye. The eye popped from its socket and landed on his cheek. Then Gunnar fell off the roof.

Skarphedin went to his brother, Grim. They joined hands and beat down the fire with their feet. But when they reached the middle of the hall, Grim fell down dead, and when Skarphedin got to the end of the hall, the whole roof collapsed with a huge crash. He was trapped between the fallen roof and the gable and could not move an inch.

Flosi and his men stayed by the fire until well after dawn. Then a man came riding up and Flosi asked his name. He said his name was Geirmund, and he was a relative of the Sigfussons. "You have done great things," he said.

"People will call them evil as well as great," replied Flosi. "But there's nothing to be done about it now."

"How many well-known people died here?" asked Geirmund.

"Njall and Bergthora died here," replied Flosi. "So did the Njalssons, Helgi, Grim, and Skarphedin, as well as Thord Karason, Kari Solmundarson, and Thord the freedman. We're not sure about others whom we don't know so well."

"You're counting among the dead a man who got away," said Geirmund. "I know because I talked to him this morning."

"Who is that?" asked Flosi.

"Kari Solmundarson," replied Geirmund. "My neighbor Bard and I met him, and Bard gave him his horse. His hair and clothes had been burnt off."

"Was he armed?" asked Flosi.

"He had the sword Fjorsvafnir [Taker of Life]," answered Geirmund. "One edge had turned blue and we said that it must have lost its temper. But he replied that he would restore its temper in the blood of the Sigfussons and the other arsonists."

"Did he mention Skarphedin or Grim?" Flosi asked.

"He told us that they were both alive when he parted from them, but that they would be dead by now," said Geirmund.

"There's little hope of peace in what you've told us," said Flosi, "for the man who has just escaped is the one who comes closest, in every respect, to being a match for Gunnar of Hldarend. You Sigfussons, and the rest of us as well, must understand that the aftermath of this burning will be so serious that many men will lose their heads, and others will forfeit everything they own. I suspect that none of you Sigfussons will dare stay in your own homes now, and for good reason, so I'm inviting all of you to come east with me. Let's face our fate together." They thanked him. Then, Motholf Ketilsson composed this poem:

> Out of all the gold-givers
> a single man survives the
> bright blaze of Njal's house,
> set by the Sigfussons.
> Now, Njal, the murder
> of the hero Hoskuld is paid for
> by fire burning brightly,
> by flames flooding the house.

"We'll have to find something to boast about other than the burning of Njal," said Flosi. "There's no glory in that."

Then Flosi climbed onto the gable, along with Glum Hildisson and a few others.

"I wonder if Skarphedin is dead yet," said Glum. The others replied that he must have been dead for a while. The fire flared up at times, and died down at others. Then, from the depths of the fire, they heard this poem being recited:

> The woman will weep,
> the golden girl shed tears,
> for the bearer of the bridge-curved shield,
> for the spirited warrior in the spear-shower.
> Spears sing in flight,
> trusty friends of wounded flesh;
> strong in spirit I advanced.
> Edges cut; in showers fell wound-giving shafts.

"Do you think Skarphedin was dead or alive when he recited that poem?" asked Grani Gunnarsson. "I'm not going to speculate about that," replied Flosi.

"Let's look for Skarphedin and the others who were burned alive in here," said Grani.

"No," said Flosi. "Only a fool like you would think of something like that at a time when men must be assembling forces all over the district. Anyone who hangs about now will be so scared later on that he won't know which way to run. My advice is that we all ride away as fast as we can." Flosi and all his men went in haste to their horses.

83. THE DEATH OF THORMOD KOLBRUNARSKALD

Olaf Haraldsson (Saint Olaf; 995–1030), was king of Norway from 1015 to 1028, and he unified the kingdom more effectively than Harald Finehair had been able to do. His harshness brought rebellion in 1028, and his attempt to regain the throne ended with his defeat and death at the Battle of Stiklestad in 1030. Before the battle, the king called the poet Thormod Kolbrunarskald to sing for him. Thormod did so and stayed by the king until his death. The following passage relates Thormod's own death.

Source: Snorri Sturluson, *Óláfs saga Helga*, in *Heimskringla*, ed. Bjarni Aðalbjarnarson, Íslenzk fornrit XXVI–XXVIII (Reykjavík, 2002), vol. 2, pp. 389–93.

233. In the battle, Thormod Kolbrunarskald stayed near King Olaf's banner. After the death of the king when the battle was at its fiercest, the men of the king's guard fell one beside the other, and most of those left standing were wounded. Thormod, too, was seriously wounded and, like all the others, retreated from the thick of the battle. Some even fled.

Now the fight called Dag's Attack broke out, and all of the king's men who were able to bear arms went there. Thormod, however, did not take part in the fray. He could not fight, because of his wounds and his weariness, but he stood beside his comrades though he could do nothing else. He was then struck in the left side by an arrow. He broke off the shaft of the arrow and walked away from the battle, back to the houses. He came to a barn, which was a large building. Thormod was carrying a drawn sword in his hand and as he went in a man coming out met him and said,

"There is a terrible noise of wailing and howling in here. It's a real disgrace that strong men can't bear their wounds. The king's men may well have advanced bravely today, but they endure their wounds very badly."

Thormod answered, "What's your name?" The man said his name was Kimbi. "Were you in the battle?" asked Thormod. "I was with the farmers," he replied, "the better side." "Are you wounded at all?" asked Thormod. "Slightly," said Kimbi. "Were you in the battle?" "I was with those who had the best of it," said Thormod.

Kimbi saw that Thormod had a gold ring on his arm. He said, "You must be one of the king's men. Give me your gold ring and I'll hide you. The farmers will kill you if you get in their way."

"Take the ring if you can," answered Thormod. "I have lost more than that."

Kimbi stretched out his hand to take the ring. Thormod swung his sword and cut off Kimbi's hand. The story goes that Kimbi bore his wound no better than those whom he had criticized earlier.

Kimbi went away, but Thormod sat down in the barn for a while and listened to what people were saying. The talk was chiefly about what each of them had seen in the battle and about the bravery of the men involved. Some praised the courage of King Olaf most, while others mentioned other equally brave men. Then Thormod recited:

> Brave-hearted Olaf made a bloody advance
> at Stiklestad. Sword thrust
> and steel spear bit.
> The king urged bold warriors to battle.
> I saw all the tree-tall warriors of Odin
> – except the courageous king –
> seek to shelter from the spear-shower,
> where most met a terrible trial.

234. Thormod left and entered a small building where there were already many badly wounded men. A woman was also there, bandaging up their wounds. On the floor a fire was burning, and she was heating water on it to cleanse the wounds. Thormod sat down beside the door. Men were coming and going as they cared for the wounded. One of them turned to Thormod, looked at him, and said, "Why are you so pale? Are you wounded? Why don't you ask for treatment?" Thormod recited this poem:

> Red I am not, but red and
> ruddy health in a man
> is what the slim, fair woman prefers.
> Few are troubled by my wounds.
> What caused this pallor,
> Generous gold-giver?
> Danish weapons that slashed deep
> and a hail of arrows that smarted.

Then Thormod stood up and walked over to the fire. He stood there for a while until the woman said to him, "You, fellow, go out and bring me the firewood that's lying outside the door." He went out and brought in an armful of wood which he threw on the floor. The woman looked at his face and said, "This man is very pale. Why are you so pale?" Thormod recited:

My paleness surprises you,
swan-white woman.
Few grow fair from wounds;
I faced the arrows' storm.
The pliant weapon, propelled with force,
pierced me through.
I fear that danger-carrying iron bit keenly,
close to my heart.

Then the woman said, "Let me see your wounds and I'll bandage them." He sat down and took off his clothes. When she had seen his wounds, the woman examined the one in his side. She noticed that there was a piece of iron buried in it, but she did not know for certain how far it had penetrated. In a stone pot she had mashed together garlic and other herbs. She boiled them up and gave them to the wounded men to eat. In this way, she found out if they had been wounded in a vital part for she could smell the scent of garlic coming from a wound in a body cavity. She brought the mixture to Thormod and told him to eat. He replied, "Take it away. I'm not so sick that I want broth."

Then she picked up a pair of tongs and tried to remove the iron, but it was stuck fast and would not budge because the wound had swollen up and there wasn't much iron sticking out to get hold of. Thormod said, "Cut through to the iron so that the tongs can grip it easily. Then give me the tongs and let me pull it out."

She did as he asked. Then Thormod took a gold ring from his arm and gave it to the woman and told her to do what she liked with it. "It is a fine gift," he said. "King Olaf gave me the ring this morning."

Thormod took the tongs and pulled out the arrow-head, which was barbed. On the barbs were shreds of flesh from his heart, some red and some white. When he saw that, he said, "Our king has fed us well: I have fat even around my heart." Then he slumped back and died. Here ends what there is to say about Thormod.

CHAPTER THIRTEEN

FROM ODIN TO CHRIST

The conversion of the Scandinavians was a lengthy and complicated process that spanned several centuries. It occurred earlier in some regions than others, and moved at different paces in different parts of the Viking world. By the twelfth century, however, the process had largely run its course in most parts of the Scandinavian world, and the Vikings had joined the mainstream of Christian European peoples. Vikings became Crusaders, and those who had once attacked churches and monasteries became soldiers of Christ.

One significant problem relates to the nature of the sources. There is no coherent contemporary narrative of the conversion of the Northern peoples, no Scandinavian equivalent to Bede's Ecclesiastical History of the English People, *to guide any examination. Few contemporary sources come to us from Scandinavians, and those that do exist are mostly from Christian writers such as Rimbert or Adam of Bremen, outsiders looking in, who were hardly unbiased observers. What Scandinavian sources there are were largely composed long after conversion, though this does not automatically make them untrustworthy. A related difficulty is that these texts are unevenly distributed across the Viking world: sources for the conversion are sparse in places such as Ireland, Scotland, Normandy, Russia, and Greenland, while in Scandinavia itself, Denmark and Norway are better documented than Sweden. Another set of problems relates to the nature of conversion as a whole: how much was conversion motivated by conscience or genuine piety, and how much by other factors? Conversion was closely associated with the state-building process; the Scandinavian kings who were remembered as being responsible for conversion are also regarded as being responsible for constructing unitary kingships in their realms. Some of the materials presented in chapter 14 on state-building — the royal monuments at Jelling in Denmark, for instance (see doc. 95) — are therefore as relevant to the theme of conversion as they are to state-making.*

84. THE CONVERSION OF THE DANES UNDER HARALD BLUETOOTH

In Denmark, conversion came in the reign of King Harald Gormsson Bluetooth, whose achievements are related first and foremost on the rune-stone that he had erected at Jelling (see doc. 95). Adam of Bremen also recounted the events surrounding the conversion of the Danish royal house to Christianity in the mid-tenth century. Very little is known of King Gorm, and it is uncertain to what extent Adam's depiction of him as hostile to Christianity should be accepted.

Source: trans. F.J. Tschan, Adam of Bremen, *History of the Archbishops of Hamburg-Bremen*, with new introduction by T. Reuter (New York: Columbia University Press, 2002), pp. 49–51, 55–57.

1.57 ... Over the Danes there ruled at that time Harthacanute Gorm [d. 958], a savage worm, I say, and not moderately hostile to the Christian people. He set about completely to destroy Christianity in Denmark, driving the priests of God from its bounds and also torturing very many of them to death.

1.58. But then King Henry [I of Germany, r. 919–36], who feared God even from his boyhood and placed all trust in his mercy, triumphed over the Hungarians in many and mighty battles. Likewise he struck down the Bohemians and the Sorbs, who had been subdued by other kings, and the other Slavic peoples, with such force in one great encounter that the rest – and just a few were left – of their own accord promised the king that they would pay tribute, and God that they would be Christians.

1.59. Then he invaded Denmark with an army [934] and in the first battle so thoroughly terrified King Gorm that the latter pledged himself to obey his commands and, as a suppliant, sued for peace. The victorious Henry then set the bounds of the kingdom at Schleswig, which is now called Haddeby, appointed a margrave, and ordered a colony of Saxons to settle there. All these facts, related by a certain Danish bishop, a prudent man, we transmit to our Church as faithfully as we have truthfully received them.

1.60 When our most blessed archbishop Unni [d. 936] saw that the door of the faith had been opened to the gentiles, he gave thanks to God for the salvation of the pagans, and more especially because the mission of the church of Hamburg, long neglected on account of the adverse times, has with the help of God's mercy and through the valor of King Henry been given occasion and opportunity for its work. Deeming nothing hard and laborious if undertaken for Christ, he determined to go in person through the length and breadth of his diocese. The entire flock of the church of Bremen followed him, as they say, saddened by the absence of its good shepherd and ready to go with him both into prison and to death.

1.61. Thereafter the confessor of God came to the Danes over whom, as we have said, the most cruel Gorm then held sway. The latter, indeed, he could not win over on account of his inborn savagery, but he is said by his preaching to have won the king's son, Harald [Bluetooth]. Unni made him so faithful to Christ that, although he himself had not yet received the sacrament of baptism, he permitted the public profession of Christianity which his father always hated.

And so, after the saint of God had ordained priests for the several churches in the kingdom of the Danes, he is said to have commended the multitude of believers to Harald. Seconded also by his aid and by a legate, Unni went into all the islands of the Danes, preaching the Word of God to the heathen and comforting in Christ the faithful whom he found captive there....

2.3. As soon as he was freed from the plots of his brothers, King Otto [I of Germany, r. 936–973] with the support of divine help executed judgment and justice unto his people. Thereupon, after he had brought into subjection to his empire nearly all the kingdoms which had seceded after the death of Charles, he took up arms against the Danes, whom his father had previously subdued by war. Bent upon fighting, they had murdered at Haddeby Otto's legates and the margrave and had utterly wiped out the whole colony of Saxons. To avenge this deed the king at once invaded Denmark with an army. Crossing the Danish frontier, which had formerly been fixed at Schleswig, he devastated the whole region with fire and sword, even unto the furthermost sea which separates the Northmen from the Danes and which to this very day is called the Ottensond for the victory of the king [Adam here attributes a campaign of Otto II in 974 to Otto I]. As he was leaving, Harald [Bluetooth] met him at Schleswig and offered battle. In this conflict, manfully contested on both sides, the Saxons gained the victory, and the vanquished Danes retreated to their ships. When conditions were at length favorable for peace, Harald submitted to Otto and, on getting back his kingdom from the latter, promised to receive Christianity into Denmark. Not long after Harald himself was baptized together with his wife, Gunnhild, and his little son, whom our king raised up from the sacred font and named Svein Otto. At that time Denmark on this side of the sea, which is called Jutland by the inhabitants, was divided into three dioceses and subjected to the bishopric of Hamburg. In the church at Bremen are preserved the royal edicts which prove that King Otto held the Danish kingdom in his jurisdiction, so much so that he would even bestow the bishoprics. And it can be seen in the privileges of the Roman See that Pope Agapetus, in congratulating the Church of Hamburg upon the salvation of the heathen, also conceded to Adaldag everything that had been granted to the archbishopric of Bremen by his predecessors, Gregory, Nicholas, Sergius, and others. To him also was conceded by virtue of apostolic authority the right to consecrate bishops as papal legates to Denmark as well as to the other peoples of the north.

2.4. Our most blessed father [Archbishop Adaldag], then was the first to consecrate bishops for Denmark: Hored for Schleswig, Liafdag for Ribe, Reginbrund for Aarhus. To them he also commended the churches across the sea in Fyn, Zealand, and Scania and in Sweden. This was done in the archbishop's twelfth year [948]. And indeed, such increase followed these beginnings of heavenly mercy, God working with them, that the churches of the Danes are seen to abound in the manifold fruits of the northern peoples from that time even to this day....

2.22. Harald [Bluetooth], the king of the Danes, noted for his piety and bravery, had long before benignantly admitted Christianity to his kingdom and held it firm until the end. Hence, also, he strengthened his rule by holiness and justice and extended his authority beyond the sea over the Norwegians and the Angles. Emund, Eric's son, then ruled in Sweden. Since he was allied with Harald, he was favorably disposed toward the Christians who came there. In Norway, Haakon [the Bad, ca 971–995] was the ruler. When the Norwegians drove him from the realm because he had acted haughtily, Harald valorously restored him and made him well-disposed to the worshippers of Christ....

85. OLAF TRYGGVASON AND THE CONVERSION OF NORWAY

Olaf Tryggvason's reign (995–1000) was brief but eventful. His conversion of Norway to Christianity was undertaken for both political and religious reasons, and however pious Olaf himself may have been, he was inflexible in the mercilessness with which he carried out his attempt to recall Norwegians to Christianity. Nonetheless, the old gods still haunted Norway and sometimes attempted to win back the men who had deserted them.

Source: Snorri Sturluson, *Ólafs saga Tryggvasonar*, in *Heimskringla*, ed. Bjarni Aðalbjarnarson, Íslenzk fornrit XXVI–XXVIII (Reykjavík, 2002), vol. I, pp. 302–23.

53. When King Harald Gormsson, king of Denmark, adopted Christianity, he sent word throughout his entire kingdom that everyone should be baptized and turn to the true faith. He himself backed the order by authorizing

force and punishment when nothing else worked. He also sent two earls to Norway with a large army. They were to proclaim Christianity in Norway. This was successful in the Vik, which was under Harald's authority, and much of the population was baptized.

After Harald's death, his son, Svein Forkbeard, went raiding both in Saxony and Frisia, and finally in England. In his absence, the Norwegians who had accepted baptism went back to making heathen sacrifices as they had done before, and as was the practice in the north of the country. When Olaf Tryggvason became king of Norway, he stayed in the Vik for much of the summer, and many of his relatives and in-laws joined him there. Many of them had been great friends of his father, and they gave him a very warm welcome.

Then Olaf summoned his maternal uncles, his step-father, Lodin, and his kinsmen Thorgeir and Hyrning. He suggested to them very earnestly that they should join him and give him their full support in establishing Christianity throughout his kingdom. He said that he would bring about the Christianization of Norway or die in the attempt.

"I shall make you important and powerful men," said Olaf, "for I have the greatest trust in you because of our kinship and our other ties." They all agreed that they – and everyone willing to follow their advice – would do whatever he asked and support him in whatever he proposed. Olaf immediately informed all his people that he would impose Christianity on everyone in his kingdom. Those who had been Christians before were the first to accept the king's bidding. They were also the most powerful of those present, and everyone followed their example.

When everyone in the eastern part of the Vik was baptized, King Olaf moved to the northern part and ordered the population there to accept Christianity. He inflicted terrible punishments on those who opposed him: some were killed, some were mutilated, and others were driven from the country. So it came about, as King Olaf had ordered, that Christianity was accepted by all the people throughout the territory formerly ruled by his father, King Tryggvi, and also in the territory of his kinsman, Harald Grenski. Thus, in the course of that summer and the following winter, everyone in the Vik was converted to Christianity.

54. In early spring, King Olaf set out from the Vik with a large army and headed west to Agder. Wherever he held a meeting with the farmers, he gave orders for everyone to be baptized. The people submitted to Christianity because none of the farmers dared rebel against King Olaf and so, wherever he went, everyone was baptized.

In Hordaland, there were many noble men descended from Horda-Kari. He had four sons: first was Thorleif Spaki [the Wise]; second came Ogmund, the father of Thorolf Skjalg [the Squinter] who was the father of Erling from Soli; the third son was Thord, the father of Klypp the Hersir [local chieftain, lord] who killed Sigurd the Snake, the son of Gunnhild; the fourth was Olmod, the father of Askel, the father of Aslak Fitjaskalli. This family was the greatest and noblest in Hordaland in those days.

Now, when these kinsmen heard the troubling news – that the king was making his way through the country from the east with a large army, abolishing the old laws, and that everyone who resisted him had to endure punishment and harsh treatment – then they set up a meeting to work out their strategy, because they knew that the king would soon be upon them. They agreed among themselves that they should all go in a great body to the Gulathing and that they should arrange to meet King Olaf Tryggvason there.

55. As soon as he arrived in Rogaland, King Olaf called an assembly and, when the farmers received the summons, they gathered fully armed and in great numbers to discuss what to do. They designated the three most eloquent men of their number to speak against King Olaf at the assembly and tell him that they would not submit to injustice even if the king ordered them to do so.

When the farmers had assembled and the meeting had begun, King Olaf stood up and at first spoke graciously to them. However, it was clear from his speech that he intended to make them Christians. He began by asking them pleasantly, but concluded by saying that anyone who opposed him and refused to submit to his commands would incur his anger and suffer punishment and harsh treatment, wherever he could lay hands on them.

After King Olaf had finished speaking, the most eloquent of the farmers chosen to answer him stood up. However, when he tried to speak, he began to cough and became so choked up that he could not get a word out, so he sat down again. Then the second farmer stood up, determined not to make a mess of his answer, even though the first man had not done too well. But when he began his speech, he stammered so much that he could not get a word out. Everyone who heard him started to laugh, and so the farmer sat down. Then the third man stood up to oppose King Olaf, but when he began speaking he was so hoarse and husky that no one could hear what he was saying, and so he, too, sat down. Then there was no one to speak out against the king, and when there was no opposition from the farmers, there was no uprising against him. In the event, everyone obeyed the king's orders and they were all baptized before the king went on his way.

56. King Olaf summoned his troops to the Gulathing because the farmers had sent word to him that they would respond to his demands there. But when both sides arrived at the assembly, King Olaf expressed a wish to confer with the chieftains first. When they had all assembled, King Olaf stated his

purpose and required them to be baptized as he had ordered. Then Olmod the Old replied.

"We kinsmen have discussed this matter among ourselves," he said, "and we have all agreed on the same course of action. If it's your intention, king, to compel us to violate our laws and to force us into submission, we will oppose you with all our strength, and let fate award the victory. If, however, you are willing to do something to further our interests, then you will succeed in winning us over to your side and we'll be your faithful subjects."

"What are you demanding of me in return for a complete reconciliation?" asked the king.

"First, that you give your sister, Astrid, in marriage to our kinsman, Erling Skjalgsson, whom we regard as the most promising young man in Norway," replied Olmod. King Olaf replied that the marriage would probably be a good one since Erling was well-born and likely to distinguish himself, but said that the decision would be up to Astrid. Later, the king discussed the affair with his sister.

"There's not much advantage for me in being the daughter of a king and the sister of a king," she said, "if I'm to be given in marriage to a commoner. I would rather wait a few years for another offer." With that, they ended the conversation.

57. King Olaf had one of Astrid's hawks stolen. Then he had its feathers plucked and sent it back to her.

"My brother is angry now," said Astrid. So she rose and went to see the king, who greeted her affectionately. Astrid said that she would like the king to make the decision on her behalf as he thought best.

"I would have thought," said the king, "that in this land I had the power to raise any man I wanted to the nobility." The king summoned Olmod, Erling, and all their kinsmen for a discussion. They talked over the marriage offer and, as a result, Astrid was engaged to Erling. Then the king called the assembly together and ordered the farmers to adopt Christianity. Olmod, Erling, and their kinsmen were prominent in supporting the king's cause and no one had the confidence to oppose them, so the whole population was baptized and converted to Christianity....

59. Then King Olaf went to North Møre with his army and converted that district to Christianity. Afterwards, he sailed into Hlad where he had the temple demolished. He removed all the treasure and ornaments from the temple and from the god; from the temple door, he took down the great gold ring which had been made on Earl Hakon's orders. Then King Olaf had the temple burned down....

62. King Olaf went to Tunsberg and convened an assembly at which he decreed that all men who were sorcerers and were known to be guilty of

practicing witchcraft and magic had to leave the country. Then the king had the neighboring settlements searched for such men and summoned them all before him. Among those who came was a man called Eyvind Kelda. He was the grandson of Rognvald Rettilbein [Straight-Leg] who was the son of Harald Finehair. Eyvind was a sorcerer and very knowledgeable about magic.

King Olaf had all these men put in one room which had been made ready for them. He had a feast prepared for them and they were given strong drink. When they were drunk, Olaf had the building set alight and the room was destroyed by the fire along with everyone inside, except for Eyvind Kelda, who got out through the smoke-hole and escaped. When he had gone a good distance, he met some men who were on their way to see King Olaf. He told them to let the king know that Eyvind Kelda had escaped from the fire and that he would never again fall into the hands of King Olaf. Moreover, as regards his magical lore, he would behave exactly as he had done before. When these men met King Olaf, they told him what Eyvind had asked them to say. The king was very annoyed that Eyvind was not dead.

63. In the spring, King Olaf traveled out along the Vik and was entertained at his large estates in the area. He sent word throughout the Vik that he intended to call out an army in the summer and travel to the north of the country. Afterwards, he went west to Agder. When Lent was almost over, King Olaf went north to Rogaland and on Easter-eve he arrived at Ogvaldsness on Kormt Island where an Easter feast was prepared for him. He was accompanied by almost three hundred men. That same night, Eyvind Kelda came to the island in a longship manned entirely by sorcerers and other kinds of magicians. Eyvind and his men went ashore and began using their magic spells. Eyvind covered them in darkness with a fog so thick that the king and his men would not be able to see them, but when they came close to the dwelling at Ogvaldsness, it became as bright as day. Then things turned out very differently from what Eyvind had intended. The darkness which he had created by magic descended on Eyvind and his men so that they could see no more with their eyes than they could with the backs of their heads and went round and round in circles.

The king's watchmen saw them, but did not know who they were. The king was told and he and all his companions rose and got dressed. When the king saw Eyvind and the others wandering around, he ordered his men to arm themselves and go to find out who these people were. The king's men recognized Eyvind, so they seized him and all the others and led them before the king. Eyvind gave him an account of everything that had happened on his journey. Then the king had them all taken to a skerry which was covered by the sea at high tide and had them tied up there. That is how Eyvind and his men lost their lives and, ever since, the skerry has been called Sorcerers' Skerry.

64. The story goes that while King Olaf was being entertained at Ogvalds-ness, an old man arrived there one evening. He wore a hood pulled down low over his face and had only one eye. He spoke very wisely and had something to say about every land. When he started talking, the king found his conversation most entertaining and questioned his guest extensively. The old man had an answer for every question, and King Olaf sat up late into the evening with him.

Then the king asked if he knew anything about that Ogvald after whom the headland and the farm had been named. The guest replied that Ogvald had been a great king and warrior and that he had worshipped a certain cow more than anything else. He used to take this cow with him wherever he went because he thought that drinking her milk every day was good for him.

"King Ogvald fought against a king called Varin and fell in the battle," continued the guest. "He was then placed in a mound here close to his farm, and stone monuments were erected, which are still standing. The cow was placed in another mound nearby." Such tales he told, and many others about kings and events from the past.

When they had sat long into the night, the bishop reminded the king that it was high time to go to bed. The king did so. But after he had undressed and got into bed, the guest sat on the footboard and again talked for a long time. It seemed to the king that as soon as one word had been spoken, he was anxious to hear the next. Then the bishop said to the king that it was time to sleep. The king did so, and the guest left. A little later, the king woke up and inquired about his guest. He gave orders for him to be called to his presence, but the guest was nowhere to be found.

Next morning, the king summoned his cook and the man who was in charge of the drink and asked them if they had seen any stranger. They replied that, while they were preparing the meal, a man came in and said that they were cooking very poor meat for the king's table. Then he gave them two thick, fat sides of beef that they cooked along with the other meat. King Olaf said that all the food must be destroyed because his guest was probably not a human being, but must have been Odin, whom heathens had worshipped for a long time. Odin, he said, would not manage to deceive them....

67. King Olaf anchored his fleet in the river Nid. He had thirty ships and a fine, large army; the king himself spent much of his time at Hlad with his retinue. When the time was approaching for the sacrifice at Maeren, King Olaf prepared a great feast at Hlad and sent invitations to Skind, and up to Gaulardal, and out to Orkadal inviting the chiefs and other great men to come and visit him. On the first evening, when the guests had arrived, there was a splendid feast with plenty to eat and drink. People got very drunk, and

afterwards everyone slept peacefully through the night. Next morning, the king dressed and heard mass, after which he had the horns blown to summon everyone to a meeting. All his men came ashore from the ships and made their way to the meeting and when everything was ready, the king stood up and spoke.

"We held an assembly at Frosta where I invited the farmers to have themselves baptized," said King Olaf, "but, in response, they invited me to sacrifice with them, just as King Hakon, Athelstan's foster-son, used to do. So we agreed to meet at Maeren and offer up a great sacrifice there. But if I am to hold a sacrifice with you, I will make it the most important kind of sacrifice that is ever offered: I will sacrifice men. Moreover, I am not going to pick slaves or villains. I will choose the noblest men as gifts for the gods. To this end, I nominate Orm Lygra from Medalhus, Styrkar of Gimsar, Kar from Gryting, Asbjorn, Thorberg from Ornes, Orm from Lyxa, and Halldor from Skerdingstead."

He named five more of the noblest men and said that he would sacrifice them too for a good year and peace; then he had the men seized on the spot. The farmers realized that they did not have the forces to oppose the king, so they asked for peace, and offered to submit to him. It was agreed among them that all the farmers who had come to Hlad would be baptized and would promise on oath to observe the true faith and give up making sacrifices. The king kept all these men at his banquet until they had surrendered their sons, or brothers, or other close relatives as hostages.

68. King Olaf advanced with his army further into the Trondheim area. By the time he arrived at Maeren, all the chiefs from the Trondelag who were most firmly opposed to Christianity had gathered there. With them were all the important farmers who had formerly offered up sacrifices in that place. There was just as big a crowd here as at the meeting in Frosta. Then the king called for an assembly, and both sides attended fully armed. When the meeting got under way, the king spoke and asked them to adopt Christianity. Jarnskeggi answered the king's speech on behalf of the farmers, saying that the farmers' wishes were still the same and they did not want the king to overturn their laws.

"We want you to sacrifice here, king," said Jarnskeggi, "just as other kings have done before you." The farmers cheered his speech loudly and declared that what Skeggi had said was what they wanted. The king replied that he would enter the temple to see how they performed their sacrifices. The farmers were pleased, and both sides entered the temple.

69. King Olaf went into the temple with a few of his men and some of the farmers. He came to where the gods were sitting, and saw Thor, the most honored of them all, adorned with gold and silver. King Olaf raised

a gold-mounted staff he was carrying and struck Thor so that he fell from his pedestal. Then the king's men rushed forward and knocked all the gods down from their pedestals. While the king was in the temple, Jarnskeggi was killed outside the temple doors by the king's men. When the king rejoined his troops, he offered the farmers two choices: to become Christian, or to fight him. After the death of Jarnskeggi, the farmers had no leader to raise their standard against King Olaf, so they made the choice to go to the king and do his bidding. Then King Olaf had everyone who was there baptized and took hostages from the farmers to ensure that they would stay Christian. After that, King Olaf sent his men all over the Trondheim district. No one opposed Christianity and everyone in the area was baptized.

76. Harek from Thjota left town [Nidaros] at the first opportunity, but Hauk and Sigurd stayed with the king and were both baptized. Harek went on his way until he arrived back home in Thjota. He sent word to his friend, Eyvind Kinnrifa, that Harek from Thjota had met King Olaf but hadn't allowed himself to be bullied into becoming Christian. He also informed him that King Olaf intended to lead an army against them in the summer. Harek advised that they should be on their guard against Olaf and urged Eyvind to join him as soon as possible.

When he received these messages, Eyvind realized that the most pressing business was to work out how they could avoid falling into King Olaf's clutches. So he set off hurriedly in a light boat with only a few men aboard. When he reached Thjota, Harek welcomed him warmly and immediately afterwards they left the farmhouse by another way and had a talk together. But they hadn't been talking for long when King Olaf's men – the ones who had accompanied Harek to the north – seized Eyvind, led him to their ships, and sailed off with him.

They did not interrupt their journey until they reached Trondheim and found King Olaf in Nidaros. There Eyvind was brought before the king, who urged him to be baptized like other men, but Eyvind refused. The king and the bishop both spoke to him courteously and tried to persuade him to accept Christianity, giving him many good reasons for doing so, but Eyvind would not be moved. Then the king offered him gifts and great revenues, but Eyvind refused them all. At length, the king threatened him with torture and death, but still Eyvind would not be moved. So the king had a basin full of red-hot embers brought in and placed on Eyvind's stomach. Soon his stomach burst open.

"Take the basin away," said Eyvind. "I want to say a few words before I die."

This was done, and the king asked, "Now will you have faith in Christ, Eyvind?"

"No, I cannot accept baptism," replied Eyvind, "for I am a spirit, given human life and shape by the magic of the Finns. Before then, my father and mother could not have a child." Then Eyvind died; he had been a great sorcerer.

86. A POET ABANDONS THE OLD GODS

According to his saga, Hallfred Vandrædaskald (the Troublesome Poet) was a court poet who found it difficult to turn his back on Odin, the god who had blessed him and his ancestors with the gift of poetry. His reluctance to convert earned him his soubriquet from Olaf Tryggvason.

Source: *Hallfreðar saga*, in *Vatnsdæla saga*, ed. Einar Ól. Sveinsson, Íslenzk fornrit VIII (Reykjavík, 1939), pp. 157–59.

1. I worshipped the quick-witted
lord of Hlidskjalf [Odin],
before everything altered
in the fortunes and fates of men.

2. All my lineage shaped lines
praising Odin's reign; I remember
precious poems, the work
of my ancestors' age;
reluctantly – for Odin's rule
always pleased the poet –
I show hostility to the husband
of Frigg, for I follow Christ.

3. Lord of heroes, I leave off
calling the raven-king [Odin]
from heathendom a god; he heaped
disgrace on man's good name.

4. Let Freyr and Freyja rage at me
– last year I left Njord's mysteries –
let mighty Thor's fury face me,
let the gods find grace in Grimnir [Odin];
with all my love I will call on Christ,
the only God and great father;

awful for me is the anger of the Son,
whose power prevails over the world.

5. For followers of the faith
of Sogn's prince [King Olaf], sacrifices are banned;
we must shun most of all the
age-old ordinances of the norns;
all men throw Odin's
tribe to the tempest;
I am forced to forsake Njord's
kin to pray to Christ.

87. THE CHRISTIANIZATION OF NORWAY UNDER SAINT OLAF

Olaf Haraldsson, or Olaf II (ca 990–1030), was the son of a minor Norwegian king. After time spent raiding in England, he seized the Norwegian throne and completed the unification of Norway begun by his great-grandfather, Harald Finehair. Part of his ambition was to spread Christianity to all Norwegians. This he did with a singular ferocity. His high-handedness caused his subjects to rebel against him, and he was forced from the throne in 1028. He attempted to regain his throne two years later, but was defeated and killed at the Battle of Stiklestad (see doc. 83).

Source: Snorri Sturluson, *Óláfs saga Helga*, in *Heimskringla*, ed. Bjarni Aðalbjarnarson, Íslenzk fornrit XXVI–XXVIII (Reykjavík, 2002), vol. 2, pp. 100–101, 177–90.

73. After King Olaf had sent Bjorn and his followers east to Gotland, he dispatched other men to the Upplands with instructions to arrange accommodation and provisions for him. They were also to let it be known that he intended to make a progress across the Upplands that winter, for it had been the custom of previous kings to spend every third winter there.

In the autumn the king set off from Borg and headed first to Vengilmark. He had planned his journey so that he could be entertained for a time in the neighborhood of the forest settlements, and he summoned all the forest dwellers to meet him there, particularly those who lived furthest from the main settlements. He questioned them closely about their adherence to Christianity, and where he found shortcomings, he instructed them in the true faith. Anyone who would not renounce heathen beliefs was severely punished. Some were banished from the country. Others had their hands or feet cut off, or their eyes put out. Some were hanged and others beheaded;

no one who refused to serve God escaped punishment. King Olaf proceeded in this fashion throughout the entire district, punishing the mighty and the humble alike. He also provided the people with priests, giving every district as many priests as he thought necessary.

When he went up to Raumarik, King Olaf had three hundred and sixty armed men with him. He soon discovered that loyalty to Christianity decreased as he traveled up country, so he continued his policy of converting everyone to the true faith and meting out terrible punishments to those who refused to obey him.

107. That autumn, King Olaf got word that the farmers of inner Trondheim had held great feasts on the winter-nights [the three days beginning winter]. There had been a great deal of drinking and all the toasts had been dedicated to the Aesir in accordance with ancient custom. He was told also that cattle and horses had been slaughtered and altars covered with their blood; sacrifices had been performed, and prayers said for a good harvest. It was also reported that everyone was sure the gods were angry because the people of Halogaland had turned to Christianity.

When the king heard this, he sent messengers to inner Trondheim to summon certain farmers whom he specified by name. One of these was Olvir from Eggja, who was named for the farm on which he lived. This Olvir was a powerful and well-born man; he was the leader of the deputation that went to the king on behalf of the farmers. When they met, the king voiced his charges against the farmers, but Olvir replied on the farmers' behalf that there had been no feasts that autumn, only social gatherings and drinking sessions and friendly get-togethers.

"As for what you've been told about what we Trondheimers say when we've been drinking, intelligent men pay no attention to talk like that, and I can't be held reponsible for the remarks of fools and drunks," said Olvir.

Olvir was eloquent and outspoken. He defended the farmers against all these accusations and, in the end, the king said that the Trondheimers themselves would have to demonstrate their loyalty to the faith. Then they got leave to go home and left as soon as possible.

108. Later in the winter, the king heard that the people of inner Trondheim had held a large gathering at Maeren and had offered up huge sacrifices there at midwinter to ensure peace and a mild winter. When the king felt he was quite sure of the facts, he dispatched messengers to the inner districts to summon the farmers to town. Once again he named those whom he considered most astute. The farmers met to discuss this message. All those who had gone earlier in the winter were very reluctant to make the trip but, in response to the farmers' entreaties, Olvir undertook the journey.

When Olvir reached town, he went straight to King Olaf and they talked together. The king charged the farmers with offering midwinter sacrifices, and Olvir asserted their innocence.

"We held Yule-tide banquets and drinking parties throughout the district," said Olvir, "and the farmers don't stint when preparing their banquets so there was plenty of ale left over, and they were still drinking it long afterwards. In Maeren there is a great estate with a big house and an extensive settlement around it. People really enjoy having large drinking parties there."

The king said little in response and appeared to be rather angry for he felt sure that he wasn't being told the truth. He ordered the farmers to go home.

"However," he said, "I'll get to the bottom of this even though you conceal the truth and refuse to admit it. And whatever you've done in the past, don't do it again."

The farmers went home and gave an account of their journey; they said that the king was very irate.

109. At Easter, King Olaf held a large feast to which he invited many of the townspeople and farmers, but after Easter, he had his ships launched. Tackle and oars were taken aboard, decks were laid, and awnings put up, and when the ships were all fitted out, they were floated at the piers, ready to put to sea.

After Easter, King Olaf sent messengers to Veradal where he had a steward named Thorald who managed his farm at Haug. The king sent word that Thorald was to come to him as quickly as possible, and Thorald did not delay, but traveled to town immediately along with the messengers. The king summoned him for a private conversation.

"Is there any truth to what I've been hearing about the conduct of the people in the Inner Trondelag?" he asked. "Are they turning to heathen sacrifices? I want you to tell me the facts as you know them. It's your duty to tell me the truth, because you are my man."

"My lord, there's something I wish to tell you first," replied Thorald. "I've moved my two sons and my wife into town and I've also brought as much of my portable property as possible. If you want me to tell you what's going on, I'll do as you command. But if I tell you, then you must protect me and my family."

"Answer my questions truthfully and I'll see to it that you come to no harm," said the king.

"To tell you the truth, sire, nearly everyone from the Inner Trondelag is heathen, even though some have been baptized," said Thorald. "It's their custom to offer a sacrifice in autumn to welcome winter, another in midwinter, and a third to welcome the arrival of summer. And this is the practice of the people in Eyna, Sparby, Veradal, and Skaun. There are twelve men who make the arrangements for the sacrificial banquets, and this spring it's Olvir's turn to organize the feast. At the moment he's very busy making preparations for it at Maeren, and all the necessary provisions are being brought there."

When the king learned the truth, he had trumpets blown to summon his troops together. Then he ordered them to board their ships. He selected steersmen and troop-leaders and told each company which ship to board. Everything was done very quickly; then King Olaf sailed inland along the fjord with 360 men in five ships. The wind was favorable and the longships made good headway. No one had anticipated that the king would reach Maeren so quickly; he got there during the night and immediately threw a cordon around the house. Olvir was captured, and King Olaf had him executed along with many other men. Then the king had his ships loaded with all the provisions for the feast and all the property – furnishings, clothes, and valuables – that had been brought there. All this was divided among the king's men as spoils of war. The king also ordered an attack on the homes of those farmers who had been most involved in the affair. Some were captured and put in irons, others fled, and some had their property confiscated.

Then King Olaf called the farmers to a meeting. Because the king had captured so many of the farmers' leading men and had them in his power, their relatives and friends decided to promise obedience to him, and there was no uprising against the king at this time. He converted everyone to the true faith, settled priests among them, and had churches built and consecrated.

The king declared that no compensation would be paid for Olvir's death, and confiscated all his property. As for the other men, the most blameworthy were executed, mutilated, exiled, or fined. Then King Olaf went back to Nidaros....

112. There was a man called Guthbrand of the Dales who ruled like a king over the valley where he lived although he was only a Hersir. In terms of power and property, Sigvat the Skald compared Guthbrand with Erling Skjalgsson, and this is what Sigvat said about Erling:

> I knew only one shield-breaker
> who came close to you;
> his name was Guthbrand; this guardian
> of men governed far and wide.
> Gold-giver, I declare that
> you two are equally great;
> he who boasts he is better
> only deceives himself.

Guthbrand had a son who comes into this story. When Guthbrand heard that King Olaf had come to Loar and that he was compelling people to adopt Christianity, he sent round a war-arrow and summoned all the Dalesmen to meet him at a farm called Hundthorp. They all came, and there were a great many of them, because Hundthorp was near a lake called Lauger and so men could get there by land or water with equal ease. Then Guthbrand called a meeting and addressed them, saying,

"A man by the name of Olaf has come to Loar intending to force us to adopt a new faith, different from the one we have held till now. He wants us to destroy all our gods, claiming that his god is much greater and stronger. It's strange that the earth doesn't open up under his feet when he says such things and that our gods allow him to go on living. But Thor has always supported us, and I'm certain that if we carry him from his place in the temple, here on this farm, then Olaf, his god, and his men will all vanish into nothing, as soon as he looks at them."

They all cheered and said that if Olaf came to Hundthorp, he would never escape alive. "And he won't dare go further south through the Dales," they said.

Then they assigned 840 men to reconnoiter northwards as far as Breida. This force was led by Guthbrand's eighteen-year-old son and many first-rate men went with him. They came to a farm called Hof and, after they had been there for three days, they were joined by a large number of people who had fled from Lesjar, Loar, and Vaga because they did not want to become Christian.

King Olaf and Bishop Sigurd left priests behind in Loar and Vaga. Then they went over Vagarost and came down to Sil, where they stayed overnight. There they heard the news that a large army was lying in wait for them. At the same time, the farmers at Breida heard about Olaf's approach and got ready to fight him. When King Olaf got up, he dressed in his war-gear and moved south along the Sil Plains. He did not stop until he reached Breida, where he found himself confronted by a large army ready for battle. Then the king drew up his forces; he himself rode at their head. He addressed the farmers and bade them adopt Christianity.

But they replied, "You'll be doing a bit more than mocking us today."

And with that, they raised a battle-cry and clashed their weapons against their shields.

Then the king's men rushed forward and hurled their spears. The farmers immediately took to their heels; very few of them stood their ground. Guthbrand's son was captured and was granted quarter by the king, who kept the young man with him. The king remained there for four days. Then he said to Guthbrand's son,

"Go back to your father and tell him I'll be with him soon." So he went back to his father and told him the bad news that they had met the king and fought with him.

"Right at the start, our whole army was put to flight, and I was taken prisoner," he said. "The king gave me quarter and told me to tell you that he'll be here soon. Now we have only a couple of hundred left out of all the men that we sent against him. So my advice to you, father, is don't fight against this man."

"Clearly, you've had the stuffing knocked out of you," said Guthbrand. "Your expedition was ill-fated, and it will be a long time before you live it down. And now you can't wait to swallow all the nonsense this man is putting about, even after the disgrace he has inflicted on you and your army."

That night, Guthbrand dreamed that a man appeared before him. He came in a blaze of light and inspired great awe.

"Your son did not have a successful foray against King Olaf," he said, "and you will fare even worse if you insist on fighting with the king, for you and your entire army will perish; wolves will drag you and your men away and ravens will tear your flesh."

Guthbrand was terrified by this dreadful vision and spoke about his dream to Thord Paunch-Belly who was a chieftain in the Dales.

"I had the same dream," said Thord.

In the morning, they had the trumpets blown to summon an assembly and announced that it would be advisable to meet this man who had come from the north with a new creed, and find out if there was any truth in what he was saying. Guthbrand said to his son, "Take twelve men and go back to this king who gave you quarter." He did so.

When they came to the king, they gave him the message that the farmers wanted to have a meeting with him, and that they wanted to arrange a truce between the two sides. King Olaf was amenable to this and they made a formal agreement to observe a truce for the duration of the meeting. After everything had been arranged, they went back to tell Guthbrand and Thord that a truce had been agreed.

The king then moved to a farm called Lidstad. He stayed there for five days and afterwards he went to meet the farmers. There was heavy rain that day. When the meeting began, the king stood up and told the farmers that the people of Leyjar, Loar, and Vagi had all become Christian and had demolished their temples.

"And now they believe in the true God who made heaven and earth and who knows all things," said King Olaf. Then he sat down.

"We have no idea who you're talking about," responded Guthbrand. "Do you call him a god when neither you nor anyone else can see him? We have a god who can be seen every day, though he isn't out today because the weather is wet. He will seem terrifying and majestic to you, and I expect that you'll be overwhelmed by fear if he comes to the meeting. But since you say that your god is so powerful, let him make tomorrow's weather overcast, but not rainy, and let us meet here then."

The king returned to where he was staying and Guthbrand's son went with him as a hostage. The king also left a hostage with the farmers. In the evening, the king asked Guthbrand's son what form their god took. He answered that their god looked like Thor.

"He's big and has a hammer in his hand. He is hollow and has a pedestal to stand on when he is outdoors. His body is adorned with lots of gold and silver, and every day he receives four loaves of bread and meat as well." After that, they went to bed, but the king stayed awake all night, praying.

Next morning, King Olaf heard mass and had breakfast. Then he went to the meeting. The weather was cloudy, but not rainy, just as Guthbrand had wished. The bishop stood up, dressed in his robes and wearing a miter on his head; in his hand, he held a crozier. He preached the Christian faith to the farmers, telling them about many miracles that God had performed. Then he ended his speech eloquently, and Thord Paunch-Belly replied,

"He certainly has a lot to say – this horned man with the curly-ended staff in his hand. And now, since you folks claim that your god performs so many miracles, ask him to make the sky bright and sunny tomorrow morning before dawn. Let's meet then and either come to an agreement about this business or else settle it in battle." With that, they parted.

113. One of King Olaf's followers was a man called Kolbein the Strong, whose family came from the Fjord district. He always wore a sword and carried a thick staff, or club, in his hand. The king told Kolbein to stand next to him in the morning. Then he ordered his men to go to the farmers' ships during the night and drill holes in them. He also ordered them to drive the farmers' horses away from the farms where they were being kept. The men did so, and the king spent the night in prayer, asking God to deliver him from this trouble through his mercy and grace.

At daybreak, King Olaf heard mass and went to the meeting. When he got there, some of the farmers had already shown up. Then they saw a great crowd of farmers making their way to the meeting and carrying among them a large effigy of a man decorated with gold and silver. When the farmers already at the meeting saw this, they leapt to their feet and bowed to the idol. The figure was placed in the middle of the meeting-area, with the farmers sitting on one side and the king and his men on the other.

Guthbrand of the Dales stood up and spoke. "Where is your god now, king? I think he must be hanging his head. And it seems to me that you and the horned fellow next to you – the one you call bishop – aren't bragging quite so much as you were yesterday, now that our god, the ruler of all, has come and is glaring at you with his piercing gaze. I can see that you're terrified and hardly dare raise your eyes to look at him. Now drop your superstitious nonsense and have faith in our god, who holds your fate in his hands." With that, he ended his speech.

The king spoke to Kolbein without attracting the farmers' attention.

"If they happen to take their eyes off their god while I'm speaking, hit it as hard as you can with your club." Then he stood up and addressed the meeting.

"You have said a great deal to us this morning. You think it's strange that you can't see our god, but we expect he'll come to us very soon. You threaten us with your god, who is both blind and deaf, and who can't protect himself or anyone else, and can't move from his place unless he's carried. I expect he'll be in for a rough time before long, for if you look eastwards, you will see our god approaching in great brightness."

Then the sun rose, and all the farmers turned to look at it. At that very moment, Kolbein struck their god so hard that it shattered and out of it leapt vipers, lizards, and mice as big as cats. The farmers were so terrified that they fled. Some made for their ships but, when they launched them, water poured in and swamped them, and the farmers could not get aboard. Those who ran for their horses could not find them.

Then the king had the farmers called back, saying that he wanted to talk to them. So the farmers returned and the meeting began again. The king stood up and spoke.

"I have no idea what all this noise and running to and fro is about," said King Olaf. "But now you can see what power this god of yours has. You gave him gold, silver, food, and provisions, and look at what sort of creatures have enjoyed it all – mice, lizards, adders, and toads. Anyone who has faith in such stuff, and won't abandon his foolishness, is making a bad mistake. Take your gold and valuables that are strewn about this field; carry them home to your wives, and never again offer them to idols of wood or stone. And now we can settle this business in one of two ways: either you adopt Christianity today or we resort to battle and let the god in whom we trust award victory to whichever side he pleases."

Then Guthbrand stood up and spoke. "We've suffered a great deal of harm because of our god and, since he couldn't help us, we will now believe in the god that you believe in."

Everyone was converted to Christianity. The bishop baptized Guthbrand and his son and left priests in the district. So the former enemies parted as friends; and Guthbrand had a church built in the Dales.

88. THE CONVERSION OF THE ICELANDERS

The conversion of the Icelanders was a largely political event, carried out as a response to Norwegian pressure. This conversion was remarkably peaceful in comparison with others in Scandinavia.

Source: *Íslendingabók*, ed. Jakob Benediktsson, Íslenzk fornrit I (Reykjavík, 1986), pp. 14–18.

7. King Olaf, the son of Tryggvi, the son of Olaf, the son of Harald Finehair, introduced Christianity to Norway and Iceland. He sent here the priest called Thangbrand, who instructed people in Christianity and baptized everyone who adopted the faith. Hall Thorsteinsson from Sida was baptized early on, and so were Hjalti Skeggjason from Thjorsardal, Gizur the White, the son of Teit, the son of Ketilbjorn from Mosfell, along with many other chieftains. However, more people argued against the faith and rejected it.

When Thangbrand had been here for a year or two, he left as he had killed two or three men who had scurrilously made fun of him, and when he arrived in Norway, he told King Olaf what had happened to him and said also that Christianity was not likely to catch on in Iceland. King Olaf was furious and, on this account, decided to torture or kill any of our countrymen who were in Norway. The same summer Gizur and Hjalti travelled to Norway from Iceland and had those men released by the king. They promised him their help in a fresh attempt to have Christianity adopted here, and they said that they had every expectation of being listened to.

They traveled to Iceland the following summer with a priest called Thormod, and, after a successful journey, arrived at Vestmannaeyjar [Westerners' Islands] when ten weeks of summer had passed. Teit used to give this account, and he was there himself.

The previous summer, it had been declared law that men were to attend the Althing after ten weeks of summer; before then, they had come a week earlier. So they left Vestmannaeyjar and traveled inland to the Althing, but they had Hjalti stay behind in Laugardal with eleven men as he had been sentenced to lesser outlawry for blasphemy at the Althing the previous summer. The reason was that he had recited this verse at the law rock,

> I won't mock the mighty gods,
> but I reckon Freya's a real bitch.

Gizur and his companions kept going until they came to the place called Vellankatli, near Olfossvatn. From there they sent a message to the Thing [here, the Althing, or national assembly], summoning all their supporters to meet them, for they had heard that their opponents intended to bar them from Thingvellir by force. Before they left, Hjalti rode up with the men who had stayed behind with him. They all rode off to the Thing and, on the way, met the friends and relatives whom they had asked to join them. The heathen men crowded together fully armed, and the sides were so close to violence that it was anyone's guess whether a battle would break out.

Next day, Gizur and Hjalti went to the Law Rock to present their case, and the story goes that it was astonishing how well they expressed themselves. However, the result was that one man after another named witnesses, and both sides, Christians and heathens, declared themselves not bound by the laws of the others. At that, they left the Law Rock.

Then the Christian men asked Hall of Sida to proclaim as their laws those that would be in accord with Christianity, but Hall got himself out of it and struck a deal with Thorgeir the Lawspeaker that he would declare what the law was to be. Thorgeir was still a heathen at that time.

When everyone returned to their booths, Thorgeir lay down and covered himself with his cloak. He lay like this, without saying a word, all that day and the following night. Next morning, he got up and sent word that everyone was to go to the Law Rock. When they had assembled, Thorgeir began speaking, and told them he considered that their affairs were in a sorry state if they could not all have the same law code throughout the land. He used many arguments to exhort them not to let this happen, saying that it would lead to trouble and that there was a strong likelihood of civil unrest, which would ruin the country. He pointed to the kings of Norway and Denmark who had carried on hostilities until their subjects made peace between them, though the kings themselves did not want to. That agreement turned out so well that, in a short time, the kings were exchanging splendid gifts and the peace held as long as they lived.

"And I think it would be a good idea," said Thorgeir, "not to leave the decision to the extremists, but to arrive at a compromise, so that each side gets something and we all have one law and a single faith. For sure, if we tear up the law, we tear up the country."

He ended his speech, and both sides agreed that they would all have a single law code, which would be what he decided to announce.

Then it was passed into law that everyone was to be Christian and that baptism was to be given to anyone in the country who was still unbaptized. From among the old laws were preserved the right to expose infants and the eating of horseflesh. Private sacrifice was still allowed, but there would be a penalty of lesser outlawry if there were any witnesses. A few years later this heathen practice was abolished like the others.

Teit told us that this was how Christianity came to Iceland. That same summer, Olaf Tryggvason died, according to Saemund the priest. Olaf fought against Svein Haraldsson, king of Denmark, Olaf Eiriksson, the Swede, and Hakon's son, Eirik, who was later earl in Norway. That was one hundred and thirty years after the killing of King Edmund, and one thousand after the birth of Christ, as it is generally reckoned.

89. THE CONVERSION OF GREENLAND

Leif Eiriksson was charged by Olaf Tryggvason with the conversion of Greenland. On his way to introduce Christianity to Greenland, Leif Eiriksson was driven off course and saw Vinland for the first time.

Source: *Eiriks saga Rauða*, in *Eyrbyggja saga*, ed. Einar Ól. Sveinsson and Matthías Þórðarson, Íslenzk fornrit IV (Reykjavík, 1935), pp. 413–16.

5. Eirik's wife was called Thjodhild. He had two sons by her, named Thorstein and Leif, both of whom were promising men. Thorstein was at home with his father, and no one in Greenland was so highly regarded. Leif had sailed to Norway and was with King Olaf Tryggvason.

However, when Leif sailed from Greenland in the summer, he and his crew were blown off course to the Hebrides. A favorable wind was a long time coming to them, and they stayed there for much of the summer....

Leif and his men sailed from the Hebrides and reached Norway in the autumn. Leif became one of King Olaf Tryggvason's retainers and was well thought of by the king, who regarded him as a highly accomplished man. On one occasion, the king fell into conversation with Leif and asked, "Do you mean to go to Greenland in the summer?"

"I do," replied Leif, "if that is acceptable to you."

"I think it may well be," said the king, "if you go there on my business and preach Christianity." Leif said that the king should decide, but he thought that it would be a difficult task to carry out in Greenland. The king replied that he could see no one better suited than Leif.

"And you'll bring good luck to the undertaking," said the king.

"It will work," said Leif, "only if I have your good luck with me."

Leif set out and, after a long time at sea, he came across land that he had not previously known. There were fields of self-sown wheat, full-grown vines, and trees of the sort known as maple. They brought back proof of all this, including some logs so big that they were used in house-building. Leif found some men who had been shipwrecked, and took them back home with him [and put them up for the winter]. In this, and in many other ways, he showed the greatest generosity and nobility when he introduced Christianity to Greenland. Forever after, he was called Leif the Lucky.

Leif made land at Eiriksfjord and went home to Brattahlid where everyone gave him a great welcome. Straight away, he began to preach Christianity and the Catholic faith. He made public King Olaf Tryggvason's message and explained how many splendid achievements and what great glory belonged to this religion. Eirik reacted coldly to the suggestion that he should abandon his religion, but Thjodhild submitted quickly and had a church built at a considerable distance from the houses. The church was called Thjodhild's Church and there she used to pray along with the others who adopted Christianity. After she adopted the faith, Thjoldhild would not sleep with Eirik, and that was not much to his liking.

90. THE CONVERSION OF ORKNEY

Once again, Olaf Tryggvason is the moving force in the conversion of a faraway land.

Source: *Orkneyinga saga*, ed. Finnbogi Guðmundsson, Íslenzk fornrit XXXIV (Reykjavík, 1965), p. 26.

12. On his return from Wendland, Olaf Tryggvason spent four years raiding in the British Isles. After that he was baptized in the Scilly Islands. From the Scillies, he went to England where he married Gyda, the sister of King Kvaran of Ireland. Afterwards, he stayed in Dublin for a while until Earl Hakon sent Thorir Klakka out west to lure him away from Ireland.

Olaf sailed east with five ships until he reached the Orkneys. There he met up with Earl Sigurd at Osmundwall, near South Ronaldsay. Sigurd, who had three ships, was just setting off on a Viking raid, but King Olaf summoned him aboard his ship, saying that he had something to discuss with him. When they met, King Olaf said to Sigurd,

"I want you and everyone who owes you allegiance to be baptized. If you don't, you will die right here, right now, and I will devastate every one of the islands with fire and flame."

When Earl Sigurd realized what a precarious situation he was in, he put himself in the king's hands. King Olaf had him baptized and took his son, Whelp, or Hound, as a hostage, and had him christened with the name Hlodvir. Then all the Orkneys became Christian.

King Olaf sailed east to Norway, taking Hlodvir with him, but Hlodvir did not live long and after his death Earl Sigurd refused to obey King Olaf. He married the daughter of Malcolm, king of the Scots, and their son was Earl Thorfinn.

91. CHRISTIANITY IN SWEDEN

Included in the fourth book of Adam of Bremen's History of the Archbishops of Hamburg-Bremen *is the following account of a Swedish convert to Christianity and Christian missions to the Swedes.*

Source: trans. F.J. Tschan, Adam of Bremen, *History of the Archbishops of Hamburg-Bremen*, with new introduction by T. Reuter (New York: Columbia University Press, 2002), pp. 208–10.

28. In that country [Sweden] there took place lately an event worth remembering and widely published because it was noteworthy, and it also came to the archbishop's attention. One of the priests who was wont to serve the demons at Uppsala became blind and the help of the gods was of no avail. But as the man wisely ascribed the calamity of blindness to his worship of idols, by which superstitious veneration he had evidently offended the almighty God of the Christians, behold, that very night a most beautiful Virgin appeared to him and asked if he would believe in her Son, if to recover his sight he would put aside the images he had previously worshiped. Then he, who for the sake of this boon would refuse to undergo nothing that was hard, gladly promised he would. To this the Virgin answered: "Be completely assured that this place in which so much innocent blood is now shed is very soon to be dedicated to my honor. That there may not remain any trace of doubt in your mind about this matter, receive the light of your eyes in the name of Christ, who is my Son." As soon as the priest recovered his sight, he believed and, going to all the country about, easily persuaded the pagans of the faith so that they believed in him who made the blind see.

Impelled by these miracles, our metropolitan, forthwith obedient to the saying that runs, "Look up, and lift up ... with your eyes and see the countries; for they are white already to harvest," consecrated for those parts the younger Adalward, whom he took from the choir at Bremen, a man who shone in letters and for moral probity. Through legates of the most illustrious King Stenkil he also fixed Adalward's see in the city of Sigtuna, which is a day's journey distant from Uppsala. But the way is such that, sailing the sea from Scania of the Danes, you will arrive at Sigtuna or Björkö on the fifth day, for they are close together. If, however, you go by land from Scania, through the midst of the Gothic peoples and the cities Skara, Södertelege, and Björkö, it will take you a month to reach Sigtuna.

29. Glowing with fervor, then, Adalward entered Sweden to preach the Gospel and in a short time led to the Christian faith all in Sigtuna and round about. He also secretly agreed with Egino, the most saintly bishop of Scania, that they should go together to the pagan temple called Uppsala to see if they could perhaps offer Christ some fruit of their labors there, for they would willingly undergo every kind of torture for the sake of destroying that house which was the seat of barbarous superstition. For, if it were torn down, or preferably burned, the conversion of the whole nation might follow. Observing that the people murmured about this design of the confessors of God, the most pious king Stenkil shrewdly kept them from such an undertaking, declaring that they would at once be punished with death and he be driven from the kingdom for bringing malefactors into the country, and that everyone who now believed would quickly relapse into paganism, as they could see had lately been the case in Slavia. The bishops deferred to these arguments of the king and going through all the cities of the Goths, they broke up idols and thereafter won many thousands of pagans to Christianity. When Adalward later died in our midst, the archbishop appointed in his place a certain Tadico of Ramelsloh, who out of love for his belly preferred even to starve at home rather than be an apostle abroad. Let these remarks about Sweden and its rites suffice.

92. CHRISTIANITY AND THE CHURCH IN NORWAY

The fourth book of Adam's History of the Archbishops of Hamburg-Bremen *includes the following discussion of Christianity in Norway.*

Source: trans. F.J. Tschan, Adam of Bremen, *History of the Archbishops of Hamburg-Bremen*, with new introduction by T. Reuter (New York: Columbia University Press, 2002), pp. 214–15.

32. The metropolitan city of the Norwegians is Trondheim, which, now graced with churches, is frequented by a great multitude of peoples. In that city reposes the body of the most blessed Olaf, king and martyr. At this tomb, the Lord to this very day works such great miraculous cures that those who do not despair of being able to get help through the merits of the saint flock together there from far-off lands. But the route is of a kind that, boarding a ship, they may, in a day's journey, cross the sea from Aalborg or Wendila of the Danes to Viken, a city of the Norwegians. Sailing thence toward the

left along the coast of Norway, the city called Trondheim is reached on the fifth day. But it is possible to go another way that leads over a land road from Scania of the Danes to Trondheim. This route, however, is slower in the mountainous country, and travelers avoid it because it is dangerous.

33. The first bishop, a certain John, came from England to Norway, and he converted and baptized the king with his people. He was succeeded by Bishop Grimkil, who at that time was King Olaf's legate to Archbishop Unwan. In the third place came the Sigefrid who preached alike among the Swedes and Norwegians. And he lived to our own age along with other equally well-known priests among the people. After their deaths, on the petition of the Norwegian peoples, our metropolitan consecrated Tholf for the city of Trondheim and Seward for those same parts. Although the archbishop took it ill that Asgot and Bernhard had been consecrated by the pope, he let them go laden with presents after he had taken pledges. Even to this day the Word of God wins through these bishops so many souls that Holy Mother Church is enjoying prosperous increase in all the provinces of Norway. On account of the newness of the Christian plantation among the Norwegians and Swedes, however, none of the bishoprics has so far been assigned definite limits, but each one of the bishops, accepted by the king or the people, cooperates in building up the Church and, going about the country, draws as many as he can to Christianity and governs then without objection as long as they live.

93. THE TRAVELS OF KING SIGURD, JERUSALEM-FARER

Sigurd Magnusson (Sigurd I, King of Norway, 1103–30) was the first European king to go on a crusade. This exploit won him the title Jorsalafari *(Jerusalem-Farer). He set out in 1107 and fought several battles in Portugal and the Mediterranean before reaching Palestine. He was with Baldwin I, King of Jerusalem, when the city of Sidon was taken in 1110. Sigurd's career demonstrates the progression from Vikings to Crusaders. From* The Saga of the Sons of Magnus Barelegs.

Source: Snorri Sturluson, *Magnússona saga*, in *Heimskringla*, ed. Bjarni Aðalbjarnarson, Íslenzk fornrit XXVI–XXVIII (Reykjavík, 2002), vol. 3, pp. 239–54.

3. Four years after the death of Magnus Barelegs, King Sigurd left Norway with his army [1107]. He had sixty ships, as Thorarin Stuttfeld says:

> At the wish of the wise
> king, there came together

> a great force faithful
> to the powerful prince,
> and sixty sleek-sided
> ships took to sea and sped
> across the waves by the will
> of gracious God.

In the autumn, King Sigurd sailed to England. At that time, the king there was Henry, the son of William the Bastard. King Sigurd stayed there over the winter, as Einar Skulason says:

> The resolute ruler sailed
> west with his warriors;
> the sea-strider [ship]
> carried the king to England.
> The war-wise prince
> rested his ship on the shore,
> waited out winter; a better
> lord never landed there.

4. The following spring, King Sigurd sailed west to France with his forces and in autumn got as far as Galicia [in Spain] where he spent his second winter. Einar Skulasson says:

> The ruler of the greatest realm
> beneath the circling sun
> spent the second winter
> in the homeland of holy St. James;
> the people's prince, I hear,
> repaid the evil earl
> for his falseness and fed
> the black swan of battle.

What happened was this: the earl who ruled that land made an agreement with King Sigurd to set up a market where he could buy food over the winter. The arrangement worked until Yule when food became scarce, for the land was barren and unproductive. King Sigurd then led his troops to the earl's castle, and the earl fled since he had few soldiers. The king seized a great deal of food and other plunder there and had it carried to his ships. Then he got ready to leave and set out westward along the Spanish coast. As he was sailing along the coast, some pirates who were looking for plunder headed toward him with a fleet of galleys. King Sigurd went on the attack in what was his first battle with heathens [Muslims] and captured eight of their galleys. Halldor Skvaldri says:

> The craven corsairs advanced
> to meet the mighty prince,
> but our king cut down
> the shield-sheltered warriors.
> Eight galleys in all were
> cleared in a quick battle;
> our lord had few losses,
> our prince took great plunder.

Afterwards, Sigurd headed for the stronghold called Sintre [Cintra] where he fought his second battle in Spain [now Portugal]. The castle was occupied by heathens who were carrying out raids against Christians, and when Sigurd took the castle, he killed everyone in it because they refused to become Christian. He also took a lot of property there, as Halldor Skvaldri says:

> I shall tell of daring deeds
> done by our gold-giver
> in Spain with his spirited
> attack on Sintre;
> for his foes,
> who refused the rule of Christ,
> it was a struggle to stand
> against the grim prince.

5. After that, King Sigurd and his fleet made for Lisbon, a large town in Spain, which is half Christian and half heathen. Lisbon separates Christian Spain from heathen [Muslim] Spain; all the districts to the west are heathen. There, King Sigurd had his third battle against heathens; he was victorious and acquired a great deal of plunder. As Halldor Skvaldri says:

> Courageous son of a king,
> your third time to triumph was
> at Lisbon when you landed
> on that southern shore.

King Sigurd and his fleet continued to head west along the coast of heathen [Muslim] Spain and proceeded to the town called Alkasse [Alcacer do

Sal] where he had his fourth battle with heathens. He took the town and killed so many people that the place was deserted. They got a huge amount of booty there. As Halldor Skvaldri says:

> War-lord, I hear how
> eagerly at Alkasse
> you fought a fourth
> brisk battle and won.

And he says this, too:

> I hear that heathen women
> sorrowed in a deserted city,
> when all the army
> was forced to flee.

6. King Sigurd pressed on with his journey and headed for Norvasund [Strait of Gibraltar], where he came across a large fleet of pirates and attacked them. This was his fifth battle against heathens, and he won. As Halldor Skvaldri says:

> Bold, you bloodied
> sword edges in the east;
> god gave you help, ravens gorged
> when you sailed through the straits.

King Sigurd sailed south along the coast of Serkland [southern Spain] until he arrived at an island called Formentera. A large number of black heathens had settled in a cave there and had built a stone wall in front of the cave mouth. They raided far and wide throughout the land and brought all their plunder to the cave. King Sigurd came ashore and made his way to the cave, which was high up in a cliff. It was a steep climb to the wall, and the cliff jutted out above it. The heathens defended the wall without fear of the Norsemen's weapons, for they could bombard the men below them with spears and rocks and, in these circumstances, the Norsemen were unwilling to attack them. Then the heathens carried costly material and other valuable items to the wall and waved them at the Norsemen, shouting at them, goading them, and taunting them with lack of spirit.

King Sigurd now came up with a plan. He had two boats hauled up to the cliff-top above the mouth of the cave and had them bound securely with thick ropes under the ribs and at the stem and the stern. The boats were then filled with as many men as they could hold and were lowered to the cave with ropes. The men in the boats threw weapons and stones at the heathens and forced them back from the wall. Sigurd and his men then scrambled up the cliff, broke down the wall, and got into the cave. The heathens retreated and the king had huge pieces of wood brought to the cave-mouth where he built an immense bonfire and set it alight. When the fire and smoke reached the heathens, some of them died and others charged toward the Norsemen's weapons; all of them were cut down or burnt. The Norsemen took the largest amount of plunder they had got yet in this campaign. As Halldor Skvaldri says:

> The battle-bold
> breaker of peace
> set sail
> for Formentera;
> the band of black warriors
> suffered sword
> and fire, before falling,
> enduring death.

And he says this too:

> War-lord, you lowered
> boats from above
> did daring deeds
> against the marauding Moors;
> peerless prince,
> you clambered courageously
> up the cliff to the cave
> with many men,

Thorarin Stuttfeld says further:

> The war-wise prince
> bade his men bring
> two black boats,
> and haul them up the hill;
> rocking on their ropes,
> the laden boats were lowered,
> brought men to the mouth
> of the cave in the cliff.

7. Then King Sigurd continued on his way until he came to the island called Ibiza. He fought and won his seventh battle there. As Halldor Skvaldri says:

> The famous lord with his fleet
> – the shield-bearer with his ships –
> came to Ibiza; keen was the glorious
> prince for peace-breaking.

After that, he came to the island named Minorca where he fought and won his eighth battle against heathens. As Halldor Skvaldri says:

> He fought a further battle,
> an eighth one after that;
> on Minorca's green grass.
> lay arrows crimsoned in combat.

8. In the spring, King Sigurd arrived in Sicily and stayed there for a long while. At that time, Roger II [1095–1154] was duke of Sicily. He gave King Sigurd a warm welcome and invited him to a banquet. King Sigurd attended the feast with a large number of men and there was splendid merry-making. Every day while the banquet lasted, Duke Roger stood at the king's table and served him. On the seventh day, however, after everyone had washed, King Sigurd took Duke Roger by the hand, led him up to the high seat and bestowed on him the title of king and the right to be king over Sicily; before then it had been ruled by earls.

9. Roger, king of Sicily, was a very powerful man. He conquered the whole of Apulia and gained control of many large islands in the Greek Sea; he became known as Roger the Mighty. His son William, king of Sicily [1154–66], was at war with the emperor of Mikligard for a long time. King William had three daughters but no son. He married one of his daughters to the emperor Henry [Henry VI, 1165–97], the son of Emperor Frederik [Barbarossa, 1122–90], and their son, Frederik [Frederick II, 1211–50], is now emperor of Rome. William's second daughter married the duke of Cyprus [?] and his third daughter married Margrit, the leader of the corsairs. The emperor Henry killed both of them. The daughter of King Roger of Sicily married Manuel, emperor of Mikligard [Manuel I Komnenos, 1118–80], and their son was the emperor Kirjalax [Kurios Alexius, Alexius II Komnenos, 1169–83]. [This genealogy contains inaccuracies.]

10. In the summer, King Sigurd sailed across the Greek Sea to Palestine. Then he rode to Jerusalem where he met Baldwin, the king of Jerusalem

[1058–1118]. Baldwin gave Sigurd a very warm welcome; he rode with him to the River Jordan and back. Einar Skulason says:

> The skald must not scant
> his praises for the prince
> whose sea-cold keel
> sailed south to the Greek Sea;
> our king came
> to anchor at Acre;
> all the prince's people
> made merry that morning.

Einar also says this:

> The courageous king
> journeyed to Jerusalem;
> no nobler prince is known
> under the high heavens;
> the gracious gold-giver
> with praiseworthy purpose
> went to wash in the
> pure water of wide Jordan.

King Sigurd stayed in Palestine for a long time during the autumn and early winter.

11. King Baldwin held a splendid banquet for Sigurd and his large following and presented Sigurd with many holy relics. A fragment was taken from the true cross on the orders of the king and the patriarch, both of whom swore on the holy relic that this wood came from the holy cross on which God himself had suffered. This holy relic was given to Sigurd on condition that he, along with twelve of his men, swore to do everything in his power to spread Christianity and to establish an archbishopric in his kingdom if he could. He swore, too, that the fragment of the cross would be kept where King Olaf rested. Finally, he swore to promote the payment of tithes and to pay them himself.

Then King Sigurd returned to his ships at Acre. At that time, King Baldwin was preparing his army for an expedition to a heathen town called Saet [Sidon?] in Syria, and King Sigurd went on the expedition with him. After a short siege, the heathens surrendered; the kings took possession of the city, and their troops got the rest of the plunder. King Sigurd turned over the whole of the city to King Baldwin. As Halldor Skvaldri says:

> Feeder of fierce wolves,
> you took the town
> – the home of heathens –
> and, great-hearted, gave it away.

Einar Skulason also speaks of this;

> The warrior will remember that
> the Dales-men's prince prevailed
> at Saet, as catapults crashed
> in a storm that shook the city;
> the reddener of the raven's beak [Sigurd]
> brought down the mighty defenses
> and swords were smeared with
> blood as the bold prince triumphed.

Then King Sigurd returned to his ships and got ready to leave Palestine. They sailed north as far as the island called Cyprus and stayed there for a time. Next, he sailed to Greece and anchored off Cape Malea with his whole fleet. He lay there for two weeks. Each day there was a fine fresh wind blowing north over the sea, but he was waiting for a good cross-wind so that he could travel with his sails spread fore and aft, since all his sails had inset panels of costly material both front and back. This was so that no one – neither the men in the bow nor those in the stern – would have to look at a plain sail.

12. When King Sigurd sailed into Mikligard [Constantinople], he kept close to the shore. The coast was lined with towns, castles, and villages, one next to the other without a break. Offshore his curving sails could be seen crowded together without a gap as if they formed a single structure. The whole population was outdoors to see King Sigurd sailing by. The Emperor Kirjalax had heard of King Sigurd's expedition and had given orders for the opening of the gate known in Mikligard as the Golden Gate. This gate is used by the emperor when he has been away from Mikligard for a long time and has won a great victory. The emperor had all the streets of the town spread with costly material between the Golden Gate and the Blachernae district, where the emperor has his finest palace.

King Sigurd told his men that they should ride proudly through the city and not show the slightest astonishment at the novel things they were seeing. And that is what they did. King Sigurd and his men rode with great pomp into Mikligard all the way to the most splendid of the royal palaces, where everything had been prepared for their reception. After King Sigurd had stayed at Mikligard for some time, the emperor Kirjalax sent messengers to ask him what he would prefer: to receive six ship-pounds of gold, or to have the emperor hold games for him at the Hippodrome. King Sigurd opted for the games and the messengers told him that the games would cost the emperor just as much as the value of the gold that had been offered.

The emperor arranged for the games in the customary manner. He and the empress held the games jointly, and their men competed against one another in everything. On this occasion, the games turned out better for the emperor than for the empress. The Greeks say that when the emperor wins more games in the Hippodrome than the empress, then he will be victorious if he goes on campaign.

13. After that, King Sigurd got ready for his journey home. He gave all his ships to the emperor, and the gilded figureheads that had decorated the king's ship were installed in Saint Peter's Church. The emperor Kirjalax gave King Sigurd a great many horses and provided him with guides for his journey through the empire. Then King Sigurd left Mikligard, but many of his men stayed behind and entered military service.

King Sigurd traveled through Bulgaria first and then through Hungary, Pannonia [part of Hungary], Schwaben, and Bavaria. There he met the Roman emperor, Lothar [Lothar III, 1075–37, then still duke of Saxony], who made him very welcome and provided him with men to guide him through the entire kingdom. Lothar also set up markets so that Sigurd and his men could buy whatever they needed. At midsummer, King Sigurd reached Schleswig in Denmark, and Earl Eilif gave him a splendid banquet.

In Hedeby, he met King Nikolas of Denmark [1064–1134], who welcomed him and accompanied him north to Jutland. There he gave him a fully equipped ship on which he sailed to Norway. King Sigurd arrived back in his kingdom to a joyful reception. It was the general opinion that there had never before been a more splendid expedition from Norway than this one. King Sigurd was twenty years old at this time and had spent three years on the journey. His brother Olaf was twelve years of age.

CHAPTER FOURTEEN

STATE-BUILDING AT HOME AND ABROAD

At the beginning of the Viking Age, Scandinavia was dominated by numerous small kingdoms or chiefdoms, although by the last period of the Scandinavian Iron Age (roughly 600–800) fairly powerful regional kingdoms had started to emerge around Lake Mälaren in Sweden, in Jutland in Denmark, and in Vestfold in Norway. As the Viking Age progressed, these nascent kingdoms were forged into the medieval states of Denmark, Norway, and Sweden. We know most about state-building in Denmark, where by about 800 CE the Danes had already created a kingdom that embraced most of modern Denmark and parts of southern Sweden and the Vestfold region of Norway. Early ninth-century Norway was divided into a number of chiefdoms and regions, and parts of southern Norway like Vestfold were under the control of Danish rulers. The medieval Icelandic saga tradition associates the unification of Norway with the Vestfold king Harald Finehair at the end of the ninth and beginning of the tenth century. For the most part, the kings who unified their kingdoms were also Christian and were, ostensibly at least, responsible for converting (or beginning the conversion of) their respective peoples. In Norway, Christianization had little place, so far as we can tell, in Harald Finehair's agenda, but Harald's role in state-building there is downplayed by modern scholars, who point instead to the Christianizing kings Olaf Tryggvason and Olaf Haraldsson (Saint Olaf) as being responsible for creating a strong unitary kingship. The fact that these so-called Vikings for Christ were also state-builders is not a coincidence, and they, like Harald Bluetooth and others, recognized the potential of Christianity, both in terms of doctrine and church organization, as a means to strengthen kingship and promote unity. For this reason the documents in this chapter may also be considered in light of the preceding chapter dealing with the conversion to Christianity.

In this period, much less is known about Sweden, which was inhabited by two peoples, the Svear and the Götar. However, by the end of the tenth and the start of the eleventh century one king was ruling both people. For a relatively brief period in the eleventh and twelfth centuries, loose "Viking empires" emerged in the North Sea and Irish Sea. Most notably, King Knut the Great (d. 1035), a grandson of Harald Bluetooth, ruled England, Denmark, Norway, and perhaps part of Sweden, while the powerful earls of Orkney, though technically subject to Norway, were formidable rulers in their own right whose authority embraced the Shetland and Orkney islands as well as the northern mainland of Scotland, the Hebrides, and the Isle of Man.

94. HARALD FINEHAIR AND THE
UNIFICATION OF NORWAY

Harald Hárfagri (Finehair) is often credited with the unification of Norway. The most detailed account of his life and reign is his saga in Snorri Sturluson's Heimskringla, *although he is mentioned in many other Icelandic sagas. Snorri describes his campaigns against a variety of other Norwegian rulers, culminating in his great victory at Hafrs-fjorðr (Havsfjord). The dates of his reign are murky and controversial. His accession is estimated at 860–880, his victory at Havsfjord at 885–890, and his death at 930–940. Whatever he had accomplished during his lifetime did not survive his death, when his numerous sons (perhaps as many as twenty!) fell to feuding over their father's revenues and title to the kingship. Accordingly, it is the Christianizing kings at the end of the tenth century and start of the eleventh (see docs. 85 and 87) who are credited with completing the unification of Norway.*

Source: Snorri Sturluson, *Haralds saga ins Hágrfara*, in *Heimskringla*, ed. Bjarni Aðalbjarnarson, Íslenzk fornrit XXVI–XXVIII (Reykjavík, 2002), vol. 1, pp. 84–122.

1. ... King Harald was a handsome man, very tall and strong, as well as intelligent and brave. He succeeded his father as king when he was ten years old and, at this time, his maternal uncle, Guthorm, assumed leadership of the royal guard and made himself responsible for governing the kingdom and commanding the army.

After the death of Halfdan the Black, many chieftains began encroaching on the kingdom he had left behind. First there was King Gandalf and the brothers Hogni and Frodi, the sons of King Eystein of Hedmark. Next there was Hogni Karuson, who overran large parts of Ringarik. Then, Haki Gandalfsson set out for Vestfold with three hundred men; he took the high road across several valleys, intending to take King Harald by surprise. Meanwhile, King Gandalf waited at Londir [Vesteroy?] with his army, planning to move it across the fjord to Vestfold. As soon as Guthorm Hertogi [commander] got wind of all this, he mustered his army, and he and King Harald moved up country to confront Haki. They encountered one another in a valley; a great battle took place, and King Harald was victorious. King Haki and many of his men were killed there, and ever since, the valley has been known as Haki's Dale.

After that, Guthorm and King Harald turned back to face King Gandalf who had arrived in Vestfold. The two sides advanced against one another, and, when they met, there was a fierce battle. King Gandalf lost most of his army, so he fled and returned to his kingdom.

When the sons of King Eystein of Hedmark heard about this, they concluded that they too would soon have a fight on their hands. So they sent word to Hogni Karuson and Hersir Gudbrand and set up a meeting at Ringsaker in Hedmark.

2. After these battles, King Harald and Guthorm Hertogi assembled their available forces and made for Uppland, traveling mainly by forest paths. They found out where the Uppland kings had arranged to meet and arrived there in the middle of the night. Before the sentries were aware of what was happening, the king's army had reached the houses where Hogni Karuson and Guthbrand were sleeping and set them alight. Hogni and Frodi got out with their men and defended themselves for a while but eventually they were both killed. With the deaths of these four kings, and through the might and prowess of his kinsman Guthorm, King Harald had now gained possession of Ringarik, Hedmark, Gudbrand's Dale, Hadeland, Toten, Romarik, and the whole of north Vingulmark. King Harald and Guthorm Hertogi were still at war with King Gandalf, but when King Gandalf died in the final battle, the fighting ended and King Harald gained possession of the kingdom as far south as the Raum River.

3. King Harald sent envoys to a maid called Gyda, the daughter of Eirik, King of Hordaland, who was being brought up in the house of a rich landowner in Valdres. Harald wanted her as his mistress because she was a very beautiful and high-spirited girl. When the envoys arrived, they delivered their message to the young woman, and she replied to the effect that she wouldn't waste her maidenhood on a king who ruled only a couple of provinces.

"I think it's extraordinary," she said, "that there is no king with enough ambition to conquer Norway and make himself sole ruler of the country, like King Gorm in Denmark and Eirik at Uppsala [in Sweden]."

The envoys thought that she answered arrogantly, and asked her what she meant by such an answer, adding that Harald was a powerful king, and a worthy match for her. But though she hadn't given them the sort of answer they wanted, they recognized that there was no immediate possibility of carrying her off against her will, so they prepared for the return journey. When they were ready and people were seeing them off, she told the envoys to take this message to King Harald: she would agree to be his lawful wife only if, for her sake, he would first conquer the whole of Norway and rule there autonomously, like King Eirik in Sweden, or King Gorm in Denmark. "For only then, I think, could he be called a sovereign," she said.

4. The envoys made their way back to King Harald and told him what the girl had said. They told him too that she was impudent and foolish and that

the king would be completely justified in sending a large force to carry her off in disgrace. King Harald replied that the girl had neither said nor done anything to merit punishment but, instead, deserved thanks for her words.

"She has reminded me of something which, strange to say, I haven't thought about before now," he said. Then he added, "I call on God, who created me and who rules the universe to witness this solemn oath: I shall neither cut nor comb my hair until I gain possession of the whole of Norway – with all its taxes and revenues – and become sole ruler there, or die trying."

Guthorm Hertogi praised his vow, and said that it was a king's duty to keep his word.

5. After that, Harald and Guthorm mustered a large army and made for Uppland. Then they went north through the Dales, and north again over Dovrefjell [a mountain range]. Whenever the king came down into a settlement, he had the men slaughtered and the buildings burned, and when news of this spread, everyone who could, fled. Some of them went to Orkadal, some to Gaulardal, and some took to the forests. Others begged for mercy and this was granted to everyone who came to the king and swore allegiance to him.

King Harald and his uncle Guthorm met no resistance until they reached Orkadal where an army had been mobilized against them. Their first battle was against a king called Gryting and King Harald won this battle. Gryting was captured, and a large part of his army was killed. So he submitted to Harald and swore allegiance to him. Then the whole population of Orkadal province submitted to King Harald and became his subjects.

6. Wherever King Harald gained control, he imposed a law giving himself ownership of all ancestral properties and forcing all landholders, both great and small, to pay him rent. Over every province, he placed an earl whose duty it was to make legal decisions and to apply the law, to levy fines and· to collect rents. Each earl was to have a third of the taxes and dues for his living-costs and expenses. He was also to have four or more hersirs under him, each of whom was to have an allowance of twenty marks. The earls were required to provide sixty men each for the royal army; the hersirs supplied twenty men each.

King Harald increased taxes and land-rents so much that his earls became more powerful than the former kings had been. When this became known throughout Trondheim, many influential men sought out King Harald and entered his service.

7. History tells us that Earl Hakon Grjotgardsson came from Yrjar [now Ørland] with a large army to support King Harald. After that, King Harald advanced into Gaulardal where he fought and killed two kings, and took

possession of their territories, Gaulardal and the Strinda district. Harald put Earl Hakon in charge of the Strinda district.

King Harald went next to Stjordal where he fought and won a third battle and annexed that district. After this, the people of the Inner Trondheim district assembled for battle. Four kings were there with their armies. They were the kings of Verdal, Skaun, Sparby, and Lower Eyin. The king of Lower Eyin also ruled Eynafylki. These four kings advanced against King Harald with their army. Harald engaged them in battle and won, killing some of them and putting others to flight. In all, King Harald fought eight or more battles in the Trondheim district and, with the fall of the eight kings, he took over the whole Trondelag....

18. News spread from the south that the people of Hordaland, Rogaland, Agder, and Thilir had united in an armed uprising and were assembling ships, weapons, and large numbers of men. The leaders of the revolt were King Eirik of Hordaland; Sulki, King of Rogaland; his brother Earl Soti; Kjotvi the Wealthy, King of Agder; his son, Thorir Haklang; and Hroald Hryg and Hadd the Hard, two brothers from Telemark.

As soon as King Harald heard this news, he assembled his army and prepared it for battle. Then he launched his ships and sailed south along the coast with many men from every district. When King Harald had got as far south as Stad, King Eirik heard about his approach. He mustered all the troops he could and headed south to meet the forces that he knew were coming from the east to support him. The entire fleet met to the north of Jadar and steered into Hafrsfjord, where King Harald was already waiting with his forces. Fierce fighting broke out. There was a long, hard battle but, in the end, King Harald was victorious, and King Eirik, King Sulki and his brother, Earl Soti, were killed. King Harald's own ship had been attacked by Thorir Haklang. Thorir was a fierce berserker and the fighting was frenzied until he was killed. After that, his ship was completely cleared of men. Meanwhile King Kjotvi fled to an island that offered natural protection, and after that, their entire army fled. Some of them escaped by ship; others leapt ashore and fled south across Jadar. As Hornklofi puts it:

> Have you heard
> how in Hafrsfjord
> a king of noble kin fought
> Kjotvi the wealthy king?
> Keen for conflict, his
> fleet set forth from the east,
> great figure-heads gaping,

prows covered with carving.

Massed aboard were men
with white shields and sharp
spears — weapons from the west —
and splendid Frankish swords;
berserkers bellowed,
— Gunnr was with them —
wearers of wolfskins howled,
shook their sharp spears.

They put their prowess to the
test, but he taught them to turn
and run, the Norse ruler
who has his home at Utstein;
he steered out his sea-steeds [ships],
when the strife started;
shields bore thudding blows
ere Haklang lost his life.

Kjotvi the bull-necked king grew
weary of war with Tanglehair
for lordship of the land,
hoped for a haven on the isle;
with asses in the air,
and heads in the hold,
the casualties crept under
rowers' benches for refuge.

Their shields shining
on backs beaten
by a rain of rocks
the wiser warriors fled;
the enemy escaped eastward,
hastened home over Jadar,
back from battle at Hafrsfjord,
their minds on mead-drinking.

19. After the battle of Hafrsfjord [885–90], King Harald faced no more
opposition in Norway. All of his most powerful enemies were dead or had
fled abroad. They had fled in large numbers, for vast areas of uninhabited

countryside were settled at this time. Among these areas were Jämtland and Hälsingland, though both already had a sprinkling of Norse settlers. During this period of unrest, when King Harald was bringing Norway under his control, outlying places such as the Faeroes and Iceland were discovered and settled. There was a large exodus to the Shetlands too. Many Norwegian chieftains fled as outlaws from King Harald, and took to the Viking life in the west. They spent the winters in the Orkneys and Shetlands, and in summer they raided Norway, inflicting a great deal of damage on the country. Many other chieftains submitted to King Harald, entered his service, and helped him run the country.

20. King Harald had now become the sole ruler of Norway. It was then that he remembered what that proud young lady had said to him. So he sent some men to fetch her and took her to live with him. Their children were Alof (the eldest), Hroerek, Sigtrygg, Frodi, and Thorgils.

23. After King Harald had conquered the whole of the country, he attended a banquet in Møre at the house of Earl Rognvald. He took a bath there and had his hair cut and combed for the first time in ten years. Earl Rognvald himself did the cutting. Harald's nickname had been Tanglehair, but now Earl Rognvald renamed him Finehair. Everyone who saw him thought that this was a very fitting name because his hair was both abundant and beautiful [see chapter 4].

95. STATE-MAKING IN DENMARK: THE JELLING STONE

Denmark's equivalent of Harald Finehair is Harald Bluetooth, the son of Gorm the Old, a ruler in Jutland in the middle of the tenth century. On the large rune stone at Jelling, a royal site associated with Gorm and Harald, Harald claimed that he "won for himself all Denmark and Norway" and made the Danes Christian. He was responsible for building some of the monuments at Jelling and is thought to be the builder of a series of fortresses throughout Denmark – possibly needed to consolidate his unification of the kingdom – as well as a substantial timber bridge at Ravning, near Jelling. The end of Harald's reign is firmly placed in the second half of the 980s, when his son Svein Forkbeard led a rebellion against him, in the course of which Harald died. The beginning of his reign is less firmly fixed.

Source of Image: Carl Christian Rafn, *Runeindskrift i Piraeus: Inscription runique du Pirée* (København: Société Royale des Antiquaires du Nord, 1856), p. 38.

Source of Transcription: Lis Jacobsen and Erik Moltke, *Danmarks runeindskrifter* (Copenhagen: Ejnar Munksgaards Forlag, 1941–42), DR 42.

Side A

haraltr : kunukR : baþ : kaurua	King Harald ordered this monument
kubl : þausi : aft : kurm faþur sin	to be carved in memory of Gorm, his father,
auk aft : þạurui : muþur : sina : sa	and Thyrve [Thorvi], his mother. [This was] the
haraltr (:) ias : sạR ★ uan ★ tanmaurk	Harald who conquered Denmark

Side B

aḷa·auk·nuruiak	and all Norway

Side C

·auk·tani·(karþi·)kristnạ	and made the Danes Christian.

96. STATE-MAKING IN DENMARK: UNIFICATION AND EXPANSION

Knýtlinga saga (The Story of the Family of Knut) *is an anonymous chronicle that was probably written in Iceland during the thirteenth century. The author may have been Sturla Thordarson, the nephew of Snorri Sturluson. The saga covers Danish history from the age of Harald Gormsson in the ninth century until the late twelfth century. This section gives an account of Harald Gormsson and the unification of Denmark, while document 97 deals with the expansion of Danish power to England.*

Source: *Knýtlinga saga,* in *Danakonunga sögur,* ed. Bjarni Guðnason, Íslenzk fornrit XXXV (Reykjavík, 1982), pp. 93–98.

1. After the death of his father, Gorm the Old, Harald Gormsson became king of Denmark. He was a powerful king and a mighty warrior who conquered Holstein in Saxony. He also ruled a large earldom in Wendland where he built Jomsborg and manned it with a large force. He paid the garrison and granted them certain rights and privileges; they held the place under his auspices. In summer, they went raiding and, during the winter, they stayed at home. They were known as the Jomsvikings.

The Lives of the Kings of Norway record that King Harald Gormsson engineered the betrayal and death of King Harald Gunnhildarson of Norway when he died at Hals in Limafjord [976 CE]. Then King Harald Gormsson invaded Norway with his army and brought the whole country under his authority. He established Earl Hakon Sigurdarson as ruler of Norway, but he himself, as king of the Danes, levied tribute from the whole country.

In the days of King Harald Gormsson, Otto the Red [Otto II, 955–983] was emperor of Germany. He made war on King Harald and ordered the Danes to convert to Christianity, but the king of the Danes, who would not adopt Christianity on any account, called out his army against Otto.

King Harald Gormsson and Earl Hakon of Norway engaged Otto in a great battle at the Danevirk, in the south of Denmark. The emperor was defeated there, but shortly afterwards he subdued the country and put Harald and Hakon to flight, driving them all the way north to Limafjord and Marsey. After this, King Harald adopted Christianity and the emperor became god-father to his son, Svein. At the baptism, Otto gave Svein his own name so that afterwards he was known as Otto-Svein. Everyone in Denmark was converted to Christianity since the emperor would settle for nothing less.

2. Styrbjorn the Strong was the son of Olaf Bjarnason, king of Sweden. In the time of King Harald Gormsson, he made a foray into the eastern Baltic, invaded Denmark, and took King Harald prisoner. So Harald gave

Styrbjorn his daughter, Thyri, in marriage and then traveled to Sweden with him. Before going ashore, Styrbjorn burned all his ships, and as soon as King Harald realized that Styrbjorn was shipless, he sailed to Lake Malaren and from there back to Denmark.

At Fyrisvellir [Fyris Plains], Styrbjorn fought against his uncle, King Eirik the Victorious of Sweden [Eirik I, ca 945–ca 995], and perished there along with most of his army, though some of them did escape. The Swedes call the battle Fyriselta [the Hunt at Fyris].

3. When King Harald Gormsson was baptized, as already mentioned, he forced Earl Hakon Sigurdarson to adopt the Christian faith, and he was also baptized along with all the men who had accompanied him from Norway. King Harald supplied him with priests and other clerics and directed him to have everyone in Norway baptized. Hakon swore that he would do so.

When the king and the earl parted, Hakon made for Norway and, en route, put the holy men ashore at Hals in Limafjord. He turned his back on Christianity and afterwards offered up huge pagan sacrifices in Norway. When King Harald heard that Hakon had rejected Christianity and raided his territory, he led his army to Norway and laid waste the coastal area, burning everything from Lindnes to Stad, except for five farms at Laeradale in Sogn. The whole population fled to the mountains and forests, taking with them whatever property they could.

King Harald and his army remained at the Solund Islands for some time. He was planning to raid Iceland with the forces he had on hand since he wanted revenge for the insulting and derisory verses leveled at him by the Icelanders. King Harald ordered a man with supernatural powers to go there in an assumed shape and tell him what he could find out about the place. The man circled Iceland in the form of a whale and later told the king that there were many monsters living there. He also said there was too much open sea between Norway and Iceland for longships to cross. When King Harald heard this, he realized that the enterprise would be hugely daunting and probably couldn't be carried out.

After his raid in Norway, Harald Gormsson returned to Denmark with his army, while Earl Hakon had all the devastated land in Norway resettled and never again paid tribute to the king of the Danes.

4. Svein, son of King Harald Gormsson, asked his father for a share in the kingdom, but his father didn't care for him much since he was the son of one of his mistresses and so he was reluctant to give him any part of the kingdom to govern. When Svein came of age, he got himself some men and ships and went raiding far and wide, at home and abroad. King Harald was enraged and gathered an army against him. Svein was joined by Palna-Toki, his foster-father, as the Jomsvikings' saga records. They headed for Sjaelland

and went up Isafjord where they found King Harald already waiting with his ships. Svein sailed to the attack immediately and there was a great fight. But then, a great number of men joined the king's army so that Svein was overwhelmed and had to flee. King Harald was mortally wounded by an arrow in the battle. He was the first Danish king to be buried in consecrated ground; by then, he had been king for eighty years: thirty years while his father, Gorm, was alive, and fifty years after that.

5. After the death of his father, King Harald, Svein became king of Denmark [Svein I, ca 960–1014]. He was called Svein Forkbeard and was a powerful king. It was in his days that Earl Sigvald and the rest of the Jomsvikings went to Norway and fought against Earl Hakon at Hjorunga Fjord in Møre. Bui Digri died in this battle, but Earl Sigvald got away. After that, the kings of Denmark lost control of Norway and shortly afterwards Olaf Tryggvason came to Norway and seized power.

King Svein married Gunnhild, daughter of Burizlaf, king of the Wends. Their sons were Knut and Harald. Next, he married Sigrid the Proud, daughter of Skoglar-Tosti and mother of Olaf, king of Sweden, from an earlier marriage to Eirik the Victorious, king of Sweden. Svein and Sigrid had a daughter called Astrid who married Earl Ulf, the son of Thorgil the Ambitious. Their sons were Svein and Bjorn. Another of Svein Forkbeard's daughters was Gytha, who married Eirik Hakonarson in Norway. Their son was the Earl Hakon who was captured by Saint Olaf at Sauthungsund.

King Svein Forkbeard was present at the death of Olaf Tryggvason [see doc. 38] at the Battle of Svold [1000 CE], as were his stepson, King Olaf of Sweden, and his son-in-law, Earl Eirik. After the death of Olaf Tryggvason, each of these three got a third of Norway.

6. King Svein was a mighty warrior and a very powerful king. He raided far and wide, both in the eastern Baltic and in Saxony to the south. Finally, he took his army west to England where he campaigned extensively and fought many battles. At this time, Athelred son of Edgar was king of England. He and Svein fought frequently; both had their victories, but Svein conquered most of England and stayed there for many years, raiding and burning throughout the country. People referred to him as "England's Devil." In the midst of the warfare, King Athelred fled the country, but then King Svein died suddenly in his bed one night and Englishmen claim that King Edmund the saint had killed him just as Saint Mercurius killed Julian the Apostate [emperor of Rome, 361–363].

97. KNUT THE GREAT AND THE NORTH SEA EMPIRE

Knýtlinga saga (The Story of the Family of Knut) records the exploits of Knut (also Cnut/Canute) the Great, a son of Svein Forkbeard and a grandson of Harald Bluetooth. Knut was born in the 990s and was a participant in his father's expedition to England in 1013, which ousted King Athelred and won Svein the kingship of England. Svein died mere months later, in February 1014, and a power struggle ensued between Knut and the English, led once again by Athelred. By the end of 1016 both Athelred and his son Edmund were dead, the English had been defeated, and Knut had been chosen as king. He added the title king of Denmark in 1019 (his brother had assumed power there on the death of Svein), and in Norway he expelled King Olaf Haraldsson (later Saint Olaf) in 1025. Olaf was slain on his return in 1030 at the battle of Stiklestad near Trondheim. Knut's shrewdness in marrying Athelred's widow, Queen Emma, in 1017, his enthusiastic support of the English church, his long and fairly peaceful reign, and his interactions with other European rulers have won him a favorable reputation as a ruler: in the judgment of the great Anglo-Saxonist Sir Frank Stenton, Knut was "the first Viking leader to be admitted into the civilized fraternity of Christian kings." His so-called North Sea Empire did not survive his death in 1035, aged only about forty years.

Source: *Knýtlinga saga*, in *Danakonunga sögur*, ed. Bjarni Guðnason, Íslenzk fornrit XXXV (Reykjavík, 1982), pp. 99–127.

7. After King Svein's death, Danish chieftains held on to the part of England they had conquered. Then fighting started again because, as soon as King Svein died, Athelred [King Athelred the Unready, ca 968–1016] came back and re-entered his kingdom with the support of Saint Olaf [king of Norway]. This is recounted in Saint Olaf's saga in the words of Ottar the Black Poet, as follows:

> Lord, you gave back his land
> to Athelred; the people's prince
> profited from your power;
> strong, you strengthened his kingdom.
> A fierce fight brought
> the kin of King Edmund back
> to their hereditary home,
> long ruled by their line.

At this time, the Danes established the housekarls [king's bodyguard] in

England. These mercenaries, who were exceptionally brave, did much of the fighting against the English.

8. Knut, son of Svein Forkbeard, was ten years old when his father died. Since Harald, his brother, was already dead, he was made king over Denmark and the whole Danish empire. The Danish chiefs who occupied the English territory won by Svein sent word to Denmark that King Knut should come west with a Danish army as reinforcement against the English. However, since Knut was still a child without experience of command, his friends suggested that he should send the army to England, appointing others to command it, and not go himself until he was older. And so that's how it came about that he stayed in Denmark for three years after coming to the throne.

When the three years were over, he levied an army for overseas. At the same time, he sent word to his brother-in-law, Earl Eirik, in Norway, asking him to muster an army and travel to England with him, for Earl Eirik was highly regarded for his courage and skill in warfare. He had been victorious in the two most famous battles ever fought in the Northlands. One of these was Svold [1000] where he, King Svein Forkbeard, and King Olaf of Norway had fought against Olaf Tryggvason and the other was at Hjorungafjord [988] where he and his father, Earl Hakon, defeated the Jomsvikings. Knut headed west to England with a huge force, as Ottar the Black relates in *Knútsdrápa* [*Knut's Praise Poem*]:

> While yet young,
> king, conqueror of fleets,
> you launched longships. No younger
> prince ever departed his homeland.
> You readied ships, bows bound
> in iron, prince. You faced perils
> And with murderous mind,
> Raised red shields against England.

He says too:

> Generous prince, the Jutes
> followed you fearlessly.
> And you, sea-king, mustered soldiers
> from Skaney for the sea-voyage.
> Above you sails swelled;
> you steered your ships west.
> Your name will be known,
> prince, for this sea-passage.

Many chiefs followed Knut to England. The most outstanding was Earl Ulf
Sprakaleggsson [Strut-Leg's Son], his brother-in-law, who was married to
Astrid, daughter of Svein and sister of King Knut. Also there were the broth-
ers Heming and Thorkel the Tall, the sons of Strut-Harald as well as many
other chiefs. King Knut reached England and sailed into the mouth of the
Humber, as they call it. Hallvard Hareksblesi recounts this in *Knútsdrápa*:

> Keen for the conflict,
> the sword-warrior set sail.
> Knut, you steered iron-stemmed
> ships forward to Fljóta.
> Overseas in England
> you moored in Humber-mouth,
> gratifying the gluttony
> of battle's bird, the raven.

As soon as Knut reached England, he went ashore and began plundering,
killing the people and burning their houses, as Ottar the Black relates:

> Great king, you gained power
> with your war-shield;
> no pleasure for you, prince,
> in the leisurely life;
> Jutes' general, you destroyed
> Edgar's line on that expedition.
> King's kin, your
> stubborn strength crushed them.

He says this too:

> Prince, while yet a youth
> you set farms aflame,
> and the fire forced men
> into the ways of war.

The local inhabitants assembled an army, marched on the Danes and engaged them in battle, as Thord Kolbeinsson says:

> The raven-rewarders [Danes],
> long loathed in the land,

> came ashore early from their ships,
> entered England.
> The farmers raised a force
> to defend their dwellings;
> the soldiers of the sword-prince [Knut]
> braved them in battle.

Lindsey was the site of King Knut's first battle in England and there was great slaughter. Then Knut captured Hemingborough and, again, many people were killed. Ottar says:

> In Lindsey's green fields you gave
> battle, brave prince.
> Danes did as they pleased
> with the conquered country.
> Slayer of Swedes,
> you made the English endure
> much misery in Hemingborough
> out to the west of the Ouse.

After that, he fought major battles in Northumberland near the Tees. Many people died there, and some escaped only to perish in the nearby fens and ditches. Then King Knut marched his army further south and was victorious wherever he went.

9. In the same summer or autumn as King Knut invaded England, King Athelred fell ill and died, having been king of England for thirty eight-years. His wife, Queen Emma, got ready to leave the country as soon as Athelred died, intending to travel west to France to meet her brothers, William and Robert, who were both earls there. Their father was Richard Richardsson, earl of Rouen, who was the son of William Longspear. He was the son of Gongu-Hrolf, who conquered Normandy; and Gongu-Hrolf was the son of Rognvald, earl of Møre in Norway.

However, King Knut's men got to hear about Queen Emma's journey and when she and her men were about to put to sea, Knut's men turned up and seized the ship with everything in it. Queen Emma was brought before King Knut, and the king and his chiefs decided that he should marry her. And that is what happened.

10. After King Athelred's death, his sons by Queen Emma were chosen as his successors. Edmund the Strong was the eldest, second came Edgar, third was Edvig, and fourth was Edward the Good [the Confessor].

King Edmund now assembled a large army and moved against King Knut. They met at a place called Sherston where they fought the most famous battle of the day with terrible slaughter on both sides. King Edmund rode right into the middle of the Danish army, coming close enough to his stepfather, King Knut, to strike him with a sword. Knut thrust his shield forward over his horse's neck, but the blow from the sword was so powerful that it cut right through the shield a little below the hand-grip and sliced into the horse's shoulders just in front of the saddle. The Danes then attacked King Edmund so furiously that he had to retreat toward his own side, but not before he had killed many Danes, though he himself was wounded only slightly, if at all. However, when King Edmund had ridden so far ahead of his men that they had lost sight of him and thought that he must be dead, the army began to run away, and, though some of his men saw him riding back from the Danes, they all fled, including those who had seen him. The king shouted loudly to his army and ordered them to turn and fight, but they acted as though they hadn't heard him. The whole army ran for it and there followed a most awful slaughter, with the Danes hunting the routed army till nightfall. Thus says Ottar the Black:

> Young prince, you felled
> English troops by the Tees.
> A deep ditch was choked with the dead,
> clogged with Northumbrian corpses.
> In the south, the inciter of strife
> disturbed the dark raven's dream.
> Svein's brave son
> brought the battle to Sherston.

11. As usual, Earl Ulf was in the front rank of King Knut's soldiers and he followed the fugitives furthest. He came to a forest so thick that for the whole night he couldn't find his way out until daylight appeared. Then, before him, on some open ground he saw a young man in his prime herding some sheep. Earl Ulf approached the young man, greeted him, and asked his name.

"I'm called Godwin," the youth answered. "Are you one of Knut's men?"

"Yes, I'm one of his soldiers," replied Ulf. "How far is it to our ships from here?"

"I'm not sure that you Danes can expect much help from us," said the young man. "In fact, you may get something quite different."

"At the moment, young man, I'd be happy if you'd just point me in the direction of our ships," replied Earl Ulf.

"You've been heading in the wrong direction entirely," said the youth. "Instead of making for the ships, you've been going inland through dense forest. And, in this area, Knut's men aren't too popular with the locals, which is understandable since they've just heard about yesterday's massacre at Sherston. If the farmers catch you, neither you nor any other of Knut's men can expect quarter, and the same goes for anyone who helps you. But it seems to me that there might be some profit to be made from you, for I don't think you're the man you say you are."

Then Earl Ulf removed a gold ring from his arm and said, "I'll give you this ring if you'll guide me to my men."

Godwin looked at him for a while and then said slowly, "I won't accept your ring, but I will try to bring you to your men. If I do manage to help you, I would rather you were under an obligation to me; if I can't help you, there is no need for a reward. But first, you must come home with me to meet my father." And that is what they did.

When they came to the farm, they went into a small living room where Godwin had a table set and good drink served. Earl Ulf observed that this was a fine, well-furnished farm. Then the farmer and his wife came in. They were good-looking, well-dressed people who gave their guest a warm welcome. He stayed there all day enjoying excellent hospitality, and toward night two good horses were saddled up with the finest harness. Then the farmer and his wife spoke to Ulf.

"I'll say farewell and place my only son in your hands," said the farmer, whose name was Ulfnoth. "If you reach your king and your word counts for anything, I'd ask you to find a position for Godwin; for, however I manage, he can't stay on here in case our countrymen find out that he has helped you to escape." Ulf promised that Godwin could join his comrades, for he was a handsome, well-spoken young man.

Earl Ulf and Godwin rode all night and arrived at Knut's ships just after daybreak. Some of the men were ashore and when they recognized Ulf, they all crowded around and gave him a welcome fit for a man who seemed to have been recalled from the dead, for he was so popular that everyone loved him wholeheartedly. For the first time, Godwin realized who his companion was.

The earl had Godwin sit next to him on the high seat and treated him exactly as he himself or his own son was treated. To put it briefly, Ulf gave Godwin his sister, Gytha, in marriage, and Ulf's strong support persuaded his brother-in-law, Knut, to bestow an earldom upon Godwin. The sons of Godwin and Gytha were Harold, king of England and the earls Tosti (called Longspear), Morkar, Waltheow, and Svein. Their descendants include many great men in England, Denmark, Sweden, and to the east in Russia, as well as the royal house of Denmark. Earl Godwin's son, King Harold, had a daughter called Gytha, who married King Valdamar of Novgorod, and their son King Harold had two daughters who will be mentioned later.

12. King Knut fought and won another major battle, this time at a town named Brentford. Athelred's sons fled, losing a large army and the Danes demolished the town, as Ottar the Black says:

> Prince, breaker of peace and shields,
> feller of Frisians,
> you brought ruin to Brentford,
> destroyed the dwellings.
> King Edmund's noble kinsman
> suffered savage wounds and
> Danish soldiers showered spears
> as the English forces fled.

King Knut fought the third major battle against the sons of Athelred at a place known as Ashton, to the north of the Danewoods. Ottar says:

> Shield-bearing Scyld's son,
> you wrought war's works at Ashton,
> where the bird of battle feasted
> on men's bloody meat.
> With sword strokes,
> prince, you won a worthy
> name, north of Daneswood,
> when you massacred many.

King Knut's fourth battle against Edmund and his brothers was fought at Norwich. It was another major battle and many men died. King Knut was the victor and the sons of Athelred were put to flight. Ottar the Black says the following:

> Generous gift-giver, who
> made mail-shirts bloody in Norwich,
> you will lose life before you
> lose courage, lord.

13. Next, King Knut led his army to the Thames, for he had heard that King Edmund and his brothers had fled to London. When he arrived at the

Thames Estuary, Earl Eirik, his brother-in-law, sailed in from the sea and they advanced together up the river with their forces. Thord Kolbeinsson says in *Eiríksdrápa* [*Eirik's Praise-Poem*]:

> The kinship of earl and king
> prospered on the path to battle;
> ships of many sizes sailed
> up the estuary;
> Earl Eirik, kinsman of kings,
> steered his ships, dark serpents
> of the sea, so close to land that the
> fields of England were in full view.

And he composed this too:

> Onward pressed the Danish prince,
> ploughed through the sea paths,
> sent his longships speeding
> to the shoals at the shore;
> the helmeted earl and Knut the king
> met joyfully that morning,
> with both men bent
> on sailing the sea ways.

In the middle of the Thames, a large fort had been built and garrisoned to defend the land against ship-borne armies coming up river. King Knut sailed up the Thames and attacked the fort, but an English fleet sailed down river from London and joined battle with the Danes. Ottar the Black says:

> Bows sang loud, swords bit,
> your attack went well against
> weapon-bearing warriors
> when your forces assaulted the fort.
> The wolf's teeth well know,
> sailor of the dark ships,
> that you gained no less glory
> in the shallows and shoals of the Thames.

14. King Knut led his whole army to London and, having set up camp, made an assault on the town, but the townsmen defended it, as is related in this poem composed by the Danish soldiers who were present:

Day after day, on the banks
of the Thames, the triumphing Valkyrie sees
flesh-tearing swords stained with blood,
and the hanged god's ravens replete;
sees the victory-seeking
prince pursuing brave townsmen,
and bloodied swords, bright as ice,
beating against British armor.

And this too:

For this day's dueling,
many an eager man
puts on the rusty, old ring-mail
we've been born and bred to;
still, we feed Odin's fowl,
the raven, with red English blood;
the skald slips swiftly
into his hammered mail-shirt.

King Knut fought many battles there, but he failed to take the town.

15. Earl Eirik led part of the army and some of the housekarls inland against the English army commanded by a great chieftain, Ulfkell Snilling. In the battle that followed, Eirik won and Ulfkell fled. Thord Kolbeinsson says in *Eiríksdrápa*:

The Gold-giver got ready
for war, west of London;
the famous sea-farer
fought fiercely for land;
blue-edged blades shivered
over the housekarls' heads
when Ulfkell endured
a staggering stroke.

Earl Eirik fought another battle against the English at Ringmere. As Thord Kolbeinsson says:

Often, the bold shield-shaker scarred
soldiers' limbs with the sword edge,
glutted grim ravens

> with bloated bodies;
> to the English, bold Eirik
> dealt death,
> reducing their ranks,
> and reddening Ringmere Heath.

Earl Eirik won this battle. Thord Kolbeinsson says more about his campaign in *Eiríksdrápa*:

> The raven-rewarders [Danes],
> long loathed in the land,
> came ashore early from their ships,
> entered England.
> The farmers raised a force
> to defend their dwellings;
> the soldiers of the sword-prince [Knut]
> braved them in battle.

16. King Knut besieged London. King Emund and his brothers defended it while messengers went to and fro between them. King Knut had married their mother, Queen Emma, and so hostages were exchanged and a truce was called to allow for discussion and the negotiation of a more permanent treaty. In the consultations that followed, an agreement was reached to the effect that the kingdom would be divided in two and that each of them would have half as long as they were both alive, but if one of them died childless, the survivor would inherit the whole kingdom unopposed. This treaty was confirmed by oaths.

King Knut paid a powerful man called Eadric Strjona to betray King Edmund and murder him, and that was how he died, even though Eadric was his foster-father and was trusted by King Edmund as he trusted himself. Afterwards, King Knut drove all the sons of King Athelred out of England. Many battles were fought because of this, but they could never raise a strong enough force to resist King Knut after the death of King Edmund. Sigvat the skald says in *Knútsdrápa*:

> Soon King Knut
> struck at the sons
> of Athelred,
> ousting them from England.

Then the sons of Athelred went to France and stayed in Normandy for a long time with their uncles Robert and William, as the saga of Saint Olaf recounts.

Earl Eirik, son of Hakon, died in England just when he was on the point of making a pilgrimage to Rome. He died when his uvula was removed and the bleeding could not be stopped.

King Knut and Queen Emma had three children. Harald was the eldest, second was Harda-Knut, and their daughter was Gunnhild, who later married the emperor Henry the Gentle, the third of his line with that name. King Knut's third son was called Svein, but his mother was Alfifa the Wealthy, the daughter of Earl Alfrun.

17. In the days when King Knut ruled England and Denmark, Olaf Haraldsson [later Saint Olaf] was king of Norway. When Olaf came to the throne, Earl Svein, son of Hakon, and Earl Hakon Eiriksson, Knut's nephew, fled the country. Earl Hakon Eiriksson traveled to England and visited his uncle, King Knut, who received him warmly. Later, hostilities broke out between King Olaf and King Knut, and Knut and Earl Hakon invaded Norway with an overwhelming force; this happened near the end of King Olaf's life. They subdued the whole country and King Knut installed his nephew, Hakon, as ruler of Norway, while he himself returned to Denmark.

When King Olaf fled Norway, he went east to Russia. Two years later, he returned to Norway and fought a terrible battle at Stiklastad [1030], against the landowners, who had broken faith with him and become his enemies. As most people know, King Olaf died there and is now sanctified; he lies in a shrine at Nidaros.

The year before the death of the king, Saint Olaf, Earl Hakon Eiriksson died in the English Sea [North Sea]. Then Svein, the son of King Knut and Alfifa, went to Norway and was appointed king of the whole country by order of his father. King Knut, also made his son, Harda-Knut, king of the Danish empire, and appointed his son, Harald, king of his considerable territories in Scotland. Knut himself, however, was over-king and was called Knut the Great, or Knut the Old. Of all the Scandinavian kings, Knut was the most powerful and had the most extensive lands.

King Knut traveled abroad on a pilgrimage to Rome and his expenditure on the journey was so vast that no one could calculate the cost in marks, and only with difficulty in pounds. As well as bringing money from his own kingdom, he also made use of the emperor's property freely wherever he wished. While King Knut was on his pilgrimage to Rome, no one who met him needed to beg for his food, for he gave everyone so much money to spend. King Knut traveled on foot from Flanders to Rome, as Sigvat the skald says:

> Few gold-givers
> will set out for the south,
> fare on foot like you,
> peerless prince.

King Knut founded a hostel where any Danish-speaker who turned up could get food and lodging for the night and, wherever he went, he distributed large amounts of money to monasteries and other important religious establishments.

18. When he returned to his kingdom in England, he came down with an illness, which showed up first as jaundice. He lay ill for a long time during the summer and in the autumn he died on 13 November [1035] in the great city of Winchester, where he is buried. He was thirty-seven years old and had been king of Denmark for twenty-seven years, England for twenty-four, and Norway for seven. It is generally agreed that Knut had more power and more extensive territories than any other Scandinavian king.

19. Knut was the most open-handed of all northern kings for, in truth, not only was he more generous than other kings in the gifts he showered on his friends every year, but also he received much more annually in taxes and dues from three kingdoms than anyone who ruled only one kingdom. Added to that, England was the richest kingdom in the Northlands.

An example of his generosity was the case of the Icelander, Thorarin Loftunga [Praise-Tongue]. He was an excellent skald who had been in the service of kings and other great men for much of his long life. When he was an old man, he went to see King Knut because he had composed a poem about him. He came before the king, paid his respects, and asked the king if he would listen to a poem composed in his honor. It so happened that the king was seated at table after dinner, and several men were standing in front of the table presenting their suits. The king listened to them first, and when they had finished talking, Thorarin said his piece, for he was not overawed by kings and had often spoken before great men.

"My lord," he said, "I'm asking you again to listen to my poem; it won't take long for there aren't many stanzas."

Knut looked at him rather angrily and answered, "No one but you has ever insulted me by composing a 'drápling' [little drápa] about me. Now get this clear: at breakfast time tomorrow, you will come here and recite a drápa [praise-poem of thirty stanzas or more] in praise of me. You will compose it in the time I have allowed you, or you're dead."

Thorarin went away and started working on a drápa about King Knut, salvaging whatever he could from the poem he had brought with him; the drápa is called *Head-Ransom*. Next morning, he recited the poem before the king and it went over very well. The king rewarded him for the poem with a gift of fifty marks of pure silver. Afterwards, Thorarin composed another drápa, called *Togdrápa*, for King Knut. Part of it went like this:

> I have richly
> repaid
> the fifty marks I got
> from war's master,
> which he gave,
> – Great bringer of death –
> for my poem,
> when I visited the prince.

King Knut presented two gold arm-rings, each weighing a mark, and a gold-mounted sword to Bersi, son of the Skald-woman, Torfa. Sigvat the skald puts it thus:

> Bersi, King Knut,
> so distinguished in deeds,
> enriched our arms splendidly
> when we met the great man;
> in his wisdom, he awarded you
> a gold mark or more, and a sharp sword;
> there was half a mark for me;
> great God himself rules all.

When King Knut died in England, there died with him the liberality of generations of Danish kings, each of whom had a more extensive kingdom than his father.

20. Knut was extremely tall and strong. He was an outstandingly handsome man, except for his nose, which was thin, high-set, and slightly crooked. He had a fair complexion and thick blond hair. His eyes were more beautiful than other people's and his eyesight was keener. He was a generous man and a great soldier; he was gallant, victorious, and exceptionally fortunate in everything concerning power and wealth. But he was not a very reflective man, and the same is true of Svein, Harald, and Gorm before him. None of them were great thinkers.

98. THE EARLDOM OF ORKNEY AT ITS ZENITH

Although technically subject to Norway, the Norse earls of Orkney were powerful rulers in their own right. Modern scholarship agrees that the Orkney earldom reached the apex of its power in the time of Earl Thorfinn Sigurdarson the Mighty (ca 1009–ca 1064), who was reckoned in Orkneyinga saga *as the most powerful earl. During his long tenure of the earldom, Thorfinn gained a reputation as a formidable warrior and was said to have subjugated nine Scottish earldoms, the Hebrides, and part of Ireland, though modern scholarship regards these claims as exaggerated. Thorfinn was also the first earl of Orkney who was brought up as a Christian. He went on a pilgrimage to Rome ca 1050 and established the first bishopric in Orkney at Birsay on the west mainland, his principal residence. The latter part of his reign was given over to the administration of the earldom. His career is outlined in the first part of* Orkneyinga saga.

Source: *Orkneyinga saga*, ed. Finnbogi Guðmundsson, Íslenzk fornrit XXXIV (Reykjavík, 1965), pp. 43, 56, 71–83.

20. Earl Thorfinn became a great leader. He was very tall and had immense strength. In appearance, he was ugly, with black-hair, sharp-features, a long nose, and a swarthy complexion. He was an energetic man, ambitious for both wealth and fame, and since he was not only courageous but also skilled in battle, he was usually victorious. When he was five years old, his grand-father, Malcolm, king of Scots [Malcolm II, ca 980–1034] gave him the title of earl and made him ruler of Caithness. When he was fourteen years old, he began making forays outside his own lands and raiding the territory of other chieftains....

Earl Thorfinn behaved magnificently in the Orkneys. He provided his entire bodyguard and many other powerful men with food and ale throughout the winter, so that they didn't have to go to an inn. In other lands, kings and earls usually provide their bodyguard with food and drink only at Yule....

[*Thorfinn's power was threatened only once, by his nephew Rognvald Brusason. The sea-battle in which Thorfinn defeated his nephew is described in document 38c. The following passage tells the story of Rognvald's last, desparate attempt to overthrow his uncle. After this, Thorfinn was never seriously challenged.*]

28. When Earl Rognvald landed in the Shetlands, he learned that Earl Thorfinn was in the Orkneys and that he had only a few men with him since he didn't anticipate trouble in the depths of winter. So, Rognvald headed south for the Orkneys without delay. Meanwhile, Earl Thorfinn was in Hrossey, un-aware of any danger. When he reached the Orkneys, Rognvald made straight

for the place where he had been told that Thorfinn was living. He arrived so unexpectedly that he and his men were able to block all the doors of Thorfinn's house before anyone had an inkling of what was happening.

It was night time and almost everyone was asleep, but Earl Thorfinn was still sitting up drinking. Rognvald and his men set fire to the house, and as soon as Thorfinn became aware of the situation he sent men to find out who was responsible for the fire. When they were told that it was Earl Rognvald who had arrived, they all leapt for their weapons, but they couldn't mount any resistance because they couldn't get outside. Before long the house was ablaze, so Thorfinn told his men to ask the earl to let them out. Rognvald allowed all the women and slaves to leave but, as for the men, he said he would prefer most of them dead. Then the people who had been spared were pulled from the building and after that the house was quickly engulfed by fire.

Earl Thorfinn tore away a piece of wainscotting from the house and jumped out with his wife Ingibjorg in his arms. The night was pitch-dark, so he got away under cover of the smoke, without Earl Rognvald's men noticing him. That very night, he rowed across to Caithness, alone in a small boat. Earl Rognvald burned down the entire building along with all the men who had not been allowed out. It didn't occur to anyone that Earl Thorfinn had not died there.

After that, Earl Rognvald traveled the length and breadth of the islands and brought all of them under his control. He sent word across to Caithness and also to the Hebrides that he was claiming all the land that had belonged to Earl Thorfinn; no one made any objection. Earl Thorfinn hid with friends in various parts of Caithness and not a whisper got out that he had escaped the burning.

29. Earl Rognvald took up residence in Kirkwall and laid in all the provisions that he would need for his winter quarters. He had a large crowd of followers and lived in great state. Shortly before Yule, Earl Rognvald and many of his men went over to Little Papey to fetch the malt for the Yule brewing. Late in the evening, as they sat around a roasting fire on the island, the man who was looking after the fire remarked that they were running out of firewood. Then the earl made a slip of the tongue. What he said was, "We'll be very old before these fires burn out." What he meant to say was, "We'll be very well-roasted before these fires burn out." He noticed his slip immediately and said,

"As far as I can recall, I've never misspoken before, but I do remember what my foster-father, King Olaf, said to me at Stiklastad, when I caught him out in a slip of the tongue. He told me that if I ever happened to mis-speak I should be prepared to die soon afterwards. So perhaps my uncle Thorfinn is still alive."

At that very moment they realized that the house had been surrounded. Earl Thorfinn had arrived. Straightaway, he and his men set fire to the house and piled up wood in front of the doors. Earl Thorfinn allowed everyone to leave except Rognvald's men. After most of the people had been brought out, a man dressed in a linen garment appeared in the doorway. Thorfinn told his men to lend the deacon a hand, but the man pressed down with his hands on the wood at the doorway, and vaulted over both the wood and the men encircling the door. He landed well beyond them and quickly disappeared into the darkness. Earl Thorfinn ordered his men to catch him.

"It must have been Rognvald who got away," he said. "No one else is strong enough to do that."

So they separated into groups and went to look for him. Thorkel the Fosterer was searching along the seashore when a dog was heard barking among the rocks beside the sea – Rognvald had taken his lap-dog with him, and the dog had given him away. They killed him there and then among the rocks, and the story goes that it was Thorkel the Fosterer who killed him. No one else would do it, but Thorkel had taken an oath to do anything that would help Thorfinn regain his power. Thorfinn and his men spent the night on the island; all the men who had gone there with Rognvald were slain.

In the morning, they loaded a cargo ship with malt. When they boarded the ship, they did not remove Rognvald's shields from the bow and they made sure that no more men were visible than had gone with Rognvald to the island. They rowed to Kirkwall and the people there thought that Earl Rognvald was coming back. So they went to meet him and most of them were unarmed. Earl Thorfinn had thirty men seized and executed. Most were retainers and friends of King Magnus of Norway, but the earl spared one of them and ordered him to go back to Norway and tell King Magnus what had happened.

30. Earl Rognvald's body was taken to Greater Papey where it was buried. The general opinion was that he had been the most popular and accomplished of all the earls of Orkney, and many people mourned his passing.... After that, Earl Thorfinn brought all of the Orkneys under his control, and no one put up any resistance. Early in the spring, news of these events reached Norway. King Magnus was greatly upset by the loss of Earl Rognvald and said that he would avenge him as soon as he could. But at that particular time, he was involved in hostilities against Svein Ulfsson, who had recently become king of Denmark. At that time too, he had just given half his kingdom to his uncle Harald Sigurdarson who had returned to Norway....

31. Earl Thorfinn now had undisputed authority over the Orkneys and all the rest of his territories.... Occasionally, he went on Viking expeditions to the west, pillaging in Scotland and Ireland. He also spent some time in

England where he was in charge of the royal bodyguard for a while.

When Earl Thorfinn heard of King Magnus's death, he sent messengers to Norway to assure King Harald of his good will and to ask him for his friendship. King Harald received the message favorably and promised Thorfinn his friendship. As soon as he received this reply, Earl Thorfinn got ready for a voyage and set off from the Orkneys with two twenty-bench longships and more than a hundred well-chosen men. He sailed east to Norway and met the king in Hordaland. Harald welcomed him warmly and gave him many fine gifts when they parted.

From there, the earl sailed south along the coast and kept going until he reached Denmark. He traveled across the country and met King Svein at Alaborg [Aalborg]. The king invited Thorfinn to stay with him and held splendid feasts in his honor. Then the earl revealed his intention of going on a pilgrimage to Rome.

When he arrived in Saxony, the earl met the emperor Henry [III] who received him warmly and gave him many rich gifts. The emperor also supplied him with many horses for his journey south. Then he traveled to Rome where he met the pope [Leo IX] and was absolved of all his sins.

After that, he made his way home and got back to his realm safe and sound. He gave up raiding and turned his attention to governing his people and lands, and to establishing laws. He resided permanently in Birsay and there he built Christchurch, a magnificent church that was the first cathedral in Orkney.

Earl Thorfinn married Ingibjorg Earls' Mother. They had two sons who survived childhood. Their names were Paul and Erlend and they were big, good-looking men who took after their mother's side of the family. They were also intelligent and good-natured and the earl loved them dearly, as did all his people.

32. Earl Thorfinn retained control of his realm until the day he died. He was certainly the most powerful of the earls of Orkney, for his rule extended over nine earldoms in Scotland as well as the whole of the Hebrides and extensive lands in Ireland. Arnor Jarlaskald [Poet of Earls] says the following:

> The folk obeyed the feeder of
> ravens from Thurs Rocks to Dublin;
> I tell the people truly
> what manner of man was Thorfinn.

Thorfinn was five years old when his maternal grandfather, Malcolm, king of Scots, gave him the title of earl, and he remained an earl for seventy [probably fifty] more years. He died shortly before Harald Sigurdar-son [d. 1066] and is buried in Christchurch, which he himself had built. The earl was deeply lamented in the lands he had inherited, but in the territories he had won by force, many people felt downtrodden under his rule. So after his death, several of these territories revolted and the people sought the protection of the chiefs who were the hereditary owners of the land. It soon became evident what a serious loss Earl Thorfinn's death was.

The following verses were composed about the sea-battle between Earl Rognvald Brusason and Earl Thorfinn [by Arnor Jarlaskald]:

> It was a disastrous day when
> the earls engaged in battle;
> many a man learned to die
> in the fierce fighting;
> men dear to me were close to killing
> one another, when war's
> flame flashed before Robery
> where many a fine man was wounded.
> The bright sun will blacken,
> earth sink under the dark sea,
> the sky will splinter,
> seas surge over the mountains,
> before a lovelier lord
> than Thorfinn
> is bred in the Orkney Isles;
> God help that guardian of warriors.

CHAPTER FIFTEEN

THE END OF THE VIKING AGE

A variety of markers have been suggested for the end of the Viking Age. These include the conversion of the Scandinavians to Christianity and their assimilation into western European religious culture (see chapter 13); the development of unitary Christian king-ships in Scandinavia, which brought the kingdoms of the region into line with other European kingdoms (see chapter 14); and military events like the defeat of King Harald Sigurdarson of Norway at the Battle of Stamford Bridge in September 1066, often cited as the last large-scale Viking expedition. A case might be made for seeing the reign of Hakon IV of Norway (1217–63) as bringing the age to an end. His Scottish expedition in 1263 was the last serious Norse intervention in the affairs of the British Isles.

Yet history seldom provides neat divisions between more or less arbitrary "ages," and because of the extensive nature of the Scandinavian diaspora it is difficult to identify a single date that has meaning throughout the entire Viking world. Moreover, as the preceding chapters have demonstrated, the Viking Age itself was not a monolithic chronological period spanning some three or four centuries but was in fact marked by a variety of distinct phases of activity, and by both continuity and change. In the end, it is probably unwise to look for a single terminal moment for the Viking Age.

99. THE BATTLE OF CLONTARF, 1014

The Battle of Clontarf was fought on Good Friday (23 April) 1014, in what is now a suburb of Dublin. The combatants were the Irish High King Brian Boru, with his Munster army, opposed by an alliance of Sigtrygg Silkenbeard of Dublin, Máelmórda mac Murchada of Leinster, and Sigurd Hlodvisson of the Orkneys, with forces drawn from the Orkneys, Hebrides, Isle of Man, and northern England, as well as Dublin and Leinster. The battle had its roots in a rebellion against Brian's ascendancy. The battle has long been regarded as significant for breaking Viking power in Ireland – a view prevalent since the Middle Ages, and fostered by the Cogad Gáedel re Gallaib (The War of the Irish against the Foreigners *[see doc. 45]) – but modern scholars are inclined to regard it as an Irish political struggle into which Scandinavians were drawn on both sides. From* Njal's Saga. *Several of the men involved with the burning of Njal died in this battle.*

Source: *Brennu-Njáls saga*, ed. Einar Ól. Sveinsson, Íslenzk fornrit XII (Reykjavík, 1954), pp. 444–60.

155. ... Then King Sigtrygg got down to business and asked Earl Sigurd to join forces with him against King Brian. The earl resisted the idea for a long time, but in the end he agreed on condition that he could marry Sigtrygg's mother and become king of Ireland if they killed Brian. His men all tried to dissuade him, but to no avail. And so they parted company with Earl Sigurd promising to join the expedition, and King Sigtrygg promising him his mother and the kingdom. It was also agreed that Earl Sigurd would come to Dublin with his entire army on Palm Sunday.

Sigtrygg traveled south to Ireland and told his mother that the earl had undertaken to join them; he told her, too, what he had promised in return. She expressed her approval but declared that they would have to muster a much larger force. Sygtrygg asked where this was to come from. "There are two Vikings lying off the Isle of Man with thirty ships," replied Kormlod [Sygtrygg's mother]. "One of them is called Ospak and the other Brodir and they are so fierce that no one can stand up to them. Go and find them and do your best to persuade them to join you, whatever their conditions."

Sigtrygg went looking for the Vikings and found them off the Isle of Man. He brought up the reason for his visit at once, but Brodir declined to get involved until King Sigtrygg promised him the kingdom and his mother. This arrangement was to be kept secret so that Earl Sigurd wouldn't find out about it, and Brodir, too, was to come to Dublin on Palm Sunday. Then Sigtrygg went home to his mother and told her everything.

Afterwards, Brodir and Ospak conferred together, and Brodir told Ospak all about his conversation with Sigtrygg. He asked Ospak to join him in the war against King Brian, saying that he had a great deal riding on it. Ospak replied that he did not want to fight against such a good king. Both of them grew very angry; they divided up their forces, with Ospak taking ten ships and Brodir twenty.

Ospak was a heathen and the wisest of men. He steered his ships into the bay while Brodir lay at anchor outside it. Brodir had been a Christian and an ordained deacon, but he had abandoned his faith and renounced God. Now he sacrificed to heathen devils. He was more skilled in sorcery than anyone else and had a mail shirt which no weapon could pierce. He was a big, strong man and his black hair was so long that he could tuck it under his belt.

156. One night a great din broke out above Brodir and his men. Awakened by the noise, they all leapt up and got dressed. Then, along with the din, came a shower of boiling blood. They protected themselves against it with their shields, but many of them were scalded. This strange happening lasted until daybreak, and one man died on every ship. Then they slept for the rest of the day.

The next night, the noise returned and once more they all sprang up. This time swords leapt out of their sheaths, and axes and spears flew up into the air above them and started fighting. The weapons attacked the men so fiercely that they had to use their shields for protection, but many of them were wounded and again one man died on every ship. This wonder went on till dawn and once again they slept all the next day.

On the third night, the uproar erupted again. This time, ravens came flying down at the men, attacking them so fiercely with their iron-like beaks and claws that the men had to defend themselves with their swords and protect themselves with their shields. This onslaught continued until daybreak, and again, one man died on every ship. Then they slept.

When Brodir awoke, he sighed deeply, and ordered his men to launch a boat, saying that he wanted to see his foster-brother, Ospak. He boarded the boat with some of his men, and when he met Ospak, he told him about all the strange things that had happened to them and asked him to explain their significance. Ospak refused to tell him until he had agreed to a truce. Brodir gave his word, but, even then, Ospak put off telling him until nightfall, for Brodir never killed at night.

Then Ospak said: "When the blood rained down on you, it was a sign that you will shed a great deal of blood, both your own and other men's. When you heard a great noise, it was a sign that the world is falling apart, and you will all die soon. When the weapons attacked you, they portended a battle.

And when the ravens flew at you it was a sign that the devils you trusted will drag you down to the torments of hell."

Brodir was too enraged to speak. He rushed back to his men and had them line up his ships across the sound and moor them to the shore with cables. He intended to kill Ospak and all his men next morning. When Ospak saw what they were doing, he swore to adopt Christianity and join King Brian and follow him to the death. He came up with a plan to camouflage his ships and have them poled along the shore so that his men could cut the mooring cables of Brodir's ships. The ships then drifted into one another while the crews slept. Meanwhile, Ospak and his men sailed out of the fjord and went west to Ireland; they did not stop until they reached Kincora. There, Ospak told King Brian everything he had learned. He accepted baptism from the king and entered his service. King Brian then mustered troops from all over his kingdom; this army was to come to Dublin the week before Palm Sunday.

157. Earl Sigurd Hlodvisson got ready to leave the Orkneys. Flosi [responsible for the burning of Njal] volunteered to go with him, but the earl would not hear of it because Flosi had still to make his pilgrimage to Rome. So Flosi volunteered fifteen of his men for the expedition, and the earl accepted his offer. Then Flosi went with Earl Gilli to the Hebrides, while Thorstein Hallsson, Hrafn the Red, and Erling of Straumey went with Earl Sigurd to Ireland. The earl did not want Harek to go with him, but promised he would be the first to hear what happened.

On Palm Sunday, Earl Sigurd and his entire army arrived in Dublin. Brodir and his troops were there already. Brodir tried to predict how the battle would go by means of sorcery. His prediction was that if the battle took place on Good Friday, King Brian would be killed though he would win the victory, and if the battle took place before Good Friday, all Brian's opponents would be killed. So Brodir advised them not to fight before Friday.

On the Thursday of that week, a man with a halberd in his hand rode up on a dapple-grey horse. He had a long talk with Brodir and Kormlod [the mother of Sigtrygg].

King Brian and his troops reached Dublin, and, on Good Friday, the Norse army came out of the town and both sides drew up in battle formation. Brodir was on one wing of the army and Sigtrygg was on the other, with Sigurd in the middle. King Brian was unwilling to fight on Good Friday, so a shield wall was thrown up around him and his army was drawn up in front of it. Ulf the Unruly was in the wing facing Brodir, while Ospak and King Brian's sons were on the other wing facing Sigtrygg. Kerthjalfad was in the centre and in front of him were the standards.

Now the two armies fell upon one another and a ferocious battle ensued. Brodir charged through the opposing ranks, killing everyone in his path;

no weapons could harm him. Then Ulf the Unruly turned toward him and struck him three times with such force that he fell on his face each time and could scarcely get up again. As soon as he regained his footing, he fled into the forest.

Earl Sigurd had a hard fight against Kerthjalfad who advanced so forcefully that he killed everyone before him. He fought his way right through Earl Sigurd's force as far as the standard and killed the standard bearer. The earl got another man to carry the standard and the battle continued just as fiercely. Kerthjalfad immediately cut down the replacement standard-bearer. Then he killed all those who were near him, one after another. Earl Sigurd ordered Thorstein Hallsson to carry the standard, and Thorstein was just about to pick it up when Amund the White said: "Don't touch the standard, Thorstein. Everyone who carries it is killed."

"You carry the standard," said the earl to Hrafn the Red.

"Carry the accursed thing yourself," replied Hrafn.

"You're right," said the earl. "A beggar should carry his own bag." So he took the standard from its pole and put it under his clothes. Shortly afterwards, Amund the White was killed, and then the earl, too, was skewered by a spear.

Ospak had fought his way through the opposing wing; he was badly wounded, and Brian's sons were both dead. King Sigtrygg fled before him and after that the whole Norse army took to flight. But while everyone else was running away, Thorstein Hallsson stopped to tie his shoelace. When Kerthjalfad asked him why he wasn't running away, Thorstein replied, "Because I won't make it home this evening since I live out in Iceland." Kerthjalfad spared his life.

Hrafn the Red was pursued into a river. He thought he could see the torments of hell below him and devils threatening to drag him down, so he said, "Saint Peter, this dog of yours has run to Rome twice already, and will run there a third time if you let him."

Then the devils let him go, and he got across the river.

Brodir saw that King Brian's army was in hot pursuit of the fleeing soldiers and that there was hardly anyone near the shield wall. So he ran out of the woods, broke through the shield wall, and struck at King Brian. The boy Tatk thrust his arm in the way, but the stroke cut off his arm and the king's head too. The king's blood splashed onto the stump of Takt's arm, and it healed immediately. Then Brodir shouted loudly, "Spread the word. Brodir has killed Brian."

Some men sped off and told the pursuing troops that King Brian had fallen. Ulf the Unruly and Kerthjalfad turned back at once. They surrounded Brodir and his men, threw tree branches over them, and took Brodir prisoner. Ulf the Unruly cut open his stomach and unwound his entrails by leading him round and round an oak tree. He did not die until all of his guts were pulled out. Brodir's men were all killed too.

When they took King Brian's body to prepare it for burial, they found that his head had grown back onto his body. Fifteen of the men who had taken part in the burning of Njal died in Brian's Battle. Halldor Gudmundarson and Erling of Straumey fell there too.

On that Good Friday morning, a strange thing happened in Caithness. A man called Darrud went out and saw twelve figures riding toward a cabin and disappearing inside. He went over to the cabin and looked through a window. He saw that there were women inside and they had set up a loom. Its weights were men's heads; its weft and warp were men's entrails; the slay was a sword, and the rod was an arrow. The women were reciting these verses:

"Darradarljod" ("Song of the Spear")

1. Wide is the warp
of slaughtered souls,
blood rains red
from the cloth-cloud;
now Valkyries weave
a web of war,
and fill out
this warp of warriors,
grey like spear-steel,
with a red weft.

2. The web is warped
with human guts
the warp is weighted
with human heads;
blood-spattered spears are
the heddle rods, the shed rod
is bound with iron bands,
the shuttle is shaped from arrows;
with our sword-beaters we strike
the wide web of victory.

3. Hild and Hjorthrimul,
Sangrid and Svipol
weave the web
with unsheathed swords;
spears will splinter,
shields shatter,
and the helmet-hunting
ax hit home.

4. Let us wind, wind,
the web of war,
which the young king fought
in former days;
let us hasten ahead,
to reach the ranks
where our friends are fighting,
trading blow for blow.

5. Let us wind, wind,
the web of war,
and follow the king
to the front,
where Gunr and Gondul,
protectors of the prince,
will see the bloody shields.
of the bold warriors.

6. Let us wind, wind,
the web of war,
where soldiers' standards
go forth to the fray,
we will not let
his life be lost;
we Valkyries are the ones
who select the slain.

7. Those who formerly dwelt
on far-flung headlands
will now be lords
of the land;

I say death will be dealt
to a powerful prince;
an earl will fall to earth
pierced by spear points.

8. The Irish will endure
everlasting anguish;
that woe will not wane
however long men live;
the web is now woven,
the battlefield blood red;
tidings of death and disaster
will spread from land to land.

9. Now it is loathsome
to look around as
clouds, crimson with blood,
spread over the sky;
the high heavens will be
deep-died with men's blood,
when the women of war [the Valkyries]
sing their songs.

10. We have spoken fine words
concerning the young king,
we have sung him songs
of victory, Valkyries' songs.
Let him who hears
the songs of the spear-women
listen and learn,
and teach them to others.

11. Let us leave here,
ride away rapidly
on barebacked horses
with swords unsheathed.

Then the women pulled down the cloth and tore it to shreds; each of them kept the piece she was holding. Darrud left the window and made his way home and the women mounted their horses and rode off, six to the south and the other six to the north. A similar event was witnessed by Brand

Gneistason in the Faeroes.

At Svinafell in Iceland, blood fell onto the priest's cope on Good Friday and he had to take it off. At Thvatt River on Good Friday, the priest thought he saw a deep sea beside the altar with many terrifying things in it; it was a long time before he could say his prayers again.

And this is what happened in the Orkneys. Harek thought he saw Earl Sigurd and some of his men. So he mounted his horse and rode to meet the earl. People saw them meeting and riding behind a hill, but they were never seen again, and not a trace of Harek was ever found.

In the Hebrides, Earl Gilli dreamt that a man came to him, saying that his name was Herfinn and that he had come from Ireland. The earl asked him what news there was from Ireland, and he answered thus:

> I was there, in Ireland,
> when brave men battled;
> swords sang out, shield met shield,
> weapons clashed in the din of war;
> I heard the fighting was fierce;
> Sigurd fell in the spear-storm,
> battle-wounds bled,
> Brian fell but won the field.

Flosi and the earl spent a good deal of time talking about this dream.

A week later, Hrafn the Red arrived and told them what had happened at the Battle of Clontarf. He told them about the deaths of King Brian, and Earl Sigurd, and Brodir, and all the Vikings.

"What can you tell me about my men?" asked Flosi.

"They all died," replied Hrafn, "except for your brother-in-law Thorstein. He was spared by Kerthjalfad and is with him now. Halldor Gudmundarson died there too."

100. THE BATTLE OF STAMFORD BRIDGE, 1066

When King Edward the Confessor of England died without heirs in January of 1066, three contenders emerged for his throne: Harold Godwinsson, earl of Wessex; William, duke of Normandy; and Harald Sigurdarson, king of Norway. The English chose Harold Godwinsson as king, but William and Harald began preparations to take the throne by force. Harald of Norway struck first, landing in the north of England with 300 ships, defeating the English at Fulford Gate and capturing York on 20 September. Five days later, Harold Godwinsson surprised Harald and his Scandinavians at

Stamford Bridge, near York, and inflicted a crushing defeat upon them. The death of King Harald Sigurdarson of Norway at Stamford Bridge is often seen as symbolizing the end of the Viking Age. It was not the last major Viking expedition overseas, but it was the end of Viking influence in England and was the last Viking expedition with a real chance of success. From The Saga of Harald Sigurdarson.

Source: Snorri Sturluson, *Haralds saga Sigurðarsonar*, in *Heimskringla*, ed. Bjarni Aðalbjarnarson, Íslenzk fornrit XXVI–XXVIII (Reykjavík, 2002), vol. 3, pp. 178–92.

83. When his preparations were complete and the wind was favorable, King Harald put to sea. He himself landed in the Shetlands, but some of his forces went straight to the Orkneys. After a short stay, Harald sailed on to the Orkneys. When he left there, he had a large force with him, including the earls Pal and Erlend, the sons of Earl Thorfinn. However, he left behind his queen, Elizabeth, and their daughters, Maria and Ingigerd.

He sailed south along the coast of Scotland and England and landed at a place called Cleveland, where he went ashore. He began raiding immediately and subdued the whole area without meeting any resistance. Then King Harald made for Scarborough and fought with the townsmen. He climbed the hill above the town, where he built a bonfire, and set it alight. When the fire was fully ablaze, they used long forks to hurl the burning wood down onto the town. House after house burst into flames until the whole town was engulfed. The Norsemen killed many people and made off with all the plunder they could get hold of. The English had no choice, if they wanted to escape with their lives, but to submit to King Harald, and so he subjugated the country wherever he went.

Then Harald headed south along the coast with his entire force and landed near Holderness where an English host had gathered against him. King Harald engaged them in battle and won.

84. Next, King Harald sailed up the River Humber and moored there, close to land. At that time, Earl Morcar and his brother, Earl Waltheow, were at York with a large army. When the earls' army came down to attack King Harald, he was at anchor in the River Ouse. He came ashore and began drawing up his forces. One wing of his army extended down to the river bank, while the other stretched inland to a dyke, where there was a broad marsh that was deep and full of water. The earls had their men advance slowly down the river, in a solid mass. The king's standard was beside the river where his line was thickest and the thinnest part of the line was at the dyke where the least reliable men were stationed. It was there, along the dyke, that the earls launched their attack. The Norse wing at the dyke gave

way, and the English followed them, thinking that the Norsemen would run away. Morcar's standard was in the lead.

85. When King Harald saw that a host of Englishmen had advanced along the dyke and was now opposite them, he had the trumpet sounded and urged on his army energetically. Then, with his standard, Land-Ravager, carried in front of him, Harald went on the offensive so fiercely that the enemy fell back in disarray. Many of the earls' men were slaughtered. The rest of the English troops quickly turned and fled, some up the river and some down. Most of them, however, jumped into the marsh, where the dead lay so closely packed that the Norsemen could cross the marsh without getting their feet wet. Earl Morcar perished there. Stein Herdisarson says this:

> People perished in the river,
> soldiers sank and drowned;
> many of young Morcar's
> finest warriors fell by his side.
> The powerful Prince Olaf
> drove foes to flight;
> they ran from the brave ruler.

Stein Herdisarson composed this poem in honor of King Harald's son, Olaf. We are told in the poem that Olaf was with his father in this battle. We hear about the same events in Harald's Stanzas:

> The fallen lay
> in the fen,
> Waltheow's warriors
> cut down by weapons;
> and so the Norse band
> keen in battle,
> could cross the fen,
> on a bridge of corpses.

Earl Waltheow and the rest of the survivors fled to the city of York. There had been terrible slaughter in the battle, which took place on the Wednesday before St. Matthew's Day [21 September].

86. As soon as King Harald arrived in England, Earl Tostig [Harold Godwinsson's brother] came north from Flanders to join him, and so the earl took part in all these battles. As Tostig had foretold when he and Harald had met previously, many people joined their ranks in England. These were Tostig's

relatives and friends, and they reinforced King Harald's army considerably. After this battle, the entire population of the neighboring districts submitted to King Harald, except for a few who fled.

Then Harald set off to capture York, positioning his army at Stamford Bridge. Since Harald had won such a great victory against powerful leaders and overwhelming opposition, the English were afraid and had little hope of resisting him. Accordingly, the townspeople decided to send a message to King Harald, offering to place themselves and their city in his hands. An agreement was reached, and King Harald and his entire army advanced toward the city on the Sunday. King Harald held a meeting outside the city, which both the king's men and the townsmen attended. The townspeople agreed to submit to King Harald and gave him the sons of the leading men of the town as hostages – Earl Tostig knew all the townspeople. In the evening, King Harald went down to his ships, very pleased with his easy victory. It had been arranged that there would be a meeting in the town early on Monday morning so that Harald could appoint governors for the city and distribute land and privileges.

That same evening after sunset, King Harold Godwinsson [king of England] entered York from the south with an overwhelming army; he rode into the town with the consent and approval of all the inhabitants. The city gates were closed and so were all the roads so that the Norsemen would not get word that the English army was in the city. The army stayed there overnight.

87. After breakfast on Monday morning, Harald Sigurdarson had the trumpet sounded for disembarking. He got the army ready and divided it into two parties, one of which was to go to the city while the other stayed behind with the ships. In each company, two out of every three men went ashore, and the third remained behind. Earl Tostig got ready to accompany King Harald ashore with his division. Those left to guard the ships were: Olaf, the king's son, Pal and Erlend, the earls of Orkney, and Eystein Orri, the son of Thorberg Arnason, who was the noblest of all the landed-men and dearest to the king. King Harald had promised him his daughter Maria in marriage.

As the weather was remarkably fine and the sunshine was hot, the men left their coats of mail behind, and went ashore taking only their shields, helmets, halberds, and swords. Many also had bows and arrows; they were all very cheerful.

But, as they approached the city, a large force came riding toward them. They saw the dust-cloud raised by the horses' hooves and, under it, they saw fine shields and bright chain mail. Then King Harald brought his army to a halt and summoned Earl Tostig to his side. The king asked him what army this could be. The earl answered that it was probably a hostile army, although it could be some of his relatives seeking mercy and friendship from the king, in return for their loyalty and support. Harald declared that they had better stay put until they could get some information about the other army; they did so. The army loomed larger the nearer it came, its weapons glittering like broken ice.

88. Then King Harald Sigurdarson spoke. "We must now come up with a good, workable plan," he said, "for there's no doubt that these are hostile forces, and that the king himself is with them."

"The first thing to do," replied Earl Tostig, "is to turn back to our ships as quickly as possible, and pick up the rest of our army and weapons. Then we'll give the enemy as hot a reception as we can, or we'll take shelter on our ships where the horsemen won't be able to get at us."

"I have a different idea," answered King Harald. "Let's put three brave warriors on our fastest horses and have them ride post haste to our men and tell them to come and help us right away. For the Englishmen must expect a fierce fight, before we admit defeat."

The earl responded that the king must decide this as he did everything else, and added that he himself had no wish to flee. Then King Harald had his standard, Land-Ravager, raised. It was carried by a man called Frirek.

89. King Harald drew up his army in a long, thin line and then drew the wings back until they met to form a large circle with an even depth all the way round. The men stood with their shields interlocking and inside the circle was the king's standard and his retinue of hand-picked men. Earl Tostig and his troops were also positioned inside the circle and he had his own standard. The king had chosen this formation because he knew that the horsemen usually charged up in small groups and then turned back immediately. The king now ordered both his own men and the earl's men to intervene wherever they were most needed.

"And our bowmen will go with us," said Harald. "If the enemy charge us, the men standing in the front rank of the circle will anchor their spear shafts in the ground and direct the points at the chests of the horsemen; the men in the second rank will aim for the chests of their horses."

90. King Harold Godwinsson had arrived there with a very large army of both horsemen and foot-soldiers. King Harald Sigurdarson then rode around his army inspecting their formation. He was mounted on a black horse with a white flash on its forehead. The horse lost its footing and the king fell off, but he got up quickly and said, "A fall is good luck for a journey."

Then King Harold of England asked the Norsemen who were with him, "Do you recognize the big man who fell off his horse, the one with the black tunic and fine helmet?"

"That's the king himself," they answered.

"He's a tall, powerful-looking man," said the King of England, "but it looks as if his luck has deserted him."

91. Twenty of the English housekarls [king's bodyguard] rode toward the Norse army. Both the men and their horses were armored. One of the horsemen said, "Is Earl Tostig in this army?"

"Yes, you'll find him here," replied Tostig. "There's no secret about that."

Then one of the riders said, "Your brother, King Harold, sends his greetings and this message: he is willing to make peace with you and give you the whole of Northumberland; he would rather give you a third of his kingdom than have you refuse to side with him."

"That's slightly different from the hostility and disgrace he offered me in the winter," replied the earl. "If this had been on offer then, many a man now dead would still be alive, and the kingdom of England would be more secure. If I accept this deal, what will he offer King Harald Sigurdarson for his pains?"

"He did say something about how much of England he would give King Harald," replied the horseman. "Seven feet of English earth, or a bit more, since he's taller than other men."

"Go and tell King Harold to get ready for battle," said the earl. "Norsemen will never be able to say that Earl Tostig deserted Harald Sigurdarson and joined his enemies when he came west to fight here in England. We are all determined to die with honor, or to conquer England." With that, the horsemen rode away.

"Who was that well-spoken man?" King Harald Sigurdarson asked the earl.

"That was King Harold Godwinsson," replied Earl Tostig.

"You kept that fact from me for too long," said the king. "Having come so close to our army, this Harold should now be beyond talking about the deaths of our men."

"True, my lord," replied Tostig. "He acted incautiously for a chief, and it might have turned out as you say. I saw that he wanted to offer me peace and great power; but I would have been his killer if I had given away his name, and I would rather he killed me than I killed him."

"He was a small man," said King Harald to his men, "but he stood proudly in his stirrups."

People say that King Harald Sigurdarson recited this poem:

> Let's advance
> In battle array
> Without body-armor
> Against blue-edged swords.

> Helmets shine, but
> I don't have a mail-shirt;
> Our armor lies
> Useless at the ships.

His mail coat was called Emma. It was so long that it hung to the middle of his calf and so strong that no weapon had ever pierced it. "That was a terrible poem," said King Harald. "I must compose a better one." Then he recited this:

> The trust-worthy woman
> bade us in battle
> not to cower behind curved shields
> fearing the din of the fight.
> She bade me bear
> my head high
> in the brunt of battle,
> where sword shatters skull.

Then Thjodolf recited:

> Though our prince himself perish,
> – that will be as God wills –
> I shall not be shaken,
> shall not abandon his young heirs;
> the sun does not shine
> on two finer future kings;
> these avenging sons of strong-willed
> Harald are two young hawks.

92. The battle began with an English cavalry charge on the Norsemen, who resisted strongly. It wasn't easy for the English to charge directly at the Norsemen because of the hail of weapons, so they rode around them instead. At first, there was no close fighting. As long as the Norsemen held their formation, the English cavalry just charged up fiercely and turned back immediately since they could make no inroads. When the Norsemen saw that the charges were ineffectual, they went on the attack and tried to put the English to flight. However, as soon as the Norsemen broke their shield wall, the English charged them from all sides hurling spears and other missiles at them. When Harald Sigurdarson saw what was happening, he hurried to where the fighting was fiercest. Many men died on both sides in the bitter

fight that followed. King Harald Sigurdarson became so enraged that he ran out in front of his troops and began laying about him with both hands. Neither helmet nor mail shirt was protection against him, and all those nearest him fled. At that moment, the English were on the verge of running away. Arnor Jarlaskald [Earls' poet] says this:

> The daring prince did not
> wear war-gear,
> yet the battle-bold king
> did not tremble in terror.
> The soldiers saw
> the blood-stained sword
> of their powerful prince
> killing King Harold's men.

King Harald Sigurdarson was struck in the throat by an arrow, and that was his death-wound. He fell, and all the men who had advanced with him were killed too, except for the men who retreated with the standard. Once again there was heavy fighting. Then Earl Tostig took up position under the king's standard, and there was a long pause in the battle while both sides drew up their lines for a second time. Thjodolf said:

> Men paid a terrible price.
> And now the troops were trapped.
> King Harald had caused them
> to make a meaningless journey west.
> The much praised prince
> lost his life,
> and the death of the daring lord
> left his people in peril.

Before the battle began again, King Harold Godwinsson offered peace to Tostig, his brother, and to all the other survivors of the Norse army, but the Norsemen cried out as one man that they would all fall dead beside one another before they would accept quarter from Englishmen. Then they raised a war-cry, and the battle started all over again. Arnor Jarlaskald says:

> Ill luck led to
> the fierce king's fall.
> Gilded spear-points did not spare
> the lord of our land.

> Not tempted by a truce,
> all the army
> of the courageous king
> chose to perish by their prince.

93. At that moment, Eystein Orri came up from the ships with his men; they were wearing their chain mail. Then Eystein seized the king's standard, Land-Ravager, and the third and fiercest phase of the battle began. Many Englishmen died in the heavy fighting and the others were on the verge of running away. This fight was called Orri's Attack. Eystein and his men had come from the ships with such haste that they were exhausted before the battle began and were scarcely fit to fight. Afterwards, though, they fought with such fury that they didn't even protect themselves with their shields as long as they could stand upright. Finally, they threw off their chain-mail, making it easy for the English to find their vulnerable spots. Some simply collapsed with the exertion and died unwounded. By late in the day, most of the Norwegian leaders were dead. As might be expected, not everyone shared the same fate: many fled and many were lucky enough to escape in a variety of different ways. The evening was dark before the slaughter was completely over.

101. THE DECLINE OF THE EARLS OF ORKNEY

By the end of the twelfth century, the earls of Orkney – who a century earlier had been all but independent rulers in the Northern Isles and mainland of Scotland with a far-reaching sphere of influence (see doc. 98) – were beginning to experience the abridgement of their power by both Norwegian and Scottish monarchies bent on consolidation of their own influence. Earl Harald Maddadarson (d. 1206) was the son of Maddad the earl of Atholl and his second wife, a daughter of Earl Hakon Paulsson of Orkney. Harald came to power amid a maelstrom of dynastic strife in 1139, at the age of five, and took sole control of the earldom in 1159. From then until the end of his life he pursued a policy of expansion and consolidation of power in the north of Scotland that brought him into direct conflict with the Scottish kings. The chief source of information on Earl Harald is Orkneyinga saga, *the later chapters of which recount the earl's conflicts with the Scottish king William I the Lion (r. 1165–1214). The dating of these clashes with the Scottish king must be worked out from other sources, but they occurred in the period between 1196 and 1201. Harald had already been deprived of Shetland in 1195 by the king of Norway.*

Source: *Orkneyinga saga*, ed. Finnbogi Guðmundsson, Íslenzk fornrit XXXIV (Reykjavík, 1965), pp. 289–98.

109. Earl Harald Maddadarson now ruled the Orkneys and was a great leader. He made a second marriage, to Hvarflod, the daughter of Malcolm, Earl of Moray. Their children were Thorfinn, David, John, Gunnhild, Herborg, and Langlif....

Eirik Stay-Brails had three sons: they were Harald the Young, Magnus Mangi, and Rognvald. These brothers went east to Norway to visit King Magnus Erlingsson [King Magnus V, 1156–84] and he gave Harald the title of earl and the right to rule over half of the Orkneys, as his grandfather Rognvald the Holy had done before him. Earl Harald the Young sailed west, and with him went Sigurd the Tiny, son of Ivar Fault, who was killed with Erling Wry-Neck at Aker. Ivar's mother was the daughter of Havard Gunnason. Sigurd the Tiny was a young man, very promising, and a flashy dresser. Magnus Mangi stayed behind with the king and died with him at Sogn.

Harald the Young and his men landed first in the Shetlands. From there, they went to Caithness and then south into Scotland to meet William, king of Scots. Harald asked the king to give him the half of Caithness that Earl Rognvald had ruled, and the king did so. From there, Harald went north to Caithness and set about gathering troops. He was joined by his brother-in-law, Lifolf the Bald, who had many noble kinsmen in the area. Lifolf was married to Ragnhild, the sister of Earl Harald the Young; he was called "Harald the Young" to distinguish him from Harald Maddadarson, who was nicknamed "the Old."

Lifolf had more influence over Harald the Young than anyone else. He and Harald sent messengers to Earl Harald the Old in the Orkneys asking him to hand over half of the islands, in fulfillment of King Magnus's promise to Earl Harald the Young. When Harald the Old heard about this, he flatly refused to divide his territory on any terms. Lifolf the Bald took part in this mission, and, before he left, Harald the Old spoke to him in a very threatening manner.

After that, Earl Harald the Old mustered a large army. Meanwhile, Harald the Young and his followers were in Caithness and they had assembled a small number of troops. When they heard that Harald the Old was gathering an army together, they dispatched Lifolf north once again across the Pentland Firth to reconnoiter the enemy. He headed west to Ranaldsey and climbed a hill where he came across three of Harald the Old's lookouts. They killed two of them but kept the third for interrogation. Then Lifolf caught sight of the earl's forces – he had many ships, most of them big. So Lifolf returned to his ship and told his companions what he had found out.

He declared that Earl Harald's army was so large that it would be folly to take him on. "To my way of thinking," said Lifolf, "we should head north today for Thurso where lots of people will join us. But if you insist on fighting Earl Harald, it is bound to be disastrous."

Then Sigurd the Tiny spoke up: "It's a black day when the earl's brother-in-law crosses the Pentland Firth and leaves his nerve behind," he said, adding that it would be a sorry outlook if they were all to lose heart as soon as they saw Harald the Old's army.

"When push comes to shove, Sigurd," replied Lifolf, "it's hard to tell who will keep his nerve. And I'm pretty sure that if it ever came time for me to desert Harald the Young, you fine fellows would be hard put to it to stay behind."

The trip to Thurso did not take place, and a little later on they saw Harald the Old's fleet sailing off Ranaldsey, so they prepared for battle. Harald the Old came ashore and drew up his considerable forces, while Sigurd the Tiny and Lifolf got the young earl's army into position. Sigurd the Tiny was wearing a scarlet tunic with the front skirts tucked up under his belt. Some of his men suggested doing the same at the back, but he told them not to bother: "For I've no intention of turning tail today," he said.

Sigurd and Lifolf were each with their own wings of the army and, as soon as they had drawn up their troops, a fierce battle began. In Harald the Old's force, there were many tough men who were really hard fighters and unusually well-equipped – men such as the bishop's kinsmen and many of the other troop leaders. Some time into the battle, Sigurd the Tiny fell fighting bravely, as befits a warrior. Lifolf did better than anyone else in the battle; the men of Caithness say that he went right through Harald the Old's lines three times, before dying heroically. When both Lifolf and Sigurd the Tiny were dead, the young earl's army took to flight.

Earl Harald the Young died beside some peat pits, and that night a great light was seen where his blood had fallen. People claim that the earl was truly saintly; a church now stands where he died. He is buried on the headland, and, on account of his virtues, many miracles have been performed there by God, as an indication that he wanted to cross over to Orkney to be with his kinsmen, Earl Magnus and Earl Rognvald.

After the battle, Earl Harald brought the whole of Caithness under his control. Then he went straight to Orkney, boasting of his great victory.

110. William, king of Scots, heard that Harald the Young was dead and that Harald Maddadarson had taken over the whole of Caithness without consulting him. The king was furious and sent messengers to Rognvald Gudrodarson, king of the Hebrides. Gudrod's mother was Ingibjorg, the daughter of Earl Hakon, who was the son of Earl Paul. In those days, King Rognvald was the greatest warrior in the British Isles. For three years he had lived aboard his warships without once coming under a sooty roof.

As soon as the king's message reached him, Rognvald raised an army from all over the Hebrides and Kintyre; he also had a large force from Ireland.

Then he headed north for Caithness and established control over the whole area. He remained in Caithness for some time, while Earl Harald stayed in the Orkneys, paying no attention to Rognvald's movements.

As winter approached, King Rognvald prepared to return to his kingdom in the Hebrides. He left three stewards behind in Caithness; one was Mani Olafsson, the second was Rafn the Lawman, and the third was called Hlifolf the Elder. Shortly after King Rognvald's return to the Hebrides, Earl Harald sent a man over to Caithness, telling him that his mission would be a success if he managed to kill one or more of the stewards.

The man crossed the Pentland Firth and traveled on until he met Rafn the Lawman who asked him where he was going. He hadn't much to say for himself, so Rafn said to him, "I can see in your face that Earl Harald has sent you here on some nasty business, but you are my kinsman, and I can't bring myself to kill you."

With that they parted and the fellow went away to find Hlifolf, whom he murdered. Then he hurried back to Orkney and told Earl Harald what he had done.

III. Earl Harald prepared to leave the Orkneys, and, when he was ready, traveled south to Thurso where he disembarked. Bishop John was in the fort at Scrabster, and when the men of Caithness saw how large Harald's army was, they realized that they could not stand up to it. They had also heard that Earl Harald was in such a foul temper that there was no saying if he would show them any mercy. Then the bishop said,

"If the earl and I meet on civil terms, then he will spare you." The bishop's view was generally accepted.

The earl's men rushed from their ships and made for the fort. The bishop went to meet the earl and greeted him pleasantly, but Earl Harald's response was to have the bishop seized, and his tongue cut out, and a knife thrust into his eyes so that he was blinded.

As he was being mutilated, Bishop John called on the holy maiden, Saint Tredwell, and when they let him go, he walked to a hillside where he met a woman and asked her for help. She saw that blood was pouring from his face and said, "Calm yourself, my lord; I'll be glad to help you." She led the bishop to Saint Tredwell's resting place and there his speech and sight were both restored.

Earl Harald then advanced on the fort and they surrendered it to him immediately. He inflicted severe punishments and imposed huge fines on the people who had been most prominent in the treason against him. Once more, he made all the people of Caithness swear allegiance to him whether they liked it or not. Then he seized all the property that had belonged to the stewards who had fled to the king of the Scots. Afterwards, he stayed on in Caithness with a large force.

112. Now, to return to the stewards, six of them decided to go south to Scotland. They met the king there at the Yule festival and were able to give him a clear account of what had happened in Caithness in the course of Earl Harald's campaign. The king was very angry about these events, and declared that he would give the stewards property worth double the value of what they had lost. On their first day with the king of Scots, each of them received twenty-five ells [an English ell is 1.143 meters] of cloth and one English mark [160 silver pennies] to cover their expenses. They spent Yule with the king of Scots in high favor.

Immediately after Yule, the king of Scots sent word to all the chieftains in his kingdom, and levied a large army from every region of the land. He led this huge army north to Caithness to attack Earl Harald and halted at Eysteinsdale, which is on the border between Caithness and Sutherland. The king's tents stretched from one end of the valley to the other, and that is a considerable distance.

Earl Harald was in Caithness when he got this news and he called out his own forces without delay. It is said that he had six thousand men, but even this force wasn't large enough to withstand the king of Scots, so he sent representatives to the king to explore the possibility of reaching a settlement. The king responded that there was no point in negotiations, unless he was awarded a quarter of the income from Caithness. On receiving this message, Earl Harald called a meeting of landowners and other leading men and asked for their advice. In view of their situation, the men of Caithness agreed to pay a quarter of their property to the king of Scots; those who had sought out the king earlier in the winter were exempted.

Earl Harald went back to the Orkneys with an agreement that he was to rule all of Caithness just as he had before Harald the Young received it from the king of Scots. During the hostilities, Thorfinn, the son of Harald, had been taken hostage by the king of Scots and blinded. Once peace terms had been agreed, the king traveled south to Scotland and Earl Harald remained as sole ruler of the Orkneys.

Toward the end of Earl Harald's life, Olaf, his son-in-law, and John Hallkelsson raised troops in the Orkneys and headed east to Norway to oppose King Sverrir [ca 1145–1202]. The man they had chosen for king was Sigurd, the son of King Magnus Erlingsson. Many high-born men from the Orkneys joined their force, which was an exceedingly strong one. At first, they were called the Islanders and then, for a while, the Gold-Legs. They fought against King Sverrir at Floravoe [in 1194] and lost. Both John and Olaf were killed there, along with their king and most of their army.

After that, King Sverrir grew very hostile toward Earl Harald, claiming that it was all his fault that an army had been raised in the Orkneys. As a consequence, the earl and Bishop Bjarni went east to Norway, where Harald submitted to King Sverrir and asked him to settle their differences. Then King Sverrir took the whole of Shetland away from Earl Harald, along with all its taxes and dues. The earls of Orkney have never regained those islands.

Harald was five years old when he was given the title of earl. For twenty-two years he was joint-earl of Orkney with Earl Rognvald the Holy and, after Rognvald's death, he was sole earl for forty-eight years. He died in the second year of the reign of King Ingi Bardarson [in 1206], and after his death, his sons John and David inherited the earldom; his son Henry ruled Ross in Scotland.

According to some writers, the most powerful earls of Orkney were Sigurd Eysteinsson, Earl Thorfinn Sigurdarson, and Earl Harald Maddadarson. After their father's death, the brothers John and David held the earldom jointly until David died of an illness in the same year as Hakon the Mad died in Norway [1214]. After that, John became sole ruler of the Orkneys.

102. THE BATTLE OF LARGS, 1263

By the middle of the thirteenth century, both Scottish and Norwegian monarchs were increasingly concerned with tightening their grip on the Hebrides, the islands off the west coast of Scotland. These islands had technically been under Norwegian control since 1098, but in practical terms they were controlled by neither power, being ruled by autonomous dynasties of sea-kings descended from Godred Crovan (d. 1095) and Somerled (d. 1164), based in the Isle of Man and the Hebrides respectively. Conflicts between and within these dynasties and the disorder that they generated were, however, a cause of concern to Scottish and Norwegian monarchs, who were both showing increased interest in the Hebrides in the early thirteenth century. When reports reached the Norwegian king, Hakon IV Hakonarson (1217–63), that the Scots had attacked the Isle of Skye in the summer of 1262, he summoned a massive levy at Bergen and set sail for the islands. His fleet, described as the biggest that had ever sailed from Norway, cruised south via Orkney and the Western Isles, but the expedition ended in disaster. Caught in an autumnal gale on the night of 30 September / 1 October off the island of Arran, some of the Norwegian ships were blown ashore at Largs, on the Ayrshire coast, and attacked by the Scots. The ensuing skirmishes between the Norwegians and the Scots are known as the Battle of Largs, and both sides claimed victory. Hakon died in the Orkneys in December, en route back to Norway, and his successor, Magnus IV, ceded the Western Isles to Scotland by the Treaty of Perth in 1266, ending four centuries of

Scandinavian influence there (although Orkney and Shetland were not acquired by Scotland until 1469). The events of 1263 are significant for more than just the cession of the Western Isles to Scotland, however. Hakon IV was one of the great medieval kings of Norway. By the time of his death he had already subjugated Greenland and Iceland. Culturally, he had made the Norwegian court comparable to other European courts, and had Latin works translated into Old Norse. Some scholars have, unsurprisingly, regarded his death as marking a transition in Scandinavian history. From Hakon Hakonarson's Saga *by Sturla Thordarson.*

Source: trans. A.A. Somerville from *Icelandic Sagas and Other Historical Documents Relating to the Settlements and Descents of the Northmen of the British Isles.* Vol. II, *Hákonar Saga, with Fragment of Magnus Saga, with Appendices,* ed. G. Vigfusson (Rolls Series: London, 1887), pp. 327, 339–55.

314. The previous summer, letters had come from the king who ruled the Hebrides. They complained bitterly about the unrest caused there by the earl of Ross, and Karnak, son of Machamal, and other Scots who had sailed out to Skye where they had burned down farms and churches, and killed large numbers of men and women. They claimed, too, that the Scots had seized little children and skewered them on the points of their spears, and had shaken them until they slipped down onto their hands, and then tossed them away dead.

They also repeated the boasts of the king of Scots [Alexander III, 1241–86], and said that he definitely meant to bring the whole of the Hebrides under his control, if he lived long enough. When this news reached King Hakon, he was very concerned and consulted his friends and advisers. But it didn't matter what advice he got ... after Yule he had conscription notices distributed throughout Norway, calling for the largest levies of men and supplies that he thought the country could bear. He summoned the whole army to meet him early in the summer at Bergen.... [Hakon then traveled to Scotland and through the Hebrides; negotiations with the king of Scots were opened]

322. ... As a result of the discussions and peace negotiations carried on between his representatives and those of the king of Scots, King Hakon decided to send messengers to meet the king of Scots face to face.... [King Hakon's envoys] met the king of Scots in the market town of New Ayr. He received them civilly, but with no great warmth. When they discussed peace, the king gave the impression that he would probably come to terms, but said that he would make up his mind and then send envoys to the king of Norway, with whatever offers seemed appropriate to himself and his council.

After that, King Hakon's men went on their way, but it was another day before the king of the Scots' envoys reached King Hakon, and peace talks began. King Hakon had made a list of all the islands off the west of Scotland which he laid claim to, and the king of Scots named certain islands that he was unwilling to give up, namely Bute, Arran, and the Cumbraes. Other than that, there was very little separating the positions of the two kings, and yet no peace agreement could be reached. As a tactic, the Scots prolonged negotiations so as to avoid arriving at any agreement at all, for the summer was almost over and weather conditions were worsening. At this juncture, the envoys went back to the king of Scots.... [Hakon decided to bring matters to a head and prepared for battle, but a storm drove some of his ships ashore].

325. When the Scots saw that Hakon's ships were being driven ashore, they rallied and charged down at the Norsemen, launching weapons at them. But the Norsemen defended themselves, using the beached cog [a large cargo ship] as protection. From time to time, the Scots attacked and just as often they withdrew. Few men were killed there, but many were wounded.

At this point, King Hakon sent some troops ashore in boats, for the storm was abating a bit. As this poem says:

> The battle-blessed
> spoiler of bright swords
> sent his eager-minded men late
> to the battle on the beach;
> the prince's people
> brought down the boastful dale-dwellers, won
> praise for their prince.

After that, the king, along with Thorlaug Bosi, went back out to his ship in a small boat rowed by his personal attendants. As soon as King Hakon's troops came ashore, the Scots fled inland. The Norsemen stayed ashore all evening and throughout the night until the approach of daybreak. Then all the Norsemen went back to their ships.

At daybreak, the men aboard the king's ship dressed and armed themselves, and the men on the other ships did the same. Then they all rowed ashore. The Scots had gone aboard the cog and taken all the property they could lay their hands on. A little later, King Hakon came ashore, with some of his nobles and a large body of men. The king had the cog unloaded and had the cargo carried out to his ship by boat.

326. When the cog was almost empty, a large number of Scots appeared; there were so many of them that most people thought the king himself must be present. Ogmund Crow-Dance was on a hillock with a company of men, and the first Scots on the scene made a feint at him and his men. When King Hakon's companions realized that the main Scottish force was approaching, they begged him to get into a boat and row out to the ships, and send them a

much larger force. The king offered to stay ashore with them, but they were reluctant to place him in such danger. So, he boarded a boat and rowed out past the island to his fleet....

[*In the meantime, the battle developed ashore.*]

There were nearly sixty men from the king's ship, and their leader was Andres Club-foot. But most people reckon that there must have been a total of eight or nine hundred Norsemen ashore. Nearly two hundred of them were on the hill with Ogmund while the rest were on the beach.

Then the Scottish army drew near, and it was a very large army indeed. Some reckon that there must have been five hundred cavalrymen, though others think that there were rather fewer than that. The Scottish cavalry was very well equipped, with mail-clad horses and some Spanish horses with armor. The Scots had a great many foot-soldiers, but they were poorly armed. Most of them had bows and Irish axes.

The Norsemen on the hill began drifting down toward the sea to prevent the Scots from encircling them. Andres Nikulasson went up the hill and asked Ogmund if he didn't think it would be wiser to go down to the beach and join the force that was already there. Ogmund took that advice. Andres told the men to go downhill, but not to rush as though they were fleeing.

The Scots attacked them fiercely, pelting them with stones. Then a great shower of weapons rained down on the Norsemen, and they withdrew, defending themselves. As they reached the downward slope of the hill, each man ran faster than the next. The Norsemen on the beach below saw this, and thought that their companions were attempting to flee, so they leapt aboard their boats. Some of them escaped to the ships this way, but most of the boats sank, and several men died. Many of the Norsemen took shelter behind the cog, while others got aboard her.

When the Norsemen coming down from the hill reached the valley between the hill and the beach, most of them took to their heels. They were ordered to turn back, and some did, but only a few.... The rest kept running and when they reached the beach, they were again told to turn back, and again some did, but not many.... This battle was both hard and one-sided for there were ten Scots for every Norseman.

All during the battle, there was such a great storm that King Hakon found it impossible to land his troops. However, Rognvald and Eilif from Naustdal rowed toward the shore in small boats. Rognvald was swept back out to his ship, but Eilif made it to land and joined the battle with several other men. They fought very bravely as did those Norsemen who had boarded boats and got to the beach. When the Norsemen began to assemble their forces, the Scots withdrew up the hill and, for some time, there were skirmishes between them, fought with spears and stones.

Late in the day, the Norsemen launched an attack on the Scots who were up on the hill, and pursued it with great vigor. As *Hrafnsmál* tells us:

> The chosen chieftains
> of the master of North-Møre [Hakon]
> sang war-songs
> before mighty men;
> the guards of the guardian
> of the highseat, hooded
> with iron advanced
> to the battle of sword-blades.
> The bright blade's
> edge bit in battle
> the unworthy enemy
> among curved red shields;
> soon the Scottish
> warriors fled the weapon
> hail from the heroes
> of our conquering king.

Then the Scots fled as fast as they could from the hill to the mountains. When the Norsemen saw that, they returned to their boats and rowed out to the ships. They had a hard time getting there because of the storm....

On the following Thursday, the king weighed anchor and moved out past the island. He was joined there by the troops he had sent to Loch Long. On the Friday, the weather was fine, so the king sent the Guests [a division of the royal bodyguard] to burn the ships which had been driven ashore. The same day, the king sailed away from the Cumbraes out to Lamlash, where he stayed for some days....

329. During the summer, the king had a great deal to worry him and many sleepless nights. There were numerous calls upon him, and his men gave him little peace. [When he came ashore at Kirkwall in the Orkneys,] he fell ill and took to his bed immediately. To begin with, the illness was not severe, and after the king had been laid up for about three weeks, his condition took a turn for the better and stayed better for three days. On the first day, he was able to get about his room; on the second day, he went to the bishop's chapel and heard mass there; and on the third day, he walked to St. Magnus's church and visited the saint's shrine. The same day, he took a bath and had himself shaved. That night, his illness intensified and he took to his bed once more; everyone thought that he was getting much worse.

In the early stages of his illness, he had Latin books read to him, but it grew difficult for him to concentrate on what the words meant, so then he had Norse books read to him day and night. To begin with, he listened to the lives of saints, and when these ran out, he had the history of all the kings of Norway read to him, one after another, from Halfdan the Black onwards.

When King Hakon realized that his condition was deteriorating, he made arrangements for gifts to be given to the men of his bodyguard in acknowledgment of their services to him. He ordered that each of them should receive a burnt mark of silver; and he gave half a mark of silver to his guests, cup-bearers, and all his other servants. He had his [silver] dinner-service weighed, except for the gilded items, and ordered that if the pure silver ran out, the dinner-service should be divided up so that everyone could have his fair share. Then he had letters written for King Magnus, explaining all the arrangements that he thought were most important.

King Hakon was anointed the night before the feast of Saint Lucy [13 December]. These bishops were in attendance: Thorgils, bishop of Stavanger; Gillibert, bishop of Hammar; and Heinrek, bishop of Orkney. Abbot Thorleif and many other learned men were present too. Before the king was anointed, the men who were with him, kissed him. While he was still capable of speech, he was asked by his confidants if he had any other son or any other offspring who could be contacted in case, tragically, he or King Magnus should die. The king was adamant that he had begotten no son except King Magnus, and no daughter that people did not know about already. By that time, the reading of kings' lives had reached Sverrir, so Sverrir's saga was begun. The saga was read day and night when the king was awake.

330. The feast of Saint Lucy the virgin fell on a Thursday, and, late in the evening of the following Saturday, the king's illness grew so much more serious that he lost the power of speech. The reading of Sverrir's saga ended close to midnight, and, just as midnight passed, Almighty God called the king away from this earthly life. [15–16 December, 1263.] This was a very great grief to everyone there, just as it was to the many others who heard about it later.

EPILOGUE

103. ADVICE FROM ODIN

Wisdom poetry is part of the cultural negotiation through which a civilization decides upon its identity. This reader closes with an example of the wisdom of the Viking Age: from Sayings of the High One (Hávamál).

Source: *Hávamál*, ed. David A.H. Evans (London: Viking Society for Northern Research, 1986), pp. 18–66, extracts.

1. Don't rush in
at any doorway;
first look round,
look left and right,
till you really know
whether a rival
is already in the hall.

38. A man mustn't
walk without weapons
even an inch from home,
because he never knows when,
as he pursues his path,
he'll suddenly need a spear.

50. The fir fails to flourish,
if it shivers shelterless,
naked of bark and needle;
thus fares the unfortunate
who lives unloved;
what point in living that life?

55. A man should be middling wise,
and never know too much;
the heart of him who sees too far
is seldom anything but sad.

70. It's better being alive
than lying lifeless;
the living man keeps his cow;
I saw a fine fire
burn bright for a rich man
while he lay dead out of doors.

76. Cattle die,
kin die
self dies too;
a good name,
if you get one,
goes on forever.

81. Praise the day when it's done,
a wife placed on her pyre,
a sword after service,
a maid when married,
ice when you're over it,
ale when you've emptied the cup.

82. Cut wood in a wind,
row boats in a breeze,
save sex for the darkness,
the eyes of day are everywhere;
sail a ship for its swiftness,
use a shield for shelter,
use a sword for severing
and a cutie for kissing.

84. A man mustn't trust
the virgin's voice,
or the woman's words;
on a whirling wheel
their feelings are formed,
their breasts founded on fickleness.

91. I put it plainly
– for I know both –
women find only fraud in men:

our well-formed words
cover the coarsest thoughts,
charming even the wisest women.

131. I advise you, Loddfafnir,
listen to my advice,
you'll benefit if you take it,
and only good will befall you;
I advise you to be wary,
but not too wary;
be wariest with ale
and another man's wife;
and third, be wary
that thieves don't outwit you.

SOURCES

Anderson, A.O. (translator)

"Martyrdom of Blathmac," from *Early Sources of Scottish History A.D. 500 to 1286, Volume 1.* Edinburgh: Oliver and Boyd, 1922; reprinted, Stamford: Paul Watkins, 1990.

Christiansen, E. (translator)

"Causes of Viking Expansion" and "Normandy Granted to Rollo," from *History of the Normans* by Dudo of St. Quentin. Woodbridge: Boydell, 1998. Reprinted by permission of Boydell & Brewer Ltd.

Cook, Albert S.

"Ibn Fadlān's Account of Scandinavian Merchants on the Volga in 922." *Journal of English and Germanic Philology* 22 (1923): 54-63. Reprinted by permission of the *Journal of English and Germanic Philology.*

Cross, S.H. (translator)

Excerpts from *The Russian Primary Chronicle Laurentian Text.* Cambridge, MA: Medieval Academy of America, 1953. Reprinted by permission of The Medieval Academy of America.

Dutton, P.E. (editor)

"Annals of St-Vaast," from *Carolingian Civilization: A Reader,* 2nd edition. Translated by P.E. Dutton. Peterborough: Broadview Press, 2004; "Abbo's Account of the Siege of Paris by the Northmen," from *A Source Book for Mediaeval History: Documents Illustrative of European Life and Institutions from the German Invasions to the Renaissance* by F.A. Ogg. New York: American Book Company, 1908; revised by P.E. Dutton, *Carolingian Civilization: A Reader,* 2nd edition. Peterborough: Broadview Press, 2004; "Life of St. Anskar," from *Anskar: The Apostle of the North, 801-865, translated from the Vita Anskarii by Bishop Rimbert his fellow missionary and successor.* Translated by C.H. Robinson. London: Society for the Propagation of the Gospel in Foreign Parts, 1921; revised by P.E. Dutton, *Carolingian Civilization: A Reader,* 2nd edition. Peterborough: Broadview Press, 2004. Copyright © 2004 by Paul E. Dutton. Reprinted by permission of the University of Toronto Press.

Holman, K.

Excerpt from *Scandinavian Runic Inscriptions in the British Isles: Their Historical Context.* Trondheim: Tapir, 1996. Reprinted by permission of Tapir Publishers.

Jenkins, R.J.H. (translator)

"Chapter 9," from *De Administrando Imperio, Volume I* by Constantine Porphyrogenitus. Edited by G. Moravesik. New revised ed., Washington, DC: Dumbarton Oaks, 1967. Reprinted by permission of the Dumbarton Oaks Research Library and Collection.

MacNiocaill, G. (translator)

Excerpts from *The Annals of Ulster (To A.D. 1131).* Edited by S. MacAirt. Dublin: Institute for Advanced Studies, 1983. Reprinted by permission of the School of Celtic Studies, Dublin Institute for Advanced Studies.

Mango, Cyril (translator)

Excerpts from "Homily III," from *The Homilies of Photius Patriarch of Constantinople.* Cambridge, MA: Harvard University Press, 1958. Copyright © 1958 by the Presidents and Fellows of Harvard College. Reprinted by permission of Harvard University Press.

Minorsky, V.

Excerpts from *A History of Sharvān and Darband in the 10th–11th Centuries.* Cambridge: W. Heffer & Sons., 1958.

Nelson, Janet L. (translator)

Excerpt from *The Annals of St-Bertin.* Manchester: Manchester University Press, 1991. Reprinted by permission of Manchester University Press, Manchester, UK.

Scholz, B.W. and B. Rogers (translator)

Excerpts from *Carolingian Chronicles: Royal Frankish Annals and Nithard's Histories.* Ann Arbor: University of Michigan Press, 1970. Reprinted by permission of the University of Michigan Press. All rights reserved.

Shetelig, H. (editor)

Excerpts from "Runic Inscriptions from Maeshowe," from *The Viking Antiquities in Great Britain and Ireland, Part VI: Civilisation of the Viking Settlers in Relation to Their Old and New Countries.* Edited by A.O. Curle, M. Olsen, and H. Shetelig. Oslo: H. Aschehoug & Co., 1954.

Tierney, J.J. (editor)

Excerpts from *Dicuili Liber de Mensura Orbis Terrae.* Dublin: Dublin Institute for Advanced Studies, 1967. Reprinted by permission of the School of Celtic Studies, Dublin Institute for Advanced Studies.

Tschan, F.J. (translator)

"Description of the Islands of the North," "Temple at Uppsala," "On Iceland," Vinland," "Conversion of the Danes under Harald Bluetooth," "Christianity in Sweden" and "Christianity in Norway," from

History of the Archbishops of Hamburg-Bremen by Adam of Bremen. New York: Columbia University Press, 2002. Reprinted by permission of Columbia University Press.

Every effort has been made to contact copyright holders; in the event of an omission or error, please notify the publisher.

The following sources are translated by A.A. Somerville:

Anglo-Saxon Chronicle
Ari Þorgilsson, *Book of the Icelanders* (*Íslendingabók*)
Book of Settlements (*Landnámabók*)
Canterbury Codex Aureus
Egil's Saga
Eirik the Red's Saga (*Eiríks saga Rauða*)
"Eirik's Poem" (*"Eiríksmál"*)
Gautrek's Saga
Grettir's Saga (*Grettis saga Ásmundarson*)
Hallfred's Saga
Hrólf Kraki's Saga
King's Mirror (*Konungs skuggsjá* or *Speculum Regale*)
Knýtlinga saga (*The Story of the Family of Knut*)
Kormak's Saga
Njal's Saga
Orkneyinga saga

Poetic Edda:
   The Goading of Gudrun (*Guðrúnarhvöt*)
   Hávamál(*Sayings of the High One*)
   The Lay of Rig (*Rígsþula*)
   The Seeress's Prophecy (*Völuspá*)

Saga of the Greenlanders (*Grœnlendinga saga*)
Saga of the People of Eyri (*Eyrbyggja Saga*)
Saga of the People of Laxdale (*Laxdæla saga*)
Snorri Sturluson, *Edda: Gylfaginning*
Heimskringla
Sturla Þórðarson, *Hákonar Saga*
Sverrir's Saga
Völsunga Saga
Voyages of Ohthere and Wulfstan

INDEX OF TOPICS

Topics are listed by document number and, in some cases, by books and sections or chapters within that document. Thus 7.11 is a reference to document 7, which is *The Life of Anskar*, and to section 11. 47.863 is a reference to document 47, which is drawn from *The Annals of St-Bertin*; 863 refers to the annal for the year 863 CE. If the topic surfaces several times within a document, no section or chapter number is given.

INDEX OF AUTHORS AND SOURCES

Authors and sources are listed by document number.

READINGS IN MEDIEVAL CIVILIZATIONS AND CULTURES
Series Editor: Paul Edward Dutton

"Readings in Medieval Civilizations and Cultures is in my opinion
the most useful series being published today."
— William C. Jordan, Princeton University